ECONOMICS, ORGANIZATION AND MANAGEMENT

Paul Milgrom
Stanford University

John Roberts
Stanford University

Prentice Hall, Englewood Cliffs, New Jersey 07632

Library of Congress Cataloging-in-Publication Data

Milgrom, Paul R.
    Economics, organizations, and management / Paul Milgrom, John
Roberts.
        p. cm.
    Includes bibliographical references and index.
    ISBN 0-13-224650-3
    1. Managerial economics.   2. Organization.   I. Roberts, John,
Feb. 11-   II. Title.
HD30.22.M55   1992
338.5'024658—dc20   91-41359
                                                                     CIP

Editorial/production supervision: Alison D. Gnerre
Interior design: Donna M. Wickes
Cover design: Mark Berghash
Manufacturing buyer: Trudy Pisciotti
Prepress buyer: Robert Anderson

 © 1992 by Prentice-Hall, Inc.
A Division of Simon & Schuster
Englewood Cliffs, New Jersey 07632

Printed in the United States of America
10 9 8 7 6 5 4 3 2 1

ISBN 0-13-224650-3

Prentice-Hall International (UK) Limited, *London*
Prentice-Hall of Australia Pty. Limited, *Sydney*
Prentice-Hall Canada Inc., *Toronto*
Prentice-Hall Hispanoamericana, S.A., *Mexico*
Prentice-Hall of India Private Limited, *New Delhi*
Prentice-Hall of Japan, Inc., *Tokyo*
Simon & Schuster Asia Pte. Ltd., *Singapore*
Editora Prentice-Hall do Brasil, Ltda, *Rio de Janeiro*

Dedicated to
Jan, Joshua, and Elana
and to
Kathy
with gratitude for their
patience, support and love

_____

CONTENTS

PREFACE

Privatization, *perestroika*, hostile takeovers, leverage, mergers and spinoffs, executive compensation, pay for performance, internal corporate reorganizations, strategic alliances, employee ownership, the S&L debacle—every day the newspapers carry stories about issues in economic organization. It is an exciting time both for students of economic organizations and for managers in these organizations, and an understanding of efficient organization can contribute greatly to the economic health of the world.

This book addresses these issues—not as isolated phenomena but by using a consistent framework of economic analysis. Although some current economics books include words like "organization" or "the firm" in their titles, this is the first textbook to deal systematically with firms and organizations as they really are and to acknowledge and analyze them in their complexity. Similarly, many management books are concerned with "organizations," but this is the first to adopt a thorough-going economic point of view and to use the powerful insights of rigorous, relevant economic theory to derive the underlying principles that are at work.

Outside of our teaching in the Economics Department and the Graduate School of Business at Stanford University, courses based on the material treated in this book are rarely found in either MBA or undergraduate economics programs. Some of our topics are included in other economics courses—for example, principal-agent theory is now occasionally taught cursorily in intermediate microeconomics courses, and the theory of the vertically integrated firm is taught in some courses on industrial organization. Nowhere else, however, are these treated with the other major issues of economic organization in a unified and systematic way. Most business and management schools offer courses that deal with many of the topics we cover, a few have courses that treat most of these topics together, and a very few of the most progressive even do so using a unified, economic approach, but without benefit of a textbook.

Our insistence on giving a unified treatment accounts for another unusual feature of the book: It is part textbook and part research monograph. For example, the treatment of problems of coordination in Chapter 4 goes well beyond anything that has yet appeared in the scientific literature of the economics profession. Academic economists studying organization have often focused too narrowly on the problem of incentives in organizations, or, even more narrowly, on incentives in relationships involving only two or perhaps three people at a time. Successful business organizations, however, are complex systems of mutually reinforcing parts, and our consistent emphasis on how the pieces of an efficient organization fit together into a coherent whole is unique to the economics literature.

The uniqueness of this book also depends on how it is used. As an economics text, our book is uniquely rich in applications of theory that are drawn from real companies and events. More than 100 examples are woven into the text, illustrating how economic principles help to explain business institutions and practices, and every major idea is introduced in the immediate context of a real-world example. As a management text, it unrelentingly applies an economic perspective in which people make self-interested choices and enter agreements only when they expect a mutual benefit. The power of this economic perspective for explaining real-world institutions and phenomena surprises many students and captures their interest. The economic slant gives management students the conceptual "hooks" on which to hang the details of the cases they study, helping them to recognize puzzles and remember lessons long after the final exam or case analysis has been graded and returned.

Why would we write a textbook for a subject where so few courses exist and with such a seemingly small audience? Over the past decade the study of contracts and business organizations has been one of the most active and fruitful areas of research in microeconomics, and the pace of new research is quickening. With the successes of Japan's unique organizations, the creation of new institutions in the formerly communist countries, the privatization of formerly publicly owned businesses in many countries around the world, the major changes in corporate ownership and governance that are still occurring, and the new emphasis on business alliances in Western countries, the importance and currency of the subject of economic organization is undeniable. The academic treatment of the principles of economic organization, however, has been fragmented, inhibiting both professors who want to teach this subject and the students who are eager to learn it. With the introduction of this book, a barrier has now fallen, and we expect a course based on the material covered here to become standard fare in the business and economics curricula.

Although we have written this book for an audience of undergraduates and MBAs, it is likely that doctoral students in various fields will find it useful as well, both for the new research it contains and because there is nowhere else to turn for a unified and systematic introduction to our subject. We also believe that practicing managers will find it useful in organizing their experiences and insights.

ORGANIZATION OF THE TEXT

We have organized the text into seven parts. The first deals with the fundamental problems of economic organization, namely those of coordinating and motivating the members of an organization to work in ways that are coherent and advance the common interests of the organization's members. Chapter 1, intended as a reading for the first day of class, illustrates these problems with a set of case studies. Chapter 2 develops the economic perspective in more detail, introducing our focus on individuals and transactions, the notion of efficiency, and the nature and classification of transaction costs. It also illustrates how these ideas are manifested in a wide variety of real institutions, both public and private.

Part II is about coordination, both by the invisible hand of prices in markets and by the quite visible hands of managers. Chapter 3 highlights the role of the price system for bringing coherence to the diverse activities of people who may be unaware even of one another's existence. We also explore the failures of the price system, but with an unusual emphasis on the economies of scale (Chapter 3) and scope (Chapter 4) that are fundamental for understanding the role of management in organizations. Alternative solutions to coordination problems are studied in Chapter 4, where we compare the price system to other systems of coordination and identify the situational factors that determine the relative usefulness of alternative systems. In this chapter we also develop the importance of complementarities among activities and the need to look at successful organizations as coherent systems of mutually supporting parts.

Part III, which contains Chapters 5 and 6, introduces the problems of contracting, information, and incentives, and gives an informal treatment of their solutions. Chapter 5 deals with contracting with bounded rationality and informational differences and incompleteness, and it also treats the problems of selecting partners and negotiating and enforcing contracts. Adverse selection is treated here as well, along with signaling and screening theories. Chapter 6 focuses on moral hazard and institutional responses to this problem of post-contractual opportunism.

Part IV, consisting of Chapters 7 through 9, provides a careful, formal treatment of some of the central methods of providing incentives efficiently. Chapter 7, which deals with risk sharing and incentive contracts, introduces a set of theoretical principles for efficient performance contracting and illustrates these principles with a series of significant applications. Whereas Chapter 7 focuses on situations in which issues of efficiency and distribution can be treated separately, Chapter 8 investigates theories in which those issues are irretrievably intertwined. Private ownership, the most pervasive and common way to provide incentives for caring for assets, is the subject of Chapter 9.

The theory of Chapters 1 through 9 is put to the test in the next seven chapters. Part V, consisting of Chapters 10 through 13, presents an economic treatment of the nature of the employment relationship, examining explicit and implicit employment contracts, compensation policies, and career paths. Chapter 10 reviews the classical theory of labor markets and more modern theories that explain why long-term employment relations predominate in every developed economy. Chapter 11 focuses on job assignments and promotions and particularly on how firms resolve the tension between assigning people to the jobs that best suit them and using promotions as a reward for past performance. The way compensation is determined puzzles almost everyone at some time in his or her life, and that is the subject of Chapter 12. Chapter 13 reviews the facts and theories about the controversial matter of executive compensation.

Chapters 14 and 15 (Part VI) treat financial decisions, particularly in investments, capital structure, and corporate control. The classical theories of finance—present value analysis, Modigliani-Miller theory, the Capital Asset Pricing model, and the efficient markets hypothesis—appear in Chapter 14, which is aimed mostly at undergraduates on the presumption that MBA students see this material elsewhere. Chapter 15 introduces students to explanations of capital structure based on information and incentive arguments and to the contentious issues at the heart of the debate around corporate control and governance.

The last part of the book comprises two chapters about the design, internal structure, and dynamics of organizations, including an examination of the boundaries and scope of business firms. One undeniable feature of organizational history is that the dominant modes of organization have changed rapidly since the onset of the industrial revolution and continue to change at a dazzling pace. In Chapter 16, we identify the problems that major organizational innovations aimed to solve and the principles that have governed past organizational choices. Chapter 17 looks ahead, emphasizing the dynamic processes that drive organization change and peering into the future of capitalist firms, national economies, and the study of the economies and management of organizations.

Use in Courses

We have used earlier drafts of these chapters as teaching notes in our undergraduate and MBA level courses at Stanford. Stanford quarters are 10 weeks long and involve 4 hours per week of class time, plus a final exam period. The undergraduate course opens with Chapter 1 on the first day, and proceeds to cover Chapters 2 through 9 and 14 through

17 with varying degrees of thoroughness. Students find the technical material in Chapters 3 and 7 to be the most demanding reading, and it pays to spend a bit more time on these chapters than on the others. We have found it useful to devote the last week of the course to case studies—either those developed by students in term papers or business school cases. Among the latter, the *McDonalds* case (*Harvard Business Review* Reprint 74410) and the *Lincoln Electric Company* (Harvard Business School case 376-028) are particularly appropriate.

In the MBA course, the principal focus of most class meetings is on case discussions. Some class time is devoted to lectures about the more conceptually demanding formulations, such as those in Chapter 7, but the other parts of Chapters 2 through 9 are used mostly as background readings that help students prepare the case analyses. Chapters 10 through 17 are assigned as specific readings in connection with particular case studies. Among the cases that we can recommend are the two classics mentioned above plus Stanford Graduate School of Business cases *Sony Corporation Enters the Entertainment Business* (S-BP265), and *Marathon Oil Company's Last Stand* (S-BP223), and Harvard cases *Analog Devices, Inc.* A (9-181-001), *Benetton SpA* (9-389-074), *Charles River Co.* (9-189-179), *Goodyear Restructuring* (9-288-046), *Lucky Stores*, A, B, and C (9-389-050, -051, and -066), *Merck & Co., Inc.*, A, B, and C (9-941-005, -006, and -007), *Natomas North America* A and B (9-184-031 and -032), *RKO Warner Home Video Inc. Incentive Compensation Plan* (9-190-067), and *Washington Post*, A and B (9-677-076 and -077). The Stanford cases are available from Case Services, Graduate School of Business, Stanford, CA, 94305-5015, and the Harvard cases from HBS Case Services, Harvard Business School, Boston, MA, 02163.

In addition, both courses make significant use of material from the daily press, especially *The Wall Street Journal* and *The New York Times'* business section, as well as *The Economist* and *Business Week*, as a basis for class discussion. It is remarkably easy to find news stories almost every day that can be meaningfully and substantively analyzed using the ideas from this book, and the use of such current material involves students and raises their level of interest.

Our Debts

This book evolved over several years of teaching courses at Stanford to undergraduates and MBA candidates, and our first debt is to these students. They challenged and debated us at every turn, comparing our economic perspective to competing ways of thinking about organizations. Without their comments, criticisms, and suggestions, this book could never have been written. Among our students, Darryl Biggar, Sandro Brusco, Xinghai Fang, Mark Fisher, Joshua Gans, William Lehr, Pino Lopomo, Jonathan Paul, Scott Schaefer, and Joel Watson commented on parts of the manuscript, devised questions and answers that we have borrowed, and generally made themselves very useful in the preparation of this text. In addition, Stanford students Aaron Edlin, Rhonda Hollinberger, and Mike Saran made suggestions that we incorporated in the final manuscript, and Chris Avery and Peter Zemsky collaborated with us in some of the unpublished research that we draw on here.

Many of our colleagues and friends at Stanford and elsewhere gave generously of their time to help us improve the manuscript in innumerable ways. For their help, we are most grateful to Masahiko Aoki, Banri Asanuma, Connie Bagley, Jim Baron, Elaine Bennett, Ted Bergstrom, Steve Durlauf, Dan Friedman, Nancy Gallini, Bob Gibbons, Avner Greif, Jane Hannaway, Mark Hodes, Bengt Holmstrom, Chuck Horngren, Mike Jensen, Pitch Johnson, Ed Lazear, John Litwack, Mark Lang, Susanne Lohmann, Anthony Marino, Peter Newman, Yaw Nyarko, Masahiro Okuno-Fujiwara, Myron Scholes, Abraham Seidmann, Ken Singleton, Grace Tsiang, Karen Van Nuys, Mark Wolfson, Barry Weingast, Robert Wilson, Ho-Mu Wu, and Mark Zupan.

The entire manuscript was edited by Rachel Nelson and produced by Alison Gnerre of Prentice Hall, who labored hard to turn our sometimes incomprehensible jargon into clear English prose. For their patience and skill, we owe them special gratitude. We also thank Whitney Blake, who got this book project off to a healthy start, and Kathleen Much of the Center for Advanced Study in the Behavioral Sciences, who provided remarkably speedy and insightful editorial advice. Debbie Johnston had the tedious but crucial job of keyboarding the corrections to our manuscript. She did her work with uncanny accuracy, freeing us to devote our time to other activities.

As we indicated above, large parts of what is reported here is new and comes from our own research. So we also owe thanks to our research collaborators, especially Bengt Holmstrom, Dave Kreps, and Bob Wilson, and to those who provided financial support for our research, including the National Science Foundation, the John Simon Guggenheim Foundation, the Center for Economic Policy Research at Stanford, and the Jonathan B. Lovelace professorship and the Robert M. and Anne T. Bass faculty fellowship at Stanford. The finishing touches were put on this book while we were Fellows at the Center for Advanced Study in the Behavioral Sciences.

Paul Milgrom
John Roberts

Part

I

THE PROBLEM
OF ECONOMIC ORGANIZATION

1

DOES ORGANIZATION MATTER?

T*he principles of organization got more attention among us than they did then in universities. If what follows seems academic, I assure you that we did not think it so.*

Alfred Sloan[1]

BUSINESS ORGANIZATION

Crisis and Change at General Motors

When Pierre du Pont appointed Alfred Sloan to head General Motors in 1921, the company was in crisis. The demand for cars had fallen in the 1920 recession, and although the firm already had huge inventories of unsold cars, the factory managers continued to produce with abandon. In response to this falling demand, Ford Motor Company had cut the price of its Model T by about 25 percent—a reduction that GM with its higher costs could not match. Trying to hold the line on prices, GM saw its sales fall by 75 percent between the summer and fall of 1920. By 1921, Ford Motor Company's Model T held a 55 percent share of the U.S. automobile market, compared to just 4 percent for Chevrolet and 11 percent for all of General Motors' brands combined. Taking relentless advantage of the huge cost advantage that came from producing a single product at very high volume, Ford was expanding its production capacity in order to increase its already dominant position in the car market.

Even apart from the immediate difficulties caused by the recession, General

---

[1] Alfred Sloan, *My Years With General Motors* (Garden City, N.Y.: Doubleday, 1964), p. 50.

Motors faced a fundamental long-term problem. It simply could not produce a car that would offer more value at a lower price than the Model T, and it was squandering the resources and capabilities it did have, as divisions like Cadillac, Buick, Oakland, Olds, and Chevrolet competed mostly with one another. What was needed first was a new, more coherent marketing strategy focused squarely on competing with Ford. Sloan's plan was as follows: GM would design different cars for different segments of the market. The Cadillac division would make luxury cars for the highest-income buyers, and the other divisions each would serve successively lower-income segments, with Chevrolet making a model that would be sold for even less than the Model T. The Model T would still appeal to some buyers, but Sloan believed that most customers would choose to buy cars that were either more luxurious or less expensive than Ford's product.

PRODUCT DIVERSITY AND DESIGN COORDINATION   There was, however, one important hitch: Carrying out this plan involved a combination of diversity of products and close coordination in design that exceeded anything that had ever been attempted before. There would need to be a variety of new car designs, new dealerships, market information about the customers in each new market segment, separate factories to manufacture each type of car, and different supplies for each factory—a huge amount of variety. At the same time, the many parts of the organization would need to be coordinated in various ways. They would have to cover the different segments of the market without competing too much with each other. They would need to share ideas about how to improve products and reduce manufacturing costs, coordinate their research and development efforts, cooperate with the supply divisions that produced major components like bearings, radiators, and spark plugs, and standardize designs enough to achieve economies of scale in parts production. Compared to Ford's one-product strategy, Sloan's segmented-market strategy required that many more decisions be made and much more information be continuously gathered and evaluated. The organization used by Ford Motor Company would be no model for the new General Motors.

    The former organization of General Motors as essentially a collection of car companies and suppliers operating without any central direction was no model either. The car divisions had failed to coordinate their parts designs, raising costs for all of them. The accounting system, which allocated costs among the producing divisions, was unable to keep accurate track of which decisions by which units raised costs and therefore failed to guide divisional managers to economize. For example, the individual divisions continued production even in the face of huge accumulated inventories of unsold cars during the recession because the system failed to assign inventory holding costs to the divisions.

GM'S MULTIDIVISIONAL STRUCTURE   Sloan studied GM's organization and decided a radical change was needed. The new organization would be a multidivisional structure with a strong, professional staff in the central office. There would be no infringement on the basic autonomy of the divisions in making operational decisions. Each separate division would make and sell a car targeted for an assigned market segment. Each would have its own managerial team with authority to make its own operating decisions. Unlike other business organizations, GM's central office would not be responsible for day-to-day operations. Instead, its primary roles would be to audit and evaluate each division's performance and to plan and coordinate overall strategy. The central office would also be responsible for the research, legal, and financial functions of the corporation. It would survey market prices to make sure that the prices used for internal accounting purposes were a good reflection of actual costs. This would enable the company to evaluate internal supply divisions on the basis of their profitability, as if each were a separate firm.[2]

Henry Ford, accustomed to being well informed about every important decision in his company, was skeptical about GM's reorganization and especially about how far its top management would be removed from its operations. He commented:

> To my mind there is no bent of mind more dangerous than that which sometimes is described as the "genius for organization." This usually results in the birth of a great big chart showing, after the fashion of a family tree, how authority ramifies. The tree is heavy with nice round berries, each of which bears the name of a man or an office. . . . It takes about 6 weeks for a message from a man living in one berry at the lower left-hand corner of the chart to reach the president or chairman of the board.[3]

However, Sloan's organization, which looked so cumbersome to Henry Ford, quickly transformed GM into a fearsome competitor. From 1927 to 1937, Ford lost $200 million, whereas GM earned over $2 billion. GM's market share grew to 45 percent in 1940, whereas Ford's once commanding share shrunk to a mere 16 percent.

The creation of a multidivisional structure not only enabled General Motors to compete successfully with its new strategy, it also set the stage for a continuing expansion of the company's product line. In the years that followed, General Motors added products ranging from trucks to kitchen appliances to its product portfolio. Such an expansion would not have been possible using the older forms of business organization. The multidivisional form that GM helped to pioneer has become a standard organizational feature of the corporate world, enabling many companies to produce a wide array of products. General Motors' new organization was well suited to its needs, but GM was hardly the last automobile company to discover the advantages of organizational innovation.

Toyota

In the early 1950s, Toyota was a small automobile manufacturer serving the Japanese market. Compared to its giant U.S. competitors, Toyota suffered from a drastic lack of capital and a tiny scale that made it impossible to match its competitors' low production costs. Although Toyota enjoyed much lower labor costs than the U.S. firms at the time, many other countries had even lower labor costs. However, none had been able to parlay these low costs into a substantial competitive advantage in what was then a high-technology, capital-intensive industry.

"Just-in-Time" Manufacturing   Like other automobile companies in Europe, Japan, and the Eastern Bloc, Toyota tried for a time to mimic the advanced mass-production techniques of its U.S. competitors. Soon, however, under the leadership of Eiji Toyoda and Taiichi Ohno, it began to develop a distinctive approach that was better suited to the scale and nature of its operations. One of the most famous of Toyota's innovations was the development of the "kanban" or "just-in-time" (JIT)

---

[2] Similar organizations were independently developed in the same era by the Du Pont Company, Standard Oil of New Jersey, and Sears. The fascinating history of the emergence of the multidivisional firm is told by Alfred Chandler in *Strategy and Structure: Chapters in the History of the American Industrial Enterprise* (Cambridge, MA: MIT Press, 1962).

[3] As quoted in Alfred Chandler, "The Historian and the Enterprise," Ninth Annual David R. Calhoun, Jr. Memorial Lecture delivered at Washington University (March 29, 1988); and Alfred Chandler, *Strategy and Structure.*

manufacturing system. This system was ideally intended to eliminate all inventories from the production process. In traditional manufacturing industries, goods processed on one machine would be held in a buffer inventory until the next machine in the sequence was ready for its operation. Inventories separating the successive stages protect each machine's operations from delays or disruptions at adjacent stages of production. However, inventory systems are subject to very large economies of scale, so Toyota could never achieve cost parity (equality) with its larger competitors if it relied on such a system.

In place of inventories, Toyota established a system of closer communication and tighter coordination between successive stages of the production process, so that each stage would be informed "just in time" when it had to deliver its product to the next stage. Without inventories to buffer the disruptions caused by defective products and broken machines, Toyota engineers had to work to improve the reliability of every step of the process. The same changes that reduced the number of interruptions in the production process often reduced the number of defects in Toyota's cars as well, as flaws were caught immediately rather than piling up in the in-process inventory. The absence of inventories also meant that Toyota had to be linked more tightly to its suppliers than were U.S. firms, communicating with them about day-to-day needs and helping them to improve the reliability of their own systems. At the same time, the need to repair broken equipment quickly caused Toyota to train its equipment operators to carry out maintenance and repairs themselves. In contrast, maintaining and repairing machines was a separate specialty with a separate job classification in the United States, and when a machine broke down, its operator stood around waiting until a repair specialist turned up to fix it.

Under Alfred Sloan's leadership, General Motors moved to take full advantage of the large scale of its operations by including the same parts in many of its different cars. By using the same chassis or engine or brakes in several models, GM could afford to develop specialized manufacturing equipment for these components, substantially reducing the production costs. In contrast, Toyota did not enjoy such scale economies and instead emphasized improving the flexibility of the equipment it did use, so that the same equipment could be quickly reset to produce different models. Given this emphasis, it should come as no surprise that Toyota had become a world leader in the use of industrial robots as early as the 1960s.

Because General Motors' specialized equipment was not easily adapted to the production of radically new designs, GM had major redesigns of its models only about once every 12 years in the 1950s and 1960s, whereas Toyota redesigned its vehicles twice as often, introducing improvements with each new design. By the early 1970s, Toyota's technological prowess in the design and manufacture of small cars had earned it a considerable share of the world market. As its sales grew, Toyota built new manufacturing plants that were much larger than those built earlier by the U.S. car companies, allowing the company to enjoy many of the scale economies that remained in the production process.

COORDINATION WITH OUTSIDE SUPPLIERS   Another feature that distinguished the Toyota organization from its North American competitors was Toyota's great reliance on outside suppliers. In contrast, GM was very highly vertically integrated. GM's huge volumes and use of the same components for many models allowed the company to utilize fully the output of efficient-sized parts factories. Furthermore, ready access to capital allowed it to produce these parts and components itself. In its early days, Toyota could not achieve efficient scale in the building of components, nor could it afford to own its own parts makers. Therefore, unlike GM, Toyota chose to rely on outside suppliers not just for its basic inputs like sheet steel, screws, and fabric for seats, but also for the more complex components and systems, such as headlamps, brake systems, and fuel-injection systems. This also opened the possibility that its suppliers then could achieve larger scale by producing for other auto manufacturers as well.

The JIT system necessitated close coordination between Toyota and its suppliers. The need was reinforced by the frequent redesign of the vehicles and the fact that the suppliers were providing high-level components that had to fit together, rather than simple standardized commodities. As a result, simple market arrangements with the suppliers became problematic. Instead of seeking numerous suppliers for each part or component and shifting business among them to induce price competition, as GM did, Toyota built long-term relations with a much smaller number of suppliers. These long-term relations facilitated communication and made the suppliers willing to face the risks of investing heavily in both skills and machinery to meet Toyota's specialized needs.

The Hudson's Bay Company

The history of the automobile industry provides a clear example of the importance of a coherent organization that is well suited to the firm's size, capabilities, and market strategy. But the importance of the details of business organization can also be seen from centuries past.

On May 2, 1670, the Governor & Company of Adventurers of England Trading into Hudson's Bay was formed as a joint stock company by a royal charter of King Charles II of England. The charter gave the company a monopoly over trade in all the lands draining into Hudson's Bay.[4] This is an immense area of 1.5 million square miles, covering much of Quebec, most of Ontario, all of Manitoba, much of Saskatchewan and Alberta, the eastern part of the Northwest Territories, parts of Minnesota, North Dakota, and Montana, and a bit of South Dakota. The area is larger than 10 Japans, 15 United Kingdoms, or 30 states of New York. The company's total legal monopoly nominally covered all trading of goods in the region, but in fact the firm was in the business of trading European manufactures to the native peoples for animal furs, and especially beaver pelts.

Now known as the Hudson's Bay Company (HBC), the firm is still in existence. It is the world's oldest commercial entity that continues its original line of business. In the late eighteenth and early nineteenth centuries, however, it was in desperate shape, being thoroughly beaten by a rival, the North West Company (NWC), that operated under a minor legal deficiency (it was violating the royal monopoly) and what should have been an absolutely debilitating technological inferiority. However, the NWC used a much more effective organizational structure and strategy that put it closer to its customers than the HBC, encouraged more flexible, effective responses to changing conditions than the older company could manage, and gave its employees stronger incentives for initiative and effort. This strategy and structure more than offset the older firm's huge cost disadvantage. Only when the HBC mimicked key aspects of the NWC's strategy and structure was it able to compete effectively.

HBC'S ORGANIZATION The stock in the Hudson's Bay Company was owned by a group of wealthy aristocrats in the United Kingdom. Management was provided from London by a committee of the owners under the leadership of one of their number,

---

[4] A well-researched and extremely readable source on these matters is Newman's two-volume history of the Hudson's Bay Company. This is the source of most of the details reported here. See Peter C. Newman, *Company of Adventurers* and *Caesars of the Wilderness* (London, New York, and Toronto: Penguin Books, 1988).

the Governor. None of these worthies ever set foot in the area of the company's actual operations during the seventeenth and eighteenth centuries, and they were often monumentally ignorant of the conditions that prevailed in the field. They recruited employees to carry out the trade in North America and paid them a flat salary. Both the general strategy that these employees were to implement and many of the finest particulars about operating decisions were made in London (along with detailed rules regarding the employees' conduct and behavior). Of course, communication between London and Hudson's Bay was extremely slow in the days of sail, especially because the bay is frozen solid for much of the year. Therefore, the lag between the reporting of information and the receipt of a response from management was frequently as long as 15 months.

The company's strategy was to build a few trading posts along the shores of Hudson's Bay and to trade only there. Native tribes near the bay were the initial customers, but they rapidly became independent middlemen, obtaining furs from more distant peoples in return for goods obtained from the company. This pattern had the usual inefficiencies of "double monopoly": The intermediaries took a significant markup for their services. However, the strategy fit well with the HBC's personnel and pay policy and with its management's preference for control. In addition, the employees in the field for the most part had no interest in leaving the relative safety and comfort of their dismal "forts" and "factories" to risk the barren wilderness in hopes of increased company profits but with no extra reward for themselves.

The North West Company

Until the surrender of French claims in Canada to the United Kingdom in 1763, the HBC faced intermittent competition from French Canadian *coureurs de bois*, independent traders from the St. Lawrence who traveled by canoe to trade with the native peoples directly on their home trapping grounds. However, the colonial authorities in New France frowned on such trade, fearing it would lure men away from farming and foster too much independence, and they taxed the returns heavily, quite often simply confiscating the furs. Indeed, the HBC itself had been established at the instigation of two such entrepreneur-explorer-traders, Radisson and Groseilliers, who tired of losing their revenues to the French government.

Once British government and commercial law came to Canada, Scottish and other English-speaking immigrants to Montreal established an effective trade based on the *coureurs de bois* model which competed with the Hudson's Bay Company. By 1779 these traders had formed a partnership called the North West Company, but even before then they had established permanent fur trade posts as far away as the Athabasca River delta, 3,000 miles northwest of Montreal.

THE NWC'S PROBLEM   The North West Company (NWC) suffered under an immense technological disadvantage, but they suffered heroically. Montreal and the Hudson's Bay forts of the HBC were approximately the same sailing distance from the source of trade goods and the market for furs in England. Montreal, however, was separated from the prime fur country by an extra 1,500 miles of trackless swamp, bare rock, and impenetrable bush. The Nor'Westers' (North West Company traders') solution was to move the trade goods to the north and bring the furs back in fragile birch-bark canoes powered by French Canadian *voyageur* paddlers. This solution was possible because the interlocking system of Canadian rivers and lakes permits travel from the Atlantic to the Arctic and Pacific Oceans with very few, reasonably short land bridges. Nevertheless, using this system presented monumental challenges.

North West Company canoe brigades would leave the fur-trading posts in the north as soon as the ice left the rivers, traveling across half the North American continent, through absolute wilderness, along fast, rocky rivers and across storm-swept lakes, often having to lug their canoes and all the goods they carried around raging rapids. Their destination was the company's inland headquarters, first located at Grand Portage on the northwest corner of Lake Superior, just south of the current border between Canada and the United States, and later moved 40 miles north to Fort William. There they would meet canoe brigades that had come up from Montreal, loaded with trade goods, via the Ottawa River and Lake Huron. The trade goods and furs were exchanged, then the Nor'Westers would retrace their paths back to the fur country, where they would spend the winter trading with the native peoples. Meanwhile, the furs would be carried back to Montreal, where they would (if the river was still open) be loaded on ships for England. As a result, there was a minimum lag of 15 to 18 months between the NWC's purchase of trade goods in England and its sale of the furs it traded for them, with 24 months a more common length of time. In contrast, trading at its Hudson's Bay forts allowed the HBC to sell furs within four to six months of buying the goods they traded for them. The difference in working capital needs, combined with that in transportation costs, should have made the HBC dominant, for its costs for importing goods were half those of its rival.

THE SUCCESS OF THE NORTH WEST COMPANY   In fact, by the end of the first decade of the nineteenth century, the NWC had seized nearly 80 percent of the trade and was immensely profitable, whereas the HBC was losing money at such a rate that its officers considered getting out of the fur business altogether. A key factor in the Nor'Westers' success was their strategy of building trading posts in the fur lands, which put them close to their customers and gave them a market advantage. But at least as important was their organizational structure, which embodied systems of incentives and decision making that encouraged the effort, imagination, flexibility, and innovation that were crucial to making the market-oriented strategy work.

The HBC was rigidly hierarchical. Rules and controls from distant London circumscribed every action and decision of its employees in the field, leaving little possibility of flexibly responding to emerging conditions. Innovation was discouraged or even punished, and performance was rewarded only by the possibility of someday gaining a promotion to the next rung of the bureaucratic ladder. Employees were chosen for their ability to withstand the excruciating boredom of their indentured terms of service by the frozen bay and for their willingness to work cheaply and follow orders. They were disciplined by floggings for breaking the company's myriad regulations.

Organized and managed this way, the HBC was no match for the NWC. The NWC was a partnership, with two classes of partners who shared in the profits of the enterprise. The senior, Montreal-based partners were responsible for acquiring trade goods and financing and for marketing the furs at the London auctions. The "wintering partners" ran the trade in the field. The two groups met annually at Grand Portage or Fort William to exchange information, set policy, and divide the profits that arose from their efforts. Operating decisions in the field were largely left to the individual wintering partners on site, who could respond quickly and imaginatively and who were well motivated by their ownership shares. Other employees were chosen for their fit with the aggressive, entrepreneurial style that characterized the North West Company and its partners. These people were given real responsibility, performance-related pay, and a serious chance to become a partner.

THE REORGANIZATION OF HUDSON'S BAY COMPANY   The HBC ultimately responded to the NWC's challenge, beginning in 1809 when new owners gained effective control of the company after its share price had fallen from £250 to £60. The response was simple: mimic their rival, build trading posts inland to compete directly with the Nor'Westers, institute a profit-sharing scheme that allocated half the profits to the officers in the field based on performance, give other employees more incentives and more freedom of action, and recruit a new class of employees who would respond to this new organizational strategy.

The Nor'Westers immediately saw the danger that the HBC's new strategy presented, for they always were painfully aware of the cost disadvantage they faced. Their immediate response was an attempted hostile takeover. They sought to buy a controlling block of shares in their rival so as to gain access for themselves to the short transportation route through Hudson's Bay. For once, being based in Canada rather than London was a disadvantage, for before they could implement their strategy, the shares in question had been purchased by the new, aggressive owner-managers and their allies.

The HBC managed to transform itself remarkably quickly from a feudal royal monopoly to an effective commercial competitor, and its inherent cost advantage became decisive. The competition continued fiercely and even bloodily for a decade, but by 1820 the NWC essentially was beaten. The competition ended in a merger that nominally treated the two rivals as equals but in fact gave control to the victorious HBC. However, the NWC's aggressive spirit survived in the merged company, which expanded its range of successful operations in the next half century across the Rockies to the Pacific and even to the Hawaiian Islands and Asia. Today, the HBC continues in the fur business, but also is a major real estate firm and the owner of the largest chain of department stores in Canada.

ORGANIZATIONAL STRATEGIES OF MODERN FIRMS

Providing incentives through compensation and ownership was an important element in the NWC's challenge and in the HBC's successful response. Design of the compensation and ownership structure continues to be an important feature of the organizational strategies of modern firms. A current example from the financial-services industry involves some interesting twists.

Salomon Brothers and the Investment Banking Industry

Salomon Brothers is a major investment bank headquartered in New York City. Like many other investment banks, Salomon was originally organized as a partnership, but it became a publicly traded corporation after the partners sold their ownership claims in 1981 to Phillips Brothers, a firm in the commodity-dealing business. In 1984, John Gutfreund, the head of the Salomon subsidiary, became CEO of the parent company, which had been renamed Phibro. The corporate name was subsequently changed to the current Salomon Inc. During the mid-1980s Salomon was reputed to be the most profitable of all the Wall Street investment banks and, on a per employee basis, the most profitable corporation in the world. Its stock sold in the neighborhood of $60 per share.

Investment banking emerged as a separate industry in the United States after 1934, when the Glass-Steagall Act prohibited commercial banks, which accept deposits and make loans, from underwriting securities as they had previously. Investment banks arose to take over the underwriting function.[5] Modern investment banks, including

---

[5] Underwriting the issue of a new security first involves the underwriter's agreeing on a price for the security with the issuing entity. The underwriter pays this price for the security, then markets it to investors. The underwriter thus bears the risk that the security will not be saleable at the agreed price.

Salomon, are involved in two main activities: corporate finance, and sales and trading. The former includes underwriting new securities issued by corporations, governments, and not-for-profits; advising on, helping with, and organizing financing for mergers, acquisitions, divestures, and financial restructurings; and advising on corporate financial policy. Sales and trading involve the trading of financial instruments (stocks, bonds, options, warrants, mortgage-backed securities, and so on) both for resale and for the firm's own investment account, and the sale of these investments to (large) individual investors and institutions.

BOND TRADING AND THE CULTURE OF SALOMON BROTHERS   Salomon Brothers always has been particularly strong in "fixed income" sales and trading. The general public tends to think of Wall Street in terms of buying and selling stocks. However, in the 1980s the real sales and trading action was in bonds, spurred by the volatility of interest rates that marked the period combined with the huge growth of the U.S. government debt and the debts of U.S. corporations and individuals. Because the price of bonds and other securities that pay a fixed rate of interest varies inversely with market interest rates,[6] volatile rates meant that bond prices could swing wildly, creating opportunities for speculation (buying or selling bonds in the hopes of realizing large profits when prices change, but risking comparably huge losses) and arbitrage (the process of buying and selling to make a nominally riskless profit by taking advantage of price disparities between markets or equivalent assets). The growth of indebtedness meant that there were a great many bonds to trade, especially after Salomon traders developed new securities that packaged together home mortgages to form tradable financial instruments. Thus, even before the explosion of "junk bond" activity centered on Michael Milken of the rival investment bank of Drexel Burnham Lambert, huge profits were being made in bond sales and trading. Salomon traders were the leaders in this business.

Bond trading is a frenzied business in which immense sums of money are at risk. Traders will buy hundreds of millions of dollars worth of bonds in a day, acting on very limited information and under extreme time pressures from competition. Each trader has a pair of telephones and spends much of the day with one in each ear, screaming orders. Tiny movements in interest rates and bond prices result in gigantic gains and losses. The risks are monumental, but the profits that come from successful trading are commensurate. The sort of people who are attracted to this work are an especially individualistic, risk-taking, competitive lot. The leaders of the firm, including Gutfreund, are former bond traders, and they have set the style of the corporate culture at Salomon Brothers. In this culture, performance as measured by profits generated is the sole source of power, prestige, status, and respect.[7]

THE PERFORMANCE-PAY SYSTEM   Salomon's compensation system for its employees, from the clerical staff through the approximately 150 managing directors and the more senior executives, involves a base salary plus an annual bonus. The bonus is determined in a fashion that approaches an individual piece-rate system. Almost every transaction is separately priced, with charges for credit risk and overhead, and the resulting profit

---

[6] Consider a bond with a maturity value of $100 that pays $5 in interest per year—a 5 percent rate of interest. Now suppose that interest rates rise to 10 percent, so that newly issued bonds with a maturity value and price of $100 must pay $10 per year in interest. Then investors will be unwilling to pay as much as $100 for the old bond, and its price will fall to a level where it again becomes an attractive investment. For a ten-year bond with a maturity value of $100 to yield 10 percent, its price must fall to $74.28.

[7] This culture is described very entertainingly in the best seller by Michael Lewis, *Liar's Poker* (New York: W. W. Norton & Co., 1989).

is credited to the individuals or departments involved. The individual bonuses then are determined on the basis of performance evaluations in which these calculated profit contributions play a key role. However, the bonus payments actually are negotiated; the bonus is not simply computed by formula from the profit contribution.

Because the bonus payments can be extremely large—million-dollar bonuses are not uncommon and the bonus is commonly two thirds of aggregate earnings—the bonus system is a key incentive device in the firm. This performance-pay system is quite elaborately defined and extensively applied by the standards of most businesses. It has very effectively encouraged Salomon's people to work extremely hard and to take great risks to increase both their own and their departments' profits. By doing so, it has reinforced the firm's fiercely competitive corporate culture.

The system has not, however, encouraged cooperation between departments. For example, if corporate bond traders obtained information that might be valuable to Corporate Finance, they might not bother to pass it on because there was nothing in it for them. It also has caused managing directors to focus excessively on their individual departments and accounts, rather than developing the firm as a whole and building its long-term success. Finally, the performance-pay system has resulted sometimes in highly dysfunctional attempts to "steal" other departments' profits.

STOCK OWNERSHIP   In May 1990 Salomon Brothers attempted to respond to these drawbacks by reforming its bonus scheme. Myron Scholes, a finance professor on leave at the firm from Stanford University, was instrumental in designing the solution.

Under the new scheme, once the individual bonus has been determined, a fixed percentage is withheld and used to buy stock in the firm. This stock is purchased in the open market, so that the capitalization of the firm will be unchanged. The stock then is held in a trust for the employee, who will not be able to withdraw it for five years. In effect, the value of each employee's current bonus is tied to the overall market value of the firm five years in the future. The plan covers all employees, although there are different percentages applied to those at the managing director level and above. It is estimated that in five years the employees will own 20 percent of the firm.

The plan won acceptance because of the incentive effects it embodies. The explicit aims were to change the culture, to encourage a long-run perspective and cooperation, and to align the employees' interests with one another and with those of the stockholder owners. It was also expected that this scheme would influence favorably the type of people who would be attracted to work for Salomon. In the long run, this "self-selection" or "clientele" effect on recruitment and turnover could be very important. Of course, the plan puts a major new element of risk into the employees' personal incomes because they no longer receive cash that they can invest as they choose in a safely diversified portfolio. Instead, they are locked into a single stock whose price might move up or down. One element in the acceptance of the plan was that the company was selling essentially for the book value of its assets at the time the program was introduced; therefore, an upward movement in its stock price was relatively likely. Nevertheless, the firm also attempted to offset the increased risk to some extent by specifying that it would buy 15 percent more stock for the employees' trust than the bonus pool would have generated.

Many companies attempt to provide incentives to employees, and especially to senior executives, through stock ownership. Employees may be allowed to buy stock at a reduced price, and executive bonuses are often paid in stock or in options that give the right to buy the company's stock in the future at a fixed price. Salomon's technique of using the trust helps ensure that the employees will actually hold on to the stock rather than sell it soon after receiving it. The intent is to ensure that employees will be concerned with the firm's long-run performance.[8] The trust also has tax advantages, because any appreciation of the price of the stock that occurs while it is being held in the trust is free of capital gains taxation.[9]

Several years' experience will be needed before we fully can judge the effectiveness of this innovation in compensation. However, the system did pass a key market test: As of 1990, announcement of the plan appeared to have raised the price of the 100 million shares of outstanding Salomon stock by between $1.50 and $2 per share from a base of $21. Thus, the plan raised the market value of the firm by between 7 and 10 percent, and the present value of the firm's profits was estimated to have risen by at least $150 million as a consequence of adopting the plan. Because the plan's direct cost to the firm is, if anything, slightly higher than the original cash-only bonus (because of the promise to buy the extra 15 percent more stock for the trust), investors in the market estimate that the new incentives' effect on revenues will be even greater than the direct profit effect.

THE CHANGING ECONOMIES OF EASTERN EUROPE

Salomon Brothers' pay reforms are an example of experimentation with ownership structure and incentive plans at the level of the individual enterprise. A much more dramatic experiment at a macro level was being carried out in the late 1980s and early 1990s in Eastern Europe, where whole economies were being redesigned.

Recent History

The world was shocked and the Western capitalist democracies were stunned in 1957 when the Union of Soviet Socialist Republics launched Sputnik, the first space satellite, and then quickly followed this triumph by putting the first man in space. Barely a dozen years before, the Soviet Union had emerged from the Second World War having suffered the deaths of 14 million of its citizens, both in battle and through deprivation, and the occupation and destruction of large portions of its territory. Before the war the Soviet economy had been rapidly industrializing under Stalin's Five Year Plans, but the progress was uneven and the Soviet economy was still relatively backward. During the war, the Soviets were forced to depend heavily on food and munitions sent by their allies, especially the United States.

The immediate postwar years saw the outbreak of the Cold War between the Soviet Union and its former allies. This conflict initially went very well for the communist side, with the installation of Soviet-dominated communist regimes in the Eastern European countries occupied by the Red Army and the adoption of communism in China, North Korea, and North Vietnam. Suddenly, the Soviet Union had demonstrated scientific and engineering prowess that seemed to exceed that of the West, and soon the Soviet leader, Nikita Khrushchev, was boasting that the economic might of the Soviet Union would bury the West. Communism, as an alternative to capitalism, not only seemed to enjoy its claims of ethical superiority but also seemed capable of producing remarkable economic progress.

By 1990, however, communism had been rejected as a total failure throughout

---

[8] It is possible, especially for sophisticated investors such as these people, to offset the lock-in effects to some degree by adjusting their portfolios. A simple way would be to sell Salomon stock short, contracting to deliver the stock at a fixed price five years hence. This would lock in a price that the employee would be able to get for the stock in the trust; therefore, the future price of the stock would no longer be of concern. The firm no doubt would be very displeased with an employee who shorted its stock.

[9] If the employee had received the stock outright at the time the bonus was earned, held it for five years, then sold it, the increased value over the period would have been a capital gain and been taxed by the federal (and perhaps the state and local) government.

most of Eastern Europe, and even the Soviet Union itself was struggling to create a market economy after 70 years of communist organization. The system simply had not produced. Living standards had been flat or falling for a decade in the Soviet Union and in most of the members of the Soviet bloc. There were constant shortages of food, housing, and all other sorts of consumer products. As a result, workers, with the implicit consent of their managers, took several hours off each day to wait in line at shops. Luck, influence, and patience were the means by which the available goods were rationed; the money that had to be paid for them was at most a secondary consideration: "We pretend to work, and they pretend to pay us." The goods that were available were relatively expensive, shoddy, and often unsafe. For example, more than 2,000 television sets a year exploded in Moscow alone, causing injuries and fires. Agricultural output, which had grown immensely throughout the rest of the world, had stagnated under state control and collectivization, and the Soviet Union had become dependent on grain imports from the West to feed its people. Meanwhile, Soviet agricultural officials annually blamed the repeated crop failures on yet another year of unusually bad weather.

Communist industry was both technologically backward and monumentally inefficient; measured total factor productivity in Soviet industry actually fell in many major sectors in the decades following the triumph of Sputnik, and Eastern Europe faced the most serious industrial pollution problems in the world. Maintaining the Cold War military competition with the United States and NATO was devouring an immense percentage of the already low Soviet gross national product (GNP), nearly bankrupting the country. Instead of the "workers' paradise" and equality that were promised, communism had delivered a repressive, totalitarian government and institutionalized privileges for the politically favored.

Building Socialism

Soviet communism found its intellectual origin in the writings of Karl Marx, a nineteenth-century classical economist. However, Marx provided no blueprint for organizing an economy along communist lines. For Marx, the triumph of communism was simply foreordained by the inherent contradictions in the capitalist system. The actual task of designing the first communist system fell initially to Nikolai Lenin, the first leader of the Soviet state that emerged after the Revolution of 1917, and then to Joseph Stalin, who ultimately succeeded Lenin and led the Soviet Union from the late 1920s until after the Second World War. It was Stalin's vision that defined the basic form for the Soviet economy: state socialism and central planning under the direction of the Communist Party.

The system that Stalin developed replaced private ownership of the means of production by collective—or, rather, state—ownership of land, buildings, machines, and other capital. Factories belonged to the communist state as representing the proletariat, and individual farms were forcibly socialized into collective farming enterprises. Private business essentially ceased to exist, except on the smallest scale. Workers were guaranteed jobs and had latitude in their career choices, but their mobility was limited and being unemployed became a criminal offense.

Prices were set by the government and left unchanged for extended periods. They therefore bore little or no connection to costs and could not serve to ration demand when shortages appeared. Prices also were not allowed to direct resources to their highest-value uses, increasing supplies of goods where there was shortage and favoring purchases from low-cost producers. Instead, a system of detailed central planning and extensive vertical information flows was instituted to replace the decentralized decision making, horizontal communications, and price-guided coordination that are characteristic of market systems. Central planners in Moscow decided how much of what goods were to be produced in each period by which factories. The plans directed where inputs were to be obtained, where outputs were to go, and what prices were to be paid. Similar systems were instituted in Eastern Europe after the communists gained control there. In Poland at one point even the production of pickled cucumbers and the number of hares that would be shot by hunters were included in the plan, although later the planning was less pervasive. In all cases, investment decisions were centralized, with capital allocated by the state. As circumstances changed and unforeseen contingencies arose that rendered the original plan infeasible, information would be passed up to the central planners who would attempt to redefine the plan and coordinate activities.

The initial intent of the socialist system was to replace economic incentives with political and moral appeals to the workers' patriotism and socialist consciousness. Pay was divorced from supply and demand—"From each according to his abilities, to each according to his needs"—and the aggregate amount of GNP to be devoted to consumer goods was determined by the planners so as to leave enough extra resources to finance the planned investments. However, whether the means of realizing the plan were administrative orders or designed economic incentives, individual self-interest intervened. This led to the sort of difficulties epitomized by the familiar (if possibly apocryphal) story of a factory meeting its target of 10,000 kilograms of nails by producing a single nail weighing 10,000 kilos. Later, when the planning and incentive systems were refined, incentive problems still arose, especially with regard to quality. A worker in a Baltic television manufacturing facility told of the rush at the end of each month to meet production targets and earn bonuses:

> We never use a screwdriver in the last week. We hammer the screws in. We slam solder on the connections, cannibalize parts from other televisions if we run out of the right ones, use glue or hammers to fix switches that were never meant for that model. And all the time the management is pressing us to work faster, to make the target so we all get our bonuses.[10]

The 2,000 exploding televisions a year in Moscow are now understandable.

THE RATCHET EFFECT   A particular incentive problem that proved to be of fundamental importance was the *ratchet effect*. The central planners were never as well informed about the productive capability of any particular factory as were the factory managers. The planners would set targets for input usage and output levels and then use the information gathered from experience to judge what would be possible in future planning periods. Those factories making their quotas were rewarded in various ways; those failing were punished. From the point of view of the factory manager, the incentives inherent in this system were especially perverse. By exceeding the quota this period, the manager could expect to be "rewarded" with a higher quota for the indefinite future, as performance expectations are ratcheted up or raised to a higher level. As a result, there was no reason ever to exceed quota. Instead, the incentives were to meet the quota barely, or even—provided a good excuse were available—deliberately miss it somewhat so that the next period's quota would be lower and easier to meet. In particular, there was an inexorable tendency to hoard resources, to hold back on effort and output, and to underreport capabilities.

These tendencies were intensified by the experience of factories and managers who responded to experiments with stronger and better incentives by increasing production, only to be accused of having defrauded the state before. These perverse

---

[10] Clive Cook, "A Survey of Perestroika," *The Economist*, April 28, 1990, 6.

incentives led to low productivity in the economy. They also burdened the planners with systematically distorted information. The task of planning even the key resource flows in the economy would have been formidable if the information being conveyed was accurate. Huge amounts of information needed to be transferred. Even employing strong simplifying assumptions about the structure of technology, the computational problems were extreme, and the problems of responding to unforeseen, emergent events were overwhelming. The factory managers' misrepresentation of productivity information and their secret hoarding of resources made the task impossible.

Beginning in the 1960s there were many attempts to reform the communist economies. Moves were made towards decentralization designed to give more decision-making authority to local planners and individual factories and to provide better incentives. None of these attempts were truly successful, although Hungary's liberalization moves following 1968 had positive effects.

The Collapse of Communism

The collapse of communism in Eastern Europe was dramatically rapid. There had been a history of worker uprisings and attempted breaks with Moscow—in East Germany and Hungary in the 1950s, in Czechoslovakia in the 1960s, and in Poland in the late 1970s and early 1980s. All had been more or less successfully squashed, often with the use of Soviet troops. Then in 1989 and 1990, within a single year following signals from Soviet leader Mikhail Gorbachev that the Soviet Union would no longer intervene in the internal affairs of the Eastern European countries, noncommunist governments appeared, the Berlin Wall came down and travel restrictions were removed, independent presses evolved, multiparty elections were held and capitalist-oriented parties were elected, communist parties were disbanded or re-formed as socialist parties, East and West Germany were united under the West German model, and experiments in moving to market economies began in the other Eastern European countries. These changes were most radical in Poland, which quite simply decided to restructure itself as a free-enterprise economy as soon as possible.

In the Soviet Union Gorbachev's policies of *Glasnost* (openness) and *Perestroika* (restructuring) were originally meant simply to reform communism and make it work better.[11] Even with these intentions, the policies met strong resistance from the entrenched party functionaries and bureaucrats. On the other side, "radicals" and noncommunists won election victories and began exerting pressure for the elimination of communism and its replacement by a market system.

THE CHALLENGES OF ADOPTING A MARKET SYSTEM   These economies face great problems in moving to more market-oriented systems. They must determine property rights and decide who will be allowed to own the currently state-owned enterprises, how title will be transferred, and what prices will be charged. They must set up capital markets and create banking, financial, and monetary systems. They have to design meaningful accounting systems so that firms can be valued and their performances judged. They need to redraft their laws to allow for new forms of economic organizations, new patterns of ownership, and new sorts of transactions. They have to find managers who can operate in a market system and compete in a world market.

---

[11] George Shultz, the former U.S. Secretary of State, is reported to have been told by his Soviet counterpart, Edvard Schevardnadze, that the Chernobyl nuclear reactor accident made the Soviet leadership more fully appreciate the need for Glasnost. The Kremlin leaders were unable to get reliable, timely information on the crisis through their bureaucratic channels. Instead they found that the Cable News Network (CNN) broadcasting by satellite from the United States was their best source of information on a major event in their own country. This drove home to top government leaders that their closed system had to be opened up for the benefit of the country.

They have to educate their populations to the new rules of the game and gain acceptance for these rules. They must decide on competition and regulatory policies and find a way to deal with the fact that simply privatizing the giant, inefficient state firms will yield a system of giant, inefficient private monopolies. They must decide how much to wean their industries from state subsidies and develop tax systems to finance government activities. They have to decide whether and when uncompetitive firms will be allowed to fail and create social-service and support systems to handle the human costs of the dislocations that their economies are sure to face, both during and after the transition.

The great difficulty in all this is that these tasks are all interdependent and in need of coordination. Private enterprise will not work without the discipline of potential failure. Output markets are of no use without input markets, including ones for capital, through which producers can obtain the resources they need. Neither of these are of much value without well-defined property rights and mechanisms for contract enforcement. All the parts have to come together and fit reasonably well for the system to work. The worst outcome might be some halfway compromise. Consider the joke told in response to criticisms that Poland's "cold-turkey" foreswearing of communism and adoption of free enterprise is too much, too soon: It was decided in a certain country to change the side of the road on which traffic drove from the left to the right, but there was concern about making too radical and rapid a switch; so as an experiment only the trucks changed sides for the first year.

PATTERNS OF ORGANIZATIONAL SUCCESS AND FAILURE

Henry Ford's account of organization missed the mark. The study of organization is not about how berries are arranged on a tree of authority but about how people are coordinated and motivated to get things done.

In these few, brief historical accounts, several patterns have begun to emerge. First, and most fundamentally, organization and business strategy can be as important as technology, cost, and demand in determining a firm's success. Despite its superior technology, greater resources, and scale advantages, Ford Motor Company under Henry Ford's management lost its battle with Alfred Sloan's General Motors. General Motors, in turn, lost market share to a smaller and technologically weaker Toyota, which labored under the same kinds of disadvantages. The Hudson's Bay Company suffered many defeats in its competition with the fledgling North West Company. The successful competitors in these stories gained advantage partly from the strategies they adopted in their markets, but a large part of their advantage also came from their innovative organizational structures and policies and especially from the match of their strategies and their structures.

Which aspects of organization matter? In these examples, incentives are one important element. The Hudson's Bay Company employees were not much inclined to show initiative and judgment when they could be flogged for their errors but got no share of any extra profits they earned for the company. At General Motors in 1920, the failure to charge divisions for the cost of the inventories they accumulated was responsible for a huge inventory build-up leading to a financial crisis. Salomon Brothers, with its many independently operating traders, originally had the incentives partly right. However, its emphasis on individual performance evaluation discouraged employees from cooperating and from sharing information with one another. Finally, the communist countries, with their ideological commitment to economic equality, ran afoul of incentives at every turn.

Another important shared feature of successful organizations in these examples is the tendency to place authority for decisions in the hands of those with information. Salomon Brothers, with two telephones and enormous discretion in the hands of its traders, is an extreme example. General Motors, with its multidivisional organization, placed product and marketing decisions in the hands of divisional managers. Toyota's decision to give responsibility and authority for machine repair and maintenance to those who operate the machines led to improved reliability. And the North West Company gained advantage over its larger competitor by operating as a partnership with the wintering partners in the field making timely decisions based on up-to-date information about local market conditions.

Although delegating authority to those with the information needed to make good decisions is an important part of good organization design, it is of little use unless the decision makers share the organization's objectives. We have already mentioned incentives as a way to align individual and organizational objectives. The additional point we want to make here is that incentives are especially important when more initiative is expected from employees. The same point, viewed from a different angle, is that delegation of authority is much more valuable when those being empowered have also been given incentives to work for the organization's objectives. It is no accident that the North West Company both relied on the judgments made by traders in the wilderness and made them partners who shared in the profits. Nor is it an accident that the traders at Salomon Brothers whose decisions can have a multimillion-dollar effect on the company's holdings are provided with both information and the incentive to use it well. Similarly, in Eastern Europe, giving more discretion to factory managers without also providing for decentralized ownership could not resolve the problems.

In the language of economics, incentives and delegated authority are *complements*: each makes the other more valuable. Evaluating complementarities—how the pieces of a successful organization fit together and how they fit with the company's strategy—is one of the most challenging and rewarding parts of organizational analysis. In our General Motors example, the reason for the multidivisional structure was to carry out Sloan's new market-segmentation strategy. The delegation of decisions to divisional managers was also combined with improved accounting information to help evaluate those decisions and with coordination from the central office to ensure that the parts of the organization were not working at cross purposes. At Toyota, an organization based on very low inventories was naturally vulnerable to disruptions at any stage in the production process and to simple changes in plans. If low inventories were to be achieved, the rest of the organization had to emphasize reliability, quick response to machine breakdowns, quick and close communications with suppliers, stable production plans, and other features that substitute for the buffer function of inventories. Toyota's emphasis on reliability fit with an emphasis on quality in its marketing, and its use of flexible equipment, necessitated by its initially small scale, fit well with its more frequent redesign of its several models.

In this book, our economic analysis of organizations is based on elaborating the several ideas that these brief histories suggest. We study **coordination**: what needs to be coordinated, how coordination is achieved in markets and inside firms, what the alternatives are to close coordination between units, and how the pieces of the system fit together. We also study **incentives** and **motivation**: what needs to be motivated, why incentives are needed and how they are provided in markets and firms, what alternative kinds of incentive systems are possible and what needs to be done to make incentive systems effective. In the last chapters, we see in more detail why these aspects of organization do matter, when we apply the principles to make a detailed study of a few important functions of the business enterprise.

EXERCISES

1.   In fast-food chains, some decisions about standards are made centrally and others are left to the individual outlet managers. Who typically makes which kinds of decisions? Why? Can you think successfully about the fast-food business by dividing the issues between coordination and motivation?

2.   Armies in battle have especially severe organization problems. What kinds of decisions are made centrally and which are left to commanders in the field? What principles dictate the division? Can you think successfully about the problems of military organization by dividing the issues between coordination and motivation?

3.   In late summer of 1991, it was revealed that beginning in February of that year, the Salomon Brothers' managing director in charge of its dealings in the markets for U.S. Treasury securities had secretly violated government rules designed to prevent any one buyer from purchasing more than a specified share of the new government debt obligations being auctioned at any one time. Moreover, senior executives at the firm had learned of these violations of the law but had failed to act on them. In the resulting scandal, four of Salomon's top executives (including Gutfreund) were asked to resign, and the future of the firm was imperiled.

One theory was that the employee who violated the rules was motivated by his competitive, aggressive nature: He bitterly resented the government's attempt to limit his actions and was determined to show them that he was smarter and tougher than they. Another was that he was motivated by greed: He wanted to monopolize the market in these government bonds and reap the rewards. In any case, his actions, and those of the senior executives who failed to stop him and report his wrong-doing, were very costly to the firm: The stock price, which had risen by almost a half in the preceding year, fell back to where it had been before, and important customers ceased dealing with the firm.

Does this episode mean that the incentive scheme described in the text was fundamentally flawed?

2

ECONOMIC ORGANIZATION AND EFFICIENCY

*[People] in general, and within limits, wish to behave economically, to make their activities **and their organization** "efficient" rather than wasteful.*

Frank Knight[1]

This book is concerned with the problems of designing and managing efficient economic organizations. The preceding chapter gives examples of the range of problems and institutions that we are considering. We now explore the source and nature of these problems and the approach we take to analyzing them.

ECONOMIC ORGANIZATIONS: A PERSPECTIVE

Economic organizations are created entities within and through which people interact to reach individual and collective economic goals. The economic system consists of a network of people and organizations, with lower-level organizations linked together through higher-level organizations.

The highest-level organization is the economy as a whole. While it is somewhat unusual to think of an entire economy as an organization, this perspective is useful because it emphasizes that the economic system is a human creation and because many of the problems that smaller, more formal organizations face exist at the economy-wide level as well. As an organization, an economy can and should be

---

[1] "Review of Melville J. Herskovits' 'Economic Anthropology,'" *Journal of Political Economy*, 49 (April 1941), 246–258, quoted by Oliver Williamson in "Mergers, Acquisitions, and Leveraged Buyouts: An Efficiency Assessment," Working Paper Series D, Economics of Organization, no. 30, Yale University School of Organization and Management (1987). (Emphasis added by Williamson.)

evaluated based on its performance relative to possible alternative arrangements. The current experiments in thoroughgoing reform of entire economic systems in Eastern Europe are prime examples of the importance of this perspective.

Formal Organizations

At the next level are the entities more traditionally regarded as organizations and the ones that are our main concern: corporations, partnerships, sole proprietorships, labor unions, government agencies, universities, churches, and other formal organizations. A key characteristic of the organizations at this level is their independent legal identity, which enables them to enter binding contracts, to seek court enforcement of those contracts, and to do so in their own name, separate from the individuals who belong to the organization.

ORGANIZATIONS AND CONTRACTING   This ability to enter contracts is critical to one of the major approaches to the economic analysis of organizations. In this view, which was first suggested by Armen Alchian and Harold Demsetz, an organization is regarded as a **nexus of contracts**, treaties, and understandings among the individual members of the organization. The firm itself is then a legal fiction that enters relatively simple, bilateral contracts between itself and its suppliers, workers, investors, managers, and customers. Without a legal entity that can contract with them individually, these people would have to fashion complex, multilateral agreements among themselves to achieve their aims.

The contracting approach to organization theory emphasizes the voluntary nature of people's involvement in (most) organizations: People will give their allegiance only to an organization that serves their interests. Furthermore, along with the ability to enter contracts come the possibilities for reform, redesign, and abandonment of the organization by rearranging contractual terms. This approach also facilitates accepting the fuzziness of organizational boundaries and the fact that organizational forms blend together. Markets and hierarchies—sometimes regarded as the major discrete alternative ways of organizing economic activity—are actually just two extreme forms of organizational contracting, with voluntary bargaining characterizing markets and strict lines of authority characterizing hierarchy.

THE ARCHITECTURE OF ORGANIZATIONS   Although the legal aspects of organization are important, a full description of organizational architecture involves many more elements: the patterns of resource and information flows, the authority and control relationships and the distribution of effective power, the allocation of responsibilities and decision rights, organizational routines and decision-making processes, the methods for attracting and retaining members and resources, the means by which new ideas and knowledge are generated and diffused throughout the organization, the adaptation of the organization's routines to reflect and implement organizational learning, the organization's expressed objectives and the strategies and tactics employed, and the means used to unify the goals and behavior of the individual members of the organization and the objectives of the organization as a whole. Various parts of our analysis focus on each of these and on how the pieces fit together to yield a coherent pattern.

Once our focus becomes the elements of organizational architecture, defining a formal organization simply by its ability to contract as a distinct legal entity can become quite inappropriate because it can easily misidentify the effective boundaries of the organization. Consider, for example, the Sony company, which is known for its innovative consumer electronics products, but also manufactures broadcast equipment, computer components, and semiconductors and owns one of the three largest record companies in the world (Sony Records, formerly CBS Records) and a major movie and television production and distribution operation (Columbia Pictures Entertainment). Sony in fact consists of the Sony Corporation, the parent organization based in Tokyo, plus subsidiary corporations around the world. Each of these subsidiaries is a separate legal entity able to enter contracts on its own, and being an employee of Sony Corporation of America or of Sony GmbH in Germany does not make one an employee of Sony Corporation. Thus, the legal-entity approach might point to viewing each subsidiary as a separate organization. Yet this accords neither with the way the world sees Sony nor with the way it sees itself and manages its affairs.

DISCRETION AND AUTONOMY FROM INTERVENTION   In these circumstances, a useful way to look at the defining boundaries of an organization is in terms of the smallest unit that is **functionally autonomous** in that it is largely free from intervention by outside parties in its affairs and decisions, over which it then enjoys broad internal discretion. Within a firm, the rightful decision makers—usually senior management—collectively have broad legal rights to order that activities be conducted as they see fit and to require that their directives be followed. Private outside parties cannot countermand these orders. Courts and government regulators may be able to intervene in some ways, but the discretion of even these public agencies is generally limited. They cannot interfere except under prescribed conditions, and then the measures they can take are limited compared to those that are available within the firm.

Using this approach, the companies that make up Sony constitute a single organization, even though they are separate legal entities. The senior managers of Sony Corporation have the power to intervene largely as they wish in the operations of the subsidiaries, even if they in fact rarely choose to do so. Thus, the subsidiaries are not separate organizations by this test. Meanwhile, no outside private party has the legal right to specify how Sony will be run, what products it will make, what prices it will charge, what pay and job assignments it will offer, how it will divide its activities among its subunits, what investments it will make, and so on. Thus, Sony stands as a separate organization.

The Level of Analysis: Transactions and Individuals

The most fundamental unit of analysis in economic organization theory is the **transaction**—the transfer of goods or services from one individual to another. The way a transaction is organized depends on certain of its characteristics. For example, if one kind of transaction occurs frequently in similar ways, people develop routines to manage it effectively. If a transaction is unusual, then the parties may need to bargain about its terms, which raises the costs of carrying out the transaction.

The ultimate participants in transactions are individual human beings, and their interests and behavior are of fundamental importance for understanding organizations. People are fundamental first in the sense of being indivisible decision makers and actors; it is people—not organizations—who actually decide, vote, or act. The actions of individuals determine the behavior and performance of organizations. Furthermore, only the needs, wants, and objectives of individuals have ethical significance. Economic organizations are judged only on the basis of how well they serve people's intended purposes. Finally, it is people who ultimately create and manage organizations, judge their performance, and redesign or reject them if this performance is found inadequate.

In analyzing how organizations emerge, how they are structured, how they function, and how economic activity is divided among them, we adopt the position put forward in the opening quotation: that people will seek to achieve efficiency in more than just the day-to-day conduct of their economic affairs. Efficiency also must exist at a systemic level, in the organization of people's activities and in the design, management, and governance of the institutions they create. Before we explore this position more fully, we need to be more precise about what we mean by *efficiency*.

EFFICIENCY

The goal of any economic organization, including the economic system as a whole, is to satisfy the wants and needs of individual human beings. We judge economic performance in terms of this goal. This approach does not imply an exclusive concern with materialistic achievement. If military dominance or national prestige is the priority, then an economy that serves these goals could be performing well by our standards. If the population were united in believing that the purpose of all human activity should be to glorify the deity, then an economic system that supported this consecration would be a good one. For purposes of our discussion, however, we assume that people primarily are concerned with regular economic goods and services. The economic system then is judged on how well it satisfies the economic needs of the population.

This approach obviously requires that we ascribe preferences to individuals. Indeed, we assume that people are equipped with measures of their welfare (called *utility functions*), that they like one situation better than another if and only if it gives greater utility, and that their economic goal is to maximize this measure of satisfaction. We explore this assumption in more detail later in the chapter.

The problem of scarcity, however, means that trade-offs typically have to be made. Increasing the utility of one person may mean having to give less to another. How then are we to measure performance? What does it mean to consider how well peoples' interests are served when these interests are possibly in conflict?

The Concept of Efficiency

The partial solution is to focus on **efficient** choices or options, by which we mean ones for which *there is no available alternative that is universally preferred in terms of the goals and preferences of the people involved*. More precisely, if individuals are sometimes indifferent about some of the available options, then a choice is efficient if there is no other available option that everyone in the relevant group likes as least as much and at least one person strictly prefers. Turning the definition around, a choice is *inefficient* when there is an alternative possible choice that would help one person without harming any other.

Note well that the efficiency criterion can never be applied to resolve ethical questions about when it is justified or worthwhile to help one person at another's expense. In some situations, such questions cannot be avoided, but efficiency will not help. Instead, appeals to other criteria that explicitly trade off one individual's welfare against another's are needed.

Note too that the efficiency or inefficiency of a choice is always relative to some specific set of individuals whose interests are being taken into account and also to some specific set of available options. This is important to remember. It is distinctly possible that a particular choice from a given set of alternatives will be efficient relative to the interests of a given group of people, but not when some larger affected group is considered. Similarly, a choice may be efficient when all the constraints that delimit the set of available options are recognized, but not when the removal of some of these makes more options available. Thus, in applying the concept of efficiency it is necessary to be clear about whose interests are counted and what alternatives are considered to be feasible.

Efficiency of Resource Allocations

Efficiency can be defined and applied at many levels, depending on the kind of choice being considered. Our first application—and the most common one in economic analysis—is to compare alternative allocations of resources. An allocation of resources A is inefficient if there is some other available allocation B that everyone concerned likes at least as well as A and that one person strictly prefers. (In this case the allocation A is sometimes said to be *Pareto dominated*[2] by allocation B.) An inefficient allocation is wasteful: by making better use of the available resources it would be possible to make some people better off without hurting anyone else. If, on the other hand, no allocation exists that is unanimously preferred to A, then the given allocation A is efficient (or *Pareto optimal*). An efficient allocation of resources is thus one such that there is no other available allocation that makes someone better off without making another person worse off.

Although the reasons for wanting an efficient allocation of resources are obvious, efficiency by itself is a weak performance criterion. First, there are typically many efficient allocations of a given collection of resources. Therefore, requiring efficiency does not pin down a unique outcome. However, we see later that under certain conditions, efficiency is a good predictor because it then implies sharp restrictions on the choices that can be made. Second, having all the potential benefits of economic activity go to an insatiable, completely selfish person would be efficient because any reallocation of resources would hurt this person and so could not gain unanimous support. Thus, to note that an allocation is efficient is hardly to recommend it on ethical grounds!

However weak efficiency may be as a predictor or as an ethical criterion, actually achieving efficient allocations is extremely demanding. At a macro level, not only must all goods be produced at the lowest possible cost, but the right mix of outputs must be forthcoming, the right levels of savings and investment must be provided, and, in general, there must be no way to increase consumer satisfaction by any reallocation of society's resources. The task of computing an efficient allocation for a complex modern economy is clearly beyond the limits of feasibility. Even with only two people, it may be impossible to determine whether there is any way of rearranging their activities to help one without hurting the other.

Moreover, even if an efficient allocation has been identified, it also is necessary to ensure that the people involved do their parts in bringing it about. The problem is that there often will be inefficient allocations that are better for one person or subgroup than is the target efficient allocation, and these people may be able to effect the inefficient outcome that they prefer.[3] Despite this difficulty, efficiency is both an important device for organizing ideas and a useful criterion for evaluating performance.

Efficiency of Organizations

Efficiency of outcomes or allocations is not, however, the key concept for the study of organizations. Instead, we are concerned about the efficiency of the organizations themselves. We assume that the fundamental objects that people care about are the

---

[2] Vilfredo Pareto was an Italian economist and sociologist who is credited with developing this criterion for problems with multiple objectives.

[3] There will necessarily be a third allocation that is efficient and that Pareto dominates the inefficient one; otherwise, the latter would actually be efficient. However, as we will see, identifying and reaching this efficient allocation may be a problem.

outcomes the organizations generate, and that organizations are to be judged on the basis of these outcomes. There are, however, several ways to do this.

A simple way is to make the comparison outcome by outcome. Consider two contracts, routines, decision processes, organizations, or economic systems, say X and Y, which both might be used in a variety of circumstances. Suppose that, in each such circumstance, Y always yields outcomes that are viewed by all the people involved as being at least as good as those that X produces, and that sometimes Y yields results that at least one person definitely prefers to the outcome under X. In this case, X is inefficient because Y does better. In contrast, a contract, routine, process, organization, or system is efficient in this sense if there is no alternative that consistently yields unanimously preferred results. In particular, an organization that always yields efficient outcomes is itself efficient.

This outcome-by-outcome comparison of organizations is quite demanding: To declare an organization inefficient, there must be another that would do better in every possible circumstance. Consequently, the resulting notion of efficiency is weak because it is easy to pass the test of not having a better alternative. Thus, there might be many efficient organizations using this criterion. Later we refine the efficiency notion, for example, by specifying that an organization is inefficient if there is another that does better for each person on average across the circumstances in which the organization operates. Such specifications narrow the class of organizations that meet the test of efficiency. Because it is now easier to find another mechanism that is unanimously preferred, it becomes more difficult to pass the test of there not being a preferred mechanism.

Regardless of which specification we employ, if achieving efficiency of allocations is problematic, realizing the systemic efficiency of organizations clearly is even more demanding. However, the notion of efficiency still provides a key organizing principle.

Efficiency as a Positive Principle

So far, we have emphasized efficiency as a normative concept, a criterion by which group decisions—including both resource allocation decisions and organization structure decisions—are to be evaluated. However, the quotation at the beginning of this chapter points in another direction. If people seek efficiency in their activities and in the ways they arrange their affairs, then efficiency can become a positive concept, with explanatory and predictive power, as well as a normative, prescriptive one.

There is good reason to expect that people will seek out and settle upon efficient choices. After all, by the definition of efficiency, if an inefficient situation is reached, then someone could propose an alternative that everyone would prefer. If the parties can bargain together effectively and can effectively implement and enforce any agreements they reach, they should be able to realize these gains. Inefficient decisions, whether about resource allocations or organizational arrangements, are thus always vulnerable to being overturned. Efficient arrangements are much less vulnerable because any proposal to change an efficient arrangement will always be opposed by someone. For this reason, we expect to find inefficient arrangements being supplanted over time, while efficient ones survive. We summarize this argument in the following efficiency principle.

> **The Efficiency Principle:** If people are able to bargain together effectively and can effectively implement and enforce their decisions, then the outcomes of economic activity will tend to be efficient (at least for the parties to the bargain).

Much of our analysis of organizations is based on the efficiency principle. We try to understand existing arrangements as efficient choices, and we interpret changes in these arrangements as efficiency-enhancing responses to changes in the environment within which the arrangements exist.

In pursuing this agenda, it is important to keep in mind the qualifications that bargaining, implementation, and enforcement should be effective. A major focus of the analysis in this book is the task of giving specific meaning to the notions of effective bargaining, implementation, and enforcement, and of identifying and analyzing conditions under which these premises might or might not be expected to hold. What factors influence the possibility and likelihood of efficient bargaining? What factors promote or impede implementation of plans and enforcement of bargains? The answers to these questions provide much of the basis for understanding actual arrangements and for analyzing possible changes.

In using efficiency as a positive concept for predictive purposes, it is especially important to be clear about the set of individuals whose interests are being taken into account in determining economic arrangements. (Recall that efficiency is always defined relative to a specific set of individuals and options.) Suppose a large group of people might be affected by some choice, but only a relatively small subgroup of them are able to communicate with one another effectively, and that they alone can reach agreements and implement and enforce them. Then the appropriate concept for predicting what arrangements will be chosen is efficiency relative to the small, effective group. The interests of people who do not take part in the decision about what choices are made are unlikely to be fully reflected in the choices. For normative, valuative purposes, efficiency relative to the larger group may still be an appropriate criterion, but it is unlikely to be predictively powerful.

THE TASKS OF COORDINATION AND MOTIVATION

A fundamental observation about the economic world is that people can produce more if they cooperate, specializing in their productive activities and then transacting with one another to acquire the actual goods and services they desire. The problem of organization then arises because when people are specialized producers who need to trade, their decisions and actions need to be coordinated to achieve these gains of cooperation, and the people must be motivated to carry out their parts of the cooperative activity. Both the existence of formal organizations and the specific details of their structures, policies, and procedures reflect attempts to achieve efficiency in coordination and motivation.

Specialization

Adam Smith's famous example of the pin factory vividly shows the benefits of cooperation and specialization and the corresponding need for coordination. Smith described how in his time (the late eighteenth century) the various stages of pin manufacturing were carried out by different people, each of whom specialized in a single task—pulling the wire, straightening it, cutting it to appropriate lengths, sharpening the point, attaching the head, and packaging the finished product—and how the resulting volume of output was many times greater than it would have been if each person involved had done all the stages alone. The crucial point, however, is that such specialization requires coordination. A single person producing pins alone turns out something useful. The time and efforts of the specialists are wasted unless they can be sure that both the people at each of the preceding stages are doing their parts in generating semifinished materials in the appropriate amounts and in a timely way, and that those at the latter stages of manufacturing are prepared to take what the people before have produced and turn it into a finished product.

The principles of specialization and coordination apply both to small, simple economies and to large, complex ones. Robinson Crusoe did not face a coordination problem when he was alone on his desert island, but once Friday entered the story, there were opportunities for gain through specialization and exchange. This meant there was also a need to coordinate the two men's actions to ensure that all the necessary tasks were done and that they were not needlessly repeated by both Crusoe and Friday. In a modern economy, the variety of tasks that are carried out is unfathomably complex. Somehow, each of these jobs must be accomplished, in the appropriate amounts, using the appropriate methods, at the right time, in the right order, and by the right numbers of the right people. Coordinating the billions of people and their choices among the infinite possibilities facing them is a mind-boggling problem. Moreover, even if a solution were somehow found that was reasonably well adapted to currently prevailing conditions, the problem would not be solved once and for all. Conditions at every imaginable level and on every possible dimension are constantly changing, and adaptation to these changes is necessary.

The Need for Information

A key problem in achieving effective coordination and adaptation is that the information needed to determine the best use of resources and the appropriate adaptations is not freely available to everyone. Efficient choice requires information about individual tastes, technological opportunities, and resource availabilities. No single person in society has all—or even a significant fraction—of the needed information. Instead, information is localized and dispersed throughout the economy. Even if the relevant information were generally available, determining what should be produced, for whom, by whom, and using what methods and materials is an overwhelmingly large and complex problem. Because this information is localized and dispersed, however, no one has the knowledge needed to make these calculations, even if they might be feasible in principle.

Two solutions are possible. Either the dispersed information must be transmitted to a central computer or planner who is expected to solve the resource-allocation problem, or else a more decentralized system must be developed that involves less information transmission and, correspondingly, leaves at least some of the calculations and decisions about economic activity to those with whom the relevant information resides. The trick with the first option is to make timely decisions while keeping the costs of communication and computation from absorbing all the available resources. The challenge of decentralization is to ensure that the separately made decisions yield a coherent, coordinated result.

Organizational Methods for Achieving Coordination

Different organizational structures achieve coordination in different ways and with differing results. As we discuss in Chapter 1, the original strategy of the Hudson's Bay Company was overly centralized. As a result, decisions were not timely and the company made poor use of local information. In contrast, the structure of General Motors was initially overly decentralized, and the company suffered from a consequent lack of coordination. In the case of Smith's pin factory, the solution was a single firm whose owner-manager specialized in providing coordination. He or she hired workers and assigned them to the different tasks, set the levels at which each was to perform, tracked performance and the external environment, and adjusted plans as needed. This individual also probably owned the capital equipment that was being used, collected the sales revenues, and paid the bills. Another solution might have been a cooperative of pinmakers, where the workers would jointly have decided on the levels of activity and the task definitions and assignments and would then have shared in the costs and revenues they generated. The older, highly decentralized system of individual craftsmen, each producing pins alone, sacrificed the gains from specialization but reduced the need for coordination. Yet another solution would have been to organize each stage of production as a separate firm and let the transactions between stages be intermediated by the market. This last alternative may sound far-fetched if we picture the person at each stage in the pin factory as a separate firm, buying input from the person/firm on one side and selling output to the next person/firm in the production line. However, the striking differences between GM and Toyota in their reliance on independent suppliers (see Chapter 1) indicate that this kind of alternative is genuine. Finally, within some modern corporations, products are sold by one division to another using *transfer prices*, and the division managers are judged on their individual division's profitability. With this system, the firm's internal organization mimics the market in many ways.

COORDINATION THROUGH A SYSTEM OF MARKETS AND PRICES   A thoroughgoing use of the market is one possible solution to the problem of coordinating economic activity. At the extreme, all transactions could be between separate individuals on an arm's-length basis, and there would be no firms or other organizations apart from the market system itself. The opposite extreme would be complete elimination of the price system under a regime of explicit central planning, with all decisions being made within a single (presumably multilevel) organization. Of course, no economic system approaches either extreme. Even in their most centralized versions, the centrally planned communist economies left many decisions to individual consumers who made their choices in part in response to prices. The market economies feature firms that interact with one another through markets but within which activity is explicitly coordinated through plans and hierarchical structures.

In fact, the system of markets and prices is often a remarkably effective mechanism for achieving coordination. Day in and day out, without any conscious central direction, it induces people to employ their talents and resources so effectively that the shortages and rationing which are familiar to residents of planned economies are deemed newsworthy events when they occur in market economies. As a practical matter, the advantages of the market system over socialist planned economies seem clear.

As we see in the next chapter, it is even possible to argue formally that no system can solve the coordination problem more effectively than a system of markets coordinated by prices. A mathematical model is used to show that in economies with certain characteristics, the allocations generated by a price system are always efficient for society as a whole. Moreover, under certain conditions, the price system achieves this result while economizing on information demands—the system requires transmitting less information than any other system capable of ensuring efficient outcomes (see Chapter 4). In an ideally functioning system of markets, all that anyone needs to know is his or her own capabilities and tastes and the prevailing prices. There is no need to transmit detailed information about preferences, technological possibilities, resource availabilities, and the like that would be needed to achieve a centralized solution because the prices summarize all the relevant information. Furthermore, when conditions change, detailed local knowledge of these changes need not be transmitted to achieve effective responses. Instead, the changes in prices again convey all the information that is actually needed for people to respond effectively.

INCENTIVES IN MARKETS   The strength of a market system with private property lies not just in its providing the information needed to compute an efficient allocation of resources in an efficient manner, however. At least equally important is the manner in which it accepts individually self-interested behavior, but then channels this behavior in desired directions. People do not have to be cajoled, artificially induced, or forced to do their parts in a well-functioning market system. Instead, they are simply left to pursue their own objectives as they see fit. Yet, at least in the right circumstances (which we explore in Chapter 3), people are led by Adam Smith's "invisible hand" of impersonal market forces to take the actions needed to achieve an efficient, coordinated pattern of choices. Workers, selfishly attempting to maximize their own individual welfare, are led to select the training, careers, and jobs where their talents and energy are most valuable. Producers, pursuing only private profits, are led to develop the goods and services on which consumers put the highest values and to produce these goods and services at the lowest possible costs. The owners of resources and capital assets, seeking only to increase their own wealth, are led to deploy these assets in socially desirable ways. Finally, consumers, seeking only to satisfy their individual wants and needs, are led to do so in the way that puts the least strain on society's resources for the level of satisfaction achieved.

All of this is based on a particular theory of markets, which posits that competition is ubiquitous, firms have little market power, and the only goods that are of significance are those that are traded in active markets. The incentives provided by real markets do not always align so nicely with the realization of social objectives. Large firms or cartels may set prices inefficiently high, leading to inefficient resource allocations. Externalities and missing markets for some goods may lead to additional distortions. The quality of goods may be hard to verify, leading some consumers to make mistakes in their choice of goods and some firms to neglect quality control in the hopes that their actions will go unnoticed. As we see in the examples of Chapter 1, similar failings plague other forms of organization as well. Organizations either must rely on individuals to ignore their own self-interests, with unsurprisingly disappointing results, or else they must devote ingenuity and resources to bring coherence between individual self-interest and the social or organizational objectives.

For example, Salomon Brothers' complex system of attributing profits and paying bonuses linked to performance is an attempt to generate within the firm the sort of incentives that are provided automatically by the market. The transferring of partial ownership to the employees is intended to give them the incentives that owners have in order to care about the long-term value of their asset, the firm. The manager and workers in the Soviet factory that produced the single gigantic nail were responding to inappropriate incentives. Their jobs were made easiest by adopting a socially wasteful production plan, and their incentives were to minimize their efforts while meeting their poorly specified quota. Such a gross inefficiency would never arise in a market system, although, as we see in later chapters, more subtle difficulties can be expected.

TRANSACTION COSTS ANALYSIS

If markets can perform so well, why then do we so often see the price system supplanted, with economic activity being organized within and among formal hierarchical structures using explicit planning and directives? More simply, why are there firms? What is their economic function? And what determines which transactions are mediated through markets and which are brought within a formal organization and made under centralized direction?

These fundamental questions were first posed by Ronald Coase. According to Coase, there are costs to carrying out transactions, and these **transaction costs** differ depending on both the nature of the transaction and on the way that it is organized. Furthermore, as suggested by the efficiency principle, the tendency is to adopt the organizational mode that best economizes on these transaction costs. Thus, transactions tend to occur in the market when doing so is most efficient, and they are brought within the firm or some other formal organization when doing so minimizes the costs of carrying them out.

This is a simple, but profound, idea. However, Coase was not very explicit about the origin and nature of these transaction costs, and without a systematic understanding of these issues, the idea is not very useful. Consequently, much of the research in the economics of organization has been devoted to giving substance and content to his idea. In fact, transaction costs are the costs of running the system: the costs of coordinating and of motivating. Thus, under the hypothesis that organizational structure and design are determined by minimizing transaction costs, both aspects of the organization problem affect the allocation of activity among organizational forms.

Types of Transaction Costs

Different organizational forms and institutional and contractual arrangements represent different solutions to the problems of coordination and motivation. These problems give rise to transaction costs, which manifest themselves differently in different contexts.

COORDINATION COSTS   Under a market system, transaction costs associated with the coordination problem arise from the need to determine prices and other details of the transaction, to make the existence and location of potential buyers and sellers known to one another, and to bring the buyers and sellers together to transact.

As an example of these coordination costs, think about the problem of exchanging financial assets such as stocks and bonds. These transactions mostly take place through organized financial exchanges, like the New York, London, and Tokyo stock exchanges. Very few markets function more efficiently than the organized financial markets, and yet the amount of resources absorbed in their operation is clearly significant. Large buildings, immense communication and computational power, and the talents of thousands of gifted people are employed in setting prices and carrying out transactions. If the often breathtaking incomes of investment bankers and security dealers are any indication of the social costs involved in employing them in this industry, the transaction costs of running these markets are very large.

In other markets, transaction costs associated with coordination include the resources that sellers expend on market research to determine buyers' tastes, on advertising and marketing expenditures to make the product or service known, and on managerial decisions determining the prices to charge. On the buyers' side, they also include the time spent searching for suppliers and for the best prices. More subtly, the transaction costs also include the lost benefits that are not realized because the matching of buyers and sellers is imperfect and worthwhile transactions fail to occur.

The transaction costs of coordination through hierarchies—whether private or governmental—are primarily the costs of transmitting up through the hierarchy the initially dispersed information that is needed to determine an efficient plan, using the information to determine the plan to be implemented, and then communicating the plan to those responsible for implementing it. These costs include not only the direct costs of compiling and transmitting information, but also the time costs of delay while the communication is taking place and while the center is determining the plan. Because this communication can never be perfect, there are also transaction costs of maladaptation that occur because decision makers have only insufficient or inaccurate information.

MOTIVATION COSTS   The transaction costs associated with the motivation problem are primarily of two kinds. The first type of costs are those associated with **informational**

incompleteness and asymmetries—situations in which the parties to a potential or actual transaction do not have all the relevant information needed to determine whether the terms of an agreement are mutually acceptable and whether these terms are actually being met. For example, the potential buyer of a new car may have difficulty determining whether the seller's claims about its economy and reliability are correct, and may wonder why the seller would want to get rid of the vehicle. Or a sales manager may have difficulty in determining whether a salesperson in the field is actually devoting full time and honest effort to the company's business, or instead is pursuing private interests on company time. In such circumstances, mutually advantageous transactions may fail to occur, because one or the other party fears being victimized, or costly arrangements will be made to protect against opportunistic behavior.

The second type of transaction costs connected to the motivation problem arise from **imperfect commitment**—the inability of parties to bind themselves to follow through on threats and promises that they would like to make but which, having made, they would later like to renounce. As an example, consider a manufacturer seeking to have a supplier make a large investment to meet the manufacturer's specific needs. The supplier must be concerned that—all promises to the contrary not withstanding—once the investment is sunk the manufacturer will try to force a lower price and other concessions on the supplier, who will then have little recourse. Recognition that threats and promises may not be kept deprives them of their credibility. Thus, far-sighted people will not rely upon them, and again there will be missed opportunities or a necessity of expending resources to facilitate commitment or protect against opportunism. The manufacturer would gain if it were possible to commit not to behave opportunistically, because then the supplier would be more willing to make the investment. Achieving such commitment may difficult, and so the investment may not be made or costly measures might need to be put in place to defend the supplier.

These problems affect both market and nonmarket organizations, although their nature and impact may differ between organizational forms. Therefore, one form may be better adapted than another for a specific transaction.

Dimensions of Transactions

According to the transaction costs approach, the variety of ways of organizing transactions found in the world reflects the fact that transactions differ in some basic attributes. Five kinds of transaction attributes play important roles in our analysis:

1. the **specificity** of the investments required to conduct the transaction
2. the **frequency** with which similar transactions occur and the **duration** or period of time over which they are repeated
3. the **complexity** of the transaction and the **uncertainty** about what performance will be required
4. the **difficulty of measuring performance** in the transaction
5. the **connectedness** of the transaction to other transactions involving other people

ASSET SPECIFICITY   One important dimension on which transactions differ is the nature of the investments that the parties to a transaction must make. When an individual consumer buys bread from a baker, neither party makes any investment with that particular transaction in mind. The baker may invest in a store and an oven, but he or she uses those assets to supply many different customers. In contrast, when a subcontractor makes wing assemblies for a particular model of Boeing airliner, it may invest in setting up a production line to make those specific assemblies. Such an investment is called a **specific investment** because it would lose much of its value outside of the specific use of providing wings to Boeing. The subcontractor would not want to make the investment unless it has a firm order from its customer, or at least reasonable assurance that an order will be forthcoming. For the same reason, an employee may not want to invest in learning the systems of a declining company where the prospects of continuing employment are poor. Transactions that require specific investments normally also require a contract or practice to protect the investor against early termination or opportunistic renegotiation of the terms of the production relationship.

FREQUENCY AND DURATION   Some transactions are one-time affairs as, for example, when a homeowner buys a house from its previous owner. Others are repeated frequently, involving some of the same parties under more or less similar conditions over a long period of time.

In the first case, one expects the parties to use whatever general mechanisms are available in the community to control their transaction. In particular, they likely will resort to a standard form contract, with any disputes between them to be resolved in court.

In the case of parties who interact frequently, one expects quite a different sort of mechanism that is specifically geared to the particulars of their relationship. For example, disputes between a supervisor and worker in a factory are rarely resolved in courtrooms. Instead, factories may set up a special grievances committee involving the union or other worker representatives, or an ombudsman may be used to hear complaints and attempt to mediate a solution. The special purpose institution is worthwhile because it can be tailored to the particular circumstances of the factory, keep down the cost of resolving disputes, and be continually improved in light of the circumstances in the particular factory. Generally, when similar transactions occur frequently over a long period of time involving some of the same parties, the one who interacts repeatedly may find it valuable to design and introduce low-cost routines to manage the transaction.

Frequency and duration also have another effect. Parties involved in a long, close relationship with frequent interactions have many opportunities to grant or withhold favors to one another. The ability to reward faithful partners and punish unfaithful ones in a long-term relationship greatly reduces the need for any kind of formal mechanism to enforce agreements between them. The parties can also develop understandings and routines that reduce the need for explicit planning to coordinate their actions. These practices can sometimes eliminate the need for formal, detailed agreements, both because the parties understand what is expected of them and because they have no need to document those understandings for outsiders to enforce. The cost savings that result can be considerable.

UNCERTAINTY AND COMPLEXITY   The standard way for two parties to organize a market transaction is to write a contract specifying what is expected from each. If the product is wheat, then the contract may simply specify that a fixed amount of a standardized grade of the grain (for example, Manitoba 1 Northern hard wheat) will be delivered at a particular date (say, April 1, 1992) and place (say, Winnipeg) for a specified price (for example, $5 Canadian per bushel). The basic contract is then very simple.

In contrast, a contract to build a power plant for an electric utility is very complicated. The utility's estimate of demand may change during construction, and the cost and availability of different kinds of fuel may change as well. The environmental impact of the facility may be unknown at the outset, and the cost of providing the necessary environmental and health and safety safeguards may be unpredictable. The right way to proceed, the length of time to take, and whether to finish the project at all are decisions that will have to be made later, after the contract is signed and execution begins. If the project is changed or delayed or terminated, there will need to be some way to determine what payments ought to be made.

Uncertainty about the conditions that will prevail when a contract is being executed together with complexity of the task make it impossible or at least uneconomical to determine in advance what should be done in every possible contingency, so the contract that is written will generally be less determinate than in a simpler setting. Rather than specifying how much of what is to be delivered when, the contract may specify who has the right to make which decisions and within what limits.

Returning to our example of a maker of wing assemblies for an aircraft, the contract between the aircraft manufacturer and the supplier might deal with uncertainty about future aircraft sales by specifying that the supplier will provide whatever number of assemblies the buyer requires according to a particular pricing formula. In return, the buyer may promise in the contract to purchase wing assemblies only from that supplier as long as the supplier is able to meet the demand. The buyer might also promise to supply advance estimates of demand that are within a fixed percentage of the actual quantities, to subsidize the purchase of specific assets used in the production, and so on.

Generally, when uncertainty and complexity make it hard to predict what performance will be desirable, contracting becomes more complex, specifying rights, obligations, and procedures rather than actual performance standards.

DIFFICULTY OF PERFORMANCE MEASUREMENT   Even when the desired performance is perfectly predictable, it may be difficult or costly to measure actual performance. For example, a person who employs a lawyer in a divorce proceeding may have no idea whether the negotiated settlement is really a good one, or whether a better lawyer could have negotiated a better deal. Similarly, the low output of a group of workers in a factory might be due to low effort, to poor materials, or to inferior methods used by the company. When a taxi that has been driven by several drivers over a period of time breaks down, the owner may be unable to tell which (if any) of the drivers has abused the car or failed to get maintenance when needed, or whether instead the breakdown is due to poor design or plain bad luck. Of course, if the taxi doesn't break down immediately, but hard use now makes future problems more likely, the cost of that abuse is nearly impossible to measure.

As these examples suggest, it is hard to provide effective incentives unless one can measure performance accurately. If the lawyer's performance could be accurately evaluated, or the factory workers' or the taxi drivers', then the consumer, factory manager, or taxi company owner could hold those parties responsible for their performance. That would presumably lead to more effort and better results.

When measuring performance is difficult, people commonly arrange their affairs to make measurement easier or to reduce the importance of accurate measurements. In our taxi example, the taxi may be assigned to just one driver, so that responsibility for any evident damage can be more easily assigned. Or, the taxi may be driver owned, so that any loss from abuse or poor maintenance (including even losses that are not immediately detectable) comes straight out of the owner/driver's pocket. Other attributes of the transaction determine which of these possible solutions is best, or even whether any of them are workable.

CONNECTEDNESS TO OTHER TRANSACTIONS   Finally, transactions differ in how they are connected to other transactions, especially those involving other people. Some transactions are largely independent of all others. For example, an office's decisions about when to buy new typewriters, where to keep its files, and which supplier to use for general office supplies hardly need to be coordinated.

Other transactions are much more interdependent. When railroads were introduced in the United States in the nineteenth century, the various railroad companies failed to coordinate their choices of track gauges (the size of the rails and distance between them). Because rail cars adapted to one gauge of track cannot be used on track laid to other gauges, the result was that goods being shipped long distances had to be unloaded and reloaded onto different cars at several points in the journey. Standardization on any one of the various gauges that were actually adopted would have been much more efficient. A similarly costly situation is still present in Europe, where Spanish rail gauges do not match those used in France. The eventual standardization of the rail gauges in the United States resulted in much quicker and less expensive shipping of goods and contributed to the development of the western parts of the country.

For a more modern example, suppose a computer maker is designing a new model of computer. It cannot deliver a working model until all the relevant components such as the memory chips, central processor, power supply, and so on are all available in sufficient quantity to begin assembly. In addition, the operating system for the computer and some of the application software must be ready; otherwise, there is nothing useful that the finished computer can actually do.

The manufacturers of the various parts and the software developers in this situation need to have their activities closely coordinated. There is little advantage to rushing the completion of a plant to assemble the computer, for example, if the other parts of the system will not be ready to go. Similarly, the amounts of the various components that the different suppliers are able to deliver must line up with one another, for there is little value to having a larger number of keyboards than disk drives. The capacities and capabilities of the machine components must be compatible with one another, and the design tolerances need to be coordinated. Failures to align capacities or to match design tolerances or to have components ready on time can be much costlier than failures to adopt the best possible design and introduction date.

When the costliest potential mistakes are of these kinds—rather than, say, failures to make effective use of local resources—we say that the transactions display **design connectedness**. Design connectedness is just one extreme; the relative costs of different kinds of mistakes can in general have any relationship.

One way that firms respond to close connectedness is to strengthen central coordination mechanisms. This may mean that there are more meetings among the people involved in the individual transactions, or that the managers in charge spend more time on oversight, or some combination of those things. A second way firms respond is to reduce the number of different people involved, so that fewer people need to be coordinated. The particular way that close connectedness is managed depends on other attributes of the connected transactions.

Limits of the Transaction Costs Approach

This transaction costs approach is appealing, and we adopt it later for some of our analyses. However, the approach cannot be correctly applied to all problems in economic organization because, without additional conditions, its fundamental argument—that economic activity and organizations are arranged so as to minimize transaction costs—is problematic. There are two main problems.

First, it is not generally true that the total costs of an economic activity can be expressed as the sum of production costs and transaction costs, where the former depend only on the technology and the inputs used and the latter depend only on the way transactions are organized. Production and transaction costs generally depend both on the organization and on the technology, which makes the conceptual separation between production and transaction costs troublesome. If production is lost due to delays in planning, is it the result of slow planning or of a technology that cannot adapt quickly to late changes in the plan? A more subtle example can be seen in the semiconductor industry.[4] Integrated circuit production is marked by increasing returns to scale and very strong learning curve effects, so that costs are lower the larger the volume of production within any facility, both in any single time period and in aggregate over time. Thus, efficiency in production would require that any particular design of a circuit be produced by a single manufacturer. For a long time, however, it was standard procedure for a company that developed a new chip to give the design to a second firm that would compete with it in producing and selling the chip. It was even common to assist this "second source" in setting up production.

This way of organizing the production of integrated circuits sacrifices production cost efficiencies for other advantages: Without a competing second source, potential users of the new integrated circuit would be reluctant to adopt it for fear that once they had become locked into its use, the supplier would exploit its monopoly position. Creating a competing second source is an effective way to achieve commitment, leading to increased demand.[5] Are the extra costs incurred a "production cost," arising because an inefficient technology is used that does not take full advantage of economies of scale, or a "transaction cost," incurred to satisfy customers that the terms of the transaction are secure? There are no unassailable answers to these questions. The lesson is that although the costs of transacting are real, they are not always easily separated from other kinds of costs.

The second problem is not with the concept of transaction costs per se, but with the notion that efficient institutions would minimize them. For example, according to Coase's postulate, employment relations can be understood as minimizing the total transaction costs involved. But why should employers minimize total transaction costs in designing their employment, compensation, promotion, supervision, and performance review systems, rather than simply the categories of costs that they themselves must bear? Some of the transaction costs surely will be borne by the employees; why should we expect the employers' choices to take proper account of these? In fact, why would they not push all the transaction costs onto the employees?

A standard answer to these questions is that competition would force employers to take account of the costs to employees. In Chapter 8, we argue that this standard answer is of limited application. But even when it does apply, having to rely on competition or other external forces to bring about efficiency would critically weaken the theory because its range of potential application would then be severely narrowed.

A more general version of this second problem is that because there are typically many quite different efficient solutions to any resource-allocation problem, efficiency alone may not be a strong enough criterion to give very specific predictions or clear explanations. Too many different patterns of organization might be compatible with efficiency for it to be a useful concept.

---

[4] See Andrea Shepard, "Licensing to Enhance the Demand for New Products," *Rand Journal of Economics*, 18 (1987), 360–68, and Joseph Farrell and Nancy Gallini, "Second-Sourcing as Commitment: Monopoly Incentives to Attract Competition," *Quarterly Journal of Economics*, 103 (1988), 673–94.

[5] The break with this practice came when Intel chose not to second-source its 80386 microprocessor. The market for this chip was judged to be secure even without second-sourcing because Intel's performance was secured by its need to compete with its own earlier chip designs, which continued to be produced by other manufacturers.

It turns out that one simplifying assumption, that is, the condition of no wealth effects discussed in the next section, takes care of this problem completely.[6] When this condition is satisfied, only one pattern of behavior is consistent with efficiency, and that is the pattern that maximizes the total value created in the transaction.

WEALTH EFFECTS, VALUE MAXIMIZATION, AND THE COASE THEOREM

In many economic decisions, the choice actually made depends on the decision maker's wealth. A poor person (or a poor country) may not have the resources to pursue some courses of action that a richer one could. Even when the same alternatives are affordable, a poorer person might still make different trade-offs than a richer one. For example, the poor person might be reluctant to take financial risks that a rich person would welcome. The changes in choices resulting from increased wealth are known as **wealth effects**.

The Value Maximization Principle

Although wealth effects can sometimes be significant, this is not always the case. In fact, the formal analysis of problems in the economics of organizations is greatly simplified when wealth effects can be ignored entirely. Moreover, it is precisely in ignoring wealth effects that such key management concepts as "creating value" become unambiguously defined.

NO WEALTH EFFECTS   We say that there are *no wealth effects* for a certain decision maker with respect to a set of possible decisions when three conditions hold. First, given any two alternative decisions y_1 and y_2, there is a definite amount of money $\$x$ that would be sufficient to compensate the decision maker for switching from y_1 to y_2 (or from y_2 to y_1). Second, if the decision maker were first given an additional amount of wealth, then the amount needed to compensate the decision maker for the switch from y_1 to y_2 would be unaffected. Third, the decision maker must have enough money to be able to absorb any wealth reduction necessary to pay for a switch from the less preferred to the more preferred option.

None of these conditions can be expected always to hold. For some people, for example, there may be no amount of money that they would accept as compensation for a serious risk of loss of life or limb, or for being forced to live far from family and their childhood homes, or to live in a culture where they cannot exercise their religious beliefs. Nevertheless, the condition that there is some monetary amount that would compensate for a change of circumstances holds widely for many of the most common kinds of business decisions.

To examine the implications and applicability of the second condition, suppose that a corporation suddenly finds itself richer on account of an unexpected increase in the value of its assets. If there are no wealth effects, then the price the corporation would demand for its goods and the returns it would demand from its planned investments would remain unchanged. In this example, the absence of wealth effects

---

[6] Like other modelers, economists use the terms *assumption* and *assume* in a different sense than they are often used in ordinary discourse. In everyday conversation, assuming something connotes believing it is true. Making an assumption in an economic model carries no such connotation. An assumption is merely a working hypothesis used to abstract from the complexity of the real economic world. The purpose of making an assumption may be to derive a good approximate prediction or to highlight a single force or effect for closer study and better understanding. Assumptions are used in both ways in this text.

seems likely to hold, at least over a broad range of wealth levels. As a second example, however, suppose a worker wins the jackpot in the state lottery. If there are no wealth effects with respect to current consumption choices, then the winner would not buy a new house, or quit his or her job, or do any of the things lottery winners normally do. Here the assumption of no wealth effects seems particularly inappropriate.

The third condition connects the decision maker's initial wealth and the changes in the nonfinancial situation that are being considered. The amount by which a worker's pay could be cut to offset his or her psychic gain in being allowed to shift working hours to miss rush-hour traffic is probably small relative to income, and the condition is likely to hold in this case. On the other hand, holding a worker in a nuclear reactor facility financially responsible for the effects of his or her mistakes is apt to run into wealth constraints, and so the assumption of no wealth effects will be inappropriate.

In general, these examples suggest that the assumption of no wealth effects is most restrictive—least likely to be valid and most likely to lead to incorrect conclusions—when the decision makers are individuals and when large cash transfers or significant changes in personal living conditions are involved. When the sizes of the cash transfers are small relative to the decision maker's financial resources, assuming that there are no wealth effects (or that they are small enough that they can safely be ignored) is more likely to be a good approximation to reality.

THE EQUIVALENT VALUE INDEX   The utility function of a decision maker who shows no wealth effects with respect to a set of decisions can be represented very simply.

Let x represent the decision maker's monetary wealth and let y be a list of all the other influences or characteristics associated with decisions that affect his or her preferences: social approval, job assignment, effort exerted on the job, and so on. An important example involves uncertain income and expenses, where x is interpreted as the certain, unconditional amount of money that will be received (or the average, expected amount) and y reflects a risky component of income. In general, the utility function takes the form $u(x,y)$, where x and y may interact in complex ways. If there are no wealth effects, however, then there is always a cash equivalent value $v(y)$ that can be assigned to the list y and the decision maker's utility function can be written in the form $u(x,y) = x + v(y)$. In other words, by adding the cash equivalent value $v(y)$ to the decision maker's wealth x, we obtain an index of personal welfare, which we may call his or her *value index*.[7] The importance of the value index is that, when it is valid, a related index—the total value of the affected parties—is an appropriate measure of welfare changes for group decision making.[8] We state the matter as follows.

> **The Value Maximization Principle:** An allocation among a group of people whose preferences display no wealth effects is efficient only if it maximizes the total value of the affected parties. Moreover, for any inefficient allocation, there exists another (total value maximizing) allocation that *all* of the parties *strictly* prefer.

---

[7] To see how the three preceding conditions relate to this formula, note first that the change in x necessary to compensate for a change from y_1 to y_2 is easily computed to be $\Delta x = v(y_2) - v(y_1)$, because for any given initial wealth M, $M + \Delta x + v(y_2) = M + v(y_1)$. The change in x to compensate for switching from y_2 to y_1 is then just $-\Delta x$. The calculated amount Δx is independent of the initial wealth, M, as the second condition requires. With a general utility function $u(x,y)$, there might be no amount Δ that would make the equality $u(M + \Delta, y_2) = u(M, y_1)$ hold, as the first condition requires, and even if there were such an amount, its magnitude would generally depend on M. Finally, as long as the initial wealth M is larger than the largest possible difference in the $v(y)$ values between two alternative ys, so that making the transfer Δx cannot require more money than the individual has, then the third condition holds.

[8] The total value is also sometimes called the total (consumer and/or producer) surplus.

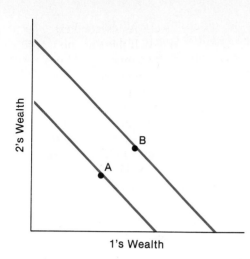

Figure 2.1: Any point like A on a line of lower total wealth is Pareto dominated by some point B on the line of highest total wealth. Points like B on the line of highest total wealth are undominated.

The Logic of Value Maximization

To establish the principle for a particular example, consider an investment decision involving two people with utility functions that satisfy the condition of no wealth effects: $U_i(x,y) = x + v_i(y)$, $i = 1,2$, where y represents inputs to be provided by the parties.[9] The investment generates total cash income of $P(y)$. We may think of $v_i(y)$ as representing the personal cost investor i bears in supplying the agreed inputs. In that case, $v_i(y)$ is a negative number for positive levels of y. The income $P(y)$ will be divided between the individuals, with x_1 being paid to individual 1 and x_2 being paid to individual 2, so that $x_1 + x_2 = P(y)$. For any particular allocation (x_1, x_2, y), *the total utility or value of the two parties is* $[x_1 + v_1(y)] + [x_2 + v_2(y)]$, which (because $x_1 + x_2 = P(y)$) is equal to $P(y) + v_1(y) + v_2(y)$. *The total value depends on y alone and not on the profit shares x.* As we vary the profit shares x_1 and x_2, the individual utilities of the two parties change, but the total utility remains fixed.

Figure 2.1 illustrates the situation. Each line depicts the possible levels of value for the two parties for any fixed investment decision y, as the profit shares x are varied. The fact that the lines are straight and run at 45° to the axes reflects the fact that total value is independent of its distribution between the parties; it is possible to move utility or value from one party to the other (via the xs) without affecting the totals. It is clear from the diagram that any point like A on a line that corresponds to lower total value is Pareto dominated by some point like B on the line of highest total value. It is also clear from the figure that no point on the line of highest total value is Pareto dominated by any point on that line or any other line. Consequently, *an allocation (x_1, x_2, y) is efficient if and only if y maximizes the total value:* $P(y) + v_1(y) + v_2(y)$.

The intuition of this result is simple: With more total it is always possible to distribute it in a way that makes everyone better off. A full mathematical proof of the proposition is developed in the exercises at the end of the chapter.[10]

---

[9] We can think of y as being the pair (y_1, y_2), where y_i is i's contribution. Then writing $v_i(y)$ rather than $v_i(y_i)$ allows the possibility that each individual's costs depend on both parties' contributions. At the same time, writing $v_i(y)$ allows that v_i depends only on y_i.

[10] In the presence of wealth effects, an allocation that maximizes the sum of utilities is still efficient, but there may also be efficient allocations that do not maximize the sum of utilities.

APPLYING VALUE MAXIMIZATION   Although this discussion is set in the context of two people making an investment, the principle itself is much more general. When preferences take the form we have described, then any decision (x,y) is efficient if and only if y is chosen to maximize the total value of the parties. Importantly, the efficiency of the choice (x,y) does not depend on the selection of x, which determines only how the fruits of the joint enterprise are shared. When the value maximization principle applies, the issue of the distribution of value is completely separable from the issue of how value is created. While this separation is not always realistic (see Chapter 8), it is often reasonable and it does always simplify the analysis of economic organization problems. For that reason, it is a good starting point for thinking about organizations.

The abstract model we have described has wide application because the variable y can be given so many different interpretations. The model can apply to people in a community who must decide on the resources y to be devoted to parks, libraries, or some other public good. It can also apply to overtime assignments (y is then the identity of the person assigned to work overtime), to water rights (y identifies the owner of the rights), to the brand of computer to be used (y names the brand), or to the location of the new office building (y specifies the location).

The Coase Theorem

In practical business situations, the way the benefits of an agreement are divided among the parties will depend, of course, on what assets each brings to the bargaining table, how patient each party is, what outside opportunities are available, and so on. Nevertheless, if the parties engage in efficient bargaining, that is, if they reach an agreement from which there is no possibility of further mutual gain, and if the value maximization principle applies, then regardless of what cash changes hands at the time of agreement, y will be chosen to maximize the total value of the parties to the agreement. Only the distribution of the costs and benefits will be affected by the strength of their relative bargaining positions, and this distribution will show up in the xs. This conclusion is summarized in a proposition that is also due to Coase:

> **The Coase Theorem**: If the parties bargain to an efficient agreement (for themselves) and if their preferences display no wealth effects, then the value-creating activities (y) that they will agree upon do not depend on the bargaining power of the parties or on what assets each owned when the bargaining began. Rather, efficiency alone determines the activity choice. The other factors can affect only decisions about how the costs and benefits are to be shared (x).

This celebrated proposition is the foundation of the transaction costs approach to the theory of the firm and other economic organizations. With the assumption of no wealth effects, the Coase theorem and the efficiency principle mean that all real activities are determined to maximize the total value of the parties, taking into account the costs of organization (transaction costs) along with all other kinds of costs. For any given plan of production specifying who is to make what with which resources (and thus the aggregate production costs that will be incurred), if we think of transaction costs as the costs of managing the transactions (including the costs of writing contracts, supervising workers, enforcing contracts, and resolving disputes), then the efficient organization for that plan is the one that minimizes transaction costs.

To understand the significance of this perspective, it is helpful to contrast it with other perspectives that have been vigorously advocated.

The Transaction Costs Approach versus Alternative Views

The transaction costs approach differs sharply from the Marxian approach. According to Marxian theorists, organizational arrangements are a reflection of underlying power relationships and class interests. In contrast, according to the transaction costs perspective, the choice of a firm's organization (y) does not depend on the a priori distribution of power between the owners of capital and the laborers. For example, in Yugoslavia, where employee control of firms has been the norm, labor hired managers who organized the factories in similar ways and instituted similar kinds of controls (even over labor) as those seen in capitalist firms.

Applied to relationships among firms and between firms and their customers, the transaction costs approach suggests that business arrangements should be understood as attempts to increase the total wealth available for sharing among the parties. Scholars trained in the Harvard school of industrial organization and antitrust would try instead to explain the arrangements as attempts by the firms to increase their ability to manipulate prices for the products they sell or the inputs or labor they buy. For example, resale price maintenance—the practice by manufacturers of limiting contractually the rights of distributors and retailers to set prices—has been attacked by members of the Harvard school as anticompetitive. The transaction costs approach suggests that it in fact may be efficiency promoting. Adherents of this approach might argue that, without resale price maintenance, discounters would free-ride off the service and customer education provided by other dealers, relying on them to provide product support but then grabbing the sales for themselves. This would drive the amount of such support below efficient levels.

The correct way to decide between competing hypotheses is to confront them systematically with detailed evidence. The observation concerning management methods in the Yugoslav firm represents an instance of this, but it is by itself insufficient. We report more of the relevant evidence later in this book.

In any case, in application, it is important to remember that the Coase theorem and its various implications depend on restrictive hypotheses regarding preferences and, perhaps more importantly, on the ability to make unlimited transfer payments between the parties. The implications do not hold when some of the parties have very limited capital with which to make payments. Thus, although it would be reasonable to apply this analysis to study the terms of a contract between General Motors and Toyota, it would be a mistake to apply it uncritically, for example, to study land tenure in a developing country or the institution of slavery in the pre-Civil War American South.

ORGANIZATIONAL OBJECTIVES

It is traditional in economics and management texts to assume that firms seek to maximize profits and, more generally, to ascribe well-defined goals to organizations and to presume that the organization acts in pursuit of these objectives. Occasionally we employ such a hypothesis in this text, when it is convenient to treat the organization as a purposeful entity. More often, however, we do *not* presume that organizations per se have goals that they seek to realize. Rather, we are careful to treat organizational decisions and actions as the outcomes either of strategic interplay among self-interested people responding to incentives designed to influence their behavior, or of collective or managerial attempts to compromise the interests of the parties affected by the decisions. Only when the value maximization principle applies is there an objective that we can ascribe to the firm that is implied by considerations of efficiency alone.

Profit Maximization

The goal most commonly ascribed to firms in economic analyses is profit maximization. It might seem at least that the self-interested owners of a firm would unanimously favor such a goal. In that case, they would attempt to design the organization to motivate its managers and employees to pursue profits. In fact, we often conduct our analyses presuming that this is the case, but the reader should remember that there are many reasons why owners might have other objectives.

First, to the extent that one of the owners is also a customer of the firm or one of its input suppliers, that owner might prefer that the firm not maximize profits in dealing with him or her, but instead favor the owner with better prices or terms. This would be a potential problem in a firm where ownership is shared between employees and outside investors, with each owning part of the claims on the firm. The inside employee-owners might prefer that the firm's managers adopt policies to protect workers' jobs, pay high wages, and provide many on-the-job benefits. Meanwhile, the outside investor-owners might prefer that the value of their investment in the firm be maximized.

Second, many of the decisions of the firm involve expenditures and receipts that are both uncertain and spread out over time. In such cases, it is common to assume that people are interested in the expected value of the discounted stream of utility they receive over time in the various uncertain future circumstances (see Chapter 12). However, just as owners differ in the likelihoods they place on the various ways future events might unfold and in the relative weights they place on income accruing in the more or less distant future, they also will disagree on which plans maximize the expected present value of profits. This is especially likely to be a problem when the firm is considering investing in a new process or product whose benefits and costs are unknown.

A partial solution to this difficulty is achieved if there are so-called **complete and competitive markets** (a concept investigated in more detail in Chapter 3). Then maximizing the market value of the firm is an appropriate goal to which the owners would agree. In this context, having complete and competitive markets means that any individual can use the financial and insurance markets to move income across time and shift it between different uncertain events, all at given prices. In doing so, the individual achieves whatever patterns of receipts he or she may like and can afford. In such circumstances, it is best to make the firm's value (evaluated at the given market prices) as large as possible, because this provides the largest amount to invest, and this amount can then be invested in light of the person's own preferences and beliefs about the future (see Chapter 12). However, markets are almost surely not complete in this sense. Thus, there are disagreements among owners about the optimal course of action for the firm, and market value maximization does not always win unanimous approval.

Third, to the extent that those making the decisions are not the only claimants on returns from the concern, they may wish to maximize their portion of the flows, rather than total returns. For example, suppose the owners are stockholders with limited liability who are at risk for the firm's obligations only up to the amount of their investments, but some of the firm's financing is via debt that must be repaid before the owners get any returns on their investments. In that case, the owners might prefer to make investments that are excessively risky rather than to maximize the value of the firm (including both the value of its debt as well as its equity). When things go well, the debtors are paid their contracted amounts and the equity holders keep the remainder. When things go badly, the debt is not repaid in full and some of the losses are thus shifted onto the debtors. Riskier investments shift more of the downside onto the debtors and leave the upside to the stockholders. Therefore, they might be preferred by the latter group, even if the increased risk reduced the value of the debt by more than it increased the value of the stock. We explore this particular conflict again in Chapter 5 in the context of the savings and loan industry.

Other Goals and Stakeholders' Interests

Of course, there are many organizations where profit maximization is clearly not the goal. Mutual insurance companies reduce the premiums paid by their policyholders through dividends (distributions of part of the excess of receipts over costs). Customer-owned cooperatives are intended to sell to their members at lower prices than profit maximization would yield. Clearly, assuming profit maximization is likely to be inappropriate for such firms. However, in each of these cases the customers (the policyholders and the co-op members) are the nominal owners, and useful analysis can be conducted using the assumption that the organization is structured to attempt to serve their interests. Similarly, in the case of a firm that is entirely employee owned such as Avis, the automobile rental company, or Egged, the Israeli intercity bus company, an examination of the employees' interests should give insight to the policies that the firm will pursue.

Even if we are willing to assume that a privately-owned firm will be designed to serve the interests of the owners, however, in whose interests is a research university run? Surely, "in the public interest" is an inadequate answer. The public consists of a multitude of people whose interests may be in conflict. Students may prefer faculty to be selected largely for teaching ability; employers may want teaching that gives students professionally applicable training and research that is geared to quick industrial application; alumni booster clubs might prefer that more resources go to generating winning athletic programs; taxpayers might want subsidies held down and only local students admitted. Generally, not-for-profit organizations have no owners in the usual sense. In such circumstances, predicting organizational form and behavior requires careful analysis of who has the power to design the organization, who can make decisions, and who can influence these decisions and their implementation.

A similar difficulty arises in firms in which the interests of **stakeholders** other than the nominal owners are given legitimacy. For example, a survey of the presidents of 100 major Japanese firms asked what the objectives of companies should be, and what their actual goals were.[11] In each case, the pursuit of shareholders' profit came a very distant fourth on the list, garnering only 3.6 percent of the responses. Asked the questions of to whom companies should belong and to whom they actually do belong (with multiple answers allowed), senior executives listed shareholders first among those entitled to ownership, but employees first among the actual owners. A survey of Japanese middle managers indicated that they viewed stockholders as only fourth in a list of those to whom companies should belong, with employees first. Shareholders came third on the middle-level managers' list of the effective owners of the firm, behind employees and management.[12]

Management in other countries also often appears to be concerned with the interests of the nonowner stakeholders, including employees, suppliers, customers, the communities in which the firm is located, and those for whom the natural environment is affected by the firm's actions. To the extent that the nominal owners cannot enforce exclusive attention to their interests in management's decisions, the

---

[11] Reported in the *Nikkei Sangyo Shimbun*, July 5, 1990. We are grateful to Masahiro Okuno-Fujiwara of the University of Tokyo for this and the next reference.

[12] Reported in *Nihon Sangyo Shimbun*, April 23, 1990. Multiple responses were allowed.

actual policies and practices of the firm are going to represent a political compromise mediated by management.

In summary, the assumption that organizations are maximizing entities with well-defined goals is one that should be made very cautiously.

MODELING HUMAN MOTIVATION AND BEHAVIOR

A central premise of economic analysis is that people (as opposed to organizations) do have well-defined interests describable by individual utility functions, and that they seek to maximize their utility. Although this assumption is far from uncontroversial, it in fact has virtually no empirical content in light of the limitless factors on which individual utility could depend.

For example, a sufficient concern both for the well-being of others and for social approval could rationalize apparently extreme self-sacrifice. There is no doubt that such factors are both real and, in some cases, immensely important. Although a narrow calculation of personal costs and benefits might usually be enough to prevent soldiers from deserting in the face of battle ("Am I more likely to be shot by the enemy or by a firing squad?"), sacrificing one's life for one's comrades seems hard to explain without appeal to altruism or to an exceedingly high regard for others' opinions of one's courage. Such factors are important even in the more mundane problems that concern us here, such as motivating workers to provide honest effort or providing incentives for borrowers not to skip out on their creditors. Furthermore, important features of many organizations can be best understood in terms of deliberate attempts to change the preferences of individual participants to make these factors more salient. As a result, organizationally desired behavior becomes more likely. This is clearly an element of leadership as it is usually understood, and it has much to do with practices of organizing semipermanent groups of workers and encouraging them to interact socially as well as at work.

Rationality-Based Theories

While admitting all this and, in particular, the possibility of intrinsic motivation, we adopt the view that many institutions and business practices are designed as if people were entirely motivated by narrow, selfish concerns and were quite clever and largely unprincipled in their pursuit of their goals. This model of human behavior incorporates the sort of rational self-interest usually assumed in standard economic models, such as that of a consumer making utility-maximizing purchases at given prices. But it goes further. It posits that people will be very sharp in discovering even subtle ways in which they can advance their interests and that they will be fundamentally amoral, ignoring rules, breaking agreements, and employing guile, manipulation, and deception if they see personal gain in doing so.

As we shall see, this assumption does have bite: It often serves to give sharp, testable predictions and explanations. Moreover, even though it is an extreme caricature to regard people as amorally motivated solely by narrow self-interest, the predicted institutions and practices are often not very sensitive to this caricature. A bank has guards, vaults, and audits because it would otherwise be robbed; this explanation of practices is unaffected by the observation that many honest people would not rob an unguarded bank. Similarly, organizations design reward schemes so that employees find it in their personal interests to work to advance the organization's goals. The fact that many employees would not instantly abandon the organization's interests even if their incentives were removed is not particularly important for our analysis.

At the same time, we do not automatically make the hyperrationality assumptions common in some economic analyses: that people are capable of instantaneous, unlimited, perfect, and costless calculation, that they can effectively and effortlessly forecast all possible eventualities and the full implications of any information or decision, and that they completely optimize in all situations. These assumptions are not just counterfactual; they also prevent understanding of many important elements of organizations. For example, organizations regularly employ **routines**—standard operating procedures and rules of thumb—for obtaining information, making and implementing decisions, and carrying out tasks. Using routines economizes on scarce and valuable decision-making resources, although it sometimes means that the decisions that are made are not the best ones that could have been reached if the problems were subjected to a full analysis rather than treated routinely. Organizational learning occurs when these routines are modified in response to new knowledge. None of this makes much sense if we assume hyperrationality.

Paradoxically, the very imperfections in the rationality of people and in the adaptability of organizations denied by many simple economic theories are necessary in proving that the rationality-based theories are descriptively and prescriptively useful. With perfect rationality, one would rarely expect to observe two organizations in substantially the same circumstances making substantially different choices, so there would be no possibility of testing what kinds of organizations perform best. For example, to test whether the commonly observed scheme of paying commissions to compensate insurance agents is an efficient method of sales incentives, we would want to compare these firms to other firms that do not provide such incentives to evaluate their performances, or possibly to the same firm using different practices at different times. It is untenable to adhere too closely to tenets of individual and organizational rationality and at the same time to claim an empirical basis for the theory. A more defensible position, suggested by Richard Nelson and Sidney Winter, is that people learn to make good decisions and that organizations adapt by experimentation and imitation, so that there is at least "fossil evidence" available for testing theories.

Nevertheless, theories based on perfect rationality and adaptability are surprisingly successful in generating explanations and specific predictions about observed institutions and business practices, and they form the main focus of this book.

CASE STUDY: COORDINATION, MOTIVATION, AND EFFICIENCY IN THE MARKET FOR MEDICAL INTERNS

The evolution of the system under which graduating medical students in the United States are matched with hospitals seeking interns and residents provides a striking illustration of a number of the themes and concepts introduced in this chapter.[13]

The practice of new M.D. degree holders taking internships in hospitals as a clinical stage in their medical education appeared in the United States about the beginning of the twentieth century. It gave the interns practical training and the hospitals cheap labor. Until graduates of foreign medical schools began seeking U.S. internships in significant numbers in the 1970s, the number of positions open in hospitals for interns always exceeded the number of students seeking internships, so competition for interns

---

[13] This section is based on two papers by Alvin E. Roth, "The Evolution of the Labor Market for Medical Interns and Residents: A Case Study in Game Theory," *Journal of Political Economy*, 92 (December 1984), 991–1016, and "A Natural Experiment in the Organization of Entry Level Labor Markets: Regional Markets for New Physicians in the U.K.," *American Economic Review*, 81 (June 1991), 415–40. See also Roth's less technical discussion, "New Physicians: A Natural Experiment in Market Organization," *Science*, 250 (December 14, 1990), 1524–28.

was intense. Of course, students differ in their overall attractiveness and in their specific appeal to different schools, so the competition was more intense for some than for others. Moreover, hospitals seeking several interns might be concerned with the particular mix of students they got, and not just with the overall quality of the individuals they attracted. They would consequently have preferences over groups of students. At the same time, students may have differing individual preferences among the hospitals at which they might intern. In sum, the final matching of students and hospitals is of great concern to all.

Various methods were used to match students and hospitals over the years. First was a scheme similar to that used in U.S. college and graduate school admissions today. Students would apply to hospitals that were seeking interns. The hospitals then ranked their applicants and offered positions to some number while telling others that they are alternates on a wait-list. The students then had to decide whether to take one of their firm offers or to wait to see if a hospital they preferred would make them a firm second-round offer. The problem was that the hospitals began competing by making their offers earlier and earlier, sometimes as early as only half-way through the students' medical school studies. This was very bad from the point of view of the hospitals, because at that stage they could learn so little about the students' ultimate performance and interests. However, each hospital still had an individual incentive to accelerate its offers to try to recruit the best students. The process was also very disruptive for the medical schools and the students' studies.

The eventual response was for the medical schools to agree not to give out information on their students until late in their careers. This moved the recruiting into the students' final year of medical school, but a new problem arose. Students who had been accepted by one of their less-preferred hospitals but wait-listed by one they liked better would hold off responding to the first hospital's offer as long as possible, hoping that they would clear the other hospital's wait-list. Again, this was individually optimal behavior by all concerned, but it meant that there were student-hospital matches that were missed but that were mutually preferred to those that actually occurred. This in turn led to students' reneging on their acceptances.

Attempts were made to overcome these problems. The chief one was for the hospitals to agree on the earliest date for making offers, for them to shorten the time given to students to make their decisions (down to as little as a twelve-hour period from midnight to noon!) and to limit communication between the hospitals and students during the period that offers were outstanding. Perhaps unsurprisingly, these measures proved futile, and the turmoil continued.

The National Intern Matching Program

In 1951, a centralized scheme was introduced by the hospitals and medical schools on an experimental basis to coordinate the matching of students to internships. The workings of the experimental version were adjusted in light of students' observations that they would do better under its rules to misrepresent their preferences among hospitals, and the revised scheme was formally instituted in 1952. Under it, students seeking internships and hospitals seeking interns first exchange information with one another, much as before. Then the students rank the hospitals in which they are willing to be employed and the hospitals similarly rank the groups of student applicants whom they are willing to take. These rankings are then submitted to a central office, which uses a specific rule (algorithm) to match students and hospitals. This new system, called originally the National Intern Matching Program (NIMP), ended the turmoil that had marked the market for interns. It has remained in place, drawing the voluntary participation of the vast bulk of hospitals and medical students (up to 95 percent of students). However, beginning in the mid-1970s there was an increasing number of married couples needing two internships in the same vicinity, and large numbers of these people sought and found matches outside the NIMP system.

The actual algorithm used to match students and hospitals is somewhat complicated, and understanding its detailed workings is not necessary for what follows. However, the basic idea can be explained simply for the (unrealistic) case in which each hospital has space for only one intern and there is an equal number of students and hospitals.[14]

The algorithm works through rounds in which it seeks to match students and hospitals on the basis of their submitted preference orders. In essence, each hospital at each round offers its position to its most preferred applicant. Students offered a place are then tentatively matched with their favorite among the hospitals making them an offer. Their names are then stricken from the submitted rankings of all those hospitals which they ranked lower than the one with which they are tentatively matched, and the process is repeated using the hospitals' revised rankings. Note that generally some students will have moved up in some of the hospitals' revised rankings, because other students whom these hospitals actually liked better have been (tentatively) matched elsewhere. This means that students who have moved to the top of some hospital's rankings will now get offers from that hospital. If they were already tentatively matched with some other hospital but prefer the new offer, the old tentative match is broken and they are (still tentatively) assigned to their preferred choice. The process then continues until everyone is tentatively assigned, at which point the assignments are made final and announced.[15]

EFFICIENCY AND STABILITY   Consider now the general case where the hospitals have multiple slots for interns and there is no presumed equality between the numbers of students and available spaces. Even in this context, the matches that the NIMP generates can be shown to be efficient in the usual sense: There is no way to reassign the students to the hospitals so as to make one of the students or one of the hospitals better off without hurting some other hospital or student. This was not necessarily true of the older systems it replaced. Moreover, the NIMP avoids many of the transaction costs that marked the older systems. The process is relatively straightforward, and most students and hospitals have accepted its results rather than trying to go around it to find mutually preferred matches.

However, in the present context, monetary transfers and "side payments" are not permitted. Thus, efficiency cannot be equated with value maximization because compensation cannot be paid. There may then be many different efficient patterns of matches. In light of this, it is especially significant that the matching generated by the NIMP can be shown to enjoy an extra property that is much stronger than efficiency in this context: the NIMP matches are *stable*. Specifically, there will never be a hospital-student pair where the student prefers the given hospital to the one to which the algorithm assigned him or her and the hospital would rather have the given student than one of the students actually assigned to it. Thus, recontracting between individual students and hospitals cannot upset the outcome of the process, even when the hospitals are free to drop people who have been assigned to them and students are free to ignore the assignment they have been given.

Stability means that the proposed assignment is not only efficient for the group as a whole, it is also efficient for every subgroup, even if that group ignores the effects

---

[14] We are indebted to Robert B. Wilson of Stanford University for this interpretation.

[15] Note that each student gets a more preferred hospital whenever his or her tentative match is changed. Thus, with only a finite number of hospitals, the algorithm eventually must cease generating changes, at which point it stops.

Table 2.1 An Example of Student and Hospital Preferences

Ranking	Student			Hospital		
	Alice (A)	Barbara (B)	Charlie (C)	Hopkins (H)	Stanford (S)	Yale (Y)
1st	Y	S	S	A	A	B
2nd	S	Y	Y	B	B	A
3rd	H	H	H	C	C	C

of their decisions on non-members. Regardless of what group of students and hospitals form to seek alternative matches, the members can never find a set of matches that involves only members of the group that is better for all of them than the match initially proposed by the NIMP. Stability is a very demanding condition. The fact that the NIMP matches are stable helps to explain the persistence of the program.

It may seem remarkable that the hospitals and medical schools were able to devise an efficient, stable system. What is perhaps more remarkable is that this scheme is ideal from the hospitals' point of view (and quite the opposite from the students' perspective).

If a hospital wants some specific number n of interns, then the NIMP algorithm actually assigns that hospital the n students it ranks highest among all the students it could ever get at one or another stable assignment (no matter how computed)! So if one stable assignment gives a hospital its first and fourth choices and another gives it its second-ranked and third-ranked students, the NIMP actually gives it its first- and second-ranked students. At the same time, each student is assigned to the hospital he or she ranks *lowest* among all those to which he or she could be assigned at *some* stable assignment.

All this presumes that the students and hospitals submit lists reflecting their actual, true rankings. In this regard, the NIMP consistently claims that there is no advantage to misrepresenting preferences. In fact, no student or hospital can gain by misrepresenting its first choice. However, it is not individually optimal for students to list their complete true preferences independent of the hospitals' rankings and the lists being submitted by other students, or for a hospital with more than one slot to fill to submit an honest list independent of the students' lists and those of the other hospitals.

AN EXAMPLE OF SUCCESSFUL STRATEGIC MISREPRESENTATION   To see how misrepresentation could theoretically be beneficial, consider an example that is remarkably simple compared to the real situation faced by actual students.[16]

Suppose there are three students, Alice, Barbara, and Charlie, and three hospitals, Hopkins, Stanford, and Yale. Each hospital wants only one student, so by the results claimed earlier, they have no reason to misrepresent their preferences. The assumed rankings are given in Table 2.1.

At the first round, Hopkins and Stanford offer positions to Alice, the most preferred student, and Yale offers one to its favorite, Barbara. Alice is tentatively matched with Stanford, which she prefers to Hopkins, and Barbara is tentatively matched with Yale. Thus, both Alice and Barbara are removed from Hopkins's rankings, moving Charlie to the top (by default as he is the only one left). At the next round, Stanford and Yale repeat their offers to Alice and Barbara, respectively, because

---

[16] We are indebted to Jeremy Bulow of Stanford University for this example.

**Table 2.2   Hospital's Revised Rankings at
Round III of the Algorithm**

Ranking	Hospital		
	H	S	Y
1st	B	A	A
2nd	C	B	C
3rd	—	C	—

each is at the top of the corresponding school's list, and Hopkins makes an offer to Charlie. All the students and hospitals are now matched, and these matches are the ones actually announced. Alice and Barbara end up with their second-favorite hospitals, but these two hospitals get their first picks.

Now suppose that Barbara misrepresents her preferences and submits a list that still ranks Stanford first, but then puts Hopkins rather Yale in second place. Tracing through the workings of the computer algorithm is much more complicated in this case (and you may prefer to skip the next two paragraphs, which describe the process), but it turns out that this misrepresentation will work to Barbara's advantage. She ends up being assigned to her first choice, Stanford.

At the first round, Alice is again tentatively matched with Stanford and Barbara with Yale. Now, however, since Barbara claims that she views Yale as third best, her name is not removed from Hopkins's list. Alice's name is, however, still taken off Hopkins's list, which now lists Barbara first and Charlie second. At the next round, Hopkins and Yale make offers to their now-favorite, Barbara, and Stanford repeats its offer to Alice. Barbara claims to like Hopkins better than Yale, so her tentative match with Yale is broken, and she is matched provisionally with Hopkins. As a result, she is removed from Yale's ranking. The revised rankings of the hospitals going into the third round are given in Table 2.2.

At the third stage, each hospital again makes an offer to the top-ranked student on its revised listing: Hopkins to Barbara, and Stanford and Yale to Alice. The tentative matches set by the computer are Barbara again with Hopkins, but Alice with her top choice, Yale. Thus, Alice is dropped from Stanford's list, moving Barbara to the top. Now, at the fourth stage, Barbara gets offers from both Hopkins and Stanford, while Alice again is Yale's choice. The computer now matches Barbara with Stanford, her first choice, and removes her from Hopkins's list. Consequently, at the fifth round, the computer matches Alice with Yale, Barbara with Stanford, and Charlie with Hopkins. This is the match that is announced.

Barbara's misrepresentation allowed her to get her first choice rather than her second, as she would have gotten by being honest. (Incidentally, it also moved Alice from her second-ranked hospital to her first.) By downgrading the hospital that ranked her first and would offer her first-round admission, Barbara manages to stay on Hopkins's list after being first matched with Yale, while Alice is dropped from Hopkins's list. Then Barbara is offered admission by Hopkins, which allows her to eliminate herself from Yale's list. This leads Yale to take Alice, opening the spot at Stanford for Barbara. Figuring out an advantageous preference misrepresentation was not obviously straightforward, since it depended on knowing the rankings of both the hospitals and the other students as well as the workings of the algorithm, but one existed.

In fact, medical students do spend time and energy trying to learn what the various hospitals are looking for, what their historical patterns of rankings have been, and what other students are likely to do, hoping thereby to figure out an advantageous way to misrepresent their preferences. However, as the example suggests, figuring out a worthwhile strategic misrepresentation is subtle and difficult. It is quite possible that students eventually give up trying to game the system and report accurately.

The Evolution and Persistence of Organizational Forms

The logic introduced in this chapter suggests that the efficiency and stability of the NIMP have contributed crucially to its survival, just as the failure of the earlier systems can be attributed to their inefficiency and instability. When an inefficient arrangement is in place, there is a general interest in supplanting it with one that will make everyone better off. When the arrangements are unstable in the sense we have discussed here, they are particularly fragile because pairs of agents have both the incentive and the ability to subvert their workings and presumably will do so.

This argument is supported by consideration of the mechanisms that have been used in the United Kingdom to address the problem of matching new physicians and hospitals there. The situation in the United Kingdom is more complex than in the United States, because there are seven regional markets, each of which has tried its own matching algorithms after a period of instability similar to that experienced in the United States before 1951. Eight of these different algorithms have been analyzed formally, of which two were found to be stable and six were not. The two stable ones are still in use, while four of the six unstable ones have been discarded.

As noted earlier, an increasing number of student couples in the United States are finding internships for themselves outside the NIMP. In terms of the theory proposed here, a reason for this is that the NIMP algorithm is not guaranteed to produce stable matches when couples look for assignments together. Thus, the recontracting problems that beset the older systems are effectively reappearing. In fact, no algorithm is guaranteed to find stable assignments in these environments, because none need exist! This suggests that instability in this market may become endemic.

Summary

There are economic organizations at many levels, from the economy as a whole to firms to units within them. Within the theory, the firm is distinguished from other, smaller units by its status as a legal entity able to enter into binding agreements with individuals. This power makes it unnecessary for the individuals to enter into a complex multilateral contract to organize their transactions and consequently makes it more likely that efficient arrangements can be negotiated.

The basic unit of analysis in economic organization theory is the transaction, where goods or services are transferred from one person to another. An important focus of the analysis is on the behavior of the individuals who transact. The main tasks of economic organization are to *coordinate* the actions of the various individual actors so that they form a coherent plan and to *motivate* the actors to act in accordance with the plan.

We evaluate organizations on the basis of how well they satisfy the wants and needs of people, that is, on the basis of their *efficiency*. Since organizations are partially designed, one can also explain features of organizations as attempts by the organization designers to achieve efficiency. The relative successes of different kinds of organization provide some of the main evidence for theories about which kinds of organization are most efficient in particular environments.

Using efficiency as a positive principle requires taking care about whose interests are being served and what kinds of arrangements are feasible. A small group that is able to bargain among its members may decide on arrangements that are efficient for themselves but that would be regarded as inefficient if the group could be enlarged. Efficiency in this sense is used to make predictions only and not to evaluate the social desirability of the agreed arrangements. In addition, arrangements that appear to be wasteful may still be efficient in the positive sense if there is no feasible alternative for the group that all would prefer.

The expansion of production in modern economies has been accomplished in large measure through *specialization*, according to which any one individual performs only a tiny fraction of the kinds of tasks required to make what he or she uses. Increased specialization implies that people become more reliant on the work of others, and the need for coordination increases. The two extreme alternative ways to coordinate are to communicate information to a central planner who makes all the important decisions or to provide individuals with the information and resources they need to make decisions that fit in with the overall plan. Both extremes are mere caricatures. Real economies all use a mix of these two approaches.

Transaction costs are the costs of negotiating and carrying out transactions. They include *coordination costs*, such as the costs of monitoring the environment, planning and bargaining to decide what needs to be done, and *motivation costs*, such as the costs of measuring performance, providing incentives, and enforcing agreements to ensure that people follow instructions, honor commitments, and keep agreements.

The way the transactions are best organized and managed depends on the basic attributes of the transaction. Five attributes have been identified as especially important. The first is *asset specificity*. When parties are called upon to make larger specific investments, they generally seek to organize in ways that safeguard those investments. Second, when one party is involved in *frequent, similar transactions* over a *long duration*, it is likely to pay that party to set up more specialized mechanisms or procedures to reduce the costs of transacting. Frequent transacting between two or more people over a long horizon allows the parties to develop understandings, reducing the need for explicit agreements, and to grant or withhold favors, reducing the need for outside enforcement of agreements. Third, *uncertainty* about the circumstances in which a transaction will occur and the *complexity* of the decisions that will be required make it hard to forecast exactly what performance will be required. This undermines the effectiveness of simple contracts and leads parties to contract over decision rights and procedures rather than over specific aspects of performance. Fourth, the *costliness of measuring performance* makes it difficult to provide performance incentives, leading the parties to seek organizations where measurement and incentive issues are of less importance. Fifth, when a transaction is *closely connected to other transactions*, that is, where failures of close fit among the transactions are quite costly compared to failures to make best use of local resources, coordination mechanisms tend to be strengthened, either by increasing managerial oversight or by arranging frequent meetings among the people responsible for the individual transactions.

In its simplest form, transaction costs theory holds that organizations are designed to minimize the total costs of transacting. The two problems with this simple theory are that the costs of transacting are not logically distinguishable from other costs, and that efficiency itself does not always imply total cost minimization. However, there is one special case where the latter problem, at least, disappears.

When individual preferences are free of wealth effects, that is, when everybody regards each outcome as being completely equivalent to receiving or paying some amount of money and when there are no a priori restrictions on monetary transfers, the efficient allocations are precisely those that maximize the total value and divide it all among the participants. This conclusion is known as the *value maximization principle*. The *Coase theorem* holds that when there are no wealth effects, all decisions about productive activities and organizational arrangements are unaffected by the wealth, assets, or bargaining power of the parties. Only the decision of how benefits and costs are to be shared is affected by these factors. This view contrasts, for example, with the Marxian view that organizations reflect underlying power arrangements and class interests and not the desire to maximize total wealth. When there are no wealth effects, an efficient organization acts as if it were an individual with a well-defined objective to maximize total value.

In the general case, the value maximization criterion does not describe how organizations behave. Organizations then may serve a variety of conflicting individual interests, rather than maximizing a single overall organizational objective. This is especially true of public organizations, like universities, with their ever-shifting balance among different social interests, but it is also true in varying degrees about business firms, where even the owners may have divergent interests.

While we do not attribute motives to organizations in general, we do attribute them to people. In the theories treated in this book, people are self-interested and opportunistic, and successful organizations must channel that self-interest into socially beneficial behavior.

◼ BIBLIOGRAPHIC NOTES

As with so many of the central concerns of economics, the problems of economic organization and organizations find their first treatment of lasting significance in Adam Smith's *The Wealth of Nations*. Although organizational issues were not a major focus of mainstream economists after Smith, important insights come from the writings of Karl Marx in the nineteenth century and especially from

Frank Knight and John Commons in the first quarter of the twentieth century. Commons in particular championed the treatment of the transaction as the fundamental unit for analysis, while Knight specifically addressed the organization of firms, and of economic activity more generally, in efficiency terms.

Ronald Coase is rightly viewed as the originator of transaction cost economics, and much of what we have reported in this chapter is an outgrowth of his classic 1937 paper in which he first developed the idea that economizing on transaction costs would determine the organization of economic activity and the division of activity between firms and markets. His 1960 paper, which develops the Coase Theorem, is another classic. It has done much to make economists aware of the power of using value maximization and efficiency as positive, explanatory principles. These papers were specifically cited when Coase was awarded the Nobel prize in Economics in 1991.

The importance of dispersed, local information for economic organization was accentuated by Friedrich Hayek in his contribution to the debate about market systems versus central planning that followed the establishment of the centralized communist system in the USSR.

Among more recent contributions, the contractual approach to organizations was championed by Armen Alchian and Harold Demsetz in seeking to explain the role of hierarchy and supervision in the firm in incentive terms. Kenneth Arrow's influential little book develops his treatment of organizations as arising when markets fail. Oliver Williamson's writings have played a major role in developing transaction cost economics. His 1985 book gives an excellent overview of his approach, which identifies asset specificity, frequency, and uncertainty as the key dimensions of transactions and which also accentuates the limits of human rationality. This latter theme was first introduced into economics by Herbert Simon, and has been developed in an evolutionary direction by Richard Nelson and Sidney Winter. Yoram Barzel, building on the contributions of Stephen Cheung, has emphasized the measurement costs dimension of transaction cost economics. The connectedness dimension and the notion of design connectedness are introduced for the first time here.

The survey papers by Bengt Holmstrom and Jean Tirole and by Williamson are valuable supplements not only for the questions in this chapter, but for many of the issues addressed throughout the book. Our paper on bargaining and influence costs is an integrated presentation and critique of the basics of transaction cost economics.

◼ REFERENCES

Alchian, A., and H. Demsetz. "Production, Information Costs, and Economic Organization," *American Economic Review*, 62 (1972), 777–95.

Arrow, K.J. *The Limits of Organization* (New York: W.W. Norton, 1974).

Barzel, Y. "Measurement Costs and the Organization of Markets," *Journal of Law and Economics*, 25 (1982), 27–48.

Cheung, S.N.S. "Transaction Costs, Risk Aversion, and the Choice of Contractual Arrangements," *Journal of Law and Economics*, 12 (1969), 23–42.

Coase, R. "The Nature of the Firm," *Economica*, 4 (1937), 386–405.

Coase, R. "The Problem of Social Cost," *Journal of Law and Economics*, 3 (1960), 1–44.

Commons, J.R. "Institutional Economics," *American Economic Review*, 21 (1931), 648–57.

Hayek, F.A. "The Use of Knowledge in Society," *American Economic Review*, 35 (1945), 519–30.

Holmstrom, B.R., and J. Tirole. "The Theory of the Firm," Chapter 2 in R. Schmalensee and R. Willig, eds., *Handbook of Industrial Economics* (New York: North-Holland, 1989).

Knight, F.H. *Risk, Uncertainty and Profit* (London: London School of Economics, 1921).

Marx, K., *Capital* (Harmondworth, UK: Penguin Books, 1976).

Milgrom, P., and J. Roberts. "Bargaining and Influence Costs and the Organization of Economic Activity," in J. Alt and K. Shepsle, eds., *Perspectives on Positive Political Economy* (Cambridge: Cambridge University Press, 1990).

Nelson, R.R. and S. Winter. *An Evolutionary Theory of Economic Change* (Cambridge, MA: Harvard University Press, 1982).

Simon H. *Models of Man* (New York: John Wiley & Sons, 1957).

Smith, A. *An Inquiry into the Nature and Causes of the Wealth of Nations* (Oxford: The Clarendon Press, 1976).

Williamson, O. *The Economic Institutions of Capitalism: Firms, Markets, Relational Contracting* (New York: The Free Press, 1985).

Williamson, O. "Transaction Cost Economics," Chapter 3 in R. Schmalensee and R. Willig, eds., *Handbook of Industrial Economics* (New York: North-Holland, 1989).

EXERCISES

Food for Thought

1.   One of the main tenets of economic analysis is that people act in their own narrow interests. Why, then, do people leave tips in restaurants? If a study were to compare the size of the tips earned by servers in roadside restaurants with those frequented mostly by locals, what would you expect to find? Why?

2.   For most large Japanese firms, a majority of the voting shares are owned by the company's major lenders (banks and insurance companies), its customers and suppliers, and related firms with whom it has longstanding relationships. How would this ownership structure affect the objectives that these firms seem to pursue?

3.   Would you expect the organization of agriculture in developing countries to be arranged in a way that maximizes the total wealth of the farmers, workers, and lenders? If arrangements do not maximize total wealth, what kind of variations would be most likely? Explain your answer.

4.   In California's fruit farms, farm workers who pick fruit are commonly organized into teams that are paid according to the number of trees that are cleanly picked. The teams themselves decide how to divide the pay among their members. What attributes of this transaction account for this arrangement?

5.   Cable television companies lay cables to individual households in the communities they serve to carry the television signal. How specific is this investment? What kind of arrangements would you expect the cable companies to make with local communities about the pricing and taxation of cable services?

Mathematical Exercises

1.   Suppose four families share a common stretch of beach and they are considering a program of improvements, including a stairway and a play structure for children. The value of spending y in total for the improvements is $5y - \frac{1}{2}y^2$ for families #1 and #2, $7y - \frac{1}{2}y^2$ for family #3, and $4y - y^2$ for family #4. What is the efficient level of expenditure on beach improvements?

2.   Continuing with the situation hypothesized in problem 1, show that if the cost of the improvements is to be shared equally, then family #4 will be unwilling to bear its share of the cost. What is the largest improvement that all the families would agree to if the cost of improvement must be shared equally? Demonstrate that the resulting expenditure is inefficiently low by finding an alternative level of expenditure and pattern of cost sharing that the families unanimously prefer.

3.   (Mathematical proof of the value maximization principle.) Suppose that there are N individuals. Person n's utility when outcome y occurs and he or she receives cash compensation of x_n is given by the utility function $x_n + v_n(y)$. Suppose that decision y generates net profits $P(y)$, which may be a positive number if we think of y as representing an investment or a negative number if we think of y as representing some public good, such as parks or roads, at a total cost of $-P(y)$. The profits are divided among the individuals with individual n receiving x_n (or paying $-x_n$). The payments must add up to the amount available, that is, $P(y) = x_1 + \ldots + x_N$. Prove that an allocation $(y, x_1, \ldots, x_N)$ is efficient if and only if y maximizes the total value $P(y) + v_1(y) + \ldots + v_N(y)$. [*Hint:* There are two things to prove. First, you must show that if an allocation does maximize the total value, then there cannot be an allocation that Pareto dominates it. Second, if the allocation does not maximize the sum, then you must show that there is another allocation that dominates it. To show the latter, take any y with a higher total value and show that the x_ns can be chosen so that the gain in total wealth is divided equally among the participants.]

4.   (Characterizing a utility function when there are no wealth effects.) Suppose that a decision maker's preferences are such that for any two decisions y and y', there is an amount of cash compensation or a cash payment such that y combined with cash compensation of $C(y, y')$ would be just as good, from the decision maker's perspective, as y' with a zero-cash compensation. Further suppose that this amount $C(y, y')$ does not depend on the level of other cash payments made to or by the decision maker. Finally, suppose that the decision maker prefers more money to less. Fix any possible decision $\bar{y}$ and define $v(y) = C(\bar{y}, y)$. Show that with this definition, the utility function $x + v(y)$ represents the decision maker's preferences; that is, the decision maker will prefer an allocation (x, y) to another allocation (x', y') if and only if $x + v(y) > x' + v(y')$. [*Hint:* Argue first that the decision maker is indifferent about having (x, y) or $(x + v(y), \bar{y})$. Therefore, for any utility function that represents the decision maker's preferences, $U(x, y) = U(x + v(y), \bar{y})$ and, similarly, $U(x', y') = U(x' + v(y'), \bar{y})$.]

3

USING PRICES
FOR COORDINATION
AND MOTIVATION

Which of these systems [central planning or competitive markets] is likely to be more efficient depends mainly on the question under which of them we can expect that fuller use will be made of the existing knowledge. And this, in turn, depends on whether we are more likely to succeed in putting at the disposal of a single central authority all the knowledge which ought to be used but which is initially dispersed among many different individuals, or in conveying to the individuals such additional knowledge as they need in order to enable them to fit their plans in with those of others.

—*Friedrich Hayek*[1]

All economies face the basic problems of determining what is to be produced, by and for whom, using what methods and resources. Even in the simplest, most primitive societies, food must be gathered, hunted or grown, clothing must be made, shelter must be provided, and so on. Of course, in primitive societies it is possible for people to do many or all of these things for themselves. However, as civilization advanced people realized that they can make more of all these produced goods using the same limited resources if people specialize their activities and if production occurs on a larger scale than would be needed to serve any single person. For example, a person who specializes in building shelters and who builds many of them can acquire specialized tools to make the job easier that would hardly be worthwhile if only one shelter were to be built. This person can also acquire experience and specialized training to improve his or her proficiency. Such a person can build more shelters, faster, with less waste of materials and better-quality construction than can individuals building shelters only for their own needs, with little or no prior experience.

With specialization comes a keen need to plan and coordinate people's activities so that effective use can be made of the limited resources at their disposal. People who build shelters for themselves may have a good idea what is needed, when, and

---

[1] "The Use of Knowledge in Society," *American Economic Review*, 35 (1945), 519–30.

where, but people who build shelters for others need to be told these things. If shelters are to be built by specialists, how many builders will be needed? How many tools of each kind should be prepared? How much lumber? And how many people should be cobblers, farmers, and so on? How much land should be planted with crops and how much used for grazing, or left fallow, or saved for parks? Even in the simplest communities, economic life demands a large measure of coordination among people.

In the modern economy, the scope of activities that need coordination is great. The amount of oil that should be pumped from Saudi Arabian oil fields depends on the characteristics of the fields, of course, but it also depends on how much gasoline, heating oil, and other products will be used by drivers, homeowners, and industries at hundreds of millions of separate locations throughout the world. It depends on how much oil is pumped in other places from Alaska to the North Sea and from Texas to Siberia as well. The changing availability of oil affects the need for refineries and drilling equipment, for cars, gas stations, and home insulation, for public transportation and highways, for electric cars, electrical generation plants, and research into synthetic fuels, among many other needs and activities. The problems of and possibilities for organizing economic activity on a world scale *are* daunting, yet they *are* carried out, every day, with no effective central control by any government or cartel and hardly any thought by the participants about their roles in the system as a whole.

If it seems surprising that the global economic system could work at all without some central coordination, it is surely even more surprising that it functions so smoothly so much of the time. In most Western nations, it is considered newsworthy when drivers cannot simply drive to the local pump to fill their cars' tanks with gasoline. In contrast, in the centrally planned economy of the Soviet Union, it is newsworthy when consumers find adequate supplies of milk and meat in the stores. Therefore, before we discuss the economics of how *managed* organizations work in Chapter 4, we first devote this chapter to the workings of unmanaged markets, in which decision makers acting without central direction and with perhaps all too little social consciousness achieve the effective coordination that often escapes more tightly controlled systems.

PRICES AND COORDINATION

Our principal purpose in this section is to begin developing the central economic model that has been used to study how markets can achieve a high degree of coordination without central planning: the **neoclassical market model**. This model is based on a particular conception of economic organization. Specifically, the economy consists of consumers/resource suppliers, whose needs and wants the organization tries to satisfy, and productive units (firms) that purchase resources (including labor services) from consumers, make the products consumers desire, and are owned by consumers (either directly or indirectly).

The needs of consumers can be satisfied in a variety of ways. If wheat for bread is in short supply this year, oats, rye, or corn can be substituted to produce a similar product. Clothing can be made from cotton, wool, or various synthetic fibers and, in many cases, consumers might not care if the garments are delivered this week or next. Even identical goods and services can be produced in many ways. Homes can be kept warm using electricity, fuel oil, natural gas, or solar power, or better insulation can substitute for energy use. Goods can often be transported to a destination by truck, train, ship, barge, or airplane. Similarly, each of the economy's resources can be put to many different uses. Corn can be used to make food or fuel. Workers can be trained to be clerks, carpenters, or computer programmers. The possibilities are almost endless.

Given the complexity of the problem of allocating resources, no single person could possibly determine an efficient allocation. To do so, one would have to first comprehend and account for all the possible activities and claims on resources that could and should be considered. Then one would have to identify feasible plans for all these activities consistent with the resources available and with the technological opportunities. Finally, from among these, one would have to identify an efficient plan. Even this last step alone demands too much to be practicable. There are simply too many facets of the economy—the different resources available, the diverse individuals with particular skills and needs, the many new technologies, and so on—that must be understood in order to check whether a particular proposed allocation is efficient. Even if the decision maker were aided by banks of powerful computers so that computation were not a problem, there would still be the need to assemble all the relevant information about production possibilities, resource availability, and individual tastes for the computers to process. Collecting the necessary data, ensuring their accuracy, and keeping them continuously up to date would be an impossible task. To organize production well, local decisions must rely to a large extent on knowledge of local circumstances. For example, decisions about how to respond when a worker gets sick or a machine breaks down are usually best handled by those directly involved.

The economic organization problem, as seen through the neoclassical lens, is to provide people throughout the economy with the information they need to make decisions that are *coherent* (that is, part of an efficient overall plan) and to motivate them to carry out their parts of the plan. The neoclassical model is a formal mathematical model consisting of a set of equations and inequalities that represents the way markets work. It can be used to prove that a system of properly determined prices can solve the organization problem. Under certain circumstances, prices provide people with all the additional information about the economy that they need in order to make efficient use of the available resources. Furthermore, if individuals and firms act out of pure self-interest, taking prices as given and maximizing their individual utilities or profits, they will be motivated to undertake exactly those activities that lead to efficiency.

Our purpose in this chapter is to study how far a simple price system can go in solving the coordination problem of economic organization. The following discussion develops the main idea in two steps. First, we solve the optimal organization problem for an example (road maintenance) in which there is a single objective (saving lives) and a single constrained resource (hours of work-crew time). We then turn to the more general theory, in which there are many consumers, each with his or her own objectives, and many limited resources, each of which is valuable and needs to be conserved. In the neoclassical model, the market simultaneously reconciles these conflicting objectives, directs resources to production, and motivates firms to produce the right products.

One Objective and a Single Scarce Resource

Suppose that you are in charge of the Department of Highway Safety for the government. Your job is to save lives by directing the resources at your disposal to projects that reduce the number of fatal highway accidents. You are limited by the number of hours available from the work crews that carry out the projects.

Reviewing your department's performance last year, you have constructed a table of some of the projects that you considered. Table 3.1 might be an excerpt from a much longer table, but it shows all the projects that were actually carried out. Thus, a total of 3,000 crew hours were expended, the maximum number available.

Last year, projects were not selected in the way that maximizes the number of lives saved. If project 2 had been eliminated and the crew hours freed were used to

Table 3.1 Life-Saving Projects (Estimates)

Project ID No.	Crew Hours	Lives Saved	Lives per 1,000 Crew Hours	Project Accepted?
5	800	4	5.00	No
4	900	3	3.33	Yes
1	800	2	2.50	Yes
6	500	1	2.00	No
2	1,300	2	1.54	Yes
3	700	1	1.43	No

carry out projects 5 and 6, an estimated three additional lives could have been saved (four lives saved by project 5 and one by project 6, instead of the estimated two lives from project 2). The supply of crew hours has therefore not been used efficiently.

Two problems make the selection operation difficult. First, because the projects are not all available for review at once, they cannot be compared to select the best ones. Second, due to the number and complexity of projects to be reviewed, staff members in several regional offices are involved in making the estimates and acceptance decisions. At the beginning of the year, you may have a pretty good idea about what kinds of projects will be available. However, you have no way to know what the specific projects will be, when they will be proposed, or which offices will evaluate them. You need to find a way to coordinate decisions made by different offices at different times during the year to assure that the most productive projects are chosen. What can you do to help your staff members make well-informed decisions?

DETERMINING THE OPTIMAL PRICE   To understand how to solve this problem, let us start with an even easier one. Suppose you knew in advance which projects would be proposed during the year. In order to maximize the number of lives saved subject to the constraint on available labor time, you would want to start by carrying out those projects that have the highest return-per-unit input, and then move from the highest-return projects to those with lower returns until the crew hours were exhausted. Otherwise, shifting labor from a project that saves a low number of lives (per crew hour) to one that saves a higher number would increase the number of lives saved without using any more crew time. Thus, you would rank the projects according to the number of lives saved per thousand crew hours required. This index of life-saving efficiency is shown for last year's projects in Table 3.1.

If the projects last year had been selected according to this index, you would have undertaken projects 5, 4, 1, and 6, at which point the 3,000 crew hours would have been exhausted. No other combination of projects in this example could save more lives given the limited availability of crew time. Note that these are precisely the projects for which the lives saved per thousand crew hours is greater than or equal to two. Your problem therefore has a very simple solution that involves communicating remarkably little information: You could simply have directed the different offices to carry out projects if and only if their indices of lives saved per 1,000 crew hours were at least two. If the offices obeyed instructions, the best allocation would have been achieved.

This example illustrates a general lesson: No matter what the list of projects, there is always a number P such that if all projects for which the index of lives saved per 1,000 crew hours is at least P are accepted and all projects with lower indices are rejected, the selected group of projects is the one that maximizes the estimated number of lives that can be saved with the available resources. Here the number P is a price, expressed in terms of lives rather than dollars, marks, or yen. The unit in which a price is expressed is not important for this analysis. What is important is that all the costs and benefits from a project be expressed in terms of a common unit so that they can be compared. In our example, 1,000 crew hours has a "price" of two lives. This means that it pays to undertake (only) those projects for which the benefit in terms of lives saved exceeds the cost of the crew hours, when the crew hours are valued in this way.

By calculating P and instructing your staff members to base their decisions on that value, the result will be coordinated project selection decisions both among offices and over the course of the year. There is no need for more detailed communication or coordination among your staff, nor does the timing of the proposals create any problems. The price P provides each staff member with all the information he or she needs in order to make the decisions that best accomplish the objectives.

Of course, in actuality you do not know in advance what the value of P should be. It will depend on the projects that actually become available during the year. If you set the value too high, you will wind up rejecting some projects that ought to have been accepted. If you set it too low, you will accept too many projects early in the year and run out of resources for better projects later in the year.

One possible solution is to estimate P on the basis of last year's experience. This may often work quite well; historically-based systems are commonly used in budgeting. If the distribution of projects varies considerably from year to year, however, an estimate of P based on the previous year's experience is likely to be inaccurate and to lead to an inefficient selection of projects. Still, it is important to recognize that any system for selecting projects will sometimes yield the wrong answers if decisions must be made before all the alternatives are known. A great advantage of the price system is that it eliminates all the other sources of waste that might otherwise be present even if all the project proposals were known in advance. More specifically, it eliminates the lack of consistency of decisions over time for a single decision maker and the lack of coordination among the several staff decision makers.

A Market-Clearing Interpretation

The method of determining the optimal price can be viewed as resulting from a market. This is an important idea because it gives us our first hint about how decentralized markets lead to the efficient use of resources.

Suppose that the project evaluators in the previous example were able to bid for the crew hour resources in an ordinary market, each with the objective of maximizing the number of the lives he or she saves minus the cost of the crew hours used. Their demands are plotted in Figure 3.1. Quantities are placed on the horizontal axis, whereas the supply of crew hours is assumed to be fixed and is represented by the vertical line at 3,000 crew hours. To determine how quantities depend on prices, find the relevant price on the vertical axis and look across to find the corresponding quantity.

Looking back at Table 3.1 we see that at any price higher than 5.00 (lives per thousand crew hours), none of the projects would be "profitable." That is, the cost of the crew hours used in terms of lives would exceed the benefit, even for the most cost-effective projects. Consequently, when the price exceeds 5.00, there is a zero demand for crew hours. At any price below 5.00 but above 3.33, project 5 would be the only profitable project, so the 800 crew hours required by project 5 are recorded in Figure 3.1 as the demand for prices in that range. At prices below 3.33 but above 2.50, projects 5 and 4 are both profitable. They require a total of 1,700 crew hours, which is therefore the demand corresponding to prices between 3.33 and 2.50 in

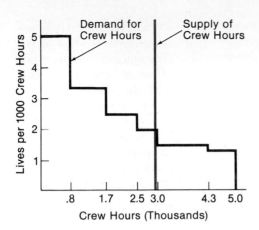

Figure 3.1: The projects that are profitable at a price like 2 where supply equals demand are just the ones that ought to be undertaken to maximize the number of lives saved.

Figure 3.1. As the price continues to fall, the demands of the various projects are added in the order listed in the table.

As the figure indicates, two (lives per thousand crew hours) is a *market-clearing price*. Simply, at this price the quantity of crew hours demanded equals the quantity available. At higher prices the demand falls short of the available supply, whereas at sufficiently lower prices there is a shortage of crew hours. At the market-clearing point, each evaluator finds it most "profitable" in terms of the specified objectives to undertake precisely those projects that are part of the optimal life-saving plan.

Extensions and Difficulties

In the preceding example, prices enable the different regional offices to work independently and yet make coherent, well-coordinated decisions. The example has many special features, however. First, there is a single scarce resource—crew hours—that limited the department's ability to save lives. Second, there is a nice match between the size of the available labor supply and the amount needed to complete the most efficient projects: Carrying out the best projects uses up exactly the available 3,000 hours. Third, the staff shares a common objective so there is no concern that some office might pursue idiosyncratic or personal goals.

Relaxing the first of these special assumptions is relatively easy. Suppose that, in place of the single constraint on the number of crew hours available, the department were limited in both the budget for materials and the number of hours available from work crews. In that case, we would conclude that two prices—one for materials and the other for work crew hours, both expressed in terms of lives—can be used to characterize the optimal plan.

As we mentioned earlier, an important characteristic of prices is that they can be expressed in virtually any units, provided that all costs and benefits are expressed in the same units. In the actual economy, prices are most commonly expressed in money terms. In this case, the plan that saves the greatest number of lives can therefore be characterized as the one that selects just those projects for which the dollar cost per life saved is less than the "dollar value" of a life.

The second special feature of the match between the size of the labor supply and the amount needed can also be removed at this point. Referring to Table 3.1, suppose that project 6, instead of requiring 500 crew hours to save one life, required 1,000 hours and saved two lives. The index of lives saved per 1,000 crew hours remains two. There is no longer enough labor to carry out this project, however, given that all higher-valued projects are still to be completed. If projects can be scaled down with both the resources used and the number of lives saved scaled down proportionately, then an augmented version of the price system still works. You would want to undertake project 6 at a 50 percent level, using 500 hours and saving one life. With knowledge of the price only, however, the office considering this project would not know that it should undertake only part of it. Thus, for marginal projects, additional communication is necessary to achieve coordination.

If the crew hours involved in individual projects are few relative to the aggregate supply of crew time, this inadequacy of prices may be only a small problem; most decisions can still be price guided, and only those that are close calls will require additional communication. If the projects are both large and indivisible, however, in that each must be completed in full or not at all, then a price system may be unable to identify the optimal solution. For example, the optimum may entail undertaking a low-valued project that fits within the available labor constraint while forgoing a higher-valued project. Communication of prices alone will then fail to allow decision makers to identify the correct selection of projects.

It is also possible to dispense with the third special feature of the single, shared objective in the context of this example. However, we instead turn to a more general treatment in which the multiplicity of individual objectives is a central feature.

THE FUNDAMENTAL THEOREM OF WELFARE ECONOMICS

We now turn to an analysis of markets in an economy that has many consumers and producers with varying individual objectives and many goods and services. Remarkably, a price system can sometimes solve the coordination problem in this context as well. Briefly, we conclude that if (1) each productive unit knows the prices and its own individual production technology and maximizes its own profits at the prevailing prices, (2) each consumer knows the prices and his or her own individual preferences and then maximizes utility given the prevailing prices and his or her income, and (3) the prices are such that supply equals demand for each good, then the allocation of goods that results is efficient: There is no other allocation consistent with the available resources and technological opportunities that the consumers would unanimously prefer.

There are two remarkable aspects to this conclusion. First, knowing only local information and the system-wide prices is enough for each producer and consumer to make the choices required for coherence and efficiency. There is no need for central planning or extensive sharing of information; coordination is automatically achieved. Second, each consumer and each firm is asked only to pursue its own interests fully and diligently; firms maximize profits and consumers maximize personal utility. Nobody is asked to use information in any way contrary to his or her narrow self-interests, and yet the whole system of behavior is coherent so that the resulting allocations of goods and services are actually efficient. The precise statement of this much celebrated conclusion has come to be known as the *fundamental theorem of welfare economics*. This theorem has a long, rich history, which dates back to its intuitive formulation in the work of Adam Smith, and includes a series of mathematical formulations developed in the nineteenth and twentieth centuries. The following formulation is a variant of a model created originally by Kenneth Arrow and Gerard Debreu.

The Neoclassical Model of a Private Ownership Economy

THE INDIVIDUAL CONSUMER Our analysis begins with a single consumer, one of many who participate in the economy. This consumer can supply his or her own labor to employers for wages. The consumer may also own stocks of consumer goods, land, commodities, or industrial equipment. Let E be a list of numbers denoting the amounts of the various goods, labor, land, commodities, and so on that the consumer owns. This list E is called the consumer's resource *endowment*.

The concept of a *list* (or *vector*) is quite important in our formal development. Each list specifies an amount for every conceivable good or service in the economy, that is, anything that any consumer or firm might ever want to buy or sell. Let G denote the number of different goods and services in the economy. A typical endowment list $E = (E_1, E_2, \ldots, E_G)$ has components specifying the amounts of farm land, wheat, labor hours, shoes, and so on that the consumer owns—one component for each of the G goods. For most consumers, many of the elements of the list are zero. The average consumer does not own rolls of newsprint, electrical generating equipment, or magnetic resonance imaging machines.

Lists can be added together. For example, if E is your endowment and E' is your neighbor's endowment, then $E + E' = (E_1 + E'_1, E_2 + E'_2, \ldots, E_G + E'_G)$ is a new list that specifies how much of each good the two of you have together.

What do consumers do with their endowments? Basically, they can sell some amounts of the different goods in the market and keep some to consume. Let S be a list of the quantities that the consumer sells of each good or service traded in the market. Of course, $S_1 \le E_1$, $S_2 \le E_2$, and so on. That is, the consumer cannot sell more of any good than he or she owns. If the consumer sells only labor and uses the income to buy other goods, then only the labor entry in the list S will be different from zero. Still, we take S to be a complete list, with an entry for each item that the consumer might possibly buy or sell.

In addition to the list S, there is a list B indicating the quantities that the consumer buys. This list has an entry for each item that the consumer might possibly buy or sell. The entry corresponding to the consumer's own labor will be zero (the consumer does not buy his or her own labor), and there may be zeroes for many other goods as well.

Of great importance to the consumer is the list P of prices at which the various goods trade. Again, there is an entry for each good, each kind of labor—everything that is traded in the market. We use the notation PB to denote the cost of buying the types and amounts of goods in the list B at the prices listed in P. We can compute PB by multiplying the price for each good by the quantity of that good purchased to get the amount spent on the individual good, and then adding these amounts up over all the goods purchased. The summation notation for this equation is $PB = \sum_{i=1}^{G} P_i B_i$. Similarly, $PS = \sum_{i=1}^{G} P_i S_i$ denotes the income the consumer earns from selling the quantities of various items listed in S.

Each consumer may also own shares of the various business firms in the economy. Let F_j be the fraction of firm j that the consumer owns. If firm j earns a profit and pays a dividend D_j, then the consumer will find his or her income augmented by the amount $F_j D_j$. Let FD denote the total income the consumer receives in the form of dividends. If there are J firms in all, then $FD = \sum_{i=1}^{G} F_j D_j$.

INDIVIDUAL CONSUMPTION PLANS   A *consumption plan* for a consumer is a pair of lists B and S indicating what the consumer plans to buy and sell. The plan is *affordable* at prices P if $PB \le PS + FD$, that is, if the consumer generates enough income from dividends and from selling labor and other goods to pay for the goods he or she plans to buy. The consumer might like to live in a mansion on Malibu Beach and drive a red Porsche, but these purchases may be unaffordable.

In the neoclassical model, the *utility* or satisfaction a consumer gets from

Table 3.2   A Description of Consumer Behavior

| Goods | Units | Price | Consumer #1 | | | |
			Endowment	Sales	Purchases	Consumption
Labor	Hours	15	2,600	2,000	0	600
Bread	Loaves	1	0	0	100	100
Autos (new)	Number	8,000	0	0	1	1
Autos (used)	Number	4,000	1	1	0	0

carrying out a plan depends only on the list of goods C that he or she consumes. This utility is denoted by $U(C)$.[2] Implicit in this notation is the assumption that consumers care only about their own consumption and not about the firms' methods of production or the consumption enjoyed by others. The model also assumes that the consumer chooses the plan that leads to the highest level of utility among those affordable at the given prices.

Table 3.2 shows the kind of data we use to describe the activities of the consumers in the economy. The first three columns in the table represent factors that are common to all agents: the goods in the economy, their units of measurement, and the prices. The next four columns represent one of the collections of lists we have described. This one is for consumer 1. The reader should imagine that the table continues with more rows below the last one, showing additional goods that can be bought and sold, and more columns, showing the data for additional consumers.

According to the table, consumer 1 is endowed with 2,600 hours of labor for the year, perhaps consisting of 50 hours per week for 52 weeks. According to the plan, the consumer will sell 2,000 hours of labor to generate income and will consume 600 hours in the form of leisure. That is, for 600 hours during which the consumer might possibly have been working, he or she will instead attend a concert or go on a family picnic, or do any number of things. Because the price of labor hours is 15, this sale of labor will generate an income of 30,000 (2,000 x 15) that consumer 1 can spend on other goods. According to the table, the consumer will also sell a used car, generating proceeds of 4,000 that can be spent on other things. The table also shows how the income will be spent. A new car will consume 8,000 units of the income, 100 loaves of bread will consume another 100, and so on.

As the table illustrates, the person's consumption of each good can be computed by starting with the endowment, adding the quantity of the good that the consumer buys, and then subtracting whatever he or she sells. That is, consumption is equal to $C = E + B - S$. The consumer normally will be a buyer of some goods and a seller of others. In either case, consumption of each good is determined by the formula just described.

The fundamental theorem makes one additional assumption about consumer tastes called *local nonsatiation*: Starting from any consumption bundle or list, there is always some good or service of which the consumer would like to have a little bit more. One consequence of local nonsatiation is that utility-maximizing consumers will always spend all of their income on something. This fact is expressed mathematically as follows:

$$PB = PS + FD \tag{3.1}$$

---

[2] Note that we do not assume here that there are no wealth effects (Chapter 2). The theorem does not require this assumption.

The left-hand side of the equation is the aggregate amount the consumer spends on purchases of all the different goods, and the right-hand side is the total income from sales and dividends.

THE FIRM   We turn next to the description of firms, or producers, in the economy. Each firm has some set of possible activities to which it can devote resources. The firm may be able to produce many different products, each in several different ways using a variety of inputs. What the firm does is summarized by what we call a *production plan*. Such a plan consists of a list O of outputs produced and another list I of inputs used. The plan is *technically feasible* if it is possible to produce the outputs O from the inputs I using the technology available to the firm. The set of technically feasible plans for the firm is denoted by T. The fact that a plan (I,O) is feasible is represented by the mathematical statement, $(I,O) \in T$, which we read as "the plan (I,O) is in T, the technologically feasible set for this firm."

Commonly, firms and consumers will be on opposite sides of any market transaction. For example, consumers typically sell labor and buy bread, whereas a bread-making firm will buy labor (and other inputs) and use it to make bread to sell. Thus, inputs for a firm often correspond to sales by consumers and outputs often correspond to purchases. In other cases, purchases and sales occur between firms, with one's output being another's input.

The neoclassical model assumes that firms are motivated by profit alone. Given the prices P, the firm's total income or revenue from the sale of its outputs is PO. The cost of its inputs, including the wages paid to workers and all other expenses, is PI. Therefore, the firm chooses the technically feasible production plan that maximizes its profit $PO - PI$. The dividend D paid by the firm is assumed to be equal to its profit $PO - PI$.

ECONOMIES AND ALLOCATIONS   Now, suppose there are many consumers in our idealized economy, each with his or her own tastes for consumption. In addition, each consumer may have a different endowment. For example, one person may be endowed with the labor of a computer programmer and another with the labor of an automobile mechanic. One may have inherited wealth, whereas another is a pauper with only his or her own labor to sell. A wide range of possibilities exists. In our notation, each individual consumer is identified by a social security number. For example, if n is the social security number identifying one particular consumer, then E^n is the consumer's endowment, S^n is his or her list of sales, and B^n is the list of things the consumer purchases. Similarly, there may be many firms with differing technologies and ownership. Firms are represented by their employer ID numbers. Firm j's plan is represented by the lists of outputs O^j and inputs I^j it will use, which must lie in its own technically feasible set, T^j.

Formally, a **private ownership economy** in our model consists of the following elements. There is a set of consumers N, together with a utility function U^n and an endowment E^n for each consumer n. There is also a set of firms J, together with a technically feasible set T^j for each firm j, and ownership shares F^{nj} for each consumer n in each firm j. An *allocation* for the economy is a consumption plan for each consumer and a production plan for each firm that together are *feasible*. A feasible set of plans is one with the following three properties:

1. Each firm is able to make the prescribed outputs from the prescribed inputs. That is, $(I^j,O^j) \in T^j$.

2. Each consumer has available the goods he or she is asked to deliver. That is, $S^n \leq E^n$.

3. The total amounts of each good planned for delivery to consumers and firms does not exceed what is available in the economy. That is, $\Sigma B_n + \Sigma I_j \le \Sigma S_n + \Sigma O_j$.

An allocation is *efficient* (or Pareto optimal) if there is no other allocation that Pareto dominates it, that is, no other allocation that all consumers view as at least as good as the given one and some consumer strictly prefers.

PRICE FORMATION   The model we are describing does not include, within its formal structure, any description of the mechanism by which prices are set and adjusted with changing conditions. Instead, it simply postulates that there are prices for each good and service that are publicly known and at which everyone believes they can transact.

In fact, there is no one single mechanism by which prices in actual economies are set. There is instead some combination of mechanisms, including stores setting posted prices for the goods they offer, commodities being sold at auction, negotiators setting wages, and so on. Which of these processes is used will vary across situations, but the results of all of them should be responsive to economic conditions.

When supplies of a good are less than the amounts that buyers want to purchase, for example, stores find it easier to sell their inventories of the good without special discounts and sales. If bidders are worried that there may be no more units for sale tomorrow, they place higher bids today. If labor negotiators feel secure that high wages will not lead to layoffs or temporary shutdowns of production, they will press for better pay. The price paid by buyers in all these circumstances tends to rise. As prices rise, buyers become less eager to buy and sellers rush to provide more goods, helping to close the gap between the quantities the sellers offer for sale and the buyers bid to purchase.

When there are excess supplies of some good, the opposite process takes place. Stores with unsold inventories put the goods on sale, bidders may find themselves bidding unopposed, and labor negotiators may worry about possible layoffs. All these factors lead to a reduction in the prices paid by buyers.

As long as there is any gap between what sellers want to supply and what buyers demand at the prevailing prices, there is pressure for prices to change to reduce the gap. Prices are constantly adjusting in response to these pressures, always aiming for a balance between supply and demand. Nevertheless, to assess the potential of the price system, we make the same kind of simplification we used to study the problem of saving lives. In the life-saving example, we supposed that the prices are known and set so as to balance the supply of crew hours with the demand for them, and we showed that the resulting decisions were optimal. Here, we suppose that the publicly-known prices are set exactly as necessary to balance supply (the quantities offered for sale) with demand (the quantities that buyers wish to purchase). This point, at which prices have no pressure to change, is called a **competitive equilibrium**.

COMPETITIVE EQUILIBRIUM   A competitive equilibrium for the economy in this model consists of a price list P that contains a nonnegative price for each good, a consumption plan B^n and S^n for each consumer n, and a production plan (I^j, O^j) for each firm j. Furthermore, these lists must satisfy three conditions. First, each consumer's consumption plan must maximize his or her utility. That is, it must give the consumer at least as much satisfaction as does any other affordable plan. Second, each firm must maximize its profits. That is, each firm's production plan must generate profits that are at least as high as those for any other technically feasible plan. And third, at the given prices, the quantity demanded of each marketed item must be equal to the quantity offered for sale. Again using the symbol Σ to represent a summation, the statement "supply equals demand" is expressed as:

$$\sum_n S^n + \sum_j O^j = \sum_n B^n + \sum_j I^j. \tag{3.2}$$

The left-hand side of Equation 3.2 is a supply list consisting of the total sales by consumers plus the outputs by firms of the various goods. For example, the quantity of oats supplied in the left-hand list is the sum of the quantities sold by individuals plus the quantities produced by farms. The right-hand side of the equation is the demand list consisting of the total purchases of the various goods. For example, the quantity of oats purchased in the list is the total of the quantities purchased by individuals, by farmers for horse feed, by bakers for bread, by breakfast-cereal manufacturers, and so on. Each purchaser is classified as either a consumer, who is maximizing the utility of consumption, or a producer, who is maximizing profits.

THE THEOREM   Now that we have identified the basic elements involved in the fundamental theorem of welfare economics, we can formally state the theorem as follows:

> **The Fundamental Theorem of Welfare Economics**: *If (P,B,S,I,O) are the price lists and plans of a competitive equilibrium, then the resulting allocation is efficient.*

A logically equivalent way to state the theorem is as follows. If (B,S,I,O) is a set of competitive equilibrium plans and (B',S',I',O') is any other set of plans that all consumers like at least as well and that at least one consumer strictly prefers, then (B',S',I',O') is not feasible.

Notice that it is only *allocations*, not prices, that we describe as efficient. Prices are the key to one system that guides people's plans and actions. It is the plans and actions alone that have physical, psychological, and ethical significance; the prices are therefore judged solely in terms of the plans and actions that result. Further, the allocation's efficiency is judged solely in terms of the consumers' preferences; profits *per se* do not count. This is in keeping with the view that organizations are in themselves without significance, but rather are created entities that exist to serve human needs.

Just as in our highway safety example, prices in the neoclassical model serve to inform the parties about what they should do. Consumers and producers do not need to know *why* prices have changed to determine how to respond to changing circumstances efficiently. For example, if fuel oil is in short supply or if a valuable new use for copper makes it desirable to economize its old uses, the prices for these goods will increase and the quantities demanded will adjust to accommodate the more limited supply.

Unlike our highway safety example, however, prices in the neoclassical model do more than just inform people; they also *motivate* them. Given the prices in a competitive equilibrium, the plan calls for each consumer to buy only what he or she thinks best, and it calls on the firm to produce only what is most profitable. Despite the variety of objectives, behavior is coherent enough so that no resources are wasted. This is the real meaning of the welfare theorem.

Finally, given prices, there is no conflict among the owners of any firm about what it should do. The only effect the firm's activities have on the owners is to contribute to their income, and all owners prefer more income to less; therefore, all will favor profit maximization.

Scope of the Neoclassical Model

The mathematical model that we have just described is quite general and allows for a large number of interpretations. The welfare theorem is true for all of them. For example, it might appear that the model allows no role for time, but this is not the case. Perhaps people will not want to consume all that they own today but will want instead to save for tomorrow. Likewise, a firm's input decisions may involve capital equipment whose useful life extends over several months or years. The neoclassical model accommodates both of these possibilities quite nicely. The goods in the model can be identified so that "oranges-today" and "oranges-next-month" are different items, and the consumer may evaluate them differently. There may then be a storage firm that can use oranges-today and warehouses-today as inputs in order to produce oranges-next-month and warehouses-next-month as outputs.

This particular interpretation permits an extension of the model in which consumers can acquire skills and change their future labor endowments. For example, individuals might have direct access to a technology which allows them to combine their endowment of raw labor time today with instruction to yield an endowment of skilled computer programmer time tomorrow.

As another example, it might appear that because "oranges-today" could be one of the goods in the model, we must assume that the same price prevails for oranges-today in Orlando and Montreal. However, because the model is abstract, we could regard oranges in Orlando and Montreal as different goods. There may be a trucking firm that can take oranges-today-in-Orlando and trucks-today-in-Orlando as inputs and produce oranges-tomorrow-in-Montreal and trucks-tomorrow-in-Montreal as outputs.

The model can also allow for uncertainty. The method here is to consider the various possible future realizations of the uncertainty in the world as defining different distinct "states of the world," and then to again reinterpret the notion of a good so that, for example, "umbrellas-when-it-is-raining" are distinguished from "umbrellas-when-it-is-sunny." Using this interpretation allows for uncertainty in production and for risky research and development (R&D) activities. For example, certain amounts of input or R&D investment today may yield high levels of output tomorrow if a fortunate state of the world should occur, and low output if the firm's productivity turns out to be low or the R&D effort is unsuccessful.

Finally, it might appear that the assumption that firms maximize profits precludes applying the model to situations in which managers are limited in the amount of information they can (realistically) process. This, too, is incorrect: Such situations can be accommodated by carefully limiting the set of feasible plans. For example, if a single manager is unable to compute the best way to allocate the labor and equipment at his or her disposal, then the plan that uses one manager and labor and equipment in that way is simply regarded as infeasible. If a better use for the same labor and equipment can be found when two managers work together, then the plan that uses two managers and the superior allocation of labor and equipment is regarded as feasible. Because the limitations on the feasible activities of firms are stated abstractly, *any* limits on what a firm can do that can be expressed as technical limits or as limits on available resources can be accommodated by the neoclassical model. The fundamental theorem of welfare economics applies for all such limits.

The neoclassical model omits any explicit treatment of the many important dimensions of transactions described in Chapter 2. Nevertheless, the model provides a useful point of departure by itemizing in such an encompassing way so many of the things that have mistakenly been regarded as obstacles to the successful operation of a price system. In purely intellectual terms, the neoclassical model is such a major accomplishment in a tradition of thinking extending back to Adam Smith that it is well worth studying and understanding.

Proof of the Fundamental Theorem of Welfare Economics

In order to prove the theorem, we must show that in a competitive equilibrium there is no other set of consumption and production plans (B', S', I', O') that is feasible, that makes no consumer worse off, and that is strictly preferred to the original plans by at least one consumer. This is accomplished by first developing the mathematical properties that such an alternative plan must have. We will then deduce that these properties contradict the premise that the original plans constitute a competitive equilibrium. Thus, we conclude that if the allocation is not efficient, it did not arise from a competitive equilibrium. As we noted, this is equivalent to the original statement of the theorem.

Suppose the consumer with index i strictly prefers his or her consumption plan under (B', S', I', O') to the competitive equilibrium consumption plan. Because the competitive plan is (by definition) the consumer's most preferred plan among those that are affordable, that consumer must have found his or her part of the alternative plan unaffordable at the competitive equilibrium prices P. We write this conclusion formally as follows: The cost of the purchases under the alternative plan for this consumer exceeds the income from sales under the plan. Mathematically,

$$PB^{i\prime} > PS^{i\prime} + DF^i \tag{3.3}$$

Every other consumer n is no worse off under the new plan. Then it must be that the net cost of the purchases minus the sales for each consumer n under the alternative plan must be no less than under the original plan, that is, no less than the dividends received:

$$PB^{n\prime} - PS^{n\prime} \geq DF^n \tag{3.4}$$

Otherwise, according to our assumption that consumers are locally nonsatiated, the consumer could have done better than at the original plan B^n, S^n by instead beginning with the plan $B^{n\prime}$ and $S^{n\prime}$ and then spending the excess $PS^{n\prime} + DF^n - PB^{n\prime}$ on something he or she likes.

Let us now add up incomes and expenditures over all the consumers. In view of Expressions 3.3 and 3.4, we find that:

$$\sum_n PB^{n\prime} > \sum_n (PS^{n\prime} + DF^n) \tag{3.5}$$

That is, using the dividends and price list of the given competitive equilibrium, the total expenditures by consumers under the new plan strictly exceeds their total income.

A similar analysis applies to firms. No firm j can be earning a higher profit under the new plan because a competitive plan is the one that maximizes profits at the prices P. That is,

$$PO^j - PI^j \geq PO^{j\prime} - PI^{j\prime} \tag{3.6}$$

Therefore, the total profits of all firms combined must have been at least as high under the old plan as under the proposed (feasible) alternative:

$$\sum_j (PO^j - PI^j) \geq \sum_j (PO^{j\prime} - PI^{j\prime}) \tag{3.7}$$

We have assumed that the firms pay out their profits to their shareholders in the form of dividends. The total dividends received by consumers under the original plan must therefore be equal to the total profits earned by all the firms:

$$\sum_n DF^n = \sum_j (PO^j - PI^j) \tag{3.8}$$

(Formally, Equation 3.8 can be derived by summing Equation 3.1 over all consumers n and then substituting the result into the market-clearing Equation 3.2.)

Because the alternative plan is required to be feasible, it must produce enough net output to meet all the planned uses for all of the goods. This requirement is represented by:

$$\sum_n B^{n\prime} + \sum_j I^{j\prime} \leq \sum_n S^{n\prime} + \sum_j O^{j\prime} \tag{3.9}$$

Observe that, unlike the others, Expression 3.9 is an inequality among lists. This means that there is enough net output of each good to meet the planned uses for that good.

To complete the proof, we must show that these inequalities cannot simultaneously be satisfied. Doing so will prove that there cannot be any feasible alternative plan that is at least as good for each consumer and better for at least one consumer. The proof is accomplished by stringing together the equations and inequalities (3.7), (3.8), (3.5), and (3.9) in that order. We first write the proof as expression (3.10) and then explain it. Notice the crucial role played by prices in this argument: All the following inequalities are stated in money terms.

$$
\begin{aligned}
\sum_j (PO^{j\prime} - PI^{j\prime}) &\leq \sum_j (PO^j - PI^j) && (a)\ by\ (7) \\
&= \sum_n DF^n && (b)\ by\ (8) \\
&< \sum_n PB^{n\prime} - \sum_n PS^{n\prime} && (c)\ by\ (5) \\
&= P\left[\sum_n B^{n\prime} - \sum_n S^{n\prime}\right] && (d)\ by\ the\ distributive\ law \\
&\leq P\left[\sum_j O^{j\prime} - \sum_j I^{j\prime}\right] && (e)\ by\ (9)\ because\ P\ is\ nonnegative
\end{aligned}
\tag{3.10}
$$

The inequality (a) says that total profits under the alternative set of production plans, evaluated using the given competitive equilibrium prices, will be no higher than those under the profit-maximizing plans. According to (b), the latter are equal to the total dividends paid to the firms' owners. Because consumers prefer their consumption under the alternative plan, the new consumption plans must be unaffordable at the competitive equilibrium prices, which is the meaning of inequality (c). In (d), we use the distributive law to regroup terms, expressing net consumer expenditures under the alternative plan as the cost of net consumer purchases under that plan, all using the original prices. For the alternative to be feasible, however, net consumer purchases cannot exceed the sum of every firm's net production of the various goods. Therefore, the value of total net consumption at the competitive equilibrium prices (or indeed at any nonnegative prices) cannot exceed the value of net production; this is asserted by inequality (e). However, that total value is just the profits under the alternative plan with which the argument began.

This string of equations and inequalities implies the nonsensical proposition that the profits of the firms under the new plan are strictly less than the profits of the firm under the new plan. Beginning with the hypothesis that the competitive equilibrium plan is not efficient, we deduced a patently false conclusion. Thus, the original hypothesis must be false: The competitive equilibrium plan *is* efficient.

INCENTIVES AND INFORMATION TRANSFER UNDER MARKET INSTITUTIONS

As we noted previously, the price system not only directs resources to efficient use, it also has other desirable properties. Given the prices, consumers are asked only to do what they perceive to be in their best interests and firms are asked only to do what is best for their owners. The market harnesses these selfish motivations and directs them to a socially efficient outcome. Thus, if the firms and consumers do take prices as given, the price system does not just provide a means to address the coordination problem. It also provides the proper motivation, and so achieves a fairly complete solution to the overall economic problem. Moreover, it does so while putting low demands on the amount of information transmission that must occur. We examine both these properties in a preliminary manner here.

Incentives in Markets

The neoclassical model assumes that producers and consumers take prices as given to them. If they do, then the coordination problem is solved. But will they find it individually optimal to take prices as given? This question cannot be addressed within the model itself because it does not contain any discussion of how prices are formed and thus of what opportunities there might be for influencing them.

If, in fact, the prices are set by the market participants themselves, it might be expected that they would reflect any market power that the participants have. In that case, the efficiency result may not hold because the exercise of monopoly and monopsony power deflects prices from their competitive levels. Moreover, even if the prices are not set directly by market participants but rather by some mechanism (perhaps an auctioneer or planner) that gathers information from the participants and then announces the appropriate prices, any individual participants whose information affects the price will generally have incentives to distort the information they provide so as to influence prices to their benefit.

A vast amount of recent research in economics, both theoretical and experimental, has focused on the behavior that is induced by the incentives that arise under various market institutions. Related studies try to determine when this behavior will lead (approximately) to the efficient outcomes identified by the neoclassical model. The theoretical work employs many different approaches, but the common conclusion is that in most economies with a sufficiently large number of participants, competition between agents will eliminate monopoly power and result in essentially competitive prices and outcomes. Furthermore, the experimental work indicates that the number of participants necessary to make a market tolerably competitive need not be unrealistically large.

Moreover, even if market incentives are not able to induce fully efficient results, market institutions when combined with private property can still be powerful engines for directing individual self-interest to produce widespread economic advance and welfare gains. As Adam Smith noted long ago, individuals pursuing only their own selfish aims are led, as if by an "invisible hand," to promote the general welfare. The comparisons of Eastern and Western Europe in the postwar period, the experience of the newly industrialized nations of Asia Pacific, and agricultural reform in China are all recent evidence of the validity of this insight.

Informational Efficiency of Markets

Friedrich Hayek's quotation that began this chapter contrasts the informational features of a system of markets with those of a system of central planning. The main difference is that the market system does not require transmission of detailed information about resource availability, consumer preferences, or technological opportunities. In contrast, a centrally planned system would seem to need such information transmission in order to compute an efficient allocation (or even a feasible one). In a market system, decisions about the use of resources are left to the individual consumers and firms with whom the local knowledge of preferences, endowments, and production possibilities resides. Only the relatively small amount of information represented by prices and by offers to buy and sell is transmitted. Indeed, a general theoretical proposition (which we examine in detail in the next chapter) shows that the competitive market system involves the minimal information transmission consistent with determining an efficient allocation of resources.

In actual market systems, more information is transmitted than simply prices. Firms seek to discover consumer preferences and plans so that they can tailor their product designs and forecast the demands that will be put on their production facilities. They also seek forecasts of macroeconomic conditions, and they attempt to discover their competitors' investment, production, and marketing plans. At the same time, they advertise the prices, characteristics, and availability of their products and that they are interested in hiring people with particular skills. They do this because consumers and potential employees want this information. As well, even in a market economy there are always government regulatory procedures that usually work through detailed rules and directives rather than through price signals. Still, prices provide much of the information that is needed, and market systems do achieve effective coordination with much less communication of nonprice information than centralized, planned systems use.

PRICES AND SOCIALISM   In the period after the Russian Revolution of 1917, there was a major debate in economics concerning the possibility of running a socialist economy efficiently. One of the first relatively precise statements of the efficiency of the outcomes of price-taking behavior in markets was developed in the course of this debate by Abba Lerner. Strikingly, however, Lerner developed his arguments to show how a socialist system, with collective ownership of the means of production, could use prices to allocate resources as efficiently as could a capitalist market economy. According to Lerner, managers of socialist firms could be directed to take prices as given and to determine quantities to equate prices to marginal costs, just as would be done in a competitive firm. The resulting quantities would then have the same efficiency under the socialist regime as those elicited under the market system. (Presumably, however, the differing pattern of ownership of resources under socialism would affect what the market-clearing prices and quantities would be.) Thus, there would be no need for the central planners to attempt the overwhelming task of determining the complete allocation to be implemented. Instead, they need "only" determine and announce the right prices.

It would take us too far afield to discuss the economics of market socialism.

One point needs to be made, however. Although properly selected prices may be able to solve the coordination problem in a system without private ownership, and although much theoretical work has gone into the study of planning procedures for determining prices to support an efficient allocation of resources, attempts to determine the proper prices in actual planned economies and to adapt them to changing circumstances have in practice encountered major difficulties. It is not just that such determinations are directly costly, although they certainly are. Perhaps more importantly, changing prices typically helps some individuals and groups and hurts others, and these distributional consequences mean that the determination of prices by governments becomes a political decision.

The consequences of distorted prices are often truly striking. For example, in Poland in the early 1980s, government bread subsidies led to severe shortages, as farmers found it more profitable to feed bread rather than grain to their barnyard animals. Similarly, in the Soviet Union in 1989, a personal computer that sold for $3,500 in the West could be sold to an industrial buyer for $145,000 at the wildly inaccurate official rates of exchange.[3] When administered prices like these fail to adjust to reflect changing circumstances, they cease to be useful guides to behavior; bread in Poland and computers in the Soviet Union were not being directed to their best uses. In this respect, a private property market system in which prices are determined by individuals using economic criteria, rather than by planners and politicians worried about the political implications of distributional effects seems to have advantages.

THE NEOCLASSICAL MODEL AND THEORIES OF ORGANIZATION

The fundamental theorem of welfare economics and the related results on incentives and informational efficiency represent an intellectual triumph that, at a practical level, is helpful for thinking about what a system of prices can accomplish. There are few economists who would argue that the neoclassical model presents even an approximately complete and accurate description of the way any modern economy works, however. Rather, the model represents an attempt to determine the scope of the hypothesis that the "invisible hand" of markets and prices is sufficient to guide the economy to an efficient outcome.

We are interested in organizations, how they arise, and how they can be efficiently run. As Alfred Chandler has observed, new organizations—especially firms—historically often were organized when people found that market outcomes were inefficient. This observation helps to guide our study. If the competitive equilibrium of the neoclassical model actually did provide a good and complete description of how markets work, there would be no need for other economic organizations. Political organizations might still arise as people attempt to capture larger shares of the benefits of joint production or to bring more concern for equity into the system, but organizations aimed at improving economic efficiency would be unnecessary. But where markets do not lead to efficient outcomes, other institutions may emerge in both the private sector and the public sector to remove, avoid, or mitigate whatever stumbling blocks are preventing simple markets from achieving efficiency. Therefore, we look for **market failures** to explain nonmarket economic organization.

Market Failures

We have already noted one aspect of market failure, namely, the possibility that firms exercising *market power* will set prices at levels other than the competitive level and

---

[3] As reported in *The Economist*, August 5, 1989, p. 44.

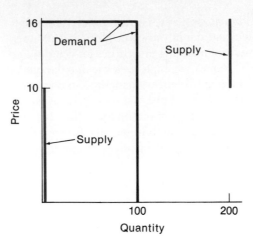

Figure 3.2: With economies of scale, the supply curve is discontinuous. The result in this case is that there is no price at which the quantity supplied equals the quantity demanded.

thereby distort resource allocations. There are other ways in which markets may fail to reach efficiency.

INCREASING RETURNS TO SCALE   One of the less obvious limitations of the competitive equilibrium is that, for some economies, it may be logically impossible for a competitive equilibrium to exist. In other words, there may be no prices at which supply is equal to demand simultaneously for all goods. This failure of existence is especially likely when there are significant *economies of scale* in some production processes, so that it is less expensive per unit to produce many units than to produce few.

For example, suppose that consumers are willing to pay as much as $16 per unit up to 100 units for some good A, but have no use for any additional units beyond this amount. Suppose that the technology for making the product requires buying a machine costing $1,000 and then using additional labor and material inputs costing $5 for each unit produced, up to the machine's capacity of 200 units. This is an example with returns to scale because the average cost of production per unit falls continuously from $1,005 if the firm produces just one unit to $10 if it produces 200 units.

Figure 3.2 shows the supply and demand curves for this particular market. At any price less than $16, consumers will want to purchase 100 units. At higher prices, they will want to purchase zero units. On the supply side, if it behaves as a competitive price taker, in the long run the firm will want to produce exactly 200 units at any price exceeding $10 and zero units at lower prices. (A price of $10 or more makes buying the machine and operating it at capacity worthwhile; a lower price would not induce the firm to buy the machine, although once it is installed the firm will produce at capacity as long as the price exceeds the short-run marginal cost, $5.) There is no price at which the quantity the firm wishes to supply is equal to the quantity that consumers wish to buy (where the supply curve intersects the demand curve). Because there are economies of scale, the supply curve is not continuous.

There is a value-maximizing solution in this example. In it, the firm produces 100 units and transfers them to the consumers. This yields $1,600 in value to consumers at a cost of $1,500. Any other plan leads to less value being created. Moreover, as long as the consumers pay the firm an amount between $15 and $16 per unit, both sides are better off than when the good is not produced. The problem is that prices alone cannot guide the firm to produce 100 units. The firm needs to know not only how valuable the good is to others in the society but also precisely how many units the consumers are willing to buy. Just as in the highway safety example earlier in the chapter, the firm needs information about quantities in addition to information about prices.

Of course, this failure of the price system in our theoretical model is not the same as a failure of firms in the real world. Farmers may base their planting on price information and price forecasts alone, but producers subject to scale economies and limited markets do keep in touch with their customers, using their sales forces to get information about quantities, qualities, desired product attributes, and much more.

Information processing for production planning is done in various ways in different countries. In centrally planned economies, the state planners provide guidance in a centralized way. In North America, firms are organized to coordinate the affairs of their various divisions. Because most firms make only limited use of the price system for organizing their internal affairs, it is reasonable to assume that the systems used in organizations require closer coordination than a price system could ordinarily provide. In Western Europe, Japan, and Korea, there is more of a sense of partnership between the government and private industry than there is in North America. A national industrial policy and systems of indicative planning may be devised to help coordinate activities among firms, both directly and by giving them common information on which to base expectations. In the developing countries of the world, a wide variety of approaches has been examined to coordinate attempts at development, with mixed results. The use of other organizational arrangements to replace the price system for purposes of coordination is discussed in more detail in Chapter 4.

EXTERNALITIES   There are various conditions under which the outcomes of market equilibria are not efficient because one or more of the premises of the fundamental theorem of welfare economics are not satisfied. We have just seen that a major failure can occur when increasing returns imply that competitive market-clearing prices fail to exist. To the extent that increasing returns are a source of market power, it may be that the market failures associated with imperfect competition are unavoidable. Externalities provide another example.

Externalities are positive or negative effects that one economic agent's actions have on another's welfare that are not regulated by the system of prices. Their presence means that inefficient levels of externality-bearing activities may result. For example, if a homeowner paints his house in pink and purple stripes, his consumption behavior might make his neighbors quite unhappy. Smoke from a nearby factory, which spoils the consumers' environment and threatens their health; investments in factories by a local employer, which benefit others by creating jobs and raising property values; inventions that provide a foundation for other inventors to build upon—all these are examples of consumption and production behavior that affect people and firms other than those making the decisions. Inefficiencies occur with externalities because the decision makers are not taking full account of all the costs and benefits associated with their choices, namely, those that accrue to other people.

MISSING MARKETS   The market failure associated with externalities may also be seen as a matter of *missing markets*: The externalities correspond to goods (or "bads") that individuals would want to buy or sell because they affect utility or production possibilities. Because these goods are not traded in competitive markets, however, no prices are attached to them and so the market system fails to guide their allocation. To illustrate further the power of the abstract formulation of the neoclassical model, we could think of having all the competitive markets that were needed, in which case the conclusion of the fundamental theorem would continue to hold. Formally, the market model could be expanded to make person A's consumption of a beautifully landscaped house one of the goods. Another good could then be created for each of person A's neighbors, who must also, in a way, "consume" A's house. These goods would be joint products: If A consumes such a house, all his or her neighbors would have to consume their corresponding goods as well. Because these are separately priced goods, however, the neighbors would make market offers to buy and sell them independently of one another and of A's choices. In a competitive equilibrium, their enjoyment of the enhanced beauty of the neighborhood would lead them to buy the goods. This would increase the total amount paid for the collection of goods corresponding to A's landscaping and would bring the higher level of beautification that efficiency requires but that would not result were A to have to pay for it with only his or her own money, time, and energy.

Of course, such markets do not typically exist. Furthermore, if they did exist, they could not reasonably be assumed to be competitive because there would be only a single buyer of each of the extra goods. We see in Chapter 9 that the efficient outcome may be achievable without all these extra markets. Certainly, however, the absence of these markets means that a system of impersonal market transactions mediated only by prices will not generate efficiency.

In fact, with this wide conception of possible markets, missing markets are the major source of market inefficiencies. We alluded earlier to the possibility of interpreting goods in the neoclassical model as being differentiated by the date at which they are available and by the particular realization of the uncertainties in the world that have occurred by that date (the "event" or "state of the world"). Of course, consumers do care about their future consumption, and there is always uncertainty about endowments, tastes, and technology. Therefore, the neoclassical model effectively assumes that there are competitive markets in which transactions can be made to buy and sell any good for future delivery at every future date, with the prices on these markets being contingent on the uncertain event as well.[4]

For example, many homeowners who have property near the San Andreas fault are concerned about being able to repair their houses after an earthquake. In the context of the neoclassical model, there would be markets in which homeowners could contract today for housing reconstruction to be done tomorrow, next year, or 22 years from now. Furthermore, for each date there would be separate markets, open today, for contingent delivery of these services depending on the fault's movements and its effect on the housing stock.

Clearly, such an extensive set of markets does not exist. Without these markets, the version of the fundamental theorem stated earlier does not apply because the assumption that everything of interest to consumers and firms is priced in a competitive market is not met. Although it is possible that enough insurance markets may exist to resolve homeowners' needs, this conclusion seems problematic. Some of the reasons a set of complete, contingent futures markets does not exist will be discussed in Chapter 5. For now it is enough to note that the absence of markets can lead to inefficiencies and market failure. It is precisely this sort of market failure that leads people to seek alternative arrangements to meet their economic needs.

SEARCH, MATCHING, AND COORDINATION PROBLEMS   In the neoclassical model, everyone is assumed to know what the prices are and where and when goods can be bought and sold. Finding a willing buyer or seller at the going price is assumed to be unproblematic. In reality, however, potential buyers and sellers may not even know of each other's existence, let alone the exact specifications of the goods and services they seek or have to offer or the terms at which they are willing to buy or sell.

---

[4] Actually, it is enough that there be securities and insurance markets that allow transfers of purchasing power across time and between possible future events. This point was first made by Kenneth Arrow, and it forms the basis for much of the modern theory of financial markets.

Acquiring this information necessitates costly *search* by one or both sides. Consumers need to search to find the best prices, firms search for potential employees, workers search for jobs, and companies expend resources finding suppliers who can meet their needs and informing potential customers about their products. This search and communication absorb resources. In addition, because these activities are costly, people do not continue searching until all the best matches are found. The difficulties described in Chapter 2 in matching medical interns and hospitals are indicative of the market failures that can arise when highly decentralized market approaches are used. The NIMP, a more centralized solution, came into being to overcome these inefficiencies.

The coordination problems that arose in the market for medical interns can also manifest themselves at an economy-wide scale. In the neoclassical model, people and firms assume that they will be able to buy or sell as much as they want in the market at the going prices. In fact, this may be reasonably descriptive of the actual situation faced by a small investor buying and selling securities on one of the organized financial exchanges. In most other markets the assumption is less accurate. People and firms are concerned about their ability to buy and, especially, sell what they want. If workers do not expect that they will be able to sell their labor, they are likely to cut back on their purchases. They may become discouraged and not bother looking for work. Meanwhile, if firms anticipate that demand will be low, they will not hire people to produce goods that they do not expect to be able to sell. Then there are few jobs, as workers feared. Further, because low employment means workers' incomes are low, demand is weak, just as firms expected. The pessimistic expectations are self-confirming: People limit their purchases because they expect others to do so, and they turn out to be right. It is possible that, in the same physical circumstances, there could be also be optimistic self-fulfilling expectations, in which firms hire and workers spend more freely because they expect others to buy their goods or labor.

The upshot is that, contrary to the conclusion of the neoclassical model, there could be multiple possible levels of economic activity that are internally consistent, with some having inefficiently low employment and output. In such a situation, it is possible that no firm has any incentive to alter its prices or wages even though sales are low and workers unemployed. Thus, the usual mechanism that neoclassical economists expect to overcome these problems may be ineffective. A version of this sort of coordination failure may also explain some of the problems of the economy of the Soviet Union. Constant shortages of goods meant there was little incentive to work hard and earn more because there was nothing to buy, and the resulting low levels of production meant that the shelves were empty.

Market Failures and Organization

In the traditional view, the presence of externalities, unemployment, or other market failures serves to justify special policies by the government, which can intervene to set right the mischief of markets. The problem with this view is that when markets fail, governments are not the only ones that can step in to set things right—individuals and firms can also take action. When a manufacturer sets up a computer department instead of buying computer services from a vendor, when an electric utility enters into a long-term contract with a coal supplier rather than purchasing coal as needed on spot markets, or when a group of homeowners bands together to provide a recreation facility for their common use, the decision makers are exercising their option to use nonmarket organizational forms to meet their needs. Private parties as well as governments can make arrangements to replace the simple price system when they are not satisfied that ordinary market arrangements have worked well.

Even though formal organizations may be seen as a response to failures of the price system, many large organizations in fact make extensive internal use of price systems to help provide coordination and motivation. We have already noted a limited version of this in the Salomon Brothers example from Chapter 1, where the profits and losses on each transaction are calculated and attributed to the individuals and groups involved. A much more thorough use of prices is found in the management systems of many multidivisional firms and a variety of other large organizations. These organizations have sought to decentralize, locating the responsibility for making many decisions at the levels where much of the relevant information resides and where the actual operations take place. Decentralization creates an acute need to ensure that the various people making key decisions have the proper incentives and that the resulting plans are compatible and coherent. Senior managers have found that many of the virtues of the price system in providing coordination and motivation hold within their organizations as well as in the market. Consequently, they have partially re-created the operation of the market within their organizations, using financial controls and performance measurement and introducing internal transfer pricing for transactions between units in the organization.

Patterns of Internal Organization in Firms

The first modern firms were organized *functionally* in a centralized fashion. The Ford Motor Company in the 1920s is an example (see Chapter 1). The head office in such firms oversaw and directed all activity, with one department responsible for finance, another for production, and still others for personnel, purchasing, logistics, sales, and marketing for the whole organization. However, this form proved to be ill suited for coordinating activity in large, multiproduct firms operating over broad geographical areas. Head-office decision makers were too far removed from crucial local knowledge about production and market conditions. Too much time and information were lost in communication between the head office and the field, and the central managers were overwhelmed with the number, size, and complexity of the decisions they faced. These problems had nearly destroyed the Hudson's Bay Company in the eighteenth century (see Chapter 1), but they became especially widespread in later times with the emergence of more large firms. The larger the firms became, the more these problems hindered effective management.

At the opposite extreme were the *holding companies* that emerged in the nineteenth century. These were extremely decentralized collections of entirely separate firms under common ownership. The head office of a holding company took little or no management role, simply collecting the profits of the constituent firms. This system worked reasonably well as long as there was no need to coordinate across units, but it could not work when there were gains to making coordinated decisions across units about investment, production, or marketing.

Several firms that faced these problems in the decades after the First World War independently introduced similar solutions to it. They moved away from functional or holding company organization and toward a **multidivisional organization**. This essentially involves creating mini-companies—divisions—within the firm, each of which is responsible for a particular product, market, region, or technology. The divisions might in turn be organized functionally, or further subdivided in a variety of ways, but the key was that a broad set of the decisions relevant to a particular unit was made the responsibility of a single division manager. However, in comparison to the extremely decentralized holding companies, the multidivisional firms had relatively strong central offices to coordinate the divisions' activities.

The companies that pioneered this form of organization in the United States included Du Pont, which set up market-based divisions to separate its explosives business from its fertilizer business; Sears Roebuck, which established separate divisions to handle stores in different regions of the country; Standard Oil of New Jersey, which had grown by encompassing increasingly diverse business activities in oil exploration, production, transportation, refining, and retail marketing; and General Motors, which (as we describe in Chapter 1) was created as a combination of independent automobile manufacturers. Each of these firms created structures to allow a measure of independence to the divisions while providing a central office that could coordinate their overlapping activities. In particular instances divisionalization thus could represent increased decentralization, as at Du Pont, or increased central coordination and control, as at GM.

Today, the multidivisional firm is the dominant organizational structure in large manufacturing firms throughout capitalist economies. Many nonmanufacturing firms and some not-for-profit organizations, including a number of universities, also employ key features associated with the divisionalized form.

Divisions can be defined in a variety of ways, even within a single firm. For example, a firm could have a defense products division (market or customer defined), a small electric motors division (product based), a biotech division (technology based) and an international division (geographic). Senior management and the head office staff retain primary roles in a number of areas, including raising outside capital, allocating resources among divisions, appointing and evaluating divisional managers, centrally coordinating the firm's overall policies, and setting its strategic direction. In the most decentralized multidivisional firms, all other activities and decisions are the province of the divisional managers, including R&D, design, engineering, procurement, personnel, manufacturing, marketing, and sales. In less decentralized firms, some of these functions reside with the head office, and divisional managers' autonomy is circumscribed on some important dimensions by centrally determined policies and directives.

Transfer Pricing in Multidivisional Firms

The performance of divisions and their managers is always measured at least partly in financial terms. Figures are developed measuring divisional cost, revenue, profit, and investment performance, and these figures are used in judging performance and in allocating rewards. They are also critical input for decisions determining where to allocate corporate capital, what products and investments to develop and back, and which executives to promote.

Within any decentralized organization, products and services are frequently supplied by one division to another. Moreover, smaller responsibility centers are often created within divisions, with financial measures employed to judge the performance of these units and their managers. These responsibility centers can be particular plants or offices or even smaller subunits. There is constant movement of products and services between responsibility centers. Therefore, the use of financial performance measures necessitates pricing these transferred goods and services. These **transfer prices** are of crucial importance to the corporation and to the divisional managers.

THE IMPORTANCE OF TRANSFER PRICES   From the point of view of the division, the prices paid and charged on interdivisional transactions can be the single most important determinant of the unit's measured financial performance. Consider an integrated petroleum company that has one division that produces crude oil, another that transports the oil to the firm's refineries, and a third that refines the crude oil into petroleum products. Crude is "sold" by the production division to the transport division, which then "resells" it to the refining division. The price in the first of these transactions determines the revenues of the production division and is a major element of the costs of the transportation division. The price in the second transaction determines the revenue per unit of the transportation division and is a major element of the costs of the refineries. Given the volume actually transferred, these transfer prices do not affect overall corporate profit, but they do determine the apparent performance of the various divisions.

However, if the division managers have autonomy over the determination of the quantities they buy and sell, either internally or in dealings with outsiders, corporate profits can also depend critically on the transfer prices. If the refinery managers are judged on their division's profitability, and if the transfer price the managers pay to the transport division is too high, they may seek to buy crude from other suppliers. If the transfer price paid by the transport division to the crude producer is too low, the latter's managers may decide to sell their output into the market, rather than transfer it within the firm. Both of these transactions may adversely affect the firm's overall profitability when the firm's profit is maximized by buying and selling internally. Even when outside sales and purchases are not an issue, if each division is free to determine how much it will buy and sell within the firm, a misspecified transfer price may make a division unwilling to transact the quantities that are needed to maximize total profits. This occurs because the transfer price makes the marginal units bought or sold unprofitable for the division, even if they are profitable for the corporation as a whole.

Badly chosen transfer prices can also misdirect corporate decisions, even when the divisional managers do not have the power to decide where or how much to purchase and sell. Altering the transfer prices can make an activity appear either highly profitable or grossly unprofitable. Unless the central executives and staff are especially careful in interpreting divisional performance measures, they may decide that a given manager is doing a much better or worse job than in fact is the case. More seriously, they may incorrectly conclude that a particular activity is highly profitable and should be expanded or that it is unprofitable and should be dropped.

TRANSFER PRICES AND MARKET PRICES   There is one special case where transfer prices that are right on all counts are remarkably easy to determine: when there is an outside market for the good or service, that market is perfectly competitive (and that would remain so even if the firm joined the market), and there are no additional costs or benefits to the corporation as a whole in using the market instead of transacting internally. In this case, adopting the outside market price as the transfer price both directs divisional quantity decisions to maximize corporate profits and provides the right signals regarding performance and investment. It makes no difference to corporate profitability whether the goods and services are bought and sold internally or externally, so long as all transaction quantities maximize divisional profits at the given market prices. Furthermore, these quantities are the ones that actually maximize corporate profits, and the competitive market prices also serve as the best available indicators of the marginal profitability of expansion or contraction. (We provide a formal proof of these claims at the end of this section.)

Of course, it is rare that these conditions will all be satisfied completely. Competitive markets for perfect substitutes for the firm's products and services are likely to be found only for standardized commodities. Thus, an international grain dealer or the manufacturer of common agricultural chemicals might find this condition satisfied, but certainly an automobile manufacturer is unlikely to find a perfectly competitive market for engines or transmissions that will fit into the company's designs.

More often, firms will have to rely on internal standard cost estimates to set

Transfer Pricing at Bellcore

A typical example of the negative effects of setting the wrong transfer prices comes from Bellcore (formerly known as Bell Labs), the research arm of AT&T, which as American Telephone and Telegraph was previously the telephone monopoly in the United States. Bellcore sells its research to governmentally regulated regional and local telephone operating companies. Bellcore discovered in the late 1980s that its highly talented and well-paid research engineers and scientists were typing their own letters, memos, and research papers or negotiating with outside typists, risking the security of internal communications, while the typing pool that was supposed to do this work was laying people off because there was not enough for them to do.

The cause of this gross misallocation of personnel was that the transfer prices paid for typing services were based on a flawed internal cost accounting scheme, which allocated too large a share of fixed company overhead to the typing unit. At their peak, the transfer prices for typing reached as high as $50 per page! The scientists and engineers, who were also subject to financial incentives, naturally chose not to use the service. As they withdrew their business, the price needed to recoup the fixed costs assigned to the typing pool rose ever higher.

This example is drawn from Edward Kovac and Henry Troy, "Getting Transfer Prices Right: What Bellcore Did," *Harvard Business Review* (September–October 1989), 146–54.

transfer prices. Still, a competitive market for a similar good may exist that can be used to help set the internal price.[6] The Bellcore case (see box) is a good example. Outside typing services were available, but they were less secure for sensitive documents, less conveniently located, and perhaps slower. Nevertheless, it was the comparison of the $50 per page price for internal typing services with the much lower outside price that indicated that something was seriously wrong.

As we see in Chapter 16, when nearly perfectly competitive markets for inputs are present, there is little reason for a firm to be **vertically integrated**, supplying its own inputs. For that very reason, the most common case for transfer pricing is where there is no market for the desired input or, if the market does exist, it is far from the competitive ideal. There may be few competitors in the market, so that prices are too high on account of monopoly power. More importantly, there may be severe transaction costs to using outside markets, which arise because of informational differences (see Chapter 5).

Without a well-functioning outside market, both determining whether the transaction should occur within the firm or across firm boundaries and establishing the appropriate price to charge internally become complicated tasks. Division managers, seeking to improve the profitability of their own divisions, have an interest then in manipulating the transfer price, perhaps by assigning overhead costs to products for which the buying division has no alternative source in order to inflate the profits reported on goods for which it faces competition.

---

[6] J. R. Gould, "Internal Pricing in Firms When There Are Costs of Using an Outside Market," *Journal of Business* (1964), 61–67.

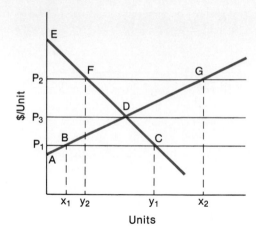

Figure 3.3: When there is an outside market, the difference in supply and demand within the firm at the market price is optimally accommodated by outside purchases or sales without adjusting transfer prices.

Transfer Pricing with a Competitive Outside Market

We claimed earlier that when a competitive outside market for its internal products exists with a market price of p, the firm maximizes total profits by setting its internal transfer price equal to p. There are two ways to go about establishing this claim. The first way is intuitive and graphical and has the advantage that it shows how large the losses are from using a different policy. The second is more abstract but has the advantage that it unifies ideas by connecting the analysis explicitly to two of the main ideas of economic analysis: the fundamental theorem of welfare economics and the principle of total wealth maximization.

A GRAPHICAL TREATMENT   Figure 3.3 illustrates the argument. In the figure, the prices P_1, P_2 and P_3 represent three possible levels of the market price. The upward sloping line is the marginal cost and supply curve of the selling division and the downward sloping one is the demand curve of the buying division. Only by coincidence would the price that clears the internal market, P_3, happen to coincide with the price determined on the outside market.

Suppose first that the outside price is low, at P_1. If the transfer price is set at the level P_3 at which internal supply and demand are equalized, what will the firm's profit be? From basic microeconomics, the demand function is the marginal revenue product of the buying division from acquiring units of the transferred product and the supply function is the selling division's marginal cost function. Consequently, the total profit enjoyed by the two divisions will be the area between the supply and demand curves, which is the area of triangle ADE. If, instead, the supply division produces x_1 and the buying division uses y_1, purchasing the excess $y_1 - x_1$ from outside suppliers in the market, then the divisional profits will correspond to the areas of the triangles ABP_1 for the supply division and CEP_1 for the buying division, so the total profit will be higher by the area of triangle BCD.

Similarly, if the outside price is the high price P_2 at which the supply x_2 exceeds the demand y_2, selling the extra supply on the market at price P_2 increases total profits by an amount equal to the area of triangle DFG when compared to transacting internally at the price and quantity where supply equals demand.

A FORMAL APPROACH   Here, we prove the claim by constructing an artificial economy and applying the fundamental theorem of welfare economics and the value-maximization principle to it. The exercise illustrates that the very same logic establishing that prices guide efficient resource allocations in markets can also be applied internally within firms, just by regarding divisions or managers as if they were consumers.

In the artificial economy, there are two goods and three consumers. The two goods are (1) the good that is transferred within the firm, and (2) money, which by definition has a price of one. The first two consumers are the two divisions (or their managers). They care only about how much of the internally produced good they buy or sell and how much money they are paid for it. We define the utility of each of these two consumers to be the total profit earned by the corresponding division. Let's denote the selling and buying divisions by the symbols S and B. If y_S is the number of units sold and x_S is the total amount received for it, we can write the selling division's utility as $v_S(y_S) + x_S$, where $v_S(y_S)$ is a negative number representing the cost of producing y_S units. For the buying division, utility can be written in the same general form as $v_B(y_B) + x_B$, but x_B is a negative number, representing the amount paid, and $v_B(y_B)$ is a positive number, representing net profits before any payment for the transferred goods. The third consumer in our artificial economy represents all the other consumers in the actual market, so we designate the third consumer by the symbol M. Consumer M has utility $v_M(y_M) + x_M$, where we specify that $v_M(y_M) = py_M$. Consequently, M is willing to buy or sell any amount of the product at price p.

What does the competitive equilibrium of this artificial economy look like? First, it must have price p, because M would want to buy or sell unbounded quantities at any other price. Given the price p, consumer S sells the amount that maximizes its utility $v_S(y_S) + py_S$ and consumer B buys the amount that maximizes $v_B(y_B) + py_B$. (Recall that y_B is a negative number.) At a market equilibrium, supply must be equal to demand; that is, $y_M + y_B + y_S = 0$. Notice that M's utility is zero regardless of how much it buys or sells at the market price p, so this market-clearing equation is consistent with maximization by consumer M. Since this is a competitive equilibrium, by the fundamental theorem of welfare economics, the allocation it specifies is Pareto efficient. Also, by construction, the value maximization principle applies, so an allocation is efficient if and only if it maximizes the total value for all the three parties. Since M's utility is always zero, regardless of the decisions y_B and y_S of the two divisions, the competitive equilibrium choices maximize the total utility of consumers B and S; that is, they maximize the total profit of the firm. If the firm sets a transfer price different from p, the result could only be lower total profits.

Notice that we have used the value-maximization principle and the fundamental theorem of welfare economics here to characterize efficient behavior *for the divisions* rather than for the actual economy as a whole. By replacing the actual consumer sector by the artificial construct M whose welfare was unaffected by the firm's decisions, we explicitly omitted their welfare from the calculation. The argument given here applies even if the fundamental theorem does not apply to the actual economy, for example, because there is a problem of monopoly power or externalities or missing markets. The kind of reasoning displayed here is quite important in the positive economic analysis of organizations and should not be confused with reasoning about the actual efficiency of the economy as a whole.

Summary

Even in the simplest situations, a team cannot work effectively unless its members act in a coordinated fashion. In a modern economy, the problem of supplying the right goods and services at the right times and places and to the right people, when production takes place over a geographically widespread area, requires a major feat of *coordination*. Moreover, the individuals involved must be *motivated* to do their parts in the coordinated plan.

Prices can sometimes be used to achieve effective organization in large-scale decision making, where decision makers are asked to value limited resources by placing a price on each resource used. In our central example, there was a price in lives for crew hours used on any project because those crew hours could be used in other projects to save lives. Furthermore, with knowledge only of the price and the characteristics of their individual projects, a decentralized staff could make decisions that taken together constitute an efficient plan for the whole organization. The prices that fulfill this function are market-like prices; they can be determined as prices at which the supply of each resource is equal to the demand.

The Arrow-Debreu neoclassical general equilibrium model is capable of representing in fine detail the complex activities of consumption and production by firms and decision makers throughout the economy. A competitive equilibrium of the model is a set of prices and an allocation of goods such that consumers are maximizing their respective utilities, firms are maximizing their profits, and the quantities that sellers wish to supply at the given prices are the same as those the buyers wish to purchase. The fundamental theorem of welfare economics holds that the competitive allocation of goods is an efficient one. At a competitive equilibrium, prices provide consumers and firms with all the information they need to know what to do, and they do not ask firms or consumers to do anything but maximize their own profit or utility. In that sense, markets can theoretically resolve both the coordination and the motivation problems. Experimental markets seem to verify that even with moderately small numbers of participants, the behavior in markets is approximately as predicted by the neoclassical model.

The neoclassical analysis also points to several problems for real economies. First, for economies with increasing returns to scale, there may not exist any prices at which supply equals demand, in which case prices alone cannot coordinate and motivate appropriate choices. Economies of scale are also associated with imperfect competition, which damages the efficiency of economic performance. Second, there may be externalities or missing markets, so that individual decision makers may find that prices do not accurately reflect social costs or that certain desired trades cannot be made. As we see in Chapter 5, some of the missing markets are absent for good reasons and are not easily restored.

Historically, one of the major reasons for the growth of the firm and certain other nonmarket institutions was that unregulated markets could not achieve efficiency. But nonmarket forms raise new problems of coordination, planning, and control. As we have seen, prices can be of great value even in internal organization to evaluate performance and guide managerial decisions.

■ Bibliographical Notes

The neoclassical model of a private-ownership economy and the fundamental theorem of welfare economics represent the culmination of two hundred years of economic research, beginning with Adam Smith's *Wealth of Nations* (1776). An account of the historical development of the theory is found in Roy Weintraub's article. The version and interpretations presented here are largely due to Kenneth Arrow and Gerard Debreu, both of whom won Nobel prizes partly for this work. The classical treatment is found in Debreu's *Theory of Value* (1959), but this volume is quite abstract and highly mathematical. More accessible treatments are found in some intermediate and graduate microeconomic theory books and in Werner Hildenbrand and Alan Kirman's book. Arrow's testimony to the U.S. Congress (reprinted in the Haveman-Margolis volume) is an especially clear exposition of the key ideas. His idea of viewing externalities as missing markets is developed in the paper in the Margolis volume.

Theoretical and experimental explorations of incentives in markets and the question of whether the competitive equilibrium approximates the outcomes of imperfectly competitive behavior are active areas of current research. Brief introductions to these subjects can be found in the articles in *The New Palgrave* by John Roberts and Vernon Smith. The low information requirements of the price system were accentuated by Friedrich Hayek in the course of the debate on the possibility of running an efficient socialist economy. Abba Lerner's proposal for market socialism and his development of the relation between price-taking behavior and efficiency are published in *The Economics of Control*. The formalization of Hayek's ideas is primarily due to Leonid Hurwicz, who gives an introduction to this topic in his paper in *American Economic Review*.

Most intermediate microeconomics textbooks treat the problems that the price system has with increasing returns, imperfect competition, and externalities. The focus on missing markets is again due to Arrow. See again his Congressional testimony referenced earlier. The importance of search was first developed by George Stigler. He was cited for this work when he won the Nobel prize. The possibility of coordination failures explaining unemployment is another active area of current research. Peter Diamond has been a leader in this work. Perhaps the most complete modeling along these lines is Roberts's paper in *American Economic Review*, but it is quite difficult and there is at present no easily accessible exposition of this work. The closest approximation may be the paper by Russell Cooper and Andrew John. The idea that organizations are a response to market failures is developed in Arrow's book.

Transfer pricing is covered in most texts on managerial accounting. The classic in the field is by Charles Horngren and George Foster.

◼ REFERENCES

Arrow, K.J. "Political and Economic Evaluation of Social Effects and Externalities," in *The Analysis of Public Output*, J. Margolis, ed. (new York: Columbia University Press, 1970).

Arrow K.J. "The Organization of Economic Activity: Issues Pertinent to the Choice of Markets versus Nonmarket Allocation," in *Public Expenditures and Policy Analysis*, R. Haveman and J. Margolis, eds. (Chicago: Markham, 1970).

Arrow, K.J. *The Limits of Organization* (New York: Norton, 1974).

Arrow, K.J. and G. Debreu "Existence of an Equilibrium for a Competitive Economy," *Econometrica*, 22 (1954), 265–90.

Cooper, R., and A. John. "Coordinating Coordination Failures in Keynesian Models," *Quarterly Journal of Economics*, 103 (August 1988), 441–64.

Debreu, G. *The Theory of Value* (New York: Wiley, 1959).

Diamond, P.A. "Aggregate Demand Management in Search Equilibrium," *Journal of Political Economy*, 90 (October 1982), 881–94.

Hayek, F. "The Use of Knowledge in Society," *American Economic Review*, 35 (1945), 519–30.

Hildenbrand, W., and A.P. Kirman. *Introduction to Equilibrium Analysis* (Amsterdam: North-Holland, 1975).

Horngren, C.T., and G. Foster. *Cost Accounting: A Managerial Emphasis*, 7th ed. (Englewood Cliffs, NJ: Prentice Hall, 1991).

Hurwicz, L. "The Design of Mechanisms for Resources Allocation," *American Economic Review* 63 (May 1973), 1–30.

Lerner, A.P. *The Economics of Control* (New York: Macmillan, 1946).

Roberts, J. "Large Economies," in *The New Palgrave: A Dictionary of Economics*, J. Eatwell, M. Milgate and P. Newman, eds. (London: Macmillan, 1987), volume III, 132–33.

Roberts, J. "Perfectly and Imperfectly Competitive Markets," in *The New Palgrave: A Dictionary of Economics*, J. Eatwell, M. Milgate and P. Newman, eds. (London: Macmillan, 1987), volume III, 837–41.

Roberts, J. "An Equilibrium Model with Involuntary Unemployment at Flexible, Competitive Prices and Wages," *American Economic Review*, 77 (1987), 856–74.

Smith, V.L. "Experimental Methods in Economics," in *The New Palgrave: A Dictionary of Economics*, J. Eatwell, M. Milgate and P. Newman, eds. (London: Macmillan, 1987), volume II, 241–49.

Stigler, G. "The Economics of Information," *Journal of Political Economy*, 69 (June 1961).

Weintraub, R. "On the Existence of Competitive Equilibrium: 1930–1954," *Journal of Economic Literature*, 21 (March 1983), 1–39.

EXERCISES

Food for Thought

1. Airline companies often try to allow for passengers who fail to show up for flights by a practice called overbooking—they sell more seats than are actually available on the flight. When all the passengers with reservations do show up, it becomes necessary to "bump" some passengers to a later flight. What criteria might be used to choose which passengers to bump? How are passengers likely to react to your proposed criteria? In recent years in the United States, it has become common to offer bonuses to passengers who will volunteer to be bumped. Evaluate this alternative from the perspectives of both equity and efficiency.

2. In many countries of the world, an attempt is made to ensure the welfare of the poorest families by subsidizing the cost of basic necessities. For example, many countries subsidize the price of bread, reducing it far below the market price. What are the disadvantages of this approach to caring for poor families? Can you identify a better approach?

3. In California, for historical reasons, city dwellers pay as much as twenty times more for water than farmers pay. What consequences would you expect to follow from such a large difference?

4.   In many colleges and universities, space in dormitories and other university subsidized housing is assigned by a complicated system based on seniority and a lottery. Why is a price system not used to assign rooms to those who value them most? What would be the advantages and disadvantages of such a system?

Mathematical Exercises

1.   In the transfer pricing problem studied in Figure 3.3, when the market price is P_1, the gain from using the outside market rather than just buying and selling internally within the firm was shown to be equal to the area of triangle BCD. Reconstruct the graph and show what portion of this gain results from increased purchases by the buying division. Show, too, the portion that results from reduced output by the selling division. If the firm has been using an internal transfer price of P_3 with no outside purchases or sales and adopts the market price of P_1, allowing outside purchases and sales, how are the measured profits of each division affected?

2.   Consider an economy with two kinds of goods that people value. We call these two goods "money" and "manna." There are also two types of people. The first type—"manna lovers"—value a combination of x_1 units of money and y_1 units of manna according to the utility function $x_1 + (3y_1 - y_1^2)$. The second type—"money lovers"—value x_2 units of money and y_2 units of manna according to the utility function $x_2 + (2y_2 - y_2^2)$. Each type of consumer is endowed with one unit of manna and ten units of money. Use the value-maximization principle to determine how manna must be allocated among the two types of consumers at any efficient allocation in this economy. What must the price of manna be (in money units) in order for there to be a competitive equilibrium in this economy? Use the first part of the problem to show that the competitive equilibrium allocation is efficient.

3.   Consider an economy with two kinds of goods, called Xs and Ys, and two kinds of people, called "X-lovers" and "Y-lovers." An X-lover who consumes x units of good X and y units of good Y enjoys utility of $2ln(x) + ln(y)$. A Y-lover who consumes x units of good X and y units of good Y enjoys utility of $ln(x) + 2ln(y)$. There are equal numbers of X-lovers and Y-lovers in the economy and each is endowed with three units of each kind of good. If the prices of good X and good Y are each one per unit, how many units of each good will be supplied or demanded by each kind of person? Use your answer to show that there is a competitive equilibrium at which the price of each good is one. Show that, in this case, the competitive equilibrium allocation maximizes the total utility of all the people in the economy. Argue that this implies that the allocation is efficient.

4
COORDINATING PLANS
AND ACTIONS

I*f there really were some basic intrinsic advantage to a system which employed prices as planning instruments, we would expect to observe many organizations operating with this mode of control, especially among multidivisional business firms in a competitive environment. Yet the allocation of resources within private companies (not to mention governmental or nonprofit organizations) is almost never controlled by setting administered transfer prices on commodities and letting self-interested profit maximization do the rest. The price system as an allocator of internal resources does not pass the market test.*

Martin Weitzman[1]

[I]t is surely important to inquire why coordination is the work of the price mechanism in one case and of the entrepreneur in another.

Ronald Coase[2]

[M]odern business enterprise took the place of market mechanisms in coordinating the activities of the economy and allocating its resources. In many sectors of the economy, the visible hand of management replaced what Adam Smith referred to as the invisible hand of market forces.

Alfred Chandler[3]

In this chapter we explore some of the many ways in which economic coordination is achieved in economies and within organizations other than through a highly decentralized system of prices and markets. We examine the characteristics of different specific sorts of coordination problems and of the mechanisms used to solve them, and we develop elements of theories to help us understand which solutions are efficient in which situations. Because the subject matter of this chapter has received less

---

[1] "Prices versus Quantities," *Review of Economic Studies*, 41, October 1974, 477–91.

[2] "The Nature of the Firm," *Economica*, 4, 1937, 386–405.

[3] *The Visible Hand: The Managerial Revolution in American Business* (Cambridge, MA: The Belknap Press of Harvard University Press, 1977), p. 1.

scrutiny from economists than other parts of the theory of organizations, the development here is less complete and the conclusions more tentative than elsewhere in this text.

In Chapter 3, we saw that a price system could sometimes solve the fundamental and immensely complex problem of coordinating the plans and actions of all the diverse decision makers in a modern economy. According to the central result developed there in the fundamental theorem of welfare economics, if prices on a complete set of competitive markets are set so that the quantities of each good supplied and demanded are equal, then the resulting allocation of resources is efficient. Moreover, the price system achieves this remarkable feat of coordination without requiring communication among individual decision makers of anything more than the summary information about the economy embodied in the prices and without requiring any individual to do other than what he or she deems to be in his or her own best interests. We also saw that sometimes the price system can be used inside firms to obtain similarly efficient results. And even though actual markets do not fully meet the assumptions of the theorem, the evidence across nations and over the years is overwhelming that a decentralized system of prices and markets based on private ownership is an extremely effective mechanism for solving the coordination problem.

Yet, as Martin Weitzman argues in the quotation that opens this chapter, formal organizations make at most quite limited use of prices to coordinate their internal activities. Indeed, as we have suggested already in Chapters 2 and 3, organizations can be thought of as arising and supplanting the market when they offer more efficient mechanisms for coordinating economic activity and motivating people to carry out the resulting plans. Given this, it would be somewhat surprising to see them rely very heavily on an internal price system. Instead, managers more usually formulate general strategies, make these operational by specifying quantitative goals, develop specific plans to realize these goals, and then direct people to carry out their specified roles using the resources they have been allocated. Routines are developed, and administrative processes and procedures are instituted to guide activity. All this is done in telephone conversations and meetings and is embodied in memos and spreadsheets. The language used is not that of prices but rather of technological, organizational and individual capabilities, quantitative performance levels, specific plans and budgets, and detailed work assignments and operations schedules. And when changing availabilities and capabilities of people and physical resources within the organization require adaptation, the signals that indicate this need and guide the organization's responses are rarely prices.

Even in market systems, there is extensive use of means of coordination besides prices. Governments in particular favor giving direct orders that specify particular actions to be taken. They set quantity limits on the pollutants that a vehicle or factory can emit, on the amounts of impurities that foods and medicines can contain, on the speed that drivers can select, and on the minimum number of years children must spend in school. They command resources directly, as in a system of compulsory military service. They provide goods and services without explicitly pricing them: roads, police services, health care, food for the needy, and so on. In some countries, including Japan and South Korea, they target industries for expansion and new technologies for development and then coordinate explicitly the realization of these plans. In the centrally planned communist economies, governments have attempted to coordinate the finest details of resource allocation through quantity plans and orders. And, during World War II, government planners in the most market-oriented economies directed the production and use of a variety of high-priority goods, including not just steel and rubber, but also sugar and meat.

Moreover, firms often do not arrange their dealings with one another as simple market transactions. For example, they may work cooperatively with their suppliers to develop together the specifications for the inputs they seek, and they negotiate complex requirements contracts under which one firm has the power to direct how much the other will supply to it. Less formally, they may share information on plans and estimated requirements. They set up joint ventures and enter other sorts of alliances, they design complex royalty agreements and franchise contracts, and they put law firms on retainer, paying them even if they do not use their services. Within these relationships, they may exchange large amounts of information and often formulate joint plans.

In Chapter 3 we explored reasons why a price system would not yield an efficient outcome and so might be replaced: increasing returns, externalities, missing insurance and futures markets, excessive search costs, and the possibility of unemployment equilibria. In this chapter we focus mostly on situations where, in principle, the price system could be used and the fundamental theorem of welfare economics would hold, and yet other mechanisms for coordination are actually employed.

Planning and coordinating economic activity never come for free. It takes real resources to plan—people with offices, files, data banks, and the computing and communication equipment to support them. In addition to the planners' time, planning demands time from production people who must fill out forms, complete reports, and answer the planners' queries. At the end of the planning process, errors inevitably still occur, both because the prices or plans are based partly on guesses and partly on erroneous, incomplete, or misleading information and because miscalculations and mistakes occur.

In actual economies, a loose mix of systems is used to coordinate and manage the various kinds of activities. What determines which system is or ought to be used in any particular set of circumstances? How can we account for Weitzman's observation that prices are often ignored in internal decision making, so that "the price system as an allocator of resources does not pass the market test"? To answer these questions, we need to study coordination problems and systems in more detail.

THE VARIETY OF COORDINATION PROBLEMS AND SOLUTIONS

Robinson Crusoe, living alone before meeting Friday, took care of all his own needs. Gathering and preparing his own food and securing his own shelter, Crusoe spent no effort coordinating his activities with those of anyone else. The need for coordination comes from specialization, in which various tasks are divided among a group of people, each of whom relies on the others for part of the job. As noted in Chapters 2 and 3, specialization creates the opportunity for enormous increases in productivity. People who specialize in a job can prepare specialized tools, gain specialized training, develop specialized methods, and exploit their accumulated experience to get more done, more quickly and with fewer resources.

The kind of coordination that is most effective depends on the nature of the task. It is helpful to distinguish among several kinds of problems to understand the kinds of solutions that are used. The most general kind of coordination problem we consider is called a **resource allocation problem**. This is a problem of allocating a fixed set of resources among various possible uses. The term resource can be interpreted broadly enough to classify virtually every kind of important economic or business decision as a resource allocation problem. In this chapter, however, it is useful to distinguish particular attributes of resource allocation problems that make one system of coordination or another especially effective.

Design Attributes

We are especially interested in problems with **design attributes**. These are problems in which (1) there is a great deal of *a priori* information about the form of the optimal solution, that is, about how the variables should be related, and (2) failing to achieve the right relationship among the variables is generally more costly than are other kinds of errors, including especially slight misspecifications of the overall pattern, as long as the individual pieces fit. In this discussion, the word design is a general term describing a system in which the pieces must fit together in a predictable way, thus narrowing the search for efficient decisions. Two common kinds of problems with design attributes are synchronization problems and assignment problems.

SYNCHRONIZATION PROBLEMS   An extreme example of a **synchronization problem** arises in the sport of crew, in which it is crucially important that each rower make his or her stroke at precisely the same moment. The coxswain solves the synchronization problem by determining a rhythm for the crew and calling out the signal for each stroke. Like most centrally directed solutions, synchronization has the disadvantage that the centrally made decision cannot be fully responsive to information of the others in the system. In this case, the coxswain can only guess how tired the individual crew members are. This could be an important disadvantage if the coxswain pushes the crew too hard early in the race, leaving them too weak for a strong finishing sprint. However, the great advantage of the system is it synchronizes the actions of the crew, making their individual efforts much more effective. The costs of not setting quite the right pace are very small compared to those of failing to have everyone pulling in unison.

Though it seems ridiculous to contemplate using prices in this context, it is illuminating to see what a price solution for this problem would be and why it would not work well. In this application, a price system would entail the coxswain telling each rower the "price" of effort, that is, how valuable a unit of extra effort at this moment would be to the team. Then, each rower would choose his or her own action, taking full account of his or her own physical condition and the summary information supplied in the form of prices by the coxswain. In principle, if the coxswain could determine the right prices and could costlessly communicate them to the crew, and if the crew could make the right decisions based on that information, the resulting level of effort would be just right. In practice, a system of prices would fare badly for various reasons. First, it would be too difficult or costly for the coxswain to obtain the relevant information from the rowers and then to determine the prices. Second, communicating the prices back to the rowers would be too difficult and too slow. Third, the crew might respond inaccurately to the prices, failing to achieve coordination even if the prices were set correctly. Finally, small errors that disturbed the synchronized rhythm of the crew would be very costly. The price system has the same advantages in this application as in others with multiple producers. It takes full account of information about the individual condition of each producer, but that advantage comes at too high a cost in this synchronization problem.

ASSIGNMENT PROBLEMS   Similar difficulties arise in **assignment problems,** in which there are one or more tasks to accomplish and there is a need for just one person or unit to do each. The coordination problem is to ensure that each task is done and that there is no wasteful duplication of effort. For example, if someone is seriously injured in an automobile accident, there typically is a need for one ambulance at the site of the accident as soon as possible. In practice, someone calls for an ambulance and then a central dispatcher assigns a particular ambulance to drive to the site. Even if the dispatchers are in constant communication with the units, they may not be fully aware of all the relevant circumstances about the location and condition of the ambulance, of surrounding traffic, or of the training and experience of the crew. In principle, the dispatchers could try to determine a system of prices to determine which ambulance could provide the best service in the most timely fashion, but in practice they just select one and send it. If the prices were set incorrectly, more than one ambulance might rush to the scene, or no ambulances might respond. A system of prices performs poorly in assignment problems because it often leads to unnecessary duplication or costly delay.

It is interesting to contrast the way decisions about the uses of ambulances are made with decisions about how many ambulances to keep available, what equipment they should have, and how the ambulance staff should be trained. These latter decisions, made in relatively unhurried circumstances, take account of people's wages and salaries as well as the prices of equipment, vehicles, and training; they also utilize estimates of the benefits of additional ambulance capacity. At higher levels of decision making, people may also take account of the opportunity value of funds used for ambulances, which might otherwise be used to hire additional police officers or to build up an emergency fund or to buy additional park land.

DESIGN PROBLEMS AND ORGANIZATIONAL ROUTINES   Our crew and ambulance examples combine several features: a sense of urgency about the decision, the extreme dependence of the optimal course of action on particular circumstances (Are the opponents ahead or behind? Is there an accident, and if so, where?), and the coxswain's and central dispatcher's substantial knowledge about the form of an optimal decision. Together these make central control an attractive alternative to a decentralized approach, as through a system coordinated by prices. However, when design problems arise repeatedly and call for largely the same solution each time, it may be unnecessarily expensive to solve each of them anew by centralized direction. Instead, established organizations set up routines that guide decentralized solutions to the recurrent design problems. For the most common kinds of demands made on the organization, no upper-management discretion needs to be exercised because those who first become aware of the demand know what to do and who to notify, without ever involving higher-level personnel. If someone notices that paper for the copy machine is getting low, then (depending on the established routine) he or she either simply orders more and leaves a sign telling others that paper has been ordered, or else he or she notifies the designated individual in the office whose job is to order more paper. With well-established routines, each part of the organization can rely on the others to do their parts. If the environment of the organization changes, however, then the same routines that were effective may become counterproductive in the new environment, and new routines will need to be devised if the organization is to continue to achieve its goals.

Innovation Attributes

Highly decentralized decision making, whether guided by prices or by organizational routines, will perform poorly whenever the optimal resource allocation depends on information that is not available to any of the people at the operating levels of the organization. Coordination problems with this **innovation attribute** are most commonly present when the organization is trying to do something that is outside its experience, such as introducing a new kind of product, entering a new market, or adopting a new approach to manufacturing. If a firm wants to consider replacing its system of buffer inventories of work-in-process at each work station with a just-in-time system (in which production is synchronized so that each station receives the necessary inputs just in time to process them), then the current production and inventory managers may not have the experience to give a well-informed assessment of the costs and benefits. The decision cannot be properly made using just the information already available in the system.

When innovation attributes are present, effectively solving the coordination problem commonly involves someone gathering or developing the needed information and then communicating it to decision makers in the organization. This task might be taken on at his or her own initiative by someone at an operating level who has recognized that the problem exists. In other cases, the task will require more resources than lower-level personnel are able to muster on their own, and higher-level decision makers will have to become involved, allocating resources and assigning people to get the needed information.

In any case, the fact that a decision requires gathering new information from outside the organization does not imply that the decision ought to be centralized. People in operating positions may be best equipped to combine new knowledge with local knowledge, or they may be better motivated to make the new system successful if they are also the ones who designed it. An effective way to handle this problem may be to educate members of the organization about the proposed alternatives and to involve them in the final decision. What is certain, however, is that a simple price system relying only on the responses of individuals using their local knowledge cannot reliably achieve an optimal plan in these circumstances.

Comparing Coordination Schemes

The sample coordination problems we have described differ from one another, and the solutions that people actually adopt vary widely. Some decisions may be extremely urgent, with little time to process information. Others may require extremely close synchronization or coordination of assignments, with little tolerance for faults. Some require only making effective use of information that is already in the organization, whereas others require the infusion of new information.

Coordination systems also vary. Certain centralized command systems demand little upward communication of local knowledge and yet they still arrive quickly at reasonable plans and communicate clearly what the operational personnel are expected to do. Others require much more upward communication, but are correspondingly more responsive to local knowledge. Decentralized systems emphasize communicating information to support local decisions, with the required volume of communication being between the two centralized extremes. When these various systems fail, they fail in predictably different ways. The price system may work too slowly or lead to duplication, or it may require too much interpretation of information by decision makers. The coxswain's call and the ambulance dispatcher's instructions are quick and their meanings are clear, but they are insensitive to local knowledge.

There are more aspects to the coordination problem than just what the means of coordination will be. The manufacturing example provides an illustration of how a system could be designed to reduce the value of close coordination while still capturing gains to specialization: The system of buffer inventories eliminates the need to synchronize production but requires costly holdings of inventories.[4]

CRITERIA FOR COMPARING SYSTEMS   We use three criteria to compare how well different systems perform in solving various kinds of economic problems. First, if all the information required by the system were reported, if all reports were made honestly

---

[4] Inventory costs include the interest on funds used to finance inventories, losses due to spoilage, theft, obsolescence, the cost of space in the storage area, and certain other costs that come from the tendency of inventories to conceal the effects of production performance that varies over time.

and accurately, and if information processing were perfect and costless, could this system achieve an efficient decision? Second, just how much communication and information does the system require to achieve its purpose? Are there other systems that could do equally well with less communication? Third, how **brittle** is the system? That is, if some of the desired information is missing or inaccurate, how badly will the system's performance deteriorate?

To compare alternative coordination systems in different settings, we rely on a cost-benefit principle: The system that should be adopted in any specific situation is the one that maximizes the net benefit, after properly accounting for all these kinds of costs. Unfortunately, the present state of knowledge does not allow us to make specific statements about which system will work best in any particular circumstance. Nevertheless, there is much of value to be learned by studying some specific problems of coordination and control and seeing how the optimal solution depends on the details of the problem.

PRICES VERSUS QUANTITIES: ASSESSING BRITTLENESS

In order to study more closely the effectiveness of different approaches to coordination, we look first at the standard economic problem of allocating scarce resources. The overall objective is to compare a system of prices with a system of centralized quantity planning in which the coordinator instructs the production units how much to produce and with what resources. However, in this context it is not sensible to ignore how prices are set (as is done in much of Chapter 3). Thus, we compare two systems: one in which the central coordinator simply specifies the production units' quantities, and another in which the center attempts to guide the units' decisions via price signals, counting on the units' managers to respond by picking the appropriate quantities. The price-based system recalls the proposal for market socialism discussed in Chapter 3. The problem could also be thought of as that of a firm attempting to coordinate internal production decisions.

Because the information available to the planner is fixed in this analysis, we use two criteria to compare the performance of the alternative systems. First, when the planner's information is perfect, does the system permit the planner to achieve an efficient outcome? Second, when the planner's information is imperfect, to what extent does the system performance fall short of the performance with perfect information? That is, how brittle is the system?

Some Examples

Suppose the planner knows the benefits accruing to any level of output from a production unit and wants to ensure that the efficient level of output is actually produced. Unfortunately, the planner may not be perfectly informed about production costs. Instead, it relies on its estimate of these costs, which may be wrong.

PERFECT INFORMATION   A sample calculation is illustrated in Table 4.1. On the basis of the planner's cost estimate, total benefits minus total costs are maximized if either 5 or 6 units are produced. If the planner directs the firm to produce 6 units, the estimated net benefit will then be 38 (total benefits of 58 minus the total cost of 20). The net benefit is also 38 if 5 units are produced, but it is no more than 36 for any other output quantity.

Still assuming that there is in fact no error in the cost estimates, the planner could accomplish the same thing by setting a price of 8 and telling the firm to produce the quantity that is most profitable at that price. The marginal benefit and the marginal cost of the sixth unit are both equal to 8. (In terms of supply and demand, the marginal benefit schedule tabulates the prices at which the quantity demanded is

Table 4.1

Number of Units	Total Benefits	Marginal Benefit	Planner's Cost Estimate			Error Scenario		
			Total Costs	Marginal Cost	Net Benefit	Total Costs	Marginal Cost	Net Benefit
4	40		5		35	17		23
5	50	10	12	7	38	20	3	30
6	58	8	20	8	38	24	4	34
7	64	6	29	9	35	29	5	35
8	68	4	39	10	29	35	6	33
9	70	2	50	11	20	42	7	28
10	70	0	62	12	8	50	8	20

In the error scenario, the planned quantity of 6 leads to a net benefit 34 out of a possible 35, but the planned price of 8 leads to a net benefit of only 20.

equal to the listed number of units, and the marginal cost schedule tabulates the same information about the quantity supplied.) At a price of 8 the firm can maximize its profits by producing either 5 or 6 units, and the outcome of the process maximizes the total net benefits.[5]

Thus, the answer to our first question is "yes" for both the price-directed and quantity-directed systems: If the planner has perfect information, then both systems result in an efficient outcome. Thus, we move to the second question: How is performance degraded by imperfect information?

IMPERFECT INFORMATION   To examine this question, suppose that the decision maker's estimate of the cost is wrong and that the actual cost characteristics are those given in the Error Scenario columns of Table 4.1. The firm will know that these are its true costs when it actually comes to carry out production, but it cannot inform the planner of the true costs before the price or quantity directive is announced.

The price or quantity to be announced is still determined on the basis of the planner's (incorrect) estimate. That is, the quantity is set at 6 and the price at 8. Also, in both cases, the socially efficient quantity to produce is 7 because that maximizes the total benefits minus the actual total costs. With a quantity of 7, the actual net benefit would be 35 (64 total units of benefit minus 29 total costs).

If the plan specifies an output of 6 units, then the net benefit will be only 34, so there is a loss of 1 unit of net benefit on account of the estimation error in this system (where a quantity is specified). In the same circumstances, suppose that the planner had tried to control the producer using a price system and had fixed a price of 8. In this case, given its actual costs, the firm maximizes its profits by producing to the point where its marginal cost is equal to 8, that is, by producing 10 units of output, yielding a net benefit of only 20.[6] The firm has responded to the price and its actual costs as efficiency requires that it should, that is, by setting output so that marginal cost is equal to price. The incorrect price has led to an inefficient quantity,

---

[5] This differs from a standard monopoly problem in that the firm here is forced to take the price as given and is not permitted to manipulate the price by varying its output decision.

[6] In this case, the firm could also maximize its profit by setting its output at 9 because it is just indifferent about producing the last unit. In the interests of clarity and simplicity, we will always use the output level where the price is equal to the marginal cost to characterize the firm's decision.

Table 4.2

Number of Units	Total Benefits	Marginal Benefit	Planner's Cost Estimate			Error Scenario		
			Total Costs	Marginal Cost	Net Benefit	Total Costs	Marginal Cost	Net Benefit
4	42		5		37	17		25
5	50	8	12	7	38	20	3	30
6	58	8	20	8	38	24	4	34
7	66	8	29	9	37	29	5	37
8	74	8	39	10	35	35	6	39
9	82	8	50	11	32	42	7	40
10	90	8	62	12	28	50	8	40

In this example, the marginal benefit does not depend on the quantity produced. As a result, the price control leads to no loss at all in the error scenario. In contrast, a quantity control leads to a loss of 6.

however. In this particular example, the loss on account of the mistake is 15 units, a much larger loss than for the quantity-directed system.

In this example, the quantity system works better, but this is not always the case. Compare the example in Table 4.1 with that in Table 4.2, in which the costs are the same but the benefit levels differ. The marginal benefit in Table 4.2 is constant at 8. In both scenarios, if the price is specified to be 8, the quantity that maximizes the firm's profits is also the quantity that is socially efficient. Therefore, the use of prices to coordinate behavior avoids any loss on account of imperfect cost estimates. If instead the planner had fixed the quantity at 6, the best level based on the estimated costs, and if the actual cost function were that shown in the error scenario in the table, then 6 units of net benefit would be lost. (Six units give a net benefit of 34, whereas the actually efficient choice of 10 yields a net benefit of 40.) In the second example, the approach of fixing prices performs better than fixing quantities.

The flat marginal benefit curve is one extreme. At the other is a marginal benefit schedule that is vertical at the relevant point, as in Table 4.3.

In this example the right quantity is 6 units, independent of which cost scenario prevails. The quantity system achieves the optimum, with a net benefit of 36. A price system based on the incorrect estimate would involve setting the price at 8, the level of (incorrectly) estimated marginal cost at the efficient quantity. However, facing a price of 8 and the costs given in the error scenario, the firm will select a quantity of 9 or 10 units, both of which give it profits of 30 ($9 \times 8 - 42$ and $10 \times 8 - 50$). The loss from using prices is either $18 = (36 - 18)$ or $26 = (36 - 10)$.

The third example recalls our discussion of ambulances. It makes little sense to call out a price and see how many ambulances arrive because the number of ambulances that will show up is too dependent on irrelevant information. If you know that you want one ambulance, you should order one ambulance. In the second example, because the marginal value of each unit is 8, the correct price will be 8 regardless of the cost function. If you know that the marginal value of output will be 8, then the best form of control is to fix the price at 8. These extreme cases are informative, but we still want to know: What general principle guides the choice in intermediate cases, such as that in Table 4.1?

A Mathematical Formulation and Analysis

To provide a more general view of when prices work relatively well, we switch to an algebraic formulation of the problem. As in our preceding examples, we study the

Table 4.3

Number of Units	Total Benefits	Marginal Benefit	Planner's Cost Estimate			Error Scenario		
			Total Costs	Marginal Cost	Net Benefit	Total Costs	Marginal Cost	Net Benefit
4	40		5		35	17		23
5	50	10	12	7	38	20	3	30
6	60	10	20	8	40	24	4	36
7	60	0	29	9	31	29	5	31
8	60	0	39	10	21	35	6	25
9	60	0	50	11	10	42	7	18
10	60	0	62	12	−2	50	8	10

In this example, the marginal benefit drops from 10 to 0 at 6 units. The optimal quantity is 6 for either cost scenario. There is no loss if a quantity system is used. In constrast, a price system leads to a loss of 26.

case where the marginal benefits and marginal costs are linear functions of the output quantity. Unlike those examples, however, we do not restrict outputs to integer amounts. Also, as in the examples, the slopes of the linear functions are assumed to be known, but the decision maker is unsure about the intercept of the cost function, so that all the marginal costs might turn out to be higher or lower than anticipated by some fixed (but unknown) amount. Suppose the losses associated with the systems of fixed prices and fixed quantities are measured in the same way as in the preceding examples, as the difference in the net benefits achieved under the particular system and the net benefits that would be achieved with correct information. In that case, it turns out that the ratio of the losses incurred depends on the slopes of the marginal benefit and marginal cost functions, as follows:

$$\frac{\text{Loss from a price control}}{\text{Loss from a quantity control}} = \left[\frac{\text{Slope of margical benefit}}{\text{Slope of marginal cost}} \right]^2 \qquad (4.1)$$

According to Equation 4.1, a price-based system of coordination leads to smaller losses than does a quantity system when the slope of the marginal benefit function is less than the slope of the marginal cost function, and the reverse ranking holds when the slopes are reversed. This qualitative conclusion matches those we had obtained in the discrete examples. (It does not quite match quantitatively because outputs were restricted to integer amounts in the examples.)

In the theory of competitive markets where firms base their quantity decisions on market determined prices and their own costs, the corresponding ratio is the slope of the firm's demand function to the slope of its marginal cost function. From the competitive firm's point of view, demand is infinitely elastic; that is, the slope of the demand function is zero. Consequently, according to Equation 4.1, its choices are best guided by the system of prices: Efficiency cannot be improved by regulating a competitive firm.

Derivation of the Formula

Figure 4.1 shows how the formula in Equation 4.1 is derived. As usual, the horizontal axis indicates quantities of output and the vertical axis indicates prices (money per unit of quantity). The downward sloping line (*MB*) is the marginal benefit curve, whereas the two upward sloping lines correspond to the marginal cost curve as estimated by the planner (MC) and in the error scenario (MC'). Total benefit corresponding to any output is then the area under the MB curve, and the total cost in either scenario is the area under the relevant marginal cost curve. The marginal benefit and estimated marginal cost curves intersect at the point $a = (Q,P)$, where Q is the efficient quantity and P the corresponding price if the planner's estimates are correct.

In the error scenario, the actual marginal cost is less than the planner's estimate by the amount d. The actual efficient quantity is then Q'. If the planner specifies a quantity of Q, what will be lost? The area of the trapezoid $QacQ'$ in Figure 4.1 represents the benefit of increasing output from the level Q specified by the planner to the optimal level Q', while the area of $QbcQ'$ represents the cost of the extra output. The difference, represented by the area of the triangle abc, is the net loss of welfare on account of the planner's mistaken quantity choice. Using the formula for the area of triangles, the welfare loss is equal to $\frac{1}{2} d(Q'-Q)$.

For comparison, suppose the planner instead specifies a price of P and the firm responds by producing the profit-maximizing quantity Q''. Compared to the optimal quantity choice Q', choosing Q'' brings extra benefits represented by the area of the trapezoid $Q'ceQ''$ and extra costs represented by $Q'cfQ''$. The extra costs exceed the extra benefits by an amount equal to the area of the triangle efc. Calculating as before, the area is $\frac{1}{2} D(Q''-Q')$.

Notice that the triangles abc and efc are similar triangles. (The marked angles at b and f are alternate interior angles and are therefore congruent. The same applies to the alternate interior angles at a and e.) It then follows that $(Q''-Q')/(Q'-Q) = D/d$: The altitudes of the triangles from vertex c are in proportion to the bases. Also, letting SMB denote the magnitude of the slope of the MB curve (the curve is negatively sloped) and SMC that of the MC curve, the diagram reveals that $d = SMC \times (Q''-Q)$ and $D = SMB \times (Q''-Q)$. Hence, $D/d = SMB/SMC$. Taking the ratio of the areas of the two shaded triangles leads to:

$$\frac{\frac{1}{2}D(Q''-Q')}{\frac{1}{2}d(Q''-Q)} = \frac{D}{d} \times \frac{(Q''-Q')}{(Q'-Q)} = \left[\frac{\text{Slope of marginal benefit}}{\text{Slope of marginal cost}} \right]^2 \quad (4.2)$$

which establishes Equation 4.1.

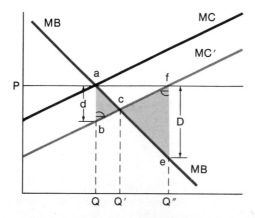

Figure 4.1: The left-hand and right-hand shaded triangles show the losses from quantity and price controls in the error scenario. The ratio of the areas is given by Equation 4.1.

Table 4.4

Number of Units	Total Benefits	Marginal Benefit	Planner's Cost Estimate			Error Scenario		
			Total Costs	Marginal Costs	Net Benefit	Total Costs	Marginal Costs	Net Benefit
4	40		32		8	28		12
5	50	10	40	8	10	35	7	15
6	58	8	48	8	10	42	7	16
7	64	6	56	8	8	49	7	15
8	68	4	64	8	4	56	7	12
9	70	2	72	8	−2	63	7	7
10	70	0	80	8	−10	70	7	0

With constant returns to scale, prices alone cannot guide the output decision.

Constant and Increasing Returns to Scale

Our discussion so far has assumed that the marginal cost of producing increases with the total number of units being made. Treating this as the long-run marginal cost, the assumption is that there are *decreasing returns to scale*. In such circumstances, if demand is large, then it is generally optimal to divide production among a number of units to keep total costs relatively low. The price system has certain extra advantages in that setting because the optimal price depends only on the aggregate or average of the producers' supply curves, while efficient quantity planning would require the planner to know the costs of each producer individually. Not surprisingly, the advantages of decentralization in economizing on information gathering and communications are greatest when efficient production requires that many producers be coordinated. We return to study how the need for communications varies among systems in the next section.

First, however, let us consider the important situation in which individual producers enjoy *increasing returns to scale* and decreasing average costs. In this case, it is inefficient to divide production among many small firms. Fewer firms could produce the same output at a lower total cost. Moreover, as we saw in Chapter 3, the criterion of maximizing profits at given prices can never be sufficient in that case to stimulate the firms to produce optimal quantities. With given prices, revenues grow in proportion to output but, with increasing returns, costs per unit fall as output increases. Thus, if the given price ever exceeds average cost, the firm would seek to increase output without bound because each additional unit of output increases total profit. The price system in these circumstances fails to meet our first criterion. It could not support an efficient plan even if there were no chance of any error in the planner's estimate of the firm's cost function.

The dividing line between the cases of increasing and decreasing returns to scale is the case of *constant returns to scale*, where the slope of the marginal cost function is zero and marginal cost equals average cost at all output levels. Applying Equation 4.1 to the case where the slope is nearly zero, the loss from a fixed-price choice is much greater than the loss from a system that fixes quantities. Our next example, presented in Table 4.4, makes the reason clear.

Setting a correct price of 8 in this example provides no guidance whatever to a profit-maximizing producer. Every level of output leads to the same level of producer profits (zero). If the price is set incorrectly, however, the results are dramatic. If the price is set to 8 when the marginal cost of production is 7 (the error scenario), then a profit-maximizing producer would expand output to the limit of its capacity. Presumably, it will also be delighted to expand its capacity. Similarly, if the price is 8 but the marginal cost is 9, the firm will drop its output to zero because it loses money on each unit produced. With constant returns to scale, the producer's responses to small price changes are too extreme for prices to be an effective instrument of controlling production.

This conclusion points out one of the most important limitations of the fundamental theorem of welfare economics. The theorem asserts that a competitive equilibrium allocation is efficient. That is, if the prevailing prices and allocation are such that supply is equal to demand for every good at the given prices, then the allocation is efficient. The problem is that, as we saw in Chapter 3, with increasing returns to scale, there may be no prices at which supply is equal to demand. Furthermore, with constant returns to scale, the price that equates the quantities supplied and demanded gives the producer no guidance about the appropriate level of production; every production level leads to an equal level of profits. As applied to Table 4.4, the theorem merely asserts that if the quantity produced at a price of 8 happens to be the one where supply equals demand (in this case, 6 units), then the outcome is an efficient one.

If several suppliers enjoy constant returns to scale over the relevant range of production levels, then an efficient plan demands that the entire order be produced by the one supplier with the lowest total cost and that the quantity ordered be adjusted so that the marginal benefit associated with the last unit is equal to that supplier's marginal cost. One way to accomplish this feat of coordination is for the suppliers to engage in competitive bidding, where each bid reflects one supplier's cost and the buyer purchases as many units as desired at the lowest quoted price. This helps to explain the common business practices of competitive bidding and requirements contracting (in which the seller agrees to supply as many units as the buyer may require at the quoted price) and suggests that these practices ought to be most common for goods produced with constant or increasing returns to scale.

Competitive bidding, of course, is a kind of market organization in which firms set prices. In the short run, the prices bid by suppliers guide the buyer's demand. In the long run, the prices paid by buyers guide the suppliers' capacity decisions. Therefore, even when constant returns to scale exist, prices still have a role to play in determining the allocation of resources.

ECONOMIZING ON INFORMATION AND COMMUNICATION

So far in this chapter we have ignored the important costs of gathering, organizing, storing, analyzing, and communicating information in a form that is useful for decision making. We now explore the extent and limitations of the idea, as suggested by Hayek in the quotation at the beginning of Chapter 3, that a system of prices is a particularly good way to economize on communication and information processing.

The Informational Requirements of Production Planning

The basic intuition regarding the informational efficiency of a price system is perhaps best illustrated by studying the problem of minimizing the cost of producing a given amount of total output in a firm with several production facilities or in an economy as a whole. Using a system in which the planned allocation is centrally determined and then implemented through quantity controls requires that the planner have huge amounts of detailed information about each individual production unit. Even finding a plan that is technologically feasible requires the center to know a great deal about the capabilities of each unit, so that it is not asked to do the impossible. Then determining how much each facility should efficiently produce out of a given desired total output requires knowing the marginal costs in each facility. Since this information is not likely to be known initially by the center, it must be communicated from the individual units. The massive planning bureaucracies that developed in the Soviet Union and other communist countries are proof of just how costly it is to gather and process that much information.

In contrast, a price-guided, decentralized system does not require communication of such large amounts of information. Individual production units will respond to given prices on the basis of their local knowledge of their technological capabilities and their costs, each producing where the common price equals its marginal cost. This means the total output is produced at minimum total cost.

This treatment, however, ignores the problem of finding the right prices that call forth the desired total output. As we noted earlier, determining the right prices requires that the price setter know only the total supply function, and this would seem to be less demanding than knowing the total production possibilities for each individual factory. But there is still a question of how the center would come to have this information. In a market system, we count on the forces of supply and demand to adjust prices. An analog in the planning context would be to think about an iterative procedure. The center would announce a candidate price, the individual units would respond with tentative production plans, and then the center would adjust the price up or down depending on whether too little or too much output was forthcoming. Then what needs to be communicated at each round is the single price and the output levels, one per plant.

An analogous scheme could be considered for quantity planning. Suppose the center announced a tentative output level to each producer, each responded by stating its marginal cost at this output level, and then the quantities were adjusted up for those plants announcing low marginal costs and down for those whose announced marginal costs were high. If the individual plants all announced the same marginal cost level, then the corresponding division of production among them would be efficient. Note, however, that each round now requires more communication than under the price-based system: an output level for each plant and its marginal cost. If there are N plants, price-based planning involves communicating $N+1$ numbers: the price from the center to the plants, and the N plants' outputs back to the center. The quantity system requires communicating $2N$ numbers. Even in this simple context, the price system requires comparatively less communication of information.

Judging Informational Efficiency

To make a formal assessment of the relative communication requirements of *any* particular system, we use the idea in the last paragraph of comparing the sizes of the messages used. However, since we want to compare more than just the sort of iterative procedures for planning production that we discussed earlier, we need to take a little different approach than used there.

THE HURWICZ CRITERION   The one widely applied approach to comparing the informational requirements of different systems is due to Leonid Hurwicz. The key idea is to consider how much information it takes to determine whether a particular plan is efficient. We then think of the planning system as based on broadcasts of augmented plans to producers and consumers. An augmented plan consists of the plan itself—input and output levels of each good for each producer and amounts of each good received or supplied by each consumer—plus possibly additional information used to check the efficiency of the plan. By "broadcasts," we mean that any information that is communicated is made available to everyone. Upon receiving the broadcast, each individual producer or consumer evaluates the plan using local information and then replies with a message, which we may take to be a "Yes" or a "No." In terms of the iterative procedures discussed previously, it is as if the center were announcing both the prices and quantities, with the firms responding "Yes" if their marginal costs at the announced output equalled the price. The whole system must be constructed so that if everyone replies with "Yes," then the resulting plan is an efficient one.

In this framework, the **Hurwicz criterion** holds that one system operates with less communication than another if the first broadcasts fewer additional variables (besides the plan itself). A system is then **informationally efficient** if no other system uses less extra information than it does to verify that a given plan is efficient.

This criterion is an imperfect measure of information used by the system. Its most significant drawback is that it does not account for how quickly different systems find an efficient allocation or for how much information they communicate in the process. Instead, it focuses only on the amount of information that is used to check whether a proposed resource allocation is efficient. So far, however, the Hurwicz criterion is the only measure of communication requirements which has been extensively and successfully analyzed.

THE INFORMATIONAL EFFICIENCY OF THE PRICE SYSTEM   Despite its drawbacks, the Hurwicz criterion does allow us to capture one aspect of the idea that the price system places particularly light demands on communication. The following theorem, which is due to Hurwicz, gives the minimum amount of information that must in general be communicated in addition to the plan to permit verification of the plan's efficiency. This amount is what is communicated in the price system.

> **Informational Efficiency Theorem**: Suppose that there is no *a priori* information about the optimal resource allocation, so that given what any single producer or consumer knows, any allocation of society's limited resources might still be efficient. Suppose too that each producer is uniquely well informed about its own productive capabilities and each consumer alone knows his or her own preferences and what amounts of various goods he or she initially owns, so that no single agent alone has the information needed to compute an efficient allocation of resources. Then any system capable of supporting an efficient resource allocation using augmented plans must communicate, in addition to the plan, at least one additional variable for each separate good or resource, minus one.

In particular, when a competitive equilibrium exists, the price system, which communicates exactly one additional variable (the price) for each good or resource after the first,[7] achieves economic efficiency with minimal communication. The price system is then informationally efficient by the Hurwicz criterion.

AN INTUITION FOR THE INFORMATIONAL EFFICIENCY THEOREM   To understand why this result is true, consider the problem of verifying whether a single producer's allocation is efficient. Producers cannot tell on the basis of their local knowledge and the proposed plan alone whether their own part of the plan is efficient because they do not know how valuable the resources might be in other uses. Because the producers are uniquely well informed about their own capabilities, nobody else can tell if the plan is even technologically feasible for the producer, let alone whether it is consistent

---

[7] The first good is taken to be the *numeraire*. The prices of all other goods can then be expressed in units of the first good. Historically, the numeraire good was often gold or silver.

with overall efficiency. Therefore, the broadcast message must convey enough information to the local producers to allow them to verify the optimality of their individual parts of the plan.

In order for the producer's specified part of the plan to be consistent with overall efficiency, the marginal rate at which the producer transforms any particular kind of input into any particular kind of good must be the same as at any other production facility in the economy that uses this input in producing the same good. (If, for example, some other factory had a lower marginal rate of transformation, then the same output could be achieved with fewer resources by increasing slightly the production of this factory and reducing the production of the other by an equal amount.) In order to determine whether these conditions hold, the producer must know what these economy-wide marginal rates of transformation are. If there is only one kind of input, then there is just one relevant marginal rate of transformation for each product. If there are many kinds of inputs, then there must be at least one additional marginal rate of transformation for each additional kind.

One number per good produced and one number for each input after the first then define a lower bound for the amount of communication that is needed to verify the efficiency of any proposed plan. As we saw earlier in this chapter and in the fundamental theorem of welfare economics in Chapter 3, this amount of communication is sufficient as well when the numbers are (relative) prices. In that case, each producer looks at the production levels specified for it, determines whether its plan maximizes its profits at the given prices, and if it does, then it responds with a "Yes." If everyone responds "Yes" and if the plans are chosen so that the supply equals demand for every kind of good, then the plans are efficient by the fundamental theorem of welfare economics.

APPLYING THE THEOREM   Of course, we do not normally think of the price system in terms of a broadcast plan. However, suppose each consumer and producer has a uniquely best choice at the competitive equilibrium prices. Then having prices "announced" and having each individual agent "respond" with the corresponding amounts that he or she wants to buy or sell involves just the amount of communication identified by the theorem. If the announced prices are the competitive equilibrium ones, the quantities balance and an efficient allocation results. Under the usual conception of how a competitive market system works, if the initial prices are not the competitive equilibrium ones, then the quantity responses will not balance. With supply not equal to demand, there will be pressures for prices to change. The new prices call forth adjusted quantities as people respond to the new rates at which they can buy and sell, and the system gropes its way along, perhaps ultimately reaching some equilibrium.

More often, however, this framework and the theorem are applied to explicit production planning problems, either within firms or at an industry or economy-wide level. One of these arises in considering situations where the coordination problem has design attributes.

Planning with Design Attributes

Notice that the hypotheses of the informational efficiency theorem rule out problems in which there are design attributes. For decisions with design attributes, there is a priori information about the nature of any efficient choice, and it may be possible to verify the optimality or near-optimality of the plan with less information than that communicated by a system of prices. In our example of the coxswain guiding a crew of rowers, it was known in advance that synchronization of the rowers' strokes would characterize any optimal solution and that failures of synchronization would be very costly to the crew. The coxswain system uses much less communication than does a system of prices, and its failures when the coxswain's judgment is imperfect are much less costly.

Problems in which synchronization is important arise frequently in business. For example, if an automobile company is designing a new car, all the parts must be designed and production facilities made ready by the target date for introducing the product. To synchronize, the new product team agrees on a product introduction date and communicates that date to other relevant parties, rather than marginal values for early completion.

It is not only timing that is communicated in this way in product development. When a new car is being developed, the engine must be designed to pull a car of a particular weight, the brakes must be designed to stop a car of that weight, and the chassis must be designed to carry that weight safely. Similar statements can be made about other attributes of the car, such as its physical dimensions. The development team coordinates its activities by agreeing on goals and objectives and on how to realize these. The language the team uses is not generally the language of prices.

Using Prices in Design Decisions   Let us emphasize that the avoidance of prices for coordinating activities in synchronization problems and other sorts of design problems is not due to any theoretical impossibility of applying a price system. Rather, it is due to (1) the unreasonable information demands that the price system makes in these kinds of problems and (2) the brittleness of the system, that is, the high cost of asynchronous behavior. To illuminate the information demands, let us consider once more how a price system would operate for a synchronization problem.

For simplicity, suppose that there are ten suppliers who must coordinate the timing of their supply activities, and five possible completion dates. Recall that goods are described not only by their physical characteristics but also by their time and place of delivery. This is a crucial point for understanding how markets and other organizations work; skis rented for two weeks in the winter are quite a different thing from skis rented for two weeks in the summer, and we should not be surprised to see sharp differences in the rental prices of the two. Applying that perspective to the synchronization problem, we find that each of the ten suppliers can supply any one of five different goods, according to whether the physical product is delivered at dates one, two, three, four, or five. Therefore, there are 50 inputs in all (five for each of the ten producers), and a price system would require a price for each of them—50 separate prices.

If the number of suppliers, possible delivery dates, or component designs are large, then the number of prices that need to be specified is also large. Nevertheless, the fundamental theorem of welfare economics does apply. *If* all the prices are set so that the coordinator would want to buy one unit of one design of each input at some particular date T and *if*, given the prices, each supplier finds it most profitable to deliver one unit of the corresponding design at date T, so that markets clear, *then* the allocation (the list of dates at which supplies of each type of component become available) is guaranteed to be efficient.

A Better Way   Determining 50 prices to solve this synchronization problem is unnecessary and wasteful. All the coordinator actually needs to know to check whether a proposed introduction date is optimal is whether the total marginal cost of introducing the product a bit earlier—taking into account the extra costs incurred by each component supplier—is equal to the marginal benefit of doing so. To check this, it suffices for the coordinator to know the marginal cost of a speed-up for each supplier, which is just ten numbers. The greater the number of possible delivery dates, the

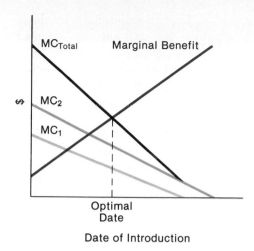

Figure 4.2: The optimal date of product introduction is the date at which the marginal benefit of faster introduction is equal to the sum of the marginal costs incurred by the two supply units.

greater the discrepancy between the minimum amount of necessary communication and the amount required by the price system.

Figure 4.2 illustrates an extreme case, for which there are only two suppliers but the product might be introduced on any of a continuum of possible dates. The downward sloping curves show the marginal cost to each component supplier of speeding up the product introduction by a small amount, given any particular target introduction date. The downward slant means that speeding up the introduction grows increasingly costly for each supplier as the planned introduction date is moved up. The total marginal cost of a speed-up for the two suppliers is determined by adding the costs for the individual units. The upward sloping curve in the figure is the marginal benefit curve. Its upward slope means that longer delays grow increasingly costly for the firm. The optimal introduction date is determined at the point where the marginal cost of additional speed-ups to the two suppliers is equal to the marginal benefit.

In this problem, to verify whether any particular list of prices leads to optimal choices, the planner would have to know what costs each supplier would incur for each possible delivery date—an infinite list of information—in order to tell which date a profit-maximizing supplier will pick. To verify the actual optimal date, however, all the coordinator needs to know is the marginal benefit of a speed-up and the two suppliers' marginal costs: three numbers in all. Taking advantage of special knowledge about the problem, the coordinator can drastically reduce the amount of communication required.

What about the cost of mistakes? In many real synchronization and product design problems, the most costly sorts of errors are failures of synchronization (as when the late availability of one component delays a large project) or fit (as when one component's incorrect tolerances cause the product to fail), and these are the ones most to be avoided. In contrast, as long as the parts fit together, small variations in the design itself are less crucial. Thus, it matters less whether the drain hole in a car's oil pan is 2 cm or 2.5 cm than that the hole and the plug are both the same size.

Because our definition of design attributes includes two characteristics—predictable elements of fit and a high cost of small errors of fit—we may conclude that the price system performs poorly for design problems on both the communication and the brittleness criteria. The usefulness of this general conclusion, however, depends on an assessment of how often real problems have both of the characteristics that we have included in our definition of design attributes.

If prices should not be used to coordinate design decisions, how should coordination be achieved? The answer is that the design variables themselves should be communicated. Each rower in the crew must know the intended stroke rate and the timing needs to be communicated to the rower. Each member of the product introduction team must know the introduction date and the weight and other key design parameters of the new car. The ambulance driver must be told which crisis to attend, when, and where. This form of control minimizes communication by the Hurwicz criterion and reduces the cost of error associated with more indirect methods. The appendix to this chapter contains a more formal treatment of design decisions, establishing that communicating the design variables is informationally efficient for the class of design decisions, just as communicating prices is informationally efficient for the class of resource allocation problems treated in the informational efficiency

COORDINATION AND BUSINESS STRATEGY

Strategic business decisions present complicated problems. Good strategic decision making virtually always requires that effective use be made of line managers' knowledge about how the operations actually work and what capabilities the business has, but they may also involve using knowledge about new technologies, new markets, new business partners, or new forms of organization about which the line managers' knowledge may be limited. In our lexicon, strategic decisions often have innovation attributes. In addition, especially in manufacturing industries, but in some service industries as well, there are important economies of scale that mitigate against completely decentralized decision making. Finally, as we argue later, business strategy decisions commonly have important design attributes. There are predictable elements of fit in any good strategy that make it important to coordinate the actions of various parts of the organization closely. All these factors work against using prices or other very decentralized means of coordination and favor direct communication and other more systematic, centralized control systems.

Scale, Scope, and Core Competencies of the Firm

As we have already seen, when there are scale economies, the efficient level of output in a firm cannot be determined by prices alone. *Operational scale* itself is a design variable. Depending on the volume of sales that a firm anticipates, it will adjust its production capacity and the size of its sales force and secure supplies and distribution equipment and facilities (such as trucks and warehouses)—all tailored to the expected scale of its operations. If the actions taken by the marketing, production, personnel, distribution, and procurement managers are to be coherent, then all these people need a shared vision of the intended scale of operations.

SCALE AND STRUCTURE   The anticipated scale of a firm's operations predictably affects more than just the scale of each part. As the GM and Toyota examples from Chapter 1 illustrate, it also determines the degree of specialization the firm should adopt. With larger operations, a firm may be able to afford more specialized equipment, more distribution outlets located nearer to customers, a larger number of plants, training programs for its employees tailored to particular circumstances, and so on. A smaller firm, operating without specialized equipment, may be more likely to rely on suppliers for many more of its components because the suppliers may be better positioned to enjoy economies of scale of their own by serving many firms. Thus, a larger firm with more specialized capital equipment may find it profitable to be more vertically integrated than would its smaller competitors. By definition, economies of scale in production allow a firm to reduce its costs compared to small-scale production, and these costs are an important element in determining the prices to be charged. Lower marginal costs, other things equal, lead the firm to charge lower prices, which increases the potential product demand, which in turn supports an increased scale of production.

Operational scale is a design variable because it meets the two conditions. It has predictable implications for the various parts of the organization, and many of the mistakes associated with incorrect perceptions of scale by parts of the organization—for example, having too few raw materials or components to keep an expensive factory operating at full capacity—can be very high. Thus, firms that are large enough to assign different management functions to different decision makers take special pains to forecast market growth, competitors' plans, technical changes, input availabilities, and so on, all so that they can use those forecasts to plan the growth (scale) of their own operations and coordinate based on these plans. By making sure that its managers share common expectations about what it is trying to do, the firm takes an important step toward coordinating their plans and behavior.

ECONOMIES OF SCOPE   Even when a firm operates at too small a scale in any individual product market to enjoy significant economies of scale, it may still enjoy them in producing components that are used in each of several products. For example, a firm like General Electric may enjoy economies of scale in producing small electric motors, using those motors to make food processors, hair dryers, fans, vacuum cleaners, and various other products. A firm like Casio may enjoy economies of scale in the manufacture of liquid crystal displays (LCDs), using them to produce calculators, wristwatches, electronic address books, and other products.

In these sorts of circumstances, the firms are said to enjoy *economies of scope*; that is, they can produce their several products together at less cost than could a group of single-product firms. Unsurprisingly, economies of scope entail all the same needs for coordination that economies of scale do. The problems are often harder, however, because coordination in planning is required among the managers responsible for different products. As Casio grew, for example, a forecast of large sales in the market for calculators led to falling costs for LCDs, making it more profitable to enter the market for wristwatches that use LCDs.

CORE COMPETENCIES   When a firm introduces new products relatively frequently, one very important kind of scale economy that it may enjoy is at the level of product development. That is, a firm may acquire generalized expertise in the important skills that are required to design and market new products in a set of related markets or in using a set of related technologies. For example, a computer maker may develop expertise in microprocessor design, display technologies, memory chips, operating systems, computer manufacturing, data communications, networking, and so on—skills that it expects to be able to apply over and over again as it continues to introduce new products. Scale economies at this level are so important in modern management theory that a new name has been coined for them: **core competencies of the firm**. In a dynamic environment, a firm's capacity to introduce new products and to manufacture them efficiently can be even more important than are the economies of scale it achieves in making its existing product line. In that setting, a strategy of developing scale economies translates into one of building the core competencies of a firm.

In an abstract sense, core competencies are just another kind of shared component, but there is an important practical difference in that the cost of building the competency is shared with a series of products that does not yet exist. Investments in new manufacturing technologies today may actually raise the costs of today's products if the old manufacturing system is well understood and well implemented. The gains to be enjoyed on account of the new system will come over a longer period, as the firm learns to use the new system, refines its methods, and adjusts the rest of its operations to take full advantage of the capabilities of the new technology. In such a case, managers need to plan for the demands of generations of products not yet even imagined. They also need to keep the price of the current products low enough to sustain a strong volume of sales, even if the company appears to be losing money on each sale, recognizing that these losses are actually an investment in the capabilities needed to produce profitable products in the future. This is just another illustration that when there are economies of scale, individual production and pricing decisions cannot be evaluated in isolation.

More controversially, the same ideas may be applied at the level of national industrial planning—a process about which many economists are skeptical but which has been used successfully in Japan and South Korea. The key first step in successful planning is to identify (groups of) industries to promote, which "fit" together with each other and with the country's existing competencies and advantages. For example, in Japan, the push to develop high-definition television (HDTV) in the 1990s is firmly grounded in that nation's strong positions in semiconductors, consumer electronics, and display technologies. To coordinate Japan's drive into HDTV, the Japanese national broadcasting company, NHK, has announced a set of technological standards that serves both to focus cooperative development efforts within groups of Japanese firms and to intensify competition among groups.

Complementarities and Design Decisions

Complementarities among a set of activities are an important source of design attributes. The standard definition of complementarity in economics is market oriented. Two inputs to a production process are said to be *complements* if a decrease in the price of one causes an increase in the demand for the other. In order to be able to employ the concept of complementarity usefully to study choices of levels of various internal activities as well as levels of input purchases, we introduce an alternative, more inclusive, definition: Several activities are mutually **complementary** if doing more of any one activity increases (or at least does not decrease) the marginal profitability of each other activity in the group.[8]

For example, where there are declining marginal costs due to learning or other kinds of economies of scale in producing a component, then the activities of producing various products using those components are complements. If General Electric's marginal cost of producing small electric motors declines with increasing volume, then the activities of producing electric fans and food processors are complementary because producing more fans makes it cheaper and therefore more profitable to produce more food processors as well.

Complementarities lead to predictable relationships among activities. A decision to increase the level of one activity will raise the profitability of any contemplated increases in levels of any complementary activities. Thus, high levels for all the elements of a group of complementary activities go together. This predictability is one

---

[8] In mathematical terms, the complementarity relationship among a group of activities can be characterized as follows. Let $x = (x_1, \ldots, x_n)$ be the levels at which the activities are conducted and let $\pi(x)$ be the resulting profits. If π is a smooth function, then the activities are mutual complements if for all $i \neq j$, $\partial^2\pi/\partial x_i \partial x_j \geq 0$; an increase in the jth activity raises the marginal return to the ith activity.

When a change occurs that makes any one of the complementary activities more profitable or less costly and encourages the firm to do more of that activity, then the marginal returns to the other activities are also increased, leading to more of those activities as well. The increased levels of the complementary activities further increase the marginal returns to the first activity, possibly leading to another round of increases in it and all the related activities.

of the two defining features of design attributes. The second feature is the high cost of failure to match or fit the parts together. This feature is a separate aspect of the problem that is not logically implied by the conditions of complementarity alone. However, we say that a group of activities is *strongly complementary* when raising the levels of a subset of activities in the group greatly increases the returns to raising the levels of the other activities. When a group of activities is strongly complementary, design attributes are always present.

The box entitled "Modern Manufacturing Strategy" describes one particular business strategy that illustrates the complementarities between particular aspects of product strategy, manufacturing policy, equipment choice, personnel and compensation policies, supplier relations, accounting methods, and more. What is most important to notice about the strategy is the coherence of its parts. The parts of the strategy that are connected are mutually supporting because they call for complementary activities. Part of the success of the modern manufacturing strategy in the 1980s and 1990s grows out of the way it takes advantage of the new technologies of the time, such as rapid, low-cost communications, highly flexible equipment, and computer-aided design, which make many of the elements of the strategy more effective and less costly.

Other manufacturing companies in other times have succeeded using other strategies, also well fitted to the available technology. In the first part of the twentieth century, for example, Ford Motor Company adopted an entirely different but equally coherent strategy that was appropriate for its time, based on producing a single product (the Model T Ford) in high-volume factories using specialized equipment and rigidly disciplined labor paid according to the job being done. This strategy reduced costs and increased the quality of the automobile so much that Ford was eventually able to capture more than 50 percent of the automobile market.

The continuing changes in technology and factory prices in the modern era, including the falling costs and growing reliability of highly automated equipment that works with no direct labor involvement, are likely to lead to further revisions in manufacturing firms' strategies.

Modern Manufacturing Strategy

One kind of strategy that has taken on a new importance in the late 1980s and 1990s is the "modern manufacturing" strategy, which is actually a whole group of similar strategies. The particular variant we describe involves producing a wide range of related products for customers with specialized needs. The firm strives to remain the quality leader in its markets with frequent new product introductions and frequent improvements of existing products.

Market behavior of this kind has implications for a wide range of activities in the organization. At the level of manufacturing, the small quantities demanded of each product prevent the company from setting up specialized production lines for each, forcing it to maintain a high level of flexibility. Because the demand for each product is small and because there are important economies of scale in inventory systems, the company will find it profitable to organize in a way that avoids holding inventories of finished products. It will eschew keeping local product warehouses and instead may even ship directly from the factory to the customers, perhaps using air freight if speed is important. In order to serve customers quickly, communications between the sales staff and the factory need to be closer than for a company that relies on finished goods inventories. Strong communications are always a key variable when products are to be completed "just in time" to meet customer demands. Since the average inventory level for a product is directly proportional to the production run, the company will want to use more frequent, smaller production runs to make its products. The use of frequent, small production runs forces the company to reset its production line more frequently to change the product being made. This makes it more profitable to use flexible production equipment, which can be quickly and easily changed over from task to task.

Frequently introducing new products adds another dimension to the strategy. Obviously, it increases the need for product designers and design engineers. It also means that equipment originally purchased to make one product will surely need to be switched to producing other products, further increasing the importance of flexibility. And it increases the importance of communications between the design team and the manufacturing department, since the product must be designed to be manufacturable with existing equipment.

The modern manufacturing strategy also affects personnel and compensation policies, supplier relations, and accounting systems in predictable ways. Short production runs mean that factory workers will frequently be changing tasks, moving from making one product to another. This tendency is compounded by the frequency of product redesigns and new product introductions. Flexible manufacturing thus requires multiskilled people who can do more than one task, and companies that adopt this strategy will often compensate workers on the basis of the skills they acquire, rather than on the basis of the particular job that they are presently assigned to do. In a system that is based on just-in-time manufacturing and low levels of buffer inventories, the rate of work at each step of the process must be in constant balance; if the molding equipment runs faster than final assembly even temporarily, inventories will accumulate. Consequently, systems tend to avoid piece-rate compensation, which would encourage workers to work at their own varying paces.

Frequent product redesign makes it important that the firm has accurate information about the cost of producing various alternative designs, both in order to make well-informed design choices and to price the product correctly. Since several products are being made on the same machine, the correct allocation of machine costs becomes an important focus of the accounting system. The variable that limits the use of machines is generally time, and so the increasing tendency among firms that use the modern manufacturing strategy is to assign machine costs to the individual products on the basis of the machine time that the product requires.

To the extent that the firm's strategy allows it to use general-purpose manufacturing equipment, it has a greater ability to rely on subcontractors to make its product in times of high demand and to invest in equipment that it cannot keep busy. Another alternative for the firm is to sell its excess capacity to other firms, that is, to become a subcontractor itself.

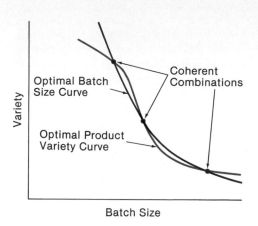

Figure 4.3: There may be several coherent combinations of batch size and product variety, but only one will generally be optimal.

Complementarities, Innovation Attributes, and Coordination Failure

When complementarities are present, the various aspects of a firm's strategy must be aligned properly for the firm's strategy to be optimal. Alignment alone is not enough for optimality, however. The parts of the strategy that Henry Ford adopted in introducing the Model T fit together well, and for a period of time the strategy worked effectively. However, as described in Chapter 1, Ford's strategy was overtaken by Alfred Sloan's strategy at General Motors, which was overtaken in turn by a variant of the modern manufacturing strategy introduced by Eiji Toyoda and Taiichi Ohno at Toyota.

Even in the absence of explicit strategic planning, the various managers in a firm may be able to adapt their choices to each other's, learning how best to pursue the firm's objectives in their own narrow domains. Figure 4.3 illustrates the possibilities for, and a potential problem with, an adaptation of this kind.

The figure portrays the decisions of two managers—a manufacturing manager and a marketing manager—in the same firm. The marketing manager chooses the number of product varieties to offer to customers, and the manager of manufacturing decides how large the batch sizes should be, that is, how many of one item to make before switching production over to another item in the product line. Suppose that each seeks to make the decision that maximizes aggregate firm profits.

Offering more products allows the firm to tailor its offerings more closely to customer needs. Then it can choose to receive a higher price for its products or to increase the number of units it sells. This benefit of increased variety must be weighed against certain costs. Holding the batch size fixed, increasing the number of varieties, raises the level of inventories proportionately. The larger the batch size, the costlier are increases in product variety and the smaller is the optimal number of products. This relationship is depicted by the optimal variety choice curve in Figure 4.3.

Similarly, given the number of different products being produced, there is an optimal batch size. Lower batch sizes increase the frequency with which the firm must incur the set-up costs involved in switching production from one product to another, but they also reduce average inventories and their costs. When the number of varieties is increased (holding total unit sales constant), the marginal inventory cost of increasing batch size rises. For this reason, increases in product variety lead to smaller optimal batch sizes. This relationship is depicted by the optimal batch size curve in the figure.

DECENTRALIZED DECISIONS AND COORDINATION FAILURE   Suppose that each manager sets the variable he or she individually controls to maximize the firm's profits, given what the other manager is expected to do. Then the marketing manager's choice will lie along the optimal variety choice curve in the figure at the point determined by the batch size this manager expects the other to select. Similarly, the production manager will select the point on the optimal batch size curve corresponding to the product variety he or she anticipates. Points where the two curves cross are ones where each manager's choice is the right one to maximize firm profits, given the other manager's choice.

As the figure shows, when the optimal variety choice is a decreasing function of the batch size and the optimal batch size is a decreasing function of the number of varieties, there can be several different combinations of product variety and batch size at which each manager's choice maximizes the firm's overall profits, given what the other is doing. Each of these combinations represents a coherent strategy. The lower right-hand intersection point can be likened to Henry Ford's strategy with the Model T—low variety and large production runs. The upper left-hand point can be likened to a "niche market" version of the modern manufacturing strategy—many varieties produced in small batches. Of course, the actual strategies involve many more choices than are illustrated in the figure, making the choice problem much more difficult.

Still, it is possible that the managers would find a coherent combination on their own, even without any explicit attempt to coordinate their decisions. For example, each might observe what the other is currently doing and adjust optimally to this choice. Such a decentralized process might converge without any communication between the managers (although it is not guaranteed to do so). In any case, it is sure to take time to reach coherence in such an uncoordinated fashion, during which the firm is operating inefficiently. Having the two managers meet and share their information would, on the other hand, seem very likely to achieve coordination on one of the coherent patterns.

There is, however, no reason to suppose that the particular coherent combination the managers arrive at will be the best one. In general, only one combination is actually profit maximizing, although this diagram does not contain enough information to determine which it is.[9] Ford's strategy was best for the auto industry in the early part of the century, while many industries now find that the modern manufacturing strategy of a broad product line combined with small batch sizes is optimal. Could the operating managers, using only the information they might normally be expected to have gained from their own experience, somehow settle on the best one? The answer is quite likely "No." Even if the managers pooled their information and attempted to make a coordinated decision, they may still not have enough information to determine which of the coherent strategy combinations is best.

INNOVATION ATTRIBUTES AND STRATEGIC COORDINATION   The key difficulty is that as the environment with its demand conditions and the costs and productivity of different technologies changes, the two curves may change more or less smoothly, and, with them, the precise description of each of the coherent strategies. Yet a small change in the curves may hide the fact that the relative profitability of the different coherent patterns has changed and so the actual profit-maximizing strategy has shifted radically.

---

[9] Determining which is best requires looking at a third factor, the total profits accruing to any pair of choices. The two curves represent "ridge lines," traces of the highest points on the profit surface in the relevant east-west or north-south direction. Depicting the height (the total profits) along the ridge lines graphically requires a third dimension. If this third dimension were shown, it would reveal that the profit surface here is like a mountain with three peaks, one at each of the intersections of the curves. Any of these might be the highest, so that the intersection point under it is the strategy pattern that actually maximizes profits.

For example, gradual changes over the years in production technologies and customer needs have not radically altered the general form of the coherent pattern corresponding to mass production. Yet in many industries these cumulative changes have made the modern manufacturing strategy much more profitable than the mass production strategy. This means that profit maximization would require a radical shift in strategy.

The operating managers may be able to use their familiarity with demand and cost characteristics to keep up with local movements in the coherent patterns, marginally adjusting their decisions to track the changes in what is best. But recognizing that a radical strategic shift is desirable is likely to require information that neither manager has, and the local adjustments they are likely to make are never going to track the global shifts in which strategic configuration is best. A shift to much smaller variety and larger batch sizes might enable the firm to use highly specialized equipment that is better tailored to the particular products being made, leading to much lower costs. Estimating the benefits of such a change would require knowledge about technologies and equipment that may be completely unfamiliar. Similarly, a shift to a much wider product line and smaller batch sizes may require much more flexible equipment and completely revised relations with suppliers, which might again be well beyond the range of the production manager's experience. Also, the marketing manager may not know how much customers would be willing to pay for more highly tailored products, or by how much sales would fall if a narrower but cheaper product line were offered.

As in this example, the overall strategic choice in the presence of complementarities is frequently a design decision with innovation attributes. The pieces of the strategy have to fit together, and the information needed to identify and choose between alternative patterns is unlikely to be available freely within the organization. In these circumstances, information must be acquired from outside the organization and assessed, a coordinated decision must be made on the design variables, and then this decision must be communicated to the affected parties. All this presents a role for central coordination and, in particular, for top management. We discuss this in the next section.

We emphasize again that the example we have been discussing involves only two choice variables, and yet complementarities still lead to potential failures of coordination. In general, the problem of selecting among multiple coherent policies becomes more difficult as the number of variables to be adapted increases and as the strength of the complementarity relations between pairs of decisions grows. Understanding the complementarities in the system makes it easier to identify potentially profitable changes of strategy and to anticipate the scope of the changes needed to implement a new strategy.

MANAGEMENT, DECENTRALIZATION, AND THE MEANS OF COORDINATION

We have seen a variety of situations in this chapter in which the price system, the quintessential decentralized coordination mechanism, is less than ideal because it is too brittle and so does not deal well with imperfect information or because it requires too much communication. When the price system fails, the search for efficiency means that other mechanisms must be adopted. Sometimes these supplement the market's operations, but often they involve the creation of formal organizations that largely supplant the market over a range of activities.

The coordination problem is not solved by merely putting a nonmarket form of organization in place, however. Instead, it is transformed into a problem of management. The ideas in this chapter are useful for thinking about the tasks of management and, in particular, the role of senior management and its staff in hierarchies. But first we need to set our terminology more precisely.

Centralization and Decentralization

We have used the terms centralized and decentralized frequently throughout this chapter, and although we have used them in a consistent way, we have not been explicit about exactly what we mean by them. We now need to be more precise.

Think about a situation in which there is a set of individuals who have various decisions to make and actions to perform. The individuals here could actually be groups if each group can usefully be thought of as performing actions and having information. A particular decision is then **decentralized** if it is left to the individuals alone to make. In contrast, a **centralized** decision is one that is made at a higher level and communicated to or imposed on the individuals. This higher level might be thought of as an individual who has the power to make the decision, as in a managerial hierarchy or under state planning. Alternatively, it could be the whole of the set of individuals meeting and acting collectively, as in a meeting or through a referendum. The centralization of a decision is a matter of degrees, depending on the level of the hierarchy involved or the number of different managers who must approve the decision.

The price system can be thought of as being fully decentralized in this sense. Individuals decide on their own how much to offer for sale and how much to try to purchase. Even the prices are determined in a largely decentralized fashion by individual decision makers. At the opposite extreme is the traditional assembly line, which, in principle, operates in a completely centralized fashion. Individuals on the line have little or no discretion about what they do and when and how they do it.

In complex organizational decisions, however, neither decentralization of all aspects of the decisions nor complete centralization is likely to be optimal. Crucial information always resides with individuals, so centralizing all aspects of a decision requires that this local information be communicated upward to the central decision makers, or else ignored. Both are costly. But leaving all decisions to the individuals who actually take the actions risks these decisions being uncoordinated. The problem is then to determine just what aspects of the overall decision ought to be left to the various individuals, what information should be communicated to assist individual decision makers, which parts of the decision should be centralized, who should make the centralized decision, and what information sources they should use. In a system with both centralized and decentralized decisions, the centralized decisions serve to define the parameters of the decentralized ones and to put constraints on the local decision makers.

The Role of Management in Coordination

The key role of management in organizations is to ensure coordination. The survival and success of the organization is crucially dependent on achieving effective coordination of the actions of the many individuals and subgroups in the organization, on making sure that they all are focusing their efforts on carrying out a feasible plan of action that will promote the organization's goals, and on assuring that the plan is adjusted appropriately to remain feasible and appropriate as circumstances change. Ensuring that the members of the organization are properly motivated is very important as well, and, as we see in later chapters, motivation problems can influence the effectiveness of coordination mechanisms. But incentives become an issue only once there is a feasible plan to be carried out and a pattern of behavior that needs to be followed.

The first step in achieving coordination is the organizational design decision discussed earlier. This involves determining which decisions are to be centralized and which are to be left to individuals and operating units, who should make the centralized decisions, and what information will be transmitted upwards to support the centralized decision making and back down to guide those who will implement the plan. The concepts developed in this chapter are useful here.

First, design variables need to be determined in a centralized fashion by a senior manager, perhaps supported by staff, or by meetings among local managers. The benefits of this centralization tend to be greatest when there are many divisions or departments that need to be coordinated. Timing and scale are examples of design variables about which explicit agreement must be reached. In the modern manufacturing strategy discussed previously, the breadth of product lines, the flexibility of equipment, and the frequency of design changes are design variables that affect the planning of several different departments and groups within the firm such as the marketing department, the manufacturing department, the engineering department, the accounting department, and the product design group. Decisions about designs need to be set and then communicated to those whose plans are affected.

While design decisions are best managed in a centralized way, most of the details of any plan are not design decisions. Efficient organization takes advantage of the knowledge of local managers and workers by allowing them considerable autonomy in implementing their parts of the plan. The modern manufacturing strategy calls for flexible equipment, but it does not specify what equipment the manufacturing department should use, how workers should be trained, what hours to work, and so on. Having management send the right messages focuses the search of individual decision makers within the firm and adds coherency to the individual efforts, adding enormously to the productive ability of the organization. Of course, the organizational design problem is itself a design problem, and must be solved in a centralized fashion.

Second, in deciding what and how to communicate, the costs of information transfer and the brittleness of the corresponding planning system become important. We have seen that sometimes prices are the efficient means to guide decisions, but that in other cases design variables and quantities should be used to guide local decisions. Again, the decision about how to communicate is a design problem that should be centralized.

Third, when complementarities lead to multiple possible coherent patterns of local decisions, then efficient choice among these requires that the decision be centralized. This need becomes even more acute when the choice involves innovation attributes, with the information necessary to identify the different coherent patterns and to evaluate their profitability not being available in the organization. In these circumstances, someone must track the external environment, collect and evaluate the information relevant to the strategic choice, and communicate the new strategic pattern to the operating levels if a change is called for. Making sure that this task is done is an assignment problem, which itself must be solved centrally. Then the determination and communication of the new strategic design again call for centralization.

SENIOR MANAGEMENT'S ROLE   Senior management and its staff usually take on these roles of determining and communicating strategy in firms. Yet, again, much of this can and should be decentralized to take advantage of local knowledge. For example, senior management need not work out all the details of how to implement a modern manufacturing strategy. Instead, having determined to make the switch, it might simply announce to the operating managers and workers that the company is going to accentuate quick turnaround, low inventories, flexibility, and meeting customers' needs in product design and that it is to achieve this reorientation by a certain date. Ideally, each division or department manager could then base his or her own plans on the assumption that the other departments would be ready as planned, determining the myriad details for implementing the plan either individually or working in groups with other managers.

These same ideas have been expressed in many ways by senior managers at various firms, but the following comment by Hewlett-Packard co-founder David Packard seems to capture the main points particularly well:

> Early in the history of the company, while thinking about how a company like this should be managed, I kept getting back to one concept: If we could simply get everybody to agree on what our objectives were and to understand what we were trying to do, then we could turn everybody loose and they would move along in a common direction.[10]

Planning at Hewlett-Packard meant sharing information until an agreement was reached about "what our objectives were" and "what we were trying to do." Once an agreement about that was reached and communicated so that everybody understood, a key part of senior management's job was largely done. It was time to "turn everybody loose" to use their local information and individual capabilities to implement the plan. The plan would serve to lend coherence to the efforts, so that everyone "would move along in a common direction."

---

[10] David Packard, quoted in M. Beer and B. Spector, *Human Resources at Hewlett-Packard*, Harvard Business School Case #9-482-125, 1982.

Summary

Much of the growth of productivity in the modern world has come from specialization. People acquire specific training to do specialized jobs using equipment and tools that are particularly well suited to the task. With the growth of specialization comes a need for coordination so that sufficient amounts of the desired products are produced by the right methods, using the best resources.

The price system is one of the main methods used in a market economy to coordinate specialized activity. According to the fundamental theorem of welfare economics, *if* market-clearing prices can be found and certain other conditions are satisfied, the market allocation is guaranteed to be efficient. The price system is not the only system with these properties, however, which raises the question: What systems of coordination are most effective and under what circumstances? To evaluate effectiveness, we introduced three criteria: (1) Can the system identify an optimal or efficient decision in the problem if perfect information is available to the coordinator? (2) How much communication does it require to identify an optimal decision? (3) If the information used is imperfect, how badly does the system performance deteriorate? That is, how *brittle* is the system?

In assessing the market system, we found that when there are economies of scale in production, market-clearing prices generally fail to exist, so the fundamental theorem of welfare economics does not apply. Generally, in these settings, a simple price system cannot guide an optimal resource allocation, even though other systems may be able to do so.

Second, the brittleness of the price system varies with circumstances. When there are only slightly declining returns to scale (compared to the rate of decrease in marginal benefits from additional production), the price system tends to be quite brittle. That is, small errors in estimating costs can lead to large inefficiencies in actual production decisions compared to those suffered by a system in which a central planner sets quantity targets. When the relationships of scale are reversed, the price system tends to perform better than a system of centrally established production targets.

In general resource allocation problems, in which nothing is known a priori about the optimal allocation, no system can identify an optimal resource allocation using less information than a system of prices uses, where communication is measured using the Hurwicz criterion. Consequently, in these general environments, if a system of prices works, then it economizes on costly communications.

Coordination problems in which there is a priori information about how the parts of the decision must fit together and in which small failures of fit are very costly are said to have *design attributes*. Centralized setting of design variables tends to reduce both the cost of errors and the amount of communication and search necessary to identify an optimal decision.

The scale of a firm's operations is a design variable. It serves to coordinate decisions about the scale of various component operations, the degree of specialization of equipment and people, the location of facilities, and so on. Forecasts of a firm's planned growth are therefore an important part of coordination in a business organization.

Economies of scale that are achieved in the manufacture of components of several products increase the need for coordination because the optimal scale of each product is an increasing function of the anticipated scale of the other products that use the same components. In this case, it is said that the products are *complements in production* and that there are *economies of scope*. When the shared input to making different products are design and manufacturing capabilities of the firm, then these shared inputs are *core competencies*. The manager of any particular product, who focuses narrowly on the costs and benefits in developing just that product, may neglect the product's important contribution to building the firm's core competencies. Apparently unprofitable investments or product decisions may actually be profitable if they preserve and extend a firm's competencies, enabling it to introduce more profitable products in the future.

Complementary activities are ones for which increases in the level of some of the activities raise the marginal profitability of the others. When complementary activities are undertaken, they must all be done together to achieve maximum effect. *Strongly complementary activities* are a common source of design attributes. In our boxed application, we identified the wide range of complementary activities that together constitute a modern manufacturing strategy.

Complementarities commonly give rise to a variety of coherent strategies. Individual managers all acting with the firm's interests in mind may get stuck with a coherent strategy that is not the best one for the firm. It takes conscious effort and centralized decision making in these cases to determine and focus attention on the proper strategy.

When the price system is supplanted by a formal organization, solving the coordination problem becomes a key task of management. The first step is to solve the organizational design problem of determining which decisions are to be centralized and which ones are to be left to individual decision makers, who is going to make the centralized decisions and what information is to be communicated upwards or obtained from outside the organization to support these decisions. Also to be determined are how the centralized choices that delimit and guide the decentralized decisions are to be communicated to the individual decision makers. This situation is itself a design problem that must be solved in a centralized fashion. Usually, solving this problem in firms is the task of senior management, as is the solution of the design problem of setting and communicating strategy.

■ BIBLIOGRAPHIC NOTES

The comparison of alternative systems of economic control was an important subject in economics following the Russian Revolution, when there was a debate about the ability of socialist economies to be as productive as capitalist ones. Among Friedrich Hayek's important contributions to the debate were his emphasis on the difficulty of communicating to a central planner all the information he or she would need to develop and implement an effective plan, compared to the much more meager information needed to run a price system. Leonid Hurwicz formalized and developed this idea, culminating in the theorem cited in the text. These analyses were generally optimistic about the potential of prices for coordination.

The first formal studies of the brittleness of alternative systems of economic control were made by Martin Weitzman, some of whose work is reported here in a simplified form. Patrick Bolton and Joseph Farrell have recently compared the costs of centralized and decentralized control systems, emphasizing the relative quickness of centralized responses to crises and the ability of centralized systems to avoid duplication of efforts. The treatment of design and innovation attributes is our own contribution, new in this book, and the treatment of modern manufacturing as a designed system is drawn from our *American Economic Review* article.

The importance of complementarities among different individual's decisions was accentuated by Jeremy Bulow, John Geanakoplos, and Paul Klemperer and Drew Fudenberg and Jean Tirole in the context of industrial competition. Our *Econometrica* paper shows how to analyze situations marked by complementarities, but it is technically very difficult. Coordination failures induced by strong complementarities have been an important theme in the recent literature on Keynesian macroeconomics (surveyed by Russell Cooper and Andrew John), but this theme has not before been systematically applied to problems in the theory of organization.

◾ REFERENCES

Bolton, P., and J. Farrell. "Decentralization, Duplication and Delay," *Journal of Political Economy*, 98 (August 1990), 803–26.

Bulow, J., J. Geanakoplos and P. Klemperer. "Multimarket Oligopoly: Strategic Substitutes and Complements," *Journal of Political Economy* 93 (1985), 488–511.

Cooper, R., and A. John. "Coordinating Coordination Failures in Keynesian Models," *Quarterly Journal of Economics*, 103 (August 1988), 441–64.

Fudenberg, D., and J. Tirole. *Dynamic Models of Oligopoly* (Chur, Switzerland: Harwood Academic Publishers, 1986).

Hayek, F.A. "The Use of Knowledge in Society," *American Economic Review*, 35, (1945), 519–30.

Hurwicz, L. "The Design of Mechanisms for Resource Allocation," *American Economic Review* 63 (May 1973), 1–30.

Milgrom, P., and J. Roberts. "Rationalizability, Learning, and Equilibrium in Games with Strategic Complementarities," *Econometrica*, 58 (1990), 1255–77.

Milgrom, P., and J. Roberts. "The Economics of Modern Manufacturing: Technology, Strategy, and Organization," *American Economic Review*, 80 (June 1990), 511–28.

Weitzman, M., "Prices vs. Quantities," *Review of Economic Studies*, 41, (October 1974), 477–91.

EXERCISES

Food for Thought

1. During World Wars I and II, even the major market economies switched to centralized forms of planning to allocate many scarce resources. Are there reasons based on efficiency to prefer such centralized planning in wartime? Are there other reasons?

2. For many years, Swiss craftsmen made the finest watches, which were powered by winding a spring by hand. The Swiss lost ground to competitors in Japan and elsewhere as more accurate, less expensive battery-powered electronic watches were perfected. What were the core competencies of watchmaking in the era of Swiss dominance and how were they changed by new technologies? What other products are made by the new watchmakers?

3. In 1987, Sony Corporation, a leader in consumer electronics (televisions, compact disk and audio cassette players, home video recording and playback machines), purchased the CBS Record Company. In 1989, Sony purchased Columbia Pictures Entertainment, one of the giants of the movie and TV production industry. In 1990, Matsushita, the world leader in consumer electronics with its Panasonic, National, and Quasar brands, purchased MCA Corporation, which makes movies, television shows, and music recordings. Why would these companies want to expand into these particular industries?

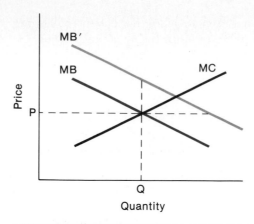

Figure 4.4: An error scenario in which the planner is mistaken about marginal benefits.

Mathematical Exercises

1.   Consider the problem of supplying an input to a division of a firm or to a firm in a planned economy. Suppose the executive or planner knows the marginal cost function for the input. This is represented by the fixed supply curve in Figure 4.4. However, the planner is uncertain of the benefit. Her best estimate of the marginal benefit curve is represented by the curve MB in the figure, and on that basis the price should be P and the quantity supplied Q. Consider an error scenario in which the actual marginal benefit is higher, as indicated by the curve MB'. Mark on the graph the quantity that would be produced using a price control in the error scenario and draw a vertical line at that quantity level. Identify the triangles with areas that correspond to (1) the loss suffered under the error scenario when Q is announced under a quantity planning system and (2) the loss suffered under the error scenario when the price P is announced and the division chooses its quantity to maximize profits. Show that the ratio of these losses with an uncertain benefit curve is just the same as the ratio with an uncertain cost curve as derived in Equation 4.1.

2.   A new product is being introduced in competition with another firm. Having the product ready for production in t months will result in net profits after the introduction of $144 - t^2$ if $0 \leq t < 12$ but will generate no profits at all if $t \geq 12$. Three departments must be ready before production can begin, and getting ready quickly is a costly matter. Department 1 can be ready in t months for a cost of $3(12 - t)$, department 2 for a cost of $4(12 - t)$, and department 3 for $5(12 - t)$. Until all three departments are ready, production cannot begin. (1) What is the optimal date t^* at which to introduce the new product, that is, the time that maximizes the net profit after product introduction minus the cost of readying the three departments? (2) What will the firm's profit be if the project is mistakenly hurried and all three departments are asked to deliver one month earlier than the optimal date? One month later? (3) What will the firm's profit be if department 1 and department 3 both are asked to be ready at the optimal time, but department 2 is asked to be ready one month earlier than the others? One month later? (4) Is the timing of product introduction in this example a *design decision*?

3.   A small community must decide how much land to set aside and improve for public parks, to be used for playgrounds, ball fields, and so on. Suppose there are one hundred families in the community and that there are no wealth effects on the families' preferences. That is, family n's utility for x_n dollars of personal savings and y acres of park land is at $x_n + v_n(y)$. If a plan to set aside and improve y acres of land at cost $c \cdot y$ is proposed with family n paying t_n in taxes to finance the project, what conditions must be checked to test the efficiency of the plan? What is the minimal amount of communication required to check whether the proposal is efficient?

MATHEMATICAL APPENDIX:
A FORMAL MODEL OF DESIGN DECISIONS

In this appendix we study a mathematical model of the problem of introducing a new product, for example, a new model car. Our principle purpose is to show that this problem indeed has the characteristics of a design decision and to establish that the informationally efficient way to handle such a problem is to announce the design attributes (rather than prices).

There are N system components that go into making the product, each of which is produced in a single, separate facility or department. In the case of a car, these would include systems like headlamps, engines, brakes, and so on, each of which is itself a complex product with many parts and many steps involved in its manufacture. We establish units so that exactly one unit of each component goes into making the final product. For example, a car requires two headlamps, so we regard a pair of headlamps as being one single unit in our formulas.

Suppose the corporation makes available a set of corporate resources for the project, and that there are k different kinds of corporate resources. There are $\bar{x}_1$ units of the first type of resource, $\bar{x}_2$ of the second, . . ., and $\bar{x}_k$ of the last. The vector $\bar{x}$ = $(\bar{x}_1, \ldots, \bar{x}_k)$ describes the corporate resources available for the project.

The allocation of these resources among the N units is denoted by the list $(x^1, \ldots, x^N)$, where $x^n = (x_1^n, \ldots, x_k^n)$ denotes the vector of resources allocated to plan and produce the nth component. Of course, the total amount of each resource allocated to the various departments cannot exceed the amount available. The factory that makes component n is ready to begin production at date t^n and with capacity y^n. In addition to the corporate resources, the factory may hire outside workers, suppliers, and contractors to do parts of the job. The total amount of outside expenditures required to design and prepare to make system n by date t^n at capacity y^n using corporate resources x^n is $C_n(x^n, y^n, t^n, z^n)$. This function C_n is a *cost function* and z^n is a parameter of the cost function that is known only by the local manager. (This means that only the local manager knows how costly it is to meet the capacity and timing objectives with a given allocation of centrally allocated resources.) We assume that it costs more to get ready earlier and to build additional capacity; that is, C_n is decreasing in t^n and increasing in y^n.

Because manufacturing a unit of the product requires one of each of the system components, the rate of sales cannot exceed the minimum of the production capacities, and sales cannot begin until the last of the system components is ready for production. Let us therefore write the revenues as:

$$\text{Gross Revenue} = R[Min(y^1, \ldots, y^N), Max(t^1, \ldots, t^N)] \qquad (4.3)$$

Revenues depend on two numbers: the amount that is produced and the date at which it is available. The first of these is equal to the minimum of the outputs of the various components and the second is the date at which the last component is ready. Naturally, R is increasing in the total available capacity and decreasing in the time to introduction of the product.

An organization seeking to maximize profits (gross revenues less the total costs incurred in all units) would want to select the allocation of the corporate resources (x), the unit capacities (y) and the readiness dates (t) to solve:

$$\text{Maximize } R[Min(y^1, \ldots, y^N), Max(t^1, \ldots, t^N)] - \sum_{n=1}^{N} C_n(x^n, y^n, t^n, z^n) \quad (4.4)$$

subject to $\sum_{n=1}^{N} x^n \leq \bar{x}$

where the inequality constraint reflects the limited availability of corporate resources.

Let us suppose that the profit expression in Equation 4.4 is concave and that the optimum involves positive amounts of each resource being used by each unit. Then, a plan (x, y, t) is optimal if and only if there exists a vector of prices p^*—one price for each resource—and numbers t^* and y^* such that the equality constraints

$$\left.\begin{array}{rcl} y^n & = & y^* \\ t^n & = & t^* \\ \partial C_n/\partial x^n & = & p^* \end{array}\right\} \qquad \text{for all } n. \tag{4.5}$$

and adding-up conditions

$$\begin{array}{c} \sum_{n=1}^{N} x^n = \bar{x} \\ \sum_{n=1}^{N} \partial C_n/\partial y^n = \partial R/\partial y \\ \sum_{n=1}^{N} \partial C_n/\partial t^n = \partial R/\partial t \end{array} \tag{4.6}$$

are all satisfied. The equality constraints say that each unit's capacity and readiness date are the same, and that the impact on costs of changing the amount of any of the corporate resources allocated to a unit is the same as at any other unit. The first adding-up condition says that the corporate resources are fully utilized. The second says that the marginal cost of adding more capacity in each unit just balances the marginal revenue from the added capacity. Finally, the last says that the marginal costs of having the output from every unit available a little sooner just balance the additional revenue that results.

Prior Information and Efficient Planning

In this formulation, it is clear that the choice of the timing and capacity variables has one of the characteristics of a design decision. Even without knowing the actual cost and revenue functions, we know in advance that at an optimum all the times t^n will be equal and similarly all the capacities y^n will be identical. There is a priori information about how these variables fit, and one consequence of this is that Hurwicz's theorem does not apply. A price system is not guaranteed to be informationally efficient.

Nevertheless, Hurwicz's basic framework still applies. We can still proceed by identifying the minimum amount of communication necessary to verify the optimality of a proposed plan (x, t, y) and checking whether a proposed coordination system achieves that minimum. For this case, the relevant extension has been derived by Fumikata Sato, who has established that, in addition to communicating the $Nk + 2$ numbers that comprise the plan itself (x, t, y), any system that can verify the plan's efficiency must communicate at least $k + 2N$ additional numbers.[11] Here is a system that achieves that bound. The central coordinator announces prices, an introduction date, and a capacity ($k + 2$ numbers). Each production department n responds by reporting what resources it wishes to purchase (k numbers) and its marginal costs for additional capacity and earlier factory readiness (2 numbers). This information allows one to check Equations 4.5 and 4.6 and so to verify whether the plan is efficient. It requires the communication of $N(k + 2)$ numbers by the N departments plus $k + 2$ numbers by the coordinator, so this system verifies the efficiency of an allocation with a minimum of communication.

---

[11] Fumikata Sato, "On the Informational Size of Message Spaces for Resource Allocation Processes in Economies with Public Goods," *Journal of Economic Theory*, 24 (February 1981), 48–69.

By comparison, any attempt to guide capacity choices and factory readiness dates using a price system would fare quite badly. For example, suppose there were $T \geq 2$ possible delivery dates. Describing a full plan would involve the Nk numbers that give the allocation of the k different corporate resources to the N plants, plus a description of the ready capacity for each of the N plants for each of the T dates, the further NT numbers. Then there would need to be a price for each of the k resources, and a price for capacity for each of the plants at each possible date. In sum, an augmented plan under a price system would involve $Nk + NT + k + NT = k(N+1) + 2NT$ numbers. This exceeds the minimum required. Indeed, if the number of possible introduction dates T is large, the amount of additional communication is similarly large, being equal to $2NT - 2(N+1)$.

The High Relative Cost of Failures of Fit

The other major attribute that defines a design problem is that failures of fit are more costly than are failures to find the right design. To see how this condition arises in the present model, let us first consider the cost of an error in which the parts fit but the design is not optimal. Specifically, let t^* be the optimal introduction time and suppose that all the t_ns are set equal to some different but coordinated date $t^* + \epsilon$. To estimate the cost of a small error, we substitute this expression for each t_n in the objective function and then take the derivative with respect to ϵ. Using the third adding up condition in Equation 4.6, we find that this derivative is zero at $\epsilon = 0$. That is, the marginal cost of an error of this kind is zero. This kind of small design error is not at all costly. Intuitively, the reason is that the product introduction date is optimally set so that the marginal cost of seeking a slightly earlier introduction is just equal to the marginal benefit. A small change from t^* to t should have a zero effect on profits, to a first-order approximation. Similarly, setting all the y^ns equal to $y^* + \epsilon$, the derivative with respect to ϵ is zero. A small error in setting y leads to a cost that is zero to a first-order approximation.

By comparison, small *errors of fit* among the variables are much more costly. Suppose, for example, that all the variables but one, say y^n, are set to their optimal values. The cost of a small error in y^n depends on whether y^n is set too high or too low.[12] When y^n is set too low, the cost is approximately (to first order) equal to the size of the deviation times the left-hand derivative of profits with respect to y^n evaluated at the optimum. When y^n is set too high, the cost is the right-hand derivative times the size of the deviation. These derivatives are:

$$\text{Left-hand derivative} = \frac{\partial R}{\partial y} - \frac{\partial C_n}{\partial y^n} = \Sigma_{j \neq n} \frac{\partial C_j}{\partial y^j} \qquad (4.7)$$

$$\text{Right-hand derivative} = \frac{\partial C_n}{\partial y^n}$$

As long as capacity is costly, these derivatives are not zero. Errors of fit incur first-order costs.

The intuitive reason for this conclusion is straightforward. When y^n is set too large, the extra capacity is useless. The loss incurred from this error is the cost of that extra capacity, as confirmed by the expression for the right-hand derivative. When y^n is too small, the limited capacity forces a reduction in the level of output with a marginal value of $\partial R/\partial y$ but also saves costs of $\partial C_n/\partial y^n$. This difference appears as the first expression for the left-hand derivative in Equation 4.7. Using the third adding-up condition in Equation 4.6, this condition can be transformed into the second

---

[12] This is because the total profits are not a differentiable function of y^n at the optimum point.

expression for the left-hand derivative. According to the second expression, the loss is just the same as if a small amount of useless extra capacity were built by all the other departments, because the shortfall in capacity at department n renders the extra capacities of the other departments unproductive.

The most important message, however, is not the particular forms that these costs take. Rather, it is that decisions concerning timing and scale are, as we have claimed, decisions with design attributes. Explicit coordination of these decisions by either a central coordinator or by committee meetings, rather than decentralized decisions loosely coordinated by prices, is predictably the norm for decisions of these kinds.

Part
III

Motivation: contracts, information, and incentives

5
Bounded rationality and private information

6
Moral hazard and performance incentives

5

BOUNDED RATIONALITY
AND PRIVATE INFORMATION

A *ny attempt to deal seriously with the study of economic organization must come to terms with the* combined *ramifications of bounded rationality and opportunism in conjunction with a condition of asset specificity.*

Oliver Williamson[1]

The preceding two chapters dealt with the problem of coordination. This chapter and the next several (Chapters 5 through 9) are concerned with the other central problem of economic organization and management: *motivation*. Motivation questions arise because individuals have their own private interests, which are rarely perfectly aligned with the interests of other individuals, with the groups to which the individuals belong, or with society as a whole. The coordination problem is to determine what things should be done, how they should be accomplished, and who should do what. At the organizational level, the problem is also to determine who makes decisions and with what information, and how to arrange communications systems to ensure that the needed information is available. The motivation problem is to ensure that the various individuals involved in these processes willingly do their parts in the whole undertaking, both reporting information accurately to allow the right plan to be devised and acting as they are supposed to act to carry out the plan.

Our analysis throughout these chapters is based on the assumption that people will do only what they perceive to be in their own individual interests. As we have already admitted in Chapter 2, this is a caricature of actual human motivation and behavior. Yet it is a powerful analytic simplification. Given this assumption, the

---

[1] *The Economic Institutions of Capitalism* (New York: The Free Press, 1985), p. 42.

motivation problem becomes one of arranging affairs so that, as far as possible, selfish individual actions take proper account not only of how the decision maker is affected by a decision, but of how others are affected as well.

This unnatural state of affairs is achieved primarily by compacts among people, who recognize their mutual interests and agree to modify their behavior in ways that are mutually beneficial. These agreements may encompass the sort of actions each is to take, any payments that might flow from one to another, the rules and procedures they will use to decide matters in the future, and the behavior that each might expect from the others. Using the language that has become standard in economics, we refer to these agreements as *contracts*, regardless of whether they have the legal status of contracts. These agreements are voluntary, they will be accepted only if the parties find them individually and mutually advantageous, they can be crafted to suit individual needs and circumstances, and in actual relationships, they may perform the same functions that formal contracts do, and more. In fact, contracts may be completely unarticulated and implicit, with no power of law behind them whatsoever.

PERFECT, COMPLETE CONTRACTS

In principle, a perfectly fashioned **complete contract** could solve the motivation problem. It would specify precisely what each party is to do in every possible circumstance and arrange the distribution of realized costs and benefits in each contingency (including those where the contract's terms are violated) so that each party individually finds it optimal to abide by the contract's terms. If the original plan were an efficient one, then a complete contract could implement the plan leading to an efficient outcome. If we start our analysis from this idealized perspective, we find that *motivation problems arise only because some plans cannot be described in a complete, enforceable contract*.

The Requirements of Complete Contracting

What would be involved in reaching and enacting a complete contract? First, the parties must each foresee all the relevant contingencies that might be important to them in the course of the contract and to which they might want to adapt the contractually specified actions and payments. Moreover, they must be able to describe these contingencies accurately so that they can unambiguously determine before the fact just what possibilities are being discussed. They must also be able to know after the fact which of the particular circumstances they considered beforehand has now actually occurred. Second, they must be willing and able to determine and agree upon an efficient course of action for each possible contingency, as well as the payments that are to accompany the actions. Third, once they have entered the contract, they must be happy to abide by its terms. This has at least two elements. First, the parties must not mutually desire to renegotiate the contract later. Otherwise, the anticipation that they will renegotiate may deprive the original agreement of its credibility and may prevent it from guiding behavior as it should. Second, each party must be able to determine freely whether the contract's terms are being met, and, if they are being violated, each must be willing and able to enforce the agreed performance.

APPLYING TO COLLEGE: AN EXAMPLE   To clarify just how severe the demands of complete contracting are, consider what would be involved in your entering such a contract with a university to become a student seeking a degree there. First, both you and the university's representatives must be able to anticipate all the various circumstances that might be relevant to the relationship in the future, and together you must be able to describe them unambiguously. This includes what subjects you might want to study in any particular term (which might depend on your experiences in previous classes and a host of other factors) and what faculty might be available to teach courses. Other potentially relevant contingencies include the condition of the job market for graduates with different degrees and training when you finish; the costs to the university of serving meals in the student cafeteria; whether an earthquake might damage the campus buildings and, if so, which ones and how much; whether a war will break out and whether you will want or need to fight; whether a drought might dry up the campus lake on which you might have wanted to sail; and whether a new scientific discovery might render what you have learned irrelevant. The list could be infinite. Each of these potentially could affect what being a student is worth to you, what having you as a student is worth to the university, and what courses of action are efficient in your dealings with each other.

Next, you and the university must figure out and agree on what to do in each of these distinct circumstances and what cash should pass from you to the university (or vice versa) in each event. Should you continue with your planned major if the professor you hate is the only one available to teach a course that is required for this major? If so, what tuition should you be charged? Should you be expected to take the same courses and pay the same fees if you turn out to be a star football player as you would if you were to be a mediocre cellist in the university orchestra or a brilliant master of the electronic games in the student union? What if you become disabled? Or one of the university's faculty members wins the Nobel prize, making your degree more prestigious? Or if the university is found liable for overcharging the government on research contracts? Or if the school's fund-raising efforts are much more successful than anticipated and it is suddenly richer than anyone ever dreamed?

It is precisely this sort of complete contracting perspective that underlies the most expansive interpretations of the theory of competitive markets, as described in Chapter 3. The goods traded in *complete*, competitive markets include state-dependent commodities like "one seat in PoliSci 101 if Professor Jones is teaching it in the spring term of my sophomore year." The competitive theory requires even more: The exchanges in competitive markets occur at publicly quoted prices; they involve commodities with well-specified, generally observable attributes and qualities; the identity and personal characteristics of the buyer or seller are irrelevant; and it is costless to determine if the agreements are being kept and to force compliance if they are not.

The Problems of Actual Contracting

In actual transactions, enacting and enforcing a complete and perfect contract is fraught with problems. Limited foresight, imprecise language, the costs of calculating solutions, and the costs of writing down a plan—collectively, the **bounded rationality** of real people—mean that not all contingencies are fully accounted for. Your contract with the university does not provide explicitly for the kinds of contingencies we described earlier, and many other contracts are similarly incomplete. In complicated relationships, contingencies inevitably arise that have not been planned for and, when they do, the parties must find ways to adapt. These adaptations introduce the possibility of **opportunistic behavior**, including reneging. For example, a university may change its course requirements, or raise its tuition unduly, or cancel its plans to build more student housing, leaving the student with little option but to meet the new requirements, pay up, and spend another year living with his or her parents.

Fear of opportunism may deter parties from relying on one another as much as they should for efficiency. For example, a farm family may be reluctant to rely on union labor to harvest a crop, fearing that a strike threat during harvest season would leave it too vulnerable to demands for wage increases. They might plant a smaller crop to allow it to be harvested by friends and family, even though a larger crop harvested by organized labor might be more efficient. In general terms, incomplete and unenforceable contracts lead to problems of **imperfect commitment**. For example, if the farmer sees that the union is not actually committed to carry out the harvest on the originally contracted terms, it will be reluctant to deal with the union.

Even if a contingency can be foreseen and planned for and contractual commitments can be enforced, one of the bargainers may have relevant **private information** before the contract is signed that interferes with the possibility of reaching a value-maximizing agreement. In the used car market, for example, sellers have better information about their cars than do potential buyers, which makes the buyers skeptical about quality. Newspapers are filled with advertisements claiming that the current car owner is "moving and must sell"—claims that are designed to make it credible that it really is a good car being sold at this bargain price. Fear that such claims are not true and that the owner wants to sell the car because it is a lemon probably sours many a worthwhile deal. This source of inefficiency is called **adverse selection**, representing the idea that the selection of cars offered in the market is determined in a way that is adverse to the interests of the buyer.

Even if there is no private information before the agreement is made, there may be inadequate information afterward to tell whether the terms of the agreement have been honored, or acquiring that information may be costly. This opens the possibility of self-interested misbehavior, and the recognition of this **moral hazard** problem limits the contracts that can be written and enforced. Real contracts are not perfect.

Consequently, the parties' individual interests under actual contracts will not necessarily be properly aligned, and this leaves room for self-interested behavior to thwart the realization of efficient plans. The motivation problem is then to overcome these difficulties to the extent possible. This involves recognizing that what can actually be accomplished is constrained by individuals' self-interested behavior and then designing the most efficient plans that recognize these **incentive constraints**. It also involves designing systems that better align individual interests, so that the constraints are looser and the available options richer. Doing so requires a detailed understanding of the various causes of imperfect contracting, of the consequences of the various sorts of contracting difficulties, and of the responses that have emerged.

BOUNDED RATIONALITY
AND CONTRACTUAL INCOMPLETENESS

The idea of foreseeing and unambiguously describing every contingency that might possibly be relevant to the agreement between you and the university is obviously ridiculous. No one could conceivably foresee every eventuality in such a complex environment. Moreover, no human language could possibly be both rich enough and precise enough to describe all the eventualities, even if they could be foreseen. Indeed, even writing down the descriptions of those events that can be foreseen and described would likely take more time than you would actually spend getting your degree!

Bounded Rationality

Real people are not omniscient nor perfectly far-sighted. They cannot solve arbitrarily complex problems exactly, costlessly, and instantaneously, and they cannot communicate with one another freely and perfectly. Instead, they are *boundedly rational*, and they know it. They recognize that they cannot possibly foresee all the things that might matter for them, they understand that communication is costly and imperfect and that understandings are often flawed, and they know that they are not likely to find the mathematically best solution to difficult problems. They then act in an *intentionally rational* manner, trying to do the best they can given the limitations under which they work. And, they learn.

UNFORESEEN CIRCUMSTANCES   As we mentioned earlier, with bounded rationality, contracts are not complete. Inevitably, contingencies will arise that have not been accounted for because they were never imagined at contracting time. Often, these gaps in the contracts are unimportant because what the parties ought to do and the costs and benefits they receive are largely unaffected by the particular circumstances. Sometimes they can have massive consequences for the parties' welfare, however. For example, in all likelihood many of the American companies that bought television network advertising time for the 1980 Moscow Olympic Games never considered the possibility that the U.S. team would boycott the games. Without U.S. athletes to cheer for, Americans were much less interested in watching the games, and the advertising time was of little value. Similarly, Westinghouse and the electric-power utilities to which it sold enriched uranium fuel for their nuclear reactors apparently did not foresee the possibility of a sharp escalation in world uranium prices when they contracted for these sales. When this actually occurred (allegedly as a result of the formation of an international cartel among the uranium-producing countries), it forced Westinghouse's costs up and led it to repudiate the contracts.

COSTLY CALCULATIONS AND CONTRACTING   Even when contingencies are foreseen, they may appear so unlikely that it is not worthwhile to describe them in detail and to agree about what to do if they should arise. This is most likely the case when the contingencies seem very improbable, when there is little experience with comparable situations that would guide the planning about what to do should they arise, when the opportunity costs of the parties' time spent writing the contract rather than doing productive work are high, and when the contingencies seem unlikely to cause large disputes if they should occur. Yet these calculations themselves are subject to error.

A recent example comes from a General Motors' panel stamping plant in Flint, Michigan. In an attempt to indicate trust in the work force and reduce regimentation and rigidity, the plant's management changed the work rules to allow employees to leave early if they had met their day's production targets. Soon some workers were leaving by noon, having done their jobs in half the time previously allotted. Outraged at paying full-time for half a day's work, management increased the production targets. The workers were left bitter, feeling that management reneged on a promise. They viewed the contract as: "Do your work at your pace, and we'll pay you the same amount as before for the same amount of output." Trust and industrial relations at the plant have deteriorated. Management certainly could have foreseen that the workers might increase their pace significantly, and even double it. But apparently management did not think it worthwhile to specify what the response would be to a doubling of the pace or to communicate it clearly. [2]

THE IMPRECISION OF LANGUAGE   A further source of contractual incompleteness is that the natural languages in which contracts are written are inherently imprecise. This means that statements describing any reasonably complex situation must be somewhat ambiguous. For example, the "commercial practicability" doctrine in contract law means that a firm that signs a contract is required to perform as agreed

---

[2] Details can be found in G.A. Patterson, "UAW and Big Three Face Mutual Mistrust as Auto Talk Heats Up,", *The Wall Street Journal* (August 29, 1990), 1A.

only when performance is reasonably possible. Just what circumstances would justify application of this provision is inherently unclear, however. In the uranium case, Westinghouse's lawyers argued that, following the huge price increase for uranium ore, delivery of the processed uranium was "commercially" impossible and therefore not required. Not surprisingly, the other side disagreed.

More generally, there is a difficult trade-off arising from the ambiguity of language: Adding numerous specific provisions to cover behavior in more distinct eventualities means that there are more boundaries that actual circumstances may lie near and more question about which provisions apply. For this reason, adding many detailed provisions to a contract can make disputes even more likely.

Contractual Responses to Bounded Rationality

People design their contracts recognizing that they cannot possibly be perfectly adapted to all possible future circumstances. Instead, they structure the best contracts they can. One possibility is to write inflexible contracts with blanket provisions that are to apply very broadly. This minimizes the costs of describing eventualities and actions and leaves little room for ex post uncertainty about what behavior is required. This in fact may be efficient for relatively simple transactions that are quickly concluded, so there is little possibility of a change in circumstances before the contract expires that would alter what actions are appropriate. Contracts reached under these circumstances are called **spot market contracts** because they govern goods or services that are to be exchanged "on the spot." For more complex transactions that extend over time, an inflexible specification of the actions to be taken is likely to be too unresponsive to changing conditions.

RELATIONAL CONTRACTS   Another possibility is **relational contracting**, which does not attempt the impossible task of complete contracting but instead settles for an agreement that frames the relationship. The parties do not agree on detailed plans of action but on goals and objectives, on general provisions that are broadly applicable, on the criteria to be used in deciding what to do when unforeseen contingencies arise, on who has what power to act and the bounds limiting the range of actions that can be taken, and on dispute resolution mechanisms to be used if disagreements do occur. For example, companies entering a relationship to collaborate on a joint research and development project do not attempt to figure out precisely what they will do in every detail as the uncertain project evolves. Instead, they each agree to give their best efforts to developing the project, to share the costs and benefits, to consult with one another as new developments occur, and to bargain in good faith when disputes arise. Such contracts can in fact work quite effectively, at least when the potential conflicts are not too great and the parties are not inclined to be too opportunistic in their dealings with one another.

The contract that governs faculty employment at Stanford University is a nice example of relational contracting. The written portion of the contract is the Stanford *Faculty Handbook*.[3] The document contains fairly explicit provisions governing such matters as the accrual of credit towards sabbatical leave, the distribution of rights to writings and patents resulting from professors' work, and the limitations on outside employment. It also states policies regarding scientific fraud, sexual harassment, and the role of a faculty member in setting a spouse's salary. On many of the most important issues to a faculty member, however, such as the determination of annual salary and teaching assignments and the criteria for tenure, it is either silent or consists

---

[3] Interestingly, neither author of this text had seen this document when he agreed to join the Stanford faculty.

largely of specific procedures to be followed in making decisions and the mechanisms for appeal.

Employment contracts, which typically delegate authority to the employer to direct the employee's actions rather than describing the work to be done in every contingency, are a response to the necessity of incomplete, imperfect contracting. When an employee is hired, he or she (implicitly) agrees to follow the employer's directions, so long as they fall within certain bounds that may be quite vaguely defined. There is no detailed bargaining about what precise actions the employee will take in various circumstances, as there would be in a world of complete contracting, although the contract (often embodied in an employee handbook) may specify some broad expectations and rules. Similarly, the employee and employer are not required to bargain with the employer over assignments and pay ex post, once the tasks that need to be carried out become known: The expectation is that the employer will tell the employee what to do. The employee's ultimate defense against unreasonable demands is to quit, and the employer's defense against refusal to take orders is to fire the employee. All this economizes on contracting costs.

In general, in situations where reasonably complete contracts are too costly or impossible, actual contracts are relational. They serve to structure a relationship and set common expectations, and they establish mechanisms that will be used to make decisions and allocate costs and benefits. This pattern of agreeing on process and procedure rather than on actions is mirrored in corporate charters. These charters specify such matters as the procedures for selecting directors and officers and, in very broad terms, their powers and the range of decisions that they may make without consulting the stockholders, but they do not go into further detail. The nature and role of contract and business law has a similar explanation. The law sets a common framework for private contracting, establishing a basis for expectations about what should or will be done in events not explicitly considered in the contract. It also sets certain default provisions that will be applied if the contract does not explicitly provide otherwise. It thereby economizes on the costs of contracting. At an even higher level, the pattern is seen again in national constitutions, which typically state broad general principles to be used in deciding issues and describe the mechanisms that are to be employed, but do not attempt to foresee the actual decisions that will be confronted.

IMPLICIT CONTRACTS   An important adjunct to incomplete written contracts are the unarticulated but (presumably) shared expectations that the parties have concerning the relationship. The importance of these shared expectations has led to their being labeled **implicit contracts**. For example, Stanford faculty members' implicit contract with the university involves their having a say in hiring decisions, their salaries being set to reflect not just the work that the market sees and rewards but also their provision of services to the institution, and their being provided with offices, some secretarial support for research, and an equal opportunity to hunt for parking spaces.

To the extent that the expectations actually are shared and commonly understood, implicit contracts can be a powerful means of economizing on bounded rationality and contracting costs. In this regard, corporate culture—seen as a shared set of values, ways of thinking, and beliefs about how things should be done—is a key aspect of the implicit contract. This view suggests why changing a corporation's culture may be difficult: Doing so means breaking old contracts and implementing new ones, all without the benefit of being able to discuss the terms of either contract very explicitly.

Implicit contracts, by their very nature, cannot be easily enforced in a court of law. There is no document, and indeed there may never even have been any oral statement of the contract. Thus, implicit contracts must rely on other enforcement mechanisms. These mechanisms are discussed in detail later in the chapter.

Effects of Contractual Incompleteness

Contracts are meant to protect people by aligning incentives. When contracts are incomplete, the alignment can be imperfect. Contracts can also be seen as a mechanism to achieve binding commitments that the parties can bank on in their planning. When contracts are incomplete and imperfect, however, they have only limited effectiveness for achieving commitment.

Concern with the possibility of being disadvantaged by self-interested behavior that an incomplete, imperfect contract does not adequately control may prevent agreement being reached in the first place. It may also inefficiently limit the extent of cooperation that can be achieved.

COMMITMENT AND RENEGING   Achieving commitment can be very valuable because it can affect other's expectations about your behavior and thereby the behavior they adopt. For example, in 1066 William the Conqueror burned his fleet behind his invasion army, cutting off its only means of retreat and committing his men to fighting. Cortes repeated this stratagem in his invasion of Mexico. This commitment deterred the opposition, who then themselves retreated. More recently, when Apple Computer introduced its Macintosh computers, it built a highly specialized plant to produce them and designed the plant in such a way that it would be very difficult to adapt it to any other use. Further, it publicized this fact heavily. By making it more expensive to drop the Macintosh than it would otherwise have been, Apple committed itself to this product and market. This could have affected the behavior of Apple's employees, who knew that they had to succeed in this market; of Apple's competitors, who would see that there was little point trying to drive Apple out of the market; and of its potential customers, who could count on Apple's continued presence in the market and its support.

Commitment runs into two sorts of problems. The simpler and more obvious one is that one side or the other may try to renege on the deal. A customer may simply not pay for services rendered, or a supplier may refuse to deliver the goods that were contracted for, perhaps because the costs of completing the contract are higher than was anticipated. Reneging is especially problematic with incomplete contracts because what should be done in various circumstances is left unstated or ambiguous and thus open to differing interpretations. Then it may be easy for you to claim that what you now want to do is what was agreed, and that no reneging is going on at all. The other party may be unsure about whether you really believe this, and so may be reluctant to label you a cheat. Moreover, even if the other party fully believes you are not living up to the agreement, the ambiguity of the contract means that it may be very hard to establish for outsiders who is misbehaving and what actual behavior is appropriate. Westinghouse argued in court that its refusal to supply uranium fuel to the electric utilities was appropriate contractual behavior. The utilities argued that Westinghouse should have to supply them at the stated prices, even if it had to absorb immense losses. Astronomical amounts were paid to lawyers in the fight over whether Westinghouse or the utilities were in the right.

When the reneging takes the form of not carrying through on the agreed actions, it may obviously affect efficiency. However, often the problem with reneging is not that it impedes efficiency directly, but rather that it affects performance indirectly. For example, a customer's paying or not paying is simply a matter of whether a monetary transfer is made from one party to the other. Under the hypothesis of no wealth effects from Chapter 2, this sort of transfer is without direct significance for efficiency. Whether the payment is made is obviously not a matter of indifference to the individual parties, however, and the fear of getting cheated may prevent an efficient transaction from ever occurring in the first place.

EX POST RENEGOTIATION   The second commitment problem is related but more subtle. In some circumstances, it may be advantageous for both parties to renegotiate the contract ex post because what was efficient when the contract was first entered may not be so once actions have been taken or further information revealed. If the parties understand at the time they are crafting the original agreement that they will later face these incentives, however, they may not be able to draft the contract in a way that generates the desired behavior.

For example, many firms use stock options to motivate executives. These options give the executives the right to buy the firm's stock at a specified price in the future. The idea is that having the options will motivate the executives to work to get the market price of the stock above the price specified in the options so that they can make money buying the stock cheaply. However, the options will not have much effect on motivation if the price at which the option can be exercised is too high relative to the market price, because the goal of getting the stock price higher than the exercise price will seem unreachable. Thus, the exercise price is typically set moderately higher than the current market price. Now suppose that after options are issued, the price of the firm's stock falls drastically. Suddenly, the options are essentially worthless to the executives and, thus, are worthless as incentives. It might then make sense to issue new options reflecting the lower stock price, and many firms have done precisely this. If the executives forecast that this will happen again in the future, however, they will not be as worried about a fall in the stock's price as they otherwise would be. This dulls their motivation to improve the stock price.

A complication is that in some contexts it will turn out ex post that to maximize total returns the original terms should not be followed, and yet one party or the other may have an incentive to insist on the inefficient completion of the contract. For example, suppose a department store chain has contracted with a knitting firm to deliver 10,000 cotton sweaters in various colors. The sweaters are worth $20 a piece to the store, and they will cost the knitter $10 each to produce. The agreed price is $15, and meeting the order will absorb the full capacity of the knitter. Then the knitter gets an order from another chain for 20,000 polo shirts. Each shirt is worth $15 to this chain and can be produced for $5, but the knitter cannot produce both the sweaters and the shirts. Efficiency requires that the shirts be produced rather than the sweaters because this yields a total value of $200,000, whereas the surplus on the sweaters is only $100,000. Thus, the original contract should be abrogated. If this possibility had been foreseen in the original bargaining, then the parties would have efficiently agreed that the shirts should be produced instead of the sweaters. If the contract was simply to deliver the sweaters at the agreed price, however, then the first chain may insist on delivery. In this case, a possible solution is for the knitter to renege on its contract and pay damages of $50,000 to the first chain for its lost profits. However, this kind of solution is problematic if the values of the various options to the different parties are not commonly known to all, because then the appropriate level of damages is hard to determine.

Investments and Specific Assets

Although even relatively simple contracts can be subject to various problems and disputes, the most commercially important impacts of imperfect commitment arise when significant investments are required, because the amounts are significant and because the benefits may accrue over an extended period of time. In economic language, an **investment** is an expenditure of money or other resources that creates a potential continuing flow of future benefits and services. The potential flow itself is called an **asset**. The kind of assets that are most familiar are physical ones, like houses or machines, which provide a potential flow of housing or manufacturing services

Terrorism, Parenting, and Commitment

The governments of many countries have announced that they will not bargain with terrorists, even when hostages have been taken and their lives are threatened. This policy is designed to *prevent* terrorism: If potential terrorists expect that the world's governments will not deal with them, even to save the lives of their citizens, then there is less gain to kidnapping or other terrorist acts.

The problem with the policy is that it requires commitment to be credible. If hostages actually are taken, then the pressures to save their lives by negotiating with their captors are immense, no matter what policies were announced beforehand. This is especially so in countries with popularly elected governments and open mass communications, where the pain and grief of the victims' relatives is seen on television and where the governments are particularly responsive to citizens' concerns. Terrorists clearly understand the incentives to renege on the policy, and this led them to take many hostages from among the citizens of democratic countries but few from undemocratic ones.

Similar, if less dramatic, commitment problems arise repeatedly for parents raising children. For the children's own good, parents want them to do various things: avoid dangerous play, study hard, save money. To encourage the desired behavior, parents use threats of punishment, ranging from "If you play on the road, you'll get a spanking you'll never forget" to "Unless you save the money yourself, you can't have a new dress for high school graduation." Of course, the parents' pain in meting out the punishment may be at least as great as the child's in receiving it. The temptation is to forgive and omit the punishment because once the misbehavior has occurred punishment brings pain with no immediate gain.

Both these examples show how concern with the future effects of not following through with the promised response to misbehavior can stiffen resolve and lead the government or parent to absorb the costs of carrying out the promise. Reputation concerns sometimes lead them to carry out their threats, even when they have an otherwise attractive temptation to renege.

over time, or financial ones like savings bonds, which yield a flow of cash returns. Many assets are not physical, however. Patents and copyrights are assets that allow their owners to demand royalties or exclusive rights to reproduce books or software programs for a certain period of time. Investments in education can create an extremely important asset, **human capital**, which leads to an increased flow of future income as well as flows of equally important, if perhaps less tangible, benefits.

The kind of investments that are most problematic in terms of the incentives they create are investments in **specific** assets, that is, assets that are most valuable in one specific setting or relationship. When the value maximization principle applies, the *specificity* of an asset is measured as the percentage of investment value that is lost when the asset is used outside the specific setting or relationship.

An important special case of specific assets are cospecialized assets. Two assets are **cospecialized** if they are most productive when used together and lose much of their value if used separately to produce independent products or services.

For example, consider the electrical power generation industry. Most electrical generating plants are located either near the customers they serve or near a source of energy. Coal-burning electrical plants, for example, tend to be located either near coal mines or near cities. The plants near cities most often receive their coal by railroad. Special rail lines are built to the mine in order to ship out their coal. These feeder rail lines are assets that are cospecialized with the coal mine itself. If the rail lines were not used to ship coal from the mine, there would be a great loss of economic value. Because coal is bulky and has a low value per unit of weight, it would probably be economically infeasible to ship the coal by means other than rail, so the mine without the rails is of greatly reduced value. Meanwhile, there is not much other use that could be made of a rail line that runs between a railroad junction and a coal mine other than to ship coal. Thus, absent the coal, the rails also are of little value. The total value of the mine and the rail line in their separate, alternative uses is much lower than is the value of the two assets when used together to provide coal to utilities.

In the case of a mine-mouth electric plant, which is located away from the city it serves and near the mouth of a particular coal mine, the mine and the plant are cospecialized assets. The mine-mouth plant relies on the output of the mine for its coal and would lose much of its value if the mine were closed. The mine would lose much or all of its value if its only customer—the generating plant—were closed. The plant and the mine in this case are cospecialized because they are far more valuable if used together to support the production of electricity than if the coal were diverted to other uses.

The problem that arises when investments are made to create cospecialized assets is that much of the value of the investment depends on the behavior of another asset owner with his or her own selfish interests. This opens the possibility of various sorts of (ex post) opportunistic behavior that endangers the investment. Mine owners who invest in expanding their mine, for example, may find themselves at the mercy of the electric utility, which might later threaten to use the plant only for backup of its nuclear or hydro-powered plants. It is not only the mine owners who need to worry about its specific investment, however. The utility owner might worry that after the plant is built, the mine owners will try to raise their price for coal. Once a mine-mouth plant is built, there is no alternative source of coal supply for the plant, so the utility owner may become vulnerable to demands for a price increase.

THE HOLD-UP PROBLEM   The general business problem in which each party to a contract worries about being forced to accept disadvantageous terms later, after it has sunk an investment, or worries that its investment may be devalued by the actions of others, is called the **hold-up problem**. The party that is forced to accept a worsening of the effective terms of the relationship once it has sunk an investment has been *held up*.

Clearly, if contracts were complete, the hold-up problem would not arise: The parties could specify the full range of circumstances that might arise and could agree on the behavior to be followed in each of these. The usual mechanisms for contract enforcement would then prevent ex post opportunism. In the present situation, you would expect that the mine and the utility, faced with the potential hold-up problem, would at least enter into a long-term contract, so that the coal price level could be determined in advance. But at what level should the price be set? The coal mine owner might be worried about increasing costs of labor and mining equipment. Should the contract include an *escalator clause*, which automatically adjusts the price of the coal when some index of mining costs rises? Should the price of coal be tied to the spot market price of coal in the general area?

How reliable must the coal supply be? If the mine owner guarantees an uninterrupted supply of coal, it will be in a weakened bargaining position when the coal miners' contracts come up for renewal. If not, the utility may worry that the mine owner will be too willing to weather a long strike. The mine and the utility have different interests.

What about future expansions? If the demand for energy increases, is the mine obliged to supply an increased amount of coal at the same price per ton? If its average and marginal cost curves slope upward, then the additional coal will be more expensive to provide. Should the price negotiations be left for later? Later, the mine will be a monopoly supplier; now, it is just one of several possible sources of coal for a new plant whose location has yet to be determined.

The hold-up problem that the coal-burning electric plant illustrates is that large, specific investments make asset owners vulnerable to opportunistic behavior by their contracting partners. This is not a problem in standard market theory where contracting is perfect and alternative suppliers are readily available. Perfect contracting implies that the parties can write adequate protections into the contract to prevent the kinds of problems that we have described. Besides, if there were many suppliers for all inputs, then there would be no need for extensive contracting. There would be no scope for price gouging because the prices would be set by a competitive market. There would be no concerns about supply interruptions because there would be alternative supplies of an identical or nearly identical input, and no worries about demand curtailment because there would be alternative uses for the asset. *It is the specificity of assets together with imperfect contracting that lies at the core of the hold-up problem*. Concern about these problems may lead to inefficiencies as firms, fearing that their investments will leave them vulnerable, refuse to make the efficient investment.

In a series of articles, Paul Joskow has investigated the nature of coal supply contracts to the electric utility industry.[4] His empirical research reveals that coal mines supplying mine-mouth plants are most frequently owned by the utility they serve and, in all other cases, have a long-term contract to supply the utility. According to Joskow, these contracts are typically quite complex, involving escalator pricing clauses of various kinds, and they do a good job of tracking the actual variations in the cost of supplying coal.

Another example of cospecialized assets can be found in the automobile industry. In the 1920s General Motors purchased their automobile bodies from an independent firm, the Fisher Body company. As the technology of automaking advanced and the car companies moved from wooden bodies to metal ones, General Motors began to design a new automobile plant to assemble their cars. In order to improve the reliability of supply and to reduce shipping costs, GM asked Fisher to build a new auto body plant adjacent to the new GM assembly plant. The plants would have no need for shipping docks; bodies would be transferred on the production line right from the Fisher plant to the General Motors plant. Fisher refused to make the requested investment, perhaps for fear that the new plant, so closely tailored to GM's needs, would be vulnerable to demands that GM might later make. The issue was eventually resolved by vertical integration: General Motors purchased Fisher Body.[5]

The hold-up problem is an example of **postcontractual opportunism**. It arises

---

[4] Paul Joskow "Vertical Integration and Long-Term Contracts: The Case of Coal-Burning Electric Generating Plants," *Journal of Law, Economics, and Organization*, 1 (Spring 1985), 33–80; "Contract Duration and Durable Transaction-Specific Investments: The Case of Coal," *American Economic Review*, 77 (March 1987), 168–85; and "Asset Specificity and the Structure of Vertical Relationships: Empirical Evidence," *Journal of Law, Economics, and Organization*, 4 (1988), 95–117.

[5] See Benjamin Klein, Robert Crawford, and Armen Alchian, "Vertical Integration, Appropriable Rents, and the Competitive Contracting Process," *Journal of Law and Economics*, 21(1978), 297–326.

Table 5.1   The possibility of grabbing creates a Prisoners' Dilemma game.

		Firm A	
		Grab	Don't
Firm B	Grab	−1, −1	−2, 3
	Don't	3, −2	2, 2

because contracts are incomplete and imperfectly specified, so that the parties to the contract can exploit loopholes to gain an advantage over one another.

A MATHEMATICAL EXAMPLE OF THE HOLD-UP PROBLEM   A numerical example will help clarify the logic of the hold-up problem. Suppose that there are two firms, A and B, which have joined together to take advantage of a business opportunity. Each firm is called on to make an investment in an asset that is entirely worthless outside of the joint venture. These assets are therefore completely cospecialized.

To keep matters simple, suppose that the project requires that each party make an investment. The cost of the investments is 2 for each party, and the gross return from the investment is 8, yielding a net benefit of 4. To capture the possibility of ex post opportunism, suppose that the division of the gross benefits between the two firms can be affected by costly actions that each takes, but that it is not possible to make an enforceable contract governing these actions. Again, for simplicity, suppose the possible actions are "grab" or "don't grab," where grabbing costs 3. If neither firm grabs, then the gross returns are shared equally and each party enjoys a net benefit of 2. If both grab, the gross benefits are again shared equally, but each firm absorbs the additional cost of 3 associated with grabbing. This yields each firm a net payoff of $4 - 2 - 3 = -1$. Finally, if one firm, say A, grabs and the other does not, then it gets all of the benefits. The grabber's payoff is then $8 - 2 - 3 = 3$, and the other's payoff is -2. These payoffs are shown in Table 5.1; the payoff table has the form of a **Prisoners' Dilemma** game.[6]

Clearly, if the firms could contract about grabbing, they would never to do that: It is costly and creates no value. If contracting about grabbing is impossible, however, what should we expect the outcome to be?

The analysis begins by considering the decision facing firm A, assuming that the specific investments have already been made. Firm B is supposed to be making its decision at the same time, so there is no possibility that what B chooses will be influenced by A's actual choice. Suppose then that A hypothesizes that B will not grab. What are A's options? If A grabs, then A receives a payoff of 3, as computed earlier. If A refrains from grabbing, then it gets only 2. Thus, if A thinks B will refrain, its own selfish interests are best served by grabbing the returns for itself. In other words, A's highest payoff in the first column of Table 5.1 is achieved by grabbing. Now suppose that A hypothesizes that B will grab. Then by grabbing as well it gets a payoff of -1, whereas its payoff is -2 if it refrains. Once again, A does best by grabbing. Because A has the same selfishly best action no matter what it

---

[6] The Prisoners' Dilemma is the most famous and most studied strategic game. For a lively introduction to the subject, see Avinash Dixit and Barry Nalebuff, *Thinking Strategically* (New York: W.W. Norton, 1991).

expects B to do, a selfish A will always grab. A parallel analysis of B's decision indicates that a selfish B would do likewise, leading to payoffs of -1 for both.

So far, the analysis is the same as for any Prisoners' Dilemma game; the difference here, however, is that the firms do not have to play. If the firms recognize the incentives that they will face after the specific investments are made, they will want to allow for these in deciding whether to invest at all. In this example, it turns out that the threat of opportunism completely destroys the incentives to invest: If the firms cannot commit not to attempt to grab more than their share of the returns, no investment takes place.

This mathematical example is so stark that one might be tempted to believe that simple morality or business ethics could overcome the problem, and indeed it sometimes does. Much of the problem is that what is honest and fair is rarely as obvious in the rich settings of reality as it sometimes seems in classroom examples, and it is tempting for people to think that what serves their own interests is honest and fair. It is too risky to rely on others to act consistently contrary to their own selfish interests unless there is something that commits them to that kind of behavior.

Achieving Commitment

We have already mentioned relational and implicit contracts as a response to contractual incompleteness. These contracts serve to set expectations and establish decision processes to deal with the inevitable unforeseen circumstances while avoiding some of the difficulties of writing explicit detailed contracts. When cospecialized assets are a factor, a common response is for the same person or firm to own both. After all, there is little concern that a firm will hold itself up! As we see later, however, this ownership solution may also incur certain costs that limit its usefulness.

Another approach is to attempt to achieve commitment by noncontractual means. This may be worthwhile, but costly. William the Conqueror and Cortes used up valuable resources—perfectly good fleets. Apple presumably spent extra on construction costs for its overly specialized plant and in return got a facility that may become obsolete sooner than it otherwise would. Yet such expenditures may be the cost of commitment.

THE ROLE OF REPUTATIONS   In other situations, concern with one's *reputation* may be an effective check on ex post opportunism, overcoming the temptations to renege or renegotiate. It may even achieve the same results as actual commitment. Bargaining with terrorists or not punishing naughty children establishes without a doubt that there is no commitment and invites further challenges. Renegotiating executive pay contracts makes less credible any claims that bad future performance will not be rewarded. Not paying legitimate bills or not fulfilling obligations also results in a reputation for untrustworthiness. In a world of costly and incomplete contracting, *trust* is crucial to realizing many transactions. Thus, the concern with getting a bad reputation that reduces future possibilities for profitable transactions can limit reneging. Effectively, it removes the incentives for opportunistic behavior by creating a cost offsetting the short-term gains of opportunistic behavior.

As we see in Chapter 8, the value of a reputation—and thus the costs incurred in building and maintaining a good one—depends on how often it will prove useful. This in turn is related to the *frequency* of similar transactions, the *horizon* over which similar transactions are expected to occur, and the transaction's profitability. The incentives to build and maintain a reputation are larger the more frequent the transaction, the longer the horizon, and the more profitable the transaction. One implication is that, in relational contracting, where there is an issue of which party should have the discretion to direct activities in unforeseen events, it should be the one with the most to lose from a damaged reputation. This is likely to be the one with the longer horizon, the more visibility, the greater size, and the greater frequency of transactions. In the employment relationship with a stable, long-lived firm, this is more likely to be the firm than the employee.

PRIVATE INFORMATION AND PRECONTRACTUAL OPPORTUNISM

Once whatever contingencies are going to be accounted for are established, the parties to a potential contract must reach agreement on a course of action and on the payments to be made. This involves some sort of bargaining.

Bargaining is a very complex process. It is also central to economic life. It was long traditional in economics to suggest that the outcomes of bargaining among small numbers of people are essentially indeterminate. Such hard-to-describe features as bargaining strength, credibility, guile, patience, and strategic insight would combine with initial conditions to determine the outcome. The efficiency principle would suggest that an efficient agreement should be reached, but predicting the actual result was too much for economic analysis.

Yet, with the hypothesis of no wealth effects, the value maximization principle means that the value-creating aspects of the agreement are determinate. Only the monetary transfers would be determined by bargaining strength and the like. Recall, however, that efficiency is defined relative to a set of feasible outcomes. What is feasible—and thus what is efficient—turns out to depend crucially on the informational conditions. When the costs and benefits of different plans to each party are known to that party alone, or when the likelihood of different possible outcomes are private information, then these *informational asymmetries* can prevent any agreement from being reached, even when an agreement would be efficient under complete information. Furthermore, even if an agreement is reached, it will not typically be efficient when judged by the standards of complete information, especially when the parties have an option not to participate.

Bargaining over a Sale

The possibility of failing to reach an agreement can arise in the simplest problems with private information about values. Consider two people, a buyer and a seller. The seller owns a unit of some good in which the buyer is interested. Each is privately informed about the value that he or she places on having the good. The buyer believes that the seller values the good either at $2 or that she finds it worthless. The seller believes that the buyer values the good at either $1 or $3. The buyer assigns a probability of 0.2 to the seller's valuing the good at $2, and correspondingly, a probability of 0.8 that it is worth $0 to her. The seller assesses a probability of 0.2 that the buyer's valuation is $1 and a probability of 0.8 that it is $3 (see Table 5.2). Of course, the seller knows what the good is actually worth to her, and the buyer knows what it is worth to him.

If the actual valuations are $1 for the buyer and $2 for the seller, it is efficient for the good to remain with the seller—this maximizes the total value. This occurs with probability $.2 \times .2 = .04$. In all other circumstances, 96 percent of the time, efficiency demands that a sale occur and the good be transferred to the buyer.

If the valuations were known, there would not be much difficulty. Both parties would know what the good was worth to the other, and if there is a value gain from transferring the good, they ought to be able to settle on some payment from the buyer to the seller that makes both parties better off.

Table 5.2 Efficient Outcomes with Different Possible Valuations

Buyer's Value	Seller's Value	
	$0 (Probability = .8)	$2 (Probability = .2)
$1 (Probability = .2)	Trade	No Trade
$3 (Probability = .8)	Trade	Trade

INFORMATIONAL ASYMMETRIES AND STRATEGIC MISREPRESENTATION   With the actual informational asymmetries, however, there are potential problems with the bargainers' trying to misrepresent their valuations to get a better price. If the buyer's actual value is $3, he might like to insist that it is only $1 in hopes of paying a lower price. If he can convince the seller that the good is worth only $1 to him, then (provided that trade occurs) he cannot be expected to pay more than $1. So, for example, by refusing any offer at a higher price, he may gain. Similarly, if the seller's value is actually $0, she might try to insist that she actually values the good at $2 so she would get a better price. Of course, misrepresentation of this sort carries the risk of the sale falling through because the parties convince each other that their valuations are $1 and $2, so that they believe there is no basis for mutually beneficial trade. This may be a risk worth taking, however.

To prevent this sort of misrepresentation, each party must do at least as well behaving straightforwardly and, in effect, "confessing" his or her actual valuation, as he or she does misrepresenting it. Further, because trade is voluntary, neither can be forced to trade if he or she does not find it personally advantageous. These conditions constrain the set of arrangements that are feasible by requiring that each party get at least some minimum amount of surplus from the transaction, where the particular amount depends on the party's actual valuation.[7] It may then be possible that there is simply not enough surplus to go around. This can prevent trade from occurring even though the buyer actually values the good more than the seller does. With private information, the full-information efficient solution may no longer be feasible.

EFFICIENT TRADE MAY BE UNATTAINABLE   To illustrate this possibility, let us take the point of view of a mediator with the power to suggest the prices that will govern exchange when the parties represent their values in particular ways. If there is no pattern of prices that a neutral mediator could identify to promote efficient trade, then there is none that the parties, with their additional interests, could find for themselves.

The problem that must be solved is to discourage the buyer from falsely claiming a low value (in the hope of getting a low price) and the seller from falsely claiming a high value. A seller who claims a value of 2 must be offered a price of at least 2, or she will refuse to participate. (Such limitations on what is feasible that arise from individuals' options not to participate are called *participation* incentive constraints.) Offering a higher price in this instance only encourages the seller to make this claim. Therefore, as Table 5.3 shows, part of any solution to this problem must entail setting a price of 2 when the seller claims a value of 2 and trade takes place. Similarly, to

---

[7] This surplus is sometimes called an *informational rent*, that is, an excess return (rent) that is received because of the individual's private information.

Table 5.3 Prices That Best Encourage Honest Reporting and Efficient Trade

| | | Buyer's Value | |
		1	3
Seller's	0	1	p
Value	2	No Trade	2

discourage the buyer from claiming a value of 1, the price should be set at 1 when that value is claimed and trade takes place.

Now, the problem is to find a price, p, to be paid when the buyer says he has a high value ($3) and the seller says her value is low ($0) that will encourage both to be truthful. Consider the seller first. If she reports honestly, she gets $1 when the buyer claims a value of $1. If the buyer is honest, this will happen 20 percent of the time. The seller gets p the rest of the time, where p is the price when the buyer's value is $3 and the seller's is $0. Thus, the seller's *expected* payoff when she plays honestly is $.2 \times 1 + .8 \times p$. If she were to claim her actual value for the good is $2, she would not trade when the buyer says his value is low, which would happen 20 percent of the time again. She would be left with the good in this circumstance, but this is worthless to her. The rest of the time she would get the price of $2 that we calculated earlier—the minimum consistent with her being willing to trade if $2 were her actual valuation, as she claims it is. Thus, her expected payoff from dissembling about her valuation is $.2 \times 0 + .8 \times \$2 = \$1.60$. Honesty pays if the first of these two expressions is larger, that is, if $.2 + .8p \geq 1.60$. This *incentive compatibility constraint* must hold if the seller is to find it worthwhile to report honestly. It implies that p must be at least $1.875.

A similar computation can be done for the buyer. If he reports honestly, he pays a price of $2 when the seller says her value is $2 and a price of p when she says her value is $0, garnering a benefit of $.2 \times (3-2) + .8 \times (3 - p) = \$2.60 - .8 \times p$. If the buyer dissembles, he trades only when the seller says her value for the good is $0, in which case he pays $1 and gets the good that is actually worth $3 to him. This would occur 80 percent of the time if the seller is straightforward about her announcement, so his expected payoff from dissembling is $.8(\$3 - \$1) = \$1.60$. To make it worthwhile for the buyer not to dissemble, we must have $\$2.60 - .8p \geq \$1.60$, or $p \leq \$1.25$.

Thus, to induce the seller to be straightforward, the price she gets when she says her value is $0 and the buyer says his is $3 must be at least $1.875, but in the same circumstance he cannot be asked to pay more than $1.25. The conclusion is that it is impossible to find any prices that always make it in the parties' individual interests to report truthfully and to trade whenever trade is, in fact, value increasing.

ACHIEVING EFFICIENCY DESPITE THE INFORMATIONAL ASYMMETRIES We conclude that, at least in this particular example with private information about values, it is not possible for trade to occur precisely when the buyer's value exceeds the seller's.[8] The

---

[8] You might object that we have not really shown this because we assumed that it was necessary to get the buyer and seller to reveal their true valuations rather than to misrepresent what the good was worth. Perhaps there is some scheme under which they do misrepresent, but trade nevertheless occurs just when the buyer's actual value exceeds the seller's. However, a remarkable result called the *revelation principle*

special characteristic of this example is that the risks to the seller of exaggerating her value to an honest buyer and to the buyer of misstating his value to an honest seller are both low: The sale will be consummated with 80 percent likelihood anyway.

If the probabilities were reversed in the example, so that the low value for the buyer and the high value for the seller both occurred with high probability (0.8 each), then it would be possible to get correct revelation and still have trade occur just when the buyer's value exceeds the seller's. For example, consider the incentives that exist if p is set to $1.50 in Table 5.3. If the buyer reports truthfully and the seller dissembles when her actual value is $0, then the seller's expected payoff is $.8 \times 0 + .2 \times \$2.00 = \$.40$, whereas telling the truth pays $.8 \times \$1.00 + .2 \times \$1.50 = \$1.10$. Honesty, in this case, is the best policy for the seller, and the same can be shown to be true for the buyer; the incentive compatibility constraints are met.

The crucial difference when the probabilities are reversed like this is that now there is a high probability (.8) that the buyer will in fact be dealing with a seller with whom there are no gains to trade unless the buyer's value is high, and similarly, the seller is likely to be dealing with a low-value buyer and so should not trade unless her value is low. This makes it more costly to dissemble, because dissembling now runs a higher risk of preventing trade. If the high-value buyer (or the low-value seller) is straightforward, he always gets to trade. If he tries to manipulate the price to his advantage, then 80 percent of the time he does not get to trade and misses out on these benefits. This makes it easier to meet the incentive compatibility constraints—they do not eliminate the full-information efficient outcome.

Incentive Efficiency

We have seen that private information sometimes, but not always, makes it impossible to achieve the full-information efficient outcome. Recall that we have defined efficiency relative to a set of people and a set of feasible outcomes. If incentive constraints are unavoidable, then we do not label the outcome as inefficient merely because a better outcome could be achieved in the absence of incentive constraints. Instead, a mechanism for determining allocations is efficient if there is no alternative method that is feasible in the presence of incentive constraints and that all the relevant parties prefer to the original mechanism. In much of the economics literature, mechanisms that are efficient when incentive constraints are recognized in this way are called **incentive efficient**. According to the efficiency principle, we ought to expect the bargainers to find incentive-efficient mechanisms. The key question then becomes how much value the parties can create for themselves when faced with incentive constraints.

INCENTIVE EFFICIENT BARGAINING WITH PRIVATE INFORMATION: AN EXAMPLE   Another example of bargaining indicates what can be accomplished. Suppose again we have a buyer and a seller, but now each party's value for the good might take on any value between $0 and $1 with equal probability. Of course, the buyer knows the true value B that he places on the good, and the seller knows her value S. Suppose the two adopt the following simple rule to govern their bargaining: They will each simultaneously name a price; if the price named by the seller is less than that named by the buyer, the sale is made at a price midway between the prices; and if the seller's demand exceeds the buyer's offer, no trade is made and the two bargainers are committed to walk away.

---

shows that this is not the case: Any pattern of outcomes that can be achieved using any mechanism that respects incentive constraints can in fact be achieved by a mechanism in which the buyer and seller report their values and are given incentives to do so honestly.

If each side named the actual value of the good to him or her, trade would immediately occur whenever there are gains from trade, that is, whenever the buyer's value B exceeded the seller's value S. It cannot be in the two parties' individual interests, however, to reveal their actual values: If the buyer is going to bargain "honestly," it is advantageous for the seller to play strategically and announce a higher asking price than her true value. Although this increases the chances that trade will not occur, the trades that are lost are ones that were hardly profitable anyway. For example, suppose the buyer is forthright but that a seller whose value is \$.50 reports a value of \$.52 instead. The only trades that will be lost on account of this misrepresentation occur in situations in which the buyer's value lies between \$.50 and \$.52 and therefore in which the price lies below \$.51, so at most \$.01 of profit is lost. On average, when a loss occurs, it amounts to just \$.005. Moreover, the chance of loss is just the 2 percent probability that the seller's value lies in the specified range, so the total expected loss from trades missed on account of the misrepresentation is $.02 \times \$.005 = \$.0001$. Against this is a price increase of \$.01 that is enjoyed whenever the buyer's value is at least \$.52, which occurs 48 percent of the time. So, the expected extra profits are then \$.0048, for a net expected gain of \$.0047 ($=\$.0048 - .0001$).

Similarly, if the seller is forthright, the buyer gains by understating his valuation. From the buyer's point of view, claiming that the value is lower than it actually is involves a chance of blocking a trade that would be profitable, but as before the cost of a small misrepresentation is tiny. More often, the misrepresentation will lead to a reduced price for the buyer, and this effect is by far the larger one: Small misrepresentations always pay.

In actuality, the calculations we have just made are not the most relevant ones. If it is going to be in the seller's interest, for example, to misrepresent her value, then the buyer ought to account for that in determining his own misrepresentation. Actually calculating the bid and ask functions that the two parties would use if they correctly forecast one another's choices is somewhat complicated, but the result that emerges is that the two will systematically bid different amounts than their true values. As a result, trade will occur if and only if the buyer's valuation exceeds the seller's by 1/4.[9] This is suggestive of a typical pattern: *When incentive constraints are important in bilateral bargaining, trade takes place only if the gains from trade are sufficiently large.*

One might hope that some other bargaining arrangement would yield greater efficiency, but this is actually not possible. In the example considered, the specified bargaining rules actually maximize efficiency subject to the constraints imposed by the private information. For example, the parties could have initially decided to continue bargaining as long as one or the other wished to do so or until an agreement was reached. The inefficiency will still be manifested, however, either in the form of costly disagreements or as a costly delay until an agreement is reached.

---

[9] To calculate the strategies that the parties will adopt if they correctly forecast one another's incentives to adopt strategic behavior, suppose that the seller expects the buyer's bid to be a linear function $b = \beta_1 + \beta_2 B$ of his true valuation and, in a corresponding fashion, that the buyer expects the seller's asking price to be a linear function $s = \sigma_1 + \sigma_2 S$ of S. Suppose too that the parties actually do decide to use rules of this form to decide how much to bid and ask. (Of course, correct revelation of their values occurs when they pick $\beta_1 = \sigma_1 = 0$ and $\beta_2 = \sigma_2 = 1$.) Then it is possible to calculate, for given assumed values of the σ's, how the buyer's expected payoff depends on his choice of β, and similarly, how the seller's payoff depends on her choice of σ for any assumed values of β. Maximizing each party's payoff with respect to its choices (by setting derivatives equal to zero) and then requiring that each correctly forecasts the other's choices yields the conclusion that $b = (1/12) + (2/3)B$ and $s = (1/4) + (2/3)S$. Then $b > s$ only if $B > S + 1/4$.

The existence of private information frequently means that some value-maximizing plans cannot be realized. Sometimes the potential gains from transacting are missed. Incentive-efficient arrangements minimize these losses, as in this example, where trade does not occur if the gains are small but does if they are sufficiently large.

Efficient Agreements with Large Numbers of Participants

Although the problem of incentives and private information can be serious even in a bilateral relationship, it becomes much more serious when the numbers of people who must agree begin to grow. When there is a diversity of interests, even moderate-sized groups often find it impossible in practice to reach a unanimously acceptable decision. In theory, with a large enough set of participants, it can be a virtual certainty that there are gains to be realized from an agreement, and yet there may be no agreement that meets the incentive and participation constraints, making it impossible to realize the potential gains.

INVESTMENT PROJECTS TO CREATE PUBLIC GOODS: AN EXAMPLE   To illustrate the underlying theoretical problem, we consider a simple decision about whether to undertake an investment project to create a public good. The cost of the project is $1 in total, no matter how many people are benefitted. Each individual either wants to have the project done, placing a value of $2 on it, or is indifferent about it, getting a value of $0 from its being undertaken. The probability that the project is valued positively by any single individual is p, a number strictly between 0 and 1. Again, each individual knows his or her actual valuation, but this value is private information. Individuals are free to drop out of the group, but if they do so they do not get the benefits of the project.

If anyone wants the project done, value maximization demands that it should be carried out because the cost is $1 and the benefit is at least $2. If the group consists of a single individual, that person will surely execute the project. Suppose, however, that there are several people. Anyone forced to pay more towards the costs of the project than it is worth to him or her can drop out of the group and avoid paying. Thus, no one can be forced to pay more than $2, and someone who claims his or her value is $0 cannot be made to pay anything. In essence, everyone must agree to the plan for it to be undertaken. The danger is that people will try to free ride off the others, falsely claiming that they value the project at $0 and hoping that someone else will pay for it.

Suppose that if $m \geq 1$ out of the N people in the group say their values are high, then the project is built, with the costs being assigned randomly to one of the m people, or that the costs are split equally among the m people voting for the project. If there are two people in the group ($N = 2$), then we can express the incentive constraint that a person with a value of $2 be willing to acknowledge that as follows:

$$p(\$2 - \$.5) + (1 - p)(\$2 - \$1) \geq p(\$2) + (1 - p)(\$0)$$

The first term on the left is the probability p that the other person will say his or her value is high (assuming honest reporting by that person), times the gain the first individual receives in this case. This gain is the $2 he or she gets from having the project done, less the expected cost to him or her, which is $.50. The second term is the probability that the other person will report a value of zero, times the gain in this case, which is the benefit of the project less its cost. So the left-hand side is the expected return from reporting honestly. If the person dissembles, then the project is built and financed only when the other person says his or her value is $2 (which occurs with probability p), in which case that other person bears all the cost. The right-hand side is thus the expected return to dissembling. The inequality says that being forthright is worthwhile. This inequality must hold if the project is to be built whenever it is value maximizing.

Solving for p, we see that p cannot be too large: $p \leq 2/3$. If p is too high, it appears too likely that the other person will volunteer to pay, and the individual under consideration cannot be induced to report his or her true valuation. It is precisely when it is likely that others would be willing to finance the project even without one person's participation that the person is most tempted to claim that he or she does not value the project and, as a result, that an efficient project will be delayed or left unbuilt.

The way to induce correct revelation is to reduce the probability that the project is carried out when the reported gains seem small. Let q be the probability that the project is carried out when only one person states that his or her value is $2. Then the incentive constraint becomes

$$p(\$2 - \$\tfrac{1}{2}) + (1 - p)q(\$2 - \$1) \geq pq(\$2) + (1 - p)(\$0)$$

Now, if $p > 2/3$, q must be less than 1 to induce truthful reporting. For example, as p approaches 1, q must approach 3/4. Thus, 25 percent of the time when someone volunteers to pay, the project is not carried out. In other words, people will sometimes free ride and not volunteer to pay for the project, even when it is actually individually worthwhile to pay for it themselves.

If there are three people, the incentive constraint (calculated assuming that the project will be built whenever it is value maximizing) gets even tougher to meet. In this case, it is

$$p^2(\$2 - \$\tfrac{1}{3}) + 2p(1 - p)(\$2 - \$\tfrac{1}{2}) + (1 - p)^2(\$2 - \$1)$$
$$\geq p^2(\$2) + 2p(1 - p)(\$2) + (1 - p)^2(\$0)$$

which requires p to be less than about 0.44. If p exceeds this value, the incentive constraint cannot be met if the project is to be built whenever its value exceeds its direct cost.

As N gets large, the incentive constraint becomes more and more difficult to meet—free riding becomes more and more tempting if the others are expected to report honestly. The essential intuition is that dissembling is costly only when the others' reports make the given individual *pivotal*—the project is built if he or she admits to having a high value for it, and not otherwise. As N gets large, it becomes a virtual certainty that someone else will value the project highly and, assuming honest reporting, will volunteer to pay for it. The cost of free riding, which is the chance that the misrepresentation prevents the project from being constructed, then becomes vanishingly small, and so misrepresentation cannot be prevented.

For example, when N = 3 and $p = 1/2$, the incentive constraints mean that the best that can be done (in terms of maximizing total expected value) is that the project is undertaken when all three or any two of the people say their values are high, but it is undertaken less than 90 percent of the time when only one person admits to having a high valuation (that is, the person is pivotal). Yet, this one person is individually willing to pay enough to finance the project.

As we discussed earlier, this analysis implies that it is not reasonable for people to assume that others will all report honestly. That recognition increases their own individual returns to honest reporting. The precise calculations are rather complex, but the conclusion for this example is that as the number of people involved in the decision becomes large, assuming that everyone behaves similarly, the probability that someone will volunteer to contribute to the project tends to a limit of approximately two chances in seven, even though it is essentially certain that funding the project is value maximizing.

Bargaining Costs

Contracting requires reaching a mutually beneficial agreement. We have just seen that private information about the values of different options can prevent reaching an agreement on value-maximizing plans. One way to think of this is in terms of **bargaining costs**, the transaction costs of reaching mutually acceptable agreements. Bounded rationality imposes bargaining costs, even in the absence of any strategic behavior. It takes time and effort to imagine and list contingencies, to determine efficient courses of action, and to settle on divisions of costs and benefits. In fact, bounded rationality means that it may be impossible to carry out these tasks completely and perfectly. The resulting incomplete contracts then give rise to further transaction costs: The costs that are incurred in achieving commitment by noncontractual methods and the inefficiencies that result from attempts to protect against imperfect commitment.

When private information is a factor, there are additional costs. These can be substantial. They can prevent agreement or delay its realization considerably. In either case, simple value maximization computed without regard to the constraints imposed by incentives is a misleading basis for prediction.

In some bargaining situations, as we have already seen, private information may completely prevent agreement even though there are significant gains to be had from trade. In fact, this possibility of private information leading to market breakdown was first noted in an even simpler market setting.

MEASUREMENT COSTS AND INVESTMENTS IN BARGAINING POSITION

In many exchanges, some important characteristic or quality of the good being traded is unknown to both the buyer or seller. For example, when an oil company buys rights to extract the petroleum on a piece of land, neither the company nor the seller typically knows how much oil will be found. Similarly, neither the purchaser or the seller of a piece of equipment, or both, may be unsure about how durable the equipment may be. Although it is conceivable that such a situation could sometimes be unproblematic—the parties might make a deal based on expected values—that is not always the most likely outcome. More often, it is possible and profitable for one or both parties to gain a bargaining advantage by investing in information about the quality of the good. For example, by becoming informed the buyer can better avoid paying a higher price for the good than what it is actually worth. Moreover, if one side has become informed, it is very likely to be in the other side's interest to absorb the costs of becoming informed as well because otherwise it will be subject to adverse selection or opportunistic misrepresentation. Thus, both sides may be led to incur the costs of measuring the good's worth.

These information costs are wasted from the standpoint of society as a whole. It is true that the information gathering will lead to a negotiated price that reflects the value more precisely, but that does not increase total wealth. A different price benefits one party only at the expense of the other. The good still ends up being transferred, just as efficiency required and just as it would have been had the information not been gathered. The costs of gathering that information are subtracted from the parties' total wealth; there is no offsetting benefit unless the information affects a productive decision or the allocation of the asset. In line with the value maximization principle, you might therefore expect businesspeople to try to devise institutions that reduce this source of waste.

The De Beers Diamond Monopoly

The De Beers group, which runs the remarkably successful world diamond cartel, uses an unusual method to sell diamonds that has been interpreted in just this way— as an attempt to reduce excessive expenditures on information.[10] Buyers indicating an interest in purchasing particular amounts of particular sizes and qualities of stones are offered a packet of stones, called a "sight," that roughly corresponds to their indicated interests. The stones are graded and sorted on the basis of their gross characteristics only, without any attempt by De Beers to estimate their value closely. The sights are offered on a strict take-it-or-leave-it basis, according to a pricing formula based on these gross characteristics. Absolutely no negotiation over the price is permitted. Also, the content of the packet is not negotiable (except for correcting errors in grading). Furthermore, failure to take the sight as offered results in the buyer's being excluded from buying from De Beers in the future.

Although elements of this arrangement may represent De Beers' exploitation of its monopoly position (it controls over 80 percent of the world diamond supply), there is little reason to expect that even a monopolist would choose an inefficient distribution scheme. From a value-maximization perspective, it makes sense to look for a competing explanation of these details in terms of efficient exchange.

Just such an explanation has been offered. If bargaining about the price and contents of a packet were allowed, then there would be incentives for the buyers to spend resources in finely examining each stone to determine the most valuable gem that can be cut from each and to estimate the values of the uncut stones that way. De Beers would have to do the same to protect itself; that is, it would have to abandon its system of using only rough grading of the uncut stones. To minimize examination costs and thereby maximize total value, however, a careful examination should be made only by the final buyer, who must actually cut the stone, and *not* by the seller or the other potential buyers. Moreover, it does not much matter which diamond retailer purchases which stone. What is most important for efficiency is that the transaction be made and that wasteful information gathering be minimized. Forbidding negotiations eliminates the incentive for buyers to incur examination costs, and the practice of withdrawing the opportunity to buy in the future prevents the "leave it" option from being used as a bargaining device to try to improve future offers. Moreover, buyers benefit from knowing that the stones they are purchasing have not been "picked over" by other potential buyers, so that examining the stones is not necessary for self-protection. Both sides enjoy savings from this system of trade.

Similar arguments have been advanced to explain the practices of prepackaging fruits and vegetables in grocery stores rather than selling them individually, of supplying warranties with products, of "block-booking" a set of movies from a given studio rather than allowing theater owners to pick and choose the films they want, and of paying percentage royalties rather than a fixed fee to book authors. In each case, the specified practice reduces or eliminates the incentives to incur costs inspecting individual items even when the efficient outcome is for trade to occur. The practices are then interpreted as examples of the value maximization principle.

---

[10] Roy Kenney and Benjamin Klein, "The Economics of Block Booking," *Journal of Law and Economics*, 26 (1983), 497–540.

Investing in Bargaining Advantages

These measurement costs are an example of the larger class of expenditures made to gain an advantage in bargaining or trade. Many such expenditures are typically unproductive, yet they are incurred because they have private value in shifting the distribution of the gains from trade. Another example comes from the international arms control arena. In the United States there have been repeated arguments for funding of enormously expensive weapons systems and the Strategic Defense Initiative ("Star Wars") on the basis that they provide "bargaining chips" in negotiations with the Soviet Union on arms control. The idea seems to be that these systems are being developed and the corresponding expenditures made not because deployment of the systems is actually worthwhile but so that they can be bargained away and leave the United States with an adequately mighty arsenal.

These investments in bargaining position carry direct costs that the bargainers may wish they could all avoid. In this regard, the time and energy so often spent haggling, posturing, and delaying agreement in attempts to influence the terms of the deal are related wastes. Moreover, to the extent that the potential contracting parties forecast that these costs will be incurred, they may be forestalled from ever attempting to reach an agreement.

ADVERSE SELECTION

Besides the incentive to misrepresent valuations, a second sort of incentive problem arising from precontractual informational asymmetries is known as *adverse selection*. The term was coined in the insurance industry. The selection of people who purchase insurance is not a random sample of the population, but rather a group of people with private information about their personal situations that makes it likely they will receive a higher-than-average level of benefit payments under the insurance policy. For example, if an insurance company were to issue an individual health insurance policy that covers the medical costs associated with pregnancy and delivery, it is a safe bet that the policy would be purchased disproportionately by women planning to bear children in the near future. Childbearing plans are a privately known, *unobserved characteristic* of the insurance buyer that has a huge effect on insurance costs. The offering of comprehensive individual pregnancy and delivery coverage is subject to such severe adverse selection that such coverages are no longer available in the United States, where most health insurance is privately provided.

In many countries, the inadequacy of private health insurance has led governments to nationalize the provision of health care, although with mixed results. In the United States, the private sector has responded by developing a new practice—group health insurance—that partially substitutes for the missing market in health-insurance contracts. In modern practice, most coverage for pregnancy and delivery benefits is supplied through employer-provided medical insurance plans, where coverage is automatic or compulsory for all members of the employee group. Because participation is not voluntary and because pregnancy and delivery benefits are packaged with other health-care benefits, the insurance company is able to insure a cross-section of the community and thus avoid adverse selection.

A second example of adverse selection arises in connection with warranties on automobiles. New cars typically come with a warranty under which the manufacturer pays for any problems (other than routine maintenance) that arise with the car over a certain period of time, such as one year or 12,000 miles. Some auto makers have experimented with selling an optional extended warranty covering nonroutine expenses over a longer period, such as five years or 50,000 miles. Insurance theory predicts that the extended coverage would most often be purchased by people who expect to put their cars to hard use, such as driving on poorly maintained roads while towing a trailer or other load in extreme weather conditions. Those who expect to use their cars to carry passengers only, on well-maintained roads and in ordinary weather conditions, would be less likely to purchase the extended warranty. Notice that an extended warranty that provides coverage for *all* buyers is relatively much less susceptible to this problem, and auto makers have recently been adopting such coverages. Thus, even though extended warranties have not been an especially popular option, several automobile manufacturers have begun to include long warranties as a standard feature on their cars. This universal coverage works better than individual coverage for the same reason that pregnancy coverage offered through employer-provided health coverage is economically viable whereas pregnancy benefits in individual policies are not.

Adverse selection is a problem of **precontractual opportunism**; it arises because of the *private information* that the insurance consumers have *before* they have purchased the insurance contract, when they are weighing whether the purchase is beneficial. A woman considering a health-insurance policy with generous benefits for labor and delivery has private information about her family plans. A driver who buys extended warranty coverage has private information about how the car will be used. These problems are additional to the moral hazard problem, according to which the availability of insurance will actually change the insured's unmonitored behavior. It is moral hazard—not adverse selection—if a family with insurance coverage for the expenses of pregnancy and childbirth is induced to have more children or to seek more extensive (and expensive) prenatal care, or if a car owner with an extended warranty is induced to take less care of the car.

Adverse selection is incompatible with the neoclassical account of markets from Chapter 3. There, in essence, all trades are with an impersonal market, and no one cares who actually takes the other side of the transaction. This is not the case with adverse selection. In the neoclassical model, each firm has a definite set of technically feasible plans. Each plan is described in terms of the things the firm must buy and sell in order to carry it out. When there is adverse selection, the resources needed to provide insurance depend not only on how much insurance is sold but also on the unobserved characteristics of the buyers. The firm cannot verify the technical feasibility of its production plan without knowing the mix of unobserved characteristics its customers will have. These depend not only on the firm's plan, but also on the insurance products offered by its competitors, on the prices of its products, and on the mix of characteristics in the population at large. In the neoclassical model, none of these things are permitted to affect the technical feasibility of a production plan.

Adverse Selection and the Closing of Markets

When the problem of adverse selection is especially severe, there may be no price at all at which the quantity of a good supplied to the market by sellers is equal to the quantity demanded by buyers. The problem is that the price must be the same to all buyers, no matter what the costs of serving them, because the costs are not observable by the seller. However, the only buyers who will pay any given price are those whose private information leads them to believe that the price is advantageous for them. These will tend to be those who—like the women planning to have children and considering insurance with maternity benefits—are most expensive to serve. If there are any administrative costs in selling the product, then the price will have to rise so high for the seller to break even that not even those valuing the product the most will find it worthwhile to buy. Any lower break-even price will attract only those who cost more to serve than the price. Thus, the market completely collapses, and it may do so even when there would be gains from trade in the absence of private information. For example, the costs of buying private maternity coverage would be prohibitive, exceeding the cost of paying directly for the medical bills.

A MATHEMATICAL EXAMPLE OF ADVERSE SELECTION   Suppose that a company offers an insurance policy for sale. Buyers' differing characteristics imply that they will receive differing expected benefits under the policy, so let x denote the expected benefit or claim payment. If the characteristic x were observed, then the insurance company would charge a higher price to consumers with higher values of x to offset its higher expected costs. We assume that x cannot be observed by the insurance company, however, so that the same price P must be offered to all potential purchasers. Suppose that, in addition to the expected receipts x, a buyer gains some value v from the pure risk reduction that the insurance policy provides. A buyer will purchase the insurance policy if the price is less than the value received: $P \leq v + x$. The set of buyers who will purchase at a price P therefore is all those whose characteristic x exceeds $P - v$.

Now we come to a critical point: How does the insurance expense that the company expects to pay depend on the price P? If there were no adverse selection, the cost of insuring an average customer would not depend on the price charged, any more than the cost of producing an average toaster depends on the selection of people who purchase it. Insurance, however, is different from toasters. For an illustration, let us suppose that the distribution of claim amounts x in the population at large is uniform between zero and $\bar{x}$, so that there are an equal number of people with any given level of expected claims x. Given this simplifying assumption, the average insurance expense is equal to the average of the amounts paid to the consumer with the lowest value of x who buys insurance ($x = P - v$) and the consumer with the highest value of x who buys insurance ($x = \bar{x}$); this average is equal to $(P - v + \bar{x})/2$. Because the people who expect relatively low collections from insurance are deterred from purchasing as the price is raised, and only those for whom $x \geq P - v$ are willing to buy, the *average* amount of the insurance expense for those customers who do buy is an increasing function of the price P, as the formula shows.

To see how this effect alters market outcomes, we describe the outcome in this hypothetical insurance market by a pair (x,P), where P denotes the market price and x the expected level of claims of the marginal customer. That is, customers who expect losses greater than x buy insurance, while those who expect lower losses do not. The average level of claims in this market is $(x - \bar{x})/2$ per customer. We suppose that the insurance company incurs a claims administration cost of c for each dollar of claims that it pays, so the average level of costs incurred by the insurer is $(x + \bar{x})(1 + c)/2$. Thus, the insurance company is willing to supply insurance to the group of buyers with losses of x or more if the price it receives is at least equal to the $P_s(x)$, where:

$$P_s(x) = \tfrac{1}{2}(x + \bar{x})(1 + c) \tag{5.1}$$

Also, the buyers will be just those whose expected claims are at least x if the price is:

$$P_b(x) = x + v \tag{5.2}$$

These two equations are plotted in Figure 5.1, using the assumptions that $\bar{x}(1 + c) > \bar{x} + v$, and that $\bar{x}(1 + c)/2 > v$, that is, that $c\bar{x} > v$. As the Figure shows, there is then no intersection of the two lines. For any given level of the price on the vertical axis, moving horizontally to the P_b line identifies the corresponding level of expected claims of the marginal insurance buyer. Then, moving vertically to the P_s line shows the price $P_s(\bar{x})$ the insurer would need to break even selling to that set of buyers. Since

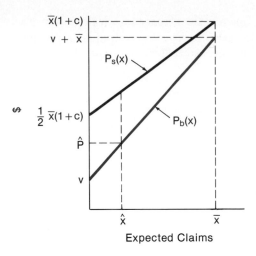

Figure 5.1: With adverse selection, there may be no price at which the insurer is willing to serve the set of customers who wish to buy insurance.

the resulting vertical move is always upwards in this example, there is no price that the insurer could charge that would break even, given the set of buyers that the price attracts. A market equilibrium in this case involves the insurer setting the price so high that nobody wants to buy, that is, the market breaks down.

The key condition for market breakdown is that $c\bar{x} > v$. For an insurance market to exist, the cost to the insurance company of administering the claims of the claimant with the *highest* expected benefits (which are $c\bar{x}$) must be no more than the value (v) that claimant expects to enjoy from the risk reduction. According to our analysis, *for a market to exist, it must be economical to provide insurance to those with the highest expected claim payments.*

Because providing insurance is costly, you might wonder whether the market fails to exist only when it would in the full-information case, that is, only when it is so costly to provide insurance for other reasons that, adverse selection aside, providing coverage is uneconomical. If an employer or government could provide mandatory coverage to the whole population, its average cost per person would be $(1+c)\bar{x}/2$, and the average benefit received by the insured people would be $v + \bar{x}/2$, so the average benefit exceeds the average cost whenever $v > c\bar{x}/2$. *For the provision of insurance coverage to increase total equivalent wealth, the cost of administering claims for the average person must be less than the benefit the average person enjoys on account of risk reduction.* Whenever $c\bar{x} > v > c\bar{x}/2$, insurance is desirable (according to the principle of total wealth maximization) but private individual insurance markets cannot survive.

The situation modeled is exactly the sort in which you might expect to find group insurance offered as an alternative to individual insurance. When adverse selection is not too severe, the advantage of individual insurance over group insurance is that it allows people to tailor their purchases to their individual tastes. When adverse selection destroys the individual insurance market, however, group insurance provides a good private sector alternative. *The failure of the market for individual insurance leads to alternative arrangements and practices in the private sector.* In some naive economic analyses, the failure of simple markets is always a valid reason for government intervention. As the insurance example illustrates, however, the private sector is continually innovating practices that avoid market failures, and these practices must be evaluated in order to decide if a government intervention can improve matters.

The model developed earlier is a variation of the pioneering adverse selection model of George Akerlof, who went further to show that the volume of trade in markets suffering adverse selection is inefficiently low, even in cases where adverse selection does not entirely destroy the market. Akerlof's model is widely known as the *lemons* model, named after its original application to the market for used cars where, Akerlof claimed, the poorest quality cars ("lemons") are the ones most often offered for sale.

Adverse Selection and Rationing

As we have mentioned a number of times, standard market theory is based partly on the premise that prices adjust until supply is equal to demand. When demand exceeds supply, the sellers will find that they can raise prices without losing sales. When supply exceeds demand, buyers can profit by holding out for a lower price. In that way, prices are driven by market forces toward the level where supply equals demand.

When there is adverse selection, however, changing the price affects not only the revenues of the selling firm but also its costs of supplying the product. As we saw in the insurance example, the average claims made against the insurance company may be an increasing function of the price charged. In a similar way, the interest rates that a bank charges can affect the selection of customers who apply for loans: Only those customers with risky investments may be willing to pay high interest rates. In that case, the bank may find it unprofitable to raise its interest rate to take advantage of excess demand. Indeed, a higher loan interest rate may actually lead to a lower return for the bank, net of the costs of default.

For example, suppose there are two sorts of borrowers, A and B, who are indistinguishable to the bank. Both have access to a single investment opportunity that requires an initial investment of $1,000,000 and which generates an expected return of 10 percent. Type A's projects are safe: They pay off $1,100,000 for sure. Type B borrowers have risky projects that have equal chances of yielding $900,000 or $1,300,000. Suppose that if the low payoff occurs, all the bank can collect is the $900,000: The borrower has no additional collateral. Suppose too that there are enough type As in the population that the bank can make money lending to all prospective borrowers at 5 percent interest, provided it does not get an adverse selection of borrowers, and that competition leads 5 percent to be the interest rate on loans. Both types will be happy to borrow, and the bank in fact does not suffer adverse selection.

Now assume that money becomes tighter in the economy and the cost of funds to the bank increases, so that the bank would need to receive just over 10 percent to be profitable while lending to a random selection of borrowers. What happens if the bank raises its interest rate to (just over) 10 percent? The safe, type A borrowers will no longer borrow, because they are certain to pay more to the bank than they can earn from their investment project. However, the risky type Bs may still be happy to borrow: If things go well, they collect $1,300,000, pay the bank $1,100,000, and make $200,000. If things go badly, they pay the bank only $900,000, netting zero for themselves. losing $100,000. The Bs thus expect a net profit of $100,000 on average, with the bank experiencing an offsetting expected loss. In this example, the bank's net earnings from its loans fall when it raises the interest rate, because the "quality" of its group of borrowers declines.

When money is scarce, the bank may often find it more profitable to use the opportunity to improve the quality of its loan portfolio rather than to charge a higher rate of interest. Joseph Stiglitz and Andrew Weiss, using this sort of reasoning, have created an adverse selection model to account for credit rationing and nonmarket means of credit allocation.[11] When there is an excess demand for loans, the bank

---

[11] They have also shown that, in some circumstances, high interest rates can induce a firm to choose riskier investments than it otherwise would. The argument is similar to one we will develop in the next

may prefer *rationing* credit rather than raising the interest rate that it charges to borrowers. The same sort of analysis can be used to explain why firms use terminations rather than wage cuts when they find their wage expenses are too high: Wage cuts are disproportionately likely to lead to quits by the ablest workers, who frequently have the best outside job opportunities.

SIGNALING, SCREENING, AND SELF-SELECTION

Sometimes the private information responsible for adverse selection may be discovered by expending effort and attention. Aptitude and achievement tests, for example, may reveal information about prospective employees, as may background checks and references from former employers. Some employers even resort to using polygraph tests. There are obvious costs and limitations to these measures, however, which limit their use and leave contracting still subject to informational asymmetries.

Often in situations marked by precontractual private information, some of the privately informed people would gain if they could make their information known. Moreover, the uninformed would gain from learning this information. For example, a worker who knows he or she is especially productive would like prospective employers to know this as well, because it would result in a better job assignment and higher pay, and the prospective employers would be glad to get the information that would allow them to identify a top prospect. Similarly, a firm that has low costs might like potential competitors to know this fact so that they will recognize that it will be a tough competitor and they will be less likely to enter its markets. A firm that has developed a new product whose quality is exceptionally high but not easily determined except through extensive experience with the product has a similar incentive. It would like to make the actual quality known to prospective buyers, who would themselves be pleased to receive the information. (Of course, they would also like to know if the quality is bad, so that they can avoid the new product.)

The difficulty is that there may be no simple, direct way to reveal the private information. In particular, self-serving claims are not likely to be credible. It is equally easy to say "I am unusually highly motivated, energetic, creative, and dedicated, and you should therefore hire me," or "You better not think about entering our market, because we are committed to it and will fight fiercely to defend it," or "New Splatto brand is the best ever, so buy it today!" whether the claim is true or false. If such claims were believed and acted on, everyone would be tempted to make them, and those who were foolish enough to believe would soon learn the error of their naivety.

However, there is still a mutual gain to be had if the desired types of the privately informed agents can make their information known. This creates incentives to find credible ways to convey the information. One way is for the uninformed to attempt to infer the private information from observable actions (or verifiable statements) of the informed. This leads to two different, but closely related, classes of strategies. These are usually called *signaling* and *screening*, with the difference between them depending on whether the informed or uninformed party takes the lead.

Signaling

In **signaling**, the privately informed parties take the lead in adopting behavior that, properly interpreted, reveals their information. The best-known example of labor

---

chapter to explain why some savings and loan associations (S&Ls) in the United States undertook very risky investments in the 1980s. When these investments failed, the S&Ls became insolvent, leading to the "S&L crisis" that is costing American taxpayers hundreds of millions of dollars. This *moral hazard* effect is additional to the *adverse selection* effect described earlier: Both effects imply that a bank that raises its interest rates will find that the quality of its loan portfolio declines.

market signaling of productivity via educational attainment is due to Michael Spence, who was the first to explore these sorts of problems systematically.

In Spence's simplest model, workers are either of high or low productivity. They privately know their own productivity, or at least are better informed about it than are prospective employers. High-productivity workers can produce, for example, $50 per hour of output net of other costs of production, and under competitive labor markets this is what they would earn if they were known to be highly productive. Low-productivity workers can produce only $20 per hour. If there is no way to distinguish between them, members of both groups will be paid the same amount, equal to the expected productivity of a randomly chosen worker. If the percentage of high-productivity workers in the population is, say, 30 percent, then the wage will be $(.3 \times \$50) + (.7 \times \$20) = \$29$. It is obvious that the high-productivity workers would like to be recognized because they are being paid less than the value of their marginal product, and employers who are overpaying the low-productivity workers and are unable to identify the high-productivity ones also would like to have the information revealed.

Now suppose that, for some reason, high-ability workers choose to acquire a distinctly higher level of educational attainment (years of schooling, difficulty of the courses taken, class standing) than do low-productivity workers, and further suppose that educational attainment is observable and verifiable. If this pattern were recognized, then employers could infer individuals' productivity from their educational achievements, and education would be a **signal** for productivity. Educated workers would be seen to be high-productivity workers and would be paid accordingly, whereas those who were relatively uneducated would be (correctly) perceived as being of low productivity and would earn the corresponding wage. The issue then is whether this sort of situation is sustainable.

The answer depends on two conditions. First, the level of education that is taken as signaling high productivity must be such that the low-productivity workers are unwilling or unable to attain it, even if by acquiring more education they could mislead employers into thinking that their own productivity was high and be paid accordingly. If this **self-selection** constraint is not met, then the low-productivity workers would attain as much education as high-ability workers, and the education signal would convey no information. The second condition is that failure to obtain the particular level of education should accurately signal that the person is not highly productive; it should not be the preferred choice of highly-productive workers. This is a second self-selection constraint.

For these two conditions to hold, it is clearly necessary that achieving a given level of education be cheaper for the high-productivity workers than for the low. If the costs are aligned in this fashion, then there will be a level of education such that the more able will be willing to pay the costs of acquiring it and the less able will not, even though gaining this level of education would lead the market to infer that their ability is high and to offer them higher wages.

The self-selection constraints ensure that the signals are *credible*. When they hold, employers can rely on the worker's signal because it will not be in the interest of those who do not have the unobservable characteristic (high productivity) to mimic those who do.

A MATHEMATICAL EXAMPLE OF SELF-SELECTION CONSTRAINTS   Mathematically, the two self-selection constraints in this example are

$$\$50 - C_L \times E_H < \$20 - C_L \times E_L$$

and

$$\$50 - C_H \times E_H > \$20 - C_H \times E_L$$

where C_L and C_H are the costs (on a basis comparable to the wage) of a unit of education to the low- and high-productivity workers respectively, and E_L and E_H are the levels of education chosen by each type. The first inequality says that low-productivity workers who mimic the behavior of high-productivity ones by choosing their level of education are worse off doing so, even receiving the high wage, than when picking E_L, being recognized as low productivity, and being paid the $20 wage. The second inequality says that high-ability workers are better off signaling than not. If $C_H \leq C_L$, these inequalities cannot both be satisfied. Only if $C_H < C_L$ can the inequalities be met and education be a credible signal for productivity.

Furthermore, for any $C_H < C_L$ there will be a level of education that the high-productivity workers would obtain to signal their private information. For example, if C_H is $10 and C_L is $20, then $E_H = 2$ and $E_L = 0$ will do. The low-productivity worker then earns a net of $50 - $20 \times 2 = $10 by mimicking and $20 by not attempting to pass as a high-productivity worker, and the high-productivity worker is better off getting the two units of education (thus receiving a net of $30) than not doing so (and getting $20). Of course, other levels of E_H and E_L will also do: For example, an E_H level of a little bit more than 1.5 and E_L of zero.

SIGNALING AND EFFICIENCY   Notice that we did not assume that educational attainment affects on-the-job productivity, although this can be incorporated into the analysis without altering the conclusion substantially (and doing so helps motivate the whole analysis). All that is required is a negative relationship between a person's cost of acquiring education and his or her productivity. According to some, this relationship might arise because productivity involves the ability to focus on boring tasks, to sit still and take directions, and to show respect for authority, and these same abilities are required to succeed in the educational system. It could also arise because inherent intellectual ability affects success both in school and on the job.

Note too, however, that although the signaling leads to the effective revelation of the private information, this does not come for free. Because of our assumptions, there is in fact no social gain to revealing the information. Thus, the expenditure on education in this example is a pure social waste! Even when we allow that education may improve productivity directly or that signaling may be valuable because it permits a better matching of workers to tasks, we will still typically find some excessive signaling—overinvestment in education—from a full information efficiency point of view. In fact, as we see in a problem at the end of the chapter, the high-productivity workers may even be worse off with the signaling than they would be if it could somehow be eliminated (although they are still better off signaling their private information than not doing so and being thought to be low productivity).

Signaling has been used extensively to explain a wide variety of phenomena. Examples include setting low "limit" prices as a signal of low costs to deter entry by potential competitors; the use of seemingly uninformative advertising with newly introduced "experience" goods (ones whose quality is not immediately evident prior to purchase) to signal their quality; the offering of product warranties and money-back guarantees as a signal of product quality; the paying of dividends by corporations to signal financial strength, even though dividends are tax-disadvantaged relative to share repurchases as a means of distributing money to stockholders; and the choice of the amount of debt versus common stock a firm issues as a signal of its financial prospects.

Screening

Screening refers to activities undertaken by the party without private information in order to separate different types of the informed party along some dimension. This is often done by offering a variety of alternatives, each intended for one of the various types of informed parties, whose choices then effectively reveal their private information. As we mentioned earlier, the self-selection constraints are crucial in achieving screening: People will choose the alternative intended for them only if it is the best for them in the set of alternatives offered, given what they know. An early application of the screening principle is the following one, which provides an explanation of the positive relationship that has often been noted between earnings and age or experience.

SCREENING AND AGE/WAGE PROFILES   It is empirically well established that pay tends to increase with age and experience. Many factors no doubt contribute to this. Some economic factors that have been suggested are: increasing skill and ability (human capital) with greater experience, greater responsibility being given to more senior employees who have demonstrated their abilities, and better matching of individual talents to job assignments as these talents become recognized. There is evidence, however, that even after accounting for these effects and controlling for them statistically, a positively-sloped age/wage profile remains: Given two workers with the same job assignment, the same responsibilities, and the same productivity, the older one will tend to be paid more. Why should this be so?

One possible answer is a general social preference or norm for paying older, more experienced workers more and younger ones less. The economic forces working against such a norm would be very strong, however. It would be in the interest of profit-maximizing firms to make attractive offers to bargain-priced young workers from firms with such a policy, and it would also be in the interest of these workers to accept.

An alternative, economic explanation due to Joanne Salop and Steven Salop is based on screening designed to reduce employee turnover. Having employees resign is costly for all firms, but it may be especially costly when, for example, the firm invests significant amounts in training workers. In such circumstances, the firm would have a special interest in attracting workers who are less inclined to change jobs. The difficulty lies in identifying those candidates with a proclivity for moving.

The screening solution is to design the employment contract so that only the desired types of workers are attracted. Suppose the firm offers to pay relatively low wages initially, with higher-than-market wages after the employee has been with the firm for an extended period of time. Such a positively-sloped experience-wage profile screens the population of potential employees because it is more attractive to workers who intend or expect to stay with the firm than to those who are less inclined to stay or who know that they will have to quit after only a short time in the job and who therefore see themselves as unlikely to collect the high wages that come with long-term employment. Note that if, in the early stages of their employment, workers in the firm are gaining experience or training that is valuable elsewhere, effective screening may require paying wages that are initially well below the going market level in order to offset the value of the training.

PERFORMANCE PAY AND SCREENING   As another example, suppose that the workers or managers who are likely to be most productive in a particular firm tend also to be those with the best outside job opportunities. Offering a performance-based pay system amounts to offering a *menu* of different contracts because it allows employees to determine their compensation by how hard they choose to work. Indeed, paying a wage that is based on measured performance tends to attract and retain the most productive job applicants and to discourage the least productive, to the employer's benefit.

Figure 5.2 illustrates the logic of this screening analysis. The workers' ability and likely contribution to the firm are measured on the horizontal axis, whereas their

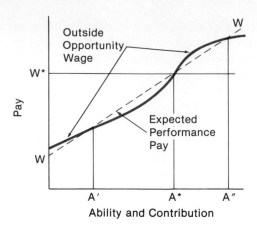

Figure 5.2: Compared to paying the fixed wage W^*, basing pay on performance attracts more productive workers to the firm and discourages less productive job applicants.

pay is shown on the vertical. The curved line shows the relationship between expected productivity on this job and any likely outside job opportunities. Our assumption that more productive workers tend to have better outside opportunities is represented by the fact that this curve is upward sloping.

If a fixed salary or wage of W^* is offered, workers of ability up to A^* will find it attractive to accept the firm's offer because that wage is more than they could earn in outside jobs. More productive workers (those with ability above A^*) would decline the firm's offer. Now suppose the firm were to introduce a performance pay system that is just sufficient to keep the wages of a worker of productivity A^* unchanged. This is shown by the upward-sloping straight line. Higher performance, measured along the horizontal axis, results in higher pay. Workers of lower productivity than A^* would be paid less, and some of them would now find it more attractive to accept jobs elsewhere. According to the figure, the workers with abilities below A' would no longer be attracted. In addition, workers with abilities in the range above A'' who were not previously attracted to the firm now will be. They now find employment in this firm attractive because they can expect to earn more under its performance pay system than in their outside job opportunities.

We will see in Chapters 6 and 7 that basing pay on measured output can also help resolve postcontractual moral hazard problems within the firm by providing incentives for workers to perform well, even when it is impossible to monitor how hard they are working. The monitoring problems make it futile to attempt to contract directly on the workers' providing a high level of effort. If their pay does not depend on their output, they then have little direct incentive to exert more than minimal amounts of effort. However, tying pay to productivity provides incentives to raise output. This effect reinforces the screening effect of differentially attracting people who are inherently more productive.

MENUS OF CONTRACTS AND EFFICIENCY   The logic of screening is also helpful for analyzing the decisions of a company that is setting prices for a whole line of related products, such as office copiers or computers. In this case, a menu of options is offered to customers, who must choose among the various products on the basis of features and price. The prices and features for each model must be chosen recognizing that they will affect the demand for other products in the line. For example, a low price on the most basic model will attract customers who would otherwise buy a more expensive model with more features. The mathematical expression of the problem is for the seller to set prices and target customer groups to maximize some objective, such as profits, subject to a set of self-selection constraints. These constraints express the requirement that prices and product features be set so that each group of customers prefers to buy the product targeted for that group rather than some other one.

Another application is in offering a menu of contracts to salespeople, where the amount of salary and the percentage commission on sales vary inversely across the menu. This has been done, for example, at IBM. The idea is that those salespeople who know that sales in their territories will be especially responsive to their efforts will select high-commission, low-salary contracts and be motivated to exert extra effort, whereas those whose private information indicates that increasing sales will be difficult will make the opposite choice. The latter group then will face less risk in their incomes and so will not have to be paid as much in expectation to compensate for bearing risk.

Similar considerations enter into the design of insurance contracts, where different policies are designed for different risk classes of buyers. In this context, self-selection is achieved by varying the extent of coverage offered. This may result in low-risk customers receiving less than full insurance coverage, whereas high-risk individuals purchase full coverage (but pay a higher amount per unit of insurance). The lack of full insurance for low-risk individuals is a cost of the informational asymmetry.

In general, achieving self-selection via screening will help overcome the informational asymmetry, but may be costly and will still leave opportunities for value creation unrealized because they are unattainable under the incentive constraints.

IMPLICATIONS

Bounded rationality and precontractual private information mean that contracts are incomplete and, at best, only constrained efficient. These represent major costs of market-like, arms'-length transactions.

In certain situations, some of these costs can be avoided by bringing the transaction under unified governance. We saw this in the hold-up problem: If a single firm owns both the cospecialized assets, the problem disappears. Similarly, the inefficiencies of bargaining between a firm and a supplier over provision of an input can be mitigated by the firm's integrating vertically to produce the input itself. There is no longer a need for contracting, there are no commitment problems with a single decision maker, and the private information that may have marked the negotiations between the supplier and the firm is not an issue any more. This solution can create other difficulties, however.

For example, if a firm chooses to make some input for itself in order to avoid the problems of bargaining with a supplier, the firm's owner may not have the time or the necessary expertise to supervise the input's production. The owner must then hire a manager. But with his or her limited time and expertise, the owner may not be able to tell if the manager is doing his or her job well. This opens the possibility of postcontractual opportunism, with the manager not working as hard as the owner would like or manipulating reports to his or her advantage. Chapter 6 deals with this phenomenon of *moral hazard*.

SUMMARY

Because real people are only *boundedly rational*, complete contracts that specify what they will do in every conceivable circumstance are impossible to negotiate and write. People's ability to make plans and contracts are limited by the existence of unforeseen circumstances, the costliness of deciding in advance what would be optimal to do in every foreseeable contingency, and the difficulty of writing down descriptions of contingencies and actions with enough precision to make writing such a contract worthwhile.

To respond to these difficulties, people write contracts that are quite different from those portrayed in ordinary market theory. They enter into *relational contracts* that specify procedures to govern how decisions will be made and disputes resolved and leave unspecified much of the substance of the relationship. Some of the contract terms are implicit and largely unenforceable in courts of law, representing understandings that exist and change with changing circumstances. These understandings are enforced by a reputation mechanism: Those who violate the understandings lose their ability to command the trust of others.

These responses, however, are only an imperfect substitute for complete contracts and do not prevent people from behaving opportunistically to seize a greater share of the fruits of the organization for themselves. Despite attempts at commitment, people sometimes renege on promises or renegotiate deals in a way that undermines the initial intent of the contract. Fear of suffering losses when a trading partner reneges may make otherwise profitable business deals sour or may cause firms to spend resources protecting themselves from opportunism by others—expenditures that are socially wasteful because they do not create value for society as a whole.

Problems of reneging are especially severe when large specific investments are required in the relationship. An *investment* is an expenditure of resources to create an *asset*, which is a potential future flow of benefits and services. The *specificity* of an asset is the fraction of the investment value that is lost when the asset is switched from its intended use to its next best use. Highly specific assets create the potential of a *hold-up problem*, in which one trading partner reneges on its contractual obligations to attempt to extract better terms from the owner of the specific asset, whose bargaining power is impaired by the losses he or she stands to suffer if forced to redeploy the asset to another use. The inability of one partner to commit not to hold up the other may prevent valuable investments from being made.

Within the firm, a reputation mechanism may help to overcome this problem. Employees are encouraged to invest in firm-specific assets, such as knowledge of the firm's objectives, routines and methods of operations, its products, customers, and organizational capabilities. The firm may protect these investments, treating employees well, in order to encourage investment by new workers and continuing investments by existing ones.

In addition to problems of bounded rationality and commitment, another source of inefficiency in contracting is private information at the time the contract is being negotiated. In the simple case of bargaining over the sale of a good, the seller may have an incentive to exaggerate the cost of producing the good in order to obtain a higher price and the buyer may have an incentive to understate the good's value, trying to obtain a lower price. These distortions may prevent the parties from reaching any agreement at all, even if the value-maximizing outcome would be for trade to occur.

When these distortions caused by incentives are unavoidable, we must recognize them in deciding which trading arrangements are most efficient. An arrangement or mechanism is *incentive efficient* if there is no other arrangement or mechanism that leads to a higher expected payoff for all parties, given the need to provide incentives to the parties to act in whatever fashion is planned.

The costs of providing incentives in bargaining can be significant even when there are only two bargainers, but they grow even larger when there are many. The problem is a *free-rider problem*: Any one bargainer may figure that a misrepresentation or refusal to contribute will have little effect on the final decision but will keep his or her costs of participation low. This effect grows with the number of bargainers and makes multiparty bargaining an especially difficult matter.

Another kind of cost that parties suffer during bargaining are *measurement costs*, which are the costs incurred to obtain an informational advantage. Institutions and practices can often be designed to minimize the opportunities for measurement or to curtail the advantages that it confers. For example, the unusual practices used by De Beers in the wholesale marketing of diamonds seem designed to reduce both the opportunity for and value of measuring the quality of diamonds.

Private information can also operate to block the efficient functioning of ordinary markets when the cost of providing services depends on privately known characteristics of the buyer or when the benefits of purchasing depend on similar characteristics of the seller. For example, the cost of providing pregnancy and maternity insurance benefits depend in part on the private plans of the purchaser regarding childbearing. The result is that the premium charged affects the selection of customers who buy, and this *adverse selection* affects the seller's costs. For example, a high-priced pregnancy and maternity plan would attract only buyers who planned a pregnancy soon, raising the insurer's average cost. In this case, the consequence of adverse selection is that there is no effective private market for individual pregnancy and maternity coverage. Similarly, in banking, raising the interest rate charged to borrowers may only lead to a poorer quality of loan applicants. Banks may instead respond by rationing credit, seeking to raise the average quality of the loans they make.

Besides rationing, the other responses in markets to selection problems include *screening* and *signaling*. Signaling is the attempt by certain individuals to communicate their private information in a credible way. For example, talented workers may acquire education as much for the value of the credential as for its direct contribution to their productivity. Screening is the design of products or contracts to attract only a desirable portion of potential customers, workers, and so on, or the design of menus of contracts to sort these parties into distinct groups. For example, offering some jobs with incentive pay schemes and others with fixed wages may tend to sort the workers. With each group of workers seeking the job with the highest likely pay, the most productive workers will tend to select the incentive pay jobs while the others opt for fixed wages.

◼ BIBLIOGRAPHIC NOTES

Nobel Laureate Herbert Simon has been the major proponent of recognizing the implications of bounded rationality for economic behavior. In particular, the explanation of the employment relation as a response to bounded rationality is due to Simon. Oliver Williamson has built extensively on Simon's insights. Victor Goldberg and Williamson have, in particular, emphasized relational contracting, as and this concept has also received significant attention from legal scholars. The survey by Oliver Hart and Bengt Holmstrom contains a valuable discussion of the implications of incomplete contracting. Williamson and Benjamin Klein, Robert Crawford, and Armen Alchian were the first scholars to emphasize and elaborate the great importance of the hold-up problem for the analysis of business institutions and practices. The importance of the general issue of commitment and renegotiation, both in contracting and in other institutions, has been repeatedly emphasized by Jean Tirole.

The importance of precontractual informational asymmetries has been one of the major themes of economic research for the last two decades. Early important contributions came from George Akerlof (the "lemons" problem with adverse selection), Michael Spence (signaling), Michael Rothschild and Joseph Stiglitz (adverse selection and screening in insurance markets), and Stiglitz and Andrew Weiss (rationing as a response to adverse selection in credit markets). The revelation principle was developed independently in various articles by a number of scholars, including Allan Gibbard, Roger Myerson, Milton Harris and Arthur Raviv, and Robert Rosenthal. Myerson and Mark Satterthwaite characterized the effects of incentive constraints with private information on the possibility of achieving value-maximizing trade. The effect of increasing the number of participants was developed by Rafael Rob, George Mailath and Andrew Postlewaite, and V.V. Chari and Larry Jones building on earlier work by Roberts.

The first complete signaling analysis of entry deterrence is due to Milgrom and Roberts. Building on ideas of Philip Nelson, we also developed the model of prices and uninformative advertising as signals of product quality. Sanford Grossman developed the analysis of warranties as signals of quality. The first model of dividends as a signal is due to Sudipto Bhattacharya. George Baker, Michael Jensen, and Kevin Murphy give an exposition of the use of performance pay as a screening device. Joanne Salop and Steven Salop developed the screening model of the age/wage profile. An exposition of pricing under self-selection constraints is given by Robert Wilson.

■ REFERENCES

Akerlof, G. "The Market for Lemons: Qualitative Uncertainty and the Market Mechanism," *Quarterly Journal of Economics*, 84 (1970), 488–500.

Baker, G., M. Jensen, and K. Murphy. "Competition and Incentives: Practice vs. Theory," *Journal of Finance*, 43 (1988), 593–616.

Bhattacharya, S. "Imperfect Information, Dividend Policy, and 'The Bird in the Hand' Fallacy," *Bell Journal of Economics*, 10 (*Spring 1979*), 259–70.

Chari, V. V., and L. Jones. "A Reconsideration of the Problem of Social Cost: Free Riders and Monopolists," Discussion Paper, Northwestern University, 1991.

Gibbard, A. "Manipulation of Voting Schemes: A General Result," *Econometrica*, 41 (1973), 587–602.

Goldberg, V. "Relational Exchange: Economics and Complex Contracts," *American Behavioral Scientist*, 23 (January/February 1980), 337–52.

Grossman, S. "The Informational Role of Warranties and Private Disclosure About Product Quality," *Journal of Law and Economics*, 24 (1981), 461–83.

Harris, M. and A. Raviv. "Allocation Mechanisms and the Design of Auctions," *Econometrica*, 49 (1981), pp. 1477–99.

Hart, O., and B. Holmstrom. "The Theory of Contracts," *Advances in Economic Theory: Fifth World Congress*, T. Bewley, ed. (Cambridge: Cambridge University Press, 1987).

Klein, B., R. Crawford, and A. Alchian. "Vertical Integration, Appropriable Rents, and the Competitive Contracting Process," *Journal of Law and Economics*, 21 (1978), 297–326.

Mailath, G. and A. Postlewaite. "Asymmetric Bargaining Problems with Many Agents," *Review of Economic Studies*, 57 (1990), 351–67.

Milgrom, P. and J. Roberts. "Limit Pricing and Entry Under Incomplete Information: An Equilibrium Analysis," *Econometrica*, 50, (1982), 443–59.

Myerson, R.B. "Mechanism Design by an Informed Principal," *Econometrica*, 51 (1983), 1767–97.

Myerson, R.B., and M. Satterthwaite. "Efficient Mechanisms for Bilateral Trading," *Journal of Economic Theory*, 23 (1983), 265–81.

Nelson, P. "Advertising as Information," *Journal of Political Economy*, 84 (1974), 729–54.

Rob, R. "Pollution Claim Settlements Under Private Information," *Journal of Economic Theory*, 47 (1989), 307–33.

Roberts, J. "The Incentives for Correct Revelation of Preferences and the Number of Consumers," *Journal of Public Economics*, 6 (1976), 359–74.

Rosenthal, R.W. "Arbitration of Two-Party Disputes Under Uncertainty," *Review of Economic Studies*, 45 (1978), 595–604.

Rothschild, M. and J. Stiglitz. "Equilibrium in Competitive Insurance Markets: An Essay on the Economics of Imperfect Information," *Quarterly Journal of Economics*, 80 (November 1976), 629–49.

Salop, J. and S. Salop. "Self-Selection and Turnover in the Labor Market," *Quarterly Journal of Economics*, 90 (November 1976), 619–28.

Simon, H.A. "A Formal Theory of the Employment Relationship," *Econometrica*, 19 (1951), 293–305.

Spence, A.M. *Market Signalling: Information Transfer in Hiring and Related Processes* (Cambridge, MA: Harvard University Press, 1973).

Stiglitz, J.E. and A. Weiss. "Credit Rationing in Markets with Imperfect Information," *American Economic Review*, 71 (1981), 393–409.

Tirole, J. *The Theory of Industrial Organization* (Cambridge, MA: The MIT Press, 1988).

Williamson, O. *Markets and Hierarchies: Analysis and Antitrust Implications* (New York: The Free Press, 1975).

Williamson, O. *The Economic Institutions of Capitalism* (New York: The Free Press, 1985).

Wilson, R. *Nonlinear Pricing* (Oxford University Press, 1992).

EXERCISES

Food for Thought

1.   We are all familiar with the experience of feeling anger when we have been cheated or otherwise mistreated, and many of us have gone out of our ways to exact retribution for such injustices, even when we expect never to see the malefactor again and we do not expect anyone else to be aware of our punishing the transgression. Apparently, we have a taste for vengeance. Most of us also seem to have a conscience, a preference for behaving honestly and fairly. Indeed, Robert Frank [*Passions Within Reason: The Role of the Emotions* (New York: W.W. Norton, 1988)] has suggested that early humans who had such preferences would have had an evolutionary advantage, so that such preferences should have become widespread as people who

were biologically "hard-wired" with these traits were more successful in competing to reproduce. What effect would the possibility that people might have such preferences have on the analyses in this chapter of commitment and bargaining?

2.   In common parlance, we often speak of "signaling intentions." For example, a firm might cut prices to signal its intent to compete fiercely to defend a market against a competitor's expansion. The idea is to deter the competitor, who would not want to challenge the first firm if it will react aggressively. The difficulty is that if the competitor does sink costs in expanding, the first firm may not find it worthwhile to fight. There is thus an issue of credibility of the signal. This problem arises whenever the signaler still has an option after the fact about what actions it will take. What means are available to give credibility to signals of intent?

3.   One of the most rapidly growing health concerns of much of the developed world is the spread of Acquired Immune Deficiency Syndrome (AIDS), with the number of reported victims growing annually at alarming rates. One of the few effective drugs to alleviate the symptoms of AIDS is AZT. Although this drug is inexpensive to produce, it is sold for a high price, earning large profits for its manufacturer at the expense of the already suffering AIDS victims. As a result, there has been a public outcry to void the patent on AZT and to allow it to be produced competitively, at lower cost. What damage might such an action cause? What protections exist for an inventor that might keep a government from seizing intellectual property? Are there any practical alternatives available to deal with the very real medical-social problem that avoid the damage you have identified?

Analytical Problems

1.   In the model of an insurance market with adverse selection, suppose that the parameters entail $c\bar{x} < v < \bar{x}(1 + c)/2$. Show graphically that there is a price at which the insurer breaks even and some people are willing to purchase insurance. What is the formula for that price?

2.   Suppose that, in the context of the example in the text of the Spence model of education as a signal, the high-ability workers are relatively more numerous, making up 80 percent of the work force, but that the costs of acquiring education and the productivities are as in the text (that is, is $C_H = \$10$ and $C_L = \$20$, while wages are $50 for the high-ability workers and $20 for the low). Determine how large E_H, the level of education chosen by the high-ability workers, must be to be a credible signal if the level chosen by the low-ability workers is 0. Show that the high-ability workers would be better off if there were no signaling (for example, if C_H were to rise to $20).

3.   The units of two neighbors in a condominium housing development, Able and Baker, overlook a small courtyard. The board of the condominium association is considering whether to plant a tree in the courtyard. The cost is $40. Everyone agrees that Able values having the tree either at $100 or at $0. The probability that the tree is worth $100 to Able is p, a number between zero and one. Similarly, Baker values the tree at either $70 (which occurs with probability r) or $0. Able and Baker are the only people who will be able to see and enjoy the tree. The board decides to ask each of them how much having the tree planted is worth to him or her personally. If both say that they value the tree then the board will have it planted and the cost shared equally between the two neighbors. If only one of them expresses a desire to have the tree planted, then it is still planted but that person is charged the whole cost. If neither claims the tree is desirable, it is not planted.

Derive the incentive compatibility constraints for each individual, and solve for the values of p and r that make it incentive compatible to offer to help pay for the tree exactly when it is actually valuable to the individual concerned. Now let q_A be the probability that the tree is planted when only Able offers to pay, and q_B be the probability that it is planted when only Baker offers to pay. If $p = 0.7$ and $r = 0.8$, what are the largest values of q_A and q_B consistent with correct revelation of willingness to pay?

4.   A used-car salesperson and a potential buyer negotiate over the price of an old car. The seller believes that the buyer values the car at $500 with probability x and at $1,000 with probability $(1-x)$. The buyer believes that the car is worth $250 to the salesperson with probability $(1-x)$ and $750 with probability x. Under what circumstances should trade occur? How does the probability of efficient trade depend on the value of x? If a mediator specifies that trade should occur at a price of p when the seller claims a value of $250 and the buyer claims a value of $1,000, derive two conditions on p that ensure that both parties will report honestly. Solve for the value of x that makes both incentive constraints exactly hold as equalities. Note that for lower values of x, trade is more likely to be efficient but it cannot always be attained. Explain why.

5.   A seller values a good at either $0 or $10. The buyer does not know what the good is worth, but knows that he values the good at $10 more than the seller does. Thus, it is certainly efficient for trade to occur, no matter what the seller's actual valuation of the good. Show that it is compatible with individual incentives for trade always to occur at a price of $10, no matter what value the seller announces. Suppose now instead that the good is worth only $5 more to the buyer than the seller. Is it possible to find prices (as functions of the seller's claimed value) so that the seller will honestly report her true value and both sides wil be willing to trade at these prices? Why or why not?

6.   Suppose X is an intermediate good in the production of a final good Y. Firm A has a patent on good X, which it produces at zero marginal cost. Firm B is considering buying a machine which it can use to turn up to 10,000 units of X into Y on a one-for-one basis. The machine costs $30,000, once purchased it cannot be resold, and it wears out completely once 10,000 units of Y are produced. Firm B can sell good Y for $5 per unit. Firm A offers to supply good X to firm B at $1 per unit once B has bought the machine.

Suppose A and B can write a binding contract setting the delivery price of good X. Will B buy the machine? What profits are earned by each firm? Suppose instead no such contract is possible. Is A's promise credible? Will B invest in the machine? What are the resulting profits?

Now suppose that A can enter into a licensing agreement with another firm, C, under which C can produce good X, incurring a marginal cost of $c per unit. Suppose that A gives C the license, and that the cost, c, is $1.01. Is A's price promise to supply B at a price of $1 now credible? Does A gain from giving away its technology? Explain why or why not. Suppose the cost c were higher than $1.01, but less than $2. What would you expect to happen now? What if c were less than $1?

6

MORAL HAZARD
AND PERFORMANCE INCENTIVES

I ncentives are the essence of economics.

Edward P. Lazear[1]

The problem with corruption is that it tends to become the Problem of Corruption. Moral issues usually obscure practical issues, even when the moral question is a relatively small one and the practical matter is very great.

James Q. Wilson[2]

Suppose that you are traveling along a highway when a dashboard light comes on indicating that your car is overheating. There is a service station nearby, so you drive your car there. The traditional analysis of this market situation is simple: There is some price to be paid to repair the problem; either you pay it and the car is fixed, or you decide to take your chances and decline to get the car serviced.

That account *might* reflect what would happen, but there are other possibilities. After beginning to work on the car, the mechanic might say, "Your radiator is shot. A new one will cost $500." If you are like most drivers, you have no idea whether the mechanic is being truthful or not. After all, it may be in the mechanic's interest

---

[1] "Incentive Contracts," in *The New Palgrave: A Dictionary of Economics*; Vol. 2 J. Eatwell, M. Milgate and P. Newman, eds. (London: The Macmillan Press, 1987), 744–48.

[2] "Corruption Is Not Always Scandalous," in *Theft of the City: Readings on Corruption in America*, J. A. Gardiner and D. J. Olsen, eds. (Bloomington: Indiana University Press, 1968), p. 29. Copyright © 1968 by the New York Times Company. Reprinted by permission.

to sell you a radiator, especially at that price. You face the same problem that decision makers in organizations frequently face: *When those with critical information have interests different from those of the decision maker, they may fail to report completely and accurately the information needed to make good decisions.* If the mechanic is lying to you, then both your interests and society's interest in efficiency are harmed. Your interests are harmed because the mechanic is profiting at your expense, and society's interests are harmed because productive resources have been wasted: A radiator that could have been repaired has instead been discarded.

Suppose that you agree to buy the radiator, wait an hour while it is installed, and then proceed down the highway another 100 miles toward your destination. You notice the overheating indicator on your dashboard lighting up again. Pulling into another service station, you learn that the new radiator was not installed correctly and it will cost you another $35 and another hour of waiting to have the job done right. *When buyers cannot easily monitor the quality of the goods or services that they receive, there is a tendency for some suppliers to substitute poor quality goods or to exercise too little effort, care, or diligence in providing the services.* Once again, both you and society are harmed. You, because you paid and waited twice for the same service, and society, because resources were wasted: It took two hours of mechanic time (and waiting time) to do a job that could have been done in one.

THE CONCEPT OF MORAL HAZARD

These problems with the sale and installation of your radiator are examples of **moral hazard**, which is the form of postcontractual opportunism that arises because actions that have efficiency consequences are not freely observable and so the person taking them may choose to pursue his or her private interests at others' expense. The possibility of this sort of misbehavior is ruled out in the neoclassical model of markets considered in Chapter 3, where it was (somewhat implicitly) assumed that the transactions that people undertake are simple exchanges of goods and services with specific, well-understood, observable attributes, and that parties to a transaction can costlessly verify whether the terms of the transaction are being met.

Insurance and Misbehavior

The term *moral hazard* originated in the insurance industry, where it referred to the tendency of people with insurance to change their behavior in a way that leads to larger claims against the insurance company. For example, being insured may make people lax about taking precautions to avoid or minimize losses. If the necessary precautions were known in advance and could be accurately measured and recorded, then an insurance contract could specify which precautions must be taken. However, frequently it is not possible to observe and verify the relevant behavior and thus it is not possible to write *enforceable* contracts that specify the behavior to be adopted. (The contract could call for the desired behavior, but how could the insurance company tell if the contract terms had been met?)

The kinds of moral hazard associated with insurance arise frequently in daily life. For example, you are likely to be much more careful in driving a rented car if you are financially responsible for all damage to the car than if you have purchased the Collision Damage Waiver and so are insured against the costs of dents and scrapes. Similarly, if you are covered under health insurance or belong to a Health Maintenance Organization (HMO), so that you are insured against all or most of the costs of visits to the doctor, you are likely to make greater use of medical services of all kinds: doctor visits, emergency room visits, prescription drugs, prenatal care, and so on. In each case, the fact that you are insured alters your behavior in ways that are costly to the insurer.

Efficiency Effects of Moral Hazard

Although the term *moral hazard* has negative connotations, not all of the changes in behavior occasioned by insurance are socially undesirable, because some social interests may not be represented in the bargain between the insurer and the insured. For example, increased prenatal visits may result in healthier mothers and babies, consistent with society's goals. Moreover, the insurance company may not suffer any losses from moral hazard if it sets the insurance premium high enough to cover the extra costs. Still, moral hazard does impair people's ability to make mutually beneficial agreements and does often interfere with efficiency.

Moral hazard in insurance presents an efficiency problem because the extra benefits enjoyed by the insured on account of his or her changed behavior will often not be worth the costs. This happens because the insured decision maker does not look at all the costs and benefits associated with his or her decisions. Moreover, the inherent nature of insurance makes this inevitable. In the car rental example, you bear the full costs of the care you exert, but if you are fully insured, then being careful brings you no extra benefits. In the health care example, you get the benefits of the extra treatment you seek when insured, but bear little or none of the costs. Thus, you will tend to go to the doctor for minor ailments whose treatment seems worth your time, even if the total costs may exceed the benefits you receive.

The incentives to alter behavior would still not be a problem if it were easy to determine when the behavior were appropriate and to prevent excessive use. This sort of monitoring is often impossible, however, or at least very costly. There is no cost-effective way for the car rental company to observe the care you take. In the medical context, you will often lack the expertise to judge whether a particular visit is necessary, and it will not generally be in the doctor's interest to report that you have made an unnecessary visit. For this reason, moral hazard is an information problem: The difficulty or cost of monitoring and enforcing appropriate behavior creates the moral hazard problem. These difficulties mean that contracting is incomplete because there is no point to writing a contract specifying particular behavior when the desired actions cannot be observed and consequently the contract cannot be effectively enforced.

In terms of standard economics, the insurance has lowered the cost to you of something you value (doctor visits, not bothering to exert great care), and you thus "buy" more. More particularly, you now pay less than the full costs of extra units and so you purchase an inefficiently large amount. Putting the issue in these terms suggests that the behavior is not especially wicked and that the negative implications in labeling it "moral hazard" may be somewhat misplaced. More significantly, it suggests that this sort of behavior—and the efficiency losses it induces—might be quite widespread. Such is indeed the case.

The Incidence of Moral Hazard

Moral hazard problems may arise in any situation in which someone (who may be a supplier, a customer, an employee, or anyone else) is tempted to take an inefficient action or to provide distorted information (leading others to take inefficient actions) because the individual's interests are not aligned with the group interest and because the report cannot easily be checked or the action accurately monitored. These problems are pervasive both in markets and in other forms of organization. Some doctors in the United States, for example, in an attempt to protect themselves from malpractice

Hidden Actions or Hidden Information?

Although moral hazard and adverse selection usually seem quite distinct in textbook discussions, in practice it may be quite difficult to determine which is at work.

A radio story in the summer of 1990 reported a study on the makes and models of cars that were observed going through intersections in the Washington, D.C. area without stopping at the stop signs. According to the story, Volvos were heavily overrepresented: The fraction of cars running stop signs that were Volvos was much greater than the fraction of Volvos in the total population of cars in the D.C. area. This is initially surprising because Volvo has built a reputation as an especially safe car that appeals to sensible, safety-conscious drivers. Volvos are largely bought by middle-class couples with children. How then is this observation explained?

One possibility is that people driving Volvos feel particularly safe in this sturdy, heavily built, crash-tested car. Thus they are willing to take risks that they would not take in another, less safe car. Driving a Volvo leads to a propensity to run stop signs. This is essentially a moral hazard explanation: The car is a form of insurance, and having the insurance alters behavior in ways that are privately rational but socially undesirable.

A second possibility is that the people who buy Volvos know that they are bad drivers who are apt, for example, to be paying more attention to their children in the back seat than to stop signs. The safety that a Volvo promises is especially attractive to people who have this private information about their driving, and so they disproportionately buy this safe car. A propensity for running stop signs leads to driving a Volvo. This is, of course, essentially a self-selection story: the Volvo buyers are privately informed about their driving habits and abilities. Unless this selection imposes costs on Volvo, however, it is not adverse selection

Both stories are at least plausible. How would you go about testing which, if either, is correct? What other explanations seem plausible?

---

suits, practice "conservative medicine," ordering tests and procedures that may not be in the patient's best interests and, in any case, are surely not worth the costs (which are borne by the patient or the insurer—not by the doctor making the decision). Some firms may find it most profitable to make shoddy or unsafe products when quality is not easily observed. Security brokers may "churn" their clients' portfolios, encouraging them to trade more frequently than they really should because each additional trade generates commissions for the brokers. Automobile dealers may fail to mention the poor resale values or the higher than average repair costs of the cars they sell. Rented apartments may be less well maintained than owner-occupied ones because the renters do not get the full benefits of their efforts at maintenance. All of these examples are drawn from ordinary market experience.

Within organizations, an office employee may spend time during the day studying for an accounting exam, thinking about a new business idea that he or she hopes to pursue, or chatting on the telephone with friends when there is work waiting to be done. Factory workers may call in sick during hunting or fishing season, and when on the job they may exert the least care and effort they can get away with. Managerial employees may exaggerate the difficulty of their assignments in order to make their performance appear more impressive, or they may denigrate others' performance in order to improve their own chances of getting a particularly desirable assignment or promotion. Division executives may adopt policies that lead to high current performance that will be rewarded by bonuses and promotions, even though these policies will ultimately destroy the long-term profitability of the divisions they will have left behind. Senior executives may pursue their own goals of status, high salaries, expensive "perks," and job security rather than the stockholders' interests, and so they may push sales growth over profits, treat themselves to huge staffs and corporate jets, and oppose takeovers that would lead to their dismissal but would increase the value of the firm.

These examples do not involve insurance explicitly, but they have the crucial feature of insurance: The decision makers do not bear the full impact of their decisions. The doctor who orders extra tests benefits in terms of the reduced likelihood of successful malpractice suits but does not pay for the costs of the tests or suffer the discomfort they cause. The employees get paid whether they work hard or not, or at least they do not suffer a decrease in pay equal to the full lost value of what they could have produced. The difficulties of monitoring are what prevents them from bearing the full costs and benefits: The stockbroker's client does not have the expertise to tell if a trade is good for him or her or just for the broker; the employee's supervisor cannot freely determine whether he or she is thinking about company business or personal matters; and the stockholders cannot easily evaluate whether a particular executive action is in their interests or not.

THE PRINCIPAL-AGENT RELATIONSHIP   Each of these examples can be cast in terms of an *agency* relationship. This term has come to be used in economics to refer to situations in which one individual (the **agent**) acts on behalf of another (the **principal**) and is supposed to advance the principal's goals. The moral hazard problem arises when agent and principal have differing individual objectives and the principal cannot easily determine whether the agent's reports and actions are being taken in pursuit of the principal's goals or are self-interested misbehavior. Agency relations in this sense are pervasive: The doctor is the agent of the patient, the worker is the agent of the firm, the CEO is the agent of the owners, and so on. As we will see later, however, moral hazard problems also arise in relationships where neither party can be considered the agent of the other but rather each is on an equal footing (as in a partnership).

CASE STUDY: THE U.S. SAVINGS AND LOAN CRISIS

The key factors giving rise to moral hazard problems—divergent interests, decision makers being insured against some of the consequences of their actions, and monitoring and enforcement being imperfect—all feature centrally in one of the most spectacular moral hazard problems of recent times, the United States "savings and loan crisis."

The Savings and Loan Industry

Savings and loan associations (S&Ls) are for-profit financial institutions that borrow money from the public in the form of deposits and then invest it by lending it out again, much like banks. The deposits of individual depositors in an S&L are insured by a U.S. federal government agency—until 1990, the Federal Savings and Loan Insurance Corporation (FSLIC). If, for some reason, the S&L could not repay the deposits, the FSLIC would. Government-provided insurance for bank deposits was instituted in the United States in the 1930s to protect depositors against bank failures. This insurance was also intended to reduce the likelihood of bank failures by eliminating "bank runs," which arise when depositors become fearful that their deposits may not be repaid, rush to withdraw their funds, and thereby bring on the failure they feared. The S&Ls, as well as the not-for-profit credit unions, were also provided with deposit insurance. The funds to pay for claims against the FSLIC came from charges levied on the insured S&Ls. The size of these premia were not linked to the riskiness of the S&Ls' portfolio of loans and other investments.

THE CRISIS IN THE 1980s   Traditionally, the S&Ls were strictly limited in how they could invest their funds, with their primary investments being residential mortgage loans to local individuals secured by the homes they owned. During the 1980s many S&Ls turned to riskier investments, including loans on commercial real estate and high-yielding but very risky corporate borrowing called "junk bonds." As the commercial real estate market collapsed in several parts of the country, borrowers ceased payments on many of their loans, and the S&Ls were left holding property they could not rent or sell. Later, defaults by some corporations on their junk bonds undercut the value of all high-risk debt, further reducing the S&Ls' assets. As well, a plague of fraud spread through the industry. This proved a devastating combination: Over 500 savings and loans slipped into bankruptcy. The FSLIC's reserves were inadequate to cover its promises to protect depositors, and U.S. taxpayers are now having to foot the bill, which is measured in the hundreds of *billions* of dollars! What led the S&Ls to make such risky investments? What led to the increase in fraud? Could it all have been prevented? Who is to blame?

THE CAUSE: MORAL HAZARD   The very design of the deposit insurance program, together with lax regulation, led to a costly problem of moral hazard in the management of the savings and loans. In brief, deposit insurance and low capital requirements (the amount of the S&L owners' own money at risk) encouraged excessive risk taking by relieving the S&Ls of the responsibility for poorly performing investments while allowing them to gain when the investments prospered. The insurance also relieved the depositors of the usual responsibility of investors to keep tabs on those who hold their money. This encouraged both risk taking and fraud. Insurance could be economically provided only so long as other regulatory policies were able to prevent the S&L managers from making reckless investments and engaging in self-dealing. In the early 1980s, however, the regulations controlling the sort of investments the S&Ls could make were relaxed. At the same time, the amount of insurance afforded to each depositor was increased and the resources devoted to enforcing the relaxed regulations were reduced. The whole system inevitably broke down.

Deposit Insurance and Risk Taking: An Example

The S&Ls made risky investments in part because the government insurance scheme made those investments profitable for the owners of the S&Ls. To see how insurance creates these incentives, let us study an example. To make the calculations simple, we set the interest rate paid to depositors at zero. The principles we deduce from this example apply to any other interest rate as well.

Suppose the owner of the S&L has full authority over how to invest the deposits. The owner can choose between two possible investments, labeled "safe" and "risky." Actually, both investments in our example have some uncertainty about their returns but, as Table 6.1 shows, the safe investment has less variation in its returns and can never actually lose money.

The safe investment requires an initial outlay of $100 and returns either $100 or $110, each with a 50 percent probability. We call it "safe" because it always returns at least the initial outlay of $100. On average, it does even better, returning the initial outlay plus $5 more.

The risky investment is a lemon. There is a 50 percent chance that it will return only $65, far less than the initial outlay of $100. On average, it loses $5. This is a

Table 6.1 Description of Investment Opportunities

	Safe	Risky
Initial outlay	100	100
High return	110	125
. . . probability	.50	.50
Low return	100	65
. . . probability	.50	.50
Expected return (gross)	105	95
Expected return (net)	5	−5

bad investment that, in a well-functioning system, would not be undertaken because it wastes social resources. As we shall see, however, the way the S&L is financed and insured can create differences of interests between the various parties whose resources are at stake, and lead the managers to undertake the risky investment.

The funds an S&L has for lending and investing come from two main sources: deposits and the capital supplied by owners. United States federal regulations in the 1980s required the owners of an S&L to provide capital equal to about 3 percent of the total value it invests. For our example, we suppose that of the initial outlay of $100 required for the investment, $97 comes from the depositors (insured by the FSLIC) and $3 comes from the owners of the S&L. The depositors have first priority on any proceeds from the investment. This means that if the proceeds from the investment are more than $97, the depositors must be paid in full. If they are less than $97, the depositors get whatever money is available, the owners get nothing, and the FSLIC pays the difference between the available funds and depositors' $97 claim.

SHARING THE RISKS   Now let us examine the distribution of the costs and benefits if the safe investment is made. The term *gross return* refers to all the income received from the investment, without regard to the initial outlay. In Table 6.2, the gross return earned by the owners is $13 if the investment works out well and $3 if it works out badly. *Net return* refers to the gross return minus the initial outlay. Because the owners have an initial outlay of $3, their net returns are either $10 or $0. In expectation, they get $5. In any event, the depositors just get their money back, netting zero (the interest they were promised), and the FSLIC neither receives nor disburses any funds.

When the safe investment is made, the FSLIC is never needed to "bail out" the S&L, that is, to help it meet its obligations. The situation is quite different when the risky investment is made, however. Table 6.3 shows how the returns on the risky investment might appear to the various parties.

Table 6.2 Analysis of the Safe Investment

	Depositors	Owners	FSLIC	Total
Initial outlay	97	3	0	100
High return (gross)	97	13	0	110
Low return (gross)	97	3	0	100
Expected return (gross)	97	8	0	105
Expected return (net)	0	5	0	5

Table 6.3 Analysis of the Risky Investment

	Depositors	Owners	FSLIC	Total
Initial outlay	97	3	0	100
High return (gross)	97	28	0	125
Low return (gross)	97	0	−32	65
Expected return (gross)	97	14	−16	95
Expected return (net)	0	11	−16	−5

The final column of Table 6.3 repeats the description of the risky investment already given in Table 6.1. The first three columns show how the initial outlay and returns are divided among the three parties. Notice that when returns are high, the owners of the S&L enjoy exceptionally high profits. In contrast, when returns are low and there is not enough money to pay the depositors' claims, the FSLIC bears exceptional costs to pay off the depositors. All the owners of the S&L lose is their $3, with the FSLIC absorbing the rest of the loss. The S&L owners benefit from risk taking, whereas the FSLIC suffers from it.

THE WINNERS AND LOSERS   The bottom line of Table 6.3 further clarifies the matter. Although this investment is a lemon overall, with an expected net return of −$5, it generates an expected net return of $11 to the owners. This is far more than the $5 the owners could expect to get from the socially preferable, safe investment. The FSLIC, which bears the losses when the investment returns are too low to cover deposits, now suffers an expected loss of $16, the difference between the owners' expected returns and the total returns on the investment. The depositors, who are insured, always get all of their money back.

According to the bottom line of Table 6.3, the expected net returns of all the parties add up to the total expected net returns of the investment. Because the depositors always get zero, each dollar of expected loss imposed on the FSLIC shows up as another dollar of expected profit for the owners! In choosing among investments with equal expected returns, the owners will prefer the riskier ones because they expect to profit most when the FSLIC's expected losses are largest.

Incentives for Risk Taking with Borrowed Funds

The financial motivation for the S&L owners to make risky investments is now clear: The riskier the investment, the higher the expected losses for the FSLIC and the greater the expected profits for the S&L. Still, our story of how the government botched its regulation of the S&Ls is incomplete. The problem is that the owners would have the same motivation to make risky investments even if the FSLIC were taken out of the picture! With the FSLIC gone, the losses would fall on the depositors instead of the government agency. Still, the owners would be the ones to benefit from the risky investment if things go well, and someone else would be left to bear the losses. Thus it might appear that if the government eliminated deposit insurance, the only thing to change would be that risks are shifted from the government agency to the depositors. *So long as investments are financed by borrowing, the borrowers will always have an incentive to undertake riskier investments than the lenders would want.* Of course, the whole point of a savings and loan institution is that depositors leave their money there for the S&L to invest; an S&L always is a borrower from its depositors, so the problem always exists. It may seem, therefore, that we have unfairly identified the FSLIC as being the root of the problem.

The Case of Seapointe Savings and Loan

Seapointe Savings and Loan was founded in 1985 in Carlsbad, California, a suburb of San Diego. Like other S&Ls, Seapointe's primary business was to make home mortgage loans. According to its business plan: "At no time will management presume to outguess the marketplace nor risk the net worth of the institution in an attempt to 'make a killing' for the sake of short-term earnings."

When Seapointe failed in 1986, however, it had never even hired a loan officer. Instead, it had sold "naked call options." That is, it had sold a promise to deliver $10 billion of bonds that it did not own, at the buyer's option, at a given future date. Selling call options is a common practice, but selling them without actually owning the bonds makes the options "naked"; it exposed Seapointe to the risk of an actual cash loss if bond prices were to rise. And rise they did, so that Seapointe was forced to pay the difference between what the bonds cost at the delivery date and the price it had promised. Seapointe lost $24 million on this one transaction—75 percent of its assets—leaving the FSLIC responsible to repay the institution's depositors. If Seapointe had won its bet and bond prices had fallen, the buyer would not have exercised its option to demand delivery of the bonds at the promised price, and Seapointe would have kept the amount it was paid for its promise. Seapointe would have 'made a killing' for its owners.

Source: Charlotte-Ann Lucas, "How an S&L Gambled Off Its Deposits Within a Year," *San Francisco Examiner* (December 2, 1990), A-1.

MONITORING BORROWERS   To gain a deeper understanding of the issues, we must look beyond the S&L industry to find related business problems. The problem of depositors who are, in effect, lenders to the S&L is by no means unique in business. Lenders exist throughout the business world. However, they take precautions to ensure that their money is not squandered, stolen, or put at unnecessary risk by those who have borrowed it. A bank that lends you money will ask you about your financial condition and about what you intend to do with the loan proceeds. It will run a credit check, demand collateral, and often require regular payments of the interest and part of the principal. If yours is a home loan, it will demand a legal interest in the property, and if it is a car loan, the bank will keep title to the car until the loan is repaid. Those who lend to firms frequently impose similar conditions. They examine the firm's financial condition and credit history, put restrictions on how their funds may be used, and often require business plans, collateral, and periodic financial statements. Correspondingly, careful scrutiny by depositors is the mechanism by which an unregulated and uninsured S&L might be kept from making irresponsible investments or defrauding its investors.

Why, then, did S&L depositors not take the same precautions as other lenders? Because doing so was costly and, anyway, the deposits were insured! The insurance itself made the depositors willing to supply huge sums to S&Ls without the usual checking of creditworthiness or monitoring of performance that accompanies other large loans. For the FSLIC to protect itself against huge losses, it thus needed to regulate the S&Ls, monitoring their activities, restricting their investments, and ensuring that they maintained adequate capital both to guard against unlucky investment outcomes and to ensure that the owners would suffer a significant loss if the organization should fail. The government failed to do this through the 1980s and suffered from the resulting moral hazard problem.

The Perverse Effect of Competition

The moral hazard problem in the S&L industry was actually intensified by the effects of competition. Normally we think of competition, which tends to drive out those executives who are unwilling to take the profit-maximizing actions, as promoting efficiency. In the context of the S&L industry in the 1980s, however, competition had a perverse effect. Many conservative S&L executives had no choice but to gamble on risky investments if they were to survive in the circumstances we have described.

Think about how the system works. The problems may have all begun with a few S&Ls that directly saw the chance to exploit the deposit insurance system by moving into more risky investments. To do so, they needed to expand their deposit base. The only quick and sure way to attract substantial new deposits is to offer higher interest rates to depositors. Thus, S&Ls seeking an influx of money to expand investments offered higher interest rates than did their competitors. The government's increasing the amount that was insured (from $40,000 per account to $100,000) made these higher rates very effective, as large investors—including many firms—deposited their money in the aggressive S&Ls.

Now, the other S&Ls began to feel the heat. Deposits were being drawn out of their doors and given to their competitors. To stay in business, some of these others also raised the rates paid on their deposits. For some, given their operating costs, these rates were higher than they were able to pay using just their normal, relatively safe investments in residential real estate. Therefore, they too were driven to riskier investments which, if they worked out well, would enable the company to pay the promised interest rates and still make a profit.

Despite the spiraling competitive pressure, some S&Ls may have held out, making only safe investments. They either offered lower interest rates to depositors and so faced a crisis of falling deposits, or they matched the competitive, higher interest rates and suffered losses as the income from their loans fell short of what was needed to pay their costs and other obligations. This became especially significant in 1979 and 1980 when a change in monetary policy by the Federal Reserve (the U.S. central bank) caused interest rates to shoot up throughout the economy. Many S&Ls had much of their money tied up in long-term, fixed-rate mortgage loans, the rates on which suddenly were less than what they were having to pay for their deposits. As well, the collapse of the real estate market in Texas when oil prices fell in the mid-1980s had a special adverse effect on the S&Ls in that state.

Many of the endangered S&Ls became prey for aggressive entrepreneurs, who bought the failing companies for low prices and tried to make them profitable by radical means—offering very high rates on $100,000 "jumbo" deposits and investing in risky commercial real estate, "junk bonds," and other similar ventures. Investors continued to place their deposits with these financially troubled companies because the deposits were federally insured.

It is easy to see how competitive pressure forced out many of the more conservative S&L executives throughout the industry. Those who were unwilling to make the risky investments were often driven out of business. The big loser was the FSLIC—and the taxpayer.

Fraud in the S&Ls

The story of the savings and loan industry as told here leaves out many important details. Risky investments that went bad did not alone deplete the capital of so many S&Ls. Outright fraud was also responsible. News accounts report that the top officers at savings and loan institutions made loans to themselves, their other companies, their friends, and their family members at reduced interest rates and without adequate collateral. They paid large dividends to investors and generous salaries to themselves and their relatives, even as their firms were sliding into bankruptcy. They concealed bad loans by lending more money to the borrowers so that they could afford to make payments on older loans. These activities are tantamount to stealing funds from the S&L, or, because of the insurance, from the taxpayers. Government investigators have found that there was fraud in at least 25 percent of the cases of S&L bankruptcy.

An analysis of the problem of fraud in the savings and loan industry would be quite similar to our analysis of the adoption of risky investments. Throughout the economy, people entrust their funds to the management of others. They protect against fraud and against excessive risk taking in the same sorts of ways: by monitoring performance, hiring auditors, writing restrictive rules into the organization's charter about what activities are allowed, and so on. They retain enough control of the management's activities to dismiss errant executives. The depositors at a federally insured savings and loan did not engage in these costly activities because the deposits were backed by an agency of the U.S. government. No private investor has an incentive to protect the federal insurance agency against fraud; the government regulators have to do that for themselves.

Who's To Blame?

This example of the S&L crisis is remarkably rich, for it involves moral hazard on the part of three distinct groups. First, and most obvious, are the S&L owners who took excessively risky investments or committed fraud. Second are the depositors who failed to monitor the S&Ls because their deposits were insured. The third group consists of the politicians—in both the legislative and the executive branches—who favored the industry at the expense of the general taxpayer. These politicians raised the amount of insurance provided by the FSLIC, thereby making it easier to attract large deposits. They relaxed the regulations on the S&Ls and did not provide for an offsetting increase in monitoring. Furthermore, when the S&Ls were first headed for financial trouble, politicians blocked the regulators from intervening to protect the FSLIC and the taxpayers. Possibly some of these politicians were motivated by a genuine belief that the actions being taken were truly in the general interest. However, the huge campaign donations made by some S&Ls to various of these politicians certainly raise the possibility that the politicians were pursuing their own interests and expected to get away with it because the public's monitoring of them is so imperfect.

PUBLIC VERSUS PRIVATE INSURANCE

The savings and loan crisis is fundamentally the result of moral hazard that arises from the existence of the deposit insurance provided by the FSLIC. Yet this insurance provides valuable social benefits as well. Small savers need not lose sleep worrying about the safety of their deposits, nor do they have to incur the very real costs of monitoring the institutions to which they have entrusted their life savings. The desirability of deposit insurance, combined with the obvious problems that the government-provided program experienced, has led some commentators to suggest that such insurance should be privately provided. There are clear difficulties in designing and implementing such a program, and the failure of a number of small private deposit insurance funds in the state of Rhode Island in 1991 may have removed some of the allure of this idea. Still, it is clear that government insurance programs do seem to have inordinate difficulties with moral hazard.

Other U.S. Government Insurance and Guarantee Programs

The crisis in the savings and loan industry is symptomatic of problems with many other government insurance and guarantee programs in the United States. Together these programs are estimated to involve insurance and loan-guarantee commitments of more than $5 *trillion*, which is almost twice the U.S. national debt and five times the level of yearly federal government spending.[3] Here are just a few examples.

THE PENSION BENEFIT GUARANTY CORPORATION   The Pension Benefit Guaranty Corporation (PBGC) was established by the Employee Retirement Income Security Act of 1974 (ERISA) with the intent, according to its advocates, of ensuring that promises of retirement benefits made to working people by their employers would be honored. The PBGC is obliged to take over plans that are terminated without sufficient funds to pay the promised benefits. It collects what it can from the company that terminated the plan and uses the proceeds to pay the pensioners. To finance the remainder, it collects a tax called an *insurance premium* that is imposed on other pension plans.

To avoid transferring huge pension liabilities to the new government agency, ERISA provided certain minimum funding standards for pensions and held employers liable in part for their pension promises. The act allowed dramatic underfunding of certain kinds of plans, however, particularly multiemployer plans run by trade unions for their own members, but also some corporate pension plans. Predictably, many of these plans aggressively expanded benefits beyond what the limited funds available could possibly justify. Later, some of these plans shut down, saddling the PBGC with the liability to pay the promised benefits.

THE FEDERAL CROP INSURANCE CORPORATION   The Federal Crop Insurance Corporation (FCIC) was established in 1939 to protect farmers against crop losses caused by the vagaries of weather. Yet the FCIC has relatively few inspectors and has been raked by fraudulent claims. Some farmers have defrauded the FCIC by claiming crop losses in one name and selling the harvest in another. Some crop insurance policies have been sold after the claimed loss occurred. In one case a claim was filed for crops that were planted 30 days after the freeze that had triggered the insurance payment.[4]

Even when fraud is not a factor, moral hazard arises. Insured farmers are tempted to take greater risks by planting less hardy or more water-hungry crops than would otherwise be prudent. If the weather turns out to be warm or rainfall turns out to be plentiful, the farmers profit; if not, the government insurance program pays.

THE GOVERNMENT NATIONAL MORTGAGE ASSOCIATION   The Government National Mortgage Association (GNMA) exists to make it easier for homeowners to obtain mortgage loans. It does this in several ways, most prominently by providing insurance to lenders against defaults on the mortgages they write. Along with the development of mortgage-backed securities (see Chapter 1) came mortgage brokers who received commissions of $30 to $45 per $1,000 of the loans they wrote, while maintaining capital of as little as $0.30 per $1,000 of outstanding mortgages.

It is profitable for these brokers to write very risky mortgages because they receive a large commission but have little capital to lose in the event of a default; GNMA

---

[3] "Government Waste: Where's Nanny?" *The Economist* (January 6, 1990), 31.

[4] Bruce Ingersoll, "Crop-Insurance Fraud and Bungling Cost U.S. Taxpayers Billions," *The Wall Street Journal* (May 15, 1989), A-1.

picks up the tab. To protect itself, GNMA specifies limits on the ratio of the loan amount to the appraised value of the property, so that it will have adequate collateral. Appraisals are subjective, however, and unscrupulous brokers have on occasion vastly exaggerated the value of properties in order to justify large loans, leading to default and large losses paid for by the taxpayer while the borrower and broker profit.

STUDENT LOANS   Student loans provide another example of how guarantees affect costs. Federal government guarantees enable many students to obtain loans on more favorable terms than would otherwise be available. Normally, when banks make loans, they take measures to ensure that the loans are collectible and they are aggressive in collecting from debtors. The incentives to ensure collectibility are blunted by government guarantees. Unsurprisingly, a huge proportion of guaranteed student loans are never repaid. Just tracking who the debtors are often exceeds the government's limited capacity to administer these loans.

Private or Public Insurance?

Although moral hazard problems are present in both government and private sector insurance programs, the problems do seem to be less severe in the private sector. In part, this is because private corporations cannot sustain such huge losses for long without going bankrupt, and they often cannot rely on the taxpayers to pay for their financial ineptitude. But the more limited difficulties with moral hazard in private insurance is not due entirely to any special merit of private insurance programs; it is partly a result of the private sector's unwillingness to undertake socially desirable insurance programs in which the costs associated with moral hazard are high.

The money-making objective of private companies is quite different from the objectives of a government agency. No bureaucrat is well positioned to eliminate an unprofitable deposit insurance program that protects the life savings of small depositors. Even a legislature would have difficulty making such a decision. Nor is it clear that elimination of such a program is socially desirable. In contrast, most private firms would have little trouble deciding to terminate the program if the losses being suffered were large.

On average, private-sector insurance programs do seem to be better managed than are their government counterparts. Some of the losses suffered by the various government programs could have been avoided by having more inspectors or tighter regulations. The "output" of inspectors, however, is not easily measured and so, especially during periods of large budget deficits, there is an attractive short-term economy to be achieved by reducing the number of inspectors on the government payroll. Short-sightedness and poor management of this sort certainly seem to have been a factor in the savings and loan crisis.

Yet moving insurance to the private sector is no cure. Moral hazard can manifest itself there in some remarkable ways as well.

Moral Hazard in Private Life Insurance

In a life insurance contract, the insured's designated beneficiary is paid an agreed-upon sum of money when the insured person dies. All life insurance contracts issued in the United States have certain standard provisions, one of which deals with death by suicide. Essentially, life insurance contracts provide that the insurance company will pay off on the policy to the beneficiary after the insured person dies by suicide only if the suicide occurs after a certain period of time has elapsed from the time the policy was issued. In the United States, this exclusion period is always either 12 or 24 months. Life insurance statistics show that the suicide rate is lowest in the twelfth and twenty-fourth months after a policy has been issued and highest in the thirteenth and twenty-fifth. The inference seems unmistakable: People postpone their suicides to allow their beneficiaries to collect the life insurance proceeds.

MORAL HAZARD IN ORGANIZATIONS

Moral hazard was first identified in the insurance context, and some of its most spectacular manifestations are still found there. For understanding organizations, however, it is important to recognize the point made earlier—that moral hazard is a very common phenomenon that affects a wide array of transactions and that attempts to deal with moral hazard account for many of the particular institutional arrangements we see, both in markets and within organizations. Indeed, the very boundary between these two forms of organization is often a response to moral hazard concerns.

Moral Hazard and Employee Shirking

An important instance of moral hazard arises in employment relationships, where employees may shirk their responsibilities. Frederick Taylor, the "father of scientific management," once wrote: "Hardly a competent worker can be found who does not devote a considerable amount of time to studying just how slowly he can work and still convince his employer that he is going at a good pace."[5]

Evidence of the importance of moral hazard in the employment relationship is the frequency with which firms give employees incentive or performance contracts. These arrangements tie the employee's compensation to various measures of performance, and are meant to motivate effort, creativity, care, diligence, loyalty, and so on. Examples include pay tied to output, such as piece rates for manufacturing workers or bonus clauses that reward unusually large numbers of touchdown passes caught by football players; pay linked to sales, such as salespeople's commissions; pay linked to productivity improvements, as under "Scanlon Plans"; and various ways of linking pay and profits, including employee stock ownership plans, the Japanese practice of paying workers an annual bonus tied to firm profitability, and many executive compensation schemes. When well designed and well administered, these sorts of arrangements can be effective in promoting the desired behavior. Although clear communication to employees of what it is that the employer values is partly responsible for this effect, direct financial incentives are the key.

To see that these arrangements are evidence of moral hazard, note that the firm is not paying directly for what the employees are supplying but instead uses a *proxy* for it. What is actually being supplied are such things as the employees' intellectual and physical effort. What is paid for are the *results* of these inputs—sales and touchdown passes, for example. The amount and quality of the employees' efforts are difficult to monitor directly, whereas the results of their efforts may be more easily observed. Thus, rather than trying to pay for unobservable effort directly, the firm attempts to motivate employees to choose to work harder or better by rewarding outcomes that are more likely when they behave in the desired way.

AIR TRAFFIC CONTROLLERS: AN EXAMPLE[6]   Air traffic controllers are charged with maintaining air safety by keeping airplanes in flight at specified, safe distances from one another. They use radar to track flights and radio to direct the pilots.

Federal government employees in the United States in the 1970s, including air traffic controllers, were covered by a disability program, the Federal Employees'

[5] Frederick Taylor, *The Principles of Scientific Management* (New York and London: Harper, 1929).

[6] This section is based on Michael E. Staten and John Umbeck, "Information Costs and Incentives to Shirk: Disability Compensation of Air Traffic Controllers," *American Economic Review*, 72 (December 1982), 1023–37.

Compensation Act. If they were unable to work because of a disability that was the result of their jobs, they were entitled to a receive a fixed percentage of their pay for the duration of their disability. This tax-free payment could be as high as 75 percent of the base salary. Given the tax rates of the period, a disabled worker might actually receive a higher take-home income under the disability program than when working.

In order to collect on a disability claim, the injury had to be shown to be both disabling and work related. The injury did not need not to be physical; stress-related disorders that prevented the employee from working would qualify. To control unjustified claims, the injury report had to be supported by a statement from a physician certifying the disability, another from the employee's supervisor describing the events leading up to the injury, prior symptoms, and the work environment, and first-hand reports from coworkers.

Air traffic controllers, whose jobs were viewed as unusually responsible and stressful, would have had a relatively easy time making a claim for disability based on nervous or emotional disability. Moreover, certain changes in 1972 and 1974 in the rules governing disability claims made claiming disability even more attractive for controllers. The 1972 changes provided for retraining for second careers for those air traffic controllers who were found to be disabled, even if the disability were not job related. The 1974 rule changes made monitoring false claims generally more difficult and made catching a fake stress-related claim especially difficult. If moral hazard were a problem among controllers, then these changes should have led to increased incidence of fake disabilities ("punching out") and an increase in claims, especially in the number of psychologically based claims.

In fact, the number of disability claims *did* rise with the initiation of each program, more than doubling in 1974 and continued to rise. The largest percentage increase following the 1972 change was in psychological and psychiatric illness, such as stress-related disabilities; it was largest by a factor of three. (Unfortunately, the data did not permit identification of the mix of claims following the 1974 change.)

More striking, however, was the apparent impact of the 1974 change on job performance. A controller who wanted to fake a claim for stress-related disability needed to show the disability was job-related to collect, and the examiners were directed to look for specific events on the job that either could have contributed to the stress or that were symptoms of the disability. This created an incentive to manufacture on-the-job incidents that could have caused the stress and that might also indicate that the employee was no longer capable of doing the job. The natural candidate here was a "separation violation," in which planes for which the controller was responsible came too close to one another.

The Federal Aviation Authority keeps track of two sorts of separation violations: System Errors and Near Mid-Air Collisions. The former represent any violations of the standard separation requirements; the latter are much more serious and directly life threatening. Because either sort of violation would do equally well for the purposes of filing a claim, a controller who did not want to cause unnecessary danger would be much more willing to generate a minor violation than a near collision. In fact, the number of Systems Errors jumped significantly after the 1974 change, but there was only a small, statistically insignificant change in the number of Near Mid-Air Collisions. Furthermore, the increase in Systems Errors tended to occur not when traffic was particularly heavy, as you might otherwise expect, but when it was relatively light and the controller could cause the "needed" violation at minimal risk.

Finally, a controller considering punching out had to decide when in his or her career to do so. Various factors, especially eligibility for retraining and an effective dependence of the amount of disability pay on years of service, made it much more attractive to punch out after five years of service. Before the 1974 changes, controllers with less than five years' experience (who presumably were relatively inexperienced and more prone to mistakes) and, to a lesser extent, those with more than ten years' experience (who were more likely to suffer from actual "burn-out") were responsible for most of the System Errors made. By 1976 personnel in the five-to-ten-year range were committing over 50 percent of the errors, although this group accounted for less than 30 percent of the total number of controllers. All this, then, is striking evidence of moral hazard.

Managerial Misbehavior

The senior executives of corporations are charged with advancing the interests of the stockholders, who are the owners of the company. They are supposed to be overseen in this duty by the board of directors, who are elected by the stockholders and who are empowered to represent them in voting on major corporate decisions and setting the executives' compensation. Thus, both the executives and the board members are considered the agents of the stockholders.

Over 50 years ago, Adophe Berle and Gardner Means argued that the dispersed holdings of stock across a multitude of small investors had created an effective **separation of ownership and control**, with no individual stockholder having any real incentive to monitor managers and ensure that the officers and board were running the firm in the owners' interests.[7] Although this claim long remained highly controversial, evidence that has accumulated indicates that managers often do fail to promote the interests of the stockholders effectively.

The problem typically is not that the executives are lazy and do not work hard enough. Corporate executives put in remarkably long hours of very intense effort. Rather, the complaint is that they pursue goals other than maximizing the long-run value of the firm. Critics claim that executives invest firms' earnings in low-value projects to expand their empires when the funds would be better distributed to the shareholders to invest for themselves. They are alleged to hang on to badly performing operations when other teams of managers could run them more profitably or even when the operations are irredeemable losers. With the connivance of their hand-picked boards, they pay themselves exorbitantly and lavish expensive perquisites upon themselves. They resist attempts to force more profitable operations, especially by resisting takeovers that threaten their jobs. All these alleged misdeeds serve the interests of the managers themselves (and perhaps the interests of other concerned constituencies, such as employees), but not the interests of the firms' owners.

Hostile Takeovers and Managerial Misbehavior   During the 1980s a wave of **hostile takeovers** occurred in the United States and to a lesser extent in the United Kingdom and Canada. A hostile takeover is the acquisition of enough of the shares in a company to give a controlling ownership interest in the firm, where the offer to acquire the firm is opposed by the target company's executives and directors. Successful hostile takeover attempts generally resulted in replacement of the target firms' senior management and the naming of new boards of directors. The buyers in these transactions were called "corporate raiders" (as well as many less complimentary things) by the managers of the target firms who fought to maintain the companies' independence. In this context, "independence" means the firms' continuing under their current managers and boards with the existing ownership. This ownership was

---

[7] Adophe Berle and Gardner Means, *The Modern Corporation and Private Property* (New York: MacMillan, 1932).

typically quite diffuse—individual small shareholders, plus pension plans, insurance companies, and mutual funds.

Many observers have interpreted the hostile takeovers as a corrective response to managerial moral hazard: The takeovers, it is claimed, were intended to displace entrenched managers who were pursuing their own interests at the expense of the stockholders. Whether this is the case or not, the huge profits that were generated in these transactions raise questions about how effectively incumbent managers were maximizing the values of the companies they ran.

The prices paid for the stock of firms in hostile takeovers in this period on average represented a 50 percent premium over the target's original market value. For example, just before Mobil Oil launched its bid for Marathon Oil in 1981, Marathon's stock was trading at $63.75 a share. Mobil offered $85, and eventually raised its offer to $126 before Marathon was acquired by U.S. Steel (now called USX). Similar premia were paid in hundreds of cases. In aggregate from 1977 through 1986, shareholders selling their stocks in hostile takeovers realized an estimated gain of $346 billion (in 1986 dollars).[8] The takeover premia appear to be evidence of managerial incompetence or moral hazard to the extent that this original market value represented the discounted profit stream that savvy investors expected the firm to generate under its original management, whereas the takeover price reflected the firm's value under the new ownership.

The takeover premia are not conclusive evidence that the managers were poor stewards, however. Perhaps there was systematic overbidding by raiders who suffered delusions about their managerial abilities or were using other peoples' money to expand their own empires. Perhaps the new owners expected to reap gains at the expense of other stakeholders (especially current managers and workers), where these private gains are not increases in efficiency but the returns to violating explicit and implicit promises. Or perhaps the stock market was systematically underestimating the target firms' prospects before the takeover attempts were launched.

We examine these issues in more detail in Chapter 15, but one feature of the takeover wave does seem to be a clear manifestation of misbehavior: The adoption of a *poison pill* provision without an approving shareholder vote.

POISON PILLS   Poison pills are takeover defenses.[9] They involve creation of special securities that give certain rights to their holders in the event that a raider acquires more than a specified fraction of the shares in the firm. Most commonly these rights are to buy shares in the target (or, if the takeover occurs, the acquiring) firm at very low prices. They work as takeover defenses because they vastly increase the cost of acquiring the firm. Although they are often labeled as "Shareholder Rights Plans" by managers trying to sell them to their shareholders (who receive some or all of the special securities), they in effect remove the ability of the owners of the firm to sell their shares to a buyer that their nominal agents—management and the board—do not like.

If the shareholders adopt such a scheme, it is largely their business, and it may well be in their best interest: Takeover defenses, if not strong enough to make takeovers impossible, may improve the stockholders' bargaining position and raise the price they

---

[8] See Michael Jensen, "Takeovers: Their Causes and Consequences," *Journal of Economic Perspectives*, 2 (1988), 21–48.

[9] For a discussion of takeover defenses, see J. Fred Weston, Kwang S. Chung, and Susan E. Hoag, *Mergers, Restructuring, and Corporate Control* (Englewood Cliffs, NJ: Prentice Hall, Inc., 1990), Chapter 20.

ultimately receive if an acquisition does occur. Boards of directors can adopt poison pills without shareholder approval, however, and they often did so during the 1980s when they (or management) became nervous about possible takeovers. Doing so seems to be simply an expropriation of the shareholders' property by those who are supposed to be looking out for and serving their interests. Moreover, the empirical evidence is that adopting a poison pill typically reduces the firm's share value, and the firms that have adopted poison pills tend to be ones where managers and board members hold very few of the company's shares.[10] This evidence further supports the view that the adoption does not serve shareholder interests.

Moral Hazard in Financial Contracts

A common sort of moral hazard problem arises when different individuals have differing claims on the financial returns from an investment. We have already seen an instance of this in the savings and loan crisis, but other examples abound and account for many elements of the form of financial contracts.

DEBT, EQUITY, AND BANKRUPTCY   Many firms are financed by a combination of **debt** and **equity**. The debt holders—banks, the purchasers of the firm's bonds, input suppliers who offer credit—are lenders. They provide cash in return for a promise to be repaid a fixed amount (perhaps with interest) at a later date. The equity holders get to keep whatever profits are left after paying the debt obligations. In a corporation, the equity is lodged with the stockholders, who elect the board of directors to represent their interests in setting policy and in hiring managers to run the firm. In a partnership or sole proprietorship, the partners or owners are the equity claimants. Absent serious managerial moral hazard, we should expect that the firm will be run in the interests of the equity holders. This is not necessarily consistent with the interests of the firm's creditors.

We already saw one form of a conflict of interest between equity and debt in the savings and loan example. Equity holders will favor riskier investments than the firm's creditors would want. The reasoning is exactly the same as was developed there: The equity holders win big if the investments work out, whereas the debt holders just get their promised fixed payment, and if the investment loses money, some of the loss may fall on the creditors who are not fully repaid.

As we also noted in the savings and loan example, lenders take measures to protect themselves against the potential moral hazard problem that arises if the firm is run to maximize the value of its stock. They do credit checks, they demand collateral, they monitor performance (in part by requiring ongoing repayment), and they may structure the loans so that they can demand immediate repayment if they get nervous about the firm's ability to pay. Moreover, in some countries, the firm's bankers are normally named to the board of directors of the corporation, where they can more easily monitor their investments. As well, the bond holders may insist on covenants in the debt contract that limit the sort of actions the firm can take and the amount of additional borrowing it can undertake.

Despite all this, sometimes the loan cannot be repaid, or at least a scheduled payment is missed. In these circumstances, the lenders can force the firm into bankruptcy. Bankruptcy can be seen as an institutional arrangement to protect the value of assets. Once a firm is forced into involuntary bankruptcy, the creditors gain many of the decision rights that normally belong to equity. This prevents more of the resources available for meeting the debt obligations from being squandered. It thus

---

[10] Michael Jensen, "Takeovers: Their Causes and Consequences," 21–48.

makes people more willing to lend money than they otherwise would be and encourages the efficient allocation of financial capital. Moreover, to the extent that managers lose in a bankruptcy—because their jobs, their perks, and their pensions may disappear—the threat of bankruptcy may serve as a check on managerial moral hazard vis-à-vis stockholders' interests.

Under U.S. tax laws, the payments that a corporation makes as interest on its debt are tax deductible, whereas dividend payments on its stock are not. Because both are payments by the corporation for the use of capital, this might suggest that the firm would gain by financing itself overwhelmingly with debt. The attendant moral hazard problem is one reason why this would not be automatically attractive, however. As the fraction of the firm financed by debt increases, there is a growing incentive for equity holders and the managers who represent them to take risks. This means that at very high levels of debt to equity, the firm will have to pay very high interest rates, put up extremely large amounts of collateral, and accord lenders extensive control rights if it is to persuade them to lend to it at all. Although this is far from a complete explanation of firms' decisions about how to finance themselves, it is an element. We will see more on this topic in Chapters 14 and 15.

OIL AND GAS TAX-SHELTER PROGRAMS[11]   In the United States in the early 1980s, many oil and gas exploration and development operations were organized through **limited partnerships**, which are hybrid contractual arrangements mixing elements of the forms of both corporations and partnerships. There are two classes of partners in a limited partnership: the *general partners* and the *limited partners*. The limited partners are in a position very like that of the shareholders in a public corporation. They take no role in managing the partnership. Rather, they simply provide the cash as investors to finance its operations, and they enjoy **limited liability**: Their financial liabilities are limited to the amounts they invest. The general partners are like the partners in a regular partnership. They make all the managerial decisions about the partnership's operations, and they have *unlimited liability* for the partnership's debts: Their personal wealth can be seized by creditors if the partnership defaults on its debts.

The federal tax laws that prevailed in the early 1980s partially accounted for the popularity of this organizational form in oil and gas exploration. The partners could often save on taxes if the limited partners paid all the costs of exploring for oil (which were tax deductible when the costs were incurred), whereas the general partners paid the costs of completing wells in which oil is found (which were "capitalized costs" for tax reporting purposes). The general partners and the limited partners would then share any revenues enjoyed when oil was pumped from producing wells.

This tax avoidance scheme is beset with moral hazard problems that arise from the difference in interests it creates between the general partners and the limited partners. The most fundamental of these results because each bears a different kind of expense and receives only a share of the revenues. If a well is found to have oil, the general partners have to decide whether to bring it to completion so it will produce. If they decide to do so, they bear 100 percent of the cost of completing the well but typically receive only 25 percent of the oil revenues, with the rest going to the limited partners. Suppose that after the exploration costs have been sunk, a well is found to have enough oil that the well-completion costs will be just 50 percent of the resulting

---

[11] This section is based on Mark Wolfson, "Empirical Evidence of Incentive Problems and Their Mitigation in Oil and Gas Tax Shelter Programs," in *Principals and Agents: The Structure of Business*, J. Pratt and R. Zeckhauser, eds., (Boston: Harvard Business School Press, 1985), 101–25.

revenues, so that the partnership as a whole would profit from completing the well. Despite the fact that completing the well would maximize total value, the general partners would not find it in their individual interests to complete the well: Their 25 percent share of the revenue is not enough to cover their 100 percent share of the cost. Furthermore, it would be very hard for the limited partners, with no role in the management of the partnership and probably no expertise in the oil business, to ensure that their interests are being given proper weight in the general partners' decisions.

A second conflict of interest arises when, as was often the case, the general partners are involved in several exploration efforts at the same time and in the same area but have differing shares in different projects. As an extreme example, suppose the general partners have another exploration project on an adjoining tract that they own outright. In that case, by shifting their drilling on the partnership's tract towards the boundaries of their own tract, the general partners can acquire valuable information about the likelihood of finding oil on different parts of their private holdings, with the cost of that information acquisition being borne by the limited partners. Similar, if less severe, problems arise when the general partner is involved in several limited partnerships but has differing interests in each. The general partner may be led to distort his or her allocation of time, effort, attention, and resources among the partnerships, favoring the ones in which he or she has the greatest interest. Again, it would be very difficult for the limited partners to monitor this sort of behavior.

A third conflict often arises when the general partners or their affiliates sell equipment or services to the limited partnership. The problem is that the general partners have an incentive to overcharge on these transactions because the limited partners pay the bills, but the general partners, who make the decisions, collect the money.

All these conflicts are clearly recognized in the industry, and the prospectuses for the limited partnerships often discuss the incentive problems very clearly and candidly. We return to this example in Chapter 7, where some of the means used to offset the incentive problems are discussed.

CONTROLLING MORAL HAZARD

In order for a moral hazard problem to arise, three conditions must hold. First, there must be some potential divergence of interests between people. Conflicts of interest will not always arise, nor will they arise on all dimensions: Different individuals' interests may naturally be quite well aligned in particular circumstances. However, conflict will occur often, if only because scarcity of resources means that what one person gets another cannot have. Second, there must be some basis for gainful exchange or other cooperation between the individuals—some reason to agree and transact—that activates the divergent interests. Up to this point, simple market arrangements would work: Divergent interests are a factor in almost all exchanges, and yet exchanges are often made successfully without being troubled by moral hazard. The critical third requirement is that there must be difficulties in determining whether in fact the terms of the agreement have been followed and in enforcing the contract terms. These difficulties often arise because monitoring actions or verifying reported information is costly or impossible. However, they could also arise even when both parties know that the contract has been violated but this fact cannot be verified by third parties (such as a court or arbitrator) who would have enforcement powers. This means that the normal market solution will be problematic, because the parties will not be able to write enforceable contracts covering all the crucial elements of the transaction. These three conditions suggest ways to deal with the moral hazard problem.

Monitoring

The first remedy is suggested by the third condition: Increase the resources devoted to monitoring and verification. Sometimes the idea is to prevent inappropriate behavior directly by catching it before it occurs. For example, U.S. corporations are not allowed to publish financial statements until they have been verified by independent auditors, prospectuses describing investments for which funds are sought from the public must be approved by the Securities and Exchange Commission, and health care insurers may have patients obtain a second opinion on a physician's recommendation for some expensive treatment if they are concerned that the treatments may be unnecessary. In other situations, monitoring is intended to decrease the probability of getting away undetected with the socially inefficient, self-interested behavior. In this case, the results of monitoring are the basis for rewards or penalties. For example, workers are often required to punch a time clock, and their pay is reduced or other punishments are imposed if they arrive late or quit early. Monitoring may also be used to support a system of rewards for good behavior.

The payment of cash rewards is itself sometimes subject to a moral hazard problem of reneging. The party who is supposed to pay the reward may misrepresent the outcome of the monitoring, claiming that the other person's behavior was not appropriate and no reward is due. This is likely to be especially easy when the criteria for judging performance are hard to describe or measure precisely, so that evaluations will tend to be subjective. Sometimes, the need to maintain a good reputation is enough to control this temptation. (Reputation effects are discussed in more detail in Chapter 8.) In other circumstances, the efficacy of monitoring may depend on generating evidence verifiable to a court that can enforce payment of the agreed rewards.

A more subtle but related commitment problem arises when punishment is due but carrying out the punishment is costly for the party who is supposed to do it. For example, if company policy requires that an employee who breaks certain rules must be fired, and a valued, hard-to-replace employee is caught in a minor violation of the rules, then the employer may be loathe to carry out the punishment and lose the employee's services. Of course, if the worker foresees that the firm will be unwilling to punish transgressions, the threat of punishment is empty.

COMPETING SOURCES OF INFORMATION   Although monitoring requires developing sources of information about the agent's truthfulness and performance, this does not always require direct expenditures of resources. One possibility is to rely on competition among different parties with conflicting interests to develop the needed information. In everyday life, competing sellers will often happily compare the relative merits of their own products against comparative defects in the competing product which the other seller would be unlikely to emphasize. The same phenomenon can occur within organizations, as for example when the navy and air force vie for responsibility for some military mission, each emphasizing its own advantages compared to its competitor. The danger with relying on competing information providers is greatest when they have some common interests that are in opposition to the decision maker's. For example, neither of two sellers of asbestos insulation was likely to emphasize the health hazards of asbestos before these became widely known.

MONITORING BY MARKETS   Managerial moral hazard is frequently alleviated by monitoring provided for free by markets. Managers of firms in reasonably competitive product or input markets who do a poor job of generating profits will face a greater probability of failure. The fear of unemployment and of carrying a reputation for having led a firm into bankruptcy may then provide managerial incentives. Similarly, the "market for corporate control" provides incentives by threatening bad corporate managers with loss of their jobs following a takeover or a successful **proxy fight**.[12]

Explicit Incentive Contracts

In some situations, monitoring actual behavior or the veracity of reports may be simply too expensive to be worthwhile. As we mentioned earlier, however, it may still be possible to observe *outcomes* and to provide incentives for good behavior through rewarding good outcomes. For example, even if it is impossible to monitor the care and skill exerted by machine maintenance personnel, it may still be possible to measure the percentage of time that machines break down. In fact, if the breakdown rate of machines were completely determined by the performance of the maintenance worker, basing pay on that rate would be a perfect substitute for basing it on care and effort. The same would be true even if other factors (such as the machines' inherent quality, the intensity and nature of their use, and the care exerted by the machine operators) also influence the breakdown rate, provided it were possible to control precisely for the effects of these other determinants of breakdown.

Unfortunately, perfect connections between unobservable actions and observed resulting outcomes are rare. More often people's behavior only partially determines outcomes, and it is impossible to isolate the effect of their behavior precisely. For example, a firm's total sales depend not only on the efforts of the sales force but also on a host of other factors: the price and advertising policy of the firm, competitors' prices and promotions, and other conditions that affect customers' demands. Rewarding on the basis of results therefore makes the salespeople's incomes dependent on random and uncontrollable factors. A similar effect arises when the outcomes *are* fully determined by the person's effort but are not measured precisely, instead being only estimated or measured with some unknown, random error. Again, incomes become subject to random variations.

THE PROBLEM OF RISK-BEARING   Most people dislike having their incomes dependent on random factors. They are **risk averse**, and would rather have a smaller income whose magnitude is certain than an uncertain income that is somewhat larger on average but is subject to unpredictable and uncontrollable variability. The risks created by incentive contracts are costly to these people. They are not as well off with a risky income as they would be receiving the same expected level of pay for certain, and they thus have to be paid more on average to convince them to accept these risks. From the employer's perspective, this extra income is a cost of using incentive pay.

Moreover, this cost can be a real one to society, one that can reduce overall efficiency. The employer often is more tolerant of risk and better able to bear it than are employees. In the extreme case, where the employer is a well-financed and widely held corporation whose stockholders keep their wealth in broadly diversified portfolios, the stockholders can be assumed to be *risk neutral*—concerned mostly with expected returns and virtually indifferent about variability in the net earnings of the firm, especially variations of the magnitude of an individual worker's performance pay. Tying workers' pay to their job performance means that a source of the variability of earnings is transferred from the owners to the workers: When things go well on the job, some of the extra returns accrue to the workers, and when things go badly, the

---

[12] The stockholders in a corporation have the right to elect the directors and to vote on certain major policy decisions at stockholders' meetings. Few stockholders ever attend these meetings, however. To allow for this, they are permitted to give their *proxy* to someone else to cast their votes on their behalf. Typically, the proxy is given to management. In a proxy contest, rival groups will attempt to win stockholders' proxies so that they can elect different directors or prevent management and the current directors from enacting a policy change that the group opposes. See Chapter 15.

impact on the owners is cushioned by the lower levels of incentive pay. However, transferring risk from the owners (who care little about the risk and benefit little from its reduction) to the workers (who may strongly dislike bearing risk) means that the total costs of the given amount of risk in the system are increased.

RISK COSTS AND INCENTIVE BENEFITS   Designing efficient incentive contracts involves balancing the costs of risk bearing against the benefits of improved incentives. Insulating risk-averse employees' pay from variations in measured job performance minimizes the costs of risk bearing, but it also eliminates monetary performance incentives. Shifting risk to the employees strengthens their incentives because their pay now depends on actual performance, but the costs of risk bearing rise as well. The efficiency principle suggests that observed contracts will tend to be efficient, subject to the constraints imposed by observability problems.

One implication of this analysis is that it is inefficient to use contracts that make risk-averse employees bear avoidable risks unless the contracts also provide useful incentives.[13] For example, consider a firm whose risk-neutral owners want to maximize profits and which has a problem motivating production workers to be productive. Because the owners care about profits, one possibility is to provide incentives for everyone by paying bonuses based on profitability. This exposes workers to income variations arising not just from their own productivity, however, but also from all the other factors influencing profits that are beyond their control: input prices and availability, the efforts of the sales force, the quality of executive decisions, variations in demand and in the interest rate the firm has to pay on its debts, the actions of competitors, and so on. In this case, it may be preferable to use an incentive plan based not on profits but on direct measures of the contributions made by individual workers or work group, such as the volume of output, the number of defects, the number of days absent from work, and so on. Even these measures expose the workers to risk, because productivity is not completely under their control, but they do insulate them from some unnecessary risks.

The basic idea behind incentive contracts is that of achieving **goal congruence**: An appropriately designed reward system causes self-interested behavior to approximate the behavior the designer wants. Alternatively, we can think of a well-designed incentive scheme as removing the conflict of interests by effectively altering individual objectives, aligning them more closely with those of the designer. We will usually think of incentives as altering rewards to increase the benefits associated with the desired behavior; for example, motivating employees' interest in profit seeking by tying their pay to profitability. However, behavior can also be modified through job design, employee involvement programs, and the provision of a better work environment, all of which reduce the unpleasantness of work and lower the costs to employees of providing effort. Requiring office workers to be at their desks during certain hours can be seen in similar terms. Because they have to be at the office, they may as well do their jobs, although if they were free to be elsewhere, they would find other things to occupy their time.

We give a (relatively) simple mathematical example of what is conceptually involved in designing an efficient incentive contract in the appendix to this chapter. In Chapter 7 we examine this issue in much more detail and develop a number of principles that can be used to understand and evaluate actual contracts and to guide contract design. Also, in Chapter 12 we examine managerial issues that arise in using incentive pay in organizations.

---

[13] The point is closely related to the adage that people should be held responsible only for things under their control. Actually, the adage with this phrasing is misleading, as seen in Chapter 7.

Bonding

In some industries, it is common to require the posting of bonds to guarantee performance. The bond is a sum of money that is forfeited in the event that inappropriate behavior is detected. For example, contractors often must post a bond that they lose if the project is not completed by the agreed date and in the agreed manner. Similarly, the capital provided by the owners of a bank or an S&L acts like a bond because in the event of losses the capital must be paid out to meet obligations. In the early 1970s, Electronic Data Systems Corporation (EDS)—Ross Perot's computer service company that was later acquired by General Motors—required trainees who resigned within three years of joining the firm to pay the firm $12,000.[14] This bonding was designed to prevent employees from receiving costly training without doing substantial work for the firm. The $12,000 amount was comparable to an engineer's annual salary at the time.

Posting a bond can be a very effective way to provide incentives, but the problem is that people often will lack the financial resources to post a sufficiently large bond. This is especially the case when the gains from cheating are large and the probability of getting caught is small, so that the bond would have to be large to give an adequate incentive. These ideas are examined more carefully in Chapter 8, but one application that sheds light on the puzzle of positively sloped age/wage profiles can be discussed here.

AGE/WAGE PATTERNS, SENIORITY PROVISIONS, AND MANDATORY RETIREMENT   As noted in Chapter 5, pay tends to increase with age and experience, even after controlling for productivity. In Chapter 5 we offer an explanation for this pattern based on inducing self-selection to reduce employee turnover. Bonding as a deterrent to employee shirking has been suggested as an alternative explanation by Edward Lazear.

Suppose that the firm can fire any workers detected shirking. We may think of workers who shirk as receiving some valuable benefit, such as a reduced level of stress or more time to pursue personal interests, which cannot be taken away from them. If workers were to post bonds of sufficiently greater value than these benefits, and if being caught cheating resulted in losing the bond, then they would not cheat. Their value to the firm would be increased by the bond and, with competition among employers, so too would be the amount they would earn. In any case, when it is efficient for workers not to cheat and shirk, the bond may allow efficiency to be achieved. If the gain from cheating is substantial, however, or the likelihood of getting caught is small, workers may not be able to afford to post a big enough bond, and the potential efficiency gain would be lost.

Suppose the firm in this circumstance makes a credible promise to the workers that, late in their careers, it will pay them more than the value of what they produce and thus of what they could earn elsewhere. If the firm pays workers less than their marginal products early in their careers, then the value of lifetime earnings and the firm's total outlay need not be affected by this scheme. As the years of high pay draw near, however, the high promised wages serve as a bond that the worker would forfeit by dishonest behavior or shirking: The wage pattern duplicates the effect of a bond. Therefore, the observed pattern of wages might be explained by a need to make workers value their jobs in order to ensure honest, hard-working behavior.

Strikingly, a mandatory retirement provision will be necessary for efficiency under this scheme. For efficiency, people should retire when the value of what they produce just equals the private cost to them of continuing working. If they were paid

---

[14] Doron Levin, *Irreconcilable Differences: Ross Perot versus General Motors* (New York: Plume, 1989), p. 46.

their marginal products, they would choose to retire at the efficient date, when the extra income just balances the increasingly high costs of continuing work. With wages late in life exceeding marginal productivity, however, some people will want to continue working too long because their pay exceeds the social value of their output. They will not retire voluntarily at the appropriate date. Thus, mandatory retirement is necessary for efficiency. Furthermore, at the start of their careers, workers would be happy to sign contracts agreeing to a mandatory retirement date, even though once it arrives they will be unhappy about being forced to stop working and earning.

This scheme also necessitates some sort of mechanism to make the firm's promise credible. The danger is that the firm will renege on its agreement by letting senior workers go once their pay exceeds their current productivity. Again, a concern with reputation may work here, but it is perhaps less likely to be effective when workers have few other employment options and so the incentives to avoid a firm that has cheated are weak. In this case, a seniority rule in layoffs can play a useful role. If the firm wants to lay off a senior worker who is earning a lot, it must first lay off all the more junior people whom it is paying less than they are worth.

Do-It-Yourself, Ownership Changes, and Organizational Redesign

Moral hazard in agency settings can sometimes be overcome by eliminating the agent and having the principals act on their own behalf. This is often impossible, however—you cannot very well be your own surgeon, for example—and in any case it sacrifices the gains of specialization.

In market settings, changing ownership patterns to bring the affected transactions within a single organization can help overcome some moral hazard problems. (We have already noted in Chapter 5 that unified ownership can be a response to inefficiencies arising from bounded rationality and private information.) For example, if a firm and a supplier are frequently involved in complex transactions that are marked by such manifestations of moral hazard as possible cheating on quality, it may be efficient for one firm to acquire the other. In that case, the differing interests (each firm's own profit) become merged, and many of the incentive problems are overcome. A simple mathematical example illustrates how this can be effective.

INCENTIVES AND OWNERSHIP PATTERNS: AN EXAMPLE   Suppose that two firms face a joint opportunity that requires both of them to make some investment. Let us denote the measured value of the investments by firms A and B by M_A and M_B. These measured amounts need not be the assets' actual values, however, and this is where moral hazard enters because the firms' wills individually decide the actual amounts they will invest. For example, a physical asset might be valued at $100 in the accounts because it cost $200 a year ago and had an estimated useful life of two years. However, the actual value of that asset today might be only $50 because new machines using a new process have made the old process obsolete. Similarly, the value of a year of an employee's time might be recorded at an amount equal to his or her wage, but the wage might not accurately reflect the employee's value to the company. The employee might be a young engineer, straight out of school, who is expected to go through a period of learning and low productivity (when one subtracts the cost of mistakes). Or, the employee might be an up-and-coming executive who has successfully managed other special projects and is more valuable to the company than others of the same rank.

Let V_A and V_B be the *actual* value to the two companies of the resources they invest in the venture. The expected revenue from the venture is assumed to be 1.5

Table 6.4   Company A's Profit Calculation

B's investment	V_B
A's investment	V_A
Total investment	$V_A + V_B$
Total expected revenue	$1.5(V_A + V_B) - 600$
A's expected revenue .... (a one-half share)	$0.75 \times (V_A + V_B) - 300$
A's net expected profit................................. (revenue minus investment)	$0.75 \times V_B - .25 \times V_A - 300$
A's profit-maximizing choice..........................	$V_A = 500$
B's expected choice	$V_B = 500$
A's expected *loss*..	$\$50$

times the actual value of the total investment minus \$600, that is, $1.5 \times (V_A + V_B) - 600$. Higher real investments lead to more revenue for the project on average.

Suppose the two companies write a contract according to which each will invest \$1,000 in the project. This can only refer to measured investments, because even if the companies were able to distinguish the values of the assets being used, there would be no objective way for a court to verify the level of unmeasured investment in order to enforce the agreement. As equal partners, the companies agree to divide the revenues generated by the venture equally. If the companies were to invest so that measured and actual values were the same, that is, so that $M_A = M_B = V_A = V_B = \$1,000$, then the investment would be profitable for both companies. The total revenues generated by the project would be $1.5 \times (V_A + V_B) - 600 = \$2,400$, which is more than the total investment of \$2,000. Each company would expect to receive \$1,200 in revenues from an investment of \$1,000, for a net profit of \$200.

Now, suppose that each company is free to choose its investment in the project so that, even though the measured value is exactly \$1,000, the actual value can be anything between \$500 and \$1,500. What choices will the companies make? Will the venture be a profitable one?

Let's look at the matter from company A's perspective. Whatever amount V_B company B actually invests, company A's expected profits will be its share of the total revenues minus its investment (see Table 6.4).

According to Table 6.4, each extra dollar of value that firm A invests in the venture yields \$1.50 in extra revenue, but A's share of that \$1.50 is just \$0.75. Therefore, A loses \$0.25 on each extra dollar of investment. A's profit-maximizing choice is to make the minimum investment of \$500, as indicated in the seventh line of the table. If A understands this calculation (and expects that B does too), then it will expect B to invest only \$500 as well. In that case, the total expected revenues of the venture will be just \$900, whereas the required investment will be \$1,000. Each firm will expect to *lose* \$50, so the investment will not be made. An apparently profitable business opportunity will be lost because A expects B to take a free ride on their investment and B expects A to do likewise.

Of course, if the two firms were to merge, and the decisions about investment were brought under a single individual who pays the entire costs and collects the full benefits, then the problem described here would be eliminated.

THE DETERMINANTS OF OWNERSHIP   As our examples related to moral hazard in employment have shown, a transaction that is "integrated" or brought "in house" does not automatically align incentives. The problem is that integration only transforms a self-interested manager who formerly worked for the supplier into a self-interested manager who works for the firm. The basic incentive problem may still need to be solved.

The upshot is that merger does not always eliminate the incentive problem that exists between separate firms. Compounding the problem is the fact that there are additional unavoidable costs to bringing previously separate activities under common direction. An important component of these are the *influence costs*, which increase with the increased potential for central control of activities in an integrated organization. Although the *influence activities* that give rise to influence costs are a form of moral hazard, they are of such importance in understanding organizations that they deserve separate treatment.

INFLUENCE ACTIVITIES AND UNIFIED OWNERSHIP

What costs are involved in bringing two separate organizations under unified direction? Why can't the merged entity do everything the separate components did and more? What are the limits, if any, on the efficient size of organizations? Why isn't all economic activity organized in a single firm?

From our discussion in Chapter 2, it is clear that the answer must be that bringing everything within a single organization involves inefficiently high transactions costs of some sort. But what are they? In fact, until recently, little attention has been given to the task of identifying the transactions costs of internal, nonmarket organization. This is a subtle matter. In actual organizations, much time and ingenuity is spent overcoming transactions costs: Witness the example of the development of the multidivisional form in Chapter 1. Moreover, a strikingly simple idea—the policy of selective intervention—undercuts many of the possible candidates that come to mind as distinctive disabilities of unified control.

Unified Ownership and Selective Intervention

Suppose it is efficient for two parts of a big organization to be independent and operate as separate entities. Then, in the original organization the center could direct the two units to conduct their transactions at arm's length as if they were not both part of a single structure. For example, when market transacting works well, why not replicate its operation within the firm, using internal, transfer pricing? Meanwhile, where there are efficiency gains to be had from deviating from the patterns of transactions that would occur in the market, why not have the central management *selectively intervene* in the operations of the component units to ensure that the gains are realized?

Following a policy of selective intervention consistently ought to mean that the unified organization can do everything the separate pieces could do, and do so at least as well. There would then be no bound on the efficient size of the organization. Why then is all activity not brought under a single firm? The logical answer must be that adhering to a thoroughgoing policy of selective intervention is impossible. But why should this policy be infeasible? **Influence activities** provide part of an answer.[15]

Influence activities arise in organizations when organizational decisions affect the distribution of wealth or other benefits among members or constituent groups of the organization and, in pursuit of their selfish interests, the affected individuals or groups attempt to influence the decision to their benefit. The costs of these influence activities are **influence costs**.

---

[15] A broader discussion of influence costs is found in Chapter 8.

Influencing Interventions

The fundamental difficulty with the policy of selective intervention is that it requires that there be a decision maker with the *power* to intervene who *collects information* with which to make decisions: These things can by themselves impose costs on the organization. The most obvious costs are the decision maker's salary and the cost of providing information to support the decision-making system, including the time that lower-level decision makers spend reporting information to the decision maker. Often more important is that individuals and units within the organization may have selfish reasons to seek unproductive interventions, and they may expend resources trying to *influence* the decision maker to bring them about. Even when the attempts fail, the resources expended in these influence activities represent a cost that brings no offsetting gain. When they do succeed in influencing the central decision maker to intervene inappropriately, there are further costs in bad decisions being made and implemented. Finally, if the organization recognizes these possibilities and adjusts its structure, governance, policies, and procedures to control attempts at influence, these deviations bring further costs. All of these are elements of influence costs.

As is evident, the magnitude of influence costs depends on the existence of a central authority, the kinds of procedures that govern decision making, and the degree of homogeneity or conflict in the interests of organization members. All this is treated in more detail in Chapter 8. Here, we focus on how influence costs limit the optimal scope of formal organizations.

When two previously separate organizations are brought under a common, central management with the power to intervene, the scope for influence increases and influence costs increase. For example, members of one unit can try to influence top management to transfer resources from the other unit to theirs. They can argue that they have better investment opportunities and so can better use the funds being generated in the other division, or that they have more valued uses for the most talented people now assigned to the other group, or that all marketing, or production, or research and development (R&D) should be consolidated in a single unit (theirs!) rather than remaining inefficiently spread over several units. The other group will have a similar incentive to defend itself and even to counterattack. It can argue that other units should be required to purchase its outputs, even though the outside market may provide superior or cheaper substitutes, because doing so helps cover corporate overhead or helps build the firm's core competencies, or it may complain that equity, morale, and ultimately productivity demand that its members be paid as well as those in another group whose members may be especially productive or may have particularly valuable skills or knowledge. Large amounts of time, ingenuity, and effort may go into these attempts at influence, and huge amounts of the central executives' time can be consumed dealing with them.

Of course, none of this would occur if there were no central authority with the power to make the proposed changes. Thus, although the merged organization may be able to achieve things that were not possible before, it also suffers costs that were not present when the parts were separate.

Influence Costs and Failed Mergers

This logic gives insight into the great frequency with which corporate mergers and acquisitions apparently fail. In a study of the diversification records of 33 large U.S. corporations between 1950 and 1986, Michael Porter found that fully 60 percent of the acquisitions in new fields of business by these firms were later divested, and 61 percent of the firms ended up divesting more of their acquisitions than they kept.[16] Although not all divestitures of previous acquisitions necessarily represent failures, even the sophisticated firms in Porter's sample had real problems making acquisitions work.

There are obviously major problems involved in attempting to integrate two different organizations with their own unique histories, their own ways of doing things, their own reporting and control systems, their own pay and benefit schemes, and so on. To focus on a pure case in which these factors should be of minimal concern, consider a pure conglomerate merger in which one firm acquires another with the intent of running it as a completely separate division, intervening in its operations only when there are clear gains to doing so. Even here, influence costs present problems that may cause the merger to fail.

TENNECO'S ACQUISITION OF HOUSTON OIL AND MINERALS   A well-documented example is the 1980 acquisition of Houston Oil and Minerals Corporation by Tenneco, Inc., which was then the largest conglomerate in the United States.[17] Houston's business was finding, developing, and bringing petroleum and mineral deposits into production. The company was very aggressive and quite successful before its acquisition by Tenneco. Tenneco's stated intent was to run Houston as a separate company, maintaining the entrepreneurial, risk-taking style that had marked it as an independent concern. In particular, it planned to maintain a separate compensation and reward system at Houston that would provide unusually large individual payoffs to professionals for successful discovery and development of petroleum reserves. (Several Houston explorationists had become wealthy with the bonuses they earned from successful explorations, and such packages were common among smaller firms in the industry.) Yet Tenneco had great difficulty developing such a plan, and it ultimately failed to do so. Within a year, more than a third of Houston's managers, a quarter of its exploration staff, and almost a fifth of its production people had left the company for better opportunities elsewhere. This severely hampered operations, and ultimately it became impossible to maintain Houston as a distinct unit within the firm.

Tenneco's costly failure to institute the intended reward policy apparently resulted from a concern for equity in pay across the organization. The Tenneco Vice President of Administration was quoted in *The Wall Street Journal* as saying: "We have to ensure internal equity and apply the same standards of compensation to everyone." Meeting this perceived need was very costly. It contributed to the exodus and to the ultimate failure of the acquisition. Failure to meet this need might well have been even more costly, however. Tenneco's 100,000 employees, jealously looking at the huge bonuses that would have been paid to the few hundred Houston professionals, might have consumed large chunks of their superiors' time with their jealous complaining and their attempts to get some of these funds for themselves. Given the relative sizes of the two groups, the overall impact on productivity at Tenneco could have been disastrous.

---

[16] Michael Porter, "From Competitive Advantage to Corporate Strategy," *Harvard Business Review* (May–June 1987), 43–59.

[17] This example is discussed by Oliver Williamson in *The Economic Institutions of Capitalism* (New York: The Free Press, 1985), p. 158. The primary source is George Getschow, "Loss of Expert Talent Impedes Oil Finding by New Tenneco Unit," *The Wall Street Journal* (February 9, 1982), A-1. The quotation in the next paragraph is from this story.

SUMMARY

The term *moral hazard* originated in the insurance industry, where it referred to the tendency of people who purchase insurance to alter their behavior in ways that are costly to the insurance company, such as taking less care to prevent a loss from occurring. Within economics, the term has come to refer to any behavior under a contract that is inefficient, arises from the differing interests of the contracting parties, and persists only because one party to the contract cannot tell for sure whether the other is honoring the contract terms. Moral hazard problems arise frequently in *principal-agent* relationships, where one party (the "agent") is called upon to act on behalf of another (the "principal"), because the agent's interests commonly differ from the principal's and the principal cannot evaluate how well the agent has worked or whether the agent has been honest.

The savings and loan crisis in the United States illustrates the problem of moral hazard and how it is most often dealt with in ordinary business transactions. The difference of interests between the owners of the S&L and the federal insurance agency (the FSLIC) arose because the owners benefited from risky investments when they turned out well, but the costs of failures are borne by the insurance agency. When the agency failed to monitor and control the S&L, this led the S&L management to make risky investments or even to engage in fraud in a way that was costly to taxpayers. Competition for depositors' funds only intensified this effect, increasing the interest rates paid on deposits and forcing more conservative S&L management to find higher-yielding—and hence usually riskier—investments.

The relation of depositors to their S&L is similar to the relationship of lenders to any other kind of firm. Normally, lenders protect their money by imposing controls and requiring reporting by and audits of the borrower. What distinguished the S&L case is that the depositors, being insured, had little reason to monitor the savings institutions, and the federal government, whose money was at risk, did not monitor on its own behalf, in part because powerful congressmen were protecting the S&Ls.

Problems of fraud and excessive risk taking similar to the S&L problem can be found in many federally insured programs. Among those described are programs insuring workers' retirement benefits, farmers' crops, mortgage loans, and student loans. Similar problems exist in private-sector insurance programs, but these tend to be less severe partly because profit-oriented insurers monitor the insured more carefully and partly because private insurers refuse to offer insurance when the moral hazard problem is too severe.

Moral hazard is not only a problem of markets, but exists in other kinds of organizations as well. Air traffic controllers seeking to collect disability benefits have "punched out," causing incidents that seemed to indicate that they suffered job-related stress and were unable to continue their duties safely. The general partners in oil and gas drilling partnerships sometimes fail to complete wells that are profitable for the partnership as a whole because their own interests differ.

Various means are available to control the moral hazard problem. One is explicit *monitoring*, which can reduce the information problem that is a fundamental component of moral hazard. A second is the use of *incentive contracts* that pay for output performance when inputs cannot be measured. *Posting a bond* that is forfeited if the agent is caught cheating can be effective in a principal-agent relationship. This bond can be implicit in the rising pattern of wages over a worker's career: A worker caught cheating after several years of employment stands to lose the high wages paid to more senior workers. Sometimes, the whole problem can be avoided by the "do-it-yourself" solution, which does not rely on an agent with differing interests. Similarly, a firm can sometimes eliminate conflicts of interest with its suppliers by integrating vertically, though this does not eliminate any individual differences of interests between the formerly independent manager of the supplier and the same person who is now an employee of the firm.

An especially important category of moral hazard is the category of *influence activities* and the associated costs, known as *influence costs*. These arise when employees divert effort to influence organizational decisions. Even if those decisions are not ultimately affected, the time, effort, and ingenuity devoted to attempts at influence are unavailable for more productive activities. Influence costs are one of the important costs of centralized control and help to explain the importance of organizational boundaries. These costs are largely eliminated when there is no decision maker with authority to make the decisions that employees wish to influence, and this condition can sometimes be brought about by creating legal or other boundaries between operating units.

■ ## BIBLIOGRAPHIC NOTES

As with so much else in the economics of organizations, the problems of misaligned incentives and what we now call moral hazard were noted and understood by Adam Smith: see his discussion in *The Wealth of Nations* of the incentives in joint stock companies (Book V, Chapter I, Part III, Article I) and of the incentives for university teachers (Book V, Chapter I, Part III, Article II). The nature moral hazard and its importance to economic analysis was made explicit by Mark Pauly in the context of an article on the economics of health insurance by Kenneth Arrow. The principal-agent model, which underlies much of the discussion in this chapter, has several early contributors, including James Mirrlees, Michael Spence and Richard Zeckhauser, and Steven Ross. More recent references are given in the next chapter. The explanation of the age/wage profile and mandatory retirement in terms of bonding is due to Edward Lazear. A useful discussion and development of Lazear's bonding model is given by Lorne Carmichael.

Adolphe Berle and Gardner Means began the debate about whether the ownership structure of the modern corporation has made it particularly susceptible to managerial moral hazard. The papers published in the *Journal of Law and Economics* [26 (June 1983)] from the Hoover Institution conference on "Corporations and Private Property" held to commemorate the fiftieth anniversary of the publication of the Berle and Means book give some flavor of current thinking on this issue, which in turn has been central to the debate over hostile takeovers. The "Symposium on Takeovers" in the *Journal of Economic Perspectives* [2(1988), 3-82] provides an overview of economists' views on this debate, which we consider in Chapter 15.

The modeling of bankruptcy as a means for effecting efficiency-enhancing changes in control is due to Phillippe Aghion and Patrick Bolton. The determinants of firms' financing decisions are treated in Chapters 14 and 15, and further references are given there.

The importance of the policy of selective intervention was emphasized by Oliver Williamson. The concept of influence costs as a major element of the transactions costs of nonmarket organization was developed by the present authors. The theory of information provided by competing sources is developed in our *Rand Journal of Economics* paper.

■ REFERENCES

Aghion, P., and P. Bolton. "An 'Incomplete Contract' Approach to Bankruptcy and the Financial Structure of the Firm," *IMSSS Technical Report*, No. 536 (Stanford, Ca: Stanford University, 1988).

Arrow, K.J. "Uncertainty and the Welfare Economics of Medical Care," *American Economic Review*, 53 (1963), 941–73.

Berle, A., and G. Means. *The Modern Corporation and Private Property* (New York: MacMillan, 1932).

Carmichael, L. "Self-Enforcing Contracts, Shirking and Life Cycle Incentives," *Journal of Economic Prespectives*, 3 (1989), 65–83.

Lazear, E. "Why Is There Mandatory Retirement?" *Journal of Political Economy*, 87 (December 1979), 1261–84.

Milgrom, P., and J. Roberts. "Relying on the Information of Interested Parties," *Rand Journal of Economics*, 17 (1986), 18–32.

Milgrom, P., and J. Roberts. "Bargaining Costs, Influence Costs, and the Organization of Economic Activity," in *Perspectives on Positive Political Economy*, J. Alt and K. Shepsle, eds. (Cambridge: Cambridge University Press, 1990).

Mirrlees, J. "An Exploration in the Theory of Optimum Income Taxation," *Review of Economic Studies*, 38 (1971), 175–208.

Pauly, M. "The Economics of Moral Hazard," *American Economic Review*, 58 (1968), 31–58.

Ross, S. "The Economic Theory of Agency: The Principal's Problem," *American Economic Review*, 63 (1973), 134–39.

Spence, A.M., and R. Zeckhauser. "Insurance, Information and Individual Action," *American Economic Review*, 61 (1971), 380–87.

Williamson, O. *The Economic Institutions of Capitalism* (New York: The Free Press, 1985).

EXERCISES

Food for Thought

1. Widespread fraud brought down some S&Ls. Does deposit insurance itself make fraud more attractive? How did the changes in regulation of the S&Ls contribute to the problem of fraud?

2. As part of a plan to rescue the savings and loan industry, in late 1988 the U.S. government encouraged private investors to purchase the assets of failing savings and loans. They offered guarantees of principal and, in some cases, interest on some of the properties taken over by the S&Ls when borrowers defaulted on loans. What effect would you expect these guarantees to have on the behavior of the new owners?

3. In automobile collision insurance and health insurance, the insurance policy often has a provision calling for a *deductible* according to which the portion of any insured loss up to some fixed limit, such as $500, is paid for by the insured person; only the excess is paid for by the insurance company. In addition, health-insurance policies often provide for *copayments* by the insured, according to which the insurance company pays only some fraction, such as 80 or 90 percent, of the medical costs in excess of the deductible, until the insured has paid some maximum amount (such as $2,000 in a year). What economic function do deductibles and

copayment provisions serve? Why do we see deductibles but not copayments used in automobile insurance policies?

4.   Farmland on which annual crops are grown is often rented, but orchards and other perennial crops are more often grown by the owners of the land. How can this be explained?

5.   In a possibly apocryphal story, a nineteenth-century English traveler in China was shocked that the oarsmen rowing the boat in which the traveler was riding were brutally whipped by a ferocious overseer if they slacked off on their rowing. The traveler was even more shocked (so the story goes) to learn that the oarsmen owned the boat and hired the overseer to beat them! How would you explain this?

6.   We attribute the prevalence of limited partnerships in oil and gas exploration to the tax advantages of having some claimants pay some of the costs and other claimants pay other cost elements. But the tax advantages might have been achieved by a regular partnership in which different partners had different forms of claims. What are the advantages then of the limited partnership form of organization?

7.   Stanford University's Honor Code forbids faculty from monitoring students during examinations. What effect would you expect this to have on student behavior? On the relationships between students and faculty?

Quantitative Problems

1.   Suppose there are two firms, Firm A and Firm B, that are considering making a joint investment in R&D. The total payoff from the project is $200 \times (V_A + V_B)^{1/2}$, where V_A and V_B are the values of the two investments. The two firms expect to share this payoff equally while each absorbs the cost V_A or V_B, of its investment. Show that the value-maximizing plans are those where the total investment of the two firms is $10,000. How much total value is created in this way?

2.   In question 1, suppose now that the firms cannot enforce a contract specifying levels of investment for each, because they cannot observe the real value of the investments that are made. Show that if Firm A expects Firm B to invest V_B, it can do no better than to invest $2,500 - V_B$. How much, then, will be invested in total? How much total value is created?

3.   Suppose that if the firms do not sign a contract, that they can develop their own versions of the research project in competition with one another. A marketable product will result for either firm provided it spends at least 35 percent as much as its competitor. If $V_A > .35 \times V_B$, then Firm A's net profit will be $200 \times (V_A - .35 \times V_B)^{1/2} - V_A$, and correspondingly for B. Show that if each firm expects the other to invest $10000/.65$, then it will choose to invest an equal amount. What will the total profits be? Would you expect the firms to reach a joint venture agreement under these circumstances?

4.   (*Forcing contracts*). In principal-agent problems of efforts provision, moral hazard is not a problem it the structure of uncertainty allows the principal to infer precisely whether the agent has failed to perform as desired. To see this, suppose in the context of the example in the Appendix that the matrix relating the probabilities of various outcomes were changed so that the high level of revenues (30) was sure to occur if the worker supplies the high level of effort ($e = 2$), but either level of effort could still happen if the low level of effort ($e = 1$) is provided. Thus, the first row of Table 6.5, corresponding to $e = 1$, is unchanged, but the entries corresponding to $e = 2$ become 0 and 1 instead of 1/3 and 2/3. Rewrite the incentive and participation constraints and show that it is possible to design a *forcing* contract that motivates the worker to work hard, supplying $e = 2$, without placing any risk on him or her. How

much is the worker paid if revenues of 10 are realized? How much when revenues are 30? What are the expected utilities of the two parties? Is there any cost in this case to effort not being observable, that is, could the parties do better if effort were observed? Would it be possible to achieve this sort of result if the low level of effort surely resulted in revenues of 10, but the high level of effort could result in either revenues of 10 (with probability 1/3) or 30 (with probability 2/3)? Why or why not?

5.   (*Selling the firm to a risk-neutral agent*). In many principal-agent problems of effort provision, moral hazard is costly if the agent is risk-averse because making his or her pay reflect the full marginal impact of his or her effort choices imposes costs on the agent that could be avoided if the risk-neutral principal absorbed the variability in incomes. Again in the context of the example in the Appendix, show that if the agent is risk-neutral, with utility function for income w and effort e of $u(w,e) = w - (e-1)$, then it is possible to acheive the same expected utilities for both parties as would result if effort were observable by having the agent bear all the risk and the principal receive an amount that is independent of the realized level of revenues.

APPENDIX: A MATHEMATICAL EXAMPLE
OF INCENTIVE CONTRACTING*

The purpose of this appendix is to develop a relatively simple example of what is conceptually required to determine an efficient contract in the presence of unobservable effort and the consequent moral hazard problem. In the next chapter we develop these matters much more fully, although with less visible mathematics. The example is a principal-agent problem. As we mentioned earlier, in the standard language of incentive theory, an *agent* is someone who does work on behalf of another person, called the *principal*. We will think of agent as a worker and principal as an employer.

Suppose the principal is risk neutral, caring only about the expected amount of money he or she receives, and the agent is risk averse and also averse to providing more than a minimal amount of effort. In particular, suppose the agent evaluates wage income and effort according to a utility function of the form $U(w,e) = \sqrt{w} - (e - 1)$, where w is the wage and e is the effort level. According to this mathematical formula, the marginal utility of income is $1/(2\sqrt{w})$, which is decreasing in the wage level. As we will see in Chapter 7, this property corresponds to risk aversion. The $(e - 1)$ term is the cost of effort, and its form reflects the idea that providing effort is costly only when effort exceeds 1 unit.

Suppose that two effort levels are possible: $e = 1$ and $e = 2$. The agent also has outside job opportunities, and to get him or her to accept employment the agent must be offered at least as much satisfaction as he or she can get working elsewhere. We model this by imposing a requirement that the job provide the agent with a utility level of at least some expected utility u, which we can interpret as the expected utility value of his or her next-best alternative. To keep the arithmetic simple, let us suppose that this minimum acceptable utility level u is 1.

The agent's efforts are assumed to help increase the revenues of the firm. Depending on those efforts, various possible levels of revenue might be received. However, the outcome also depends on random factors that neither the principal nor the agent can observe or control. Table 6.5 gives the probabilities of the possible outcomes for each level of effort. For example, when $e = 1$, Revenue is 10 with probability 2/3 and 30 with probability 1/3.

With $e = 1$, the expected revenues are $(2/3) \times 10 + (1/3) \times 30 = 50/3$, whereas lifting the effort to $e = 2$ raises the expected receipts to $(1/3) \times 10 + (2/3) \times 30 = 70/3$. Effort is productive in raising the probability of the good outcome and thus the expected receipts.

If e were observable and the parties wanted it set at 2, the solution would be for the contract to specify that $e = 2$ and that the agent be paid enough to get him or her to agree to take the job when he or she provides $e = 2$, and to be paid nothing if the agent picks $e = 1$. Because the contract calls for a fixed wage w if the agent provides the required effort, the agent bears no uncontrollable risk; the income will be w for sure. The revenues, of course, remain random, but this risk is borne entirely by the risk-neutral principal. This allocation of risk is efficient. Putting any variability in the agent's pay would necessitate compensating him or her for bearing risk, whereas the risk-neutral principal is indifferent about the risk. The pay needed to get the agent

---

* Those who are not familiar with the theory of expected utility and decisions under uncertainty might prefer to skip this Appendix until they have studied these topics, which are developed at the start of Chapter 7.

**Table 6.5   Probability of Outcomes For
Differing Levels of Effort**

Revenue

Action	R = 10	R = 30
e = 1	p = 2/3	p = 1/3
e = 2	p = 1/3	p = 2/3

to agree to the contract is determined by the utility function and the minimum available elsewhere:

$$\sqrt{w} - (e - 1) = \sqrt{w} - (2 - 1) \ge 1, \quad \text{or} \quad w \ge 4$$

So long as the pay is at least 4, the agent will not prefer to take a job elsewhere. Because the principal has no reason in this model to give the agent any more than necessary, the principal gets an expected return net (of the pay to the agent) of $(70/3) - 4 = (58/3)$.

In contrast, if the principal wants only the low level of effort, this can be achieved at minimum cost by paying 1 in either event. This puts no risk on the agent. It again gives the agent an expected utility of 1, but $(47/3)$ to the principal. Thus, the wage cost of the extra effort is $4 - 1 = 3$, both to the principal and to "society," whereas it raises expected receipts by $(20/3) > 3$. Thus it is worthwhile to require and pay for the higher level of effort.

In any case, if e is observable, then regardless of the desired level of e, the efficient contract protects the worker from having to bear any uncontrollable risk while, if the high level of effort is efficient, the contract requires the agent to work at the higher level but compensates him or her for it.

Things are different when only the level of revenues, but not the level of effort e, is observable. In this case, the principal cannot effectively insist that the agent take a particular level of effort. Effort is not observable, and revenues are not fully determined by effort, although they are responsive to it. Revenue levels of 10 and 30 are both possible no matter what the agent does, so a bad outcome might be attributable to bad luck rather than shirking, and a good outcome might occur by sheer good luck regardless of what the agent does.

If a high level of effort is desired but the agent is averse to working that hard, the way to motivate high effort is to pay more for a good outcome than for a bad outcome. This requires exposing the agent to some income risk.

If the principal wants $e = 2$, then the agent's expected utility when he or she picks $e = 2$ must exceed that when he or she slacks off and picks $e = 1$. Let y be the amount the agent receives under the incentive contract when the outcome is 10 and z be the pay when the receipts are 30. Then the agent's expected utility in picking $e = 2$ is

$$(1/3)(\sqrt{y} - 1) + (2/3)(\sqrt{z} - 1)$$

(where we have used the probabilities that correspond to the high level of effort in evaluating the expected wage), whereas his or her expected utility from picking $e = 1$ is

$$(2/3)(\sqrt{y} - 0) + (1/3)(\sqrt{z} - 0)$$

In this expression we used the probabilities corresponding to $e = 1$. For the agent to

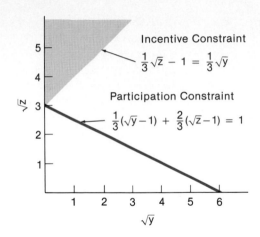

Figure 6.1: In this example, the point $(0,3)$ satisfies both the incentive and participation constraints at least cost to the principal. Note that the graph is expressed in terms of the *square roots of y and z*.

be willing to pick the higher effort level, the first of these expressions must be at least as large as the second:

$$(1/3)(\sqrt{y} - 1) + (2/3)(\sqrt{z} - 1) \geq (2/3)(\sqrt{y} - 0) + (1/3)(\sqrt{z} - 0)$$

This expression is called an *incentive compatibility constraint* in the formal theory of incentives. It represents a constraint on the design of a compensation scheme when the principals want to elicit a high level of effort. Note the parallel with the incentive compatibility constraints that arise in problems with precontractual private information (see Chapter 5). As there, the constraint relates the utility of the agent when he or she acts in the desired fashion to that when he or she misbehaves and it thereby limits the arrangements that will work.

With a bit of algebra, the incentive constraint is transformed into the following simpler form:

$$(1/3)\sqrt{z} - 1 \geq (1/3)\sqrt{y} \qquad (6.1)$$

According to Equation 6.1, the pay for the good outcome must sufficiently exceed that for the bad in order to compensate the agent for providing the extra effort that makes the good outcome more likely.

Another kind of constraint on the design of compensation is called the *participation constraint*. The terms of employment, taken together, must provide the agent with at least as much utility as that available in outside opportunities. Otherwise, the agent will not agree to *participate* by accepting employment. Recall that for this example, we assume the expected utility of outside opportunities is 1. Then, the participation constraint is:

$$(1/3)(\sqrt{y} - 1) + (2/3)(\sqrt{z} - 1) \geq 1 \qquad (6.2)$$

The principal's problem is to find the values of y and z that satisfy these constraints and give the maximum expected returns net of pay to the agent. Furthermore, both y and z must be positive: The agent cannot (in this example) be made to pay the principal when things go badly.

The two constraints are graphed in Figure 6.1. The values of y and z that meet the incentive constraint (6.1) are those above the upward-sloping line, whereas those that satisfy the participation constraint (6.2) are above the downward-sloping line. The shaded area represents the values of y and z—the pay levels for bad and good outcomes—that both attract the agent to take the job and motivate him or her to perform as desired. Because the principal's net return is largest when the expected pay to the agent is smallest, the best contract from the principal's point of view is $y = 0$,

$z = 9$. This meets both constraints and gives the principal an expected return of $(1/3)(10 - 0) + (2/3)(30 - 9) = (52/3)$.

The agent is no better off than he or she would be if e were observable, whereas the principal's payoff has fallen from (58/3) to (52/3) because the expected wage paid the agent has risen from 4 to 6. The additional expected wage merely serves to compensate for the risk the agent faces. Thus, the unobservability of effort and the consequent moral hazard has an efficiency cost. In this case, the cost arises from having to load too much risk on the agent.

We also need to make sure that it is actually worthwhile to provide incentives to get the agent to select the high effort level. If instead the principal decided to settle for $e = 1$, then there would be no need to use incentive payments. Paying the agent a constant wage of 1—independent of the outcome—would provide the agent with just enough expected utility to get him or her to agree to the contract. Because it would put no risk on the agent, this pay scheme minimizes the costs of employing him or her. Of course, with the agent's pay unaffected by the outcome, the agent will minimize his or her effort provision and pick $e = 1$, as planned. This yields a payoff to the agent of 1 again, and to the principal of $(2/3)(10 - 1) + (1/3)(30 - 1) = (47/3)$. Because this is less than the payoff when $e = 2$ is induced, motivating the higher effort level is worthwhile.

This, of course, is just one example. In other examples, trying to motivate a high level of effort is inefficient because the costs of loading enough risk on the agent to provide the requisite incentives exceed the gains from the higher level of effort. Moreover, this can happen even when a high level of effort would be optimal with full observability and no moral hazard. In the present example, taking the receipts in the good event to be 20 rather than 30 yields such a case. It is also easy to concoct other examples with several possible effort levels where the solution is to give up on trying to induce the level of effort that would be optimal without the observability difficulties, though it is still worthwhile to provide incentives for some effort beyond the minimum conceivable. In these cases, the inefficiency manifests itself both in the agent's bearing risk that he or she would rather avoid and that the principal is better equipped to face, and in the level of effort induced being less than is desirable.

Designing real incentive contracts involves much more complex issues than this example can reveal. Some of these are developed in the next chapter, and more are explored in Chapters 8, 12, and 13.

Part

IV

EFFICIENT INCENTIVES: CONTRACTS AND OWNERSHIP

7

RISK SHARING
AND INCENTIVE CONTRACTS

8

RENTS AND EFFICIENCY

9

OWNERSHIP AND PROPERTY RIGHTS

7

RISK SHARING
AND INCENTIVE CONTRACTS

W*ell, then, says I, what's the use you learning to do right when it's troublesome to do right and ain't no trouble to do wrong, and the wages is just the same?*

Huckleberry Finn[1]

In Chapter 6, we examined how insurance of various forms can combine with difficulties of monitoring actions or verifying information to blunt individual incentives. We also surveyed a number of responses to such moral hazard problems. Among these were *incentive contracts*, under which individual incentives are strengthened by holding people at least partially responsible for the results of their actions, even though doing so exposes them to risks that could be more easily borne by an insurance company. In this chapter, we develop a detailed theory of the nature and form of efficient incentive contracts in the presence of moral hazard, establishing a number of general principles that can be used to understand, evaluate, and design such contracts. Although we develop this theory largely in terms of employment contracting and performance pay, the principles are broadly applicable to a wide variety of institutional contexts.

INCENTIVE CONTRACTS AS A RESPONSE TO MORAL HAZARD

In both theory and practice, there are more options open to society than to insure a risk fully or not to insure it at all. Actual insurance contracts are also incentive

---

[1] The Adventures of Huckleberry Finn, Mark Twain (1884).

contracts: They have provisions that restrict and condition claim payments in ways that provide better incentives than full insurance without removing the essential part of the insurance coverage. The deductible clause that is common in homeowners' fire and theft insurance policies requires the policyholders to bear the initial part of any loss they may incur while still protecting them against large financial losses. Health-insurance policies often require copayments, according to which the insurance pays only a fraction of the costs, with the rest being borne by the insured. Automobile insurance is experience rated, so that those who are responsible for traffic accidents pay higher rates. These features are designed to encourage the insureds to take care and to deter their excessive use of the insurance. For example, the copayments on emergency room visits are set so that, rather than automatically rushing to the emergency room, a patient will wait to be treated in the doctor's office for illnesses and injuries that are not extremely urgent. In this spirit, the policy may provide no coverage at all for treatments that are considered to be elective, such as cosmetic surgery other than that which is necessary to repair damage caused by an injury. As these examples make clear, insurance contracts are designed with profound attention for the need to reduce the waste caused by moral hazard.

Similar moral hazard issues must be faced when devising compensation contracts for employees in a firm. Here, too, there is a balance that needs to be struck between providing incentives and insulating people from risk. To provide incentives, it is desirable to hold employees *responsible* for their performance; this means that employees' compensation or future promotions should depend on how well they perform their assigned tasks. As we will see, however, holding employees responsible typically will involve subjecting them to risk in their current or future incomes. Because most people dislike bearing such risks and are often less well equipped to do so than are their employers, there is a cost in providing incentives. *Efficient contracts balance the costs of risk bearing against the incentive gains that result.*

Sources of Randomness

If employees were always able to perform as required and if it were easy to determine precisely whether they have behaved as they were supposed to, having pay depend on performance would not generate any risk-bearing costs. An employee could choose whether to perform appropriately or not. Appropriate behavior would be compensated as agreed; inappropriate behavior would go uncompensated and might be penalized. Higher levels of required performance would be associated with higher pay to compensate for the additional effort that the employee is called upon to expend, but there would be no risk in the employee's pay because the outcome is completely under the employee's control.

In most real situations, however, attempts to impose responsibility on employees for their performance do expose them to risk because perfect measures of behavior are hardly ever available. For example, if the employee is expected to give expert advice on some matter, it may be impossible to determine whether the advice is based on the best available information and analysis and whether the recommendations are actually designed to promote the employer's interests, or whether the employee has acted selfishly or deceptively. When care and effort are wanted, it may equally be impossible to determine if employees are doing what they should or slacking off. In these kinds of situations, even though the quality of effort or the accuracy of information cannot itself be observed, something about it can frequently be inferred from observed results, and compensation based on results can be an effective way to provide incentives. Piece rates are a prime example: Rather than trying to monitor directly the effort that the employee provides, the employer simply pays for output.

However, results are frequently affected by things outside the employee's control that have nothing to do with how intelligently, honestly, and diligently the employee has worked. Sales at a fast-food restaurant may be lower than expected due to the outlet manager's lack of creativity in devising promotional efforts or negligence in supervising the staff, but the low level may also be caused by other factors. Road construction could have made the location less accessible to customers. The opening of a competing restaurant nearby could be to blame. Population growth may have been less than forecast. In the case of a franchise, the franchisor's failure to provide attractive menus or timely deliveries of food could be responsible. Or some combination of these and other factors might be at work. Similarly, if an aircraft crashes, pilot error may be to blame, or poor maintenance, or a design flaw in the craft itself, or a bolt of lightning, or an air traffic control error, and so on. When rewards are based on results, uncontrollable randomness in outcomes induces randomness in the employees' incomes.

A second source of randomness arises when the performance itself (rather than the result) is measured, but the performance evaluation measures include random or subjective elements. For example, the way an employee is evaluated may depend on his or her supervisor's subjective perception of the employee's attitude towards the job and behavior towards other workers. Employees may see this sort of evaluation as a source of risk because it is based partly on elements outside the employee's control. A worker's performance may be evaluated by sporadic monitoring, and these random observations may not give a perfect reflection of the actual quality of the work. In either case, the imperfect evaluation of performance induces randomness in rewards.

A third source of randomness comes from the possibility that outside events beyond the control of the employee may affect his or her ability to perform as contracted. Health problems may reduce the employee's strength and ability to work, concerns about family finances may make it impossible to concentrate effectively on the tasks at hand, or weather or traffic conditions may render meeting a regular schedule impossible. Thus, performance itself becomes random, and so too does performance-based compensation. Consequently, making employees responsible for performance subjects them to risk.

Balancing Risks and Incentives

It might be possible to insulate employees from these risks by making their compensation absolutely risk free and unrelated to performance or outcomes. In that case, however, the employees would have little direct incentive to perform in more than the most perfunctory fashion, because there are no rewards for good behavior or punishments for bad. As we will see, both here and in Chapter 12 (where we examine compensation issues more specifically) effective contracts balance the gains from providing incentives against the costs of forcing employees to bear risk.

The same considerations arise in many other business transactions. The size of the crop produced by a sharecropper is influenced by weather and pests as well as by the sharecropper's own skill and effort. Traditionally, landowners make part of the sharecropper's compensation proportional to the size of the crop. This arrangement provides helpful incentives that induce the sharecropper to plant drought- and pest-resistant varieties, to irrigate and care for the crops, and so on. However, it also exposes the sharecropper to the risks of a poor harvest—a risk that is at least partially outside his or her control. Similarly, in the United States, a lawyer who sues for damages on behalf of a client often receives a contingency fee (a percentage of the damage award or settlement). This system provides the litigator with an incentive to work hard on behalf of the client, but because the outcome of the lawsuit is not entirely under the litigator's control, both the litigator's income and the client's are uncertain.

Although all of these cases share certain common features, the accuracy of the performance assessments that can be achieved and the need for and possibility of risk sharing or insurance vary from case to case. Because of these differences, the institutions and practices that best balance risk and incentives also vary.

The conclusion that arrangements should vary from case to case is too vague to be of any use to managers or interest to economists. Fortunately, we can do better. The principles developed in this chapter make it possible to reach a relatively subtle understanding of how *optimal* practices can be designed that trade off the value of protecting people from risk against the need to provide them with incentives.

In order to analyze how rational people respond to incentives in insurance-like contracts, we must first examine how rational people behave and interact in risky situations. This involves three steps. The first is to describe the risks precisely, using the language of statistics. Then, we describe how rational people, acting individually, can choose consistently among risky choices and how varying individual attitudes toward risk taking can be incorporated into the analysis. Finally, we examine how groups of people can share risks and form insurance pools, being careful to quantify the benefits of insurance coverage. Given this background, we then examine how people respond to incentives in risky situations. This then allows us to develop the principles of efficiently designed incentive contracts.

DECISIONS UNDER UNCERTAINTY AND THE EVALUATION OF FINANCIAL RISKS

The first element we need is a theory of decisions under uncertainty. There are, in fact, a number of rich theories addressing this subject in great generality, but for our purposes it is enough to consider the special case in which the risks are financial. The first step is to describe the financial risk. We do this using two ideas familiar from statistical theory: the concepts of **mean** and **variance**. These terms are defined in the appendix to the chapter. Here, we illustrate their meaning by computing the mean and variance in an example.

Computing Means and Variances

Recall that the mean or expected value of a random income is simply the expected amount of income, computed as the weighted average of the possible values that income might take on, with the weight on each value being the probability of that value occurring. The relevant calculations are illustrated in Table 7.1.

The table shows a hypothetical situation in which there is an investment for which the returns are zero with probability one half, $3,000 with probability one third and $6,000 with probability one sixth. The *mean* or *expected value* of the return is $\frac{1}{2}(\$0) + \frac{1}{3}(\$3,000) + \frac{1}{6}(\$6,000) = \$0 + \$1,000 + \$1,000 = \$2,000$. In the table, the calculation works by multiplying the entries in columns 1 and 2 to obtain column 3, and then summing the column. Having higher probabilities on higher values increases the mean.

The *variance* of income is a measure of its variability or randomness. It is computed in columns 4 and 5 of the table. In column 4, we take each possible value, subtract the mean (to get a measure of how far the particular value deviates from the expected value), and square the result (so that terms greater than the average that result from higher-than-expected incomes do not cancel out the negative terms that result when income is less than expected). In column 5, these squared variations are multiplied by the corresponding probability. Summing the column gives the variance. In the example, the variance is $\frac{1}{2}(0 - 2,000)^2 + \frac{1}{3}(3,000 - 2,000)^2 + \frac{1}{6}(6,000 - 2,000)^2 = \frac{1}{2}(4,000,000) + \frac{1}{3}(1,000,000) + \frac{1}{6}(16,000,000) = 5,000,000$. (The units are "dollars squared.") If income is certain, then the variance is zero, because the income never deviates from its expected value. Increasing the probability of very high and very low values tends to increase the variance.

Table 7.1 Sample Computation of Mean and Variance

1 Probability	2 Return	3 (1) × (2)	4 (Return − Mean)^2	5 (1) × (4)
1/2	0	0	4,000,000	2,000,000
1/3	3,000	1,000	1,000,000	333,333
1/6	6,000	1,000	16,000,000	2,666,667
		Mean = 2,000		Variance = 5,000,000

Certainty Equivalents and Risk Premia

One of the main hypotheses we employ in this chapter is that most people are *risk averse*; that is, they would prefer receiving a certain income of $\bar{I}$ to receiving a random income with expected value $\bar{I}$. The amount the person would be willing to pay to make the switch is the **risk premium** associated with the random income. The magnitude of the risk premium depends on both the riskiness of the income and the individual person's degree of risk aversion. The amount that is left after the risk premium is paid is the **certainty equivalent** of the random income. It is the amount of income, payable for certain, that the person regards as equivalent in value to the original, random income.

One of the central results of decision theory is that the certainty equivalent can be estimated by a simple formula: $\bar{I} - \frac{1}{2}r(\bar{I})Var(I)$, where $\bar{I}$ and $Var(I)$ are the mean and variance of the random variable I, and $r(\bar{I})$ is a parameter of the decision maker's personal preferences called the **coefficient of absolute risk aversion** for gambles with mean $\bar{I}$. The mean in this formula is the mean income, and the amount subtracted from it in the formula is the risk premium; it is equal to one-half times the coefficient of absolute risk aversion times the variance of the income. According to the formula, the risk premium is proportional to the coefficient of absolute risk aversion: People who are more risk averse according to this measure are willing to pay proportionately larger risk premiums to avoid a given risk. If the coefficient of absolute risk aversion is zero, then the person is unwilling to pay any premium to avoid the risk. Such a person is called **risk neutral**. A person is risk averse when the coefficient of absolute risk aversion is positive. The amount $\bar{I} - \frac{1}{2}r(\bar{I})Var(I)$ that is left in expectation after the risk premium is deducted is called the person's certain equivalent income or the certainty equivalent of the random income I.

If there is no uncertainty regarding the level of income, then $Var(I) = 0$; the only value that income actually might take on is $I = \bar{I}$. Then, the formula yields the sensible result that the person is as well off with the nonrandom income I as with a certain amount that is equal to I: The thing is as good as itself. When I does vary (so $Var(I)$ is positive) and the person is risk averse (so $r(\bar{I})$ is also positive), the risk premium is positive. This means that he or she would be willing to accept a lower amount than $\bar{I}$ to avoid the risk. More precisely, the risk premium, $\frac{1}{2}r(\bar{I})Var(I)$, is the amount that the person would pay to have the certain income $\bar{I}$ for sure rather than face the uncertainty in I.[2]

---

[2] The estimate of the certainty equivalent given in this formula is good when the variance is not too large or the coefficient of risk aversion is small. In terms of the example in Table 7.1, where the mean income was $2,000 and the variance was 5,000,000, the formula becomes $2,000 - 2,500,000r(\bar{I})$. This approximation is reasonable only for values of r in the range of .00008 or less (corresponding to a risk premium of 200); when $r \leq .0008$, it yields the nonsensical answer that the individual would be indifferent

Risk Premia and Value Maximization

Our analysis in this chapter uses the value maximization principle, which in the context of uncertainty asserts that an arrangement is efficient if and only if it maximizes the total certain equivalent wealth of all the parties involved. Recall from Chapter 2 that the premises needed to derive the principle are (1) that each person has enough wealth to make whatever payments might be called for under any relevant contract and (2) that each person has a well-defined willingness to pay for any given product or service and the amount of this monetary valuation does not depend on his or her income level. As discussed in Chapter 2, these are strong and often unrealistic assumptions, but they greatly simplify the analysis and enable us to separate analytically the effects of the level and variability of income from all other effects on the matters of interest. In the context of uncertain income, the second assumption is reduced to this: The risk premium that a person would pay to eliminate a given amount of variance must not depend on the expected level of income $\bar{I}$. In view of the risk premium formula, this means that $r(\bar{I})$ must not depend on $\bar{I}$. Throughout the rest of this chapter, we make that assumption and write r instead of $r(\bar{I})$. With this assumption, the crucial formulas become:

$$\text{Expected Income} = \bar{I}$$
$$\text{Risk Premium} = \tfrac{1}{2}r Var(I)$$
$$\text{Certain Equivalent} = \bar{I} - \tfrac{1}{2}r Var(I)$$

We use these formulas to calculate the benefits of insurance and the costs of the risk bearing that is required to provide incentives.

RISK SHARING AND INSURANCE

One of the most fundamental facts about the economics of risk is that when several people are facing statistically independent risks, then by sharing the risks among themselves they can greatly reduce the cost of risk bearing. Two risks are **statistically independent** if knowing the realized value of one risk gives you no information about the value that the other will achieve. For example, the amount you won or lost per dollar invested in the state lottery today does not give you any reason to change your estimates of the likely returns in the stock market tomorrow. In contrast, for risks that are not independent, knowledge of one *is* useful in predicting the other. For example, the prices of gold on the London and New York markets are both random, but they tend to move together under the influence of arbitrage (buying in one market and selling in another to make a riskless profit). Thus, knowing the price in London tells you something useful about what the New York price is likely to be, and so the two risks are not independent. This **principle of risk sharing**—that sharing independent risks reduces the aggregate cost of bearing them—is the basis of all financial insurance contracts.

How Insurance Reduces the Cost of Bearing Risk

In modern economies there are many kinds of institutions to assist people in sharing risks. One important group consists of the insurance companies. Having many policyholders, the insurance companies can spread risks very widely, enabling the companies to reduce individual risks greatly. If the risks are independent and the number of policyholders quite large, the risks are effectively eliminated and insurance works very well. For example, the risk that you will suffer an automobile accident is

---

between the gamble and getting a negative income for sure. In using the approximation, we thus assume that the variance of the uncertain income is not too large relative to the individual's risk aversion.

very nearly independent of the risk that any other particular person will do so, therefore automobile insurance is a feasible enterprise. Insurance companies specialize in evaluating individual risks and, by pooling the risk-bearing capacity of policyholders and (sometimes) shareholders, they reduce the cost of the risk bearing to negligible proportions. Pooling independent risks also has the additional advantage of making the insured losses statistically predictable. An insurance company can ask each insurance policyholder to pay a price for insurance equal to the expected amount of the loss, plus a margin for expenses and profit, and can be reasonably sure that the aggregate premium income together with a proportionately small reserve fund will enable it to pay for whatever losses may be suffered, even in a bad year.

Some kinds of risks, however, are so large and pervasive in their impact that they cannot be made negligible by sharing and they cannot be managed by traditional insurance arrangements. (Technically, the risks that people bear in this case are not statistically independent.) For example, an oil price increase would have such widespread effects, reducing the effective incomes of most people in oil-consuming countries, that no amount of risk sharing among those oil consumers can insulate them from the loss. Risks of this general kind are shared through other markets, especially the financial markets. By purchasing stock in companies that own oil reserves, for example, an investor who is especially vulnerable to oil price increases can arrange to have an offsetting profit if oil prices increase. Financial markets allocate many other kinds of risks, as well. For our purposes, an important example is the investment risks that are taken by firms, such as those associated with a new technology. The risk of failure of the technology is borne by shareholders in the company that develops it, and this capacity for risk sharing reduces the firm's cost of financing the investment, helping to promote technical change.

Efficient Risk Sharing: A Mathematical Example

Suppose that there are two people, A and B, each of whom has some risk associated with his or her income, where these risks are independent. Let I_A and I_B represent their random incomes, with means $\overline{I}_A$ and $\overline{I}_B$ and variances $Var(I_A)$ and $Var(I_B)$, and let r_A and r_B denote their coefficients of absolute risk aversion. In view of our earlier assumption, the value maximization principle applies. Consequently, every efficient risk-sharing contract maximizes the total certain equivalent income of all the parties, and every such contract is an efficient one.

If the parties make no special arrangements, then the total cost they suffer on account of risk bearing, that is, the total risk premium, is $\frac{1}{2}r_A Var(I_A) + \frac{1}{2}r_B Var(I_B)$, which is the sum of the two individual risk premia. Suppose that the parties instead agree on a risk-sharing contract with party A receiving a fraction α of the income I_A and ß of the income I_B (and thus of the risks associated with the two uncertain incomes.) In addition, suppose A receives a cash transfer of γ for the risk-sharing services provided. (This transfer might be positive or negative, but it is independent of the actual, realized incomes.) Party B receives the remaining share of each risk and makes the cash payment γ. After this agreement, A's income will be $\alpha I_A + ßI_B + \gamma$ and B's will be $(1 - \alpha)I_A + (1 - ß)I_B - \gamma$. This is a feasible agreement because the total income each party receives always adds up to $I_A + I_B$, the amount available. With this agreement, the *total risk premium* of the two parties is:

$$\text{Total Risk Premium} = \tfrac{1}{2}r_A Var(\alpha I_A + ßI_B + \gamma) + \tfrac{1}{2}r_B Var((1 - \alpha)I_A + (1 - ß)I_B - \gamma)$$

$$(7.1)$$

Because the total certain equivalent income of the two parties is equal to the mean income, $\overline{I}_A + \overline{I}_B$, minus the risk premium, the efficient arrangements are those that minimize Equation 7.1.

Using identities about variances (see Formula 7.18 in the appendix), Equation 7.1 is a quadratic function of α and β. The total risk premium is minimized when $\alpha/(1 - \alpha) = \beta/(1 - \beta) = r_B/r_A$. For example, suppose $r_A = 2$ and $r_B = 4$. The higher value for B's coefficient of absolute risk aversion indicates that B finds bearing risk more onerous than does A. Indeed, the risk premium that B attaches to any given risk is twice the amount A would pay to avoid the risk. In these circumstances, we might expect that A would bear more of the risk than would B. Evaluating the solution, we see that $\alpha/(1 - \alpha) = \beta/(1 - \beta) = 2$, so $\alpha = \beta = \frac{2}{3}$ and $(1 - \alpha) = (1 - \beta) = \frac{1}{3}$: A does in fact bear most of both risks. Moreover, A bears the same share (two thirds) of both.

To formulate the general principle that applies here, it is helpful to think in terms of different peoples' capacity to bear risk. We measure this by introducing the notion of risk tolerance. Someone with a coefficient of absolute risk aversion of r will be said to have **risk tolerance** of $1/r$. Notice that in the preceding example, A's share of each risk is equal to A's share of the total risk tolerance ($\frac{2}{3} = \frac{1}{2}/(\frac{1}{2} + \frac{1}{4})$).

These calculations actually reflect a general principle that can be shown to hold for any number of people and any number of financial risks: *When risks are shared efficiently, the share that a party bears in each risk is the same and is equal to his or her share of the total risk tolerance of the group.* Moreover, when risks are allocated efficiently, the total risk premium comes out to be:

$$\text{Total Risk Premium} = \tfrac{1}{2} Var(I_A + I_B)/[(1/r_A) + (1/r_B)] \tag{7.2}$$

Equation 7.2 resembles the formula for the risk premium charged by a single decision maker. It says that when risks are shared efficiently among a group of people, the total risk premium is the same as if the total risk were borne by a single decision maker whose risk tolerance is the sum of the members' individual risk tolerances. In the preceding numerical example, $(1/r_A) + (1/r_B) = \frac{1}{2} + \frac{1}{4} = \frac{3}{4}$. This formula, too, is general; it can be shown to hold for any number of people and any number of financial risks. With efficient risk sharing, the group is less risk averse than the people comprising it and so the costs of bearing risks can be reduced.

When individual risks are independent, these facts imply that sharing risks can be a very effective way to reduce the cost of risk bearing. For example, if there are n people, each with an income with variance v and each with the same coefficient of risk aversion r, and if each bears the income risk separately, then the risk premium will be $\frac{1}{2}rv$ per person. If the people share the income risks efficiently, then each will have a $1/n$ share of the total risk. The variance of the total risk is $V = nv$, so the variance of an individual $1/n$ share is $V/n^2 = v/n$ (see Formula 7.18 in the appendix again). Therefore, by sharing risks, each person's risk premium is reduced from $\frac{1}{2}rv$ to $\frac{1}{2}rv/n$. When n is large, even substantial financial losses can be reduced to economic insignificance by sharing them efficiently across the group.

Optimal Risk Sharing Ignoring Incentives

For both insurance companies, with their wide base of policyholders, and publicly traded corporations, with their wide base of shareholders, it is reasonable to suppose as a first approximation that the total risk tolerance of the company is infinitely larger than the risk tolerance of any individual policyholder or employee. As we mentioned earlier, an institution or person with infinite risk tolerance is said to be risk neutral: The coefficient of absolute risk aversion is zero and so the risk premium for bearing any risk is also zero. Applying our general propositions to the case where risks are to be shared between a risk-neutral insurance company and a risk-averse insurance policyholder or between a large, risk-neutral employer and a risk-averse employee, we find that the optimal share of the risk to be borne by the insurance buyer or employee is zero. Efficient risk sharing requires shifting all the risk onto the risk-neutral party, who suffers no cost in bearing the risk.

This conclusion, however, depends on ignoring the incentive problems for insurance and employment created by the condition of moral hazard.

PRINCIPLES OF INCENTIVE PAY

The general problem of motivating one person or organization to act on behalf of another is known among economists as the *principal-agent problem*. This problem encompasses not only the design of incentive pay but also issues in job design and the design of institutions to gather information, protect investments, allocate decision and ownership rights, and so on. However, we focus our discussion in this chapter principally on the issues surrounding incentive pay, and we set our discussion of incentives in the context of employment. The principal in this case is the employer, who wants the employee (the agent) to act on his or her behalf.

Basing Pay on Measured Performance

As we discussed in the introduction to this chapter, there are many situations in which providing incentives requires that employees' pay depend on their performance. Essentially, if the employees' direct provision of effort, intelligence, honesty, and imagination cannot be easily measured, then pay cannot be based on these and any financial incentives must come from basing compensation on performance. Efficient risk sharing, in contrast, requires that each person in society should bear only a tiny share of each risk, without regard to its source. In particular, individuals should be insulated against the randomness that would enter their pay by basing it on measured performance. Therefore, performance-based compensation systems cause a loss from inefficient risk sharing. The money value of the loss is equal to the risk premium associated with the actual compensation system minus the risk premium that would be associated with efficient risk sharing. Firms that use performance-based compensation hope to recoup this loss (and more) by eliciting better performance from their employees.

There are various reasons why incentives might be needed to elicit top-notch performance. Some employees may find their work distasteful and may neglect it unless they are held responsible for achieving results. Even when employees are hard workers who like their jobs, they may still have priorities that are different from those of their employer. For example, without compensating incentives, managers might be tempted to be too generous to their subordinates in granting raises and time off, or to hire the children of relatives and friends, to spend lavishly on a pleasant work environment or on fancy accommodations when traveling on business, to use company resources for community projects that raise their personal status, to devote excessive efforts to projects that advance their careers or that are especially interesting or pleasant, and so on.

To analyze these possibilities in a model, we suppose that the employee must exert an effort e at personal cost $C(e)$ to serve the interests of the employer. The effort e represents any activity that the employee undertakes on behalf of the firm, and the cost $C(e)$ can represent the unpleasantness of the task, foregone perquisites, lost status in the community, or anything else that the employee gives up to serve the employer's interests. For tasks that are pleasant, the "cost" can be zero or even negative.

The effort e is assumed to determine to the firm's profits: Profit $= P(e)$. It is sensible to assume that greater effort leads to higher profits. It is not necessary for the employer actually to know the functional relationship between effort and results; instead, the P function can be thought of as the employer's *subjective* estimate of the productivity relationship. If the relationship between profits and effort is random, then $P(e)$ should be thought of as the expected value of profits when effort level e is expended.

It may be impossible for anyone to observe an employee's direct effect on profits, but it is that effect, in principle, that the employer cares about. For example, the employee may be a sales representative whose efforts lead to no sales today but create a good impression that brings customers back in the future. The employer may care about the impression that is created, without actually being able to tell either how hard and how skillfully the employee has tried to impress customers or how many customers have actually been favorably impressed.

The general point here is that compensation can vary systematically only with things that the employer can observe. The employer cannot pay more to sales representatives who are particularly effective in creating a good impression if it is impossible to tell who they are. In addition, even some observable indicators may not be suitable bases for compensation. It may be possible, in principle, for the manager to photograph the faces of customers as they leave the store and pay compensation based on how many faces were smiling. What makes this possibility seem so absurd is its manifestly subjective nature. What is a "smiling" face? To base a compensation formula on something that is not objectively measurable is to invite disputes and unhappiness among employees.

A Model of Incentive Compensation

For our first formal model of incentive compensation, we assume that the effort level e that the employee chooses can be understood to be a number—for example, energy expended or hours worked. As we have already noted, if e were directly observed, there would be no difficulty in providing adequate incentives; the employer could make pay contingent on satisfactory performance without exposing the employee to any risk. We therefore suppose that the effort e cannot be directly observed. We shall suppose, however, that the employer can observe some imperfect indicators of e, that is, indicators that provide some information about e but are contaminated by random events beyond the control of the agent. For example, measured output might provide such a signal: It is related to effort, but many influences beyond the employee's control also affect the realized output. In addition, the employer may be able to observe other indicators of factors, such as general economic conditions, that are not controlled by the employee but that do affect performance.

Suppose that the indicator of effort can be written in the form $z = e + x$, where x is a random variable, and that a second indicator is y, where y is not affected by the effort e but may be statistically related to x, the noise between e and the observed z. Note that e and x are not separately observed; only their sum, z, is observed, and many different combinations of e and x yield the same level of observed z. Thus, high effort might be offset by bad luck, or low effort might be masked by good fortune.

For example, if the employee is the sales manager for some product, z might be a measure of total sales for the product (which depends on sales effort, e, and random events, x, such as realized demands) and y might measure total industry demand, which is correlated with the potential demand in the markets where the employee manages sales and thus with realized sales. To keep our formulas as simple as possible, we suppose that x and y are each adjusted to have mean zero. Then, the expected level of sales is just the effort level. In terms of the example, instead of making y the industry demand, we could make it the amount by which industry demand differs from a forecast value.

The class of compensation rules that we study are those that are linear in the two observations, that is, ones that can be written in the following form, where w stands for wage:

$$w = \alpha + \beta(e + x + \gamma y) \tag{7.3}$$

Compensation thus consists of a base amount, α, plus a portion that varies with the observed elements, z and y. We use β to measure the **intensity of the incentives** provided to the employee, so that one contract will be said to provide "stronger incentives" than another if the first contract specifies a higher value for β. The justification for this language is that if the employee increases his or her effort choice e by one unit, then according to Equation 7.3, expected compensation increases by β dollars, so higher levels of β bring greater returns to increased effort.

The parameter γ indicates how much relative weight is given to the information variable y (as compared to $z = e + x$) in determining compensation. If γ is set at zero, then y is not used in determining compensation. Given any value for γ, the term $z + \gamma y$ gives an estimate of the unobservable e. One of the principle issues in contract design is to determine how much, if any, weight to give to y in this estimate, that is, to determine the level of γ.

As an example of such a contract, suppose α is \$10,000, β is \$20 and γ is 0.5. Then expected pay is \$10,000 + \$20e, because the expected values of x and y are zero. If the employee sets e equal to 100, the expected pay becomes \$12,000 (= \$10,000 + \$2,000); if e is set at 200, the expected pay is \$14,000. Unless there is no real uncertainty, however, x and y will often not take on their expected values, and so pay will deviate randomly from its expected level. If x is more favorable than expected, say taking on the value 100, whereas y is less favorable, taking on the value -400, then the observed values are $z = e + 100$ and $y = -400$. Now an effort level of $e = 100$ brings pay of \$10,000 + \$20(100 + 100 + 0.5(-400)) = \$10,000, and an effort level of 200 brings pay of \$12,000. Of course, if x and y take on different values than those just specified, the compensation again will differ. For example, with $e = 100$, $x = -100$ and $y = 100$, pay is \$11,000, whereas effort of 200 with these same levels for the random factors brings an income of \$12,000. Thus, pay varies not just with the employee's effort, but also with the random events represented by x and y, and this randomness imposes risk on the employee (unless β is zero).

THE LOGIC OF LINEAR COMPENSATION FORMULAS   The restriction to linear compensation formulas such as the one in Equation 7.3 is not always sensible. The ideal form of the compensation rule in any circumstance depends on the nature of the efforts required and on the available performance measures. Linear compensation formulas are quite popular, however, and so we take a brief diversion from our main analysis to consider when such schemes might work especially well. The considerations that arise in this discussion should serve as a reminder that incentive compensation issues are very complicated ones and not all of the relevant issues are represented in our simple mathematical models.

Linear compensation formulas are commonly observed in the form of commissions paid to sales agents, contingency fees paid to attorneys, piece rates paid to tree planters or knitters, crop shares paid to sharecropping farmers, and so on. Linear formulas are not the only ones used, however. For example, sales agents are sometimes paid a bonus for meeting a sales target. As compared to a system of sales commissions, a reward for meeting a sales target has the disadvantage that the sales representative loses any special incentive to make additional sales after the target is reached or after a poor start leaves the target hopelessly out of reach. Commission systems apply a uniform "incentive pressure" that makes the agent want to make additional sales regardless of how things have gone in the past. In selling, because incremental sales are typically equally profitable for the firm after either a slow or a fast start, this uniform incentive pressure is appropriate (in fact, optimal).

Partly as a result of efforts by firms to avoid the problem just described, when sales targets are used they are often set to cover short periods of time, so that the periods during which incentives are too low are not extended ones. This makes the compensation of additional sales efforts more nearly equal over time. The sales representatives themselves can be expected to respond to time-varying incentives by advancing or delaying the closing of sales until the period when the compensation rate is highest. To the extent that the sales representatives succeed, they have effectively arranged for all sales to be compensated equally, that is, they have converted what is nominally a sales target system into something closely resembling a system of commissions proportional to sales.

Beyond this, of course, linear systems have the advantage of being simple to understand and administer. A scheme that employees cannot understand or that cannot be administered as intended cannot provide the desired motivation.

TOTAL WEALTH UNDER A LINEAR CONTRACT   An employee's ability to bear risk is negligible compared to the employer's whenever the employer is a large or medium size enterprise. For this reason, it would be optimal—incentive issues aside—for the employer to bear all financial risks, leaving the employees fully insured against all sources of fluctuation in their incomes. However, removing all compensation risk also removes all the employee's direct financial incentives to increase profits by providing effort. What is wanted is an employment contract that balances the need for risk sharing against the need to provide incentives.

Actual employment contracts involve a large number of terms, but we wish to focus on only those few dealing directly with incentive pay. Therefore, we will characterize a contract by a list of parameters $(e, \alpha, \beta, \gamma)$ that specify what level of effort e the employer expects to elicit and how the employee is to be compensated on the basis of performance. The employee's certain equivalent wealth from such a contract is the expected compensation paid minus the personal cost to the employee of supplying effort minus any risk premium: $\alpha + \beta(e + \overline{x} + \overline{y}) - C(e) - \frac{1}{2}r\text{Var}[\alpha + \beta(e + x + \gamma y)]$, where $\overline{x}$ and $\overline{y}$ are the mean levels of x and y and r is the employee's coefficient of absolute risk aversion. Recall that, to simplify formulas, we had assumed that both $\overline{x}$ and $\overline{y}$ are zero. Using the formulas about variances in the appendix, we find that the employee's certain equivalent income consists of expected income minus the cost of effort and minus a risk premium for the income risk the employee bears:

$$\text{Employee's Certain Equivalent} = \alpha + \beta e - C(e) - \tfrac{1}{2}r\beta^2\text{Var}(x + \gamma y). \quad (7.4)$$

The employer's certain equivalent consists of the expected gross profits minus the expected compensation paid:

$$\text{Employer's Certain Equivalent} = P(e) - (\alpha + \beta e) \quad (7.4\text{a})$$

Implicit in this is a hypothesis that the employer is approximately risk neutral.

Notice that the employee's certain equivalent consists of α plus a function of the other variables (β, γ, e) and the employer's consists of $-\alpha$ plus another function of those variables. That is, each party's equivalent wealth consists of a money term plus a term that depends on all the other aspects of the decision. By transferring money from one party to the other, one can raise one party's certain equivalent and reduce the other's by an equal amount. This is precisely the no wealth effects condition that we described in Chapter 2; we can therefore apply the value maximization principle. It follows that any efficient contract must specify the parameters so that they maximize the sum of the certain equivalent incomes of the two parties. That sum is

$$\text{Total Certain Equivalent} = P(e) - C(e) - \tfrac{1}{2}r\text{ß}^2 Var(x + \gamma y) \qquad (7.4\text{b})$$

Equation 7.4b specifies what is to be maximized.

INCENTIVES FOR EFFORT AND CONTRACT FEASIBILITY   The next step is to specify which choices of contracts are feasible. After all, it would be ideal to ask the employee to work hard without having to provide any incentives or make the employee bear any risk! We require, however, that the employer be realistic: The level of effort the employer expects must be compatible with the incentives that are provided to the employee. Although the anticipated effort level of the employee is part of the contract, the actual effort level cannot be directly observed and is chosen later by the employee, with his or her own interests foremost in mind. To be realistic, we (and the employer) must therefore determine how the employee's choice of effort e will depend on the other parameters (α, ß, γ) of the contract.

Equation 7.4 provides the key to the answer. Suppose that the costs of providing effort vary smoothly with the level provided and that the cost of effort increases at an increasing rate or, in other words, the marginal cost of effort to the employee is rising. Then, the level of effort that maximizes the employee's certain equivalent income in Equation 7.4 is the level that makes the derivative of that expression equal to zero, that is,

$$\text{ß} - C'(e) = 0 \qquad (7.5)$$

Equation 7.5 is called an *incentive constraint* and must be satisfied by any feasible employment contract. It says that employees will select their effort levels in such a way that in their marginal gains from more effort equal their marginal personal costs. The gain is the increased pay, and a unit increase in effort brings an expected increase in pay of ß; the marginal cost is C', the rate at which the personal cost of effort increases as the level provided increases.

An employment contract is therefore efficient if and only if the choices (e, α, ß, γ) are ones that maximize the total certain equivalent in Equation 7.4b among all "incentive-compatible" contracts, that is, among all contracts that are consistent with Equation 7.5 and thus realizable or feasible. It is useful to solve problems of this kind in two steps. In the first step, we fix the effort e at some level and ask how the parameters α, ß, and γ are optimally chosen then. This is called the **implementation problem** of obtaining the specified level of effort in the most efficient fashion.

It is evident from Equation 7.5 that fixing e also amounts to fixing ß at $C'(e)$ if we are actually going to get the employees to provide the specified effort level. In Figure 7.1, to raise the effort level that the employee will choose to provide from e to $\overline{e}$ necessitates increasing the intensity of incentives from ß to $\overline{\text{ß}}$. The difference in the intensity of incentives needed can be computed as the difference in the desired effort levels times the slope of the marginal cost-of-effort curve, C''.

Also, from Equation 7.4b, we see that α does not affect the total certain equivalent at all (it determines only how the total is divided between the two parties). Thus, putting aside any requirement that both parties be willing to agree to the contract (which would limit the possible values of α to ensure that each's expected welfare was sufficiently high), we see that the efficiency of the contract does not depend on the choice of α. As for γ, it is clear that the total certain equivalent is maximized when γ is chosen to make $Var(x + \gamma y)$, the variance of the estimate of e, as small as possible because this minimizes the risk premium—the costs of imposing risks on the employees to generate incentives.

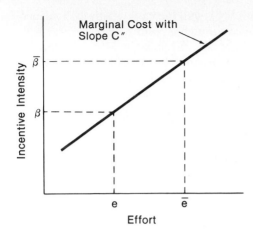

Figure 7.1: Increasing effort provided from e to $\bar{e}$ requires increasing ß to $\bar{ß}$, where $\bar{ß} - ß = (\bar{e} - e)C''$.

The Informativeness Principle

This last result—that γ should be chosen to minimize the variance of $x + \gamma y$, the estimate of e—is a special case of a more general principle.

> **The Informativeness Principle.** In designing compensation formulas, total value is always increased by factoring into the determinant of pay any performance measure that (with the appropriate weighting) allows reducing the error with which the agent's choices are estimated and by excluding performance measures that increase the error with which effort is estimated (for example, because they are solely reflective of random factors outside the agent's control).

As applied to our particular model, a measure with low error variance serves as a better basis of performance pay than a measure with higher variance. Thus, y should be included in the determinants of pay if and only if there is some value for γ that makes $Var(x + \gamma y)$ smaller than $Var(x)$, the estimate that results when y is ignored and γ is set at zero. The optimal value for γ is determined by minimizing $Var(x + \gamma y)$.

Using appendix Equation 7.18, we see that $Var(x + \gamma y)$ equals $Var(x) + \gamma^2 Var(y) + 2\gamma Cov(x, y)$, where $Cov(x, y)$, the **covariance** of x and y, is a statistical measure of how x and y are related and vary together. Minimizing this expression with respect to γ yields the result that γ should optimally be set at $-Cov(x, y)/Var(y)$.

If x and y are independent, then $Cov(x, y)$ is zero. In this case, γ is optimally set equal to zero. This reflects the fact that with x and y independent, knowing y tells us nothing about x and so gives us no better estimate of e: There is no point in simply adding noise to the performance measure. If x and y are positively related, as they might be if x reflects the conditions in a specific market and y is a measure of general market conditions, then $Cov(x, y)$ is positive. Then γ should be negative. Good general market conditions (positive levels of y) likely mean that conditions were also good in the specific market (positive x). Therefore, a greater portion of any given level of the observed performance $z = x + e$ is likely to reflect good luck (high x) rather than good effort (high e). Similarly, if y is low, x was also likely to be low, and a given z signals a higher level of effort e. A negative value for γ takes account of these likelihoods by increasing pay when general conditions are bad and decreasing it when they are good. Meanwhile, if x and y tend to move in opposite directions from one another, so that a low y is likely to correspond to a high x and vice versa, then $Cov(x, y)$ is negative and γ is optimally positive. A high y then signals that the given, observed level of z was likely obtained despite a low level of x, and therefore a high y is evidence suggesting a high level of e, which is rewarded through a positive value for γ.

Also note that as the variance of y increases, the magnitude of γ optimally decreases. Larger values of $Var(y)$ mean more "noise"—less reliable information—and the optimal choice of γ takes account of that by giving less weight to the signal. Even if y is an extremely unreliable measure, it will still optimally be used, but it will be given very little weight, affecting pay significantly only when it takes on an extremely large or small value.

APPLICATION: COMPARATIVE PERFORMANCE EVALUATION   In applying the informativeness principle, consider the practice of **comparative performance evaluation**, according to which the compensation of an employee (typically a manager or executive) depends not just on his or her own performance but on the amount by which it exceeds or falls short of someone else's performance. Debates about this practice often revolve around the issue of controllability: As a matter of principle, it is argued, an employee's compensation should not depend on things outside the employee's control because that is perceived as unfair and because it appears to make the employee bear an unnecessary risk. So when is comparative performance evaluation a good idea? When would it be better to base the compensation of the employee only on his or her own performance?

To phrase this issue in the terms of our theory, suppose the measured performance of the employee depends on the employee's efforts, on random events that affect that employee only, and perhaps on other factors that affect all similarly situated employees. For example, the employee's measured performance might depend on the difficulty of the task, which is similar to that of the tasks assigned to other workers. Or, if the employee is a manager, the profitability of his or her unit might depend on what happens to oil prices, or interest rates, or the general level of demand in the industry. Each of these factors could be expected to have a similar effect on the profits earned by other similarly situated units.

To formalize all this, suppose there are two managers, A and B. Suppose the performance measure for manager A can be written in the form $z = e_A + x$, where e_A is the effort of manager A and x is the sum of two independent components: $x = x_A + x_C$. In this expression, x_A is a random component that affects A's performance only and x_C is a random component that affects both A's and B's performances. (The subscript C stands for this "common" source of randomness.) Similarly, B's performance measure takes the form $y = e_B + x_B + x_C$, where x_A, x_B, and x_C are independent sources of randomness. Is it better to compensate manager A based on the *absolute* performance measure $z = e_A + x_A + x_C$ or on the *relative* performance measure $z - y$, which is equal to $e_A - e_B + x_A - x_B$?

The informativeness principle directs us to the error variances attached to each compensation scheme. The variance of the first (absolute) performance measure is $Var(x_A) + Var(x_C)$, whereas the variance of the second (relative) is $Var(x_A) + Var(x_B)$ (again, see the formulas in the appendix). The relative performance measure therefore has lower variance and is to be preferred if and only if $Var(x_B) < Var(x_C)$. In other words, if the randomness that affects performance is predominantly due to a common effect, such as oil price increases or the unknown difficulty of the task, and if the variation in performance due to random events that affects particular people is smaller than the variance of the common element, then comparative performance evaluation is better than individual performance evaluation because it enables the employer to eliminate the main source of randomness in evaluating performance. If the reverse relation holds ($Var(x_C) < Var(x_B)$), however, that is, if common sources of randomness that affect both employees have smaller effects than does the randomness that affects individual employees, then it is better to base compensation on an absolute standard of performance.

Of course, in general, neither purely absolute nor purely relative performance evaluation is most efficient. As the informativeness principle establishes, some mix of absolute and comparative performance evaluation is generally preferred to either extreme form. In fact the relative weights to be placed on $e_A + x_A + x_C$ and on y can be computed from the principle.

APPLICATION: DEDUCTIBLES AND COPAYMENTS IN INSURANCE   In automobile insurance, *collision* coverage is insurance that pays the owner of an automobile when his or her own auto is damaged in a collision. *Comprehensive damage* coverage is insurance that pays for damage to the person's automobile when it is stolen or damaged by other means, such as by a falling tree in a storm. Both of these kinds of coverage usually work by specifying a *deductible*, which is the portion of the loss that the insured person must pay before any payment is due from the insurance company.

Suppose that the owner of the car can, by driving carefully, parking in a garage, keeping the car doors locked, and so on, reduce the probability that the car will be stolen or damaged. That is the kind of effort that the insurance company would want to elicit. In the case of a collision or a theft, however, the owner has no control over the size of the loss that would be suffered. In that case, the size of the loss provides no information about the care taken by the owner. Therefore, according to the informativeness principle, the owner's contribution toward any loss should not depend on the size of the loss but only on the most informative performance indicator, which is the fact that a loss has occurred. So, in an optimal insurance contract, the owner's contribution should not depend on the size of the loss but rather should be a fixed amount per accident, which is very nearly the terms of a standard auto insurance contract. (We say "very nearly" because if the loss is smaller than the deductible, then the amount the insured owner pays does depend on the size of the loss.)

It is helpful to contrast the practice in automobile insurance with the practice in health insurance and health-care plans, where it is common to require copayments from the consumer for any services used. A consumer's choices about when to visit the doctor, whether to seek urgent care or to wait for a regular appointment, and so on, are all choices that affect the total level of cost incurred. The total level of cost incurred therefore provides information about how effectively the agent—in this case the consumer—has conserved scarce health-provision resources. As the theory predicts, the payments made by a health-insurance consumer therefore varies directly with the cost incurred by the health care provider.

The Incentive-Intensity Principle

The next step in the general analysis of incentive contracts is to determine how intense the incentives should be. In this step, we fix the information weighting parameter γ at whatever level the contract specifies (whether optimal or not) and let V $= Var(x + \gamma y)$.

> **The Incentive Intensity Principle**. The optimal intensity of incentives depends on four factors: the incremental profits created by additional effort, the precision with which the desired activities are assessed, the agent's risk tolerance, and the agent's responsiveness to incentives. The formula for the optimal intensity is: $\beta = P'(e)/[1 + rVC''(e)]$.

According to the incentive intensity principle, there are four factors that interact to determine the appropriate intensity of incentives. The first is the profitability of incremental effort. There is no point incurring the costs of eliciting extra effort unless the results are profitable. For example, it is counterproductive to use incentives to encourage production workers to work faster when they are already producing so much that the next stage on the production line cannot use their output. According to the incentive intensity principle, the optimal intensity is proportional to the profitability of incremental effort, provided the other three factors remain unchanged.

The second factor is the risk aversion of the agent. The less risk averse the agent, the lower the cost he or she incurs from bearing the risks that attend intense incentives. According to the incentive intensity principle, more risk averse agents ought to be provided with less intense incentives.

The third factor is the precision with which performance is measured. Low precision corresponds to high values of the variance V, which according to the formula means that only weak incentives should be used. It is futile to use wage incentives when performance measurement is highly imprecise, but strong incentives are likely to be optimal when good performance is easy to identify.

The final factor is the responsiveness of effort to incentives, which is inversely proportional to $C''(e)$ (see Figure 7.1). For example, an employee working on a fixed rate production line cannot increase his or her own output in response to piece rate incentives. According to the incentive intensity principle, incentives should be most intense when agents are able most able to respond to them. Generally, this happens when they have discretion about more aspects of their work, including the pace of work, the tools and methods they use, and so on. An employee with wide discretion facing strong wage incentives may find innovative ways to increase his or her performance, resulting in significant increases in profits.

Mathematical Derivation of the Optimal Incentive Intensity

Figure 7.2 illustrates the trade-offs that determine the optimal intensity. The intensity, ß, is measured on the horizontal axis and its marginal benefits and costs on the vertical axis. The downward-sloping line records the net marginal benefit of increasing the intensity of incentives. The net marginal benefit of extra effort is $P'(e) - C'(e)$. To determine the net marginal benefit of extra incentives, the marginal benefit of effort must be multiplied by the rate at which extra effort is supplied for each extra unit of intensity. That rate, as we have previously seen, is $1/C''(e)$. Since the agent will choose e so that ß $= C'(e)$, the net marginal benefit is $(P'(e) - C'(e))/C''(e) = (P'(e) - ß)/C''(e)$, as shown in the Figure. The transaction cost associated with setting effort intensity ß is the risk premium $\frac{1}{2}rVß^2$, with associated marginal cost $rVß$, as plotted in the Figure. The optimal intensity of incentives occurs at the point where the marginal benefit and marginal cost are equal.

To find the optimal intensity by direct maximization, write the total certain equivalent for any fixed value of e and ß as $P(e) - C(e) - \frac{1}{2}rß^2V$, by Equation 7.4b. From the incentive constraint of Equation 7.5, we know that ß $= C'(e)$, so the objective can be rewritten as:

$$\text{Total Certain Equivalent} = P(e) - C(e) - \tfrac{1}{2}rC'(e)^2V \qquad (7.6)$$

Equation 7.6 gives a clear picture of the benefits enjoyed and costs incurred for any given level of effort. The benefit term in this equation is just the profit $P(e)$, but the cost has two components: the direct cost $C(e)$ incurred by the agent plus the transaction cost $\frac{1}{2}rC'(e)^2V$ of providing the requisite incentives.

The optimal level of effort e under the contract is found by differentiating the

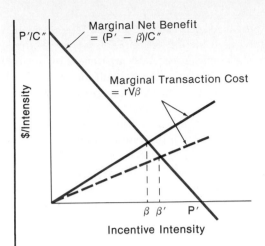

Figure 7.2: The optimal intensity of incentives balances the direct net marginal benefits of increasing ß against the marginal transaction cost.

total certain equivalent with respect to e and setting that derivative equal to zero: $0 = P'(e) - C'(e) - rVC'(e)C''(e)$. Using Equation 7.5 again, we can replace $C'(e)$ by ß in this expression to obtain: $0 = P'(e) - ß - rVßC''(e)$. Solving this for ß results in the formula given in the incentive intensity principle.

APPLICATION: INCENTIVES FOR JAPANESE SUBCONTRACTORS   Two recent studies have been performed that compare the recommendations of the incentive intensity principle with the actual contractual practices used to compensate subcontractors who supply parts or components for large Japanese automobile and electronics firms.[3] In Japanese practice, the amount paid by a manufacturing firm for its inputs depends on the actual costs as measured in the supplier company's accounting records, rather than being a contractually fixed price. If the target level of cost is $\overline{x}$ and the actual cost incurred is x, then the supplier is paid $x + ß(\overline{x} - x)$. That is, the manufacturing firm pays the actual cost incurred plus a fraction of the difference between the target cost (which is negotiated to include an allowance for profit) and the realized cost. This adjustment is an incentive term. If the supplier's actual cost is less than the target, it gets to keep some of the savings. If its costs exceed the target level, then the manufacturing company absorbs some of the difference. Thus, if the actual cost x is less than the target , the subcontractor earns an extra profit of $ß(\overline{x} - x)$; if it is more, then $ß(\overline{x} - x)$ is negative, which means that the subcontractor pays a penalty for its poor performance.

To analyze this case, notice that an effort that reduces costs by 1 yen also adds 1 yen to the manufacturing firm's profit, so we may take $P'(e) = 1$. Consequently, the theory recommends that $ß = 1/(1 + rVC'')$. The researchers rearranged the terms in this equation to obtain $1/ß - 1 = rVC''$. Taking logarithms of both sides of the new equation leads to an equation that the researchers could test using linear regression analysis:

$$log(1/ß - 1) = log(r) + log(V) + log(C'') \tag{7.7}$$

The ideal would now be to use data on ß, r, V and C'' from different contracts to estimate the empirical relationship among these variables. Then one could test statistically whether the empirical relationship was the one predicted by the theory.

---

[3] S. Kawasaki and J. McMillan, "The Design of Contracts: Evidence from Japanese Subcontracting," *Journal of Japanese and International Economies*, 1 (1987), 1327–49; and B. Asanuma and T. Kikutani, "Risk Absorption in Japanese Subcontracting: A Microeconometric Study on the Automobile Industry," forthcoming in the *Journal of Japanese and International Economies* (1991).

However, the available data did not provide direct information on all these variables.[4] In such a situation, the next best thing is to identify instruments for the theoretical variables of interest, which are $log(r)$, $log(V)$ and $log(C'')$. An *instrument* for a variable is another variable that (1) can be observed, (2) varies directly with the actual variable of interest, and (3) is uncorrelated with the other variables of interest.

To test Equation 7.7, the researchers first estimated $1 - ß$ by dividing the variation in the supplier's profits over time by the variation in their costs. These estimates were then used to tabulate $log(1/ß - 1)$ for the various firms in the sample. The risk aversion r was assumed to be inversely proportional to various measures of the size of the firm, such as the number of the firm's employees. Size variables therefore were used as instruments for $log(r)$ in the equation. The variance V in costs was estimated by determining the trend in costs and then computing the variation in actual costs around the trend over time. In theory, C'' should be inversely proportional to the scope for performance improvement by the agent. The researchers supposed that the scope was proportional to the firm's value added in the production process (in the Kawasaki and McMillan analysis) or to the firm's responsibility under the contract for supplying technology and designing parts and production processes (in the Asanuma and Kikutani analysis). These value-added and responsibility measures were used as instruments for C'' in the actual estimation. With only these instruments for the actual variables of interest, all that could be hoped for is that the signs of the coefficients in the estimated equations would be the same as predicted by the theory: The intensity of incentives $ß$ should be greater for firms with more employees, more value added, and less variability in year-to-year performance. The empirical findings were consistent with these predictions.

The tests we have described represent only weak evidence in support of the theory. The equation whose coefficients were finally estimated was not the exact one predicted by the theory, and the instruments used are not beyond criticism. Moreover, the estimation procedure did not test whether there were other variables affecting actual choices of $ß$ that were not predicted by the theory and, if so, how important those other variables were for understanding incentives. Nevertheless, the evidence obtained is consistent with the theory: Incentive contracts for Japanese suppliers do appear to depend on the considerations identified by the theory in the general way that the theory predicts.

APPLICATION: INCENTIVES IN OIL AND GAS TAX SHELTER PROGRAMS   Another study has tested the incentive-intensity principle in the context of the organization of oil and gas tax shelters in the United States in the early 1980s.[5] At that time, many drilling operations were financed by limited partnerships. As you recall from Chapter 6, under the federal tax laws that then prevailed, the partners could often save on taxes if the limited partners paid all the costs of exploring for oil (which were tax deductible when the costs were incurred), whereas the general partner(s) paid the costs of completing wells in which oil was found (which were "capitalized costs" for tax reporting purposes). The general partner and the limited partners would then share any revenues enjoyed when oil was pumped from producing wells.

A problem with this tax-reduction scheme is that it created a difference in in-

---

[4] Kawasaki and McMillan used data reported in *MITI's Census of Manufacturers (The Firm Series)* and *Surveys of Industries.* Asanuma and Kikutani limited their attention to Japanese automobile manufacturers, from whom they could obtain somewhat more detailed information.

[5] Mark Wolfson, "Empirical Evidence of Incentive Problems and Their Mitigation in Oil and Gas Tax Shelter Programs," *Principals and Agents: The Structure of Business,* J. Pratt and R. Zeckhauser, eds. (Boston: Harvard Business School Press, 1985), 101–27.

terests between the general partner, who controlled the partnership's activities, and the limited partners because each bore a different kind of expense. If a well were found to have oil, the general partner had to bear 100 percent of the cost of completing the well, but typically received only 25 percent of the oil revenues. Suppose that after the exploration costs have been sunk, a well were found to have only enough oil that the general partner would need to have a 50 percent share of revenues to recover the well-completion costs. Then, it would not be in his or her interest to complete the well, even though the full revenues would more than cover the completion costs.

Several of the prospectuses used by the general partners to attract investors described the problem quite candidly. According to one:

> A situation may arise in which the completion of an initial well (the majority of the costs of which are capitalized costs) on a prospect would be more advantageous to the limited partners than to the general partners. The situation would arise where a completion attempt on an initial well, the majority of the costs of which are paid by the general partners, could apparently result in a marginal well which would return some but not all of the completion cost incurred by the general partners but would return revenue to the limited partners.[6]

The conflict of interest described here is likely to be most severe when many of the wells being drilled are "marginal" prospects. If the well that is found is a gusher, then even the 25 percent of revenues accruing to the general partner would make completion of the well highly profitable. The general partner seen as the agent of the limited partners, therefore, is most likely to be responsive to completion incentives—to have his or her behavior positively affected by explicit incentives—when many of the wells to be completed are marginal ones. No explicit incentives for completing wells are necessary when they are very productive, and giving such incentives would not have much effect on the general partner's behavior. Economic theory predicts that the contracts that are actually used should be responsive to this difference in completion incentives.

To test this theory, the researcher divided drilling programs into three types: exploratory programs, developmental programs, and balanced programs. *Exploratory drilling programs* were ones in which wells were drilled in new areas, where the greatest likelihood was that no oil would be found but any wells that were found were unlikely to be marginal. In these programs, the conflict between the general and limited partners' interests in completing wells was likely to be small, and the general partners' completion decision was likely to be little affected by any special contractual incentives. Some 96 percent of the money invested in these exploratory drilling programs in the sample was in contracts that were designed to minimize taxes, with no special allowances to improve the general partners' completion incentives. *Developmental drilling programs* were ones in which all drilling occurred in an area that had been previously explored and where oil was known to be present, but where no more major finds were expected. Many developmental wells turn out to be marginal wells, so we should expect that the general partner would have been quite responsive to incentives to complete these wells. The researcher found that only 23 percent of the money invested in these programs was in contracts that provided no completion incentives. For *balanced drilling programs*, which contained a mix of exploratory and developmental wells, the corresponding figure was 37 percent.

This evidence provides a useful test of one aspect of the incentive-intensity

---

[6] *Prospectus of the Hilliard Fund* (1982), 22, as quoted by Wolfson.

principle. The impact of any given monetary incentive on the agent's behavior varies with circumstances, and the principle predicts that incentives will be more intense and more often incorporated into contracts when the agent's responsiveness to them is high. The evidence in this case generally confirms the prediction of the principal-agent model: Incentives are provided when they are likely to make a difference.

The Monitoring Intensity Principle

So far, we have assumed that the measurement of performance is outside the scope of the model; that is, the variance V with which efforts are measured has been treated as outside the employer's control (other than through the determination of γ). Often, however, it is possible for an employer to improve measurement by devoting resources to that objective. For example, in a factory, the number of workers per supervisor could be reduced to allow closer monitoring, or more quality-control tests could be made. For service workers, customers could be interviewed to learn whether they were satisfied with the service. In a telephone ordering or service operation, call-counting and timing equipment could be installed or supervisors could listen in on incoming calls to see how well they are handled. All of these things are costly, but all improve the employer's information about how employees are performing.

To investigate how much should be spent on monitoring, suppose that the variance of the performance measure can be controlled at a cost. Let $M(V)$ be the minimum amount that must be spent on monitoring needed to achieve an error variance as low as V. It is generally costly to reduce the error variance, so we suppose that M is a *decreasing* function—settling for a larger V entails lower monitoring costs. We also suppose that the marginal cost of variance reduction is a rising function, that is, $M'(V)$ is increasing. Rewriting Equation 7.4b to include the cost of the resources that are spent on measurement, we have:

$$\text{Total Certain Equivalent} = P(e) - C(e) - \tfrac{1}{2}rV\beta^2 - M(V) \qquad (7.8)$$

The relationship between e and β is still determined by the incentive constraint Equation 7.5, which is unaffected by the introduction of costly measurement. We may therefore hold e and β fixed and choose V to maximize the expression in Equation 7.4b. Taking the derivative of Equation 7.8 with respect to V leads to:

$$-\tfrac{1}{2}r\beta^2 - M'(V) = 0 \qquad (7.9)$$

According to this equation, the marginal cost of reducing V, which is $-M'(V)$—a positive number—must be equal to $\tfrac{1}{2}r\beta^2$ at the efficient solution.

> **The Monitoring Intensity Principle:** Comparing two situations, one with β set high and another with β set lower, we find that V is set lower and more resources are spent on measurement when β is higher: When the plan is to make the agent's pay very sensitive to performance, it will pay to measure that performance carefully.

The determination of V is illustrated in Figure 7.3. The downward sloping curve gives the marginal cost of reducing the variance with which performance is measured. Because the risk premium is $\tfrac{1}{2}r\beta^2V$, the marginal cost of variance changes is depicted in the figure by a solid line at level $\tfrac{1}{2}r\beta^2$. When the incentive intensity is reduced from β to $\bar{\beta}$, the chosen level of V increases: Fewer resources are spent on measurement.

There may appear to be some circularity in our several observations. In the incentive-intensity principle, we claim that β should tend to be set large when V is low. In the last paragraph, we claim that firms should try to reduce V when β is large.

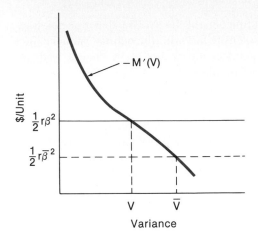

Figure 7.3: The optimal level of measurement equates the marginal cost and marginal benefit of variance reduction. Less intense incentives lead to higher V (less measurement).

Which causes which? Do intense incentives lead firms to careful measurement, or does careful measurement provide the justification for intense incentives?

The answer is that, in an optimally designed incentive system, the amount of measurement and the intensity of incentives are chosen together: Neither *causes* the other. However, setting intense incentives and measuring performance carefully are *complementary* activities in the sense described in Chapter 4; undertaking either activity tends to make the other more profitable.

Figure 7.4 illustrates the situation. The two solid lines in the figure depict the two relationships between measurement and incentive intensity just described. One of these lines specifies the optimal intensity of incentives ß for any particular measurement variance; the other specifies the optimal variance for any particular intensity of incentives. Notice that both lines slope downward. According to the incentive-intensity principle, ß falls when the variance V rises. Similarly, according to the monitoring intensity principle, V falls as ß rises; it pays to measure more carefully (lower V) when incentives are intense. The point where the two lines cross determines the optimal combination; it is the point where V is chosen optimally for the given intensity of incentives and ß is selected optimally for the given measurement error.

The dotted line in Figure 7.4 shows how ß would depend on V in different circumstances, in which P' was higher or C'' lower. According to the incentive-intensity principle, these changes would lead to higher levels of ß for any fixed level of V. That change is represented in Figure 7.4 by the dotted line lying to the right

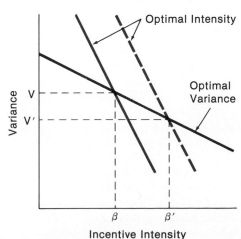

Figure 7.4: An increase in P' or a fall in C'' leads to more intense incentives and more measurement (less variance).

of the original line determining ß as a function of V. Notice that the point of intersection of the new optimal incentive-intensity line with the optimal variance line is lower and to the right of the original point of intersection. The change leads to sharper incentives and lower variance (more monitoring).

The Equal Compensation Principle

Now we enrich our conception of behavior in the firm to recognize that most employees do more than one thing as part of their jobs. When there are several activities being conducted, the employer will be concerned that employees allocate their time and efforts correctly among the various things that need to be done. This complicates the problem of providing incentives.

For example, suppose that the marketing representatives for a company making specialty steel alloys perform several kinds of activities: They solicit business from new customers, provide problem-solving services and advice to customers about how to use the company's alloys, gather information about competitors' marketing activities, and report about possible new products that might sell well. Of these several activities, the easiest one to monitor is direct sales efforts, because it leads immediately to measurable sales. Some of the other activities also lead to sales, with some time lag: Keeping customers happy is likely to increase the representative's sales over a period of time. If there is high turnover in the sales jobs, then the information about how well customers are being served may not be available in a timely enough fashion to use for compensating the responsible representative. Finally, some of the activities, such as monitoring competitors' moves, are much more difficult to evaluate than is simple sales performance. If the firm were to compensate the marketing representatives based primarily on the accurately measured current sales figure, that might induce a distortion in their behavior, causing them to switch efforts toward the immediate high-payoff activity of generating sales and away from the activities necessary to keep customers happy and the firm well informed. If that sort of behavior led eventually to a loss of customers and declining sales, the representative could seek another job, proudly displaying the sales performance he or she achieved in the first job. A related problem might arise for the salespeople in a department store, who might be tempted to maximize immediate commissions by pressuring a customer to buy a more expensive product than necessary, leading to dissatisfied customers and lower future sales for the store, not only of that one department's products but also of products sold in other departments.

Alternatively, suppose that a fast-food chain wants its outlets to be profitable but also wants them to contribute to the chain's reputation for cleanliness, fast service, and hot, fresh food, because that reputation enhances sales at *other* outlets. These profit and reputation goals can be in conflict. For example, a fast-food chain outlet along a highway where many of the customers visit only once would suffer little loss of profits if its hamburgers were sometimes cold and its bathrooms dirty, but the chain's other stores might lose business on that account. If the chain compensates the store manager on the basis of sales alone, the manager would be unlikely to take full account of the effects of his or her actions.

These observations lie behind our fourth principle of incentive contracting and compensation.

> **The Equal Compensation Principle**: If an employee's allocation of time or attention between two different activities cannot be monitored by the employer, then either the marginal rate of return to the employee from time or attention spent in each of the two activities must be equal, or the activity with the lower marginal rate of return receives no time or attention.

The equal compensation principle imposes a serious constraint on the incentive-compensation formulas that can be effective in practice. In particular, if an employee is expected to devote time and effort to some activity for which performance cannot be measured at all ($V = \infty$), then incentive pay cannot be effectively used for any other activities that the individual controls. The use of straight salary compensation for managers can often be justified on these grounds.

MATHEMATICS OF THE EQUAL COMPENSATION PRINCIPLE   Suppose the employee does two different things, signified by levels of effort e_1 and e_2. We will think of these levels of effort as time devoted to two activities, and we assume that the cost incurred by the employee is an opportunity cost: It is time that becomes unavailable for other, more pleasant or rewarding activities. It then makes sense to write the cost as depending only on the total effort, not on its division between the two tasks: $C(e_1 + e_2)$. The employer measures performance by observing the indicators $e_1 + x_1$ and $e_2 + x_2$, where x_1 and x_2 have expected values of $\overline{x}_1$ and $\overline{x}_2$.

Suppose that the employer pays the employee according to a linear compensation formula based on the two indicators: The wage paid is then $w = \alpha + \beta_1(e_1 + x_1) + \beta_2(e_2 + x_2)$. How should α, β_1, β_2, e_1, and e_2 be chosen?

To take incentives into account in the problem, we first examine the employee's objective given this compensation rule. A self-interested employee will choose e_1 and e_2 to maximize his or her certain equivalent income:

$$\text{Employee's Certain Equivalent} = \alpha + \beta_1(e_1 + \overline{x}_1) + \beta_2(e_2 + \overline{x}_2) - C(e_1 + e_2) - \tfrac{1}{2} r Var(\beta_1 x_1 + \beta_2 x_2) \quad (7.10)$$

For this problem, we suppose that the effort is restricted to a nonnegative number: $e_1, e_2 \geq 0$. If e_1 is strictly positive, then at the maximizing choice for the employee, the derivative of Equation 7.10 with respect to e_1 must be zero, so $\beta_1 = C'(e_1 + e_2)$. Similarly, if e_2 is strictly positive, then $\beta_2 = C'(e_1 + e_2)$. The analysis of the employee's incentives alone thus establishes that β_1 must equal β_2 if each tasks is to receive some attention.

APPLICATION: COST CENTERS AND PROFIT CENTERS   As the models make clear, an important part of the problem of designing incentives is to determine what the employee will be responsible for, that is, what measures will be used to evaluate performance as a basis for compensation. As an example, consider the problem of providing incentives to the manager of a manufacturing facility. One approach might declare that the manager is responsible only for the costs incurred in the factory, on the theory that the manager has little control over revenues. In that case, we say that the factory is a *cost center*, and the accounting systems should be set up to assess accurately the costs attributable to the factory. Another approach declares that product quality and speed of delivery are important to sales, so that it is a mistake to encourage the manager to focus on cost control at the expense of these factors. Thus, sales performance might be given some weight in determining the manager's compensation.

To represent these issues in terms of our theory, suppose that the two activities to which the manager might contribute are cost reduction and revenue generation. If sales revenues are subject to random variations that are outside the manager's control and statistically independent of the randomness that affects costs, then the cost of providing incentives of strength β to the manager for revenue generation is the risk premium: $\tfrac{1}{2} r\beta^2 Var(\text{Revenues})$. The equal compensation principle implies that if the factory manager is to be provided with sales-generation incentives at all, then it is futile to do that in a half-hearted way: The incentives need to be of the same strength as those for manufacturing cost control. If the β associated with cost control is to be large, then the β associated with revenue generation must be large as well, and therefore quite costly (in the sense of its leading to a large risk premium). Then, the factory is a *profit center*, to which revenues and costs are both attributed in determining performance.

Cost centers and profit centers are not the only alternatives, however, nor is either likely to be the best alternative in the situation we have described. The firm should actively seek ways to make production managers responsible for what they each control without making them responsible for the performance of the sales force, which they do not control. For example, if quality control and delays in the factory are the chief concerns, then the firm could devise new measures of manufacturing performance, such as the average time from order to delivery and the number of products returned as unsatisfactory. According to the informativeness principle, these measures are superior to measures based on dollar sales because they provide a more informative assessment of the manufacturing manager's actual contribution to the sales effort. As we observed earlier, the firm gains most by improving the measurement of variables that figure most heavily as a basis for compensation.

The equal compensation principle suggests another possibility as well: The manager could be paid a salary with no explicit incentive component. This would be a plausible course of action when manufacturing quality control is important but hard to assess accurately. Of course, the manager will still understand that promotions and pay increases will depend on how superiors assess his or her performance, but at least this solution avoids the distortions in allocation of time and effort and the randomness in compensation brought about by an incentive compensation plan based on arbitrary measures of performance.

This analysis of cost and profit centers focuses only on the issue of compensation. Before leaving this example, however, it is helpful to recall that the actual organization design problem is more involved than that. Managers who are given responsibility for profits, for example, are commonly given broader decision authority than those responsible just for costs or sales. Determining a manager's compensation amounts to deciding what he or she is responsible for, and that decision should be made together with decisions about the scope of the manager's authority.

APPLICATION: INCENTIVES FOR TEACHERS   The equal compensation principle can be applied to the recent public policy debate about whether it would be helpful to provide cash incentives for teachers to improve elementary and secondary education. Proponents of cash incentives argue that they would be helpful in focusing teachers on their tasks and motivating them to be innovative in the search for effective ways to train their students.

Opponents of the incentives for teachers, however, have a cogent response. The measures that have been used in the past to evaluate teaching performance for elementary school age children are tests of basic skills, and teaching these is just one part of a teacher's job. Children are also expected to learn social skills, oral expression, and creative thinking, and to build confidence that prepares them for the harder challenges to be faced in later years. Teachers who are compensated based on tests of basic skills alone would be tempted to neglect these other aspects of the job. They might also be led to teaching the most docile students, whose performance scores are easiest to improve, while neglecting students who have more trouble learning. In one instance in South Carolina in 1989, a teacher was caught teaching the answers to the actual test, a copy of which had been illicitly obtained. Compensating teachers based on test scores motivates teachers to help students test well, rather than to help students learn.

According to the equal compensation principle, if it is desirable to have teachers devote some efforts to each of several activities and if it is impossible to distinguish efforts on the various different activities, then all these kinds of efforts must be compensated equally. If social development, oral expression, or creative thinking cannot be accurately measured, then the only realistic options are to remove the responsibility for teaching them from the teacher or to pay the teacher a fixed wage, with no element of incentives pay.

It is a good idea to remember that responsibilities and compensation should really be determined together. In the case of teachers, for example, one proposal is to install a system of specialist teachers who are compensated based on student test scores but who are not responsible for other aspects of student performance.[7] This would not, by itself, solve all the potential problems we have described, but it would allow performance incentives and still ensure that attention is paid to developing the very important "higher thinking skills" in young students. The general point to remember is that by determining the job design and the compensation together, one can sometimes solve problems that cannot be solved by compensation policy alone.

APPLICATION: ASSET OWNERSHIP   The equal compensation principle also makes it possible to give a careful treatment of some important issues in the theory of employment and asset ownership. We represent ownership by supposing that at the end of a period of production, the owner of the asset may take it and employ it in other uses. For example, if the employer is the owner of a machine (the asset), he or she can assign the job of production and the use of the asset to another worker, whereas if the worker owns the asset then he or she can employ it on his or her own behalf or on behalf of another employer. What kind of incentives are optimal and who should own the asset?

Assets are notoriously hard to evaluate accurately and objectively. That is why accountants generally report adjusted historical cost figures for asset valuations rather than attempting to account for asset values on the basis of the asset's physical condition (unless deterioration is obvious), its fair market value, or its productivity. The value of a business automobile, for example, is accounted for by its purchase price less an allowance for depreciation, even though its actual value depends on its mileage, physical condition, and so on. Production machines are accounted for in a similar way, even if hard use or changes in production methods has made their actual value lower.

We represent the idea that assets are hard to value accurately in our model by the following assumption: Although the *actual* value of the asset, $A(e_1) + x_1$, is an increasing function of the effort e_1 that the worker devotes to maintaining and improving the asset (and of random factors x_1), accounting measures of asset values do not reflect those efforts and so cannot be used to provide incentives. Only the direct output of the production process, which is $e_2 + x_2$, is observed by the parties and can serve as a basis for compensation. Therefore, we may write the compensation paid to the worker in the form $\alpha + \beta(e_2 + x_2)$.

Suppose that there is some level of total effort $\bar{e}$ that the employee is willing to provide even in the absence of any cash incentives, although this level might be lower than the employer would like to see provided. The efforts e_1 and e_2 devoted to each of the two activities cannot be observed, however. Should the firm induce greater effort by setting β positive and thereby inducing more production effort e_2?

If the firm owns the asset, then the worker's certain equivalent compensation is $\alpha + \beta e_2 - \frac{1}{2}\beta^2 rVar(x_2) - C(e_1 + e_2)$. If β is positive, the worker's optimal choice of e_1 is always zero. This is just an application of the equal compensation principle:

---

[7] Jane Hannaway, "Higher Order Skills, Job Design, and Incentives: An Analysis and Proposal," working paper, Stanford University, 1991.

Because the marginal return to the agent from efforts devoted to maintaining or increasing the asset's value is always zero, the worker will devote no efforts to that activity ($e_1 = 0$) unless the returns to other activities are also zero. When the worker is an employee and maintenance of the asset is important, we find (in this model) that it is optimal to pay a fixed wage with no incentives for output performance ($ß = 0$). Then the worker will set $e_1 + e_2 = \overline{e}$ and presumably will be willing to allocate this total amount of effort as the firm directs.

The other possibility is that the worker may own the asset. In that case, the worker's certain equivalent compensation is the sum of the asset's expected value (which depends on e_1) and his or her expected compensation, less a risk premium that reflects both the uncertainty in the asset's value and that in the worker's pay, as well as the cost of effort: $A(e_1) + \alpha + ße_2 - \frac{1}{2}rVar(x_1 + ßx_2) - C(e_1 + e_2)$. As the owner, the worker has a built-in incentive to care for the asset; he or she keeps any value that is created when the asset is well cared for. In order to motivate the worker also to pay some attention to production, it is necessary to set $ß > 0$. Then, with positive returns to both types of effort, the worker will choose to provide more total effort than $\overline{e}$—the amount he or she would provide as an employee with no pay incentives for working harder.

To summarize, if it is important that time and effort be devoted to both producing and maintaining the asset, then incentive pay should always be used for workers who bring their own tools ("independent contractors"), but it should never be used for those who use the firm's tools ("employees"). In practice, incentives are used more extensively for independent contractors than for individual employees, as our analysis suggests they should be. The analysis also suggests that independent contractors will work harder than employees, devoting more effort both to caring for the asset and to being directly productive. They will also earn a higher average income to compensate for the extra work they do and the greater risk they bear.

Finally, we come to the question: Who should own the asset? A detailed study of asset ownership is contained in Chapter 9, so we are brief here. In the model just described, if the worker owns the asset, then the worker bears risk both from the randomness of asset returns and from the errors in performance measurement, which add $\frac{1}{2}r(ß^2Var(x_2) + Var(x_1))$ to the total risk premium. Against this must be weighed the fact that the ownership of the asset and increased incentives for the production activity will elicit a higher level of effort. A cost-benefit calculation that balances these considerations must be done to determine which arrangement is likely to be more successful. Certain general principles are evident, however. Increases in the worker's risk aversion or in the variance of asset returns or in the variance of performance estimates in the production task all add to the risk premium that is incurred when the employee owns the asset, making the ownership solution less valuable. If there are many ways to improve performance, then the employee's efforts are especially likely to be responsive to incentives (represented in our model by the assumption that C'' is small). Increases in the worker's scope for action tend to favor having the worker own the asset. As we see later, there are a number of other considerations involved in assigning asset ownership efficiently that are not represented in this simple conceptual model.

Intertemporal Incentives: The Ratchet Effect

An especially thorny problem in real incentive systems is how to set the standard by which performance is to be evaluated. In terms of our model, this means that the mean of x is unknown, so that the mean measured performance corresponding to any fixed level of effort in any performance measurement period is uncertain. If the estimated mean value of x is $\overline{x}$, then the expected level of performance is $e + \overline{x}$ and the corresponding expected pay is $E = \alpha + \beta(e + \overline{x})$. If the intended expected compensation is E, then the value of α that will be set is determined by rearranging that equation to obtain: $\alpha = E - \beta(e + \overline{x})$. Increasing the estimated value of $\overline{x}$ therefore leads to changes in the fixed component of the incentive formula. The magnitude of the effect is proportional to the incentive intensity β. Setting the standard too high will lead to consistently low levels of pay, perhaps leading to low morale and quits. Setting it too low will lead to happier employees but also to consistently higher levels of pay and lower net profits than would otherwise be possible.

There are just three reasonably objective ways to set a performance standard. The first, which is used frequently only for routine clerical or production tasks, is to have engineers perform *time-and-motion studies* to determine, in detail, how a certain operation is most efficiently done and how long it should take. For example, an engineer might use a stopwatch to determine how long it takes a microfilm operator working at normal speed to load film into the machine, process documents through it, and rewind, catalog, and store the film in the appropriate area. Conducting such studies is costly, and the studies themselves can become obsolete quickly if the job is one where workers can learn and adopt new techniques as they accumulate experience. The second way is to use the performance of other people in similar jobs, that is, to use *comparative performance evaluations*, which we analyzed earlier in the chapter. The third way is to use the *past performance* of the same person in the same job. However, basing standards on past performance penalizes good performance and rewards bad. If workers foresee this possibility, very negative consequences can emerge.

The tendency for performance standards to increase after a period of good performance is called the **ratchet effect**. The term was originally coined by students of the Soviet economic system, who observed that managers of Soviet enterprises were commonly "punished" for good performance by having higher standards set in the next year's plan or, even worse, in the next quarter's plan (see Chapter 1). There are widely known instances of Soviet factory managers who responded to newly installed incentives with massive gains in productivity, only to be denounced on the grounds that their improved performance was proof that they had previously been lazy or corrupt. The ratchet phenomenon is even much older than this example: In a traditional interpretation of the Jewish Passover story, the Egyptian Pharaoh held a brick-producing contest among the Hebrew slaves and used the results as a standard to set a much higher daily production quota.

THE IMPACT OF THE RATCHET EFFECT   The "ratcheting up" of standards in response to good performance is not merely unfair, it can be unproductive: If workers foresee the way future standards will depend on current performance, they may refuse to cooperate with efforts to improve productivity. Soviet managers, who are well aware of the ratchet effect, have often been reluctant to institute changes that could radically reduce costs, despite promised incentive payments. Similarly, in the United States, the traditional animosity of labor unions toward piece rates may be explained by the concern that employers, once they have discovered the rates at which highly motivated employees can work, will set a higher standard, leading to lower average pay or to the same average pay for harder work.

There are situations in which there can be efficiency reasons for basing current standards on past performance, but these arise when there are different employees doing the work in different periods. According to the informativeness principle, it is desirable to use all available information that might reduce the variance in the measurement of second-period performance. First-period performance will often give useful information of this sort. The issues here are really identical to those that arise in the case of comparative performance evaluation, though in this case the comparison is across time periods in the same job rather than across workers at the same time in different jobs.

Using information from past performance lowers the variance with which second-period effort is measured. According to the incentive-intensity principle, the parties will therefore tend to set the incentive term, ß, higher in the second period than they otherwise would, taking advantage of the reduced variance. The theory thus predicts that when the parties write contracts for one period at a time and when past performance embodies useful information for evaluating future performance, incentives will become more intense over time, as the parties utilize past experience to incorporate more accurate performance expectations in their contracts. Because higher levels of ß induce higher levels of effort, the actual effort levels elicited from the worker will also rise over time.

The argument using the informativeness principle is only correct, however, if there is a new occupant in the job in each period. If the same worker is to do the job in each period, then the parties would be better off if they could commit initially to a contract that elicits the same level of effort in each period. This point is subtle, and establishing it will necessitate use of the formal model. The essential source of the inefficiency, however, is that if the worker anticipates that standards in future accounting periods will depend on past performance, then it becomes more difficult or costly to provide him or her with incentives to perform well in the early accounting periods. The example of the Soviet factory managers whose incentives were destroyed by the fear of increased performance standards illustrates the underlying logic of this argument. Because the problem could, in principle, be avoided if the parties could commit themselves in advance not to rely too heavily on past performance for standard setting, we classify it as a problem of *imperfect commitment*.

The Mathematics of the Ratchet Effect

To study the ratchet effect more closely, let us suppose that an employee works for two periods and exerts effort e_1 in the first period and effort e_2 in the second, but that the contract that is used in the second period is the one that appears optimal at that time, given the available information. Suppose in addition that each of these effort levels is observed only imperfectly: The employer observes only $z_1 = e_1 + x_1$ in the first period and $z_2 = e_2 + x_2$ in the second, where the observation errors in the two periods are assumed to have equal variances and to have means equal to zero. We may write the employee's incentive pay in the first period as $\alpha_1 + ß(e_1 + x_1)$, that is, a constant component α_1 plus an incentive component that is proportional to an unbiased estimate of the employee's effort.

It is reasonable to suppose there is a positive correlation between x_1 and x_2: A high level of x_1 means that a high value of x_2 is likely. This would occur if some of the same factors that contribute to a high level of measured performance in the first period also contribute to high measured performance in the second. Then the parties can use the observed performance in the first period to get an estimate $\hat{x}_2$ of x_2, the part of second-period performance that is beyond the employee's control. This estimate of x_2 can then be used to get a better estimate of the employee's actual effort in the second period. That is, the parties may define a standard $\hat{x}_2 = \gamma + \delta(e_1 + x_1)$ and form an adjusted estimate of the employee's second-period performance of the form $\hat{z}_2 = z_2 - \hat{x}_2$ $= e_2 + x_2 - \hat{x}_2$.

What makes this seem beneficial is that if δ and γ are chosen well, then $Var(x_2 - \hat{x}_2)$ is less than $Var(x_2)$: The adjusted measure eliminates part of the performance variation that is beyond the worker's control and provides a more accurate portrayal of his or her actual performance. Then the informativeness principle indicates that this estimate should be used in the contract. For example, if a retail chain bases each store manager's pay partly on the level of sales at the store, then it seems only fair (and efficient) that those stores in good locations should have to meet a higher sales target. Surely, there is no more generally accurate way to determine the quality of a location than by looking at the past record of the store's sales, and that is just what the proposed standard achieves.

If the employee's second-period pay is given by the same sort of function as in the first period—a constant term plus an incentive term that rewards higher estimated effort—then the employee's total compensation over the two periods is $\{\alpha_1 + \beta_1 (e_1 + x_1)\} + \{\alpha_2 + \beta_2[e_2 + x_2 - \gamma - \delta(e_1 + x_1)]\}$. Collecting terms allows us to rewrite this as

$$\text{Total Compensation} = \alpha_1 + \alpha_2 + (\beta_1 - \delta\beta_2)(e_1 + x_1) + \beta_2(e_2 + x_2 - \gamma) \tag{7.11}$$

Note, however, that the coefficient of e_1 in Equation 7.11 is not the nominal contractual amount, β_1, but rather the smaller amount $\beta_1 - \delta\beta_2$. This is the ratchet effect at work. The direct return—in terms of first-period pay—to extra effort in the first period is β_1, but higher first-period effort increases the standard in the second period by δ. It thus reduces the pay accruing in the second period for any choice of second-period effort by $\delta\beta_2$. If the same employee occupies the job in both periods, then the anticipation of first-period performance being used in the second period reduces effective first-period incentives. Thus, it makes sense to define the "effective incentives" β_1^E and β_2^E by $\beta_1^E = \beta_1 - \delta\beta_2$ and $\beta_2^E = \beta_2$.

In terms of the effective incentives, the total certain equivalent wealth can be written as

$$\text{Total Certain Equivalent} = P(e_1) + P(e_2) - C(e_1) - C(e_2) - \tfrac{1}{2}rVar(\beta_1^E x_1 + \beta_2^E x_2) \tag{7.12}$$

An efficient contract maximizes this expression subject to the incentive constraints, $\beta_1^E = C'(e_1)$ and $\beta_2^E = C'(e_2)$, that determine the worker's effort choices. Using properties of the variance (see the formulas in the appendix), Equation 7.12 can be rewritten as

$$\text{Total Certain Equivalent} = P(e_1) + P(e_2) - C(e_1) - C(e_2) - \tfrac{1}{2}r[(\beta_1^E)^2 Var(x_1) + (\beta_2^E)^2 Var(x_2) + 2\beta_1^E\beta_2^E Cov(x_1, x_2)] \tag{7.13}$$

where $Cov(x_1, x_2)$ is a measure of the way the two measurement errors tend to move together. Recall that we have assumed that $Var(x_1)$ and $Var(x_2)$ are equal. Both Equation 7.13 and the incentive constraints are symmetrical with respect to time: They would be essentially unchanged if we were to change each e_1 into an e_2, each e_2 into an e_1, each β_1^E into β_2^E, and each β_2^E into β_1^E. Thus, if there is a unique total wealth maximizing contract, it must treat the two time periods symmetrically. That is, it must have $e_1 = e_2$ and $\beta_1^E = \beta_2^E$.

In contrast, we saw that when the parties cannot commit in advance to the second-period contract terms and instead act optimally in the second period given what has already transpired, they will set $e_2 > e_1$: Incentives are made more intense over time.

OVERCOMING THE RATCHET EFFECT   The parties would be better off if they could commit to hold the line on incentives, not using the first-period performance to adjust second-period performance standards. In that case, the contractual and effective incentives would be the same. This policy is in fact in place at some companies. The Lincoln Electric Company is famous for its extensive use of incentive contracts and, in particular, piece rates. Lincoln has for decades maintained a policy that once a piece rate has been set, it will not be changed unless the equipment is changed or new work methods are introduced. In this case, a new time-and-motion study will be done, and the resulting standard will remain in effect even if realized performance later suggests that it is too low. If the standards are set too low, then the Lincoln workers may earn a lot of extra money, but their incentives to work hard are never threatened.

Why don't more companies adopt such a system? There are many reasons, not least of which is that it is so difficult for a firm to commit itself not to use available information.[8] Even if the parties agree in advance not to use the information embodied in the first-period performance and set contract terms accordingly, there will still be efficiency gains after the fact to renegotiating the contract and using the information. Lincoln Electric has managed to commit to its policy of maintaining standards by applying piece rates widely throughout its organization, developing expertise at doing time-and-motion studies, building a reputation for applying its "no revisions" policy consistently, and tuning the rest of its policies so that they are consistent with a piece-rate system.

Our characterization of the ratchet effect as a problem of commitment also helps us to understand how *self-employment* arrangements and *ownership* can sometimes alleviate the problem. A self-employed person sells goods or services directly to customers. If the industry is competitive, then the performance standards are the comparative ones set by the marketplace, and a person's good performance does not lead directly to higher future standards. Similarly, someone who owns an asset can be assured of keeping whatever gains accrue from showing how to use it effectively. Of course, the problems of risk sharing often make the ownership solution impractical, and self-employment is infeasible in many situations.

Within companies, job rotation is another device that can be used to alleviate the ratchet effect. By assigning people to various jobs over time and using previous jobholders' performance to set the standard, the current jobholder is not penalized for a job well done. Job rotation also may bring benefits in improved morale and greater flexibility in production. Its costs, however, are in potentially reduced efficiency, as workers have less opportunity to gain experience in any task.

MORAL HAZARD WITH RISK-NEUTRAL AGENTS

The main thrust of this chapter has been to study principal-agent problems where motivating agents by making them bear part of the risk is costly because the agents are risk averse. From an analytical perspective, we can organize our study of other aspects of the theory by assuming away the risk-sharing problem and studying principal-agent theory with a risk-neutral agent, that is, one whose coefficient of absolute risk aversion is equal to zero. In that case, no risk premium is ever incurred, regardless of how the risks are shared. So, the agent can be perfectly motivated at zero cost by setting $\beta = 1$, that is, by making him or her bear the entire risk. For a manager-agent running a firm, this is very much like having the manager buy the firm and

---

[8] There may be other reasons that have little or nothing to do with incentive issues directly. For example, in a multistep production process, there may be little value to having one worker proceeding faster than the others, so the firm may not want to encourage every individual worker to work as fast as he or she individually can.

enjoy all the profits and suffer all the losses. In the case of automobile insurance, it amounts to having drivers paying full cash compensation to those who they have damaged. There are several reasons, however, why a solution of this kind would often be unworkable, and each of these points to a factor that makes the moral hazard problem more difficult to resolve.

Problems with the Risk-Neutral Agent Scenario

When is making the risk-neutral agent responsible for all financial losses not a workable solution? First, the solution will fail whenever the agent lacks sufficient funds. A manager may simply be unable to guarantee payments for the business's expenses with personal funds, and a driver may be unable to pay for damages from a serious accident. Arrangements in the economic world are often made with these limits in mind. Public policy toward drivers generally requires that automobile owners have insurance or show some other evidence of financial responsibility before their cars can be licensed. In the private sector, vendors are frequently unwilling to extend trade credit to a company with little working capital, for fear that their bills will never be paid.

A second case where making the agent bear the risk is not workable is when the risk is a nonfinancial one and is therefore difficult or impossible to transfer. There is no way for a careless or drunken driver to undo the injuries or death that may result from an automobile accident simply by paying damages, or for a negligent blood bank to bear the suffering of a recipient of AIDS-tainted blood, or for a company that dumps toxic or radioactive waste to eliminate the genetic damage done to victims simply by paying a cash penalty. All of these examples pose important problems for public policy, but the principles that arise are not the kind that are most helpful for understanding the institutions and practices of the business world. So we merely note that these problems do limit the theory and pass on.

ADVERSE SELECTION IN THE PRINCIPAL-AGENT PROBLEM   A third case in which "selling the firm to the manager" is not a workable solution is when the principal and the agent cannot agree on a price, for example, because the market is disrupted by adverse selection. This variation is well typified by the case of an employee of a department store chain who invents a new consumer product. Being no expert at marketing, the employee negotiates with the chain to market the product. What kind of arrangements should the employee make for marketing the product?

The employee in this case is the principal who is trying to negotiate a contract to motivate the agent (the department store chain) to market the product. Unlike our earlier examples, this is a case in which the agent is much more tolerant of risk than is the principal, so efficient risk sharing would dictate that the agent bear (almost) all the risk, and efficient incentives for marketing effort by the agent would seem to lead to the same conclusion. If these were the only factors involved, the efficient solution would be to sell the rights for the product to the department store chain, which would then bear all the market risk. Furthermore, as the owner the chain would be motivated to work as hard as necessary to extract all the potential value from the product.

However, there is another element that may block this easy solution—the element of adverse selection. In this case, the chain is an expert marketer who may be much better informed than is the employee/inventor about the market potential of the product. If the rights are to be sold to the chain, how will the price be determined? The chain will refuse the principal's offer whenever its estimate of sales is low and will accept the offer when its estimate is high. Therefore, the inventor can only successfully sell the rights for a price that is lower than the expected profitability of the product.

An alternative procedure would be for the inventor to keep the right to the product and demand royalties from the chain, that is, a payment proportional to the number or value of the units sold. In that way, the inventor can mitigate the adverse selection problem because the employer could be expected to accept a royalty contract regardless of its private information about the sales potential of the invention. It only has to pay an amount proportional to its actual sales. There are two problems with this option too, however. First, the inventor is made to bear too much risk, and, second, the department store chain, which no longer receives all the profits from sales, will be inclined to expend too little effort promoting sales of the product.

Another way that the employee/inventor might try to avoid the problem of distorting the chain's incentives while receiving some royalties is to base the royalties on profits rather than on sales. In that way, the chain would be motivated to incur the right amount of costs to maximize profits because its share of cost is the same as its share of the revenues. The drawback of this scheme is that the accounting for expenses is in the hands of the chain, and the employee/inventor ought to expect that the accounts will be manipulated to reduce royalty payments. Indeed, in the 1980s and in 1990, there were well-publicized lawsuits by film makers and actors against Hollywood studios that had agreed to pay a percentage of profits on movies or television shows, only to claim that there was little to share. In a celebrated case, actor James Garner sued over his rights to royalties from *The Rockford Files*, one of the most successful television shows in history. According to the accounting procedures used by the studio, however, the show never earned a profit.

The formal analysis of efficient contracting when there is both moral hazard and adverse selection is quite complex. The inventor's best policy in the situation we describe depends on his or her risk aversion, on the importance of motivating the chain to promote the product aggressively and how that importance depends on circumstances, and on the quality of the chain's sales forecasts, among other variables. Although the theory has little to say about the *details* of the solution, it has much to say about the form. In a broad range of cases, the best the inventor can do is to offer the chain a choice between purchasing the full rights to the invention at a relatively high price or paying a lower price plus royalties proportional to sales. The actual prices and royalties will depend on the parties' relative bargaining power, but the inventor should anticipate during the negotiations that the chain will want to own the rights when it forecasts high sales and to pay a royalty when its forecasts are less optimistic. If the chain insists that the rights are not worth much, then the inventor should insist on receiving royalties instead of a fixed payment, even though this may cause the chain to promote the product less effectively. By selling the invention outright when its value is high, the inventor motivates the chain to promote sales vigorously in that case and so increases the value of the invention.

The case of the inventor and the chain store is important because the problems that arise and the pattern of analysis are similar to those in many other business settings. The key characteristic of these settings is that there is one party that has superior information about costs and that needs to be motivated to work hard. For example, in setting procurement policy, governments (and firms) depend on suppliers to supply appropriate information about costs and recommendations about product design and also to work hard to build quality into the products supplied. In the regulation of utilities, the public utility commissions rely on the regulated firms both to supply information that will be the basis for price decisions and to work hard to keep costs as low as possible.

Do all these variations invalidate the general principles presented earlier in the chapter? They do not. Although such principles as the informativeness principle and the equal compensation principle are derived from and phrased in terms of a particular conceptual model (in which agents are risk averse and must be motivated to undertake personally costly effort), both can be rephrased to hold over the whole range of variations described here. Of course, the general principles cannot, by themselves, substitute for analysis of particular cases, but they do provide a useful guide across a wide range of applications.

SUMMARY

Most people in the economy dislike bearing risk. The cost of risk bearing can often be reduced by sharing the risk among a group of people. If the group is large and the risks that different people contribute are statistically independent, this procedure can virtually eliminate the cost of bearing these risks. Insurance companies exist primarily to perform this economic function. Some kinds of risks, however, are not easily insured, principally because they are risks that affect many people simultaneously (such as environmental risks and energy shortages) and so would threaten the capital of any insurance company. These kinds of risks are managed and shared through other institutions, with the securities markets playing a prominent role when the risks are expressible in money terms.

Principal-agent problems are situations in which one party (the principal) relies on another (the agent) to do work or provide services on his or her behalf. When agents' actions cannot be easily monitored and their reports easily verified, the agents have greater scope to pursue their own interests rather than the principal's. Then, to provide incentives for the agents to behave in the principal's interests, it is necessary to arrange for them to bear some responsibility for the outcomes of their actions and therefore to bear more risk than would otherwise be desirable.

Several principles govern the design of optimal incentive contracts. The *informativeness principle* says that the cost of providing incentives increases with the variance of the estimator of the employee's effort. An optimal incentive contract should base the employee's compensation (or the insured's contribution to cover a loss) *only* on the minimum variance indicator of the employee's behavior. This principle is applied to illuminate issues of comparative performance evaluation and the use of deductibles in automobile insurance and copayments in health insurance.

The *incentive-intensity principle* says that the strength of incentives should be an increasing function of the marginal returns to the task, the accuracy with which performance is measured, the responsiveness of the agent's efforts to incentives, and the agent's risk tolerance. This principle is useful for explaining variations in the strength of incentives among Japanese subcontractors and among general partners in certain oil and gas drilling programs.

The *monitoring intensity principle* states that more resources should be spent monitoring when it is desirable to give strong incentives. This principle is the mirror image of the observation that more accurate performance information leads to higher optimal incentives, which is part of the incentive intensity principle. Measuring performance carefully and providing intense incentives are complementary activities, which should be found together.

The *equal compensation principle* holds that if an employee's allocation of time and effort between alternative tasks cannot be monitored by the employer, then the marginal returns earned by the employee in any tasks to which he or she actually devotes effort must be equal. Providing strong incentives for a portion of an employee's activities can cause the employee to cut back his or her efforts in other activities. This principle informs comparisons of cost centers and profit centers, policy debates about the provision of incentives for elementary and secondary school teachers, and analyses of asset ownership patterns.

The *ratchet effect* refers to the practice of basing performance targets on past performance in the same activity. Although such a practice would seem to be consonant with the informativeness principle because it bases performance goals on one of the best available indicators of possible performance, it also imposes certain costs. If the occupant of the job does not change over time, then the effect of the ratchet is to punish yesterday's good performance by setting higher standards today. In modern capitalist economies, ownership and self-employment are two principal means by which a person who performs well can guard against being subjected to the ratchet effect.

There are various factors not included in our models that would make the principal-agent problem more difficult to resolve. One is that the agent may lack sufficient capital to pay penalties for losses that he or she causes. A second is that some losses are essentially nonfinancial losses that cannot be easily compensated using cash. A third is that the agent may have private information that makes it more difficult for the principal and the agent to agree on contract terms.

■ BIBLIOGRAPHIC NOTES

The economic theory of decisions under uncertainty has its origins in Daniel Bernoulli's eighteenth-century writings. This theory was put on a sound logical foundation in the 1940s through the collaborative efforts of the mathematician John von Neumann and the economist Oskar Morgenstern. A modern treatment of this theory has been presented by David Kreps. The refinements contributed by Kenneth Arrow and John Pratt (and reviewed in the appendix) made it possible to apply the von Neumann and Morgenstern theory to analyze risks that are specifically financial in nature. Their work led to the formulas for risk premia and certain equivalents that we have used. The theory of risk sharing and insurance was built on these foundations in the 1960s by Karl Borch and Robert Wilson.

The modern theory of incentives was begun in the 1970s by various authors who explored what optimal incentive compensation contracts might be like in a variety of different applications including: insurance (Michael Spence and Richard Zeckhauser), sharecropping (Joseph Stiglitz), tax policies (James Mirrlees), and managerial compensation (Robert Wilson and Stephen Ross). Stephen Shavell and Bengt Holmstrom originated the informativeness principle, which was later generalized in the work of Sanford Grossman and Oliver Hart. Milton Harris and Artur Raviv also made early important contributions to understanding the nature of efficient contracts. The ratchet effect has been analyzed by Martin Weitzman, David Baron and David Besanko, and Xavier Freixas, Roger Guesnerie and Jean Tirole. The problem of renegotiation of principal-agent contracts was first studied by Mathias Dewatripont; see also the contributions by Philippe Aghion, Dewatripont, and Patrick Rey and by Drew Fudenberg and Jean Tirole. Our discussions of optimal linear incentive contracts and the other principles of incentive pay borrow heavily from the work of Bengt Holmstrom and Paul Milgrom.

There were many contributions to incentive theory in the 1980s focusing on the case where there is a tension between the needs to alleviate adverse selection and moral hazard. In addition to a number of those listed above, leading contributors to that theory were Joel Demski, Jean-Jacques Laffont, Preston McAfee, John McMillan, Roger Myerson, Michael Riordan, and David Sappington. Their theories were often set in the particular situation of a government regulator (principal) trying to regulate a utility (agent), or a procurement officer (principal) trying to negotiate a complex contract with a supplier (agent). The principles that have emerged from these analyses, however, have wide application.

■ REFERENCES

Aghion, P., M. Dewatripont, and P. Rey. "Renegotiation Design under Symmetric Information," mimeo, 1989.

Arrow, K. J. *Essays in the Theory of Risk Bearing* (Chicago: Markham, 1970).

Baron, D., and D. Besanko. "Regulation and Information in a Continuing Relationship," *Information, Economics and Policy*, 1 (1984), 267–330.

Baron, D., and R. Myerson. "Regulating a Monopolist with Unknown Costs," *Econometrica*, 50 (July 1982), 911–30.

Bernoulli, E. "Specimen theoriae novae de mensura sortis," *Commentarii Academiae Scientiarum Imperialis Petrepolitanae*," (trans) "Exposition of a New Theory on the Measurement of Risk," *Econometrica*, 22 (January 1954), 23–36.

Borch, K. "Equilibrium in a Reinsurance Market," *Econometrica*, 30 (July 1962), 424–44.

Demski, J., and D. Sappington. "Optimal Incentive Contracts with Multiple Agents," *Journal of Economic Theory*, 33 (1984) 152–71.

Dewatripont, M. "Renegotiation and Information Revelation over Time in Optimal Labor Contracts," *Quarterly Journal of Economics*, 104 (1989), 589–620.

Freixas, X., R. Guesnerie, and J. Tirole. "Planning Under Incomplete Information and the Ratchet Effect," *Review of Economic Studies*, 52 (1985), 173–92.

Fudenberg, D., and J. Tirole. "Moral Hazard and Renegotiation in Agency Contracts," *Econometrica*, 58 (November 1990), 1279–1320.

Grossman, S., and O. Hart. "An Analysis of the Principal-Agent Problem," *Econometrica*, 51 (1983), 7–45.

Harris, M., and A. Raviv. "Optimal Incentive Contracts with Imperfect Information," *Journal of Economic Theory*, 20 (1979), 231–59.

Holmstrom, B. "Moral Hazard and Observability," *Bell Journal of Economics*, 10 (1979), 74–91.

Holmstrom, B. "Moral Hazard in Teams," *Bell Journal of Economics*, 13 (1982), 324–40.

Holmstrom, B., and P. Milgrom. "Aggregation and Linearity in the Provision of Intertemporal Incentives, *Econometrica*, 55 (March 1987), 303–28.

Holmstrom, B., and P. Milgrom. "Multi-task Principal-Agent Analysis: Incentive Contracts, Asset Ownership and Job Design," SITE Working Paper #6, Stanford University, 1990.

Kreps, D. *Notes on the Theory of Choice* (Boulder, CO: Westview Press, 1988).

Laffont, J. J., and J. Tirole. "Using Cost Observations to Regulate Firms," *Journal of Political Economy*, 94 (June 1986), 614–41.

Laffont, J. J., and J. Tirole. "The Dynamics of Incentive Contracts," *Econometrica*, 56 (1986), 1153–75.

McAfee, R. P., and J. McMillan. "Competition for Agency Contracts," *Rand Journal of Economics*, 18 (1987), 396–7.

Mirrlees, J. "An Exploration in the Theory of Optimum Income Taxation," *Review of Economic Studies*, 38 (1971), 175–208.

Mirrlees, J. "Notes on Welfare Economics, Information, and Uncertainty," in *Essays on Economic Behavior Under Uncertainty*, M. Balch, D. McFadden, S. Wu, eds. (Amsterdam: North-Holland Publishing Co., 1974).

Mirrlees, J. "The Optimal Structure of Incentives and Authority within an Organization," *Bell Journal of Economics*, 7 (1976), 105–31.

Pratt, J., "Risk Aversion in the Small and in the Large," *Econometrica*, 32 (1964), 122–36.

Riordan, M., and D. Sappington. "Information, Incentives and Organizational Mode," *Quarterly Journal of Economics*, 102 (1987), 243–64.

Ross, S. "The Economic Theory of Agency: The Principal's Problem," *American Economic Review*, 63 (1973), 134–39.

Shavell, S. "Risk Sharing and Incentives in the Principal and Agent Relationship," *Bell Journal of Economics*, 10 (1979), 55–73.

Spence, A. M., and R. Zeckhauser. "Insurance, Information and Individual Action," *American Economic Review*, 61 (1971), 380–87.

Stiglitz, J. "Incentives and Risk Sharing in Sharecropping," *Review of Economic Studies*, 64 (1974), 219–56.

Stiglitz, J. Incentives, Risk and Information: Notes Towards a Theory of Hierarchy," *Bell Journal of Law, Economics and Organization*, 6 (1975), 552–79.

von Neumann, J., and O. Morgenstern, *The Theory of Games and Economic Behavior*, (Princeton: Princeton University Press, 1944).

Weitzman, M. "The Ratchet Principle and Performance Incentives," *Bell Journal of Economics*, 11 (1980), 302–8.

Wilson, R. "The Theory of Syndicates," *Econometrica*, 36 (January 1968), 119–32.

Wilson, R. "The Structure of Incentives for Decentralization," in *La Decision* (Paris: Centre Nationale de la Recherche Scientifique, 1969).

EXERCISES

Food for Thought

1.   In the late 1960s and early 1970s, when McDonalds (the fast-food chain) was undergoing a period of very rapid expansion in sales, it considered a variety of different compensation systems for its managers. The company wanted to encourage its managers to increase sales, control costs, and maintain the company's standards of quality, service, and cleanliness. It also wanted local store managers to hire and train people who could become managers of new outlets, which were being added to the chain at a rapid pace. What difficulties would you expect this situation to pose for McDonald's management? What would you expect to occur if a local outlet manager's compensation were based primarily on sales growth? On outlet profits? What kind of compensation plan should McDonald's adopt? How would you expect the compensation formula to change as McDonald's moved into its next phase, with fewer new outlets being opened in North America?

2.   A common complaint of university students is that professors seem too remote and uninterested in teaching them. How do university systems of compensation, promotion, and tenure contribute to the problem? Is the problem likely to be more severe for tenured or untenured faculty? Why do universities often have rules restricting outside consulting activities?

3.   Use Figure 7.2 to determine both how the level of monitoring and the

intensity of incentives would change (1) if the total cost of monitoring were to fall by a fixed amount and (2) if the marginal cost of monitoring were to fall.

4.   Unlike specialty stores, department stores sell a wide array of products to a single group of customers, and are often especially interested in maintaining their reputations for servicing their customers well. How might this consideration affect the compensation of department store sales personnel compared to the salespeople at specialty outlets?

5.   Suppose a Canadian subsidiary of a British company assembles a product using inputs manufactured in Canada. Under what conditions should the manager of the British firm be responsible if a change in the foreign exchange rate raises the cost in pounds sterling of purchasing the inputs, causing losses to result? Under what conditions should the manager not be held responsible?

6.   In 1989 the NBC television network in the United States announced a new way of compensating the local television stations affiliated with the network. These independently-owned stations carry NBC programs during "prime-time" evening hours from 8:00 to 11:00 p.m. NBC earns its revenues by selling advertising time to national advertisers whose ads appear during the network's shows. The amount NBC gets for its advertising time depends on the number of viewers its programs attract. The number of viewers watching a particular station (and thus the network's programs) during prime-time depends in part on the number of people who are attracted to watch the non-network programs that the station shows before prime time. These viewers tend to stay with the channel that they started watching on a given evening. NBC's innovation was to begin paying its affiliates in part on the basis of the number of viewers that they attracted for their early-evening programming, such as local news, rather than just on the size of the audiences that watched the prime-time network programs on the station. Analyze this plan in terms of the principles developed in this chapter.

Mathematical Exercises

1.   Suppose that a group of people A, . . ., Z share an income risk I, in proportion to their risk tolerances. For example, individual A bears a share $\rho_A/(\rho_A + \ldots \rho_Z)$ where $\rho_A = 1/r_A$, and so on. Show that A's risk premium in this case is $\frac{1}{2}\rho_A Var(I)/(\rho_A + \ldots \rho_Z)^2$ and hence that the total risk premium borne by all the members is $\frac{1}{2}Var(I)/(\rho_A + \ldots + \rho_Z)$—the same as the risk premium that would be required by a single person whose risk tolerance is $\rho_A + \ldots \rho_Z$.

2.   Consider the case of two people, A and B, with incomes I_A and I_B, and suppose that they enter a risk sharing contract so that A's income is $\alpha I_A + \beta I_B + \gamma$, with B receiving the balance. The total risk premium for this arrangement is given by Equation 7.1 in the chapter. (a) Expand this equation into one expressed in terms of $Var(I_A)$, $Var(I_B)$, and $Cov(I_A, I_B)$. [Hint: Your answer should be a quadratic function of α and β.] (b) To find the values of α, β, and γ that minimize this expression, take the derivatives of the expression with respect to α and β and set the derivatives equal to zero. Show that the solution of these three equations has $\alpha = \beta = \rho_A/(\rho_A + \rho_B)$, where $\rho_A = 1/r_A$ and $\rho_B = 1/r_B$ are the two risk tolerances. (c) Use mathematical induction and the results of this and the preceding problem to show that regardless of the number of people, person 1's share of each risk should be the same as his or her share of the total risk tolerance of the group.

3.   In the text we compared the advantages of relative performance evaluation against an evaluation based solely on the employee's own performance. Here we consider all combinations of the two as well. Thus, suppose manager A's measured

performance is $e_A + x_A + x_C$ and B's measured performance is $e_B + x_B + x_C$, where x_A, x_B, and x_C are independent sources of randomness. Suppose it is proposed to base manager A's compensation on his or her own performance minus δ times some measure B's performance. Find the value of δ that minimizes the variance of the performance measure. How does this value change with changes in $Var(x_A)$? Changes in $Var(x_B)$? Changes in $Var(x_C)$?

4. Suppose an entrepreneur can select among investment projects that all cost the same amount but differ in their risk-return characteristics. The set of available projects is described by a curve giving the highest available expected net return (after subtracting the initial cost of the investment) corresponding to any given variance in the returns. Let this curve be $m = 2v - (\frac{1}{2})v^2$, $0 \leq v \leq 2$, where m is the mean return and v is the variance of returns. Thus, the entrepreneur can achieve a riskless return of $m = \$0$, essentially by not investing, while the maximum expected return is attained by selecting a project with $v = 2$, which yields an expected return of 2. What project will the entrepreneur choose if he or she must bear all the returns (positive or negative) alone and he or she has a coefficient of risk aversion of $r > 0$, so that his or her preferences are given in certain-equivalent form by $m - (\frac{1}{2})rv$?

Now suppose that it is possible to share the risk of the investment with an outside investor who has a coefficient of risk aversion of s. What is the investment choice that maximizes the total certain equivalent? How should the risk be shared? Could this be achieved by selling an ownership claim in the entrepreneur's firm to the investor in such a way that the investor will be willing to pay enough that the entrepreneur is better off selling this share?

5. A risk-averse entrepreneur is considering selling stock in his or her company to the public. He or she will continue to manage the firm after it "goes public." The entrepreneur gets utility from income, x, and from the consumption of on-the-job perquisites, c, according to the utility function $u(x, c) = \bar{x} - \frac{1}{2}var(x) + 100c^{\frac{1}{2}}$, where $\bar{x}$ is the mean of the income x and $var(x)$ is its variance. The uncertain profits of the firm are $Y - c$: each dollar spent on perquisites reduces profit by a dollar. The variance of Y, (and thus of $(Y - c)$), is σ^2, which we assume to be greater than 2,500. The entrepreneur is currently the sole owner of the firm, receiving as income the firm's profit. What level of perquisites will he or she choose?

Now, suppose the entrepreneur sells a fraction α of the firm to risk-neutral investors, retaining $(1 - \alpha)$ for him- or herself. Thus, the entrepreneur receives as income whatever amount the investors pay for this fraction of the firm, say $M(\alpha)$, and then gets his or her share, $(1 - \alpha)(Y - c)$, of the random profit. The variance of his or her income is thus $(1 - \alpha)^2\sigma^2$. What is the relationship between α, the fraction of ownership the entrepreneur sells, and the level of c he or she will subsequently choose? Does this choice maximize total value (the expected utility of the entrepreneur plus that of the investors)? What will be the expected profit as a function of α?

Assume that competition among investors leads them to pay an amount for any given ownership share equal to the profits they expect to receive. How much will the entrepreneur receive from selling a fraction α of the firm if investors correctly anticipate the level of c that the entrepreneur will choose after selling that fraction of the firm? What is the realized level of expected utility for the entrepreneur from selling a fraction α of the firm if the investors have correct expectations? What is the best level of α for him or her to pick? Could the entrepreneur gain by binding him- or herself not to increase c as α changes?

Mathematical Appendix

This appendix consists of two parts. The first is a review of statistical concepts. The second derives the approximation reported in the main text regarding the certain income that is equivalent, from the decision maker's point of view, to a given random (uncertain) income.

Review of Statistical Concepts

The set of possible outcomes in a statistical problem is represented by a **sample space** S. A **random variable** x is a function that associates with each element $s \in S$ a real number $x(s)$. For example, the elements of S may be the books on a bookshelf and $x(s)$ may specify the number of pages in the book s. In a coin-tossing problem, the elements of S may be sequences of heads and tails and x may be some statistic, such as the one that assigns to each sequence $s \in S$ the number of heads that occur in the first ten coin tosses. With the sample space S comes a **probability mass function** p that assigns a probability $p(s)$ to each element of $s \in S$. The probability mass function is used to compute such probabilities as $Prob(x = 11)$—the probability that the random variable x takes the value 11.

Each random variable x has a *mean* denoted by $\overline{x}$, also called its **expectation** and denoted $E[x]$. The formula for calculating expectations is:

$$E[x] = \Sigma_{s \in S} p(s)x(s) = \overline{x} \tag{7.14}$$

Each random variable also has a *variance* given by:

$$Var(x) = E[(x - \overline{x})^2] = \Sigma_{s \in S} p(s)(x - \overline{x})^2 \tag{7.15}$$

Variance is one measure (among many possible measures) of the degree of randomness of x.

Given two random variables x and y, the **covariance** of x and y is:

$$Cov(x, y) = E[(x - \overline{x})(y - \overline{y})] \tag{7.16}$$

Notice that $Cov(x, x) = Var(x)$.

Given two random variables x and y and two real numbers α and ß, we can form a new random variable $\alpha x + ßy$, which for each possible outcome s takes the value $\alpha x(s) + ßy(s)$. Its expectation can be computed from those of x and y by the following formula, which can be derived from Equation 7.14:

$$E[\alpha x + ßy] = \alpha E[x] + ßE[y] \tag{7.17}$$

Using Equations 7.14–7.17, we can derive the formula:

$$Var(\alpha x + ßy) = \alpha^2 Var(x) + ß^2 Var(y) + 2\alpha ß Cov(x, y) \tag{7.18}$$

The two random variables x and y are *(statistically) independent* if for all numbers α and ß, $Prob[x = \alpha \text{ and } y = ß] = Prob[x = \alpha] \cdot Prob[y = ß]$. Statistical independence represents the idea that knowing the value of one of the variables provides no information about the value of the other. If x and y are independent, then $Cov(x,y) = 0$, so by Equation 7.18, $Var(x+y) = Var(x) + Var(y)$.

Evaluating Financial Risks:
Certain Equivalents and Risk Premia

Expected utility theory establishes conditions under which a decision maker will rank risky prospects according to their associated expected utilities. Let u be a function that assigns to each monetary outcome x a utility $u(x)$. Then, representing prospects by random variables, the expected utility of prospect x is $E[u(x)]$. Let us compare this prospect with a certain prospect, that is, one that yields the payment $\hat{x}$ with probability 1. The certain prospect will be preferred if $u(\hat{x}) > E[u(x)]$; the risky prospect will be preferred if the reverse inequality holds. When the decision maker is just indifferent between the two prospects, then $\hat{x}$ is called the certain equivalent of the prospect x.

The crucial formula for our applications is the following approximation:

Approximation. Suppose that u is three times continuously differentiable, that $\overline{x} = E[x]$, and that $u'(\cdot) > 0$. Then, approximately, the certain equivalent is:

$$\hat{x} \approx \overline{x} - \tfrac{1}{2}r\,(\overline{x})\mathrm{Var}(x) \tag{7.19}$$

where $r(\overline{x}) = -u''(\overline{x})/u'(\overline{x})$.

Derivation. According to Taylor's theorem, for any z,

$$u(z) = u(\overline{x}) + (z - \overline{x})u'(\overline{x}) + \tfrac{1}{2}(z - \overline{x})^2 u''(\overline{x}) + R(z)$$

where $R(z) = u'''(\hat{z})(z - \overline{x})^3/6$ for some $\hat{z} \in [\overline{x}, z]$. We assume that this remainder term is negligible. Hence we write, approximately,

$$u(z) \approx u(\overline{x}) + (z - \overline{x})u'(\overline{x}) + \tfrac{1}{2}(z - \overline{x})^2 u''(\overline{x}) \tag{7.20}$$

Substituting x for z in Equation 7.20 and computing the expectation, we find, approximately,

$$E[u(x)] \approx u(\overline{x}) + E[x - \overline{x}]u'(\overline{x}) + \tfrac{1}{2}E[(x - \overline{x})^2]u''(\overline{x})$$

But, $E[x - \overline{x}] = E[x] - \overline{x} = \overline{x} - \overline{x} = 0$, so approximately,

$$E[u(x)] \approx u(\overline{x}) + \tfrac{1}{2}E[(x - \overline{x})^2]u''(\overline{x}) \tag{7.21}$$

We expect that the certain equivalent $\hat{x}$ will be close to $\overline{x}$, so we approximate its utility differently, also using Taylor's theorem,

$$u(\hat{x}) = u(\overline{x}) + (\hat{x} - \overline{x})u'(\overline{x}) + \dot{R}(\hat{x}) \tag{7.22}$$

where, $\dot{R}(\hat{x}) = \tfrac{1}{2}u''(\hat{z})(\hat{x} - \overline{x})^2$ for some $\hat{z} \in [\overline{x}, \hat{x}]$. Because we apply the approximation only when $\hat{x} - \overline{x}$ is small, we again treat the remainder term as negligible. For a certain equivalent, we have $u(\hat{x}) = E[u(x)]$. So, combining Equations 7.21 and 7.22, we have, approximately,

$$(\hat{x} - \overline{x})u'(\overline{x}) \approx \tfrac{1}{2}E[(x - \overline{x})^2]u''(\overline{x}) \tag{7.23}$$

This may be expressed in the form

$$\hat{x} - \overline{x} \approx \tfrac{1}{2}\cdot[u''(\overline{x})/u'(\overline{x})]\cdot E[(x - \overline{x})^2] = \tfrac{1}{2}\cdot r(\overline{x})\cdot \mathrm{Var}(x) \tag{7.24}$$

which establishes the Approximation (7.19).

8

RENTS AND EFFICIENCY

R*eputation said, "If once we sever, Our chance of future Meeting is but vain; Who parts from me, must look to part for ever, For Reputation lost comes not again."*

Charles Lamb[1]

Highly paid labour is generally efficient and therefore not dear labour, a fact which though it is more full of hope for the future of the human race than any other that is known to us, will be found to exercise a very complicating influence on the theory of distribution.

Alfred Marshall[2]

WHEN DISTRIBUTION AFFECTS EFFICIENCY

Up to this point, almost all of our analysis has been founded on the value maximization principle (Chapter 2), which holds that if the condition of no wealth effects is satisfied, then an arrangement is efficient for the parties involved in an agreement if and only if it maximizes their total equivalent wealth. The no wealth effects condition requires (1) that the individual parties evaluate all the benefits they receive and all the costs and risks they must bear as being equivalent to some cash transfer, (2) that these evaluations do not depend on the amount of wealth that the parties hold, and (3) that people are able to make timely payments in whatever amounts may be required to divide up the benefits of the transaction without affecting the cost or feasibility of any other aspect of the transaction. Where the value maximization principle applies, efficient arrangements are those that maximize total wealth, regardless of how that total is shared.

Even though it is rare for the no wealth effects condition to be satisfied completely and precisely, it still provides a useful starting point for many analyses. It may be approximately correct in some circumstances, and even when it is not, it allows a

---

[1] "Love, Death and Reputation," stanza IV.

[2] *Principles of Economics*, 8th ed. (London: Macmillan, 1920), 423.

very useful simplifying separation between the issues of distribution and efficiency. However, there are many cases in which wealth effects are so important that concerns for distribution and efficiency cannot be analyzed separately without greatly distorting the facts. For example, in developing countries, workers with higher wages might eat healthier, more nutritious diets, giving them more energy and higher productivity levels. For such workers, paying low wages would limit the volume or quality of the work they can do, and so paying higher wages increases the total wealth that can be created. This consideration is too important to ignore, especially in the poorest countries.

Even in developed countries, the distribution of wealth might affect the cost or feasibility of some kinds of transactions. For example, according to our analysis of incentive contracting in Chapter 7, if the agent is risk neutral then the moral hazard problem can be completely avoided by having the agent receive the full returns to his or her actions. With a risk-neutral agent, there is no need for risk sharing and no gain to removing any of the risk. The solution is for the principal to receive a constant amount, independent of the outcomes generated by the agent's actions, with the agent bearing the full variability in income. Where the agent is a manager of a firm, this solution involves selling him or her the firm. Unless the agent's income or wealth is sufficiently high, however, he or she may be unable to raise the funds necessary to buy the operation. The value maximization principle then does not apply because the parties cannot make the necessary transfers.

A closely related difficulty arises in the question of who should own the tools or machines a worker uses (see Chapter 7). Consider the case of a long-distance truck driver. The driver can significantly affect the value of the truck by the care he or she exerts in driving and maintaining it. If the efficient solution is for the driver to own the truck so that he or she is strongly motivated to protect its value, then efficiency cannot be achieved unless the driver can afford to own it. Again, the principle does not apply in this case. The resulting inefficiency raises the possibility that the total wealth created might be increased by allowing the workers to receive a larger share of the income they generate so that they can afford to buy the truck.

Limits on a party's ability to pay cash damages are another common reason for distribution and efficiency to be linked. For example, financial penalties are used much less often than simple theory would suggest. Such theory notes that financial penalties are especially efficient means of providing incentives because the penalty is only a transfer: The loss to the penalized individual is offset by a gain for the one receiving the penalty payment. In contrast, other forms of punishment (jailing, whipping, ostracism, death) involve actual net reductions in total welfare—the punished person is hurt, and no one has an offsetting gain. However, fines and financial penalties are of hardly any use to punish a borrower who has gone broke and defaulted on a loan. Similarly, cash penalties are hardly ever used in employment contracts, except sometimes for employees with very large incomes relative to the damage that their misbehavior can do. For example, professional athletes' contracts commonly grant management the right to assess fines for breaking team rules, but similar clauses are much rarer for factory workers. When cash penalties are limited, other details of the transaction may have to be manipulated to provide suitable incentives to the parties.

Influence activities also represent an instance where the distribution of costs and benefits affects efficiency (see Chapter 6). Costs are incurred in trying to shift organizational decisions so that they favor one group or another, and no direct aggregate benefit results.

When the value maximization principle fails to apply, the way the total wealth generated by a project or venture is shared can affect other aspects of the transaction, such as who is hired to do a job or what technology is used. In developing countries, for example, if workers with higher incomes are more productive because they are better nourished, and if the wages paid to workers are so low that nourishment is problematic, then employers may choose to hire workers from wealthier families, even though a worker from a poorer family may be better matched to the job in terms of skills and work attitude. Of course, hiring wealthier workers exacerbates the problem of income inequality and contributes to the much discussed "cycle of poverty." Similarly, wealthier drivers who own their trucks may earn much more than do other drivers, further increasing the wealth differences between them. These examples also illustrate the important possibility that private parties may agree to arrangements that are technically inefficient when distribution affects productivity.[3]

A host of new issues and questions are raised when wealth effects are important. One group of questions concerns how to provide effective incentives when cash penalties for bad behavior are impossible. For example, how do lenders manage their loans when borrowers may default and the loan may become uncollectible? How do firms motivate workers when fines cannot be used? Other questions concern how the wealth created by a venture will be shared. For example, how does the legal system manage the competing claims on a firm's resources that are made in bankruptcy proceedings when payment of all claims is impossible or when it would so damage the firm as to lead to a reduction in total wealth? How do parties determine compensation levels when compensation may affect efficiency? A third class of questions concerns the sources and consequences of inequality within organizations: How do wages and perquisites vary across jobs within a single firm? How does the firm manage the resulting competition for the good jobs? These types of questions are examined in this chapter.

EFFICIENCY WAGES FOR EMPLOYMENT INCENTIVES

Suppose that an organization needs to rely on the good and honest behavior of some employee. The organization may be a police department relying on its officers to reject all attempts at bribery, an oil company relying on the captains of its tankers to stay alert and sober on the job, an investment company relying on its analysts to investigate alternative investment options with diligence, or a marketing division relying on its salespeople to entertain customers and not family or friends. Suppose, too, that (perhaps because of wealth limitations) the only effective means available to discipline an employee suspected of cheating is to terminate his or her employment. Our first question is: What determines whether the threat of termination of employment is an effective deterrent against cheating? Our answer is that the employee's incentives depend on what the employee stands to gain by cheating if undetected, how likely cheating is to go undetected, what wage the employer offers, and what other market opportunities the employee may have. A simple model based on one developed by Carl Shapiro and Joseph Stiglitz will help to make the point clear.

The Shapiro-Stiglitz Model

Let w be the wage the employee is paid in his or her current job (say, $50,000), and let $\overline{w}$ be the wage the employee could get if he or she looked for another job in the market after being fired from the current job (say, $40,000). The wage $\overline{w}$ is assumed

---

[3] An arrangement is **technically inefficient** if there is another arrangement that produces more with the same total amount of resources. In this example, a transfer of wealth from the rich family to the poor one, which increased the productivity of the poor worker, would increase technical efficiency. The initial arrangement, however, is still Pareto efficient; the proposed alternative is not Pareto superior because it would leave the wealthy family less well off.

to be discounted to take into account the cost of searching for a new job, including any period of unemployment during the search, the cost of submitting applications, and so on. Let g be the amount that the employee could gain by cheating on the job, regardless of whether he or she is detected. This gain might take the form of income from bribes, increased leisure from working shorter hours than agreed, material gain from redirecting business resources to benefit family and friends, or simply reduced pressures from responding less diligently to organizational demands and crises. Let p be the probability that the cheating, whatever form it may take, is detected. Let N be the multiplier to express the long-term value of this relationship, adjusting for both interest and the number of periods during which the worker is employed by the firm if not caught cheating. If the employment relation lasts only one period and is never repeated, then $N = 1$. If the employee is hired from time to time and expects to be rehired in the future only if he or she has never cheated the employer, then N is larger than 1. If there is a continuing employment relation between the worker and the employer, then N may be much larger than 1.

Putting ethics and morality aside momentarily, it will serve the employee's narrow personal interest to cheat if

$$g > p(w - \overline{w}) N \qquad (8.1)$$

that is, if the gain from cheating exceeds the probability that the cheating is detected times loss of income from being fired.[4] For example, if g is $1000 and p is .05, then cheating earns $1000 but incurs an expected cost of only $.05(\$50{,}000 - 40{,}000) = \$500$, so cheating is profitable. The amount $w - \overline{w}$ is called the *rent* that the employee earns from the job: The excess of earnings in the current job over opportunities elsewhere. The possibility of earning this rent makes the job and the prospect of being rehired in the future valuable to the employee and makes being fired an outcome to be avoided.

Despite the pure, self-interested calculation that we have ascribed to the employee, we do not argue that ethics and morality do not matter. Few people are either devils or saints. Most do not always cheat when cheating is profitable, and most sometimes succumb to the temptation to cheat, perhaps by convincing themselves that what they are doing is not really dishonest. Considerations of right and wrong certainly do enter into many peoples' decisions and affect their behavior. Nevertheless, experience suggests that the amount of cheating that goes on in an organization is responsive to the incentives for cheating. Moreover, when cheating goes unpunished, it breeds more of the same: Once some people are seen to be cheating, an "everybody does it" attitude may infect an increasing fraction of the organization's employees. In that way, an initial failure to provide the right incentives may lead to an epidemic of cheating spreading throughout the organization.

Even for the most honest people, repeated and substantial temptations to cheat combined with ambiguity about what is right and wrong are likely to result in occasional cheating. Incidents like those where religious leaders are caught diverting donations to their own personal use should be enough to convince even skeptics that material temptations affect the behavior of people in every kind of position. An organization can best forestall cheating by making it unprofitable, that is, by setting its monitoring intensity p and its wage w to ensure that the expected loss of wages from cheating, $p(w - \overline{w})N$, exceeds the gain from cheating, g.

This analysis shows one reason why highly paid workers may be more diligent

---

[4] This formula assumes that the employee's options beyond the horizon embodied in N are not affected by whether or not he or she is caught cheating, so that the gain from being with the firm is realized solely over the period represented by the multiplier N.

and productive than are similar workers earning a lower wage, as suggested by the quotation from Alfred Marshall in the beginning of the chapter: Highly paid workers have more to lose by cheating, so they find it in their interests to behave honestly.

MANAGING DISTANT TRADING AGENTS   The idea that high wages encourage honest behavior is an old one. Thomas Macaulay, describing the efforts of Lord Clive to control corruption among English civil servants employed by the East India Company in India around 1765, wrote: "Clive saw clearly that it was absurd to give men power and to require them to live in penury. He justly concluded that no reform could be effectual which should not be coupled with a plan for liberally remunerating the civil servants of the Company."[5] Lord Clive undertook vigorous efforts to change the standard of behavior among civil servants but recognized that his efforts could not be fully effective unless the civil servants found it in their individual interests to adhere to the new standard.

A similar system of high compensation was used by the Maghribi traders in Fustat (old Cairo) in the eleventh century.[6] These merchants, who shipped goods across the Mediterranean to Sicily and other destinations, involved the whole merchant group in ostracizing cheaters. This system made a good reputation a most precious commodity that merchants would go to great lengths to preserve. Mathematically, involving the whole group in the punishment can be seen in terms of decreasing $\overline{w}$—making the outside opportunities less attractive because no one else in the group will employ a cheater—or in terms of increasing N—increasing the multiplier because not only the opportunities to represent the cheated trader were lost, but also those opportunities to represent other traders. Either of these makes cheating less attractive. The extensive web of social relations among the traders, which allowed them all to be quickly informed when an agent cheated, made this system of group sanctions even more effective by increasing p.

Macaulay's emphasis on power corresponds to a high value of g in our model; powerful civil servants were able to extort the locals, to sell favors, and so on. Moreover, the remoteness of the regions in which these civil servants operated made this behavior hard to monitor. In terms of our model, p is small. As expression 8.1 shows, when the gain g is large and the chance p of being caught cheating is small, then only by paying a large premium over the worker's opportunity wage can proper incentives be provided: "it was absurd to give men power and to require them to live in penury."

Theoretically, the smallest wage that can deter cheating is $w = \overline{w} + g/(Np)$, which exceeds the opportunity wage by the amount $g/(Np)$. This wage is called an **efficiency wage**; it is set higher than market-clearing wages in order to motivate the employee to work more *efficiently*. By paying an efficiency wage, the company established a financial reward for honest behavior from its employees, and so discouraged them from cheating.

EFFICIENCY WAGES VERSUS INCENTIVE PAYMENTS   In view of our analysis of incentive payments in Chapter 6, you may wonder why explicit incentive payments are used in some circumstances and efficiency wages in others. That question surely merits more study, but a preliminary answer can be given now.

In our analysis, when incentive contracts are feasible, they have been calculated

---

[5] Thomas Babington Macaulay, "Lord Clive," in *Macaulay: Poetry and Prose* (Cambridge, MA: Harvard University Press, 1967), 355–57, as quoted by Robert Klitgaard in *Controlling Corruption* (Berkeley: University of California Press, 1988), 81.

[6] Avner Greif, "Reputation and Coalitions in Medieval Trade: Evidence on the Maghribi Traders," *Journal of Economic History*, 49 (1989), 857–82.

to be the optimal form of contract. Efficiency wage contracts are to be preferred when explicit incentive contracts of the type we have described in Chapter 7 are *not* feasible. There are several possible reasons that incentive contracts may not work. The simplest is that the employee may be unable to get by on the low levels of income that might be generated by the incentive contract when the signals of performance are low or to pay the fines that the contracts sometimes require. This is analogous to our introductory discussion about why ownership might be infeasible even when it is optimal—the would-be owner might be unable to finance his or her purchase. It would be possible to raise the portion of the employee's pay that is not performance dependent so that he or she can always afford the contractual payments and so that the performance incentives are maintained. This may be too expensive for the employer, however, who may prefer an efficiency wage approach.

The second reason incentive contracts may not work is that an efficiency wage scheme can utilize subjective performance evaluations in a way that is problematic for a system of incentive pay. When performance evaluations are subjective, the employer may be tempted to underrate performance in order to reduce the required incentive payment. In anticipation of that, the employee must be less responsive to any promised incentive payments. The problem is one of *moral hazard* on the part of the employer, whose assessment of employee performance cannot be objectively verified. With the efficiency wage scheme, however, the employer pays the same wage of *w* to any employee in the job. The employer cannot save wage payments by dismissing an employee (assuming the employee has to be replaced), and he or she would be reluctant to dismiss a good employee anyway. The efficiency wage scheme thus solves the employer's moral hazard problem.

UNEMPLOYMENT AND OUTSIDE OPPORTUNITIES   An apparent problem is that firms using efficiency wages must pay high wages relative to employees' outside opportunities, but it is impossible for all firms to pay high wages relative to one another. One possible escape from this dilemma is that there be unemployment: A worker who loses a job is not immediately able to find another and so suffers a loss, even though once he or she finds employment again, it is at the same high wage as before. Shapiro and Stiglitz in fact accentuate this possibility. High wages reduce the aggregate demand for labor, creating unemployment that allows all firms to have high wages relative to their employees' outside opportunities. Of course, the output that could have been produced by this "reserve army of the unemployed" represents a social cost.

Another possibility that resembles patterns in the Japanese economy has been suggested by Masahiro Okuno-Fujiwara. At least the largest Japanese firms focus their hiring on new graduates, and these firms offer lifetime employment to the male workers they recruit who are recent graduates from schools or universities. There has traditionally been very little job changing, at least among the people with permanent jobs in major firms, and these firms have rarely hired people more than a very few years out of school. Of course, the Japanese economy is generally perceived to operate extremely efficiently, with high levels of productivity and little unemployment.

Suppose that firms focus their hiring on new entrants into the labor force, and suppose that once workers join a firm, they stay there for their whole careers. If no one ever cheats and is fired, then there will never be mid-career workers looking for employment. Because workers never observe mid-career people being hired, they might reasonably conclude that there is no market for such people. As a result, being fired would mean permanent unemployment, and this prospect is so dismal that it deters cheating completely. Thus, the high levels of effort and honesty associated with efficiency wages could be achieved without the social cost of unemployment.

Any detailed consideration of whether the theoretical possibility identified by

Okuno-Fujiwara has actual relevance to explaining the Japanese economy's performance would take us too far afield. However, a theoretical criticism of the possibility of a full-employment, no-cheating equilibrium should be noted. As Okuno-Fujiwara himself noted, this equilibrium is very fragile. If there were, for whatever reason, mid-career people looking for jobs, then (at least in terms of the formal model) there is no reason for firms to discriminate against such people. They would be hired, and this would presumably upset this expectations-based equilibrium.

Interestingly, there has been a widely noted increase in the number of managers and professionals changing jobs in recent years in Japan. A major element in this increased mobility has been the entrance of international firms to the Japanese market, especially commercial and investment banks. They have sought to hire skilled Japanese nationals and have been especially successful in attracting those who have studied abroad for MBAs and law degrees. It will be interesting to see what will happen if this pattern begins to spread to Japanese firms.

A Mathematical Example:
Comparative Statics for Efficiency Wages

In the Lord Clive example, the company's response was not simply to pay larger premiums—it intensified monitoring of the employees as well. Lord Clive brought in outsiders to audit and inspect local practices, being on the lookout for bribery and favoritism. Our goal in this section is to study a mathematical representation of how monitoring intensity and wage incentives are used together to provide incentives when monitoring is costly. We then study how changes in a parameter describing the problem affects the optimal solution.

Let $M(p)$ be the monitoring cost incurred in every accounting period when the probability of detection is p. If the company wants to deter cheating, it can minimize its total cost in each period by choosing its wage and monitoring policy to solve:

$$\text{Minimize } M(p) + w$$
$$p, w$$
$$\text{subject to } p(w - \overline{w})\, N \geq g \tag{8.2}$$

Equation 8.2 is called a **minimum cost implementation problem**. Assuming that the company wants to encourage (*implement*) a particular kind of behavior and to deter cheating, the problem is to determine the least costly way of doing so. The objective being minimized in expression 8.2 is the cost that is incurred during each period of employment, and what keeps the company from paying a low wage and doing little monitoring is the *incentive constraint* expressed in the second line of the expression. It is clear that the company will not pay a higher wage than is minimally necessary to provide incentives. Therefore, at the optimal solution:

$$w = \overline{w} + \frac{g}{Np} \tag{8.3}$$

Substituting that into the objective in expression 8.2 yields:

$$\text{Minimize } M(p) + \overline{w} + \frac{g}{Np}$$
$$p \tag{8.4}$$

At the optimal solution p^*, the first derivative of expression 8.4 with respect to p must be zero and the second derivative must be nonnegative. That is,

$$O = M'(p^*) - g/p^{*2}N \text{ and} \tag{8.5}$$
$$O \leq M''(p^*) + 2g/p^{*3}N \tag{8.6}$$

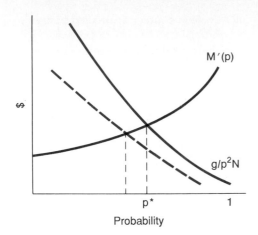

Figure 8.1: The optimal probability of detection, p^*, decreases when N increases.

To see how the solution depends on the parameter N, consider Figure 8.1. The horizontal axis measures p, the probability of detecting cheating. The vertical axis measures dollar returns. According to Equation 8.5, at the optimum we must have $M'(p^*) = g/(p^*)^2N$. The right-hand side of this expression is the change in the optimal efficiency wage as p increases. It is plainly decreasing in p. This is the curve that falls from left to right in the figure. The left-hand side is the increase in monitoring costs as p increases. It might be rising or falling, but expression 8.6 says that if it is falling, it does not fall as fast as the right-hand side falls. In the figure we have shown the first case. The solution is at p^* in the diagram, where the two curves intersect.

Now suppose N, the number of periods the employee might work for the firm, increases. This plainly decreases $g/(p^*)^2N$ for any value of p, which in the figure appears as a downward shift in the curve. The new intersection point is the solution with the higher level of N. It corresponds to a lower value of p, as the figure shows. *As the potential length of a relationship increases, there is more trust and less direct monitoring because the gains from the relationship are larger and so the incentives to cheat are less severe.*[7]

In an exercise at the end of the chapter, the reader is asked to demonstrate the additional proposition that the optimal wage $w^*(N)$ also declines with N provided that M' and M'' are positive. *A longer horizon on the relationship reduces the surplus that must be received in any particular period to deter cheating.*

The next step in the formal analysis is to check whether implementing the desired behavior is worthwhile. Let $\pi(b)$ be the gross profit earned if the behavior b is implemented, and let $C(b)$ be the corresponding minimum cost, as determined from the implementation problem. We can then build on the earlier analysis to study the problem of maximizing $\pi(b) - C(b)$ by choice of the behavior b. There is little to be said about this problem in general except that, other things being equal, the higher the cost of implementing any particular behavior the less likely it will be that the behavior will be optimal.

The actual problem faced by any real company is much more detailed than this simple problem indicates, involving choices of who to hire, what to motivate, how to monitor, and much more. These questions are considered in more detail in Chapters 10 through 13. The formal analysis conducted here analyzes only that part of the company's problem that we have called the minimum cost implementation

---

[7] Because we employed the extra assumption that p^* is differentiable, we have proved only a special case of this proposition, but it can be shown to be true quite generally.

problem, which is the problem of determining how to encourage a specified behavior at the least cost.

One way to test the significance of the analysis would be to examine how pay levels are affected by the kinds of variables used in the minimum cost implementation problem. That would entail finding surrogates for g, M, and N and examining whether increases in g and M' and decreases in N are associated statistically with larger relative wages. A more intuitive test of the correctness and significance of the theory can be deduced from the second step of the theory, in which the firm chooses what kind of behavior to encourage. If the effects we describe here are important, then observation of real organizations ought to show that the optimal choice is often to set standards of behavior that would be inefficient if enforcement were costless but that are easier to monitor and enforce than the seemingly more efficient behavior.

This prediction does seem to accord well with a variety of actual practices. For example, many firms prohibit making personal telephone calls on business phones and during business hours. In principle, it might seem better if the company policy permitted only important personal calls to be made, but that policy would be hard to enforce. It would be costly (and perhaps unacceptable to employees) for the firm to monitor the *content* of personal calls to judge their importance. Furthermore, because importance is such a subjective matter, judgments of importance are subject to abuse. A policy that proscribes all personal calls (except, perhaps, when special authorization is obtained) is far less costly to enforce. For another example, rather than trying to limit the costs incurred on business travel to those that seem justified, many companies allow their employees to spend any amount up to a prespecified limit, knowing full well that the employees will eat fancier dinners and rent finer cars as a result. These extra expenses come to be regarded as the ordinary perquisites of business travel. A plausible explanation of that policy appears to be that it is just too costly to determine what level of expenses actually is reasonable for any particular business trip and to limit employees accordingly.

A Marxian View of Efficiency Wages

A Marxian version of this same theory has been suggested by Samuel Bowles. According to Bowles, capitalists will tend to invest excessive amounts in monitoring workers because increases in the probability of detection p make it possible to pay lower wages w while still satisfying the constraint that employees are motivated not to cheat. Although wages paid to workers represent a cost to the firm, they do not represent wasted resources for society; they are merely a transfer from capitalists to laborers. On the other hand, monitoring expenditures are not a mere transfer. Monitoring consumes real resources, including supervisory time, trips to the field, record keeping, and so on. Indeed, the factory system itself, which brings together workers to do their jobs in a common facility when the work might be performed at home, has sometimes been explained by Marxian historians as a wasteful system that emerged to improve the monitoring of workers by their capitalist employers. If higher wages were paid to workers, Bowles argued, then fewer resources could be devoted to monitoring and the resources saved could be used to increase the production of valuable goods. Therefore, capitalist modes of production are inefficient, utilizing excessive resources for the task of monitoring workers.

Bowles's argument has some interesting elements that merit further attention. At its core, the argument is founded on the correct idea that issues of distribution and efficiency cannot be completely separated. Nevertheless, this Marxian argument is too incomplete to be really convincing. Recall that efficiency wages provide incentives by paying a high *relative* wage, that is, a wage that is high relative to other market opportunities. Even in a socialist economy, it is not possible for all workers to receive a high relative wage, that is, a higher wage than the average for the economy unless, as suggested earlier, there is unemployment or highly limited labor mobility. A uniform increase in wages for workers in the economy would transfer income from the owners of capital to the workers, but it would also leave relative wages unchanged and so would not reduce the need for monitoring. Indeed, if socialism were to bring with it a greater concern for income equality among workers, leveling the wages across industries, then it would require *more* monitoring in the old high-wage industries than the capitalist system it replaced.

Moreover, socialism is not just about how the benefits of production are divided but also about who should own the means of production. As we have already seen, private ownership of productive assets can sometimes have enormous advantages, and these are not taken into account in the Marxian argument just described.

Despite these weaknesses, Bowles's analysis does establish that Marx's claim that expenditures on supervisory personnel by capitalists are partly motivated as a way of transferring income from workers to capitalists, and this has some warrant in modern economic theory. It is also important because it opens some common ground for a dialogue between modern economic theory and Marxian theory.

Additional Aspects and Applications of Efficiency Wage Theory

The efficiency wage model that we have described analyzes the situation of a particular principal and agent, without regard to how the agent is chosen or how incentives vary over the agent's career. In this section we offer several examples to illustrate some of the relevant issues.

ADAM SMITH'S ACCOUNT OF MERCHANT HONOR   Adam Smith emphasized the role that the frequency of commerce had on a merchant's incentives. His account matches nicely with the comparative statics exercise we did earlier, focusing on how the variations in N among countries affects incentives and behavior of their merchants:

> Of all the nations in Europe, the Dutch, the most commercial, are the most faithful to their word. The English are more so than the Scotch, but much inferior to the Dutch, and in the remote parts of this country they [are] far less so than in the commercial parts of it. This is not at all to be imputed to national character, as some pretend; there is no natural reason why an Englishman or a Scotchman should not be as punctual in performing agreements as a Dutchman. It is far more reducible to self-interest, that general principle which regulates the actions of every man, and which leads men to act in a certain manner from views of advantage, and is as deeply implanted in an Englishman as a Dutchman. A dealer is afraid of losing his character, and is scrupulous in observing every engagement. When a person makes perhaps 20 contracts a day, he cannot gain so much by endeavoring to impose on his neighbors, as the very appearance of a cheat would make him lose. When people seldom deal with one another, we find that they are somewhat disposed to cheat, because they can gain more by a smart trick than they can lose by the injury which it does to their character .[8]

According to Smith, the greater a merchant's volume of business, the greater the incentive to act honestly in order to protect his or her valuable business reputation.

---

[8] Adam Smith, *Lectures on Justice, Police, Revenue, and Arms*, Edwin Cannan, ed. (New York: Augustus M. Kelley, 1964).

REPUTATIONS AND THE MAGHRIBI TRADERS   The cost of providing incentives using reputations also depends on the other opportunities that the parties may have. An agent whose outside opportunities would remain good even if caught cheating has relatively little to lose from cheating, so motivating that person tends to be costly. On the other hand, an agent whose business opportunities lie with a small group of principals who communicate among themselves must worry that actions that damage his or her reputation will result in the loss of a large volume of valuable business. These agents are more likely to resist temptations to steal or cheat, even if the wage for the particular job is low. In other words, it is less costly to motivate these agents than to motivate agents with better outside opportunities.

The example of the Maghribi traders cited earlier illustrates this point.[9] The evolving pattern of agency arrangements among traders in the western Mediterranean in the eleventh century can be attributed in part to the changing costs of motivating different kinds of agents. In the ninth and tenth centuries, when the volume of trade was lower and the reliability of communications was poorer, merchants commonly traveled with their own goods. Relying on a personal agent was hazardous, because the agent "could easily have disappeared with the capital or cheated in business conducted in far-off markets where none of his associates had any control."[10] By the eleventh century, however, an extensive network existed in the Muslim Mediterranean by which merchants provided references for one another, so that the loss that any single merchant stood to suffer from a loss of reputation grew much larger. As a result of these changes, the merchants found it more economical to rely on overseas merchant-agents. The merchants in towns A and B would entrust their goods to one another for sale rather than relying on a personal agent from the originating merchant's home port. This change may be explained at least in part by the reduced cost of ensuring the honesty of the overseas agent. An economic analysis that focuses on resource costs alone cannot give an adequate account of these evolving trade relationships.

CAREER PATHS IN FIRMS   Career paths are another element that was missing from our simple efficiency wage model. Our simple model gave only minimal attention to the role of time by incorporating the number of times N that the worker expects to be employed. In a more complete model—one in which the incentives for loyalty, honesty, and hard work are provided by the promise of high *future* wages—a pattern of pay that is rising over the worker's career provides incentives more effectively. Many companies have virtually institutionalized a career pattern in which, for successful workers, earnings rise throughout the worker's career, perhaps eventually reaching a point where they exceed the worker's marginal product. Early in a worker's career, when his or her accumulated investment in the company and in his or her career is low, the worker is placed in a job of low responsibility, where the work is relatively more routine and easily monitored and errors can be corrected. After the worker is better trained, has invested in learning the specific business, and when the reward for this diligence is nearer at hand, then the worker is assigned to less routine tasks that may also be more difficult to monitor. We saw earlier in this chapter that high pay is a substitute for close monitoring, so the relationship between pay and responsibility is just as expected. (Note that this analysis is complementary to the explanation of the pattern of rising wages with experience in terms of screening offered in Chapter 5 and the bonding explanation given in Chapter 6.)

---

[9] This account is based on Avner Greif, *op. cit.*

[10] C. M. Cipolla, *Before the Industrial Revolution* (New York: Norton, 1980), 198, as quoted by Greif.

PRODUCT REPUTATIONS AND BRAND NAMES   We have emphasized the applications of efficiency wage theory to the incentives for employees, agents, or business partners to behave honestly. The principles we have described have broader application than that, however. Benjamin Klein and Keith Leffler have emphasized that thin profit margins are the enemy of quality in markets for goods and services, too, because they tempt individual producers to cut their quality and earn higher profits until consumers recognize the change. The firms could then exit the market. If the product is recognizable by consumers, however, and if the product margins are high, the value of staying in the business can outweigh any short-run profits from degrading the product quality.

Where competition keeps prices relatively low or where certain products are replaced so frequently that customer dissatisfaction with the old product is irrelevant, brand names that cover a whole product line can provide another way to establish a reputation for quality. A homeowner may buy this year's model of a Black and Decker drill if he or she is satisfied that last year's model, purchased by neighbors, was of good quality and if the power screwdriver of the brand that the homeowner purchased two years ago is still working well. The reputation value of a brand name leads profitable firms with established brands to work hard to maintain quality.

REPUTATIONS AS CONTRACT ENFORCERS

Successful commerce requires that businesspeople be able to count on one another to honor their agreements and, as the Adam Smith quotation emphasizes, the reputation mechanism has long been one of the most important mechanisms for ensuring that contracts are honored. In this section, we examine this idea in more detail. We conduct this part of our analysis using *game theory*, which makes it possible to examine more systematically limitations of simple incentive systems and how some of those limitations can be overcome by more complex and sophisticated arrangements.

The Elementary Theory: Reputations in Repeated Transactions

As discussed in Chapter 4, for many kinds of business transactions—those that take place over an extended period of time in particular—conditions arise for which no plans have been made. Transactions can be classified according to how decisions are made in these circumstances. In *spot market* transactions, there are no long-term agreements and little likelihood of significant changes in circumstances before the contract is executed. When the unexpected does occur, the parties bargain among themselves about how to respond. An alternative to spot markets is to establish a relational contract, for example, a **hierarchy** or **authority relation** in which a manager evaluates the facts and alternative courses of action and then instructs the other parties on what to do. Sometimes, long-term contracts allow one party to exercise discretion without establishing an authority relation. For example, a homeowner may delegate some degree of authority to a remodeling contractor to make decisions about how the remodeling job should be done.

These abstract descriptions of contracting practices apply to many concrete situations. When a person becomes an employee of a firm, he or she typically agrees to accept whatever direction is given within somewhat nebulous "customary limits" in exchange for a fixed hourly wage or for a salary. The employee's supervisor is the one with authority. The supervisor can exercise discretion in assigning tasks, and the employee must rely on the supervisor to do so fairly. In our home remodeling example, even if the contract is unusually precise, it will not specify what the contractor should do if rain delays the start of work, or if fixtures that were selected from a catalogue are no longer available, or if the dimensions on the drawings contain an error. The

MacRents:
Efficiency Wages in the Fast-Food Business

An empirical implication of efficiency wage theory is that a decrease in the intensity of supervision will result in an increase in the optimal efficiency wages. The fast-food restaurant business offers a test of this prediction.

The fast-food business in the United States involves a number of chains: McDonald's, Burger King, Wendy's, Jack in the Box, Kentucky Fried Chicken, Arby's, and Roy Rogers are among the most familiar. Each of these has large numbers of outlets, some of which are owned and operated by the parent firm, and some of which are owned and managed by independent businesspeople operating under franchise agreements.

The two types of outlets appear very similar. They have the same menus based on the same recipes, they are architecturally and technologically similar, they are geographically similar, they draw employees from the same local work forces, they have similar pricing policies, and so on. However, the franchise units are managed by their owners, who set the wages, fringe benefit levels, and work rules and conditions in their individual outlets, make their own hiring and firing decisions, and claim the profits and losses of their operations. In contrast, the company-owned restaurants are managed by salaried employee-managers, with wages and benefits being set by district managers.

A key part of the outlet manager's job is to monitor and train the assistant managers and supervisors as well as the actual nonmanagerial staff of the restaurant. Standard incentive arguments would suggest that a franchisee, who collects the residual profits, will be much more highly motivated to monitor intensively and train effectively than will a salaried manager. (The fact that franchises tend to be about five times more profitable than company outlets supports this view.) In turn, efficiency wage theory then suggests that the company will choose to pay higher wages to the workers in its outlets than will franchisees in theirs. The higher wage makes the job more valuable and losing it more painful. This offsets the lower probability of being fired for cause that results from weaker monitoring and so reduces the amount of surliness, carelessness, absenteeism, shirking, theft, on-the-job drunkenness, and so on from what they would otherwise be.

The technology and delivery systems of the fast-food business have been chosen to minimize the chance that a bored teenage worker can cause any great problems. This suggests that the effort the manager devotes to the supervisors and assistant managers may be especially important and that the efficiency wage differential for these employees in the company outlets should perhaps be relatively higher than the differential for regular employees.

These predictions are supported by data from two surveys of fast-food restaurants (one of workers and supervisors in a sample of McDonald's, Kentucky Fried Chicken, Arby's, and Roy Rogers outlets in 1982, the other of managers in a sample of McDonald's, Burger King, Kentucky Fried Chicken, and Wendy's restaurants in 1985). In the first survey, employees hired into a given job started at essentially the same wages in both types of outlets, but the wages grew much faster over time for the supervisors in the franchise outlets than for those in the company-owned stores and somewhat more rapidly for nonmanagerial workers. The result was that earnings for supervisors were a sizeable 8.9 percent higher in company restaurants and a statistically (if not economically) significant 1.7 percent higher for full-time nonmanagerial workers. The second study examined only starting wages, but the company restaurants were only two thirds as likely to start new employees at the minimum wage as were the franchise outlets. Moreover, company-owned outlets provided more generous fringe benefits, further increasing the pay differential. The biggest difference in benefits was in the provision of free meals. Preventing employees from helping themselves to a free meal is very difficult to control. If it is difficult to induce sufficiently careful monitoring to prevent employees from stealing food, it may be best simply to permit it explicitly.

Based on Alan B. Krueger, "Ownership, Agency and Wages: An Examination of Franchising in the Fast Food Industry," Working Paper 3334, National Bureau of Economic Research (1990).

homeowner must rely on the contractor to react appropriately to the inevitable sequence of unforeseen conditions that were not specified in the original contract. In each of these situations, at least one party (and frequently both) must rely on the honesty and good will of the other.

The disputes that arise in these situations are often connected with ambiguity about what kinds of discretionary behavior are honest or appropriate. To start analyzing the problem, however, let us suppose that *although it is not possible to specify what to do in any particular situation, it is possible for parties close to the transaction to determine whether the person with authority has done "the right thing."* It is this two-part assumption that characterizes our "elementary theory." The assumption implies that we are examining a situation in which detailed contracts cannot be written, making legal enforcement difficult, but in which the parties themselves have enough information to evaluate each other's past behavior, which is a basic requirement of any system of reputations.

OFFERING TRUST   We use the box shown below to describe abstractly a transaction opportunity that may occur repeatedly. At each round—that is, each time the transaction opportunity arises—one party, called the *offeror*, can offer to trust a second party, called the *decision maker*. The formal structure of this interaction is represented in the box, which describes a **normal form game** with two players. The box shows that each player has two **strategies** at each round. The offeror's strategies are to offer

	Decision Maker	
Offeror	Honor Trust	Don't Trust
Offer Trust	V, V	−L, V + G
Don't Offer	0, 0	0, 0

trust or not. The decision maker's strategies specify what he or she plans to do *if trust is offered*. The entries in the box show what the payoffs will be for each combination of strategies. If trust is offered, the decision maker must then decide whether to honor that trust by behaving fairly. The box describes the parties' payoffs. The first number in each cell of the box describes the offeror's payoff, whereas the second describes the decision maker's. If no trust is offered, no transaction occurs and both parties earn a payoff of zero. If trust is offered and honored, then both parties receive a valuable payoff of V. However, there is a short-run temptation for the decision maker not to honor trust; by not honoring, he or she receives an extra payoff of G in that round. In that case, the offeror suffers a loss of L and would have fared better if he or she had not offered trust and had instead settled for a payoff of zero. We assume, of course, that V, G, and L are positive numbers.

It is important to interpret the numbers here correctly. Zero is simply a value that we have assigned arbitrarily to whatever the two parties might do if they do not share trust—the number itself has no significance except as a baseline from which other values are measured. That the value V is positive means that honored trust is more valuable to both parties than whatever happens if trust is not offered at all. The larger V is, the more the parties have to gain by offering and honoring trust. That G is positive means that the decision maker has something to gain in the short run by dishonoring trust. For example, if the decision maker is shamed by behaving dishonorably, the other gains are large enough to offset this shame. That L is positive means that offering trust entails a risk: The offeror has something to lose.

Suppose now that this normal form game were to be played only once. According to game theory, which posits that each player is self-interested, we predict that the offeror will not offer trust and the decision maker will plan not to honor trust in case it is offered. The self-interested decision maker, if given the opportunity, would surely prefer to earn $V + G$ by dishonoring trust than to earn just V by honoring it. The offeror, recognizing the decision maker's incentives and knowing that he or she is self-interested, would therefore choose to avoid the loss of L by not offering trust. The result is that each party receives a payoff of zero, missing the opportunity to obtain payoffs of V.

REPEATED DEALINGS AND THE NASH EQUILIBRIUM   Despite this unfortunate outcome, the game-theoretic solution does seem to be a reasonable description of what might happen if the situation we have portrayed were to arise among strangers who meet only once, especially if the temptation G and the potential loss L are large. If the two players are people who encounter one another in this sort of circumstance frequently, however, they might be expected to develop some way to overcome the problem of trust and enjoy the fruits of the honored trust outcome. For example, the decision maker might say to the offeror: "I would like you to trust me once to test my honor, and you would be wise to do that. After the test, base your expectations about me not on some arbitrary, pessimistic theory about how a stranger might play this game, but on how I prove myself in action. If you do offer trust, I promise always to honor it. We both know that if I should ever fail to honor your trust, you would never trust me again. For that very reason, it will actually be in *my* interest, as well as yours, to honor your trust, for only by doing so can I earn your continuing trust, which I have good reason to value."

Is this speech believable? To check its logic, suppose that earning a payoff of X every time the parties meet in the indefinite future has the same value for the decision maker as does a one-time payoff NX today. The magnitude of the number N depends in part on how frequently the parties expect to meet and on the interest rates that they face.[11] What can we expect to happen if the offeror believes the self-interested decision maker's speech and acts accordingly? If the decision maker does not honor the offeror's trust, the decision maker gains G immediately when he or she cheats but will never be trusted in the future. If the decision maker does honor trust in each period, he or she will earn a payoff of NV instead. If NV > G and each party expects the other party to behave as described, then neither party could do better by deviating from the prescribed behavior. The offeror cannot gain by withholding trust: He or she expects the trust to be honored and therefore expects a payoff of V per period by offering trust, compared to 0 per period if the trust is witheld. The decision maker cannot gain by dishonoring trust: He or she expects a payoff of V per period, which is valued at NV if trust is honored in each period, but only G < NV if trust is dishonored today, for then trust will never again be offered. In the language of game theory, this situation in which no party can gain by making a unilateral deviation from the prescribed behavior is called a **Nash equilibrium**.

For a pattern of behavior to be a Nash equilibrium, it means that *if* the parties all expect this pattern of behavior, then it is in the individual interests of each to adhere to the pattern. In many situations, especially ones where people have little experience, there is no reason to suppose that people will have the same expectations about behavior or that their expectations will be correct. If (1) all the players in the game do have the same expectations, (2) those expectations are correct, and (3) the players act in their individual best interests given their expectations, then the combination of strategies is a Nash equilibrium.

One important difficulty with using a Nash equilibrium to predict social behavior is that there may be more than one. In the game we have portrayed, a second Nash equilibrium strategy combination is for the offeror never to offer trust and the decision maker never to honor it. A third possible Nash equilibrium is for the decision maker to promise to cheat only every second time that trust is offered and for the offeror to offer trust at every round as long as the decision maker never cheats in two successive rounds. If L < V and the rounds are frequent, neither player can gain by changing his or her strategy, so this strategy combination is also a Nash equilibrium. The hypothesis of Nash equilibrium rules out some patterns of behavior but does not always lead to a unique prediction about what the outcome will be.

REPUTATIONS   Let us return now to the first Nash equilibrium that we described, in which the offeror continually offers trust for as long as the decision maker continues to honor it. We studied this situation assuming that the offeror at each round is the same person, but that is not really necessary for the analysis. If the decision maker faces a series of different offerors who each offer trust only if the decision maker honored trust when it was last offered, then the decision maker's calculation about whether to honor trust is exactly the same as if there were a single offeror. One might say that in each transaction, the decision maker honors trust in order to encourage future trading partners to offer trust or, in other words, to maintain his or her *reputation for honesty*. In the world of business, a reputation for honesty can be valuable because it can attract trading partners. In addition, if it is possible but costly to write detailed contracts, a good reputation can often allow the decision maker to avoid that expense as well as the use of costly and error-prone legal contract enforcement mechanisms.

---

[11] If the game is to be played an infinite number of times, the interest rate that players can earn on their investments is r per period, and the players meet at intervals of t periods, then $N = 1/[(1 + r)^t - 1] + 1$. Lower interest rates (smaller r) or more frequent meetings (smaller t) lead to larger values for N. See Chapter 14 for additional details of how to make present-value calculations.

Trench Warfare in World War I: The "Live and Let Live" System

In economic applications, we usually emphasize the *financial* returns that accrue to earning others' trust. Sometimes, the most significant returns are not financial at all. A remarkable example of valuable trust among enemies is the "live and let live" system that developed between battalions of opposing armies along the trenches of the Western Front in World War I. Although the commanders of the opposing German and Allied armies wanted the troops to shoot to kill, the soldiers often behaved differently. Trust and reputations explain how this came about.

In the trench warfare of WWI, the same opposing battalions faced each other for long periods of time. Deadly fire from one side could be reciprocated by the other side. Although many of the soldiers in opposing battalions in any war would prefer to avoid exchanges of deadly fire, they cannot trust the other side to withhold its fire because each side has a strong interest in destroying the enemies' fighting capabilities. In WWI, however, the daily exchange of fire between entrenched battalions in a war of attrition offered a rare opportunity. Daily interactions could make it a Nash equilibrium for the two sides to fire in earnest only if fired upon. To achieve this outcome, each side had to demonstrate to the other its ability to retaliate if the other side initiated deadly fire, as well as its willingness not to use deadly fire without provocation.

In many parts of the front, the soldiers did achieve such a truce while still making it appear to their commanders that they were shooting at the enemy. According to Robert Axelrod's account, "During periods of mutual restraint, the enemy soldiers took pains to show each other that they could indeed retaliate if necessary. For example, German snipers showed their prowess to the British by aiming at spots on the walls of cottages and firing until they had cut a hole. Likewise, the artillery would often demonstrate with a few accurately aimed shots that they could do more damage if they wished."

Eventually, the Allied commanders uncovered these tacit truces and took steps to end them. They initiated a series of commando raids on the German trenches that brought retaliation from the Germans and more retaliations by the opposing Allied soldiers, until the accumulation of fire made the "live and let live" system untenable.

Source: Robert Axelrod, *The Evolution of Cooperation* (New York: Basic Books, 1984).

Ambiguity, Complexity, and Limits of Reputations

Although it may not be possible to specify in advance in an enforceable contract how the decision maker should behave, it may nevertheless be possible for those involved to decide afterward whether the parties had behaved honorably. This assumption is sometimes problematic, however. In many cases, if it really were easy to decide what constitutes honorable behavior, then it would be easy for courts to settle disputes at low cost.

In reality, perceptions of circumstances frequently come into conflict, and parties differ about just what is "the right and honorable thing to do." Even when parties agree about the circumstances, they may disagree about what can be done or what is likely to be effective. For many kinds of decisions, it is not possible to try out each alternative to see what the consequences would have been.

The problem we have described is compounded if there is more than one party offering trust. As difficult as it may be for a single party to know whether another has acted fairly, it is even more difficult for an outsider to the transaction to assess what has happened when there has been a dispute. In a simple reputation system, that is precisely the task that faces a whole series of outsiders to the transaction. The cost and difficulty of making those judgments, and the need for them to be made repeatedly by a series of outsiders undermines the effectiveness of a system of trust based on reputations alone. Various institutions and practices have arisen to restore some of the lost effectiveness.

CORPORATE CULTURE   One way to enhance the effectiveness of a system of reputations within a group is to construct or evolve a set of workable principles and routines that create shared expectations for group members. In a large organization, the principles would help guide managers in making decisions as well as providing a set of clear expectations for everyone in the organization. Sometimes, routines evolve with no far-reaching purpose in mind, but simply represent patterns of action that have worked well in the past. In other instances, the principles take the form of explicit rules promulgated with a clear purpose in mind. For example, the San Francisco Forty Niners football team has a rule that a player in the starting lineup who becomes injured and misses some games is always entitled to return to his starting role upon recovery, regardless of how well the substitute plays in his absence. The rule is designed to keep injured players from concealing injuries. The team surely faces temptations to make "exceptions" to the rule—especially when the substitute plays very well—but exceptions would undermine the players' trust in the coaches. Without the rule, the notion of fair treatment would be far more ambiguous. What is the "fair" thing to do if the substitute plays especially well?

At Nordstrom, the department store chain, one rule is that merchandise returned by customers is always cheerfully accepted without requiring proof of purchase. To teach this rule, a story is told to trainees of a salesperson accepting without question a customer's return of an old, badly worn set of automobile tires, even though Nordstrom has never sold tires! The story helps to establish a rule that everyone can understand and makes clear to trainees the strong commitment to customer satisfaction that is a hallmark of Nordstrom's operations.

From this perspective, corporate culture is the set of routines for decision making and shared expectations that employees are taught and the stories and related devices used to convey those expectations. In Chapter 4 we emphasized the role of routines and shared expectations for coordinating action within the organization. Here we emphasize a different function: The culture provides a set of principles and procedures for judging right behavior and resolving inevitable disputes. Because the principles have to be simple to be communicated effectively to newcomers to the organization and because they have to be adapted to work in the typical circumstances that the organization faces, no one culture can work well for all organizations. This helps make some limited economic sense of the "clash of cultures" explanations that are often cited as a reason that two organizations with very different styles or histories experience difficulty when they try to merge their operations.

REPUTATIONS AND THE LAW   Robert Ellickson has taken the culture argument even further, claiming that even in modern times, in stable communities, the need to maintain a good reputation is more powerful than are legal sanctions in settling community disputes.[12] He reports that in Shasta County, California, a ranching and agricultural area, the principles actually used to compensate for damages caused by stray livestock, for example, are not those imposed by the relevant laws, but instead are ones that were evolved over generations in the local community. There is no legal enforcement of the rules of neighborly relations—just the perceived need by residents to maintain a good, trustworthy image in the local community.

In fact, most contractual disputes never reach a court of law. The parties work out informal ways to resolve their differences, and these mechanisms are supported at least as much by reputation considerations and by the expectations of future gains as by the threat of legal action.

THE "END GAME" PROBLEM   A major constraint on reputational enforcement mechanisms is that the horizon over which the relationship is expected to continue must be relatively long if the value of the reputation is to exceed the gain from cheating. We saw this in extreme form in the previous game: If there is only a single interaction, then trust will not be extended because it is sure to be violated. Thus, if there is a last time the parties will interact, and the parties know they have reached this point, they will fail to achieve the gains that are potentially available. Moreover, if they know they are approaching the end of the relationship, the returns to maintaining a reputation are seen to be small and may not be enough to prevent trust from being violated. In these circumstances, other mechanisms may have to come into play if inefficiency is to be avoided.

One possibility is to move to more formal incentive mechanisms. For example, it has been suggested that concern with their reputations and their consequent career opportunities is a major check on managers' temptation to behave opportunistically. As a manager approaches retirement age, however, these career concerns ought to weigh less heavily. Thus, it may be advisable to increase the use of explicit incentive pay for managers as they approach retirement. A recent study by Robert Gibbons and Kevin Murphy found exactly this pattern in the compensation of a large sample of corporate chief executive officers (CEOs) in the United States.[13] Total compensation of the CEOs in this sample became more responsive to their firms' stock market performance as they neared their retirement ages.

Another kind of solution to the **end game problem** is the sale of businesses. The founder of a business, nearing retirement, finds it valuable to maintain the reputation of the business to attract a higher price from potential buyers. This can lead the business to act as if it had a much longer horizon than its founder or its executives.

The end game problem is also commonly experienced by companies in bankruptcy. Bankruptcy attorneys commonly observe that the customers of bankrupt businesses claim that the goods delivered in the last days of operation are of inferior quality and refuse to pay full price for them. With the bilateral relationship nearing its end, attitudes toward payment harden, and disputes to be resolved in court become more likely.

The Advanced Theory: Reputations Aided by Institutions

One of the ways that people enhance the effectiveness of a system of reputations is by narrowing the range of people with whom they do business. Frequent transactions

---

[12] Robert Ellickson, "Of Coase and Cattle: Dispute Resolution Among Neighbors in Shasta County," *Stanford Law Review*, 38 (February 1986), 623–87.

[13] Robert Gibbons and Kevin Murphy, "Optimal Incentive Contracts in the Presence of Career Concerns," mimeo, University of Rochester (1990).

if they are all of similar magnitude allow trust to flourish. In modern societies, however, people have specialized occupations and specialized skills. Many specialists, such as plumbers, furniture repairers, or automobile salespeople, interact with individual customers relatively infrequently. Buyers may purchase frequently from the same sources, but the availability of competing suppliers still creates impersonal transactions that are hardly better than the outside alternatives.

Business and legal institutions of various sorts can help to fill the gap. Legal institutions replace the system of reputations altogether. Parties who rely on the legal system count on the threat of a lawsuit, rather than that of a bad reputation, to ensure full compliance with the contract's terms. The legal system, however, has many disadvantages for contract enforcement. Because it is a general system, it relies on general rules that may be poorly tailored for the particular industry where the dispute arises. Legal procedures are often cumbersome, time consuming, and expensive. Furthermore, legal rules based on historical precedents may be unresponsive to changing technologies and other changing realities. Judges and juries may often lack the expertise to evaluate industry disputes based on technical issues well enough to apply legal rules appropriately. In international disputes, courts sometimes lack the authority to enforce their decisions. Also, throughout history, corrupt and biased judges and outside political influences have added to the costs and the apparent randomness of court rulings.

For all these reasons, private institutions have frequently been more important than legal ones for establishing standards of behavior, ensuring contract compliance, and resolving disputes. Often, the private institutions work by buttressing the reputation system itself.

FROM MEDIEVAL PRIVATE JUDGES TO MODERN RATING AGENCIES   In Europe, before the rise of the nation-state, merchants developed a system of private laws—the *lex mercatoria*—and employed private judges to resolve disputes. The merchant law often differed from the generally prevailing church law on the same issues. Merchants at the time depended on one another for many services, such as security while traveling or assistance in handling goods in foreign ports. Good standing in the community of merchants was essential to conducting business. The system of merchant law provided an evolving standard of behavior that was more responsive to merchant needs than was the church law. The system of private judges making pronouncements about disputes greatly simplified a third-party merchant's problem of interpreting a dispute between two other merchants to reach a judgment about their respective reputations. The crucial tasks of *deciding* who is right and *communicating* to other merchants the identities of offenders were handled effectively by this system.[14]

Throughout history, many devices have been used to inform the public when a merchant is no longer in good standing. In colonial America, the stock and pillories were used to make a public display of merchants who violated commercial law. In the eighteenth and nineteenth centuries, when whalers from different countries met at sea, they would have a party called a "gam," where the captains of the vessels would exchange information about many things, including disputes with other whalers that needed to be settled. Whalers in the United States, concentrated as they were in a few seaside communities, needed no such practices to keep informed about one another. The whalers' system of community enforcement of norms based on repeated interactions was so effective in its early years that there are no recorded cases of property disputes among whalers going to court, even though the issues of who owns

---

[14] See: Paul Milgrom, Douglass North, and Barry Weingast, "The Role of Institutions in the Revival of Trade: The Medieval Law Merchant," *Economics and Politics*, 2 (March 1990), 1–23.

a whale are quite subtle.[15] (Should it be the first to sink a harpoon? The first to secure a flag in the whale? Can a ship harvest a whale that has been killed and flagged but is floating free or must it allow the killing ship to come make the harvest?) Only in the late nineteenth century, when petroleum products began to replace whale products did the legal system become involved in whaling disputes. At that time, rents in the whaling industry began to decline and time horizons for whalers became shorter—effects that combined to undermine the community-based system of reputations.

In modern times, the local Better Business Bureau will mediate complaints by customers against local businesses and report information about complaints against local merchants and craftsmen. Similarly, credit bureaus report information about past loans and whether they were properly repaid, and consumer agencies report survey information about various matters, such as how satisfied consumers are with the handling of their insurance claims at various companies. Disseminating this information strengthens incentives for reliable behavior. Merchants are motivated to settle complaints made through the Better Business Bureau to preserve their good reputations. People are more eager to repay loans knowing that a faulty credit rating will prevent them from borrowing again on favorable terms. A similar logic applies to insurance companies.

BOYCOTTS AND EMBARGOES: INTERNAL DISCIPLINE   The main characteristic of institutions that work by enhancing the reputation system is their reliance on sanctions delivered by individuals. If applying sanctions is costly, some individuals may refuse to comply, undermining the effectiveness of the system.

Medieval merchant guilds in northern Europe were bodies made up of all the foreign merchants trading in a single town.[16] A major difficulty these traders faced was that the cities in which they traded did not always carry out their contractual agreements, for example, to protect the traders against theft by locals. The only significant response that the merchants had was to refuse to trade in the offending town, but this ran into the free-rider problem noted earlier. In the major trading centers of northern Europe, especially Bruges, the trading merchants came from many different cities, and this made enforcing embargoes especially difficult. Moreover, towns faced with an embargo would try to encourage traders to free ride by offering them especially attractive deals. The guilds can be seen as an institution through which merchants coordinated their responses to cities that reneged on trading agreements.

In 1280, following a dispute over Bruges's responsibility to provide physical protection for the merchants, the guild of merchants trading in the city attempted embargo, transferring their trade to Aardenburg. The embargo, however, was defeated when Bruges offered special terms to merchants from various towns who found the absence of competing traders to their liking. In response to such failures, the town guilds united under the new, more encompassing organization—the Hansa, or Hanseatic League. If the Hansa declared an embargo on a city and traders violated the embargo, then their home city itself might be put under embargo or the offending traders might be refused access to goods from other member towns. Following another dispute, in 1358 the Hansa endorsed another embargo of Bruges, and the city responded again by offering special terms to Hansa member Cologne and nonmembers

---

[15] Robert Ellickson, "A Hypothesis of Wealth-Maximizing Norms: Evidence from the Whaling Industry," *Journal of Law, Economics, and Organization*, 5 (Spring 1989), 83–97.

[16] These guilds should not be confused with the more familiar crafts guilds, which were organizations of all the producers of a particular good in an area, for example, the weavers guild in London.

such as Kampen. With its strong internal discipline, however, the embargo was eventually successful and Bruges honored the trade charter.[17]

There is a danger of misinterpreting this historical episode as a mere distributive dispute, in which one party's gain is the other's loss. Actually, institutions like the Hansa which help to enforce agreements perform an important efficiency-enhancing function that helps to account for their emergence and survival. From the host city's point of view, the very ability to renege on agreements is also an *inability to commit to honest behavior*. That inability can be very damaging. In 1283 King Edward I of England, reflecting on the broken promises of security for foreign merchants in his country, observed that "many merchants are put off from coming to this land with their merchandise to the detriment of merchants and of the whole kingdom."[18] In modern times, as in history, people can find it valuable to establish arrangements, practices, and institutions that narrow their options or enable others to enforce contracts against them because those very arrangements make them a more reliable and trustworthy business partner.

RENT SEEKING, INFLUENCE COSTS, AND EFFICIENT DECISION ROUTINES

Rents and Quasi-rents

So far, we have developed the argument in primarily nontechnical language, speaking about the economic profits of a firm or about the high wages of the worker. In economics journals, however, the general principles are most frequently couched in terms of *rents* and *quasi-rents*. A **rent** is the portion of earnings in excess of the minimum amount needed to attract a worker to accept a particular job or a firm to enter a particular industry. For example, a worker who ranks jobs only on the basis of wages and who is offered a job at wage rate w earns a rent of $w - \hat{w}$ if $\hat{w}$ is the highest wage he or she can earn in any alternative employment. Similarly, if a price of $\hat{p}$ would be just sufficient to attract a firm to produce in some market, and if the quantity the firm sells is q, then the firm earns rents of $(p - \hat{p})q$, provided the actual price p that it can charge is greater than $\hat{p}$. Notice that the price $\hat{p}$ is the same as the average total cost of operating in the industry, including the opportunity cost of capital as well as the costs of all the other fixed and variable factors used by the firm. Rents typically arise because of scarcity, whether natural or induced. In 1990, for example, baseball pitcher Roger Clemens was given a contract calling for him to be paid $21.5 million over a period of four years, in each of which he would probably not pitch in many more than 40 games. There is surely a large element of rent in this pay. Clemens receives this rent because his talent is in very short supply. In turn, his employers, the Boston Red Sox, can pay him this much because they are earning rents from their exclusive franchise to present major league baseball in New England.

A **quasi-rent** is the portion of earnings in excess of the minimum amount needed to prevent a worker from quitting his or her job or a producer from exiting its industry. Whereas rents are defined in terms of decisions to enter a job or an industry, quasi-rents are defined in terms of the decision to exit. If the wage $\overline{w}$ would be just sufficient to keep an employee at work at a particular job, taking into account such costs as

---

[17] See Avner Greif, Paul Milgrom, and Barry Weingast, "The Merchant Guild as a Nexus of Contracts," unpublished working paper, Stanford University (1990).

[18] *English Historical Documents*, David C. Douglas, ed. (Oxford: Oxford University Press, 1955), 420.

those of searching for a new job and those of acquiring any needed new skills, then the employee's quasi-rents are $w - \overline{w}$. The employee will exit (quit and seek a new job) precisely when the quasi-rents are negative. He or she will value the job and want to keep it when the quasi-rents are positive. Similarly, in the standard theory of markets, a firm will exit an industry only if the price does not cover its average variable costs, which we may call $\overline{p}$. If the actual price p is higher, then the firm earns quasi-rents of $(p - \overline{p})q$ on its output q.

To understand the difference between rents and quasi-rents, let us compare the entry and exit decisions for the firm. Because the price p that is just sufficient to make entry profitable is equal to the *average total cost*, whereas the price $\overline{p}$ that is sufficient to make exit unprofitable is just the *average variable cost*, it must be true that $\overline{p} \leq p$. That is, it is possible for a firm to earn quasi-rents even when the initial decision to enter the market leads to only normal profits and even when it yields less than normal profits. *The difference between rents and quasi-rents arises from the presence of costs that must be incurred to enter the market but that cannot be salvaged by an existing firm that chooses to exit.* For this reason, quasi-rents are always at least as great as rents.

Rents and quasi-rents are useful for analysing different kinds of decisions. In the theories described in this chapter, it is quasi-rents—what the agent stands to lose if forced to exit—that plays the central role. Although rents can exist only fleetingly in a competitive economy, quasi-rents are much more common. They are created whenever specialized (nonsalvageable) investments are made and so have the potential to be widely useful for providing incentives.

Rent Seeking in the Public and Private Sectors

We have seen how rents can help support efficiency, but their presence can also create incentives to expend resources attempting to reallocate the rents. This is typically a pure cost with few or no counterbalancing benefits.

Governmental decisions to grant monopolies, determine rates for utilities, or establish tariffs or other trade barriers can create rents or quasi-rents for firms. Firms attempt to capture these rents for themselves, rather than having them go elsewhere. They do so both by participating legitimately in the political and regulatory processes and, sometimes, by paying bribes. The result is a costly public policy problem, both because the attempts sometimes lead to distorted decisions and because so much valuable time and energy is spent in a process that results only in transfers, not in actual social gains. Activities that serve no social function other than to transfer rents or quasi-rents have been called *rent seeking* and *directly unproductive profit seeking* (DUP) when they occur in the public sector, and the costs of resources used and decisions distorted are *influence costs*.

According to some analysts, influence costs are one of the largest costs of big government. When there are many decisions being made and each has large redistributive consequences, then many of the brightest and ablest people in society will find it most remunerative to spend their time trying to influence those decisions, either pursuing their own individual self-interests or those of their clients. This causes many of the inefficiencies of public decision making. Resources are expended by private parties (often through their elected representatives) solely to affect the distributive impacts of public decisions, as when huge lobbying efforts are mounted to win a cable television franchise, and efficiency is sacrificed for distributive or political ends, as when a federal facility is sited in a key congressman's district rather than where it will do the most good. Direct governmental expenditures are just the tip of the iceberg: The resources expended by others to influence judges and juries, legislators and regulators, inspectors, auditors, standards boards, purchasing agents, tax authorities, and other government employees may far exceed those expended by the government itself on making and even on implementing the decisions that are influenced.

The reason the size of government enters into the analysis is that larger governments have larger agendas, more decision makers, and more issues to resolve. The opportunities for influencing governmental decisions grow along with the size and scope of government. This does not mean that anarchy is the optimal form of government; the presence of costs does not deny the possible existence of still larger benefits. Moreover, private sector decision making may sometimes reflect too *narrow* a set of interests, so that only the public sector can fairly and efficiently determine some matters.

The notion that factional politics is costly is hardly a new one. James Madison wrote in *The Federalist* two centuries ago, "the causes of faction cannot be removed, and . . . relief is only to be sought in the means of controlling its effects."[19] The economic theory of organizations offers a set of principles to evaluate alternative means. It allows people to decide in a discriminating way what kinds of organizations are best suited for what kinds of decisions, depending on the nature of the interests that need to be resolved, and what kinds of decisions ought not to be made at all by any central authority.

QUASI-RENTS AND INFLUENCE ACTIVITIES IN ORGANIZATIONS   Scholars have paid far less attention to the influence costs that are incurred within firms, unions, trade associations, and other private-sector organizations, largely because classical economic theory denies the existence of any rents within those organizations that can be appropriated by influencing decisions.

In the classical theory, there are no good jobs and bad jobs. The wage that workers are offered is just the same as they could earn in any other similar job in that firm or any other firm. Given any two jobs that require the same qualifications, if one job were universally regarded as more pleasant or a better route to future promotions, then the only way to attract workers to apply for the bad job would be to pay a higher wage. Thus, if being a steeplejack is dangerous, it will pay more than some safe job, and if being a garbage collector is unpleasant, it will command premium wages.

If wages were really determined in this way, there would be no problem of organizational politics. People would not care much about decisions made by employers because any change that affected employees would be exactly compensated in the wage payments they received. In reality, however, employer decisions do affect the employees' welfare. There are quasi-rents within organizations, and organizational politics can consume real resources as each party battles for a larger slice of the organizational pie. We introduce this idea somewhat informally in Chapter 6, but here we give it a much fuller development.

For organizations that are already formed, quasi-rents are created whenever employees are called upon to make specific investments in their jobs. In the efficiency wage theory discussed earlier, firms may be led to pay higher-than-market wages to motivate workers in jobs where good performance is especially important and monitoring is difficult. Firms may offer higher-than-market wages to attract applications from superior workers or to reduce turnover among key employees or experienced workers who have received specialized training or developed special customer or supplier relationships. Rents or quasi-rents may be created when firms train workers

---

[19] From essay 10 by James Madison in *Federalist Papers: A Collection of Essays Written in Support of the Constitution of the United States*, by Alexander Hamilton, James Madison, and John Jay (New York: New American Library, 1961).

in skills that are of value to other employers because the trained workers will later be able to demand higher wages or to move to a new employer for a higher wage.[20]

One effect of all these rents is to make individual workers care about their job assignments within firms. There will be good assignments and bad assignments, "dead end" jobs and "fast-track" jobs, positions in which pay is high, and others in which it is much lower. Someone will be assigned to Paris, Texas, and someone to Paris, France. However, it is not only the job assignment decisions that affect employee welfare.

THE VARIETIES OF INFLUENCE ACTIVITIES   Two conditions are necessary to make influence costs likely. First, a group of decisions or potential decisions must be made that can influence how the benefits and costs in an organization are distributed and shared. Second, the affected parties must have open channels of communication to the decision makers during the time period when decisions are being made, as well as the means to influence them. The first of these conditions is often unavoidable in organizations. Who will be given the promotion to a key job with higher pay, perks, and status? Will resources be allocated to one division's projects or to another's, where access to these resources means the winner will grow, thus offering job security and better opportunities for advancement for its people? Should the corporation undergo a **leveraged buyout**, in which the management group borrows extensively to buy back the company's shares, so that management owns the firm? Leveraged buyouts greatly increase the firm's debt-equity ratio and the value of the remaining equity but reduce the value of any existing debt by making it riskier. Should an outside subcontractor be used, when doing so may move good jobs outside the firm? Will an internal reorganization be instituted that promises efficiency gains but that will require layoffs for some employees and the need to learn new ways and a loss of power for others?

In such decisions, the potential winners and losers will seek to influence the outcome, expending both their own resources and, if they can, the resources of the organization in the process. For example, the candidates for promotion may take time from their current responsibilities to improve their apparent qualifications for the good job, or they may attempt to curry favor with the bosses. The proponents of a project may devote their efforts to building the best possible case for investing in that project, hiding the potential difficulties and focusing on the upside, while at the same time trying to undercut competing proposals. The potential gainers and losers in the refinancing may spend millions of dollars on investment bankers, consultants, lawyers, and advertising, trying to influence the outcome. Those threatened by the subcontracting proposal may concoct self-serving arguments about reliability, *ex post* opportunism, or morale. Those fearing the reorganization will resist the change by hiding or distorting information, withholding cooperation, and attempting to frighten others into becoming allies. All this is essentially a political competition for rents and quasi-rents. As such, it parallels the phenomenon of rent seeking in the public sector.

Employees are not the only ones affected by the firm's decisions. Stockholders' returns are affected by a wide range of decisions, including investments, wage levels, dividend policy, mergers, and pricing. For lenders, the security of their loans will depend on the riskiness of the firm's investments, the wages it pays to workers, and the dividends it pays to shareholders. A firm's decisions about the design and placement of its factories can affect community housing values, traffic, and environmental quality; its choices of suppliers can affect the distribution of wages and profits among

---

[20] Many of these conclusions depend on the existence of some limitations on workers' abilities to borrow or to post a bond.

the potential suppliers, and its pricing policy affects both competitors and customers. There are frequent disputes about which of these interests are legitimate ones that ought to be weighed in the decision-making process. Is a small community entitled to block a decision by the area's largest employer to close its local factory? Are its downtown stores and their employees entitled to protection when a discount chain opens up on the edge of town? Should neighbors be allowed to demand compensation or mitigating measures when the expansion of a community medical center intensifies traffic problems in one particular neighborhood?

Organizational Design: Optimizing Influence Activities

So far, we have emphasized the costs involved when interested parties participate in decisions, but that is only half the story. Good decision making requires information about the concerns of affected parties, about what options are available, and about the likely consequences of each option. The first kind of information is best obtained directly from the people who are affected. These same people are also frequently the most highly motivated to seek out good alternatives, gather evidence, perform analyses, and forecast consequences. Competition among interested parties with opposing interests may offer the best chance for all the relevant facts and desirable alternatives to be effectively advocated. Provided the decision maker is incorruptible, these flexible processes offer the best hope for well-informed decisions, the effect of which is to raise the total value available to be shared.

We have thus identified two main elements that must be balanced in a cost-benefit analysis to determine the best decision-making process for particular kinds of decisions. Opening a decision process to participation by individuals whose own interests are at stake increases influence costs, and these costs are greatest when the decision redistributes large amounts of wealth or value among the parties. These costs must be balanced with the improved information and analysis that accompany more participation. We examine the ways in which these costs can be mitigated and the hypothesis that decision processes are often designed to balance these two effects in order to make the most effective decisions at the lowest possible cost.

LIMIT COMMUNICATION   Much influence activity takes the form of politicking: arguing one's case, often strenuously and disingenuously. An obvious way to try to control such activity is to ignore or forbid it. This is not always easy, however. A dean can tell a department chair that he or she will not hear further complaints about needing more faculty positions ("slots"), but the chair might make an appointment ostensibly to discuss another matter and renew the campaign. The dean can attempt not to listen and even order the chair to drop the subject, but many of the costs have already been incurred.

One effective way to foreclose communications is to ensure that parties do not have the information they need to politic effectively. For example, individual salary information is often kept secret in organizations because if salaries were widely known, lower-paid people could argue more easily for raises by comparing their own performance with the worst-performing of the well-paid employees. Moreover, once a salary decision is made, it is not generally subject to appeal. As a general principle, *to limit the time wasted in rent seeking, rent-distributing decisions should be made once and for all*. Once made, the debate should be ended and the matter closed.

The widely deplored unresponsiveness of bureaucracies and of personnel departments in particular can be interpreted in this light. Line managers frequently complain that Personnel is more interested in rules and salary curves than in attracting, keeping, and motivating quality employees. Personnel managers cannot even be reached by phone when an important matter comes up because they are always in meetings with one another, concocting new ways to keep the people who do the real work from doing what needs to be done. But suppose Personnel were to respond to every claimed need for relaxation of hiring procedures and every demand that somebody had to receive a special raise or promotion or else be lost to the company. In that case, employees, realizing that their supervisors can get special deals for them, would have every reason to campaign for them. As it is, the managers can respond that they would love to do something for the employee, but Personnel will not permit it, and so the employee's incentives for influence activities are blunted. Requiring people to work through bureaucratic channels has a similar effect by raising the costs of special pleading.

Requiring openness in a democratic society means that foreclosing communication is not so easily available in the public sector, and this may explain why influence costs are so high there. Regulatory commissions must hold public hearings, and their decisions are subject to court review and legislative oversight. Anyone is free to appear before these hearings and to appeal to the courts and to the political system if they do not get their way. Furthermore, the courts, which have the power to intervene in many private transactions, have in recent years become open to new lines of argument that further increase the scope for influence.

Controlling influence by limiting communication is costly because useful information is often cut out as well. Much influence activity involves mixing self-serving information in with valuable reports. Knowing what competing firms are paying is useful, and the only way to get such information may be from employees who are campaigning for a raise. Refusing to listen to the entreaties means eliminating the source of pay information as well, and, as a result, the quality of decision making is degraded.

LIMIT THE DISTRIBUTIONAL IMPLICATIONS OF DECISIONS   One clear way to limit competition for rents is to equalize their distribution across potential competitors, or at least to limit the possible differentials. As in the Houston-Tenneco example from Chapter 6, this leads to a policy of narrower differences in pay and benefits than outside market conditions or productivity considerations might indicate. For example, it was long standard in law firms to pay all partners of a given seniority the same amount, independent of their specialty or the revenues they generated for the firm.[21] This policy reduced conflict over the distribution of profits and probably encouraged partners to devote time to activities that were in the long-run interest of the firm but did not result immediately in easily attributable revenues. The cost of the policy is that the informational and incentive roles of rewards are muted by closing differentials. In law firms, the costs have been manifested in high revenue-producing partners leaving to form their own firms or to join others that have more results-oriented pay schemes. In recent years, the seniority pay system has been breaking down under these pressures.

The policy of pay equity is most likely to be worthwhile when the potential for damaging influence activities is greatest. An empirical study of pay dispersion within 1,805 university, college, and junior college academic departments provides useful evidence of this.[22] As argued previously, increased knowledge of individual pay levels

---

[21] Ronald Gilson and Robert Mnookin, "Sharing Among Human Capitalists: An Economic Inquiry into the Corporate Law Firm and How Partners Split Profits," *Stanford Law Review*, 37 (January, 1985), 313–92.

[22] Jeffrey Pfeffer and Nancy Langton, "Wage Inequality and the Organization of Work: The Case of Academic Departments," *Administrative Sciences Quarterly*, 33 (1988), 588–606.

increases the likelihood that differentials will lead to politicking. Departments whose members frequently interact socially and in which people frequently collaborate rather than work alone should feature much closer communication among department members, including communication about pay. They should then be more susceptible to influence costs and should adopt narrower differentials than experience and productivity (and, presumably, outside market opportunities) would generate. Public universities often are required to make pay levels public, whereas private universities are not. Therefore, public institutions should, under the theory, have narrower pay differentials. Furthermore, communication is more difficult and information is less likely to be dispersed thoroughly in larger groups, so small departments ought to show less disparity in pay. Finally, a participative, democratic governance structure within the department, as opposed to a more autocratic one in which a chair makes the key decisions, presents more opportunities for costly politicking and so might be expected to be associated with smaller differentials. In fact, each of these factors did show up in the study as statistically significant: Pay dispersion was narrower in democratically run departments, in smaller ones, in public institutions, and in departments with extensive communication among members.

More generally, a policy of protecting individuals and groups from adverse consequences of organizational decisions can actually promote efficiency. This may take the form of giving individuals or groups a direct say in what is going on and being done, although this **participatory management** approach risks opening up the system to extra influence. An alternative is to require that changes will not be instituted unless they benefit everyone. Moreover, it may be worthwhile to pass over some value-creating opportunities if they would too adversely affect some of the organization's members, because the apparent value may be completely lost in influence activities. This may even extend to breaking up the organization.

DECENTRALIZE AND SEPARATE UNITS   Influence activities are possible only when there is a central authority with the ability to affect the distribution of costs and benefits between individuals or units. One extreme solution is to remove the central authority. Thus, for example, when the energy price increases of 1973 made aluminum production in Japan uneconomical, Mitsubishi Chemical, Sumitomo Chemical, and Showa Denko all decided to contract or eliminate their aluminum production operations.[23] The difficulty with such moves is that the affected division will try to resist, making claims on corporate resources to keep it going or at least to slow the pace of disinvestment. This was a special danger in the context of the Japanese system that encourages consensus decision making and consultation. The solution was to **spin off** the aluminum operations, that is, to create new companies separate from the parent companies with no claim on the parent companies' resources. In that way, the opportunities for influence and the attendant costs were greatly reduced.

STRUCTURE DECISION PROCESSES TO LIMIT INFLUENCE ACTIVITIES   In some situations it is possible to protect efficiency from distributional conflict by separating the efficiency aspects of decisions from their distributional consequences. For example, airline companies do not have much reason to care which cabin attendants are assigned to which flights; all that matters is that all the flights are covered. The attendants themselves do care, however, and if management were to make the assignments there would be vast opportunities for trying to influence the decisions. The solution adopted

---

[23] James Abegglen and George Stalk, Jr., *Kaisha: The Japanese Corporation* (New York: Basic Books, 1985), 24–25.

is to let the attendants themselves choose among the flights that must be covered in order of seniority. This separates the efficiency and distributive aspects, and, by basing it on seniority, puts the distributive aspect of the decision beyond management's control and thus frees the decision from incentives to exert influence. (The same process is used in assigning pilots, copilots, and engineers, although here it can have an efficiency cost when it results in the least experienced pilot, copilot, and engineer being teamed together in charge of a flight.)

More generally, setting immutable rules and establishing decision-making procedures that must be followed can reduce influence. For example, a firm policy of not responding to outside job offers reduces the incentives to seek offers as bargaining tools. The cost is that valued employees may be lost in this way. Similarly, to limit politicking, promotions may be made purely on the grounds of seniority and past performance, even when this is largely irrelevant to judging who would be the best person for the job. But then people may be placed in important jobs for which they are ill qualified, and better people passed over. The famous Peter Principle ("People are promoted to their levels of incompetence")—a tongue-in-cheek description of a real organizational tendency—is a natural outcome of this process.

Highly structured decision routines are very common in personnel matters like the route assignment decision described earlier. In determining annual raises, firms often allow the employees to fill out a self-evaluation and perhaps to meet briefly with their supervisors to discuss their performance, but they rarely permit any more influence than that. The main cost of measures like these that prevent rent seeking is that they limit the information available to decision makers. However, a well-designed decision process can often generate adequate information while incurring relatively low influence costs.

Tenure decisions for university professors provide an example. Typically, an academic department will have a limited number of slots for tenured faculty members.[24] Untenured professors are reviewed after some period (typically six years) to determine if they are qualified for tenure. Both the candidate for tenure and the other untenured professors have a direct interest in the decision, and these interests are often conflicting because of the limited number of slots. Because the other untenured professors normally have little information that is not already available to the tenured faculty, they normally play no role at all in the decision process. The candidates themselves usually play only a small role, perhaps by providing a statement concerning their teaching and research as well as copies of their course syllabi, teaching ratings, and published books and papers. The tenured professors, who have less reason to be threatened by a new tenure appointment, read these materials, solicit the opinions of outsiders, and vote on a recommendation to the university administration.

The tenured professors do have an interest, though, in expanding the size of their department, in order to encourage smaller classes, have more colleagues with whom to discuss their research, and spread administrative work among more people. Given university budget constraints, one department can grow only at another's expense. To limit rent seeking by departments, the university administration typically fixes the number of tenure positions in advance and has a slow and arduous procedure for revising the number of positions allotted to each department. *The process is structured to limit opportunities for rent seeking while still acquiring the necessary information to make a well-informed decision.*

The policy long followed at Hewlett-Packard, the California-based instruments and computer company, of allowing divisions to pursue essentially any reasonable

---

[24] The question of why there is tenure is taken up in Chapter 11.

research and development projects they wish, but requiring them to finance their projects out of funds they generate themselves, is also understandable as a response to influence costs. The policy prevents the divisions from attempting to persuade central management to draw resources from other divisions. This saves in terms of both the costs of these efforts and the costs of other divisions' defending against them, but it limits the opportunities to undertake worthwhile projects.

In the Houston-Tenneco example, a major complaint of the Houston exploration people (besides the pay level) was the frustratingly slow bureaucratic pace and the timidity of decision making at Tenneco compared to what they had known at Houston. Yet again this policy may have been appropriate to the large concern, where influence was a greater potential problem and so institutional checks on it were more valuable.

Product and Pricing Decisions   It is helpful to compare these processes used for personnel assignments and salary decisions with those of a different kind of decision: the determination of how a product should be designed and priced. Product design and pricing decisions are crucial ones for any organization, being important determinants of marketing success. Nevertheless, these decisions often have only minor redistributive effects within the organization (except when there are competing product-design teams, employees are probably unlikely to have a large personal stake in any particular design). These decisions commonly are made using an open committee process in which the decision makers acquire information from as many sources as possible and are free to exercise discretion over a wide range of possibilities. Moreover, the decision is typically open to reconsideration if new information comes to light. Finally, unlike tenure decisions, pricing decisions are typically delegated to middle managers with little oversight by their superiors. The comparatively unstructured product pricing and design decisions stand in stark contrast to the highly structured personnel decisions. The difference is attributable to the absence of any serious distributive consequences of pricing and design decisions.

Many other examples of highly tailored decision processes can be found in business practice. In selecting a supplier for some product, such as production equipment or office computers, the firm may ask the potential suppliers to make proposals or sales presentations, indicating how the product would work and why they would do better than those supplied by competitors. This process may reveal issues or information about potential applications that the firm had not contemplated and so lead to another round of questioning. The sales representatives might be limited to make formal presentations and to answer questions. After they leave, a more open-ended discussion among insiders can take place. Once a decision is made, it is unlikely that it could be reopened by any claim of new information by a seller, but it might be reopened by an insider if he or she had important new information, for example, about changing needs. The process as a whole is tailored to allow useful information to be contributed by the interested parties who are best informed while controlling and reducing the time wasted in excessive attempts at influence.

Influence Costs and the Legal System

Before legal systems throughout the world developed a set of rules to govern commercial transactions, merchants introduced their own sets of rules and their own private courts to render judgments in disputes among themselves. These rules evolved over time to meet the changing needs of commerce. The rules of the English merchants were eventually incorporated into the English common law, where they continued to evolve into the modern business law used in much of the world today. The "law and economics" movement seeks to interpret the existing system of commercial, contract, and bankruptcy law as *efficient* solutions to the problems of doing business; it also seeks to identify better solutions to these problems.

CHAPTER 11 BANKRUPTCY   The complicated bankruptcy law of the United States provides many examples of detailed rules that are intended to enhance efficiency. One such rule is the distinction between liquidation and reorganization in bankruptcy. When a company is **liquidated**, its assets are sold and the proceeds are divided among the company's lenders and creditors. Liquidation is usually forced on the firm by its worried creditors who are trying to protect what value is left in the firm. However, liquidation is not always the best option for companies that are unable to pay their debts or for their creditors.

In 1990 Bud's Ice Cream of San Francisco, a national distributor of premium ice cream, found itself in financial trouble due to management and distribution problems. Although the company was unable to pay its debts, its production facilities, skilled employees, and strong brand name were attractive to potential buyers, who believed they could overcome the company's problems and restore its profitability. When Bud's petitioned the bankruptcy court for **reorganization** under Chapter 11 of the U.S. bankruptcy code, its creditors were prevented from seizing assets that were promised as collateral. An orderly process was then instituted for determining how the remaining value in the company could be maximized and how the results should be divided among the various claimants.

Without this option, there would have been a free-rider problem among Bud's creditors, who would each have been tempted to demand immediate payment of its claims or to seize some of Bud's assets in the hope of being paid quickly, before there was no cash or collateral left. This competition among the creditors, combined with an understandable refusal by others to provide new credit, can destroy a company—an outcome that can eliminate jobs and harm employees, suppliers, customers, and creditors alike. By using Chapter 11 bankruptcy, production in the company's facilities can continue uninterrupted and the brand name can be preserved, avoiding the waste that accompanies the liquidation of a company with valuable but fragile assets, such as brand names or employee organization. In Chapter 11 bankruptcy, the various creditors form a committee to make arguments to the court concerning their mutual interests. This eliminates some of the most destructive kinds of rent-seeking competition among the creditors and allows the group to recoup as much as possible from the loans they had made. The resulting negotiations under court supervision make it less likely that a single recalcitrant creditor could block a deal to sell the company to new owners, making an efficient agreement more likely.

We can illustrate how the rules in the bankruptcy code are designed to preserve value by considering how the priorities for the payment of the firm's debts are set. For a company like Bud's Ice Cream, doing business requires supplies of cream, sugar, fruits, flavorings, and other ingredients, as well as materials for boxes and packaging, cash for workers and shippers, power for refrigeration equipment, and so on. Bud's must acquire these supplies and services and it must ship its goods before it is paid by its customers. Therefore, the company relies on many of its suppliers to help finance its operation by trade credit; that is, these suppliers don't demand payment for the goods and services that they supply until 30 days or more after they make delivery. If the bankruptcy rules gave priority to debts incurred before the Chapter 11 petition was filed, then once a bankruptcy petition was filed, suppliers might withhold their supplies, for fear that they would never be paid for their new shipments. Refusals of that sort would prevent the company from doing business, destroying whatever remains of its value. Actual bankruptcy law takes that problem into account by giving a higher priority to those who supply new credit *after* the bankruptcy petition is filed so that, from their perspective, it is quite likely that the trade credits they provide will be repaid.[25] At the same time, to protect the interests of existing creditors, the court commonly limits the company's ability to make nonroutine investments, raise wages, or pay dividends to owners.

CORPORATE OFFICERS' AND DIRECTORS' LIABILITY   Another area of law that is interesting to examine in light of the influence costs theory is that regarding the liability of corporate officers and directors. In the mid-1980s in the United States there was a change in the way courts interpreted these laws. When the directors of a company resisted a takeover attempt, either thwarting the attempt completely or eventually settling with another company for a lower price, or when they accepted a takeover bid that some shareholders believed was too low, suits were filed holding the officers and directors of the company personally liable for the shareholders' losses. Earlier, the courts had adhered to a **business judgment rule,** according to which the court respected the business judgments of directors even if the results of their decisions turned out badly, with few exceptions. Directors could be held liable only if they were shown to be "disloyal" or "negligent" in their decision making. This business judgment rule was eroded by an increasingly inclusive interpretation of the word "negligent." One result of the changing standards was an "insurance crisis" in which insurance companies refused to offer coverage against the growing risk of lawsuits, which in turn deterred many qualified people from accepting positions as directors of public companies. Most states reacted to this crisis by changing their laws to restore protection for officers and directors, for example, by changing the standard so that behavior must be shown to be "reckless" rather than merely "negligent" before damages can be awarded—a change that its proponents say will reduce wasteful rent seeking by both shareholders and their lawyers.

Participatory Management

One of the recent trends in management practice has been the growing emphasis on participatory management, a style of management that encourages participation by a wide range of employees at various levels in making all sorts of decisions: product improvements, changes in the production line and the organization of work, training methods, and so on. Although this practice has gained increasing attention among American firms, their Japanese counterparts have applied it to more levels of the organization with their emphasis on **quality circles,** groups of employees who make suggestions to improve productivity and product quality, and other similar management techniques. The openness and the attendant access that employees have to decision makers raises the risk that these techniques might be undermined by individual rent seeking. How, then, do these organizations avoid incurring excessive influence costs?

In Japanese firms, the system of lifetime employment with narrow pay differentials between ranks and with both pay and responsibility tied closely to seniority makes it difficult for employees to gain large personal advantages by any kind of politicking. Indeed, the larger risk is that employees who seek their personal interests may be branded as disloyal and lose the benefits their tenure would normally bring. Lifetime employment has a second benefit: It assures these employees that any labor-saving innovations that they recommend will not cost them their jobs. The long period of growth of Japanese companies has further contributed to the sense of security that

---

[25] The actual rules governing the priority of various classes of creditors are quite complicated. The class of **secured creditors** (those to whom collateral was promised) has a relatively high priority. **Unsecured creditors** for whom the debt was incurred after the petition is filed have a lower priority, and a still lower priority is assigned to unsecured creditors whose debt was incurred before the bankruptcy petition.

their employees share. For a growing firm, jobs may be best protected by ensuring that the company's costs are low enough to allow the growth to continue. In comparison, when output in a company is shrinking, the interests of capitalists and laborers in finding labor-saving, cost-reducing production methods may become sharply divergent, leading to much higher influence costs.

Furthermore, for Japanese managers, frequent job rotation, lifetime employment, limited outside opportunities, narrow pay differentials, and the relative homogeneity of their backgrounds all contribute to a sense that what is good for the management group as a whole is good for each individual manager. This is an attitude that limits rent seeking and contributes to the impressive responsiveness of Japanese firms to changing circumstances. These mutually supporting pieces form a coherent whole. The participatory decision-making system, the pay structure, the promotion criteria, and the lifetime employment policies are mutually complementary, and the construction of the system is a design decision where the pieces need to fit together properly. When one element is disturbed, however, great costs can result.

For example, consider the situation that prevailed in the late 1980s after Sony Corporation, the Japanese electronics firm, purchased an American record company, CBS Records, and an American movie and television production and distribution firm, Columbia Pictures Entertainment. Sony hoped to combine its strength in entertainment delivery hardware (such as compact disk players, video cassette recorders, and television receivers, including the emerging High-Definition Television technology) with CBS Records' and Columbia's strength in entertainment software (musical albums, new movies, television shows, plus an enormous library of older films from Columbia) to better exploit the complementarities across these segments of the entertainment business. To attract management talent to Columbia, however, Sony paid Columbia's two top managers much higher salaries than the norm in Sony, more in fact than all the parent company's senior managers put together! Top executives at Sony soon found themselves spending hours every day answering complaints by managers from the parent company and its "hardware" subsidiaries who felt they should be paid comparably with the people in the entertainment subsidiaries.

In terms of costs to the organization, the time spent by top executives talking to unhappy managers is only the tip of the iceberg. Surely, the managers themselves spent many hours talking among themselves and thinking about how best to present their arguments. The total cost suffered by an organization like Sony that relies on extensive internal communications must have been substantial.

EMPLOYEE STOCK OWNERSHIP PLANS (ESOP)   In the United States, companies often attempt to involve their workers more deeply in decision making. One of the ways to lessen the differences in interests between workers and capitalists is the **Employee Stock Ownership Plan,** commonly known as the ESOP (pronounced "ēsop"). By making employees shareholders, firms with ESOPs hope to make the workers as a group more accepting of organizational changes, more willing to be flexible in accommodating labor-saving arrangements, and more forthcoming with suggestions about how to improve operations. Management publications often emphasize the role of "listening to employees" and "making employees feel involved" in assuring the success of ESOPs. This advice accords well with influence cost theory. The benefits of any wealth-creating changes must be systematically shared among the "members" of the organization to deter their blocking the change to protect themselves, and, better yet, to inspire their cooperation in promoting the value-creating change.

SUMMARY

Reputations have economic value to the extent that they make it easier for their possessors to engage in work, trade, or other valuable activities. An activity is valuable if it generates *quasi-rents*, returns in excess of what could be had in other activities. These quasi-rents are commonly created by costs associated with changing businesses, jobs, or careers, such as the cost of moving or of specific training. The desire to keep one's current job or customers forms the basis of market incentives for hard, honest work and high-quality products. This incentive to acquire and maintain a good reputation is stronger the more frequently the reputation is useful and the longer the horizon over which it may be used.

When there are no specific investments being made, firms may sometimes use *efficiency wages*—wages higher than the worker's opportunity wage and which therefore consist partly of a *rent*—in conjunction with monitoring of the worker to provide incentives for good behavior. Incentives and monitoring are *substitutes* in the implementation problem; a higher wage can be used to offset poorer monitoring opportunities. However, this fact does not imply that improved monitoring always leads to lower wages. Instead of substituting monitoring for wages, the firm may find it more profitable to seek a higher level of performance from the worker when monitoring becomes easier.

The Marxian view is that capitalists waste resources on unnecessary monitoring in order to keep wages low. This criticism is problematic, however, because incentives depend on *relative* wages: Even a socialist economy cannot pay high relative wages to every worker.

People who wish to be trusted can benefit from establishing a reputation of honoring trust. Reputation, operating without the assistance of specialized institutions, is effective only when the reputed behavior is something that can be directly observed by others who rely on the reputation. It is therefore most effective in a long-term bilateral relationship in which the parties are aware of one another's past behavior. It is more problematic in a large merchant community because outsiders to a transaction can rarely know who is right in any business dispute. To overcome this problem, merchants long ago developed practices and institutions that establish standards of behavior, discover facts, and resolve disputes. In modern times, credit bureaus, Better Business Bureaus, and corporate cultures can all be partially understood in these terms, although these institutions sometimes have other functions as well.

An additional problem for the reputation mechanism is that it may not be in the third parties' interests to participate in sanctions against disreputable trading partners. Historically, institutions have arisen to maintain discipline in the application of sanctions. An example is the Hansa, a coalition of merchant guilds ("kontore") in northern Europe, that arose in the thirteenth century to enforce discipline among merchants in applying sanctions to cities that reneged on their promises.

End games pose another problem for a reputation mechanism. People nearing retirement or firms nearing the end of a contractual relationship have less need to maintain the good will of their contracting partners, and they may then seek other ways to enforce their agreements.

The existence of rents and quasi-rents tempts people to spend resources competing for them. To the extent that these expenditures are wasteful, they are called *influence costs*. These costs tend to be greatest for those decisions that have the large redistributive consequences, whereas the benefits of influence activities are greatest for complex decisions that have a large impact on the organization's overall objective and that are facilitated by a free flow of information. Influence costs are created by efforts of affected parties to manipulate decisions. These may include employees, suppliers, customers, shareholders, communities, and so on, depending on whose interests are potentially affected.

Organizations cope with influence costs by tailoring their decision processes to the kind of decision being made, limiting interested parties to contributing only the most relevant information, making contentious decisions final and not subject to review, and softening the impact of change by spreading it equitably among organization members. For some kinds of decisions, rigid bureaucratic rules can actually be optimal, if the total value created by improving decisions is small compared to the total costs of influence that would be attempted. For this reason, the distribution of a fixed pay pool is usually managed under a rigid set of procedures, whereas the setting of other financial variables, such as product prices, is frequently more informal. In one example, aluminum companies were separated from their parent companies during the contraction of the Japanese aluminum industry to insulate the parent and its subsidiaries from influence by the aluminum divisions. Generally, the extent to which any party is allowed to participate in a decision depends on the information and analysis the party is able to contribute and on the degree to which the decision might redistribute resources, pay, or perquisites to that party. Influence costs can also be reduced by rules that protect the interests of members of the organization and by sharing the benefits of any changes with them.

The legal system provides many opportunities for influence activities, but some legal institutions appear to be designed with the objective of reducing influence costs in mind. Certain bankruptcy rules and corporate directors' liability rules are examples.

When worker participation in decision making is desired, a system of pay equity and benefit sharing helps to reduce influence costs. The Japanese personnel policies seem especially conducive to constructive participation by workers, and firms with ESOPs in the United States find it more attractive to include a wide group of workers in company decision making.

The problem of influence seeking is widely thought to be more costly for decisions made in the public sector than for those of the private sector. One reason is overlapping political jurisdictions, which allow interested parties to pursue their interests (or require them to defend their interests) in many different forums. A second reason is the inability of democratic governments to make final decisions that are not subject to continuing review by affected constituents.

■ BIBLIOGRAPHIC NOTES

As our opening quotation from Alfred Marshall suggests, the idea that rent distribution can affect efficiency is by no means a new one in economic theory, though it had not received much emphasis in modern theory before 1980. Papers by Carl Shapiro and by Benjamin Klein and Keith Leffler about how rent flows provide firms with an incentive to build and maintain a reputation for product quality, as well as the efficiency wage model by Carl Shapiro and Joseph Stiglitz discussed in the text initiated the modern theory. Samuel Bowles and Masahiro Okuno-Fujiwara have extended the Shapiro-Stiglitz analysis in important directions also discussed in the text.

Organization behavior scholars have emphasized the importance of corporate stories and culture: see the book by Joanne Martin or the volume edited by Peter J. Frost, Larry F. Moore, Meryl Lewis, Craig Lundberg, and Martin. Among economists, David Kreps has emphasized the role of reputations in organizations as a substitute for contracting and especially the roles of organizational routines and culture in establishing expectations and standards of behavior. Jacques Cremer has also contributed importantly to this line of work. The analysis of reputations and trust in the text makes use of game theory, a set of ideas and methods that have had a major impact on economic modeling and analysis in recent years. Recent treatments of this subject that are relatively accessible to those without extensive technical and mathematical backgrounds are given by Avinash Dixit and Barry Nalebuff, by Robert Gibbons, and by Eric Rasmusen. The formal, game-theoretic modeling of the dynamics of reputation formation and its implications was initiated by Kreps and Robert Wilson, by the present authors in our 1982 paper, and by the four of us together.

Gordon Tullock was the first economist to emphasize the role of rent-seeking behavior, which has been applied to analyze the cost of big government by many others. Many of the classic papers in the field are collected, with additional new material, in the volume by James Buchanan, Robert Tollison, and Tullock. The present authors introduced the first studies of influence processes in firms and how they are optimally managed: See the paper by Milgrom and our 1988 and 1990 papers.

REFERENCES

Bowles, S. "The Production Process in a Competitive Economy," *American Economic Review*, 75 (March 1985), 16–36.

Buchanan, J., R. Tollison, and G. Tullock. *Toward a Theory of the Rent-Seeking Society* (College Station, TX: Texas A&M University Press, 1980).

Cremer, J. "Cooperation in Ongoing Organizations," *Quarterly Journal of Economics*, 101 (February 1986), 33–49.

Dixit, A., and B. Nalebuff. *Thinking Strategically* (New York: W. W. Norton, 1980).

Frost, P., Louis L. Moore, C. Lundberg and J. Martin, eds. *Reframing Organizational Cultures* (Newbury Park, CA: Sage Publications, 1991).

Gibbons, R. *Game Theory for Applied Economists* (Princeton, NJ: Princeton University Press, 1992).

Klein, B., and K. Leffler. "The Role of Market Forces in Assuring Contractual Performance," *Journal of Political Economy*, 89 (1981), 615–41.

Kreps, D. "Corporate Culture and Economic Theory," *Perspectives on Positive Political Economy*, J. Alt and K. Shepsle, eds. (Cambridge MA: Cambridge University Press, 1990), 90–143.

Kreps, D., and R. Wilson. "Reputation and Imperfect Information," *Journal of Economic Theory*, 27 (August 1982), 253–79.

Kreps, D., P. Milgrom, J. Roberts and R. Wilson. "Rational Cooperation in the Finitely Repeated Prisoners' Dilemma," *Journal of Economic Theory*, 27 (August 1982), 245–52.

Martin, J. *Cultures in Organizations: Three Perspectives* (New York: Oxford University Press, 1992).

Milgrom, P. "Employment Contracts, Influence Activities and Efficient Organization Design," *Journal of Political Economy*, 96 (1988), 42–60.

Milgrom, P., and J. Roberts. "An Economic Approach to Influence Activities in Organizations," *American Journal of Sociology*, 94 (Supplement) (1988), S154–S179.

Milgrom, P., and J. Roberts. "Bargaining and Influence Costs and the Organization of Economic Activity," *Perspectives on Positive Political Economy*, J. Alt and K. Shepsle, eds. (Cambridge, MA: Cambridge University Press, 1990), 57–89.

Milgrom, P., and J. Roberts. "The Efficiency of Equity in Organizational Decision Processes," *American Economic Review*, 80 (May 1990), 154–59.

Milgrom, P., and J. Roberts. "Predation, Reputation and Entry Deterrence," *Journal of Economic Theory*, 27 (August 1982), 280–312.

Okuno-Fujiwara, M. "Monitoring Cost, Agency Relationships and Equilibrium Modes of Labor Contracts," *Journal of the Japanese and International Economies*, 1 (June 1987), 147–67.

Rasmusen, E. *Games and Information* (Oxford: Basil Blackwell Ltd., 1989).

Shapiro, C. "Premiums for High Quality Products as Rents to Reputation," *Quarterly Journal of Economics*, 98 (1983), 659–80.

Shapiro, C., and J. Stiglitz. "Equilibrium Unemployment as a Worker Discipline Device," *American Economic Review*, 74 (June 1984), 433–44.

Tullock, G. "The Welfare Costs of Tariffs, Monopolies and Theft," *Western Economic Journal*, 5 (1967), 224–32.

EXERCISES

Food for Thought

1. Firms that employ skilled workers are very conscious about the wages being paid by other employers and where they fit in the distribution of wages. In fact, there are thousands of surveys done each year (and sold to businesses) of the compensation being paid in different areas and industries to different types of employees. Is this consistent with labor being hired in a competitive market of the type usually modelled in standard microeconomics texts, in which firms hire workers up to the point where the wage equals the marginal product of labor? How else could you explain this phenomenon?

2. In Chapter 5 we described the "Market for Lemons"—the possibility of market breakdown under adverse selection that may occur when sellers are better informed than buyers about product quality. Could repeated dealings and reputations help alleviate this problem? How? What difficulties do you see in relying on reputations to overcome adverse selection? What institutions might facilitate the workings of reputations in specific contexts?

3. In many countries, corporations whose shares are publicly traded are required to have their financial statements audited by independent accountants who check whether the financial information being provided by management to investors is accurate and has been prepared following accepted methods and procedures and who then publicly attest to their findings. The auditors are generally chosen by management (perhaps subject to nominal stockholder approval). Audit work provides a major source of income for accounting firms. Generally, each accounting firm has many clients that it audits: Even when it might be technically feasible for a relatively small accounting firm to audit a large corporation's records, there seems to be a reluctance for corporations to use audit firms when a single client would represent too much of the accountant's business. Instead, a handful of extremely large accounting firms typically do almost all the auditing of large corporations, with each having many corporate clients. How do you account for this?

4. The proper level of salaries for public officials is often a matter of debate.

bureaucrats cash in on their connections by becoming high-paid lobbyists. Recent U.S. proposals call for tying pay increases to limits on these activities. Discuss the efficacy of such a plan.

5. In university decision making, the boards of trustees often receive reports from students and faculty members, but these groups are rarely represented directly on the boards themselves. How can this pattern be explained? What difficulties would you expect to attend such representation?

6. Describe the respective interests of the customers, employees, suppliers, competitors and local governments in a firm's decision to move operations from its current location to a newer, more efficient plant. What would be the advantages and disadvantages of representing each of these interests in a group responsible for making the decision?

7. In 1991 Eastern Airlines, which had attempted a reorganization in bankruptcy, finally filed for liquidation, stopping its flights and selling its assets. Among the airline's creditors at the time were customers who had paid for tickets. According to the value-maximization criterion, should customers be offered a high priority to have their tickets refunded? Why or why not?

8. In 1990, Quaker Oats Co. spun off its troubled Fisher Price toy subsidiary by distributing shares in the new company to Quaker's own shareholders. According to company officials, the reason for the change was to allow Quaker to concentrate management attention on its basic food business. (Multidivisional companies often lavish more attention and resources on some subsidiaries than on others.) Why would Quaker have to turn Fisher Price into a separate business to achieve that result?

Mathematical Exercises

1. In the context of the efficiency wage model, suppose that N is given by $(1 - \delta^t)/(1 - \delta)$, where δ is a discount factor giving the value today of a dollar to be received a year from now and t is the number of years the worker anticipates remaining with the firm. Thus, N is a measure of the horizon over which the employee is concerned, appropriately discounted. Suppose the worker expects to be employed for 5 years, that is, $t = 5$, and evaluates future income using $\delta = 0.9$, so that N is approximately equal to 4.1. The worker's opportunity wage $(\overline{w})$ is \$20,000 per year, and he or she can make an immediate gain of \$3,000 by leaking the firm's trade secrets to a competitor. The firm can monitor the worker to prevent this, but doing so is costly: raising the probability p of catching misbehavior by an amount Δp costs \$1,500Δp.

Formulate the firm's problem in selecting the monitoring intensity p and the wage w and solve for the optimal values.

Suppose now that the threat of a takeover or bankruptcy endangers the employee's future with the firm, so that the employee now expects to be employed only one more year. Will the contract you found above still deter cheating? Why or why not?

More generally, show that in the efficiency wage model, a lengthened horizon allows providing incentives with a lower wage. That is, show that the optimal wage level $w^*(N)$ is a nonincreasing function of N provided the marginal cost of monitoring is positive and increasing in p, that is, provided $M'(p) > 0$ and $M''(p) > 0$ for all p.

2. Suppose there is some chance that a noncheating employee will voluntarily leave the firm for reasons unconnected with the amount of the wage. What effect will this have on the probability of cheating for any given monitoring intensity and wage? What will be the effect on the optimal wage?

3. In the efficiency wage model, suppose there is some probability q that the

this have on the probability of cheating for any given monitoring intensity and wage? What will be the effect on the optimal wage?

3.   In the efficiency wage model, suppose there is some probability q that the worker will appear to be cheating, even though he or she has actually worked hard and honestly. Determine the proper efficiency wage in that case.

4.   In the discussion of the game of offering trust in the text, it was shown that if the game is being played only once, then trust will not be offered and, if it should be offered, it will not be honored. Suppose instead the two parties know they will interact exactly twice. Would trust be offered and honored in the second, final interaction? Why or why not? If the parties anticipate this and trust is offered in the first round, will it be honored? Why or why not? [Hint: Will honoring trust affect behavior at the last round?] Will trust then be offered? By this logic, what would happen if the parties knew they would interact exactly three times? Any arbitrary, but finite and known number of times? Do you find this to be a credible prediction about how people actually would behave? Why or why not?

5.   Suppose instead that each time the parties interact, there is a probability $p > 0$ that they will interact again, and, correspondingly, a probability of $(1 - p)$ that this will be their last interaction. Then at any point, the probability that they will interact twice more is p^2, the probability of three more interactions is p^3, and so on. Suppose the parties are interested in the expected value of the total payoffs they receive. Thus, each seeks to maximize the sum of the payoff at the current round, plus p times the payoff that accrues if they interact again, plus p^2 times the payoff if they should interact a third time, plus p^3 times the payoff from a possible fourth interaction, and so on. In summation notation, the objective of each party i is to maximize $\Sigma p^n u_{in}$, where n runs from 0 (the current round) to infinity and u_{in} is the payoff to party i at the corresponding round. Show that so long as the payoff V to each party when trust is offered and honored is strictly larger than the payoff when trust is not offered (which we set equal to zero in the text), then for any values of the gain G to abusing trust and loss L to having trust not be honored there is a value of p that makes it Nash equilibrium behavior to offer trust and honor it at each round. What threats and punishments can be used in achieving this outcome? [Note: for any number Δ, $\Sigma p^n \Delta = p\Delta/(1 - p)$.]

6.   Alternatively, suppose there is a chance p that the party who can honor or abuse the trust is "trustworthy," that is, that he or she would always honor trust, even if it were offered in a single interaction. The person who can offer trust cannot directly tell if the other party is trustworthy, but, of course, a single instance of abusing trust that has been offered demonstrates that the individual is not trustworthy. Show that if L is not too large relative to p, then if the parties are going to interact only twice, it will be equilibrium behavior for trust to be offered in the first interaction and for it to be honored, even if the person actually is not trustworthy and will not honor trust if it is offered at the last round. [In doing so, first calculate how large p must be to make it worthwhile to offer trust in a single interaction. Now suppose that trust has been offered at the first interaction and consider the options of the party who must decide whether to honor the trust. Suppose that honoring the trust results in the other person going into the last round still believing there is at least a chance of p that trust, if offered, will be honored. Show that if p is large enough, trust will be extended at the second round if it was not abused at the first. Now show it is worthwhile to honor the trust at the first round. Finally, recognizing that trust will be honored at the first round if p is large enough, determine whether it will be offered.]

7.   Consider a firm employing two risk-neutral individuals, A and B, each of whom can choose to exert unobservable effort at a personal cost of c to finding new investment projects that increase the value of the firm. Suppose that if either individual

exerts effort, there is a probability $\frac{1}{2}$ that he or she will develop a project, and that this probability is unaffected by whether the other person tries to generate a project and also whether he or she is successful. Thus, if only one invests, there is a probability of $\frac{1}{2}$ of a project being generated. If both invest, there is a probability of $\frac{1}{4}$ that A succeeds and B does not, a probability of $\frac{1}{4}$ that B generates a project and A does not, a probability of $\frac{1}{4}$ that neither will generate a project and, finally, a probability of $\frac{1}{4}$ that both will generate projects. Only one project can be adopted, even if both A and B find projects. A project results in an increase in value of \$1.

Determine, for each level of c, whether it is efficient to have none, one, or both of the two people seek to develop projects.

Suppose now that c is sufficiently small that it is efficient for both to attempt to develop projects and that this fact is known to the managers of the firm but the exact value of c is not known. Derive a scheme for paying employees and directing their efforts that motivates them to behave in the value-maximizing fashion, no matter what the actual level of c. Recall that, because the firm cannot observe the employees' effort choices, it cannot pay them directly for exerting effort. Instead, all it can do is make the payments depend on whether or not one or both of the employees generated a project. Also, suppose that the amounts to be paid cannot in any circumstance exceed the actual value created, and that the payments to each must always be non-negative. Are rents created for the employees by this scheme? How are they distributed?

Now suppose that the scheme you designed is in place but that employee A can unobservably lower the chance that B will successfully develop a proposal from $\frac{1}{2}$ to $(1 - 2s_A)/2$ by expending a personal cost of $(s_A)^2/2$ on sabotaging B's efforts, and similarly for B. Suppose each must decide on whether to sabotage the other before they know if any efforts they have exerted will result in projects. Will the two employees find such activities worthwhile, given that they have already chosen to exert the effort necessary to develop projects? Interpret the result. Foreseeing these incentives, will the employees be motivated by the contract to provide effort to develop proposals?

9

OWNERSHIP AND PROPERTY RIGHTS

E conomic growth will occur if property rights make it worthwhile to undertake socially productive activity.

Douglass C. North and Robert Paul Thomas[1]

The institution of *ownership* accompanied by secure property rights is the most common and effective institution for providing people with incentives to create, maintain, and improve assets. Examples of the effectiveness of ownership incentives are all around us. Many of the relative inefficiencies of the communist countries of Eastern Europe and Asia have been attributed to the lack of private property, which dulled incentives to maintain assets, to innovate and take risks, and to create new wealth (see Chapter 1). On a more familiar level, people tend to take better care of their own cars than they do of cars they rent from Hertz or Avis. They drive their own cars more carefully and protect them better from theft. Similarly, since Avis was purchased by its employees, the employees reportedly work harder and use more ingenuity in their jobs than they did before. In fact, however, Avis's employee-ownership plan raises many questions, most fundamentally: What does it mean for a group of people to "own" an asset? and What does it mean to "own" so complicated an asset as a firm?

Throughout this chapter, our analysis assumes that there are no wealth effects. With this assumption, the value maximization principle applies (see Chapter 2).

[1] *The Rise of the Western World: A New Economic History* (Cambridge, MA: Cambridge University Press, 1973), 8.

Efficient arrangements are then simply the feasible arrangements that maximize the total value received by the parties involved.

THE CONCEPT OF OWNERSHIP

Economic analyses of ownership have concentrated on two issues: the possession of residual decision rights and the allocation of residual returns.

Residual Control

The concept of ownership is complicated, even for simple physical assets. A person who owns something has certain rights and obligations concerning its use. For example, if you own a car, you are free to drive it (provided that you have a license and obey the traffic laws), to park it (in a legal parking space), to paint and decorate the car (provided that you keep the windows clear and do not offend the public morality too greatly), to choose where and how often to have it serviced (provided that you obey the emissions control and safety laws), to lend it to others for driving (if the borrower is a licensed driver), to transfer your rights to another party (either permanently through gift or sale or temporarily through rental), and so on.

Similarly, if you own a company, you have the right to hire and fire its employees (subject to legal limitations on discrimination and wrongful discharge and the terms of any employment contracts), to determine the products, prices, and policies of the company (subject to regulation), to transfer the profits or other resources of the firm to your personal account (subject to the tax laws and any restrictive clauses in the company's loan agreements or other contracts), and so on. For economic analysis, it is often useful to interpret "owning an asset" to mean having the **residual rights of control**—that is, the right to make any decisions concerning the asset's use that are not explicitly controlled by law or assigned to another by contract.

If ownership means having residual control, then its importance must derive from the difficulty of writing contracts that specify all the control rights. Suppose that for some particular business relationship it were cheap and easy both to write and to enforce *complete contracts*—ones that specify what everyone is to do in every relevant eventuality at every future date and how the resulting income in each such event should be divided. In that hypothetical situation, there would be no unforeseen contingencies, no eventualities for which plans had not been made, no unexpected gains or losses, and no difficulties in ensuring that the agreed actions and divisions of income would be implemented. Residual rights would mean nothing then because no rights would be left unspecified. Nothing would be residual. People could still write contracts that looked like ownership and assigned ownership rights. One party's required actions in various contingencies would not be explicitly specified but instead would be left to that party to decide. Furthermore, that party's payments under the contract would simply be what was left after others were paid their due. Such contracts would have no particular advantages, however, because the parties could also write contracts that specified everyone's actions and payoffs explicitly.

In fact, as we argued in Chapter 5, complete contracts are generally impossible for transactions of any significant complexity that occur over a period of time longer than a few days. Complete contracting requires freely imagining all the myriad contingencies that might arise during the contract term, costlessly determining the appropriate actions and division of income to take in each contingency, describing all these verbally with enough precision that the terms of the contract are clear, arriving at an agreement on these terms, and doing all this so that the parties to the contract are motivated to follow its terms. Presuming all this were possible, the resulting document would, for any but the simplest arrangements, be unimaginably long. Of course, each of the presumed conditions is probably impossible on its own, and their conjunction is certainly so. It is impossible to imagine all the various possible contingencies that might develop, let alone enumerate and describe them. Figuring out in advance the optimal thing to do in each of these cases would require superhuman abilities. Arriving at an agreement on the resulting contingent plans would require lifetimes, even if there were no fundamental conflicts of interest between the parties. Furthermore, no language could ever be sufficiently precise to specify the contract terms unambiguously, with no scope for disagreement. Finally, the problems of informational asymmetries can plague contracting (see Chapter 5). The unavoidable conclusion is that contracts are necessarily incomplete. Consequently, arrangements that leave all control rights that are not otherwise assigned to a single, distinguished individual (eliminating the need to negotiate and reach agreement for every unplanned event) enjoy significant cost advantages.

Although the notion of ownership as residual control may be relatively clear and meaningful for a simple asset like an automobile, it gets much fuzzier when applied to something complicated, like a large organization. Large organizations bundle together many assets, and who has what decision rights may be ambiguous. Just what rights have been contracted away and to whom? An incomplete contract may be unclear on this point. For example, do the directors of a firm have the right to decide to accept a takeover offer without soliciting competing bids?[2] Who has the rights to make a decision that necessarily affects several different assets with possibly different ownership? Can a partner in a law firm accept an unsavory client who will bring in lots of revenues but whose association with the firm may sully the other partners' reputations? Such decisions may be especially controversial when both the physical capital of the firm and the human capital of its members are involved. We examine this matter in more detail later in looking at the ownership of a corporation.

An additional complication is that the rights that come with ownership vary among countries and over time. A firm's owner may have the right to hire employees but not the right to lay them off or fire them at will. In the United States, the traditional doctrine allowed employers the right to fire employees "at will," but this right has been whittled away by court decisions requiring that terminations be only "for cause." The allocation of such rights is important. For example, without the right to make layoffs when demand is slack, owners will find it more expensive to hire new workers than they otherwise would, perhaps leading to lower levels of employment overall. At the same time, if efficient production requires that workers invest in firm-specific skills, then changes that protect their investments, like improved grievance procedures or employment guarantees, make them more likely to invest in acquiring those skills.

Residual Returns

The legal notion of ownership involves more elements than just the control rights we have described. One particular control right, the right of possession, is often emphasized as marking ownership. Its main economic consequence is that it allows the owner to refuse use of an asset to anyone who will not pay the price the owner demands. That makes it possible for the owner to receive and keep the residual returns from the asset. These may be direct, current cash flows or changes in the future flows, which then are reflected in changes in the current value of the asset.

---

[2] In the Pritzger purchase of Trans Union, the board neither solicited outside bids nor sought the opinion of an investment banker on the firm's value. It ended up losing a landmark stockholder lawsuit, *Smith* v. *Van Gorkum*, 488 A.2d 858, 876 (Del. 1985).

Such returns are the basis of a notion of ownership used in earlier economic analyses of firms. According to this notion, the owner of a firm is the **residual claimant**—the one who is entitled to receive any net income that the firm produces. That is, the owner is entitled to whatever remains after all revenues have been collected and all debts, expenses, and other contractual obligations have been paid. Net income is conceived of as the **residual return**—the amount that is left over after everyone else has been paid.

Like residual control, the notion of residual returns is intimately tied to contractual incompleteness. Under complete contracting, the division of the wealth in each eventuality would be specified contractually, and there would be no returns that could usefully be thought of as residual.

Just as the allocation of residual control can be fuzzy in the case of firms (because rights of control of different categories of decisions may be poorly specified or may lie with various parties), the notion of residual returns is fuzzy as well. One problem is that the recipients of the residual returns may vary with the circumstances. When a firm is unable to pay its debts, increases in its earnings may have to be paid to the lenders. In those circumstances, the lenders would be the residual claimants. The success or failure of the firm may affect the market's perception of its managers' abilities and thereby their future opportunities and incomes. Thus, the managers become residual claimants on a portion of the total returns. Firms may pay bonuses, increase workers' pay, and promote more workers into higher-ranking, higher-paying jobs in good times rather than in bad. None of this is contractual, so arguably at least some of the workers then share in the residual returns of the firm.

For these reasons, ownership of something as complicated as a firm is a tenuous concept. Our examination of firms in this book is founded mostly in more detailed analyses of which individuals and groups make decisions, with what information, and by what decision processes. For simpler assets, however, the notions of residual control and residual returns are a good basis for beginning the analysis.

Pairing Residual Control and Returns

Tying together residual returns and residual control is the key to the incentive effects of ownership. These effects are very powerful because (at least in simple cases) the decision maker bears the full financial impact of his or her choices.

Suppose a transaction involves several people supplying labor, physical inputs, and so on. If some of the parties involved receive fixed amounts of value specified by a contract and there is only one residual claimant, then maximizing the value received by the residual claimant is just the same as maximizing the total value received by all the parties (see Figure 9.1). If the residual claimant also has the residual control, then just by pursuing his or her own interests and maximizing his or her own returns, the claimant will be led to make the efficient decisions. When it is possible for a single individual to both have the residual control and receive the residual returns, the residual decisions made will tend to be efficient ones. In contrast, if only part of the costs or benefits of a decision accrue to the party making the decision, then that individual will find it in his or her personal interest to ignore some of these effects, frequently leading to inefficient decisions.

The perspective of residual rights and residual returns illuminates the now-familiar question of the incentives of an owner of a car versus those of a renter. One important attribute of the rental transaction is the extreme *difficulty of performance measurement*—the virtual impossibility of establishing exactly how much the car's value has depreciated during any particular rental (Chapter 2). For this reason, the rental company is unable to base its charges on its actual costs. Instead, it bases them on the things it can observe (such as days and hours of the rental, miles driven, and

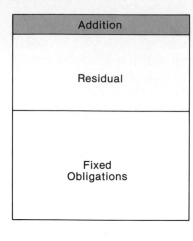

Figure 9.1: When some obligations are fixed, adding to the residual return or value is the same as adding to the total, so the residual claimant maximizes total value.

obvious collision damage). Such a charge is necessarily less than perfectly sensitive to any single actual use and its effects, so careful use is not fully rewarded and rough use is not fully charged. The one who decides on how the asset is actually used—the renter—has residual control (for a time) but is not the residual claimant. In contrast, the owner of a car receives both the residual control and the residual returns. If you exercise your right not to maintain your car, then you suffer the diminished services it provides and the reduced selling price it eventually commands. For more general assets, as long as performance measurement is imperfect, a user who does not receive the residual returns is unlikely to take the value-maximizing level of care in maintaining its value and even more unlikely to do much to add to the asset's value.

Several of the examples in Chapter 1 illustrate the power of assigning residual rights of control and residual returns to the same people. The North West Company's wintering partners had broad rights to make decisions in the field, and as partners they collectively claimed the profits that resulted from their actions and decisions. This was the key to their succeeding against the Hudson's Bay Company despite the latter's huge cost advantage. The bonuses at Salomon Brothers are an attempt to replicate "high-powered" market incentives inside the firm, and the experiment with paying the bonuses partially in stock is an attempt to make Salomon's people look at the right asset—the firm as a whole—rather than just their own departments.

We have also seen examples where a misalignment of residual rights and returns have caused trouble. The residual claimant to the returns from an enterprise in a communist system is the state, but the residual decision makers are effectively the enterprise manager, the workers, and the bureaucrats in the ministry overseeing it. None of these has any great personal stake in the value of the enterprise. Another example comes from the U.S. savings and loan industry, discussed in Chapter 6. Those who had the right to control the S&L's investments also had the right to keep any profits earned but were not obligated to make good on all losses. That combination of rights and obligations created an incentive for risk taking and fraud that was not effectively countered by other devices during most of the 1980s.

Properly combining the two aspects of ownership—residual control and residual returns—provides strong incentives for the owner to maintain and increase an asset's value. Indeed, in one of the classic papers on the economics of organization, Armen Alchian and Harold Demsetz treat the essential nature of the firm as a matter of creating this linkage. They consider a situation with **team production**, in which output is the joint product of several workers' contributions and the outputs attributable to any individual are difficult to define and certainly hard to observe. This creates an incentive problem of shirking that, were individual output observable, could be easily overcome by giving each worker title to what he or she produces. A solution in this case is for one member of the team to undertake a specialized function—to *monitor* the other workers and to have the authority to expel members of the team who perform unsatisfactorily and replace them with new members. Alchian and Demsetz then raise a crucial question: "But who will monitor the monitor?" Their solution is for the monitor to be motivated by receiving the residual returns. The result is what economists call the **classical firm**—an organization in which a boss hires, fires, and directs workers who are paid a fixed wage. The boss receives the residual returns. Notice that this form of organization only can emerge if property rights are tradable; it must be possible to assign residual control and residual returns to the person best suited to be boss.

Although ownership creates strong individual incentives, that does not necessarily mean that a system of private ownership is always efficient for society as a whole. Having a single decision maker bear all the risk in an asset's value may be incompatible with efficient risk sharing and may, in any case, be impracticable if the amounts are large. In other situations, increasing the value of a particular asset may be best accomplished by undermining competitors, setting monopoly prices, or polluting the environment—all activities that bring about inefficiencies.

A prominent school in economic, legal, and historical scholarship has argued that these limits on the advantages of business contracting, although real, are absent in the great majority of business transactions. The chapter-opening quotation is an example of the kind of thinking that characterizes members of this school. They suggest that a system of clear, enforceable, tradable property rights will tend to generate socially efficient outcomes. This position is important to the study of organizations for two reasons. First, it suggests that once appropriate property rights are established, there will be a natural tendency for arrangements to evolve toward an efficient pattern as people rearrange their affairs to capture the mutually available gains. This in turn has important implications for interpreting observed patterns, especially once they have persisted for some time. Second, even if you reject the conclusions of this school, the pattern of analysis does provides a useful framework for understanding business contracts.

THE COASE THEOREM RECONSIDERED

According to the model of competitive market equilibrium presented in Chapter 3, any allocation resulting from the competitive market process is efficient: If a complete set of markets exists, if behavior on these markets is competitive, and if markets clear, then there is no way to reallocate resources that would benefit everyone. The conditions of this theorem are really quite restrictive, however. Certainly they give only weak formal support to the position that any real-world market system with private-property rights is likely to promote economic efficiency. Nevertheless, economists adhering to the Coasian view would argue that the conclusion that free exchange leads to efficiency can be extended far beyond the formal purview of the competitive model. Their arguments utilize the Coase theorem and the efficiency principle discussed in Chapter 2.

Recall that the efficiency principle states that if people are able to bargain together costlessly and can effectively implement and enforce their decisions, then the outcomes of economic activity will tend to be efficient (at least for the parties to the bargain). The Coase theorem states that if the parties bargain to an efficient agreement (for themselves) and if their preferences display no wealth effects, then the value-creating activities that they will agree upon do not depend on the bargaining power of the parties or on what assets each owned when the bargaining began. Rather, efficiency alone determines the activity choice. The other factors can affect only decisions about how the costs and benefits are to be shared.

We saw in Chapters 5 and 6 that the premises that people can bargain, implement, and enforce their agreements are not automatically valid. There can be significant transactions costs that arise from bounded rationality, private information, and unobservability of actions. Fully value-maximizing agreements, therefore, may not be reachable. At best, all we can hope for in such circumstances is some sort of constrained efficiency that is limited by the difficulties of foreseeing, describing, and planning, as well as by the need to provide incentives.

Another set of problems may prevent efficient agreements, even when none of these other factors are important. These have to do with whether there are clear, enforceable property rights that can be transferred easily. If there are not, then again, efficiency may not be realized. If no one clearly owns a valuable asset, then no one has an incentive to guard its value properly. If property rights are not tradable, then there is little hope that assets will end up with those people who can make the best use of them and so value them most. If property rights are not secure, then owners will not invest great amounts in assets that they may lose with no compensation, or they may sink valuable resources into protecting their claims.

These responses to insecure property rights give an efficiency cost to theft, which at first glance might seem to be only a transfer without any direct efficiency consequence. The reluctance to invest when property rights are insecure results in inadequate maintenance and development of assets. Car owners in large cities who refrain from installing radios in their vehicles for fear that they will be stolen are foregoing a transaction that would be valuable if their rights were secure. More importantly, there is some suggestion that the threat of government expropriation without adequate compensation has hindered investment and development in parts of the Third World. Meanwhile, the resources sunk into protecting assets from theft bring no direct social returns. Security guards and burglar alarms are therefore considered social waste.

Ill-Defined Property Rights and the Tragedy of the Commons

One of the saddest incentive problems resulting from untradable, insecure, or unassigned property rights is known variously as the **common-resource problem**, the **public-goods problem**, the **free-rider problem**, and the **tragedy of the commons**. The idea is that when many people have the right to use a single shared resource, there is an incentive for the resource to be overused and, correspondingly, when many people share the obligation to provide some resource, it will be undersupplied. When the residual returns to an asset are widely shared, no one person has a sufficient interest to bear the costs of maintaining and increasing its value. In such cases, concentrating the ownership rights can lead to increased efficiency. Fishing rights provide a good example of this phenomenon.

THE ECONOMICS OF OCEAN FISHERIES   In order to maintain the stock of fish in a given area of the oceans, a large enough proportion of each generation must survive for breeding. Next year's population is, over the relevant range, an increasing function of this year's. However, when large numbers of people all have the right to fish commercially in the same area without effective limits on the amount each can take, there is a danger of overfishing, with too many fish being taken to permit the population to recover. Any single boat owner who limits his or her catch (and income) to preserve the overall population bears all the costs of forebearance. Meanwhile, the benefits are spread over all the boats fishing the area that will have a larger harvest next year, with only a small fraction of the gain going to the one who conserved. Moreover, modern fishing methods have made it technically easier to harvest immense numbers of fish, so overfishing is an increasing danger.

There are a variety of ways in which assignment of ownership or property rights might alleviate this problem, including group ownership and single ownership. (In order to make such assignments, many countries have been claiming control of the fisheries up to 200 miles off their coasts, even while disputing others' rights to do the same.)

The Group Ownership Approach   One way to combat the problem of overfishing would be to vest a fishery association made up of the members of the local fishing fleet with the exclusive right to control the fishery. This would include rights to determine who may fish in the area, the total catch size, and various rules affecting the methods of fishing, such as the hours or seasons when fishing is permitted, the mesh size of nets, and so on. Individuals could then be assigned rights to partake in the total allowed catch in various ways. For example, they could share the total realized catch equally, or each could be assigned a quota limiting the number of fish he or she can take.

The relative advantages of this kind of arrangement are easy to see. The individual rights provide incentives for each boat to gather its catch efficiently because any extra resources used or time wasted are costs the boat's owner bears alone. As a group, the association has a collective incentive to safeguard the fish population. In fact, from the group's point of view, the most advantageous fishing arrangements may be those that maximize the joint profits of the fishermen, taking into account the full effect that this season's harvest has on future harvests. Of course, the association also may have an incentive to limit the catch in order to drive up fish prices, but in many regions that is only a trivial problem because consumers have so many close substitutes for the local fish. In that case, the catch that maximizes the present value of the fleet's net income is the socially efficient one.

This scheme is not without its problems, however. First, it may be costly to keep out interlopers who would want to fish although they have no right to do so. The fact that the state might bear most of the costs of enforcing the association's property right in no way changes this.

Second, there may be severe moral hazard problems among the individual members of the association, depending on how the catch is shared. If a quota is used, with each boat keeping the revenues from the fish it brings in and paying the costs of catching them, there will again be an incentive for overfishing by cheating on the quota. However, these incentives will be somewhat attenuated by the fact that the benefits of conservation are divided among a smaller group. Moreover, enforcing quotas may be easier in the limited group because monitoring fishing seasons and inspecting catch sizes and types of nets is simplified when all the boats operate out of the same few harbors. Furthermore, the possibility of denying fishing rights to anyone caught cheating provides incentives for obeying the rules. Still, resources must be expended to enforce the rules.

In contrast, if each association member is given a fixed share of the total catch, then the incentives are to cut back on effort, crew sizes, and so on, because all the savings accrue to the individual but the costs in terms of a smaller catch are spread over the whole fleet.

A third difficulty with vesting the fishing rights with the fleet as a group is that there may not be unanimity among the members about the appropriate rules to govern the exploitation of their fishery. Fishing boats differ in their costs of fishing, and their owners may vary in their expectations about future fish prices and their outside job opportunities, which together govern how rapidly they think it appropriate to harvest the fish population. They may also have differing ideas as to what rate of fishing the population can sustain. These differences mean they will disagree about possible policies. Then all the costs of political group decision making will be incurred, and the inefficiencies we discussed in Chapter 5 may be incurred.

Single Ownership   An alternative that avoids this problem of inefficiencies is to assign the rights to a single individual—presumably, but not necessarily, one of the members of the fishing fleet. This is the "single-owner" solution that works so well for ordinary items like automobiles, houses, and furniture. When applied to fishing rights, it has all the same general advantages as the system that allows the community to determine the size of the total catch and fishing rules. The single owner would have reason to be concerned about the next year's fish harvest and to avoid the overfishing that would destroy it. Like the fishery association, he or she would have good reason to weigh the advantages of catching extra fish in the present season against the cost of a reduced future harvest. With these factors in mind, the owner of the fishing rights would choose seasons, mesh sizes, and so on, to maximize the (present value of the) profits to be earned during the period of ownership.

The major problem with assigning all the rights to one person is deciding who the lucky one should be. Rotating the rights among the possible candidates from year to year would be terribly inefficient; it would encourage overfishing because the current holder of the rights would not gain at all from preserving the population for the next year. Another possibility would be to auction the rights to the highest bidder and compensate the losers by distributing the proceeds of the auction among them. This would ensure the most efficient use of the rights, especially if the winner can then charge others for use of the rights or can hire others to help gather the catch (and, in either case, can induce efficient behavior from them), because the winner will be the one for whom the rights are most valuable. Because the value of the fishing rights varies from person to person, however, perhaps in unmeasurable ways, it would be difficult to determine appropriate individual compensation for the lost rights. This again opens the process to the inefficiencies of bargaining under private information and may make it very difficult to win agreement for the plan.

PETROLEUM DEPOSITS AND AQUIFERS   The analysis of fishing rights is a very particular one and does not apply exactly to any other situation. Still, the basic patterns in the analysis of attention to detailed specifications of rights, to the sorts of options available, and to the incentives involved all arise repeatedly in analyzing other problems. Two closely related situations concern underground pools of petroleum and ground water.

An underground petroleum deposit can stretch for a great distance under the earth's surface. If ownership rights are not established over the pool, we have a free-rider problem closely paralleling that with the fisheries: Each party tries to draw oil out quickly so that the others do not get it all first. This excessive pumping raises the costs of extracting the oil and leads to a too rapid exhaustion of the resource. In fact, the common practice is to assign mineral rights to any petroleum located under a piece of the earth's surface to the owner of the land above. Often this means that different parties may hold the mineral rights to different pieces of land above the same pool. These rights give the parties title to any crude oil that they draw to the surface through wells dug on their properties. However, a well sunk into any point in the pool tends to draw crude from across the whole deposit as the petroleum flows, albeit slowly, to the region of reduced pressure. This means that if different interests have rights to draw oil from a single pool, there is still a tendency toward rapid extraction. All this is exacerbated by the possibility of sinking a well on one piece of property but drilling on an angle so that it hits the petroleum deposit under another's land. The results can be disasterous—Iraq's anger about Kuwait's alleged overpumping and poaching in oil fields straddling the two nations' border was a major element leading to the Persian Gulf War of 1990–1991.

Very similar problems arise with underground aquifers. These pools of underground water in porous rock formations may stretch over hundreds of miles. Aquifers are a major source of water for drinking and irrigation. In the western United States, a number of aquifers are being drawn down much more quickly than they are refilled by natural seepage from the surface. The problem is just as with fisheries or crude oil: No one owns the aquifer, so no one guards it properly. It is especially acute in California, the only western state with no program of ground-water management. Except in two small areas with regional controls, anyone who sinks a well can take as much water as comes out. In 1991 California farmers were expected to draw down the amount of water in the aquifers by 4.9 trillion gallons.[3] The results are subsidence of the ground surface—some areas in the city of San Jose sank eight feet before local controls were instituted—as well as pollution of the aquifers by seepage of sea water and pollutants. There is also the potential that the dried-out porous structure will collapse, permanently destroying the aquifer.

OWNERSHIP PROBLEMS IN THE SOCIALIST COUNTRIES   Some of the reforms that took place in China during the 1980s (before the bloody crackdown of 1989) can be understood in similar terms. Factories in China have been mostly either state owned (by the national government) or collectively owned (by the factory workers or the community). No single individual was held accountable for performance in these factories. Indeed, employment and wages were protected in China, and the authority of factory managers was limited. As in many other communist countries, losses incurred by these factories were covered by interest-free "loans" from the state, but in practice these loans were seldom repaid. They represent a subsidy paid (through taxes) from profitable factories to unprofitable ones.

Attempts to hold Chinese factory managers accountable without creating a managerial class have led to experiments with rotating managers. According to our analysis, these were doomed to failure for the same reasons that the rotating property rights solution to the overfishing problem cannot succeed. Managers with short tenure will avoid making expensive investments in new equipment, R&D, worker training, and so on, because the benefits of these investments are enjoyed only by others at a later date. Chinese reformers have also raised the possibility of using long-term factory leases patterned on the long-term leases on Chinese farms. These were seen as an ideologically safe way to transfer effective ownership rights to private parties and thereby provide incentives. Their effects on agricultural productivity have been very positive.

In 1990 a struggle emerged in the Soviet Union over President Gorbachev's proposals to grant long-term leases to tenant farmers in order to reinvigorate the notoriously inefficient farm sector of that economy. Ideological resistance to that reform centered on the belief that long-term leases are really just a disguised form of private ownership of the land. Yet until something is done to improve individual accountability for performance, it seems unlikely that Soviet farms can become as productive as their western counterparts.

Untradable and Insecure Property Rights

One of the essential aspects of ownership rights for ordinary goods is that they can be bought and sold. According to the Coase theorem, assets will then tend to be acquired by those who can use them best. If a person owns goods or rights that are more valuable to his or her neighbor, then there is a price at which the two would both find it profitable to trade, and the goods move to where they are most valuable.

Ownership rights are not always transferrable, however. This can interfere with

---

[3] Lisa Lapin, "Subterranean Ocean Could Be Drying Up," *San Jose Mercury News* (April 7, 1991), A-1.

efficient resource use because the assets then do not get put to their best use (unless by chance they are assigned to those who value them most). A second problem arises when property rights are insecure, so that they might be restricted or lost at some future point without fair compensation being paid. Insecure rights weaken the owner's incentive to invest in developing and maintaining the asset because there is always the danger that both the asset and the returns it generates will be lost. We discuss both these problems in the specific context of water rights in California, although the features of the analysis can be widely applied to show how patterns of ownership and legal doctrines concerning owners' rights affect the efficiency of economic performance.

WATER USE IN CALIFORNIA   The state of California is largely a desert, although this fact is often forgotten, masked by the state's population of 30 million and its position as the eighth-largest economy in the world with one of the world's largest and most productive agricultural industries. In most parts of the state, rain falls only during the short winter season, and the natural vegetation is adapted to the arid climate. Winter snowfall in the mountains of northeastern California normally provides a huge annual water runoff, however, most of which naturally would flow into the Pacific Ocean via the rivers draining into the Central Valley, through the delta of the Sacramento River, and into San Francisco Bay. This runoff, diverted by dams, reservoirs, aqueducts, and pipelines, provides most of the water used by farms, residents, and industry throughout California. Although 75 percent of the state's water is located in the northern part of the state, 75 percent of the population is in the southern part.

For many years, residents of northern California have been concerned about the damage done to the environment by withdrawing so much water from the natural flow patterns. Reduced water flowing into the Sacramento River delta has allowed salt water from the ocean to reach further inland, wreaking havoc with natural habitats and luring lost whales far inland. The water flow into the San Francisco Bay from melting snow in the mountains cleanses the bay and keeps it from becoming stagnant and accumulating pollutants; reduction in the water flow reduces the cleansing action, harming the environment of the bay. Compounding the environmental problems, droughts in northern California in the late 1970s and 1980s have endangered water supplies to industries and urban residents there while water continued to flow to the southern half and agriculture. Many urban and suburban Californians look with envy on the water rights afforded farmers.

Approximately 85 percent of the water actually used in California is employed in agriculture, nearly all of it for irrigation. All other industries, as well as all residential use, account for only the remaining 15 percent. Agriculture, however, represents only about 3 percent of the state's aggregate output of goods and services. The water delivered to farmers comes from various sources, some quite expensive, overseen by a variety of federal, state, and local public agencies.

PROPERTY RIGHTS FOR CALIFORNIA WATER   Water rights for farmers vary considerably throughout the state of California, depending on the source of the water. Some farmers have inherited extremely valuable rights to have huge quantities of cheap water delivered to them. Water for farming from the federal Bureau of Reclamation sells for $10 to $15 per acre-foot, and the cheapest subsidized water sells for as little as $3.50 per acre-foot, even though it may cost $100 to pump this water to the farmers.[4] At these prices, it is economical to grow cotton and rice in the desert, and California farmers produce large amounts of both crops (and receive subsidies to do

---

[4] An acre-foot is the amount of water necessary to cover 1 acre to a depth of 1 foot, or about 325,800 gallons. It is the standard unit of measurement for water in such contexts. As a basis for comparison, the average suburban California household uses about half an acre-foot annually.

so). Meanwhile, households in Palo Alto pay about $65 for the same quantity of water, and some urban water users pay as much as $230. The most desperate nonagricultural communities along the Pacific coast of California have gone so far as to build desalination plants to obtain potable water from the ocean at a cost of approximately $3,000 per acre-foot.

How much of the cheap water is used? One agricultural use alone, irrigating pastures for grazing cows and sheep, used 5.3 million acre-feet of water in 1986.[5] This is enough water to cover the District of Columbia to a depth of 1,250 feet! It is also more water than was consumed by all the households in the state for all purposes, including filling swimming pools and hot tubs, watering lawns, and washing cars. Yet the industry of raising cattle and sheep on irrigated pasture in California had gross revenues for that year of less than $100 million.[6] Plainly, devoting so much water to such a low-value use is possible only because the water used to irrigate pastures is sold so cheaply.

THE LIMITED TRADABILITY OF WATER RIGHTS Why then does the water not flow to higher-value uses? Part of the answer is that many farmers' right to the water is limited and not freely transferrable. Farmers are not generally allowed to sell their water to the highest bidder.

What would happen if these ranchers and farmers owned the full rights to buy particular amounts of cheap water and then could resell the water (or the right to buy it cheaply) to others? Suppose, as most evidence indicates, that the marginal acre-foot of water really is more valuable to residential and industrial users than to farmers and ranchers. (Why else would they pay $3,000 for an acre-foot of water that a farmer gets for $3.50?) In that case, some farmers and ranchers would find it profitable to cut back their production, change the crops they raise to less water-intensive ones, or switch to more efficient methods of irrigation. They could then sell rights to the water they would save to other users who value it highly. According to the Coase theorem, efficient use of water is what should be expected if water rights are secure and tradable.

Water rights in California are not assigned in that way, however. The rights are not transferrable. Thus, the farmer will use water until the marginal units are worth only the low price he or she pays, while at the same time those marginal gallons would be worth much more to someone else.

In fact, the incentives may be even more perverse than this. For those receiving the cheapest water, there is sometimes a "use it or lose it" rule: If a farmer is entitled to use a certain number of acre-feet of water but uses less, perhaps by switching from cotton to fruit orchards, then his or her claim to the water is lost. To the extent that having an assured supply of cheap water in the future is valuable, the farmers might use up their full allotment even when it is worth less to them at the margin than the price they are required to pay.

The problem is related to the one that often arises when water is rationed in urban areas. In times of drought, users may all be required to cut back equally. So, for example, if a family conserves water when supplies are plentiful, then in a drought year it will be asked to reduce its water consumption from a small base. This can be done only at great personal hardship. Meanwhile, another family that has been wasteful finds it easy to reduce its use by the required fraction or amount. It is not hard to see that these systems for allocating water on the basis of past water consumption

---

[5] Marc Reisner, "The Next Water War: Cities Versus Agriculture," *Issues in Science and Technology* (Winter 1988–89), 98–102.

[6] To put this in figure in perspective, Stanford University currently receives about twice this amount in donations each year.

create incentives for wasting water. (We encounter this same sort of problem in Chapters 1 and 7. There, the tendency of organization planners to base this year's performance standards on last year's actual performance creates the ratchet effect that leads to lower levels of performance-enhancing efforts.)

INSECURE WATER RIGHTS   As we already mentioned, making existing rights transferrable would potentially improve matters. Farmers would sell their cheap water to city dwellers or industries who value it more, and both parties would be better off as a result. Alternatively, the water rights could be given to the city dwellers, perhaps collectively, city by city, and these people could sell them to the farmers if the value of the water in raising food exceeded that in washing cars or other urban uses. The Coase theorem says that this initial assignment of rights is immaterial to whether efficiency will be achieved, so long as the rights are well defined, secure, and tradable. The great problem is to find a politically palatable way to change water rights so that this limited resource can be used more efficiently.

Simply assigning rights to cheap water to farmers would be problematic. As one California legislator put it, "Taxpayers have spent billions of dollars to develop the water resources, the canals, the dams, for these farmers. Now to suggest that the farmers can turn around and sell that water for a profit is a major insult to the taxpayers."[7] Many farmers in fact oppose making water rights transferrable, fearing that any alteration in the current arrangements would ultimately result in loss of their water rights without any compensation.

WINDS OF CHANGE   In 1991, as California entered its fifth consecutive year of drought and major cities struggled with severe water rationing, legal barriers to water trade between farming and urban uses began to crack. The Los Angeles Metropolitan Water district was particularly active in designing novel arrangements. Where possible, it paid some farmers to let their fields lie fallow during drought years, in return for which the district could take unused waters. It also invested in improvements in the nearby farm counties' aqueducts, reducing water lost to evaporation, leaching, and leakage, and receiving in return the extra water made available by these projects.

The story of California water rights told here illustrates several themes of this book. Nontradable property rights lead to inefficient uses of resources, making institutional change desirable. However, legislative attempts to reform the laws about water rights also open the issue of the how extra value created by the reforms are to be distributed. The resulting influence costs are very high, and the threat to existing farmers has led many people to oppose any proposal for value-increasing reforms. Furthermore, the large number of people affected and the variety of their interests makes it more difficult to reach a mutually agreeable bargain. The costs and difficulty of bargaining block application of the efficiency principle, allowing an inefficient arrangement to persist for many years. Nevertheless, the increased cost of the inefficiency during a period of drought brought new, stronger pressures for permanent change in California, perhaps to a far more efficient system.

Bargaining Costs and the Limits of the Coase Theorem

A key premise of the Coase theorem is that the costs of arriving at and enforcing an efficient agreement are low. From this follows the conclusion that resources will be allocated efficiently, even in the absence of competitive markets and regardless of the initial allocation of property rights or distribution of bargaining power. In this section

---

[7] Representative George Miller, as quoted in Lisa Lapin, "Perestroika for Water: Drought Inspires Revolution," *San Jose Mercury News*, (February 3, 1991), A-1 and A-14

we investigate reasons why there might be significant impediments or costs to reaching and executing efficient agreements and examine the nature of these "bargaining costs." This discussion relies heavily on the material on bounded rationality and private information as discussed in Chapter 5.

Identifying the major sources of bargaining costs serves three functions. First, it helps us to identify where to expect inefficiencies to be found. Second, it helps to explain a whole range of practices and institutions, including those that arise to minimize bargaining costs and certain government regulations that seem designed to achieve as much as possible in an environment where bargaining among individual citizens would be too difficult, complex, or costly to be a realistic possibility. Finally, it lays a foundation for the new theory of law and economics. If the allocation of property rights does affect value, then one possible objective for the law of property rights is to assign them in a way that creates value.

Legal Impediments to Trade

Some of the most obvious impediments to trade are legal ones. In our discussion of water rights, we have seen how unassigned, ill-defined, nontransferrable, insecure, or unenforceable property rights can stifle efficiency. To the extent that the political and legal systems are supposed to determine and protect property rights, the inefficiencies arising from faulty property rights are traceable to these spheres. Moreover, the political and legal systems sometimes deliberately erect barriers to exchanges when it is believed that allowing certain trades would be morally undesirable. The U.S. Constitution's ban on involuntary servitude not only prevents a person from selling himself or herself into slavery but also has been interpreted as limiting some less drastic long-term labor contracts. You are simply not permitted to transfer your property rights in your person, even if you believe that the deal being offered is a good one. The limitations or outright prohibitions on the sale of certain chemicals (such as alcohol, cocaine, LSD, and heroin), books and videos (pornography and seditious material), and personal services (prostitution and assassination) also have a largely moral rationale.

In other cases, various factors might interfere with consummating a mutually profitable bargain to transfer property rights, even when such a bargain might exist and be ethically acceptable. These impediments and the responses to them provide a basis for understanding some aspects of efficient institutions.

COSTS OF AGREEMENT AND ENFORCEMENT   There are various costs of agreement and enforcement. First, there are simply the costs of determining, writing, and enforcing an agreement in a world of bounded rationality, imperfect communication, private information, observation and verification difficulties, and opportunism. The relevant parties have to be identified. They must reach agreement on the basic physical relationships that tie actions to outcomes and determine a set of plans in light of the model of the environment. Then the actions that each party is to take and the distribution of the resulting returns must be determined, accepted, and specified with sufficient clarity that all can understand them and know what to do and what to expect. Finally, some mechanism must be put in place to enforce the agreement and to resolve disputes.

In some situations these costs are small compared to the benefits that result: Transactions do get made! In others, however, they may be large or even overwhelming. For example, it would be quite costly for the passengers on an aircraft to negotiate whether the flight should permit smoking. If smoking is not permitted, should smokers be compensated for being deprived? How should compensation be determined? For example, should the person who complains loudest get the largest payment? Think of the opportunities for misrepresentation: Nonsmokers might even claim to be smokers to get compensation! Who should pay the compensation—the airline or the nonsmokers? If it is the nonsmokers, how much should each of them pay? How is this to be determined? Alternatively, if smoking is permitted, should nonsmokers be compensated? Should they be charged less by the airline because they are putting up with a foul atmosphere? What prevents a smoker from paying the lower fare then surreptitiously lighting up?

As another example, it would be overwhelmingly costly for all the drivers and pedestrians in even a small community to trade rights governing road use, such as who can drive how fast, who has the right-of-way at intersections, and so on. If there were no costs of enforcement, a value-maximizing agreement would generally treat different citizens differently. Drivers with superior driving abilities and a taste for fast cars might be permitted to drive faster (and might be required to pay for that right), whereas others might be required to drive slowly and yield the right of way to all concerned. However, there are too many parties affected for them to successfully negotiate and enforce rules and compensating payments. Even determining an efficient contract would involve immense costs and would most likely be impossible. Which drivers under which conditions should be allowed to drive at which speeds? To which other drivers and pedestrians must they yield right of way and under which conditions? When and for whom is the benefit of parking in a traffic lane worth more than the costs in terms of danger and congestion that are imposed on others? How is all this to be determined? Moreover, the costs of enforcing the agreement would be immense. Is the car approaching me being driven by A, to whom I should yield at this time of day at this corner, or by B, who should yield to me? Was that A who drove by at an efficient 85 miles an hour, or B, who is supposed to drive at 25?

To economize on these transaction costs, people seek other organizational solutions. Airlines make rules about smoking on aircraft, and governments about safe driving practices, even though, in fact, a driving speed that is safe for one driver may be too fast for another. A similar analysis justifies the creation of laws that specify how property owners must maintain the public sidewalks crossing their properties and the damages that must be paid if the laws are violated and an injury results, for example, if a passerby slips on the snow of an unshoveled walk. The laws governing product safety can be analyzed similarly. These laws mostly specify rights that are not tradable; a person often cannot accept a lower safety standard for a product in exchange for a lower price. One reason for this is to prevent private recontracting that would involve excessive costs in enforcement (borne in part by the government through its system of courts).

IS EVERYTHING WE SEE EFFICIENT?   A common objection to the argument that these costs are impediments to efficient agreement is that the costs of negotiating and enforcing contracts are, in fact, *costs*, and should be treated as such. If these costs are recognized, apparent inefficiencies then disappear because the reason a "better" outcome was not achieved is that the transaction costs of achieving it are too high. This line of argument has some appeal: It seems inappropriate to ignore the costs of running the organization, especially when the organizational structure is a choice variable. Furthermore, in cases like the smoking and traffic law examples, where the problem arises frequently, people may devise rule-making or law-making institutions that are intended to resolve the situation at low cost. In its most optimistic form, the hypothesis becomes not just that ownership patterns tend to be efficient in terms of the usual measures of costs and benefits, but that economic activity generally is organized so that the excess of benefits over total costs (that is, the total value) is maximized.

This hypothesis, although provocative and informative, is surely wrong. For example, suppose that two firms would suffer a pretax loss by merging their businesses but would enjoy an aftertax gain. Would they merge? To do so would be inefficient because the total profits (before tax) would fall. The reason for merging would be simply to reduce the government's share of the profits. Since the government is not likely to be an active partner in these negotiations, the merger most likely will go through because the outcome is efficient for the firms even though it is not efficient for society as a whole.

A similar problem arises whenever there is multilateral bargaining with one bargainer who cannot realistically participate in the negotiations. It may also arise when there are multilateral bargains when all can participate; two or more bargainers may gang up on the third in an inefficient way to hold him up more "efficiently." For example, firms may negotiate an agreement to raise prices above their competitive levels. That outcome benefits the firms, but consumers will be damaged by the conspiracy. Furthermore, the firms' gain is less than the consumers' loss from the price increase. Because of the costs to the consumers of participating in the agreement or of enforcing any agreement they might negotiate, however, there is no assurance that the ultimate agreement will maximize total value.

Despite these difficulties, transaction costs are relatively low in many situations. Thus, in the following chapters, where we examine the application of these ideas to a range of managerial and organizational problems, we assume that private arrangements tend to be efficient for the parties involved, at least given the information-based incentive constraints. More importantly, we assume that when significant transaction costs impede private contracting, people seek and often find innovative, sophisticated institutional arrangements that minimize or completely avoid these costs.

Transaction Costs and the Efficient Assignment of Ownership Claims

When transaction costs are low, the Coase theorem holds that the initial assignment of property rights is irrelevant to efficiency, so long as the rights are clearly assigned, secure, and transferrable. When there are significant impediments to efficient bargaining, however, it may be crucially important that these rights be assigned properly initially. Otherwise, with little prospect of private bargaining reassigning these rights effectively, they can end up being very badly allocated. Of course, in well-functioning societies, the initial assignment of property rights is typically a task of government.

CREATING, ALTERING, AND ASSIGNING PROPERTY RIGHTS   Even the most ardent advocate of *laissez faire* (noninterference) would likely concede a role for government in protecting property rights. However, governments also create new property rights where none were defined before and modify and transfer existing rights.

Governments create property rights, for example, through the patent, trademark, and copyright laws. These give title to the realization and expression of ideas to their creators. The holders of a patent can use the courts to prevent others from using their invention without compensation; the authors of this book had to get the permission of the copyright holders to use the various quotations that appear in this book. These property rights in fact result in short-term inefficiency. The use of your idea by someone else does not wear it out, use it up, or deprive you of its use. Once the idea is created, it is efficient to have it employed as widely as possible because there is no opportunity cost to its further exploitation. This solution would mean that inventors and developers would receive only a tiny fraction of the returns to investments, however. This would remove much of the incentive for creative and innovative activity, and the long-term impacts would be devastating.

Governments also often alter or remove existing property rights. In the 1970s

California changed the property rights of the owners of oceanfront property. These owners are now extremely limited in the ways they can develop their properties, and they have to provide access through their private land to the public beaches. In another recent example, new buildings in increasing numbers of political jurisdictions are now required to be accessible to people in wheelchairs. The property owners cannot choose to develop their properties as they might prefer and would formerly have been able to do. Similarly, people formerly had the right in the United States to smoke in the designated sections of commercial aircraft on domestic flights or, rather, the airlines had the right to permit this behavior on their planes. This right has been removed by a recent federal law: Smoking is now forbidden on domestic flights, even if everyone on the flight is a smoker. (In the interests of efficiency, however, the flight crew is still permitted to smoke: The lawmakers were concerned that nicotine deprivation would adversely affect the pilots' performance.)

ASSIGNING RIGHTS EFFICIENTLY: POLLUTION   At one time people essentially were free to pollute the environment to get rid of their wastes, without charge. Although no document gave them a clear legal right to do so, no party had a property right to the air and water that the polluters used: No one person could go into court and sue because a town's sewage was being dumped into the river that passed his or her house or because the air he or she breathed was full of toxic matter. In any case, this initial situation was not efficient because it led to serious environmental degradation: filthy air, contaminated soil, and poisoned water; acid rain that is killing forests and lakes far from the pollution sources; and global warming and destruction of the ozone layer that may threaten continued life on the planet. Arguably, these costs far exceed the gains to the polluters from dumping wastes into the environment rather than not creating them or disposing of them in other ways.

One possible solution would be to assign a clear property right to the polluters. The Coase theorem asserts that if bargaining were costless, this would lead to an efficient solution. In fact, however, the results are very likely to be inefficient. Polluters with clear rights to pollute would presumably be willing to sell their rights if the cost of disposing of their wastes in a more environmentally friendly way were less than the price they were offered for their rights. Those who are harmed by pollution place some value on having a cleaner environment, and if they could bargain costlessly with the polluters, they would presumably strike a value-maximizing deal that would result in the efficient amount of pollution. The transaction costs of carrying out this exchange are tremendous, however, and they make the value-maximizing bargain unattainable.

What are the sources of the bargaining costs? First, the problem of identifying the affected parties is very great, given the uncertainties about the long-term effects of various sorts of pollution. When these effects cross national borders, the problems become even more severe. Next, the free-rider problem among the victims of pollution is overwhelming. To know whether it is worthwhile to eliminate a particular source of pollution, we must determine the values that all the affected parties put on having the pollution gone. If the parties will be asked to pay according to what they say it is worth to them, they will have an incentive to free ride by underreporting, hoping that others will foot the bill. If they will not have to pay more when they say that they would benefit greatly from less pollution, then they will overstate their gain to ensure that the transfer takes place. The difficulties of achieving value-maximizing agreements with private information about valuations, especially when there are large numbers of people involved, suggest that this bargaining is unlikely ever to lead to transfers of pollution rights, even when they would be efficiency enhancing. Finally, there would be the costs of monitoring the agreement to ensure that the polluter was not cheating.

In these circumstances, assigning rights to polluters would not lead to an efficient outcome. It is better to lodge the rights to the environment with the public at large and to have the government enforce these rights through the legal and regulatory systems.

The Ethics of Private Property

Thus far we have treated property rights solely as a matter of economic efficiency, but the institution of private property has ethical significance as well. On the one hand, supporters of market systems see private property as a fundamental right, not just an expedient mechanism for generating incentives. On the other hand, many people worldwide believe that private property is fundamentally immoral. As the nineteenth-century socialist P.J. Proudhon succinctly put it: "Property is theft!" This view still has wide acceptance today. As well, in some cultures, the idea of private property is quite circumscribed, and some religions forbid private property altogether. Among many of the native peoples of North America, the idea that someone could somehow "own" the land was unimaginable, while Hutterites practice christian communism, living together in very successful farming communes in Manitoba, Saskatchewan, and North Dakota, with all material goods held in common.

Even when the institution itself is not fundamentally questioned, ethical issues arise. Pharmaceutical patents are necessary if private parties are to be willing to take the risks and absorb the costs of developing new drugs. The holder of a drug patent has the legal right to set the price at which the drug is offered for sale. Does anyone have a moral right to charge immense amounts for insulin, however, without which diabetics can die, or for AZT, which in the 1980s and early 1990s was the only drug available to help those afflicted with AIDS?

Property rights are also a major point of conflict between the industrialized world and the less developed nations. New technologies permit mining the deep ocean bed, but only the developed countries have the resources to exploit this opportunity widely. To encourage and protect the immense investments that are involved, it would make economic sense to create property rights to the sea bed. The oceans have not been considered to be the private property of anyone, however, or the territory of any nation—if they belong to anyone, it is to all humanity. What right do rich corporations and rich nations have to appropriate them, especially when the poor of the world cannot compete? Similar issues arise with communications satellites. These must be put into geosynchronous orbit so that they are constantly above a particular point on the earth's surface. The number of such orbits is limited. As the developed world appropriates more and more of these by parking satellites in them, fewer are left for the rest of the world's peoples who cannot now afford to appropriate slots for themselves.

These examples raise additional ethical issues about how anyone ever came to own any physical property if the earth's physical resources are regarded as initially the common heritage of all humanity. Ethicists have taken a variety of approaches to this question, some emphasizing human rights and fairness with little regard for questions of efficiency. A detailed comparison of these ethical approaches are beyond the scope of this book, but students should be aware that the possibility of creating value for everyone, provided the values are distributed in a way that is not too unfair and that shows proper regard for inalienable human rights, is an important part of the justification for creating the institution of private property.

The box describing the privatization process in Eastern Europe, in which formerly state-owned companies are transferred into private ownership in the hope of increasing total value, highlights some of the ethical tensions and practical problems associated with this process.

Privatizing Industry

In recent years a number of governments have "privatized" industries that were previously state owned, transferring ownership to private investors. For example, Japan has privatized its rail and telecommunications systems, and the United Kingdom has privatized huge portions of its industry: airports, water-distribution systems, seaport operations, airlines, railroads, aircraft and armaments manufacturing, petroleum and gas exploration, production, refining and marketing, telecommunications, automobile manufacturing, trucking, and more. In these cases, privatization was usually achieved by creating shares in the companies and selling the equity to the public through investment banks and brokers, often at prices that were much less than their estimated market value.

In Poland, Hungary, and Czechoslovakia, where industry generally was state owned under communism, the noncommunist governments in the early 1990s faced special problems of how to convert industries to private ownership. One difficulty was that often there was only a single producer of any given product in each of these countries, and the governments were leary of creating private monopolies. A second problem was that many of these industries were dependent on (implicit) state subsidies, and there was concern that they would not survive as private entities and that their failure would create economic hardships. One of the thorniest problems, however, was how to allocate the ownership claims in the firms that were to be privatized.

One possibility was simply to create shares in the companies and give them to their current employees. Other citizens, who were also previous nominal owners, objected to this. Giving shares to everyone was another solution, but this would dilute the ownership tremendously. This would not be a problem if there were well-functioning capital markets with low transaction costs through which people could then sell their shares, but such markets did not exist. Moreover, it was very hard to figure out what a share in one of these enterprises might be worth. The accounting systems in use were totally inadequate, and in any case, the figures they did generate were based on the largely irrelevant prices that had been set by the planners under communism. This made it unreasonable to expect that the markets would be very efficient if they were created. It also made selling the shares, as was done in the United Kingdom and Japan, problematic. Investors would be worried about overpaying, and the governments would be fearful of a political backlash if the shares turned out to have been grossly underpriced. A final concern was that foreigners, who were more experienced and sophisticated businesspeople and investors, might end up owning all the good properties.

Because the importance attached to these different problems varies among countries and industries, no single technique is always best, and governments ought to adapt their techniques to the firm's situation. For example, small, domestic firms might best be sold in auctions excluding foreign investors, whereas large employers with outdated equipment might be sold cheaply to any foreign firm willing to invest capital to save jobs. Privatization in Eastern Europe is a continuing experiment in institutional design.

As seen previously and in earlier chapters, the way ownership rights are assigned and protected can affect the efficiency of contracting. Incomplete contracts, bargaining costs, moral hazard, and influence costs can all be sources of inefficiency in business relationships, and the assignment of ownership rights can affect the magnitude of each of these problems and the possibilities for creating value.

In this section, we seek to develop a more systematic theory of who should own a particular asset. Such a theory should be of value in understanding existing arrangements, in predicting what sort of ownership patterns will be adopted in different circumstances, and in guiding decisions about setting ownership of particular assets. Our approach is to develop the theory of value-maximizing asset arrangements based on the attributes of the underlying transactions in which the asset is used.

Asset Specificity and the Hold-Up Problem

The most important attribute of transactions for studying asset ownership is the asset-specificity attribute. We discussed the specificity issue in Chapter 5, but its importance justifies recalling that discussion.

Assets are *specific* to a certain use if the services they provide are exceptionally valuable only in that use. A railroad line that carries a mix of passenger traffic and cargo with various destinations and that also carries products from a particular factory is not specific to the factory. A spur line that carries cargo to and from an isolated factory is specific to that factory, however, because it would be worthless (except for its scrap value) in any other use. The *degree of specificity* of an asset is defined to be the fraction of its value that would be lost if it were excluded from its major use. When two assets are both highly specific to the same use, maximizing value requires using both together in that use. The two assets are then said to be *cospecialized*.

Specificity and cospecialization are important because they give rise to the hold-up problem. When an asset is specific to a particular use, as the railroad spur is specific to serving the factory, the owner of the specific asset can be held up. The factory owner might insist on especially low rail rates, threatening to ship the factory's output by truck if the the railroad owner does not accede to that demand. The threat is a powerful one because the rail line is highly specific and would lose almost all its value if the threat were carried out. Thus, the spur-line owner might indeed be forced to make concessions to the factory. If the factory's product is too large or heavy to ship by truck, however, then the assets of the line and the factory are cospecialized, in which case each side wields a potent threat against the other. Any breakdowns in bargaining will lead to large costs on both sides.

A hold up itself has no effect on total value. In our example, unless bargaining costs are high, the Coase theorem implies that the factory owner and the railroad owner will agree on some value-maximizing shipping arrangement. The direct effect of the hold up by the factory owner is simply that the railroad owner receives less of the total value and the factory owner more; efficiency itself is unaffected.

Despite this, hold ups are not innocuous and can lead to value-destroying consequences. The railroad owner, for example, fearing the possibility of a future hold up, might not invest in the specific asset. The fear of hold ups can deter people from investing in highly specific assets, reducing the total value to be shared. This is the real social cost of the hold-up problem.

THE OWNERSHIP SOLUTION Economic theory predicts that an efficient organizational structure will protect the investments of those who would otherwise be deterred from making the most important, value-creating investments. The obvious solution for the factory and the spur line is for the factory to own the tracks. Two other examples of hold ups from Chapter 5 are mine-mouth electrical generating plants, which rely on an adjacent coal mine for their coal supplies, and the Fisher Body plant, which was to be set up as a dedicated facility to serve General Motors only. In each case, the problem was the reluctance of one or both parties to make large specific investments for fear of the hold-up problem. Fisher Body, for example, might have built a more expensive plant that was not dedicated to General Motors but that could be easily switched over to serve other customers. The extra investment might have been inefficient, but it would have protected the company from being held up. Similarly, an electric-generating plant located near a coal mine might be built to accept a wider array of coal grades than the mine produces, so that the utility company would be less reliant on the output of the mine. In each case, the danger is that unnecessary costs may be borne and value destroyed by attempts to protect against a hold up. General Motors resolved its difference with Fisher Body by purchasing the company, and mine-mouth electric-generating plants in the United States usually own the coal mines that serve them. The box on computer hardware and software contrasts the different approaches taken within the computer industry to the problem of managing specific investments.

Generally, when an asset is specific to a particular use, the hold-up problem for that asset can be avoided by having the user own the asset. Central to this theory is that there will be a tendency for specific assets to be owned by those who use them and for two cospecialized assets both to be owned by the same person or organization.

Despite its considerable importance, this "tendency" prediction can only be tentative because it ignores other attributes of the transaction. Indeed, the prediction itself can be ambiguous, and its two parts can even be inconsistent with one another when there is more than one specific investment. For example, the railroad spur is specific to both the factory it serves and to the main rail trunk line to which it connects. To whom should this doubly cospecialized asset belong?

In this particular case, the correct answer would probably be governed by the attributes of the related shipping transaction. If rail rates on the main trunk line are regulated by the government and the shipper is required to accept shipments at these predetermined rates, then there is less danger of the factory being held up by the railroad if the factory invests in the spur line, but there may be a danger of the railroad being held up by the factory in the reverse case. For example, shipment by truck may be an alternative, or the factory may be only marginally profitable and considering shutting down. Therefore, the factory should own the spur line in this case. The hold-up analysis is central to analyzing ownership, but its application requires a more detailed evaluation of the context, which involves studying other attributes and related transactions.

Uncertainty and Complexity

If all relevant contingencies can be forecast and planned, then a contract specifying what is required can be a good alternative to ownership. In our railroad and factory case, for example, the railroad might lease the spur line to the factory for a fixed amount per year over a term of many years. Provided the only important hold-up possibility for the rails is the rental price, this could be a fully satisfactory alternative to ownership by the factory. For relatively simple transactions, long-term leases are often a good substitute for ownership.

A similar example is the use of farm land for growing annual crops such as wheat. The investments made by the farmer in any one particular growing season such as preparing the soil, planting, fertilizing, and so on are highly specific, but the transaction itself is simple. The landowner might want to sell the land eventually for some kind of development, or build a house on it, or farm it alone. The owner is unlikely to lose much if he or she changes his or her mind on one of these questions

Computer Hardware and Software

Computers, the operating systems needed to make them function (such as UNIX™, DOS™, OS/2™), and the applications programs (statistical packages, word processors, database systems, and so on) that allow people to use the machines are often cospecialized to one another. For example, Apple Macintosh computers use a different operating system than do personal computers from other manufacturers. This means that applications programs have to be specially written to work on a Mac. Similarly, programs to be used with Tandem Computer's machines are specialized to this hardware and its operating system, which in turn are useless without the programs for running automatic teller machine systems for banks, doing transaction processing for stockbrokers, and carrying out the other applications where the "failsafe" characteristics of Tandem's machines are so important.

In these situations, the relationships among the producers of software, operating systems, and hardware are very important. Apple produces its own operating system rather than entrusting it to an outside company. It initially also wrote many of its own applications programs, first using Apple employees and later experimenting with a separate subsidiary, Claris Corporation, to produce software. Tandem has alliances with a variety of software houses that produce different programs for its machines, and it is very concerned with their success, although it currently takes no ownership position in these other companies.

In contrast, many manufacturers make personal computers that are "IBM compatible," meaning that they use the same operating system (Microsoft Corporation's DOS) as does IBM's Personal Computer line and that application programs that will run on an IBM will run on these machines too. This means that the software is not specialized to any one machine, and applications programs for IBM-compatible machines are produced by a huge number of different firms. There are typically no special relationships or arrangements between the software producers and IBM, and the hardware manufacturers usually do not produce software for these machines. Given that only Microsoft produces DOS, however, these machines and the applications programs are specialized to DOS. As would be expected, IBM and Microsoft have worked very closely together.

In 1990 the relationship between IBM and Microsoft became strained. The point of contention was the new OS/2 operating system jointly developed for IBM's new personal computer lines. IBM wanted to push forward with attempting to make OS/2 the new industry standard, whereas Microsoft preferred to stick with DOS supplemented with its Windows™ software, which is graphics-oriented (like the system on the Macintosh) and allows users to access several applications packages at once.

Because IBM's profits in the personal computer market depend on its ability to introduce idiosyncratic products, whereas Microsoft can thrive as long as IBM compatibles do well, the two firms have different interests. IBM's management ought to have anticipated this potential for a conflict of interests and arranged contract terms to mitigate the conflict when it negotiated its software development deal with Microsoft.

but cannot act on the decision during a single growing season, however. Therefore, a relatively simple contract that transfers rights to use the land for farming to a renter for a particular season is a good substitute for having the farmer own the land, at least in terms of protecting the farmer from having his or her specific investments subjected to a hold up. The terms of the contract might specify what is to be planted and make the rent dependent on this because some crops deplete the nutrients in the soil more rapidly than others, but this is not a major difficulty. The fact that the bilateral relationship between the farmer and the landowner is repeated over a period of years also provides an incentive for each to treat the other fairly, for example, for the farmer to avoid depleting the land.

The situation with fruit orchards, vineyards, and other perennial crops is very different. There, the farmer's investment is expected to last for a long period of time, during which complicated decisions about crops, soil, and other uses of the land may have to be made. Spelling out all these contingencies in a long-term contract would be impossible. The investment and the land are still highly cospecialized—physically separating the land from the trees or vines would be very wasteful—but this time a long-term contract is less satisfactory. We expect to find that farmers of these kinds of crops are much more likely to own the land they farm than are farmers of annual crops. Evidence from the state of California is consistent with this distinction.

Frequency and Duration

The longer the period over which two parties might interact, the more difficult it will be to foresee and contract for all the relevant contingencies and the less likely is a pure, arm's-length contracting solution to be satisfactory. This means that some other governance structure including common ownership may be preferred, especially when the fixed costs of creating the solution can be spread over more individual transactions. However, the long horizon also means that reputations may be more effective as control mechanisms. Which predominates is a matter of the specifics of the case.

In both the North American and Japanese automobile industries, the manufacturers buy many parts and systems from outside suppliers, while making others themselves. The largest U.S. producer, General Motors (GM), has been much more vertically integrated than Toyota, the largest Japanese producer, with GM producing much more in house than does its competitor. The parts, components, and subassemblies that GM produces in house tend to be highly specific to GM.[8] For the parts it does obtain outside, GM has usually relied on short-term, arm's-length contracting. It sets detailed specifications and selects suppliers on the basis of competitive bidding, signing them to simple, fixed-price contracts. Winning this year's contract is no guaranty of getting any business next year, however. The number of firms supplying GM is in the thousands. Toyota has only a few hundred suppliers. They often provide complex components that they design themselves and that are quite specific to Toyota's models. The relationships between Toyota and its subcontractors are close, complex, and long term. They are marked by extensive sharing of information and costs and by Toyota's active involvement in advising its subcontractors, although Toyota often has no ownership interest in these firms.[9]

All this is consistent with the theory. As the theory predicts, the bargaining costs on purchasing complex, specialized components in outside, arm's-length negotiations are too high for it to be a viable method of arranging repeated transactions, and in

---

[8] David Teece and Kirk Monteverde, "Supplier Switching Costs and Vertical Integration in the Automobile Industry," *Bell Journal of Economics*, 13 Spring 1982, 206–13.

[9] Banri Asanuma, "Japanese Manufacturer-Supplier Relationships in International Perspective: The Automobile Case," Working Paper No. 8, Faculty of Economics, Kyoto University (1988).

each case an alternative was sought. At GM, the solution was one of ownership: GM makes a large fraction of its own components. At Toyota, the solution was to establish long-term relationships with a smaller number of key suppliers who would make a wide array of components and systems and would be rewarded or penalized for their performance when additional contracts were awarded for the next car model.

Although both systems are responses to the same problems, they are not equally effective. By the mid-1980s, GM had begun adapting aspects of the Japanese system to its own operations. GM reduced the number of its suppliers, bought whole systems (such as a seat) instead of components (such as springs, seat frames, padding, and covers) and established closer supplier relations, to the point of allowing certain suppliers to participate in the design of the next model.

Difficulty of Performance Measurement

Even when assets are not highly specific, the assignment of ownership can still matter. There is an easy way to provide proper incentives when a nonspecific asset is used by a single person to produce marketable output: That person can be made the owner, both having the residual control and being the residual claimant. In this way, the person will have a proper interest in maximizing the residual value of the asset. This solution also has disadvantages, however. Two important disadvantages are accentuated in Chapter 7. The first is that transferring ownership also transfers the risk of fluctuations in the value of the asset to the single individual, who may find the risk very costly to bear. The second disadvantage arises when the person who cares for the asset also has other responsibilities in which performance is difficult to measure. By the equal compensation principle, these other responsibilities will be neglected unless strong enough incentives are established for it to be worthwhile for the asset owner to devote some effort to them. When performance in the other responsibilities is difficult to measure, these incentives are costly and represent an added cost of transferring asset ownership.

An alternative to the ownership incentive is the kind of incentive that we studied in Chapter 7: the use of explicit performance-based pay. This alternative requires attempting to measure the person's performance in caring for the asset. Compared to transferring ownership, the disadvantage of this system is that it incurs an added cost (for the measurement itself) and still leaves the agent facing risk—in this case the risk associated with measurement errors. Generally, when it is relatively inexpensive to measure performance accurately and when the risks associated with asset ownership are relatively large, it is better to base compensation on measured performance than to shift ownership. When care is especially difficult or costly to measure and the risks of asset ownership are not too great, then the ownership solution should be preferred. When the problem of motivating the person to honor his or her other responsibilities is great, the best system may be to avoid offering any formal financial performance incentives.

Finding the best ownership pattern is more complicated when the value of an asset can be affected by several different people. Consider the organization of a small shipping company that collects orders and dispatches truck drivers to carry the loads to various destinations. Is it more efficient for the truck drivers to own the trucks or for the shipper/dispatcher to own them? The answer depends on whose behavior most affects the value of the trucks and how hard it is to measure performance in those dimensions. If a single driver or team uses each truck to make cross-continental trips, with the truck being serviced on the road by the driver or whatever mechanic he or she can find, then the dispatcher's behavior is likely to have little effect on the value of the truck, whereas the driver's behavior would be important. Meanwhile, the driver's use of and care for the truck are hard to measure, so the value-maximizing allocation of ownership rights would be to make the driver the owner.[10] If the truck is used for local deliveries on several shifts, however, with several drivers using each truck and all service work performed by mechanics in the company garage, then the individual trucker's incentives become less important (he or she no longer makes maintenance decisions) and ownership becomes less effective for providing the trucker incentives (because the cost of a poorly operating truck is shared among those who use it). At the same time, the behavior of the shipper/dispatcher, who hires the mechanics and drivers, provides equipment for the garage, and so on, becomes a more important determinant of the truck's condition. Ownership should then lie with the dispatcher. The theory therefore predicts that there will be different ownership patterns depending on the way the truck is used and maintained. Ownership will be assigned in each case to the person whose hard-to-measure actions have the greatest effect on the truck's value.

Connectedness

Few real businesses conduct just one kind of transaction using just one kind of asset. We must study ownership issues in terms of the connections among the various transactions and assets. We have already seen an example of multiple connected assets in our discussion of the railroad spur line and the factory. The line is specific both to the factory and to the railroad trunk line. A complete analysis depends on assessing both connections. When there are multiple assets, each specific to some common uses, determining the optimal assignment of rights can become very complex.

The general principles remain the same, however. Ownership rights should be structured with a concern to minimize the distortions in investment decisions caused by the hold-up problem. Notice that the theory does *not* say that the transaction should be structured to minimize the amounts lost by individuals in the hold ups. These amounts are not accorded any weight themselves in the efficiency calculation because they have no direct effect on total value. Hold ups are accounted for only indirectly, through their effect on the investments that people are willing to make.

A second factor influences this choice. When the assets or the services they yield are strongly complementary, so that a higher level of one significantly increases the value of the others, there may be multiple patterns of investment in each asset that are mutually consistent with one another, forming coherent patterns, and yet only one of these distinct patterns actually maximizes total value. As seen in Chapter 4, this sort of situation necessitates explicit coordination among those choosing the amounts of the various assets or activities, even when all the decision makers are pursuing the same objective (as they would when all the assets are under common ownership and no moral hazard problems intervene between the owner and the decision makers). When the decision makers have divergent interests, the coordination problems become much more difficult because incentive problems can interact with them. This suggests that, other things being equal, strongly complementary assets should be brought under common ownership.

Of course, this last suggestion is subject to the qualification that has been applied several times before: Sometimes alternative sophisticated governance structures can be excellent substitutes for ownership, and these alternatives may avoid some of the influence costs of ownership. Thus, the assets of Toyota's subcontractors are likely to be complementary with Toyota's own assets. For example, Toyota's just-in-time system is essentially infeasible unless its suppliers have adopted a system that allows them to

---

[10] In recent years, the introduction of the tachograph, a measuring device for use in trucks to keep an accurate record of driving times and speeds, has significantly changed this equation. The device makes it easier to measure performance and reduces the advantages of having drivers own their own trucks.

be ready to deliver on a moment's notice. This means that close coordination is necessary. It is evidently achieved between Toyota and its subcontractors across organizational boundaries, despite the lack of common ownership.

Human Capital

Finally, we turn to one of the most important kinds of assets in any advanced industrial economy: workers' and managers' skills and knowledge. A person's skills and knowledge are assets that can only be owned by the person alone. In the absence of slavery, workers are not free to transfer ownership rights permanently to someone else.

The nontransferability of human capital is problematic when those skills are specific to an organization or physical assets. A team of people working together may well develop cospecialized skills and knowledge: familiarity with one another's habits, a common language to describe the local goings-on, knowledge of organizational routines, and so on. Simply allocating ownership rights in the organization or its physical assets cannot protect the personal investments of all the workers. Some of the arrangements that do protect them are described in Chapters 10 and 11.

The impossibility of transferring ownership of human capital assets also leads to an important question: In whose interest should firms be run?

OWNERSHIP OF COMPLEX ASSETS

We have just seen some elements of a theory of what would constitute an efficient allocation of ownership rights. We now return to the discussion of ownership itself to reexamine the fundamental idea and to question whether ownership is an effective means of providing incentives in all kinds of organizations and for all kinds of assets. We have treated ownership as possession of residual control, including the right to dispose of the asset or appropriate all or part of its value for personal use. This notion is fairly clear-cut in the case of most simple, discrete assets held in sole proprietorships, like the truck ownership example discussed earlier. In richer situations with more complex assets, however, complications arise.

Owning Complex Return Streams

If the payoffs from an asset are not one-dimensional (essentially, if all returns are not money), then there may be different residual elements associated with each dimension. For example, if two professors form a partnership to write a text together, then there are a variety of rewards. During the writing, each learns different things and suffers different costs, and in fact their families may suffer more than either author. Once they have finished, there are royalties from the sales. In addition, there is the effect of the prestige of each author in the profession and within his or her department. Presumably each will teach from the book, and this will have some effect on the success of their courses and the status they enjoy among their colleagues and students, as well, perhaps, as on their salaries. Finally, the success or failure of the book will influence the ability of the authors to negotiate better contracts on future books, either separately or together.

The royalties received on this enterprise are transferable cash payments. The effect of the book and of the students' reception to the courses on salaries are monetary but very hard to measure, as are the effects on future contracting opportunities. How much of each author's raise is due to the book and its impact? The other costs and returns are nonmonetary, not easily transferable, and indeed, extremely hard to identify and quantify, even when they accrue to the authors personally rather than to their families. Moreover, the returns are only partially responsive to the efforts of either coauthor, because responsibility and credit are shared. In effect, both partners are residual claimants, but on different, imperfectly transferable streams. Even if we decide that both authors own the book (although the publisher may well have the copyright), does either then have optimal incentives to work on it?

That such a simple venture gives rise to such complications is surely suggestive that many business transactions will be at least equally complex. A manager who carries out a particular project gains expertise that is of unknowable value in the future. The returns from the project are not just the revenues and costs that the firm records and that generate residuals that may be ultimately claimable by the stockholders but also the effect on the manager's future earnings opportunities. These may never be observable to the firm or even to the manager. Are they not residuals then? Who then "owns" the project?

Who Owns a Public Corporation?

The concept of ownership becomes even more problematic when we consider the complex agglomerations of assets that make up the modern corporation. Is there any single individual or recognizable group with effective ownership rights over the bundles of assets that are Ford, Toyota, Fiat, Hyundai, Hudson's Bay Company, Salomon Brothers, Sony, British Airways, IBM, Apple, or any of the other giant corporations that are the unique characteristic of the organization of economic activity in the late twentieth century?

STOCKHOLDERS   Nominally, and by law, the stockholders own a corporation. Their rights are in fact quite limited, however. Stockholders can vote to change the corporate charter, they can elect the directors and (except where a "classified" board with fixed, overlapping terms is in place) remove them by majority vote. They usually have the right to vote on substantial "organic" changes, such as mergers in which the company disappears or the sale of most of the corporation's assets. That is it. The stockholders cannot set the dividends that are paid out to them, they have no role in investment or acquisition decisions, they do not hire the managers or set their pay, and they have no say in setting prices. In other words, they have no direct rights in deciding any of the multitude of issues that are crucial in running the business. Of course, by electing the directors, who are empowered to hire and fire management and to make or ratify all major management decisions, the stockholders can indirectly affect the decisions that are made. Furthermore, if the directors they elect do not follow their wishes, the stockholders can replace them as the opportunities arise. Yet, this is quite removed from the control associated with the idea of ownership of a simple asset like a truck.

Recall, however, that the formal definition of residual rights runs in terms of decisions and returns that are not explicitly vested elsewhere by contract or law. One could then argue that, in buying the shares in the firm, the stockholders contractually assigned the rights to make most decisions—including the crucial decisions about the distribution of the returns from the asset they "own"—to someone else. They are still the owners; they just happen to have written contracts that leave them few residual rights. This resolution is not satisfactory, however. Stockholders' rights are not residual; instead, they are strictly delimited and enumerated.

DIRECTORS   If any group could be considered to have residual control in a corporation, perhaps it might be the board of directors. It is they who have the power to set dividends; to hire, fire, and set the compensation of the senior executives; to decide to enter new lines of business; to reject merger offers or instead approve and submit them to the stockholders; and so on. In the United States, the authority of the board of directors is buttressed by the "business judgment rule," according to which the courts basically will not second-guess the directors' business decisions.

If the directors have residual control, however, they certainly do not have claim to the residual returns. If the corporation is liquidated, the receipts are distributed to the stockholders once debts and taxes are paid, and the directors are not free to appropriate the profits for their own use.

Moreover, two recent developments in the United States have rendered uncertain just what contractual and legal obligations a U.S. corporation's directors may have and thus what decision rights are residual. First, the rapidly changing legislative and case law surrounding directors' obligations in the context of changes in corporate control (mergers, acquisitions, and so on) means that directors really cannot be sure just what rights they have. The skyrocketing cost of director's liability insurance is evidence of how unsettled these matters are. Second, the emerging social notion of "stakeholders" having a claim on the corporation means that politically, if not legally, the freedom of the corporation to act as its directors might wish is circumscribed in as yet ill-defined ways.

MANAGERS AND EMPLOYEES   Beyond this is the question of whether, even in the context of regular operations, the directors (or the stockholders) really can have residual control. A right that cannot be exercised is of little significance. Furthermore, for most purposes, the directors must rely on the officers of the firm to provide them with the information needed to make decisions. By controlling the flow of information to the board and setting the agenda, the senior executives may have effective control of many of the decisions that are nominally controlled by the board. Moreover, many critics argue that the board members are effectively chosen by the senior executives and are totally beholden to them. The shareholders may elect the board, but they almost always simply elect the slate of candidates on the proxy statement sent out by management, and effectively management decides who is nominated.

Yet the officers in turn are dependent on the corporation's employees to develop the information in question and to carry out the decisions that are made. Many a senior manager's plans have been thwarted by the resistance of lower-level employees. Perhaps these employees are really the residual decision makers.

All this calls into question the usefulness of the concept of ownership as residual control in the context of the large corporation. Note too that the idea of the owners being those with residual claims is not fully satisfactory. First, if the residual claimants are not in a position to control the decisions that affect the value of the asset, then the incentive properties that have been claimed for ownership are certainly weakened. Second, as we have already seen, it may be impossible to identify any individual or group that is the unique residual claimant or, indeed, to identify the benefits and costs accruing to any decision and so compute the residuals.

Finally, if the situation is murky in the case of a for-profit corporation, how does the concept of ownership apply to a university, a church, or another nonprofit organization? In such organizations, no private parties have a right to appropriate the residuals after debts are paid. Instead, residuals must remain in the organization, and if the organization is dissolved, any remaining funds go to the state. If there is a residual claimant, it would seem to be the state, but surely the state does not have the residual control in such an organization any more than it does in a for-profit organization.

Whose Interests Should Count?

Proponents from both sides of an odd coupling of interests argue that companies, and especially publicly held corporations, should not be run simply in the interests of their stockholder/owners. The parties to the alliance are, on one hand, the managers and employees of the corporations, often backed by the companies' suppliers and the governments of the localities where these companies have operations, and, on the other, a variety of academics and activists who believe that the pursuit of profits is either socially inappropriate or immoral. Both groups are apt to characterize stockholders as uninvolved, absentee owners with no allegiance to the firm and no concerns but their narrow selfish interests in short-term financial gains. They are either unworthy of having their interests predominate or incapable of realizing where their long-term interests actually lie. Instead, the company should pursue social aims (usually those favored by the activists) or should care for the interests of the people who are actually involved in the organization (usually the position of the stakeholders).

Against these positions is another discomforting alliance made up of investors, both private and institutional (mutual funds, insurance companies, pension funds, financial intermediaries), along with the the investment-banking and stock-brokerage industries, as well as a set of free-market economists. This alliance argues that maximizing the value of the firms enhances economic efficiency. Entrenched managers, self-interested employees, noncompetitive suppliers, and incompetent governments who argue for paying attention to other concerns simply want to escape the discipline of the market and use the owners' resources for their own ends. Having managers pursue anything other than maximization of the value of the firms entrusted to them is to invite calamitous self-serving moral hazard. What results is that the managers will simply pursue their own interests, perhaps adjusted to account for the interests of their allies.

There is surely not space enough to resolve this dispute here. However, we can offer observations based on the ideas we have already developed, and we return to these issues in Chapter 15.

EXTERNALITIES AND CORPORATE SOCIAL RESPONSIBILITY   In a system of complete, competitive markets, the arguments for running the firm to maximize profits or the value of the firm are largely unassailable (see Chapters 2 and 3). Similarly, if bargaining costs are low and property rights are well established, secure, and tradable, so that the Coase theorem would apply, there would be no basis for complaint about a firm pursuing the interests of its stockholders. Unfortunately, we do not live in such a world.

In actuality, the decisions that are made in firms can affect many different people in ways that the market does not adequately mediate. Externalities such as pollution are one example. A firm that chooses to pollute may increase its value at others' expense, and this course of action is unlikely to promote overall efficiency when we cannot count on the mechanisms of bargaining to ensure that the firm recognizes the full costs and benefits of its actions. Similarly, if the firm is dealing with unsophisticated, badly informed customers, it might gain while decreasing efficiency by selling them shoddy or even dangerous goods.

In such situations, a socially responsible course of action may be more efficient. The question is whether asking for such behavior, even if realistic, might not bring unintended consequences. Suppose that the firm's managers are directed to promote social efficiency. Do they have the information to do so? How are they to learn of the costs and benefits to other parties of various courses of action when there are neither prices nor explicit bargaining with the affected parties to guide them? How is all this to be monitored effectively, and by whom? Who has the information and the incentive to tell if managers who are not pursuing profits are behaving appropriately or are instead serving their own interests?

SPECIFIC ASSETS AND STAKEHOLDERS' RIGHTS   In Chapter 8 we discussed how quasi-rents can arise within firms and how different business decisions can affect the distribution of these returns among employees. Employees are not the only ones affected by the firm's decisions, however. Obviously, stockholders' returns are affected by a wide range of decisions, including investments, wage levels, dividend policy,

Japanese Corporate Ownership and Responsibility

In recent years, Japanese corporations have enjoyed immense commercial success. Japan is a country almost without the usual natural resources—few significant mineral and ore deposits, no domestic petroleum reserves, very limited farm land—and its human and physical capital stock was devastated less than 50 years ago in World War II, when Japan became the only country ever to suffer a nuclear attack. It now is one of the great economic powers, and (depending how one converts yen to other currencies), it may be the richest industrial economy per capita in the world. More than in most developed countries, Japan's large corporations seem to dominate its economic organization.

Japanese corporations are structured somewhat differently than are those in other developed capitalist economies, and the basic principles that guide them seem to be different as well. A typical Japanese board of directors is made up almost exclusively of full-time employees of the firm. According to a 1991 study of 100 of the "best" companies in Japan, only 19 had any directors who were not employees, and of the 2,737 directors of these companies, only 55 were outsiders. Even these might be the firms' bankers or the heads of wholly owned foreign subsidiaries. In contrast, among major U.S. firms, 75 percent of the directors are outsiders, and the ratio is almost as high in the United Kingdom. The stock in these Japanese firms is, to a large extent, in the "friendly hands" of affiliated companies, suppliers, customers, or banks with long-term relationships with the firm. More than 80 percent of the largest firms have a majority of their stock in friendly hands. These owners will not sell a firm's stock under any sort of normal conditions, nor are they at all likely to participate in a proxy contest. In other countries, stock is more often in the hands of investors who may have no other business connection to the firm. The executives of major Japanese corporations have typically spent their entire careers in their companies, and there is little possibility of a senior executive being lured away from one major firm to another. No managerial labor market enforces discipline on them.

In whose interests are Japanese corporations run? Their structure would hardly suggest that it is the stockholders' interests alone that are being served, although the profits that are generated have been handsome, and the Nikkei Stock Index of the share prices of the top firms has climbed to remarkable heights.

A distinguished student of the Japanese economic system, Masahiko Aoki, has described the Japanese corporation in terms of the managers' mediating between the interests of different groups—particularly employees and investors (who, under the Japanese system, may include suppliers and customers).* But what weights do managers give to these various groups' interests?

Two surveys reported in a Japanese newspaper, the *Nikkei Sangyo Shinbun* (April 23, 1990, and July 5, 1990) are informative in this regard. The first concerned the attitudes of Japanese middle managers; the second dealt with the attitudes of the presidents of major Japanese firms.

Both groups were asked to whom the firm should belong, that is, presumably, in whose interests should it be run, and to whom they actually do belong. Multiple answers were allowed, so that the idea of there being multiple legitimate claimants could be expressed. Middle managers ranked shareholders third on the first question, with only two-thirds of the respondents naming the nominal owners as having a right to have their interests be taken into account. The most frequently named group were employees, followed by society as a whole. Further down the list were customers and management. Regarding the issue of in whose interests they believed firms actually were run, the middle managers again ranked employees first and shareholders third, with management now in second place. Interestingly, fewer of the respondents mentioned shareholders in their answer to this second question than to the first.

The senior executives were more oriented to the stockholders, mentioning them most frequently on the first question. Still, the number mentioning employees was almost as large (80 percent versus the 87 percent mentioning shareholders), and most company presidents in fact indicated that the firm should belong to both groups, with society as a whole also getting many mentions. On whose interests actually were served, the most common answer was employees, with shareholders coming second. Again, most of the presidents mentioned both groups, but a full 20 percent indicated that shareholders interests did not count in running the firm.

*Masahiko Aoki, *The Cooperative Game Theory of the Firm* (Cambridge: Cambridge University Press, 1984).

mergers, pricing, and many others. The security of creditors' and lenders' claims will depend on the riskiness of the firm's investments, the wages it pays to workers, and the dividends it pays to shareholders. A firm's decisions about the design and placement of its factories can affect community housing values, traffic, and environmental quality; its choices of suppliers can affect the distribution of wages and profits among the potential suppliers; and its pricing policy affects both competitors and customers. There are frequent disputes about which of these interests are legitimate ones that ought to be weighed in the decision-making process. Is a small community entitled to block a decision by the area's largest employer to close its local factory? Are its downtown stores and their employees entitled to protection when a discount chain opens up on the edge of town? Should residential neighbors be allowed to demand mitigating measures or compensation when a medical center expands its facilities, increasing local traffic with its attendant noise, parking problems, and traffic safety issues?

With incomplete markets and imperfect bargaining, the way various interests are weighed in decisions can have consequences for the efficiency of the economic system that must not be ignored. For example, in the plant closing decision, investments by workers and others in houses near the factory may lose much of their value if the factory were to close. Such investments are cospecialized with the plant. Efficiency then requires that the homeowners' interests be given some weight in this decision. Similarly, the workers may have invested in firm-specific human capital that is, by its very nature, cospecialized with the plant. Closing the plant destroys the value of these investments. The township as a whole may have invested in roads, sewage-treatment facilities, schools, and other assets whose value depends on the plant's continued operation.

The presence of these cospecialized investments suggests that, at the time the investments are being made, it would be in the mutual interest of the firm and of employees, homeowners, local government, and other stakeholders to devise some way to protect stakeholders against opportunism by the firm, perhaps by agreeing to restrictions on plant closings. Protection of this sort would encourage stakeholders to invest in building these cospecialized assets, which also benefits the firm by making a larger labor force available. Because there would need to be so many parties affected, it is unlikely that bargaining among them all could lead to an efficient solution, and it may be better to have laws instead that settle the rights of the parties in advance.

SUMMARY

In economic terms, ownership is distinct from other forms of contract only where contracts determining specific decision rights over an asset and assigning its returns are imperfect and incomplete. Then, ownership may be identified with the right to exercise *residual control* where the contract is silent about decision rights, or with the right to receive any *residual returns* that remain after contractual obligations are fulfilled. For simple assets, it can be advantageous to have as many decision rights as possible vested with the person who receives the residual returns, for in the process of maximizing his or her own personal returns, that person will also generally be led to maximize total value.

When ownership rights are tradable and the conditions of the Coase theorem apply, the initial allocation of property rights does not affect the efficiency of arrangements because the rights will be traded as necessary to restore efficiency. When rights are not tradable, however, they may wind up in the wrong hands. The limitations on the trading of water rights in California provides an example. Water is frequently directed to certain low-value uses (such as growing rice) when farmers who are entitled to cheap water cannot trade their rights to cities who value the rights more highly. Similarly, when rights to an asset are insecure, the owner may not find it worthwhile to preserve and enhance the value of the asset because he or she may not be permitted to enjoy the benefits of those efforts.

Some assets are commonly shared within a community. The result is often what is widely known as "the tragedy of the commons," in which the shared resource is abused by members of the community because the costs of the abuse are widely shared. We analyzed this problem in connection with local fishing rights and found that similar analyses apply to aquifers and petroleum deposits. In the fishing rights case, various ownership patterns could be tried to improve matters. The community could own the asset, but unless the community was homogeneous such a solution could lead to large influence costs. Also, the problem of monitoring compliance to the community's rules must still be solved. Individual ownership provides another alternative, but that may lead to distorted incentives if the returns to the asset cannot be directed entirely to the owner. In socialist countries, even farms and factories are often treated as shared resources and accordingly are not properly maintained. The Chinese experience (especially with private agriculture) during the decade of the 1980s demonstrates how ownership incentives can powerfully improve individual performance.

When property rights are secure and tradable and bargaining costs are low, the Coase theorem suggests that people will trade rights until the new pattern of ownership is efficient. Some argue that we should presume that observed patterns are always efficient when we account for all the relevant costs because untraded rights simply indicate that the exchange was not worth the cost that would have to be incurred. When the agreements being made between two (or more) parties affect others who do not participate in the bargaining, however, it is not generally true that any trade must be value increasing. It could instead simply be appropriating value from the nonparticipants. In circumstances like these, there can be important advantages to simply assigning property rights to those who are likely to value them most highly.

Property rights in the modern world continue to change, with rights to clean air, intellectual property, sea-bed minerals, beach access, fishing rights, and broadcast bands being examples. The rights to use new drugs serve to remind us that the assignment of ownership rights has ethical and distributive aspects in addition to its efficiency ones.

When bargaining costs are low, the theory predicts that actual ownership rights will come to be assigned efficiently. When an asset is highly *specific* to a particular use, meaning that it is much less valuable in its next-best use, then there are gains to assigning ownership to the final user in order to avoid the hold-up problem. In the *hold-up-problem*, the user threatens not to use the asset in order to extract better terms from the owner. The reason hold ups are a problem is that they discourage investments in highly productive specific assets. When two assets are both specific to the same transaction, they are *cospecialized*, and the theory predicts they will usually both be owned by the same party. *Difficulty of measuring performance* in maintaining an asset favors transferring ownership to the asset user, but a similar difficulty in measuring performance in other important responsibilities may make transferring asset ownership unwise.

Other attributes of the transaction also affect the value-maximizing ownership pattern. Simple transactions may be managed by nearly complete contracts, in which case the hold-up problem is of only minor importance. A lease of the asset, for example, may be a good substitute for ownership. Long durations of the asset and complexity of the transaction make these alternatives less effective and favor the ownership solution mentioned previously.

Human capital poses a special problem because (1) it represents a large fraction of the capital of any advanced industrial country, (2) it is generally not tradable, and (3) it is quite commonly cospecialized with the human capital of other people. Complex organizational arrangements are often devised to protect investments in human capital (see Chapter 10).

Although the concept of ownership seems reasonably clear in many of the cases discussed here, the concepts of residual control and residual returns that define ownership are actually quite elusive. For large corporations, we argued that there is really nobody who owns both the residual returns and the residual control necessary for ownership to work as the simple theory describes. For nonprofit organizations, there is nobody with a right to collect the residual returns and, therefore, we would say, no owner. In the case of this book, there are various kinds of returns, not all financial, and these come in different proportions to the two authors and the publisher: There is no single residual claimant.

Despite these qualifications, ownership is clearly the most common and effective means to motivate people to create, maintain, and improve assets, and its importance in practical business life would be hard to overstate.

◼ BIBLIOGRAPHIC NOTES

As with so many other parts of the economic theory of organization, Ronald Coase made the initial modern contribution to the economic analysis of property rights, emphasizing that the ability of parties to trade and contract lies at the center of the theory. The economic analysis of property rights has since attracted the attention of a large number of scholars: The volumes by Yoram Barzel and Harold Demsetz give an introduction to the work of two of the more prominent of these. Useful discussions of current thinking about the Coase theorem are provided by Robert Cooter and Joseph Farrell.

The importance of residual returns for the theory of the firm was developed more fully by Armen Alchian and Demsetz; residual control as a virtual definition of ownership was championed by Sanford Grossman and Oliver Hart. Oliver

Williamson, Grossman and Hart, and Hart and John Moore have contributed especially importantly to the analysis of efficient ownership patterns.

The importance of specific investments was first developed in the context of human capital theory by Gary Becker and was elaborated in the theory of the firm by Williamson and by Benjamin Klein, Robert Crawford, and Armen Alchian.

■ REFERENCES

Alchian, A., and H. Demsetz. "Production, Information Costs, and Economic Organization," *American Economic Review*, 62 (1972), 777–97.

Barzel, Y. *Economic Analysis of Property Rights* (Cambridge: Cambridge University Press, 1989).

Becker, G.S. *Human Capital: A Theoretical and Empirical Analysis, with Special Reference to Education* (New York: Columbia University Press, 1964).

Coase, R. "The Problem of Social Cost," *Journal of Law and Economics*, 1 (1960), 1–44.

Cooter, R. "The Coase Theorem," *The New Palgrave: A Dictionary of Economics*, J. Eatwell, M. Milgate, and P. Newman, eds. (London: The Macmillan Press, 1989), Vol. 1, 457–60.

Demsetz, H. *Ownership, Control, and the Firm* (Oxford: Basil Blackwell, 1988).

Farrell, J. "Information and the Coase Theorem," *Journal of Economic Perspectives*, 1 (Fall 1987), 113–30.

Grossman, S., and O. Hart. "The Costs and Benefits of Ownership: A Theory of Vertical and Lateral Integration," *Journal of Political Economy*, 94 (August 1986), 691–719.

Hart, O., and J. Moore. "Property Rights and the Nature of the Firm," *Journal of Political Economy*, 98 (December 1990), 1119–58.

Klein, B., R. Crawford, and A. Alchian. "Vertical Integration, Appropriable Rents, and the Competitive Contracting Process," *Journal of Law and Economics*, 21 (1978), 297–326.

Williamson, O. "Transaction-Cost Economics: The Governance of Contractual Relations," *Journal of Law and Economics*, 22 (1979), 233–61.

EXERCISES

Food for Thought

1.   Foster City, California, is a city that was built largely on land reclaimed from the San Francisco Bay. In the early 1960s, when the homes were built there, the developer made the unusual arrangement of selling only the houses to the purchasers while retaining ownership of the land, collecting a lease payment equal to about 5 percent of the value of the land on a 30-year lease on each property. Between 1964 and 1989 land values in Foster City rose by about 5,000 percent, that is, by a factor of about 50. In 1989 the Foster organization announced that it planned to increase the lease payments proportionally when the leases were renewed. In response, the homeowners formed an organization and hired a lawyer to prevent the huge planned rent increase. Discuss this situation in terms of the theory of cospecialized

assets. Who is being held up? What inefficiencies, if any, would you expect to result from this unusual arrangement?

2.   Many firms rent office space from others under contracts that run for periods of about 5 years. Typically, the renter owns the furniture and equipment used in the office and is responsible for maintaining it, but the owner of the building is responsible for maintaining the common areas (hallways, lobby, grounds). The building owners own the windows, but the renter may own the window treatments (draperies, blinds). The building owner is responsible for maintaining the electrical system and air conditioning, but the renter may be responsible for decorating and painting the walls. How can you account for this pattern of ownership rights and responsibilities? What kinds of companies would you expect to own their office space rather than to lease it?

3.   In the late 1980s the United States and Japan became embroiled in a dispute over the use of huge "drift nets" to catch fish in the Pacific Ocean. These are nets that may be as much as 40 miles long and are allowed to drift in the water, catching whatever comes into them. What kinds of economic and moral issues would you expect to arise in these talks? What kinds of enforcement issues would be most difficult to resolve? Why?

4.   Ownership patterns vary around the world, even within free market economies. In the United States and Canada, when a house or apartment is sold, the kitchen cabinets are almost invariably sold with it. In Europe, the opposite is often the case, with kitchen cabinets being treated as furniture. What differences in kitchen design would you expect to find between Europe and North America? Discuss whether these differences cause or are caused by the different ownership patterns.

5.   Two main systems of water rights exist in the United States. According to one system, downstream water users are entitled to an uninterrupted flow; according to the other, the first users are entitled to continue their use at historical levels, but they forfeit their rights if they reduce their actual usage. What difficulties would you expect in trying to modify each of these systems to make water rights tradable?

6.   Publishers of even the smallest daily newspapers usually own their own presses, but even the largest book publishers normally contract their printing jobs to independent printers. What accounts for this difference in who owns the printing presses?

7.   When airline flights are overbooked in the United States, an auction is sometimes held to see which passengers are willing to transfer to a later flight in return for compensation. The compensation is determined by the lowest price needed to induce the required number of people to give up their seats. This seems to work fairly well. Would a bidding system work for deciding whether a flight should permit smoking? Why or why not?

8.   When Neil Armstrong first stepped on the moon in 1969, he claimed it on behalf of the United States for all of humanity—the moon is not U.S. territory. The earlier tradition back on Earth was for Western European explorers to claim any country they "discovered" for their monarchs, even if there were obviously people inhabiting the lands already. What are the economic merits and disabilities of each pattern? What of their ethics?

9.   Condominiums and housing cooperatives have become increasingly important institutions in the United States in recent years. Condominiums are now common in most states, and co-ops are a major feature of the New York housing market.

Condominiums are multifamily living units—usually apartment buildings—in which each resident owns his or her individual living unit plus a share of the common areas: the grounds, hallways, exterior structure, etc. Ownership of a unit entails membership in the condominium association, which makes policy decisions, collects fees to maintain and improve the common property, and contracts for maintenance and other services. The association operates under rules that are subject to majority votes, with voting power allocated either by ownership share or equally, one vote per unit. Owners are generally free to sell their units (and, with them, their shares in the common areas) to anyone, although the association may have a right to match any offer and buy the unit. Owners typically obtain their own individual mortgage loans to finance purchase of their separate units.

In a housing cooperative, the members all own the whole building together, and individuals then obtain long-term leases from the co-op for particular residential units. The residents are, then, collectively their own landlord. Because no individual owns any particular piece of the building, mortgages are obtained by the co-op. Further, individuals are not free to sell their interests to anyone they please: the co-op members must approve any new members. Decisions are again made by the members collectively, although they typically would delegate such questions as interior decoration to the individual tenant-members.

What do you see as the relative merits and deficiences of each of these patterns of ownership? How do they compare with investor-ownership under which the tenants rent their units?

Part

V

EMPLOYMENT: CONTRACTS, COMPENSATION, AND CAREERS

10
EMPLOYMENT POLICY AND HUMAN RESOURCE MANAGEMENT

11
INTERNAL LABOR MARKETS, JOB ASSIGNMENTS, AND PROMOTIONS

12
COMPENSATION AND MOTIVATION

13
EXECUTIVE AND MANAGERIAL COMPENSATION

10

EMPLOYMENT POLICY AND
HUMAN RESOURCE MANAGEMENT

[Classical economic theory's] way of viewing the employment contract and the management of labor involves a very high order of abstraction—such a high order, in fact, as to leave out of account the most striking empirical facts of the situation as we observe it in the real world.

Herbert Simon[1]

In advanced economies, labor earnings typically account for about two thirds of national income. In the service industries, which constitute an increasing share of economic activity, expenditures on labor are proportionally even more important. At the same time, the share of direct labor expenses in the total costs of modern manufacturing firms has fallen relative to older patterns. Nevertheless, employees' efforts, skills, knowledge, creativity, and dedication are perhaps even more crucial to manufacturing firms today than previously. Devising and implementing effective policies to attract and retain good people, to help them develop to their potential, to utilize their skills and knowledge, and to inform, motivate, and reward them are thus among the most important tasks that managers face. These **human-resource** policies and the way they are managed have tremendous effects both on the success of the organization and on the quality of life that the organization's members experience.

Our approach to human-resource and compensation issues is the one we have taken throughout this book: We assume rational and largely self-interested behavior; we presume that people seek efficient solutions to the problems they face; we examine efficiency explanations for the institutions and practices we observe; and we look to identifiable transaction costs to account for divergences from efficiency. For much of

---

[1] "A Formal Theory of the Employment Relationship," *Econometrica*, 19 (1951), 293–305.

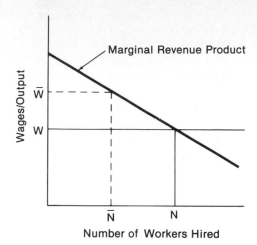

Figure 10.1: In the classical economic model, the firm hires workers until the wage paid to the last worker is equal to that worker's marginal revenue product. Lower wages lead firms to hire more workers.

the analysis, we further simplify by assuming that there are no wealth effects and then apply the value maximization principle.

This purely economic approach may seem seriously incomplete when applied to human-resource issues. After all, we are discussing people and the relationships among them. People get satisfaction from their work and from a job done well. They often define themselves in terms of their jobs, identify with their employers, and judge their self-worth in terms of their success at work. The relationships among people working together are social, not just economic. Assuming a cold-blooded economic calculus thus may seem to be a vicious caricature, and its use might seriously misdescribe actual employment relations and misdirect policies.

All these objections may be correct but, as we will see in this and the following chapters, an economic approach has great value in helping to organize issues and understand phenomena and in imposing discipline on our analysis.

THE CLASSICAL THEORY OF WAGES, EMPLOYMENT, AND HUMAN CAPITAL

The study of labor markets, employment, and wages is a major element of standard neoclassical economics. Although this approach has serious deficiencies in explaining a variety of actual practices, it is still worthwhile highlighting some of its central features.

Wages and Levels of Employment

In the classical economic analysis, the conditions of supply and demand at any time determine the levels of employment and wages. Firms in such a world have no discretion over the wage levels paid to their workers. Instead, firms take the wages of different classes of workers as given by market conditions and decide how many workers of each type to hire. As illustrated in Figure 10.1, a firm's optimal policy is to hire additional workers of any one type until the last worker's marginal revenue product—the incremental income that hiring the worker brings to the firm—is just equal to the wage rate. Until this level of employment is reached, additional workers contribute more to revenues than they do to costs, and so it is worthwhile to hire more people.

The hiring decisions made by all the buyers of labor combine to determine a demand curve for labor of each type. Workers' decisions about whether to seek employment at the going, market-determined wage or instead to go to school, stay home to raise a family, travel, start a new business, and so on, determine the corresponding supply curves. The market wages for each type of worker are set by the interaction of supply and demand in the usual way.

Workers in any world described by this model would be highly mobile, staying with an employer only if that employer offered the workers a more preferred combination of wages, hours, job location, and so on, and otherwise moving—possibly every day—to the employment where their skills and effort are most highly valued. Firms would raise and lower their employment levels frequently as shifting demand for their product changed the workers' marginal revenue products. Wages and overall employment would fluctuate with changing market conditions as well, with the two continually adjusting to keep the marginal revenue product of each type of worker ever equal to that type's wage.

Human Capital

Workers' productivity is not solely a function of their innate strength, dexterity, intelligence, and the amount and quality of the physical capital that they have to use, but also of their **human capital**. Human capital refers to the knowledge and acquired skills a person has that increase his or her ability to conduct activities with economic value. Examples of human capital are a carpenter's ability to build a staircase and a lobbyist's contacts and knowledge of the workings of government. Human capital is most often acquired by experience or through training by others who already have the requisite skills. It is the factor that differentiates raw labor power from skilled expertise at some task or job and is a crucial determinant of productivity.

It is useful to distinguish between **firm-specific** and **general-purpose** (or **nonspecific**) human capital. The former includes skills and knowledge that are valuable only in the context of a particular firm, whereas the latter involves skills and knowledge that increase the person's productivity when working for any of several different employers. Examples of firm-specific human capital include knowledge of the idiosyncracies of the particular firm's machinery or its accounting system, the special terminology and decision procedures used in the firm, and the needs of the firm's customers. Examples of general human capital include knowledge of how to operate a type of machine or prepare accounting statements, a familiarity with general business terminology and procedures, and general skills in sales and marketing.

In a labor market with no specific human capital, no firm would ever invest in training workers to improve their general-purpose human capital. Such training would only increase the workers' market-determined wages, reflecting their increased productivity and value to other employers. There would be no payoff for the investing firm. In contrast, workers would have reason to develop general human capital that makes them more productive and valuable to a variety of potential employers because that would lead to higher earnings for themselves. A farm worker, for example, might learn to harvest fruit more efficiently, but could not expect much training from the farmer. Similarly, a young manager might pursue an MBA degree at night, but his or her current employer would be unlikely to help pay the tuition.

It might seem worthwhile for an employer to invest in workers' specific human capital, that is, in knowledge and skills that are valuable only in this specific firm. There is no market pressure to pay workers more for these skills because they do not increase the workers' value to other employers. There is little reason for the workers to make such investments, however, and unless they stay with the firm for an extended period, the firm itself will gain only a small fraction of the potential benefits of the investment. For example, an itinerant farm worker has little reason to invest in learning about the peculiarities of a particular farmer's fields or equipment, and the farmer gains little by investing in training about those things. When workers are highly mobile, the levels of investment in firm-specific human capital are apt to be quite low.

Defects of the Classical Model

Some labor markets do seem to operate in much the way the classical model describes. An example is the market for itinerant farm workers, who move from employer to employer as new crops are ready for planting or harvesting. For many other occupations—especially ones with highly trained workers—the actual markets seem to work very differently. Pay levels fluctuate much less than would be predicted by the classical model; pay cuts, in particular, are quite rare. Actual turnover and worker mobility are limited relative to the predictions of the model: After an initial period early in the average worker's career when mobility is high, workers frequently continue to work for a single employer for a period of many years. Firms do not adjust employment levels so frequently as the classical theory would suggest, and they often eagerly sponsor training programs for their employees that augment both general and specific human capital. Meanwhile, employees invest in acquiring skills and knowledge that are valuable only in the firms currently employing them, and they do so expecting that they will be rewarded. Simply put, the elementary classical model presents a very poor description of employment relations in advanced economies.

LABOR CONTRACTS AND THE EMPLOYMENT RELATIONSHIP

To begin understanding some of the features of actual labor markets and employment policies, it is useful to consider the nature of the relationship between the employer and the employee.

Employment as a Relationship

The conclusion that pay equals productivity at each point in time is based on the idea that labor is bought and sold in spot markets, where a given wage payment purchases a given, observable amount of a particular, well-specified kind of work to be performed at a given time and place and under given conditions. Such markets do exist. The vast bulk of the transactions for labor services, however, are mediated by complex contracts that cover longer, often indefinite periods of time. These contracts often uncouple pay and productivity. They are incomplete and involve important implicit elements, and they assign significant authority to the employer. Instead of a simple, arm's-length market transaction between buyer and seller, most employment actually represents a complex, long-term *relationship* between the employer and employee. We seek in this section to understand some of the reasons for and consequences of these relationships.

Employment Contracts

The employment contract is typically quite imprecise. The employees agree that—within limits that are rarely completely described and only partly understood—they will use their minds and muscles to undertake the tasks that the employer directs them to do, perhaps using the methods that the employer specifies. The employer agrees to pay the employees. The range of actions that might be requested or required is unclear. Future compensation and even the criteria used to determine future pay and promotions are unspecified. The mechanisms to be used in case of dispute are not stated, nor are the penalties for most possible violations of the contract. Yet these are among the most important contracts that any of us enter throughout our lives.

Union contracts are more explicit on all these dimensions, but in some countries, including the United States, they cover only a fraction of the work force. This in itself puts into even sharper focus the questions of why most employment contracts are incomplete and largely implicit and why they give such discretionary authority to the employer.

The incompleteness, the implicit nature, and the shape of the employment contract are all responses to the impossibility of complete contracting. The factors preventing complete contracting are discussed in earlier chapters. Briefly, they involve the difficulties of foreseeing all the events that might possibly arise over time and the appropriate actions to take, the difficulties of unambiguously describing these events and actions even if they could be foreseen, and the costs of negotiating acceptable explicit agreements over these many terms even if they could be described. Union contracts attempt to specify terms more fully and explicitly. They are notoriously costly to settle, and the rigidities that they impose are a frequently noted source of inefficiencies. The usual employment contract instead is much more a **relational contract**: It frames the relationship, specifying broad terms and objectives and putting in place some mechanisms for decision making when unforeseen events occur.

AUTHORITY IN EMPLOYMENT RELATIONS   The decision-making mechanism in the employment contract is basically that the boss can order the employee to do anything that is not explicitly forbidden by the contract's terms or by law. Strikes and formalized grievance procedures aside, the employee's only real recourse is to quit, which he or she is typically free to do at any time. At the same time, at least in the United States and many other industrialized countries, the employer is basically free to fire the worker when and if he or she wishes: Employment is "at will."

The usual Marxian explanation for this pattern is that the employer has all the power in the bargaining, and the contractual relationship that emerges simply reflects this distribution of power, maximizing the employer's gains by exploiting the employee's weakness. However, many detailed aspects of the contract can be understood better as attempts to increase the total value of the relationship.

First, in any particular circumstance it is often efficient that one party clearly have the residual decision-making authority. Otherwise, the costs of bargaining will be incurred whenever a situation arises that was not covered explicitly by the contract. These costs, in the form of delay or failure to reach agreement, could be fatal to the success of the organization. Imagine what would happen if the employer and employees had to bargain anew every time a new order came in, a shipment was late, or a machine broke down. If assigning all the authority to one party presents too great a danger of harmful opportunism in some circumstances, then the efficient contract will provide for alternative governance procedures—either different decision-making processes that involve more parties or constraints on the decision maker's allowable choices. In most circumstances, however, the efficient solution is for the authority to rest with a single party: Someone needs to be the boss.

Note that this argument applies even when there is a single employee. When multiple employees are involved, and their tasks must be coordinated, there is a second advantage to having one person with decision-making authority. Even if the boss were not needed actually to coordinate the employees' actions—they might be left to determine the plan of action by themselves—having someone who has the power to specify and enforce a plan if the employees cannot agree among themselves and who is responsible for the plan's success contributes to achieving the desired coordination.

Second, it is often desirable that the same party have the residual decision-making authority in all events not explicitly foreseen in the contract. Otherwise, events would have to be described with sufficient precision to specify who has the authority. It is possible that events could be described well enough to permit this, although the contract still would not spell out the actions to be taken in these events.

Indeed, the bankruptcy laws essentially take this form: Residual decision-making authority shifts to the court-appointed trustee in any event where bankruptcy occurs. Nevertheless, there are advantages to having a unique residual decision maker at any one point in time.

The third issue is: Who should have the authority and be the residual decision maker? There are two angles to take on this, each relating to a particular theory of what a firm is.

THE FIRM AS A NEXUS OF CONTRACTS   One theory views the firm as a legal fiction— a contracting entity that serves to economize on the number of bilateral contracts that are needed to coordinate activity. Actual work and decisions are carried out by individual people who rely on one another. It would be costly and wasteful, however, for every pair of workers to have their own contract and for there to be contracts between each worker, supplier, and customer. Instead, each party enters a single contract with the legal fiction that is the firm, economizing on information and contract expenses. If the actions of N different individuals need to be coordinated to achieve potential benefits, then there would have to be $N(N - 1)/2$ separate bilateral contracts to link all the parties directly. By creating a "firm," only N contracts must be written, one between each individual and the firm. The difference in the number of required contracts grows very rapidly as N increases. With $N = 5$, the difference is $10 - 5 = 5$; with $N = 50$, the difference is $1,175$; and with $N = 500$, the difference is $124,250$. With imperfect, incomplete contracting and costly communication, there are then coordination advantages to having the representative of the firm decide what is to be done when unforeseen circumstances arise because the firm is the unique entity that is a party to all the contracts.

This still leaves open the issue: Who should appoint the boss? The arguments in Chapter 9 regarding the efficient allocation of ownership suggest that in many circumstances it is appropriate that the owners of capital (or the owners' agent) have the residual decision-making power. But which capital? The decisions that are made under the employment contract will affect the value of both the human capital and the physical capital being used in the firm. If the workers' human capital is at greater risk, then it would be efficient to give them the residual decision power. This is effectively done in many human-capital intensive businesses. For example, university professors have the ultimate decision-making power in regard to academic matters in their institutions, and many accounting, consulting, architectural, and medical-practice firms are organized as partnerships so that the owners of human capital have the residual decision rights. In most employment relationships, however, most of the risk is arguably borne by the owners of the physical capital, and it is then efficient to give them the decision power.

THE FIRM AS A BEARER OF REPUTATION   A second, complementary theory views the firm as a reputation bearer. A major potential motivation to treat others fairly is to build and maintain a good reputation that will facilitate future dealings. As we saw in Chapter 8, the value of a good reputation increases with the number of times it may be used. Thus, if one party to a relationship has a longer horizon than another, the first party, when put in a position of power, will have a stronger incentive to build and maintain a reputation with the other parties for using power well. This argues for giving the residual decision power to whichever party to a relationship has the longer horizon.

A firm generally can continue in existence after any of the individuals originally involved in it are long gone. For example, the Hudson's Bay Company is over 300 years old. Further, it seems reasonable that reputations can attach to firms rather than just to individuals. There are books listing firms that are considered to be good places to work. Firms also have reputations for making good- or bad-quality products, and credit reports are issued partly based on the individual firm's past financial record. Then a firm, with its potentially unlimited lifetime, would have much stronger incentives to act in a way that builds and maintains a good reputation than any mortal person. This incentive would be accentuated by the greater frequency of dealings within any given period of time that a firm would have relative to most individuals. A firm that behaved well would have a good reputation to which would attach a stream of rents; one that acted badly would get a bad reputation and would be less valuable.

Of course, the firm itself does not take the actions that lead to a reputation, nor does it have use for the rents that accrue to a good reputation. People act in the name of the firm, and it is they who value the resulting rents. Thus, we are apparently back up against the regrettably short horizons of individual mortals. If, however, those who are in a position to influence the reputation of the firm can sell their claims on the rent stream that attaches to a good firm reputation, then they will have an incentive to make sure the reputation remains unsullied. This is true whether they affect the reputation directly by their own actions or indirectly by determining the incentives of those who do act in the name of the firm. Thus, both the decision power and the ownership of the rents should attach to those who can most easily and effectively transfer their claims at full value.

In most contexts, this would seem to be the investors in the firm, whose claims take the form of marketable securities, rather than, say, laborers who would need to sell their jobs to transfer their claims. This is another reason why the boss as the person with the power to make decisions in unforeseen eventualities should very often be the representative of the providers of physical capital, rather than the providers of labor.

Implicit Contracts

Although the written employment contract is quite incomplete, it is supplemented by unwritten, often completely implicit understandings. These implicit contractual terms govern many of the crucial elements of the employment relationship, including pay, work assignments, and employers' and employees' duties to one another. They are not expected to be enforced by the courts or other third parties. Rather, they are intended to be **self-enforcing:** They are structured so that the parties have incentives to abide by them for fear of the consequences of violating the agreement. As described in Chapter 8, the incentives in self-enforcing agreements require that each party receive a stream of rents from the relationship, so that each will be hesitant to do anything that endangers its continuation.

For agreements to be enforced by courts or other outsiders, these third parties must be able to understand the agreement and verify how the contracting parties have behaved, so that they can determine accurately whether the contract was violated. For self-enforcement, it is necessary only that the affected parties understand their obligations to one another, that they can observe each other's behavior, and that each party enjoys a sufficiently large stream of rents from the contract. The weaker informational conditions of self-enforcing contracts tend to enlarge the scope for implicit contracts over explicit ones relying on court enforcement.

As a simple example of how an implicit contract might work, suppose a firm and its workers would like to agree that the workers will work especially hard and that the firm will pay them a bonus at the end of each period if they do so. The workers can always violate the contract by not working hard, and the firm can violate it by falsely claiming that the workers have shirked and then refusing to pay the bonus that has been earned. Even if the firm and the workers observe the actual effort level, court enforcement requires that the workers be able to prove that they actually worked at the agreed level when the firm claims they shirked. Similarly, the firm must be able to prove that the workers shirked when they claim they did not.

For a self-enforcing, implicit contract to work, it is enough that neither party be able to gain from cheating. The workers' principal threats are to quit or to refuse to continue working hard. For these threats to deter the firm from cheating, the arrangement must be beneficial for the firm as well; that is, the firm must be getting rents or quasi-rents from the arrangement that it would lose if the arrangement were terminated. On the workers' side, shirking and not receiving the bonus must be worse than working hard and being rewarded, so the bonus must at least offset the costs of the extra effort. Moreover, the workers always have the option of quitting and going elsewhere, so adhering to the contract must pay them more than (or at least as much as) this alternative. Thus, in total there must be a strictly positive surplus from the agreement, and each party must share in it.

Note that it is the prospect of future gains from maintaining the relationship that provide the incentives under the implicit contract. This in itself gives a reason for employment relationships to be enduring, long-term ones.

THE ROLE OF FIRM-SPECIFIC HUMAN CAPITAL   This arrangement requires the existence of rents or quasi-rents. Rents are likely to be competed away in any long-term relationship but quasi-rents, which represent a normal return on past investments, can be lasting. The returns on investments in firm-specific human capital might be a source of the needed quasi-rents. Once a firm has trained its workers in firm-specific skills, the workers will be more valuable to the firm than new replacement workers would be. Thus, as long as they are not paid the full value of the extra output of their firm-specific human capital (and note that there is no market pressure to make them receive this extra value), the firm would earn a quasi-rent from their continued employment that might be enough to deter its cheating and having them quit. Meanwhile, as long as the workers do at least as well working hard and receiving their bonuses as they would by shirking or quitting and going elsewhere, they will have no reason to violate the implicit contract.

Risk Sharing in Employment Relations

In the classical model of labor markets, worker incomes can fluctuate substantially over time. Workers are constantly paid their marginal products, which change not just with their personal conditions but also with the state of demand faced by firms and the prices and productivity of other inputs. This arrangement is inefficient in the normal case where workers are risk averse. Moral hazard and adverse selection impede shifting these risks to those outside the employment relationship, and, to some extent, within it as well. Nevertheless, such risk sharing can and does take place.

EMPLOYMENT AND INCOME SECURITY   The firm's owners will often be in a position to take on some of this risk, insuring the workers' incomes against random fluctuations. Indeed, one of the earliest contributors to the theory of the firm, Frank Knight, argued that the shifting of risk and authority to the employer was the defining characteristic of the firm. The entrepreneur takes the income risk, pays the employees a fixed wage, and then takes the decision-making power to protect against moral hazard.

If the firm can be treated as risk neutral (perhaps because it is owned by investors with well-diversified portfolios), then, other things being equal, it should seek to insulate the workers fully against income risk. This provides a value-creating service for the employees while imposing no cost or risk premium on the risk-neutral firm. The expected pay level can be reduced without harming the workers if the firm takes on some of the risk they would otherwise face, and so both sides can gain.

If the firm is risk neutral and the workers' preferences between income and leisure exhibit no wealth effects, then the firm should also insulate the workers against the effects of unemployment (because with no wealth effects, any kind of risk is equivalent to some income risk, and we have already seen that it pays to insure income risks completely). In this special case, the workers' utilities are made independent of any shocks to their productivity or the fortunes of the firm. The pay-productivity link would be almost completely broken: At the time of hiring, pay would be linked to *expected* productivity, but afterwards there would be no attempt to match pay to realized productivity.

Even in this special case, full insurance does not mean that everyone always works and there are no layoffs. If realized productivity is low, then the optimal amount of labor to use (defined by the equality of the marginal product of work and its marginal disutility to the worker) is also low. There would be waste in maintaining high levels of employment because what would be produced would not be worth the cost. In that case, not everyone may be called in to work, and if the firm faces a permanent reduction in its need for workers, some will be let go. However, those who are not working because of temporary layoffs are still paid by the firm: The pay level makes them as well-off not working as they would be if they had to work and incur the cost of effort. Further, any workers let go will receive severance payments that make up for the loss of their jobs. Thus, those who are working and those who are laid off would be equally well-off under this ideal contract.

INCENTIVE PROBLEMS AND PARTIAL INSURANCE   The prescription that firms fully insulate workers against income risk obviously is not followed in actual employment relationships. There is some insurance, but it is only partial. It is important to understand why this is the case.

The hypothesis that firms are approximately risk neutral is most applicable to the kinds of random events that affect individual workers independently. For such individual shocks, the firm can act much like an insurance company, balancing out the losses incurred by some employees with the gains experienced by others. However, as we argue in Chapter 7, insurance cannot work for all kinds of risks. In particular, changes in such factors as general economic conditions, interest rates, or energy prices have such widespread effects that the firm cannot be risk neutral with respect to those. Moreover, if the company has limited access to financial capital, the possibility of bankruptcy or of disruption in valuable investments makes it costly to insure workers against the kinds of events that affect the overall prospects of the firm. Under efficient arrangements, the workers will have to bear at least some portion of these kinds of risks.

This fact creates a problem, however, when the firm has better information about its financial health and prospects than do the workers or their unions. The firm's management may be tempted to exaggerate financial difficulties in order to justify paying lower wages to workers. To prevent this, contracts or bargaining must be arranged so that the firm bears a cost of some sort for claiming the kind of hard times that lead to lower wages.

If there is a union, one possibility is that the firm might have to weather a strike to verify its claim. The strikes that have sometimes followed management demands for wage reductions at troubled airlines in the United States are examples. Firms are often more willing to weather a strike when anticipated demand is low because the opportunity costs of a reduced level of operations are lower than they would be if times really were good. Thus, such a willingness may be a credible signal of the firm's information and assertion that times are hard. An alternative is that the firm may have to engage in layoffs to convince workers that times are hard and wage concessions

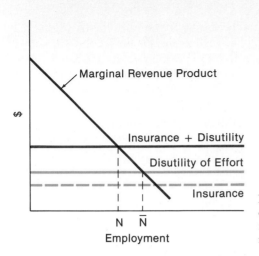

Figure 10.2: The efficient level of employment is $\overline{N}$, but, with unemployment insurance, the firm and workers can do better for themselves by choosing the lower level, N.

are needed. Once again, when anticipated demand is actually high, it may be too expensive for the firm to reduce its work force just to feign financial difficulty, so layoffs can be a credible signal that anticipated demand is low.

In each of these cases, the firm provides only partial insurance to workers against fluctuations in their incomes and employment. Even when a risk-neutral government agency provides unemployment insurance, however, full insurance may be impeded by a moral hazard problem. As illustrated in Figure 10.2, the firm may be able to collude with the employees by laying them off and allowing them to collect unemployment insurance, thereby increasing their total value, even when layoffs would not otherwise have been the outcome.

Another possible source of incomplete insurance is the desire to provide incentives to workers. We have seen in Chapters 6 and 7 and will see again in Chapters 12 and 13 that providing effort incentives may require the workers to bear some risk. This would also prevent completely insuring them against productivity shocks if the effects of these shocks on measured performance are not freely distinguishable from the effects of variations in effort. Alternatively, effort incentives may be provided by workers receiving efficiency wages that exceed their outside opportunities as long as they are not caught shirking and by their being fired otherwise. If the technology for monitoring is imperfect and sometimes results in a hard worker being incorrectly labeled a shirker and fired, then insurance is obviously incomplete.

One of the biggest problems with any attempt to insulate workers fully from risk, however, is that they may behave opportunistically. To be fully insulated means not only that the worker's wage does not fall during hard times or when the worker is found to be of low ability, but also that it does not rise during good times or when the worker is found to be of high ability. In the latter case, however, there is a danger that the workers may quit to pursue higher wages elsewhere. In practice, it is easier to protect workers from the risk of bad times and low ability than to collect a share of the benefits they may receive when times are good or their abilities turn out to be higher than expected. This too limits the possibilities for employers to insure workers' incomes.

PARTIAL INSURANCE AND AGE-WAGE PROFILES   The ideas we have just described have been used to provide another explanation of the observed positive relationship between age or experience and pay. Suppose that individual workers' abilities are initially unknown both to the workers and to all their potential employers, but that high-ability workers are more likely to produce larger output (however measured). Over the course of the workers' careers, observations of their performance then generate information about their abilities. Each instance of good performance increases the likelihood that the workers are really of high ability, and bad realized results reduce this estimate of their talent. If the workers were always paid according to their (estimated) productivity, their pay would vary up and down as the estimate of their abilities moved with their realized performance. Bearing this risk is costly to the workers, and efficiency would call for all the risk to be shifted to the firm if it is risk neutral. This would result in the workers' pay being made independent of their estimated ability and productivity.

This complete risk-transfer solution is feasible only if both the employer and the employees can commit themselves to it. The employer must be able to promise not to lay the employees off or to reduce their wages if their productivity turns out to be low, and the employees must be able to commit not to quit in favor of better-paying jobs if their productivity turns out to be high. In practice, the firm is likely to be better able to make such a commitment by using its reputation as a bond. The workers would usually have more difficulty making such commitment in any credible way because they have less use in their business dealings for a reputation as one who does not quit. Another way to achieve commitment that is sometimes effective is to write a legally binding contract. However, a long-term labor contract that binds the workers to the firm and prevents them from quitting might not be enforceable in the courts, which might treat the agreement as an unlawful slavery contract.

Predictions. Whatever the reason, if the workers cannot commit themselves, then the complete risk-transfer solution is not possible. The most complete risk transfer that can be achieved is for the employer to make a commitment not to lay the workers off or to reduce their wages. If an implicit contract of this kind described actual arrangements, what patterns would we expect to see in earnings data?

First, the workers' observed level of wages would never fall. They would however, rise when the workers were particularly successful and the market's estimate of their ability rose. These wage increases might be accompanied by job changes, if the highly valued workers were bid away by other employers, but they need not be if the current employers meet the competition. Thus, wages would tend to rise over the workers' careers, even though their (actual but imperfectly observed) productivity remains the same over their lifetimes.

As well, when workers do get raises or accept new jobs, their new wages will be less than their currently estimated marginal productivity. The reason for this is subtle. Competition among employers will mean that when a worker is hired, his or her expected future wages over the period of employment must be equal to his or her expected marginal product. For workers who prove to be especially productive, future wages will increase to match. For workers who perform poorly, however, there will be no wage reductions, so the firm will be paying more than the worker's marginal product. Consequently, according to the model, the firm will, on average, overpay its older, long-term workers. Because pay must equal marginal product over the worker's career, it follows that, on average, the firm pays its younger, newer workers less than their marginal products. In effect, the difference between estimated marginal product and wage is an insurance premium paid by younger workers to guard against future wage reductions.

An additional prediction is that for any given age and estimated level of ability, wages will tend to be higher for workers with more experience and especially for those with longer job tenure in the same firm. This happens for two reasons. One is that the longer the worker's employment history, the less uncertainty there is about his or her productivity and the lower the insurance premium that is deducted in determining the worker's offered wage in any new job. The second reason, which reinforces the first, is that a worker with longer tenure in the same firm is more likely to have had his or her productivity overestimated since his or her last job change and consequently to be paid more than his or her currently estimated marginal product.

Finally, for any given level of experience and estimated ability or productivity, wages will tend to be higher for older workers with fewer years remaining to retirement. Once again, the reason is that the implicit insurance premium is lower for older workers because there are fewer remaining years during which the employer may have to subsidize the wage of the worker if he or she proves to be relatively unproductive.

These predicted features have been found in the data relating to pay in the United States and several other countries. Pay cuts are rare, although raises are not. Wages do rise with age and with experience, even after controlling for productivity. Finally, wages tend to vary more among workers as their experience increases. [2]

MANAGING AN EMPLOYMENT AND INCOME SECURITY PLAN   These analyses show that by (even partially) insuring workers' incomes, the firm can reap gains in the form of lower expected pay levels for any level of performance required from the workers. Against this gain must be balanced the costs of providing this insurance. These may be significant if the firm is not fully risk neutral, and they are especially painful when business turns bad but the firm cannot reduce costs by wage cuts or layoffs. Income insurance turns labor into a fixed cost that cannot be avoided in economic downturns. There is also the possibility that insuring incomes will mean divorcing pay and realized productivity and that this will have bad incentive effects. These matters are addressed in more detail in Chapter 12.

Despite this, many firms do seek to provide a measure of insurance. For example, the "Big Three" U.S. automobile manufacturers—General Motors, Ford, and Chrysler—bargained with the United Auto Workers union in the 1980s for changes in work rules that enhanced flexibility and productivity. In return, the auto companies promised unprecedented income insurance: Combining state-provided unemployment benefits with firm-provided funds, laid-off hourly workers would receive up to 85 percent of their regular take-home pay for up to three years, unless they were called back to work or found other jobs. Because even the most enjoyable job involves certain costs, such as the expenses of commuting, meals away from home, wardrobe, child care, and so on, the 85-percent income guarantee amounts to essentially full insurance against the loss of take-home pay. In the first months of the economic downturn that hit in mid-1990, more than 100,000 Big Three auto workers were put on temporary or indefinite layoff and began receiving these benefits.

Of course, the extent to which employees are willing to accept lower wages in return for an income guarantee depends very much on the credibility of the promise. This in turn depends both on the firm's willingness and ability to carry out the promises. For example, in the recession at the start of the 1980s, the Big Three did not fully meet their promises to supplement their workers' state unemployment benefits because the funds they had set up for this purpose had run out and they were unwilling or unable to tap other sources of money for this purpose. Going into the recession of the early 1990s, the auto firms had accumulated much larger reserves to meet their new contractual guarantees. However, there was some question of their ability to make the payments if the recession proved to be especially deep or extended: General Motors alone lost $1.4 billion dollars in the last quarter of 1990, and together the Big Three lost another $2.33 billion in the first three months of 1991. [3]

---

[2] J.L. Medoff and K.G. Abraham, "Experience, Performance and Earnings," *Quarterly Journal of Economics*, 95 (1980), 703–36.

[3] For more details see Gregory A. Patterson, "Hourly Auto Workers Now on Layoff Have a Sturdy Safety Net," *The Wall Street Journal* (January 29, 1991), A-1.

Some firms attempt to avoid layoffs altogether. Large companies in Japan follow this practice for their permanent employees (both blue collar and white collar workers), and the Japanese automobile companies have extended this policy to the hourly workers in their U.S. production facilities. When weak demand necessitates production cutbacks, temporary and part-time workers are let go, but the regular employees continue, although early retirements may be encouraged. To keep the workers busy, training and preventative maintenance activities are increased, and, if necessary, the firm may increase its in-house production of parts that are normally purchased from suppliers. Lincoln Electric Company, the most successful U.S. manufacturer of welding equipment, is another example of a firm with a no-layoff policy. It maintained employment in the severe recession of the early 1980s, but only by assigning production workers to such activities as repainting the factory. Such a demonstration of commitment can be crucially important to the workers' believing the firm's promises.

Borrowing and Lending in Employment Relationships

Just as the firm can use its superior risk-bearing ability to insure workers' incomes profitably, so too can it use any superior access that it may have to capital and other markets on their behalf and thereby realize a mutual gain. If the firm can borrow more, or at better rates, than can its employees, it may be efficient for the firm to lend them money to allow them to consume in advance of income receipts. For example, Stanford University lends money to its faculty to finance buying homes in the very expensive housing market near the university. Another example comes from professional partnerships, such as law firms and multiple-practitioner medical practices. In these firms, new partners have to buy into the partnership, but it is common for the firm to lend the necessary funds to those selected for partnership. In law firms this is usually accomplished through a simple loan. In medical practices, the new partner is sometimes expected to buy his or her share of the accounts receivable over five years, so that in effect the other partners lend the new partner money over this period. In towns dominated by a single employer, it was common for a company-owned store to extend credit to employees against their paychecks for purchases of food and clothing. Popular accounts of this practice often accentuate the difficult plight of a worker heavily in debt to the company store. Nevertheless, because these workers probably lacked access to other sources of credit, the loans may well have enhanced efficiency.

Instances of the firm investing for its employees because of better access to the capital markets are less common. In many countries, however, pensions are tax-favored forms of receiving income: No income tax is due on amounts paid by the firm into pension funds, nor are the earnings of these funds taxed as received, although withdrawals after retirement are taxed as they are made. These tax-code provisions favor the firm's paying some part of compensation in the form of pension-fund contributions, in essence saving on behalf of the employees. Deferred compensation, under which some of the money earned in one year is paid out in later years, also involves an element of the firm's saving on the workers' behalf. Both of these also have the effect of increasing the strength of the links between the employer and employees.

RECRUITING, RETENTION, AND SEPARATION

With employment being a complex, long-term, multifaceted relationship rather than a simple market transaction, both sides will be particularly careful to avoid entering the relationship with an inappropriate partner, and, once it is entered, both will be concerned with maintaining and building the value of the relationship. Still, mistakes will be made in the initial matching of employers and employees, and circumstances may change the value of the relationship for either or both sides. Thus, both must also be concerned with ending the relationship when (and only when) this is appropriate.

From the employer's side, these concerns are the focus of **human-resource management**. Managing the organization's work force and maintaining the value of the relationship with the employees is a central task of management—not just of those specifically employed in the Personnel Department, but of all managers. The chapters that follow examine two central issues in managing human resources: job assignments and promotions (Chapter 11) and motivation and compensation (Chapters 12 and 13). Here we first address aspects of the problems of selecting and recruiting new employees, of retaining them once they are hired, and of severing the employment relationship when the time comes to do so.

These are very broad issues: A full-scale treatment can absorb several full graduate courses. Obviously, we cannot attempt such a treatment here. Instead, we focus on the difficulties imposed by the inevitable differences that occur in the information available to (potential or actual) employers and employees. These informational asymmetries are especially a problem in recruiting, where each side has information about itself that the other does not have but that is important for judging the quality of the potential match.

Recruiting

Organizations face an ongoing need to recruit new members. The decision about the number and sort of people to recruit depends on the organization's strategy, its technology, and its forecasts about the future.

Forecasts enter on both the supply and demand side. The demand side is fairly obvious: A firm anticipating rapid growth will see a need for more people. Thus, the U.S. investment banks expanded rapidly through the first half of the 1980s, expecting that the new products they were able to develop and market in the wake of financial-market deregulation and the growing business opportunities associated with corporate takeovers and restructuring would lead to greater needs for professional staff. The crash of the stock market in 1987 and the decline of merger and acquisitions activity in 1989 cooled their hiring significantly, and in fact led many of them to reduce employment.

Consideration of the supply side is important too. For example, some universities began heavily recruiting faculty members in the late 1980s and early 1990s, even though they had no immediate need for more staff. They did so because they anticipated that the impending retirement of the large number of faculty hired in the expansion of higher education in the late 1950s and early 1960s, combined with no apparent growth in the supplies of new faculty being trained, would yield consequent labor-market tightness in the mid-1990s.

The strategy and technology of the organization also have some fairly straightforward implications for recruiting. A dance company has little use for electrical engineers, for example, whereas a firm that has adopted what we have called a "modern" manufacturing strategy has a need for production workers who are able to master multiple tasks and who can take individual responsibility for diagnosing problems and responding to them.

The cost of firing or laying off employees is a significant element in the decision about how many to hire. These costs are affected both by the firm's strategy and by public policy (see the box entitled "Public Policy Toward Layoffs"). A firm that has a policy of lifetime employment for its workers will be more reluctant to take on new employees in the face of what might prove to be a temporary need than would one

Public Policy Toward Layoffs

In various Western European countries, a firm that lets workers go is obliged by law to pay them generous severance payments. For example, in France, Israel, and Norway, a worker with ten years of service is entitled to a year's pay on severance, and in Italy the figure is 20-months' pay. In Sweden, the introduction of new legal restrictions on layoffs in the early 1970s was accompanied by rises in both vacancy rates and unemployment in firms. Another study of Western Europe found that similar laws reduce employment and labor-force participation and tend to increase unemployment. The study also suggests that increases in the severance-pay requirements were responsible for a significant part of the increase in unemployment that has been experienced in a number of Western European nations during the 1970s and 1980s. Although neither study addressed the effect of these laws and regulations on the formation of new firms, it might be hypothesized that by raising the costs of failure, they discourage start-ups.

There has been an active public debate in the United States concerning the responsibilities of firms to employees in the context of mass layoffs and plant closings such as those that followed some of the hostile takeovers of the 1980s. There was a push for legislation at the federal level to require a firm contemplating a plant closing to give workers six-months' advance notice. Employers successfully resisted, and the proposal did not become law. Their arguments were that such public announcements of strategic intentions would be exceedingly costly because competitors would learn their plans. As well, customers, fearing for the firm's viability, would be induced to seek other sources of supply. Further, the firms argued that if such notice were valuable, workers could bargain for it in the negotiations between individual firms and their employees.

Sources: Eugenia Kazamaki, *Firm Search, Sector Shifts and Unemployment* (Stockholm: Swedish Institute for Social Research, 1991), and Edward Lazear, "Job Security Provisions and Employment," *Quarterly Journal of Economics*, 105 (1990), 699–726.

that has no such policy. This presumably has an effect on the hiring of permanent employees in major Japanese firms, which are reknown for having such policies. The rapid expansion of the Japanese economy over the last several decades, however, may have dampened this effect by reducing concerns about the possible need to cut employment.

At the same time, guarantees of long-term employment or protection in the event of layoffs are attractive to risk-averse workers and thus help to attract people to the firm. Job security was a major element in the collective bargaining between the U.S. automobile manufacturers and the United Auto Workers union in their negotiations during the 1980s. The practice of such firms as IBM, Hewlett Packard, and Lincoln Electric of avoiding layoffs has helped them in recruiting. Yet for some occupations, a willingness to take risks is an important asset, and firms in such businesses should be concerned about attracting people who are very risk averse. This raises the problem of attracting the right sort of applicants.

ATTRACTING APPLICANTS   The first step in attracting applicants is making the organization and its needs known to potential members. Sometimes the problem is in making them aware of the existence of the organization and the sort of opportunities it offers. For example, in the 1980s business schools worldwide faced a continuing shortage of faculty. In the North American business school faculty labor market, the number of net openings in any given year generally was twice the number of people entering the field from graduate schools. This gap persisted despite the schools' offering salaries and working conditions that would seem extremely attractive. Academic-year starting salaries for new faculty in the top U.S. business schools for 1990 were in the range of $7,000 per month, with higher figures in some specialties (such as accounting and finance). Teaching loads were low (perhaps four hours of actual classroom teaching per week for 30 weeks per year), generous research support was provided, and the prospects of eventually receiving tenure appeared good. It appears that the schools did not do an adequate job of making the opportunities they offered known to the relevant population. In other situations, however, the problem can actually be an excess of applicants, as the box on applications to MBA programs illustrates. In such situations, it can be useful to encourage self-selection among the applicants, so that only those with the qualities the firm seeks will be attracted to apply.

SELF-SELECTION AND SCREENING IN RECRUITING   Simply making what the organization offers and what it expects known to the relevant group can induce some self-selection among potential applicants. This can sometimes be a by-product of other policies. The very clear image that IBM long projected of white shirt and dark suit with somber tie always in place very effectively informed potential employees about the firm, so that those who were attracted were the sort of people the company wanted. However, policies can also be designed with the specific intent of affecting self-selection.

Recall that the basic idea in screening is for the relatively uninformed party to design policies or procedures that induce the informed to make choices that effectively reveal their private information. In the present context, the privately informed parties are the potential applicants, who know more than does the firm about their work and risk attitudes, their abilities and interests, their long-term plans, and various other personal factors that are of interest to the firm as a potential employer.[4] The choices they make are simply whether or not to apply for a given opening. The idea is for the firm to design aspects of its policies and structure to attract application from the sorts of people it wants while discouraging those it does not want.

We have seen examples of this in earlier chapters. Pay that is linked tightly to performance will be most attractive to those who know (or believe) themselves to be unusually productive because they expect that this pay system will reward them exceptionally well. Another example of screening is the use of seniority-based pay to discourage applications from people who know that they are likely to leave the firm after a relatively short time. Initially workers are not paid as well by a firm using this strategy as they would be elsewhere, but they are compensated for this shortfall later in their careers with pay levels that exceed their market opportunities. Only those who intend to stay will be willing to join a firm using such a policy.

Other aspects of human-resource policy can help promote self-selection. For

---

[4] Certainly the employer has private information about its characteristics that the applicants do not have: what sort of people it is seeking; what job responsibilities, training and pay it will offer; what the opportunities for promotion are; and what sort of experience it will be to work at this firm. However, the applicant typically will be able to gather this information from observing the firm, talking to present and former employees, and reading publications, and the firm's concern with its reputation can limit any incentives it might have to conceal or misrepresent this information.

MBA Student Admissions

In the late 1980s the leading graduate programs in business in the United States each received many more applications for admission from well-qualified people than they could possibly accommodate in their MBA classes. For example, Harvard regularly got at least eight applications for each place in its program, and Stanford got about a dozen applications for each place in its class. The various schools take some pride in attracting so many exceptional candidates, and they use increases in the number of applications they receive as a competitive selling point. Yet, there is a sense in which a huge number of applicants for each place is evidence that the schools are not doing a good job recruiting students!

Handling and selecting from among all these applications is a monumental task for the schools. Each application must be logged in, checked for completeness, read and evaluated by several people, and compared with others. The candidates who are to be offered admission must be selected and notified, and the others must be informed about their being rejected. These are not the only costs: For the bulk of the applicants, the time and effort they and their references put into their applications comes to nought.

To minimize these costs, the ideal solution would be for each school to do such a fine job of communicating what it seeks in its applicants that the only ones who actually apply are the ones who would be admitted from the current pool and would accept the offer to enroll. Of course, communicating all this would be outrageously costly, especially because each school aims to assemble the best *class* it can, which is not necessarily made up of the people with the top test scores and grades. Many schools' admissions criteria involve not only academic performance and ability but also managerial experience and promise and the individual's contribution to the diversity of the class.

A subtle point is that even if perfect self-selection could be achieved in this context, the schools would still need to examine all the applications. If they did not, but instead simply counted on self-selection and accepted the students as they applied, then the students would not be motivated to self-select.

example, the benefit policy can be used to promote self-selection, as when a retail clothing store offers employee discounts. The discounts tend to be most attractive to those who are especially clothes conscious, and these people in turn are perhaps more likely to be effective salespeople for fashion wear. The box on military service academies offers another example.

SELECTION CRITERIA AND SIGNALING   Once candidates have been identified, the problem arises of choosing among them. Again, informational asymmetries can beset the process. If the firm has done a good job of indicating what it seeks and what sort of opportunities it offers, then anyone who applies wants a job. Not all applicants will be equally desirable, however, and the employer must sort among them. Clever interviewing and testing techniques designed to elicit the information that the applicants have and the firm needs may help overcome these informational difficulties and promote good hiring decisions. Signaling may be also useful.

The example of signaling in the labor market via educational attainment is

Self-Selection at Military Academies

The three U.S. military service academies (at West Point, Annapolis, and Colorado Springs) require their students to serve a term of active duty in the military after graduation. A common explanation for this practice is that it is simply a way of making the students repay the costs of the university educations they received at government expense. If this explanation were correct, one would expect to find that service academy graduates are paid less than those who join the armed forces after completing a university education on their own, which is contrary to the facts of the case.

An alternative explanation is that the military wants to attract applicants who have a genuine interest in a military career, regardless of their abilities to pay for a college education. The danger in offering a free education with no obligation of military service is that some applicants may apply in order to receive the free education, even though they have no real interest in military careers. Students without a genuine interest in a military career are likely to be discouraged from applying by the regimentation of the academies and the military service requirement.

discussed in Chapter 5. It explains why firms might select employees on the basis of educational attainment or previous work experience, even if these are not directly relevant to the job at hand, provided they are correlated with factors that are of interest. For example, although the specific skills and knowledge gained in the last year at the average high school may rarely be directly relevant on the job, many employers will consider only graduates for employment because they perceive drop-outs as likely to be unmotivated, undisciplined, or less able. Even such minor factors as dress and demeanor in an interview can be signals. So long as those who have the attributes that the firm seeks find it less costly or more beneficial to signal than do those without the attributes, then signaling can arise and be useful to the firm.

Signaling arises from a correlation between observed choices and unobserved characteristics. For example, high-productivity workers might signal their status by their educational attainment. However, screening might also take place on other, nonchoice variables if these are (believed to be) correlated with the unobservable attributes the employer values. For example, if a prestigious school's admissions office is thought to be especially effective in identifying talented individuals, then employers may rationally be willing to give special consideration to those the school has admitted.

SCREENING AND EMPLOYMENT DISCRIMINATION A related idea has been advanced to explain discrimination in employment on the basis of attributes that are not directly relevant to job performance: personal appearance, nationality, sex, ethnicity, and race.

A popular explanation for such discrimination is simply that the employers are bigots who fear or despise members of the groups against whom they discriminate. An argument against this explanation is that there would be profit opportunities in hiring talented people from the groups suffering discrimination. These people have more limited opportunities and so can be attracted more easily than can members of the favored groups. Thus, employers who practice discrimination should be at a competitive disadvantage compared to those who do not, and discrimination should not be viable if competitive pressures are reasonably strong. A similar objection applies to explanations based on prejudice by members of the majority work force. This kind of prejudice can explain workplace segregation, with prejudiced workers banding together in segregated workplaces, but it cannot explain the systematically lower wages paid to members of the disfavored groups.

One response to this criticism is that even if the employer is not personally prejudiced, customers may be. Then it may be economical to serve this taste. If this is to be the explanation of widespread discrimination, however, there must be very widespread bias in the population. Otherwise, it would not be profitable to pander to it so generally. Such a pattern certainly is possible but hard to reconcile with popular support for public policies aimed at fighting employment discrimination.

An alternative explanation of discrimination is based on screening ideas. Suppose that employers believe that some important but not freely observable determinants of success are more likely, for example, to be held by men than women. Then the employers may favor male applicants over female ones who have otherwise identical observable characteristics. If the employers believe that the relative probabilities of success are sufficiently in the males' favor, and if determining whether an applicant actually is qualified is costly, they may even refuse to seriously consider women applicants at all.

This pattern of behavior may be morally repugnant. It is, however, rational behavior if the perceived correlation between sex and the likelihood of success is great enough. The probability of finding a female applicant who is actually competitive is thought to be so small as to not be worth the cost of considering female applicants individually. Unfortunately, if all the relevant employers hold such beliefs, then women never get hired for these positions. Then, *even if the beliefs are completely groundless*, no disconfirming evidence ever is generated because women never get a chance to prove the beliefs are wrong. Thus, the baseless beliefs survive, and with them, the unjustified discrimination.

This discrimination is not just unfair; it is also inefficient because the women's talents are not being put to their best use. This analysis points to the potential value of equal-opportunity programs that require good-faith consideration of all applicants and of affirmative-action programs that require special efforts be made to identify and consider applicants from disadvantaged groups.

Although this sort of discrimination may be rational given the employers' beliefs, the beliefs themselves may be inconsistent with the underlying facts. It might seem, therefore, that the discrimination would not survive a little experimentation, for that would reveal the true state of affairs. Suppose, however, potential employees need to make investments in skill acquisition and that these investments are not freely observable by employers. Then a pattern of discrimination can differentially affect the incentives for investment. The members of the group discriminated against may not expect to receive a full chance to benefit from the skills they acquire and so will not be as willing to invest as those in the favored group. Consequently, the two groups actually do end up being differentially qualified, and the experiments rationalize the discrimination: The bias is self-confirming.

Retention

The costs of recruiting are reason enough to be concerned about retention. Moreover, other things being equal, experienced employees will tend to be more valuable.

HUMAN CAPITAL AND TURNOVER   Either through explicit training or as a by-product of being with the firm, experienced employees will have gained both general and firm-specific human capital. General human capital is valuable in a broad set of employment relationships, and so the worker must be fully compensated for the increased productivity that it brings. Workers' general-purpose human capital thus makes them more valuable but also more costly, so that overall they are no particular bargain. In contrast, firm-specific human capital is valuable only in the particular employment relationship. It can take many forms: knowledge of operating procedures in the firm, of local information sources, of locally specialized language usage, and of customer, supplier, coworker, and machine idiosyncracies; special skills in tasks peculiar to the firm; and membership in the social networks within the firm and between the firm and its suppliers and customers. All of this increases the worker's productivity in the firm. Yet because this capital is of little value outside the firm, it need not be fully compensated, and workers with more firm-specific capital will tend to be a bargain.[5] In losing these workers, the firm also loses the rents and quasi-rents that they generate. Finally, losing a visible employee to a competitor may be taken (both by insiders and outsiders) as a signal that the employee had some bad news about the firm, its prospects, and its competitive position. This can make it harder to recruit and to retain others.

One important response is simply to pay the workers for (at least some part of the value of) their firm-specific human capital, even though there is no direct competitive pressure to do so. Paying workers more than their competitive opportunities not only reduces costly turnover, it also encourages them to develop valuable firm-specific human capital, and it can provide the basis for an efficiency-wage system that leads employees to value their jobs and gives them incentives to work hard at them (see Chapter 8).

OUTSIDE OFFERS   An important issue in retention arises in deciding whether and how to respond to outside offers that employees may receive. If the employer can tell how valuable the outside offer is to an employee, then it can choose to match the outside offer if the employee is sufficiently valuable or otherwise let the employee go. So long as the employers know how the employee will respond, a bidding process between competing employers would lead to a total value-maximizing solution.

This information condition, however, is not likely to be satisfied in reality. Any job has certain nonpecuniary benefits and costs whose values are subjective, known only by the employee. Besides, people may form personal attachments to their coworkers or communities; they may have pride or pleasure in their work and want to see projects through to completion; they may value a firm's style, prestige, or corporate culture; they may have private estimates of the firm's prospects and how these will influence their own futures; or they may simply find one sort of job more or less pleasing to do than another. Given these uncertainties, it is very difficult for the firm to evaluate an outside offer to one of its employees, and so it cannot easily tell what it will take to match the offer. An incentive then arises for the employee to shop for offers and to engage in disingenuous bargaining about how attractive these offers are. This sort of behavior can be quite costly.

The Nonmatching Option.   At the opposite theoretical extreme, when the firm knows the employee's productivity in the firm but has no information about the value of outside offers, the best policy is simply to pay a fixed wage and never respond to outside offers. The fixed wage is higher than what would be offered if there were no threat of outside offers, with the extra amount being in the nature of an insurance payment against having to incur the costs of losing the employee. It will be greater the larger are the losses incurred if the employee leaves.

The great difficulty with this policy is that it requires commitment. Suppose a valued employee comes in with an offer for more than he or she is currently being

---

[5] Of course, the firm may have had to pay for the creation of this capital at an earlier time when the investment was being made, so the returns it gets now are not necessarily the result of exploitation.

paid but much less than he or she is worth to the firm. The employee indicates that he or she did not seek the offer and would rather stay than go, if the firm will only do something about the pay. Refusing to deal in these circumstances is very hard because there are clear gains to both the firm and the employee if he or she is given a raise and stays. Dealing, however, deprives the no-response policy of any credibility it may have had. One hope may lie in responding secretly. The idea would be to explain to the employee the costs of having the no-response policy fail, tell the employee that he or she is nevertheless too valuable to lose, and ask the person not to tell fellow employees that he or she is staying because of receiving the raise. Regardless of the ethical questions this raises, it is a dangerous policy to lie to employees and to ask them to lie to one another.

A closely related strategy is to respond with valuable noncash compensation. At many universities, for example, outside offers to professors are sometimes met by promises of more control in departmental decisions, being named to a prestigious research chair, better laboratory support, and so on. For individuals whose complaints are salary alone, these responses set no unfavorable precedent, yet they can be very effective in helping to retain valuable personnel. At the same time, control and research chairs, by their very nature, cannot be granted to everyone, so granting these to one professor does not establish a clear precedent that others can follow.

Encouraging Outside Offers.   Other organizations follow a diametrically opposed strategy. They normally give minimal raises to everyone, and the only way to get a good raise is to come in with an outside offer. This policy is used by some economics departments and business schools where research is especially highly valued relative to teaching.

The information conditions are, once again, the key to determining when such a strategy may be useful. Evaluating research is notoriously difficult for everyone, but most especially for administrators, and yet what a faculty member's research is worth is likely to be much the same among institutions of comparable rank. The home institution typically begins with only very imprecise information about what a faculty member is worth. An outside offer from a close competitor reveals how highly other comparable institutions value the professor's work. If the university's own estimate confirms the competitor's view, then matching may be an appropriate response. At the same time, if competitors are unwilling to make an attractive offer to the professor, that is evidence that he or she is already overpaid and no exceptional raise is merited.

The problem with this scheme is that it forces talented people to spend time seeking outside offers. This is costly for the university, costly for the offeror, and may lead to the professor actually accepting the offer and leaving the university.

MOBILITY COSTS   A person who changes jobs incurs costs of several kinds such as finding and evaluating another job, negotiating a new employment contract, breaking social links, disrupting family life, and finding a new place to live and new schools for the children. He or she may also suffer financial penalties imposed by the previous employer. There may be **golden handcuffs** on the employee—large amounts of deferred compensation and unvested pensions that will be lost by the departing employee. Sometimes explicit bonds may be forfeited on leaving the firm. Changing jobs will only be worthwhile for the employee if the new job is sufficiently better than the old one to compensate for these transaction costs of moving.

It might seem that the employer would want to institute such penalties because they aid retention—employees can be retained at lower wages than would otherwise be needed. The value maximization principle and the Coase theorem suggest a different analysis, however. It would be inefficient for the employer and employee to agree to any contract in which the employee is discouraged from moving when the

Deferred Compensation and Retention at BellSouth

BellSouth is the fastest growing and most profitable of the regional telephone companies, or "Baby Bells," which resulted from the court-ordered breakup of the AT&T/Bell system, which had dominated the U.S. telephone industry until the 1980s. BellSouth provides local telephone service in the southeastern region of the United States, and it is also a factor in the fiber-optics and cellular telephone industries nationally.

BellSouth reportedly employs an interesting deferred compensation scheme to encourage employees to stay with the firm and adopt a long-term view. Under this scheme, employees can place up to 25 percent of their pay into a special account. The company then augments the employee's contribution. If the employee retires from the company, either at the normal retirement age or by taking mutually agreed early retirement, then the account pays off at more than twice the market rate of interest. On the other hand, if an employee quits, the interest is computed at simply the market rate. The difference can be immense, especially for more senior people: Differences of hundreds of thousands of dollars are possible.

The moving costs that this scheme creates would seem to be an effective means of limiting turnover, especially among people who have been in this plan for long periods. Notice that the scheme provides the firm with an opportunity to reduce the pay of more senior people relative to what it might otherwise have needed to pay. Whether the firm exploits this opportunity or, if not, how it commits itself not to, are interesting issues for study.

value created in the new job is greater than in the current one. Penalties for quitting would make the initial job offer less attractive to the worker and require that other compensating benefits be paid. This will be worthwhile only when the penalties discourage value-reducing job moves.

Separations

Just as a firm may need to attract new employees, it will sometimes need to reduce employment, either permanently because of long-term shifts in its demand for labor or temporarily because of transient shocks that affect productivity. The firm also may have an interest in releasing particular employees who are not working out, even when they would like to stay. At the same time, workers who find that their jobs are a poor match for their talents and interests may want to leave. Such **separations** of employees are important for realizing labor-market efficiency, even in the context of a general pattern of long-term employment relationships.

EFFICIENT SEPARATIONS AND SURPLUS SHARING   A major difficulty with achieving efficient separations is that the party initiating the separation may not have the proper incentives to take full account of all the costs and benefits involved in the decision. As we have already noted, a successful employment relationship typically requires that both the employer and the employee be receiving at least as much from the relationship as from their next-best alternatives and that overall there is a strictly positive surplus being generated. Now suppose now that circumstances change, and one side finds that the relationship is no longer advantageous. For example, the employee may find a better job elsewhere. Then he or she will want to quit if the excess of benefits received in the new job over those in the current employment are larger than are the private costs of moving. This calculation, however, ignores the fact that quitting would destroy the surplus that the current employer enjoys in the relationship. Similarly, the employer's decision about firing an employee will take account of only the employer's gains and losses, and not those that the employee experiences.

One might think that a properly structured system of separation payments could overcome these difficulties. The party initiating the separation would have to make a payment to the other that offsets that party's loss of surplus, and so he or she would internalize the full costs and benefits. There are several informational impediments to a solution of this kind, however.

One problem would be determining the appropriate size of the payments. The value of the relationship to each party is not likely to be freely known by the other, and so the problems of bargaining with privately-known values will arise. Even if these are avoided by settling for some standardized payment levels that do not depend on individual valuations, a second problem arises. If different payments to be made depend on whether the separation is a quit or a layoff, then the distinction can quickly become blurred. An employer can often make an employee's life so miserable at work that he or she just has to quit, or an employee can misbehave so badly that the employer sees no choice but to fire the offender, and yet third parties cannot tell who is to blame. This makes a separation payment system very problematic because it will not be clear who should pay whom.

SENIORITY AND LAYOFFS   Many firms have a policy of "last-in, first-out" on layoffs: The workers with the least seniority are let go first. This is frequently written into union contracts, but some nonunionized firms follow this policy as well.

Firms would voluntarily adopt this policy if more experienced workers were more productive relative to their wages than less experienced ones. As we have noted before, however, the evidence is that the reverse is true: Wages increase faster with experience than does productivity, so that inexperienced workers are paid less than their marginal products whereas older ones are paid more. Thus, the direct incentives would seem to be to lay off the older, more experienced workers first.

Although these incentives are present, following them would undermine the policy embedded in the increasing experience/wage profile. We have seen a number of reasons for adopting this pay pattern, including providing effort incentives and limiting turnover. Both are accomplished by paying workers less than their marginal products early on, then making it up to them later in their careers by pay that exceeds productivity. If workers feared that they would be laid off once they started earning more than their marginal products, they would never enter into such (implicit) contracts. Thus, firms have an incentive to build reputations for keeping on older, more experienced workers, even when they seem overpaid relative to younger people who are let go.

The threat to this policy is that the firm may be tempted to induce the senior employees to quit, and others may not be able to tell that it really was the firm that initiated the separations. Of course, a pattern of senior workers quitting and bitterly denouncing the firm would eventually harm the firm's reputation, but this threat might still not be enough to protect the workers fully. This may be one reason why unions so often demand strict seniority policies, not only in layoffs but also in job assignments and other aspects of job arrangements that the employer might be able to manipulate to affect employees' welfare on the job.

AMBIGUOUS SEPARATIONS AND HUMAN CAPITAL INVESTMENTS   Suppose there is an opportunity to invest in general (nonspecific) human capital, but that employees cannot afford to absorb the costs of this training themselves.[6] An obvious solution would be for the employer to finance its employees' training investments but then to recoup the cost by paying a wage less than the employees' marginal product for some period of time. The problem is that another firm might be willing and able to make an attractive job offer that destroys the arrangement. A financial penalty of just the right magnitude would discourage the employee from leaving just to capture the value of the training, but would still permit the employee to leave if he or she really were more valuable to the other employer.

Thus, for example, some firms that underwrite their employees' study for graduate degrees formally *lend* them the tuition. The company then forgives the debt if the worker stays with the firm for a predetermined period after graduation. The loan may, however, become payable in full if the employee quits before the requisite period has expired.

This solution carries the risk that it may limit efficiency-enhancing job changes unless the employee has accumulated enough money to pay the penalty or the new employer is willing to finance the employee's buyout from the old employment contract. This does happen, of course, but now the new employer has to worry about recouping its investment. A further potential problem is that the scheme may be subject to moral hazard on the part of either the original employer or the employee if it is hard for outsiders to distinguish which party initiated a separation.

To see the difficulty, suppose that the penalty is set prior to the investment being made, that the employee has agreed to continue working for a period after completing the training at the same wage as before, and that the investment turned out badly, so that the employee's productivity was not in fact increased. There would be an obvious problem if the employer could fire the employee in these circumstances and collect the penalty, so suppose that the penalty is structured to become payable only if the employee quits. Still, it may be possible for the firm to induce a quit, and outsiders may be unable to tell who is actually responsible for the separation. Then the firm earns nothing on the unsuccessful investment if the employee stays on but receives the penalty if it can induce a quit. The obvious incentive is to drive the employee out. Of course, fear of this outcome may deter the employee from investing in the acquisiton of the human capital.

Similarly, if the employee can persuade the firm to fire him or her after the investment worked out well, but outsiders cannot tell that the separation is really a quit, then he or she receives the full benefits of the investment in higher wages in a new job, and does not have to pay the penalty. This deters the firm from financing the investment.

CASE STUDY: HUMAN-RESOURCE POLICIES IN JAPAN

A properly constructed human-resource management policy is a system that must fit together, with the various parts being mutually consistent and supporting. It must also fit with the strategy and structure of the organization. Examination of some of the characteristic features of the personnel policies employed in successful large Japanese firms reveals such complementarities.

Hiring and Retention

Two policies have been most frequently noted in discussions of human-resource practices in major Japanese firms: long-term employment guarantees for so-called

---

[6] This condition is not necessarily inconsistent with the absence of wealth effects at the time the initial employment contract is signed.

permanent employees, and recruiting of permanent employees only at the early stages of their careers. Although these two features are actually not uniquely Japanese (as we will see in Chapter 11), they do appear to be carried further in Japan than elsewhere. It is extremely rare for a major Japanese firm to dismiss a permanent employee and similarly rare for one of the leading firms to hire someone at other than one of the lowest, entry levels.

The first clear effect of these policies is in reducing turnover. A widespread policy of hiring only at the bottom means that there are unlikely to be attractive job opportunities in other major firms for experienced, mid-career employees. Meanwhile, smaller firms do not usually offer as attractive compensation as do large ones. They also give fewer advancement opportunities, have less job security, and are less prestigious places to work. These limited opportunities for moving from major firms both make retention easier and simultaneously reduce the costs that employees would otherwise incur in monitoring the market for better opportunities. However, such a system would load too much employment risk on employees if they did not have job security: Being let go would not just mean losing this job, but also being very unlikely ever to find a comparable new one. The permanent-employment policy mitigates this danger, and so it supports the hiring policy: The two are complementary in the language introduced in Chapter 4.

Protecting Interests of Permanent Employees

Still, the limited opportunities for Japanese permanent employees to move to comparable jobs with other major employers means that much of their incomes are quasi-rents: Large amounts could be taken away without pushing the employees' pay below the levels available in their next-best alternatives and inducing wholesale resignations. This would present a constant temptation in a firm that was run solely in the interests of investors, and the employees' fear of this potential opportunism would then make them leary about committing to a major firm. The control structure of Japanese firms, which gives considerable power to the employees as a group, enables them to protect their valuable employment rights.

In fact, in many ways it appears that the employees are residual claimants on the Japanese firm's assets and have residual decision-making power at least on a par with the investors in the firm. The typical firm's board of directors is made up almost exclusively of senior managers who have spent their whole careers in the firm. Senior executives see the interests of the employees as being as worthy of consideration as those of investors, and they believe that employees' interests actually do guide policy to a very important degree. Decision-making power is pushed down the managerial hierarchy, often right to the shop floor, where worker groups are responsible for determining how they will do the tasks they face, where employee suggestions are eagerly sought and acted on, and where an individual has the right and duty to stop the assembly line if a problem arises. Policy is formulated at the lowest possible levels and becomes adopted and moves up through the hierarchy only by gaining concensus support. Employees receive a large percentage of their incomes in the form of bonuses that are tied to the overall performance of the firm. Meanwhile, only a small part of the firm's cash flow is paid out to investors as dividends, with the bulk being reinvested in the firm to permit its continued growth and ensure its survival.

TRAINING   This system, in which employees need not fear for their jobs, expect to share in the fortunes of the firm, do not anticipate leaving for another employer, and have a say in the directions the firm will take, encourages them to invest in firm-specific human capital. This is further encouraged by the policy of paying blue-collar workers not for the particular jobs to which they are currently assigned, but instead for the skills they have acquired from a list established by the firm. At the same time, low mobility allows the firm to finance the acquisition of even general-purpose human capital without fear that employees will use it to obtain higher-paying jobs with a different employer. This may explain why Japanese firms pay significant numbers of their employees to get graduate degrees in business and law at the firm's expense, whereas European and North American firms rarely do so.

With high levels of firm-specific human capital, the decisions taken by the firm place risks on employees' human assets that are comparable to those borne by investors' physical capital. Protecting the value of this human capital then requires that employees' interests figure into the firm's decision making. This gives further reason for employees' involvement in decision making, as well as for the policies of promoting the survival and growth of the organization.

Assignments, Promotions, and Consensus   An environment of economic and technological change means that a firm's employment needs will be changing too. In this context, a guarantee of long-term employment would be tremendously expensive if the firm could not reassign workers to new tasks as the needs arose. Thus, a system of permanent employment differentially favors the sort of flexible work rules for which Japanese firms are known. Moreover, to the extent that high levels of human capital facilitate such adjustments, investments in training enter as a supporting element in yet another way.

Within the major Japanese corporations, promotions are very much based on seniority. A new white-collar recruit can expect to spend at least a decade with the firm before being considered (along with the others in the same cohort, who entered the firm together) for a promotion. Then members of any experienced cohort are evaluated for further promotions only after more senior people have had their chances. Pay is tied to seniority as well, with individual merit or performance pay being rare. Also, the differences in pay levels between ranks are typically smaller than in European firms and much smaller than in North America. These systems would be infeasible if there were an active outside labor market that could bid up the pay of star performers. Thus, the promotion and pay policies rely on the practice of hiring only at the bottom.

The system of decision making by consensus requires that large numbers of individuals have a role in decisions and that all affected parties be allowed to make their views, interests, and concerns known. This would leave the organization very susceptible to extreme influence costs if pay and promotions were less a matter of seniority and more sensitive to apparent qualifications and merit. In addition, the policy of promoting growth, even at the possible cost of reduced investor returns, helps ensure that there will be good opportunities for promotion when the time comes, and this too helps control influence activities and promotes effective concensus decision making. The policy of reinvesting most of the cash flow also limits the competition among groups and business units within the firm for the resources needed to develop their projects. If the resources were more limited and internal projects had to compete with paying the money out to investors, those inside the firm would campaign much more intensely for their interests. Finally, the standard policy of moving people around within the corporation, rather than having them build their careers in a single function or unit, also contributes to their taking a broad view of their personal interests that is more in line with overall organizational success, and this too helps control influence activities.

To coordinate and manage this complex system, the personnel department must be able to track employees effectively, ensure that their careers are developing properly, and assign them where they are most valuable. This is a crucial and complicated task that involves managing an important and valuable resource bearing directly on the welfare of an important group of residual claimants. Thus, the personnel function is accorded great respect in a major Japanese corporation, and it is able to attract among the best employees in the organization.

We argue in Chapter 4 that extensive complementarities among the parts of a system is one of the hallmarks of a coherent strategy. Japanese human-resource policies are a good illustration of this general principle.

SUMMARY

In classical economic theory, workers are treated as inputs to production; wages are determined in the market, just like any other input price, and labor turnover is frequent. Although this is a satisfactory approximation of the market for some unskilled workers, it is not an accurate account of markets for most others. When the development of specialized skills is important or the costs of changing jobs is high, wages are no longer fixed by the market and can be set to help fulfill a variety of human-resource objectives, including attracting and holding the right people, developing effective skills in the work force, motivating people, and insulating them from excessive risk.

Employment relationships are complicated, and the contracts describing them are highly incomplete. The details of the work that is to be done are most often determined by a boss in whom authority is vested. Most often the boss is appointed by the suppliers of physical capital. One possible explanation is that the physical assets are more vulnerable to appropriation than human capital, and assigning ownership to physical capital alleviates the hold-up threat. A second possibility is that the ways that bosses make decisions determine the reputation of a firm, and it is important that the builders of that reputation be able to capture some of the value they create by selling it when they separate. Because human capital is not normally transferable, but physical capital is, it is efficient to attach authority and reputational value to the transferable physical-capital shares.

Human-resource policies can create value by insulating workers against the risks associated with business fluctuations and uncertainties about their own ability. Any such protection reduces the workers' incentives to invest in improving their own abilities, and the firm itself may be unable to bear all the risks associated with business fluctuations. In addition, employees may often be unable to commit not to collect the benefits of favorable fluctuations. If the employer is committed to maintain employment without cutting the employee's wage while paying an amount equal on average to the employee's expected marginal product over the course of his or her career, then (1) wages never fall but remain constant or climb over time, (2) more experienced workers are paid more on average than are equally productive workers with less experience, especially for experience in the same job, and (3) older workers are paid more on average than equally productive and equally experienced younger workers. Employers can sometimes also create value by saving or borrowing on behalf of their employees.

Recruiting activity by firms is a function both of the firm's anticipated needs and its estimates of future availability of appropriately trained workers. Once a firm has decided how many of which kinds of workers it wants, it informs potential candidates, attracts the right class of applicants, and then hires those whom it has selected. The design of the job, including wages, responsibilities, and promotion opportunities, all affect the numbers and kinds of workers who will apply. Once applications are made, firms use a variety of indicators to decide whom to examine most closely and whom to hire. A pattern of discrimination against certain groups of workers at this stage (identified, for example, by race or sex) can discourage disadvantaged workers from acquiring skills or applying for skilled jobs, leading to a self-reinforcing pattern of discrimination.

Once a worker has been hired, the problem is to keep those workers who are best suited for the job while encouraging separations (quits or layoffs) that increase value. A difficulty in this is that if the rents or quasi-rents generated by the employment relationship are shared between the the firm and the employee, neither may have the proper incentives to account for the losses the other would suffer in a separation. Seniority rules may be useful in protecting more experienced and older workers against opportunistic dismissals, particularly when the firm has adopted pay policies that lead to paying senior workers more than their marginal products while paying junior workers less. A major complicating factor in any system of separation payments is that it may be difficult for third parties to determine who has really initiated a given separation. This difficulty also can interfere with the firm's financing an employee's investment in human capital.

The distinctive human-resource management policies of major Japanese firms have attracted much attention in Europe and North America. These policies in fact form a coherent whole, with the principle elements mutually supporting one another and other aspects of the firms' strategies and structures.

■ BIBLIOGRAPHIC NOTES

The application of standard microeconomic theory to labor markets is discussed in any intermediate microeconomic theory text. Gary Becker is most responsible for developing the theory of human capital, but many authors have recognized its significance and the concept is now a cornerstone of the economics of labor.

Herbert Simon introduced the idea of employment as a relationship into economics and explained the crucial features of the employment relation as responses to the necessary limitations on contracting that follow from bounded rationality. Oliver Williamson, Michael Wachter and Jeffrey Harris developed these ideas further. See also Williamson's books. Relational contracts in general have been explored by Victor Goldberg. The conception of the firm as a "nexus of contracts" was put forward by Armen Alchian and Harold Demsetz, while David Kreps developed the treatment as the firm as a bearer of reputation.

The idea of implicit contracts was introduced by Costas Azariades, Martin Baily, and Donald Gordon in the context of trying to explain wage rigidities for macroeconomic purposes. The theory has been developed extensively since, with particular attention to the possibilities for the firm to insure workers' incomes and employment under various assumptions on the legal enforceability of contracts. Many of the key papers were published in a special issue of the *Quarterly Journal of Economics* [98 (1983)]. A relatively nontechnical survey of the area was provided by Sherwin Rosen, while Oliver Hart has surveyed implicit contracts when there are informational differences between workers and firms. Hart and Bengt Holmstrom offer another useful survey that covers agency models and models of incomplete contracts as well. The model of implicit partial insurance contracts and wage dynamics is due to Milton Harris and Holmstrom.

References on screening, signaling, and self-selection are given in Chapter 5. The analysis of discrimination based on screening was developed by Kenneth Arrow, George Akerlof, and Michael Spence. The extension to treat human capital investment is developed by Shelly Lundberg and Richard Startz and by Sharon Oster and Paul Milgrom. Milgrom also showed conditions under which it would be optimal not to respond to outside offers.

Masahiko Aoki provides an excellent discussion of Japanese firms' policies and practices and extensive references. James Baron provides a constructive critique of economic analyses of the employment relation from the vantage point of research in sociology and social psychology.

■ REFERENCES

Akerlof, G. "Discriminatory Status-Based Wages Among Tradition-Oriented, Stochastically Trading Coconut Producers," *Journal of Political Economy*, 92 (1985), 265–76.

Alchian, A., and H. Demsetz. "Production, Information Costs, and Economic Organization," *American Economic Review*, 62 (1972), 775–95.

Aoki, M. "Toward an Economic Model of the Japanese Firm," *Journal of Economic Literature*, 28 (March 1990), 1–27.

Arrow, K.J. "Models of Job Discrimination," *Racial Discrimination in Economic Life*, A.H. Pascal, ed. (Lexington, MA: Lexington Books, 1972).

Azsariadis, C. "Implicit Contracts and Underemployment Equilibria," *Journal of Political Economy*, 83 (1975), 1183–1202.

Baily, M. "Wages and Employment Under Uncertain Demand," *Review of Economic Studies*, 41 (1974), 37–50.

Baron, J. "The Employment Relation as a Social Relation," *Journal of the Japanese and International Economies*, 2 (1988), 492–525.

Becker, G.S. *Human Capital: A Theoretical and Empirical Analysis, with Special Reference to Education* (New York: Columbia University Press, 1964).

Goldberg, V. "A Relational Exchange Perspective on the Employment Relationship," Working Paper No. 208, Department of Economics, University of California, Davis (1982).

Gordon, D.F. "A Neoclassical Theory of Keynesian Unemployment," *Economic Inquiry*, 21 (1974), 431–49.

Harris, M., and B. Holmstrom. "A Theory of Wage Dynamics," *Review of Economic Studies*, 49 (1982), 315–33.

Hart, O. "Optimal Labour Contracts Under Asymmetric Information: An Introduction," *Review of Economic Studies*, 50 (January 1983), 3–36.

Hart, O., and B. Holmstrom. "The Theory of Contracts," *Advances in Economic Theory: Fifth World Congress*, T. Bewley, ed. (Cambridge: Cambridge University Press, 1987).

Lundberg, S., and R. Startz. "Private Discrimination and Social Intervention in Competitive Labor Markets," *American Economic Review*, 73 (1983), 340–47.

Kreps, D. "Corporate Culture and Economic Theory," *Perspectives on Positive Political Economy*, J. Alt and K. Shepsle, eds. (Cambridge: Cambridge University Press, 1990), 90–143.

Milgrom, P. "Employment Contracts, Influence Activities, and Efficient Organization Design," *Journal of Political Economy*, 96 (1988), 42–60.

Milgrom, P., and S. Oster. "Job Discrimination, Market Forces and the Invisibility Hypothesis," *Quarterly Journal of Economics*, 102 (August, 1987), 453–76.

Rosen, S. "Implicit Contracts: A Survey," *Journal of Economic Literature*, 23 (1985), 1144–75.

Simon, H. A. "A Formal Theory of the Employment Relationship," *Econometrica*, 19 (1951), 293–305.

Spence, A.M. *Market Signalling: Information Transfer in Hiring and Related Processes* (Cambridge, MA: Harvard University Press, 1973).

Williamson, O. *The Economic Institutions of Capitalism: Firms, Markets, Relational Contracting* (New York: The Free Press, 1985).

Williamson, O. *Markets and Hierarchies: Analysis and Antitrust Implications* (New York: The Free Press, 1975).

Williamson, O., M. Wachter, and J. Harris. "Understanding the Employment Relation: The Analysis of Idiosyncratic Exchange," *Bell Journal of Economics*, 6 (1975), 250–78.

EXERCISES

Food for Thought

1.   A recent study found that workers who were laid off generally received lower wages once they found new jobs.[7] However, the gap between the old and new wages differed systematically across various groups and by the cause of the layoff. White-collar workers suffered relatively large declines compared to blue-collar workers, and unionized blue-collar workers suffered the smallest declines. Also, workers who had been in their previous jobs only a short period of time suffered relatively smaller losses than those who had been with the employer for a longer period. Finally, those who had lost their jobs because of plant closings experienced smaller wage reductions than those who were laid off while their former place of employment stayed in operation. How might you account for these patterns?

2.   According to a study by a researcher at Boston University,[8] only 13 U.S. firms with more than 1,000 employees have explicit policies never to institute a general layoff: Delta Airlines, Digital Equipment, Federal Express, IBM, S.C. Johnson, Lincoln Electric, Mazda, Motorola, National Steel, New United Motor (NUMMI), Nissan, Nucor, and Xerox. Why do you think that so few firms have adopted such a policy? Other firms, although apparently not having an official no-layoff policy, in fact appear to follow such a policy. For example, Hewlett Packard has consistently avoided layoffs, putting everyone on part-time work if necessary when business was especially slow. What advantages and disadvantages might there be to this approach?

3.   Using 1980 data from 250 of the largest U.S. employer-provided pension plans, Edward Lazear[9] found that the present value of the pension received by the average worker with 40 years of experience with the firm from which he or she retired at the normal retirement age was $79,476. If the same worker took "early retirement" and retired 10 years earlier, he or she would get pension benefits with a net present value of almost twice as much: $158,225. This was despite the fact that the worker would have been with the firm a shorter time and so would have "earned" less pension and also the fact that the employee's final pay (to which pension benefits are often tied) would have been lower. These policies obviously encouraged early retirement. How would you account for them? Now that employers in the U.S. can no longer force mandatory retirement, would you expect that the extent to which they encourage people to retire earlier would have increased or decreased?

4.   German law mandates that the workers in a large corporation, although they

---

[7] Robert Gibbons and Lawrence Katz, "Layoffs and Lemons," National Bureau of Economic Research working paper 2968 (1989).

[8] Fred Foulkes, quoted in Milton Moskowitz, Robert Levering, and Michael Katz, *Everybody's Business* (New York: Doubleday, 1990), 593.

[9] Edward P. Lazear, "Pensions as Severance Pay," *Financial Aspects of the U.S. Pension System*, Orley Ashenfelter and Richard Layard, eds. (Chicago: University of Chicago Press, 1983).

hold no ownership position, have the right to elect half of the firm's directors. This institution is termed "codetermination," and its original intent was to ensure that workers' interest, and not just investors' concerns, were considered in corporate decision making. Under what conditions would efficiency argue for such a system? Apparently, investors' interests still seem to dominate. How would you account for this?

5. Actuaries perform the crucial task in the insurance industry of estimating the time paths and probability distributions of costs and revenues that attach to different insurance contracts. Becoming an actuary involves passing a series of rigorous examinations that are set by the professional actuarial society. Usually these are taken over several years, during which time the prospective actuary is working for an insurance company in the actuarial department. The skills and knowledge that these tests measure are general human capital which the market rewards highly. Yet insurance companies give large amounts of time off to their employees to study for these examinations. Passing an exam usually results in a significant pay increase and often in a promotion. How do you account for these patterns?

6. Motorola, the U.S. electronics firm, reportedly has a policy that once an employee has been with the firm for ten years, if his or her employment is to be terminated, the president of the company must dismiss the employee in person. What would be the point of such a policy?

7. Major Japanese firms appear to do much more pre-employment screening and testing of applicants than firms in other countries. How would you account for this? Japanese firms that have set up production facilities in the United States have continued this practice. In part because the standardized aptitude and intelligence tests that are sometimes used as part of this process are alleged to be biased in favor of those of European or East Asian ethnic backgrounds, the extensive screening has led to complaints of racial discrimination in employment. What should be the public policy in this context?

11

INTERNAL LABOR MARKETS, JOB ASSIGNMENTS, AND PROMOTIONS

T*o find men capable of managing business efficiently and secure to them the positions of responsible control is perhaps the most important single problem of economic organization on the efficiency side.*

Frank H. Knight[1]

In the developed economies, most people are in long-term employment relationships with their current employers. The practice of *nenko*, or lifetime employment, in large Japanese corporations is a familiar example, but stable, near-lifetime employment is widespread elsewhere as well. For example, it has been estimated that in the early 1980s the typical U.S. worker was in a job that would last about eight years, with a quarter of the work force being in jobs that will last 20 years or more.[2] For workers over 30 years of age, 40 percent were in jobs that would last at least 20 years. In fact, job tenures of more than 15 years are apparently more common in the United States than in Japan,[3] and jobs lasting 20 years or more are somewhat more common in the United Kingdom than in the United States.[4] Workers in such long-term employment relationships expect to make a career with the firms

---

[1] *Risk, Uncertainty and Profit* (Chicago: University of Chicago Press, 1985). First published in 1921.

[2] Robert Hall, "The Importance of Lifetime Jobs in the U.S. Economy," *American Economic Review*, 72 (September 1982), 716–24.

[3] Kazuo Koike, "Japan's Industrial Relations: Characteristics and Problems," *Japanese Economic Studies*, 7 (Fall 1978), 42–90.

[4] Brian G. M. Main, unpublished paper cited by Hall, *op cit*.

now employing them, and many hope to rise through the ranks in their firms via promotions.

Their employers share these expectations. They normally hire new people into the firms only at a limited number of "ports of entry" that are often lower-level jobs; they fill vacancies by reassigning or promoting members of the current work force; and they expect that workers will stay with the firm over the long haul, moving along fairly well-defined career paths within the firm.

INTERNAL LABOR MARKETS

Long-term employment relationships, limited ports of entry for hiring, career paths within the firm, and promotions from within are key features of **internal labor markets**. An internal labor market consists of an employer and (some particular group of) its long-term employees. There may be more than one internal labor market within a single firm, each involving different groups of workers. For example, the hourly employees at each of a company's several plants might constitute a separate internal labor market, with the managerial employees in the firm as a whole making up yet another. Each internal labor market interacts on only a limited basis with the general, external labor market: Mobility into and out of the internal labor market is limited in practice, and the conditions in the outside market exert only a muffled influence on job assignments and compensation within the internal labor market. Rather than simply and directly reflecting general market conditions, an internal labor market largely operates according to its own administrative rules and shared understandings.

Labor Market Segmentation Patterns

The concept of internal labor markets was first developed in economics in the early 1970s by Peter Doeringer and Michael Piore. Since then, numerous economists, sociologists, industrial relations experts, and organization behavior scholars have developed and used the idea in studying employment patterns and policies.

Not all workers are in internal labor markets. To understand employment patterns and the prevalence or absence of internal labor markets in different contexts, Doeringer and Piore distinguished *primary* and *secondary sectors* in the economy. Internal labor markets are common but not universal in the primary sector, whereas they are absent from the secondary sector. Instead, the secondary sector is marked by short-term employment relationships that hold no promise of promotion and where wages are fully determined by market forces. The secondary labor market includes unskilled, manual-labor, blue-collar jobs; low or unskilled service positions (janitors, check-out clerks, waiters); low or unskilled white-collar positions (office mail-room workers, filing clerks); and migrant, part-time, and seasonal workers. Other jobs, such as skilled blue-collar work, most white-collar positions, and technical, managerial, and professional employment, are in the primary sector.

Not all primary sector jobs are in internal labor markets. For example, a medical doctor in private practice is not usefully thought of in any internal labor market. Still, he or she is certainly not in the primary labor market that is characterized by low skill levels, low earnings, easy entry, job impermanence, and low returns to education or experience. Most white-collar workers, most skilled blue-collar workers, and most professionals and managers, however, are in internal labor markets in the primary sector.

Later scholars have refined the notion of the primary sector, subdividing it in various ways according to differences in such factors as the level of entrance standards, promotion and turnover rates, the criteria for promotions, and the forms of control.

For example, Richard Edwards divided the sector into "independent" and "subordinate" subsectors, with the latter containing most semiskilled blue- and white-collar jobs and the former including supervisory and managerial jobs, professional positions, and crafts work where workers maintain a considerable degree of independence.

As noted, there may in fact be several internal labor markets within an individual firm. Rarely do blue-collar, production workers move into white-collar jobs, except perhaps by being promoted to supervisory positions. Movement between lower-level office jobs and managerial positions is also rare. Yet within each group the firm can offer extensive *job ladders*, with different rules and procedures for determining compensation and promotions and different mechanisms for control and motivation.

FAIRNESS AND EFFICIENCY   Obviously, most people would prefer a job in the primary labor market to the secondary, and a position in the independent primary submarket would usually seem preferable to one in the subordinate submarket. Thus, the assignment of people to different parts of the labor market can be approached as primarily a justice or equity issue. It may just not seem fair that some jobs, such as migrant agricultural labor, should offer so little in pay, security, and future promise and yet involve backbreakingly hard work.

The demands made by jobs in the different sectors differ substantially, however, and, unfortunately, not everyone is qualified for the really good jobs. People who do not have good jobs and seem to deserve better might perform very poorly if they were actually put into jobs for which they lack the skills and abilities. Thus, fairness is not the only issue; efficiency matters too.

A more practical question is whether the way people are divided among segmented labor markets reflects and promotes efficiency or, instead, retards efficiency while also offending on fairness grounds. If the initial assignment of people to jobs is determined by race, class, or sex, by personal influence or political connections, or by random chance, then it is hard to believe that efficiency is being well served. Furthermore, the limited mobility between internal labor markets then perpetuates the misallocation. If, however, the assignment is reflective of relative abilities and skills, then at least efficiency is being served.

Pay in Internal Labor Markets

A feature typically identified with internal labor markets is some insulation of compensation decisions within the firm from external market forces. This insulation cannot be total, of course. At a minimum, the firm must compete with other employers at the ports of entry. More generally, workers will have outside options of some sort throughout their careers. In addition, the employer may be willing to hire at relatively senior levels from outside if the costs of filling a job from within are too far out of line. For example, if a pressing need suddenly develops for employees with expertise in a new technology, the firm may hire people with the needed knowledge and skills from outside rather than attempting to develop the requisite expertise internally. Or a company in distress may look outside for a new CEO to bring fresh ideas and leadership that may improve the firm's fortunes. In such situations, the firm will have to pay market wages to attract the new people. Nevertheless, for many workers, wages are insulated to a large degree from outside market forces, helping to reduce the income risks that workers bear and to make it possible to use wage policy to achieve other objectives.

JOB CLASSIFICATIONS AND PAY   In this context, it is often claimed that in internal labor markets, "wages attach to jobs rather than to individuals." The idea is that there will be a fairly narrow range of pay specified for any job in the internal labor market. What any particular employee is paid is then determined primarily by his or her job

Table 11.1   Stanford University 1990 Job Classifications and Monthly Pay Ranges

Range Number	Examples	Min	Max
B7	Office Assistant I; Medical Asst.I	1414	2071
B8	Nursery Aid	1485	2174
B9	Secretary I; Off.Asst.II, Sports Asst.I; Med.Asst.II	1558	2285
B10	Sctry.IS; Accounting Asst.I; Library Specialist I	1639	2405
B11	Sctry.II; Off.Asst.III, Sports Asst.II; Med.Asst.III	1717	2523
B12	Sctry.IIS; Acct.Asst.II; Lib.Spec.II	1807	2654
B13	Editor I	2197	2789
B14	Sctry.III; Off.Asst.IV; Acct.Asst.III; Lib.Spec.III	1985	2929
B15	Sctry.III (Premium)	2088	3082
B16	Administrative Assistant ("A.A.") I; Legal Secretary	2197	3231
B17	Graphic Composition Supervisor	2304	3393
B18		2423	3560
B19	Patient Test Technician Specialist	2547	3745
B20		2673	3931
B21	Medical Technologist	2813	4122
B22	Senior Medical Technologist	2950	4336
B23		3098	4553
B24		3252	4782
C4	Student Services Officer ("SSO") I; Editor II; A.A.I	2179	3302
C5	Assistant Librarian; Accountant I; A.A. II	2406	3766
C6	SSO II; Assoc.Libr'n; Acct'II, Editor III; A.A.III	2668	4225
C7	SSO III; Libr'n; Acct't III; Editor IV; Manager I	3043	5080
C8	Senior Libr'n; Acct't IV; Manager II	3550	5856
C9	Manager III	4280	6685
C10	Manager IV	5034	7797
N11	Manager V	6667	OPEN

assignment rather than by actual individual productivity or opportunity costs. There is some evidence for this. Certainly, at least for lower-level jobs, many firms have very explicit salary scales, and the only way to get a raise once an employee's pay hits the top of the scale is to get a promotion.

Stanford University's practices on job classifications and pay are illustrative of many large employers. Nonunion staff positions at Stanford are classified into 27 levels ranging from B7 to B24, C4 to C10, C99, and N11. (There is an even richer, more complex classification of the jobs covered by collective bargaining.) Jobs in the B classification are "nonexempt" positions under U.S. government regulations. People in these positions fill out time sheets and must be paid overtime for work beyond their normal work week. Jobs in the C and N ranges are "exempt" positions that do not carry overtime rights. These are usually professional, supervisory, or managerial positions. Examples of some jobs in each class and the minimum and maximum monthly wages for each are shown in Table 11.1.[5]

Jobs are classified according to a determination of the skills required and responsibilities involved. Thus, for example, there are six different secretarial job levels: Secretary I, IS, II, IIS, III, and III(Premium). Each involves a higher level of qualifications and responsibilities. Different sorts of jobs are classified as being in the same range if they are determined to involve similar skill requirements and

---

[5] No examples are given for the highest nonexempt (B) levels because no actual jobs are currently classified at these levels.

responsibilities. For example, the jobs of Secretary III, Office Assistant IV, and Accounting Assistant III are considered comparable and so they are classified the same (B-14). The pay levels attached to a classification level are set at least in part in response to market forces and are adjusted annually. However, differential market demand and supply conditions faced by candidates for different jobs are not supposed to affect the classification of the jobs, at least in the short run. Instead, they are to be accounted for by adjusting the amount paid to people in different jobs within the specified range.

Once in a job, individual workers may receive raises up to the maximum salary for that job's classification. Typically, the total amount of these raises in any year is controlled by the central administration, but their allocation among employees is determined by lower-level supervisors. Raises beyond the maximum salary can be achieved only by being promoted to a job with a higher classification or by having one's current job reclassified. Thus, a Medical Assistant I (a B-7 job) might be promoted to Medical Assistant II (B-9) and then to Medical Assistant III (B-11). Similarly, a Manager I might win promotions up to Manager V. These patterns are common to most large organizations with formal personnel systems, and not at all unique to Stanford.

CAVEATS AND QUALIFICATIONS   Despite all this, the idea that wages attach to jobs in internal labor markets must not be taken too rigidly. First, even within the context of a job classification scheme there can be significant differences in pay between people assigned to the same job. At Stanford, for example, the maximum salary corresponding to a given job classification is on the order of 50 percent more than the minimum for that rank, and the maximum at one level exceeds the minimum several grades higher. This leaves quite a bit of room within any single job classification for merit pay linked to productivity and for pay differences that reflect seniority or other factors, such as special individual needs or arrangements.

Second, many Japanese firms that have internal labor markets employ a "dual hierarchy."[6] Wages are determined not by task assignment or rank in the familiar reporting and authority hierarchy (the person's job), but by what skills the workers have acquired and their performance—their places in the second, "rankings" hierarchy. Thus, two employees with very different assignments may be paid the same, perhaps even when one is superior to the other in the reporting hierarchy, because they have the same positions in the ranking hierarchy. Similarly, two people doing the same job but at different positions in the ranking hierarchy can be paid quite differently. Managing this dual hierarchy is a complex task, and this helps account for the central role, high prestige, and access to the most talented employees that the Personnel Department has in a typical Japanese corporation. Increasingly, North American and European firms with internal labor markets have experimented with and adopted similar policies, paying for skills rather than for the actual job being done. This approach is especially favored in organizational systems which put a premium on workers' being willing and able to move between multiple tasks quickly and smoothly in response to changing conditions.

THE RATIONALE FOR INTERNAL LABOR MARKETS

Long-term employment means limited job mobility, at least across organizations. Yet the ease and speed with which labor moves to its most productive use has often been

---

[6] For more details, see Masahiko Aoki, *Information, Incentives and Bargaining in the Japanese Economy* (Cambridge: Cambridge University Press, 1988), especially chapter 3.

seen as a major determinant of economic efficiency and growth. What then accounts for the prevalence of internal labor markets with their pattern of more-or-less permanent employment? And how can we explain their other features: limited ports of entry, job ladders and promotion from within, and wages that are at least partially attached to jobs rather than being determined by individual productivity?

Long-Term Employment

At least three distinct factors contribute to the efficiency of long-term employment relations of the sort we see in internal labor markets. These are the increased opportunities to invest profitably in firm-specific human capital, the greater efficacy of efficiency wage incentive contracts in long-term relationships, and the enhanced ability to make an accurate assessment of an employee's contributions to long-term objectives by monitoring performance over a longer period of time.

FIRM-SPECIFIC HUMAN CAPITAL   Firm-specific human capital is knowledge, skills, and interpersonal relationships that increase workers' productivity in their current employment, but are useless if the workers leave to join other firms. Other things being equal, workers who have acquired firm-specific human capital will be more efficient in their current employment than elsewhere. Thus, there will be a greater tendency for them to stay with their current employer than would otherwise be the case. Furthermore, long-term employment *encourages* the development of productive, firm-specific human capital: long-term employment and investment in firm-specific human capital are complements. Unless both the firm and its workers can expect the employment relationship to continue, there is little incentive to make costly investments in acquiring firm-specific knowledge and skills. Moreover, even human capital that is a free byproduct of working in the firm—such as the interpersonal relationships that facilitate working together effectively—will not develop unless the employment relationship covers an extended period.

EFFICIENCY WAGE CONTRACTS   The effectiveness of efficiency wages, reputation mechanisms, and implicit, incomplete contracts increases when people take a longer-term view, and this is encouraged by long-term employment. Consider, for example, an efficiency-wage scheme under which workers keep their jobs and receive supercompetitive pay if they perform but lose their jobs if they are caught shirking. This requires the possibility that employment relationships may extend over many periods. A longer horizon also makes reputation considerations more powerful because it allows more opportunities to benefit from a good reputation or to suffer from a bad one. This can be important in enforcing implicit contracts.

ASSESSING CONTRIBUTIONS TO LONG-TERM GOALS   For a team of fruit pickers whose job is to pick trees cleanly, performance can be easily and quickly measured: count the number of cleanly picked trees. There is no advantage to waiting to assess the picker's performance. At the opposite extreme, it is very difficult to evaluate a manager's performance in selecting the new technologies in which to invest until some time, perhaps a long time, has passed. It is difficult to provide incentives for long-term performance to someone whose employment lasts for only a short time.

This time lag before good performance indicators become available can pose a double problem for some kinds of managers—who participate in making investment decisions and are also in charge of decisions that affect short-term performance. As we have seen, the equal compensation principle requires that efforts in making short-term decisions and long-term ones be compensated equally at the margin if a manager is to devote some effort to both. In a short-term relationship, offering incentives for short-term performance would make the long-term incentive problem worse, because it would encourage managers to focus on immediate performance objectives while neglecting the long term. To mitigate this problem, the firm might have to weaken incentives for short-term performance as well. Thus, inability to measure long-term performance can degrade incentives for all kinds of performance.

Promotion Policies

Promotions serve two roles in an organization. First, they help assign people to the roles where they can best contribute to the organization's performance and success. Second, promotions serve as incentives and rewards. These conceptually distinct roles are sometimes in conflict, which creates difficult management problems but helps account for many observed organizational practices.

PROMOTION POLICIES AND JOB ASSIGNMENTS   Higher-level jobs in the hierarchy typically demand higher levels of knowledge or skill and involve assignments and responsibilities where successes are more significant and mistakes or failures are more costly. Assigning people who actually have the requisite qualifications and talents to these jobs is very important. Often, however, it is difficult to tell immediately which jobs are most suitable for a newly hired employee, although the best match is more easily discerned after the employee has been working at the firm for some time. In that case, promoting employees currently in lower-level positions becomes the efficient mechanism for filling specialized and higher-level jobs. In other cases, the qualities needed in higher-level jobs may be acquired only through experience in the organization. This is especially likely where knowledge of operating procedures, technology, other employees' skills and temperaments, and customers' and suppliers' characteristics is important. Again, promotion is the efficient mechanism in these circumstances.

MANAGERIAL HIERARCHIES   Decision making, supervision, and leadership at higher levels in managerial hierarchies have more impact than do those at lower levels because the jobs are designed that way. The lowest-level managers and supervisors are given responsibility for the most routine kinds of tasks. They are expected to consult with their superior managers for advice on nonroutine matters outside their own experience, especially for any decisions that can have a major effect on the firm's performance. Further up the hierarchy, managers are accorded greater responsibility and greater discretion. Whereas the impact of a district manager's decisions is largely limited to the performance of that district, the decisions of top management influence the success of the whole firm. This pattern has potential implications for the assignment of people of differing ability levels to jobs. The key issue is whether increasing the effort, experience, ability, and talent levels of the person assigned to a job is greater or less at different levels in the hierarchy.

Given the way managerial jobs are usually structured, it is in fact important to have more productive people in higher-level jobs. In standard economic language, the marginal returns to increasing either the effort provided by a manager or the level of talent, ability, and relevant experience that he or she brings to bear will be greater the further up the manager is in the hierarchy. This in turn means that the firm will want to put harder-working and more talented managers in higher level positions, with the very best people at the top. Again, to the extent that these characteristics are more easily discerned among current employees than among outsiders or are developed primarily through experience in the organization, promotion becomes the efficient way to fill higher-level positions.

PROMOTIONS AND OUTSIDE LABOR MARKET COMPETITION   To some extent, outsiders to the firm rely on the promotion process to help them identify the ablest workers. Those

Bias in Promotions: Favoring Star Performers

An apparent form of unfair discrimination comes in promotions when those who have done well early in their careers are favored at later rounds. For example, they may be given better opportunities to show themselves to good advantage, more resources to work with, or the benefit of the doubt in interpreting their performance. Those who have gone to the right schools and done well there get the jobs with the best chances for advancement, and then those whose early performance on the job impresses the bosses get the breaks on later assignments. The same phenomenon is found in seeded athletic tournaments, where the highest-ranked players are given the easiest early matches. In the job context, such bias may seem to reflect unfair favoritism. However, it also has certain advantages when the objective is to identify the ablest workers.

As an illustration, consider a situation where a firm is trying to decide which of two employees to promote into an important job. Initially each is as likely as the other to be the better choice. The firm has the choice of observing their performance either once or twice, and the performance at each stage gives information on qualifications for the job. Finally, suppose that all the firm can observe is which employee performed better at each round. Then if the two are treated the same at the second round of observation, independent of which one did better at the first round, the firm gains nothing from having the extra observation on their performance!

To see this, note first that if the firm observes the candidates' performance only once, then it will optimally assign the one with the better performance to the job. Now suppose the second observation is available and that the second round is not biased in favor of the winner of the first round. Then the firm has an optimal decision rule that ignores the second period information, namely, promote the winner of the first round. This clearly is the right thing to do when the same individual does better at both rounds. When one individual wins at the first round and the other at the second, then there is at least as much evidence favoring the first-round winner as favoring the second, so it again pays to promote the first-round winner. The opportunity to compare the employees again in a fair contest, or in one biased in favor of the first round loser, has no informational value.

Suppose instead that the firm makes it easier for the winner of the first round to win the second as well. Then, the firm's optimal decision will be to promote the winner of the second round, so the second round does have informational value. If the purpose is to identify the best candidate, then it is optimal to bias the second round in favor of the winner of the first round.

Based on Margaret Meyer, "Learning from Coarse Information: Biased Contests and Career Profiles," *Review of Economic Studies*, 58 (January 1991), 15-41.

who are promoted, presumably, are those who have performed well in their previous jobs. Holding their ability fixed, promoted workers have better outside job opportunities than do unpromoted ones. They therefore have to be paid a higher wage. This has two effects. First, promotions are practically always accompanied by pay increases. Second, because a productive worker must be given a raise when he or she is promoted, there may be some desire on the part of the firm to delay promotions and reduce the number of job categories in order to maintain its information advantage over outsiders. This temptation to withhold promotions may be especially great with workers who are not already highly visible to outside employers, perhaps because they are not well connected in the social networks of businesses outside the firm. Promoting these people makes them more visible and increases the wage they must receive and the chances of losing them. In contrast, there is little point in trying to hide workers who are already quite well known outside.

PARALLEL JOB LADDERS   The comparisons we have been describing, between two successive levels of management or two kinds of secretaries or machine operators, apply only when the successive ranks in the hierarchy entail similar kinds of tasks. The best salesperson may not have the skills needed to be an effective sales manager, even if his or her intimate knowledge of the product and market would be a great benefit in the supervisory position. Similarly, it would be a strange coincidence if the best teacher and researcher on a faculty were also the best candidate for dean. This fact presents a special problem when the role of promotions as incentives and rewards is recognized. Many an excellent engineer has been promoted to be a mediocre manager, and others who would have been even worse managers but were passed over for promotion have become disaffected or unmotivated. Tying pay to rank, as is standard in internal labor markets, exacerbates these difficulties. In response, a number of companies have recently been experimenting with separate career ladders for scientists and engineers that do not require them to move into management in order to get ahead. Examples are Analog Devices, Inc., which makes equipment for manufacturing semiconductors, and 3M Company, the makers of Scotch® tape, Post-It® notes, and thousands of other products. IBM is another example. It has had some extremely distinguished scientists make their entire careers in the company, winning promotions and advancement without ever moving into management. Other firms, however, believe that it is desirable for senior engineers and scientists to become involved in management because they see this experience as helping to ensure that those who discover and implement new technologies will also be sensitive to business needs.

PROMOTIONS AS INCENTIVES AND REWARDS   It is clear that promotion opportunities play a major role as an incentive device in most hierarchical organizations, either in place of direct monetary incentives or in concert with them. This fact in turn helps explain the common policy of normally hiring only at a limited number of ports of entry that are usually low-ranking positions in the hierarchy. Suppose employees constantly had to worry that none of them would get promoted the next time there was an opening and that instead an outsider would be brought in above them. Then their incentives to work hard to win the promotion might be severely blunted because the chance of winning the prize would be much less.

The extensive use of promotions as incentive devices presents a puzzle, however. It would seem that promotions are a very blunt tool, at least compared to direct monetary incentives. Promotions are discrete, whereas monetary rewards can be varied continuously as required. Promotions can go to a few people at most, whereas presumably everyone can be given monetary incentives. Furthermore, promotions for even the best people must be relatively infrequent. In contrast, monetary rewards and punishments can be meted out as frequently as desired. Promotions also create competition between employees, which may be dysfunctional when cooperation and teamwork are important. Finally, as noted in the preceding section, there can be serious conflict between the role of promotions as incentive and reward devices and their role in assigning people to jobs. Promoting as a reward for good performance in the current job can result in the famous "Peter Principle." This tongue-in-cheek principle holds that people in organizations always get one promotion too many: They keep getting promoted until they finally reach their "levels of incompetence"—jobs they cannot do well—and then spend the remainder of their careers doing those jobs. It is easy to see how this could happen under a system in which promotions are simply a reward for good performance. Why then is there such reliance on promotions as rewards?

Of course, if pay attaches to jobs through some routine administrative process that is not responsive to individual skills, abilities, or performance, then the only effective way to award performance pay is to promote those who perform well to higher-paying jobs. This is not an adequate answer to the question, however, because it presupposes that pay has to be attached to jobs rather than to individuals.

TOURNAMENTS   Providing incentives by promoting the best performers to higher-paying jobs is a particular kind of comparative performance evaluation. The workers are effectively ranked on the basis of their relative performance, and the winners get promoted whereas the losers are passed over. Given the pay at each level, this system creates a *tournament*. Just as in golf or tennis tournaments or the league playoffs in various team sports, the amount a person receives for winning depends only on how well he or she does relative to the other contestants and not on any absolute measure of performance. The only performance information needed or used in a tournament is the relative, *ordinal* information about who did better, not some absolute, *cardinal* information about the amount by which an employee's performance exceeded some absolute standard.

In many circumstances, only ordinal, relative information is available in a timely manner and at a reasonable cost. It may be quite easy to determine and agree about which of a group of people is doing the best job. At the same time, it would be extremely difficult to specify just how well each is doing in some absolute sense. This may be especially likely when the jobs involve many different elements that are hard to describe and to specify in advance. Yet this cardinal information may be needed under any system that tries to reward performance by finely-tuned pay adjustments. In these circumstances, tournaments may be the only effective method of providing incentives. Consider three examples:

- The faculty in a college may easily agree that student A in a difficult field of study is doing better than is student B, who is following an easy course of studies, even though B has higher grades overall. There is no apparent way to specify how well each is doing absolutely, however, or even how much better A is doing than B. Still, it is clear which student should get the award as the outstanding graduate.

- Secretary A works for someone who requires a multitude of services to be done quickly and accurately with skill, intelligence, and discretion. Moreover, A regularly helps others in the office with their assignments. Secretary B's boss requires only that the phone be answered and that an occasional letter be typed. Although both secretaries do everything that is asked of them in exemplary fashion, A is clearly working harder than is B. There is no question about which of the two is more deserving of a promotion. However, assigning a numerical measure to their contributions in a manner that could be used

Incentives In Tournaments: Golf

A recent empirical study has shown that effort and performance in tournaments are sensitive to the size and distribution of the prizes. This study found that higher prizes lowered the scores in men's professional golf tournaments: raising the total prize money by $100,000 (in 1984 dollars) lowered each player's score on average by 1.1 strokes over a 72-hole tournament. Most of this effect occurred in later rounds of the tournaments when the players are more likely to be tired and so find maintaining concentration more difficult. Also, players' final-round scores responded to the strength of the incentives they faced. Because the monetary gain to finishing first rather than second is much greater than the gain to finishing second rather than third (and similarly for all other places), there is a greater marginal return to a player's lowering his final round score by a stroke when he is among the leaders after the first three rounds than when he is back in the pack. In fact, those with a greater return to effort of this sort did do better in the final round, even when other factors influencing their scores are controlled for statistically.

Based on Ronald G. Ehrenberg and Michael L. Bognanno, "Do Tournaments Have Incentive Effects?" *Journal of Political Economy*, 98 (December, 1990), 1307–24.

to determine pay levels in a performance-pay formula would be very difficult, expensive, and subject to dispute.

- Executive A has taken a failing division that was subject to severe foreign competition and long-term labor problems and restored it to marginal profitability while investing in new products that seem to hold real promise for the future. Executive B has overseen the continued generation of cash by a division that produces a high-demand product for which there is little competition. By all the standard financial measures, B's division outperformed A's. It might have been possible to design individual performance contracts that provided appropriate monetary incentives for the two executives in their differing assignments, but doing so would certainly have been hard; determining that A has done the better job and should be the one promoted is much easier.

A second reason for using tournaments to provide incentives arises when there is a large common element to the uncertainty that affects the relationship between people's effort choices and their measured performance. For example, the actual sales made by individual salespeople may all be affected in a similar fashion by the same unobserved market factors, such as the actions of competitors or the market's acceptance of a new product. We applied the informativeness principle in Chapter 7 to show that comparative performance evaluation in general can be useful when observing how one agent has performed. This allows a better inference to be made about how much effort another has expended. When there is a large common element affecting each agent's performance, looking at relative performance can effectively eliminate the common factors and so permits better inferences about who has worked hard. This in turn allows the same incentives to be provided with less risk being placed on those being motivated. This possibility may help explain the popularity of sales contests in motivating salespeople.

A third advantage of tournaments arises when management or owners may be tempted to renege on performance payments that have been earned, saving money by claiming that performance was lower than it actually was and that only low performance bonuses are due. For this to be a serious problem, it must be difficult for employees to observe one another's performance (so that implicit contracts are not effectively enforceable) and for third parties to verify performance (so that arbitration cannot resolve the problem). In these circumstances, it may still be possible to observe whether the promised tournament prizes have been awarded. A tournament, in which the prizes to be awarded are fixed in advance, then provides management with a means to commit to paying for performance. Without such commitment, the possibilities for eliciting good performance by (incredible) promises are more limited.

A potential disadvantage of tournaments arises when there are opportunities for collusion among the employees. If rewards depend only on relative performance and not on absolute performance levels, then the expected returns to each individual are the same if everyone agrees to take things easy as if they all work hard. Of course, taking things easy saves them the cost of effort and represents a tempting possibility for the workers.

A second difficulty is that it may be as easy for a contestant in a tournament to get ahead by sabotaging others' performance as by honest effort. This obviously creates inefficiency.

Even putting these problems aside, theory suggests that for tournaments to provide efficient incentives, the prizes must be appropriately adjusted. In internal labor markets the prizes are the extra pay attached to the higher-level job as well as the opportunity for winners to compete for the next promotion. This means that pay and promotion policies need to be determined together. Before discussing this, we consider some of the reasons why pay might attach to jobs.

Pay Attached to Jobs

As mentioned earlier, because a policy of promotions based on performance helps competing employers to identify the firm's most talented and hard-working employees, promotions ordinarily require giving raises, even when the new jobs are not more difficult. This might explain why pay tends to rise within a hierarchy, but it does not explain why pay is not more tied to individual performance or characteristics.

MEASUREMENT PROBLEMS   One reason for attaching pay to jobs arises when performance and productivity are very difficult to measure with any accuracy or even to describe in sufficient detail. This is especially likely to be the case for staff positions in large, complex organizations, where it is hard to determine who has contributed what to the organization's performance. In such cases, the value of one person's contribution depends heavily on others' actions and decisions and on factors that may have been unforeseen at the time any explicit performance contracts would have had to be written. Attempting to pay for performance in these circumstances may actually amount to little more than a random pay policy. Similarly, paying for skills is of little value if skill levels are hard to observe and measure or, even more, if it is hard to foresee and evaluate the skills that may be useful.

Another option would be individual salary bargaining with each employee. This could be extremely inefficient, however, because the bargaining costs could be quite high. Moreover, unless those doing the bargaining for the firm are given incentives that make them very good representatives of the firm's interests, there may be additional problems. Supplying the proper incentives to the bargainers is also problematic, however. How is the firm to tell if its bargaining representative overpaid an employee or if the representative was bargaining too hard and losing people that the firm wanted? How can it even inform the bargainers what behavior it wants from them?

DECENTRALIZED PAY DETERMINATION   A further possibility might be to give responsibility to individual managers for pay determination. This alternative is attractive because local managers are apt to be relatively well informed about their subordinates' abilities and contributions. It might work well, provided the managers have effective incentives that cause them to internalize the costs and benefits of their compensation decisions.

Achieving such motivation will be difficult in many circumstances, however, especially when the manager's performance itself is hard to measure. Unless the manager has profit-and-loss responsibility, there will be little reason not to be overly generous with pay. Moreover, doing performance reviews is often unpleasant work, as is allocating raises. Managers tend to avoid doing these tasks, and when they do carry out reviews they find it difficult to make sharp distinctions between their employees and to give low ratings to any but the worst of them. Most employees end up being evaluated highly, and so the rankings carry little useful information.[7] The problem is that the individual managers bear the (personal) costs of assigning low ratings, and it is difficult to compensate them for these costs. In fact, to the extent that the system by which the managers are evaluated rewards employee development, the managers may in effect bear extra costs when they grade employees as poor performers.

Moreover, to the extent that the firm has interests in employment and pay that go beyond the purview of the individual manager, further problems arise. One such case arises when the firm wants to be able to transfer employees among jobs with different supervisors, as is common in internal labor markets. Unless the managers' contracts lead them to value their employees' acquiring human capital that is valuable to the firm at large, but not to the specific function the employee is currently doing, they are not going to encourage employees to make such investments. Furthermore, unless managers are rewarded when their subordinates are promoted or reassigned, they may be tempted to hide their best people. For this reason, IBM and some other large companies evaluate their managers on the number of their employees who are promoted or hired away by other units in the company.

Influence costs present another reason to avoid discretion in determining pay levels. If similar jobs across the firm are paid similarly and by largely administrative decision, there is little room for politicking about pay. If there is substantial discretion in determining pay, however, influence costs can become very large as employees lobby for better pay, using comparisons with those in other units. Of course, there may still be influence exerted to affect job classifications and thereby the pay received. This will arguably be more limited, however, because the opportunities for effecting a change are more limited.

PAY RANGES   The common system for pay determination in internal labor markets can be seen as a response to these difficulties of specifying and measuring performance and of giving full discretion on pay determination to local managers. The usual solution is that pay ranges are established for different jobs, and then the pay awarded to each individual employee is determined on the basis of the supervisor's evaluation of the employee's merit. Often the managers of different units are given limited budgets for annual raises, so the pay increase that can be awarded to any individual employee is further constrained.

Table 11.2 illustrates these points using the 1991 Simon and Schuster Salary

---

[7] See Chapter 12 for a more extensive discussion of performance evaluation.

Table 11.2   Simon & Schuster, Inc.
    1991 Merit Increase Matrix
    Percentages Represent Maximum Merit Increase Guideline

PERFORMANCE RATING	Location in FY'91 Salary Range				
	Below Minimum	Lower Third	Middle Third	Upper Third	Above Maximum
1: Outstanding (10% of total)	8.0–12.0%	7.0–10.5%	6.0–9.0%	5.0–7.0%	4.0–6.0%
2: Exceeds requirements /above expectations (30% of total)	7.0–10.5%	6.0–9.0%	5.0–7.5%	4.0–6.0%	0.0–3.0%
3: Fully competent (45% of total)	6.0–9.0%	5.0–7.5%	4.0–6.0%	0.0–3.0%	0.0%
4: Needs improvement / below expectations	0.0%	0.0%	0.0%	0.0%	0.0%
5: Unsatisfactory	0.0%	0.0%	0.0%	0.0%	0.0%

Increase Guidelines. Notice that there are target percentages for the numbers of individuals to be assigned to each performance category. Giving managers a role in setting individual pay allows them to use the information they have on performance. Simultaneously, the specified pay ranges attached to jobs and the limited budgets for raises restrict the managers' discretion and so help control the possible incentive problems that giving discretion creates.

At the same time, when the pool of money available for raises is small, the possibilities for rewarding employees differentially on their relative merit are often quite limited. Even if the worst performers are given no raises, the funds available may permit giving only a few dollars more than average to the best people. With so little effectively at stake, the managers have even less reason to take the task of performance appraisal very seriously and to incur the costs of sharply and accurately differentiating among employees.

Internal Labor Markets as Systems

The arguments presented so far to explain the various features of internal labor markets—long-term employment, limited ports of entry, the use of promotions to fill vacancies, pay attaching largely to jobs and only secondarily to individual merit—are not mutually inconsistent, and in fact many of them involve complementary elements. Because we have made these arguments in a piecemeal way, however, you might expect to find great diversity in the practices of actual firms, depending on the severity of the problems internal labor markets are intended to resolve.

In reality, firms operating in a wide variety of differing circumstances have implemented internal labor-market systems sharing many of the characteristic features we have discussed. This suggests that these features are part of a coherent *system* comprised of mutually supporting elements to solve a universal problem, and we should seek to understand them accordingly.

Unfortunately, our understanding of internal labor markets is not yet sufficient to allow us to explain them in a fully systematic fashion, accounting for all their major features in a unified way. Some first steps in this direction have been made, however.

INTERNAL LABOR MARKETS, SHIRKING, AND SELF-SELECTION   One of the more successful attempts to explain many of the characteristic features of internal labor markets as

Rat Races and Career Concerns

Many professions seem to be characterized as a "rat race," with people working much harder and longer hours to keep up with the pack (and maybe get a little ahead) than apparently makes sense by any rational calculation of social costs and benefits. For example, lawyers, management consultants, and university faculty often put in 70- or 80-hour work weeks, sacrificing their social lives, their families, and even their health for their jobs. The rewards in these jobs are high, but it seems unlikely that the last hours these people put in each night yield sufficient extra output to justify the costs. Similar phenomena seem to arise in the case of students studying "too hard" to gain admission to the prestigious universities in Japan and the *grandes ecoles* in France—the students would all be better off if they competed less intensely, and it is not clear that society would be the worse off if they relaxed somewhat.

Why does this inefficient pattern of behavior persist? Why doesn't someone—an employer, for example—put a halt to the rat race? Doing so would increase efficiency, and presumably the employer could then capture some of the resulting gains, perhaps by having to pay less to attract and keep people.

One possible explanation focuses on information problems. It is rational for employers to take high levels of past and current performance as an indicator that future performance levels will also be high if the performance depends partly on some persistent but unobserved personal characteristic, which we may call "ability." Performance in any period also depends on effort exerted and on random factors, but employers cannot observe whether an instance of high performance reflects ability, effort, or luck. The result is an extra incentive to work hard because higher performance today leads to higher employer estimates of ability and thus to higher expectations about future performance and higher future pay.

Notice that these incentives to work too hard are strongest early in one's career, for two reasons. First, that is the time of greatest uncertainty about actual workers' abilities and, therefore, the time when workers have the greatest opportunity to influence employers' perceptions. That is also the time when the length of the remaining career is longest and so when the benefits of any perceived increase in ability has its highest value. Later, when a person's reputation is stabilized by repeated observations of performance, it will be harder to alter perceptions of ability, and the benefit of an improved reputation will be shorter lived.

Of course, employers understand these incentives and, in making their inferences about ability, they should allow for the fact that younger people will be working exceptionally hard early in their careers and less hard later. Even though at an individual level, hard work does lead to more favorable evaluations and estimates of the employee's ability, the extra effort does not systematically bias employers' perceptions of employees' abilities. If some individual dropped out of the rat race, cutting back on effort, this individual reduced effort level would not be observed. Then, the lower level of resulting performance would be incorrectly interpreted as evidence of low ability, not as the result of the person's selecting a lower, and more efficient, level of work intensity. No one individually finds it worthwhile to stop racing, even though the result is socially wasteful.

Based on Bengt Holmstrom, "Managerial Incentive Problems: A Dynamic Perspective," in *Essays in Economics and Management in Honour of Lars Wahlbeck* (Helsinki: Swedish School of Economics, 1982). See also George Akerlof, "The Economics of Caste and of the Rat Race and Other Woeful Tales," *Quarterly Journal of Economics*, 90 (November 1976), 599–617.

a unified response to a universal problem identifies two key problems faced by the firm. The first is to motivate employees to supply effort when the actual level of performance is observed by the firm's managers but is not verifiable by third parties. The lack of verifiability means that it is infeasible to tie pay to performance directly via any explicit contract that would be enforceable by the courts. The second problem arises because individual employees alone know just how difficult it is for them to achieve any given level of performance. Efficiency requires that those who are more able should perform at a higher level, and the problem is then to induce them to do so.

A system with many of the features of internal labor markets can theoretically solve these two problems simultaneously. Suppose the firm sets up the following system. It defines a hierarchy of regular jobs, plus an entry position. Attached to each job is both a pay level and a standard of performance required of those in the job, with higher-level jobs offering more pay and demanding higher performance. Under competitive pressure, the wage in any job will have to equal the extra value created by a worker who meets the specified performance standard for the job. However, because performance is not verifiable, the firm agrees that it will pay the specified wage to any worker holding a particular job in any time period, independent of the employee's actual performance. This arrangement is enforceable by the courts because whether the person was assigned to a particular job and whether he or she was paid the agreed amount are assumed to be verifiable. If the worker does not perform to the required level, however, he or she is fired (after getting his or her paycheck). Workers who do perform are kept on for another period.

All hiring is into the entry-level position. Those who perform very poorly in this position are paid and let go, but those who do better are promoted into a regular job. Generally, an employee in any job in the ladder who performs up to a predetermined standard (higher than that needed to keep the job) is promoted to the next level, with its higher pay and higher demands. Even in the period in which the employee wins a promotion, however, he or she receives only the pay guaranteed in the current job.

EQUILIBRIUM BEHAVIOR   How will employees behave in the system just described? Provided that the requirements of a job are not too demanding relative to the employee's abilities and that the pay is sufficiently high, the employee will choose to work hard enough to meet the standards set for the job. To do otherwise would result in being fired, leading to a loss of a high-wage job. Moreover, meeting any given standard will be easier for abler people. Therefore, these people may find it worthwhile

More Rat Races

A problem with the rat-race story as told earlier is that in many situations, the effort that people put in is at least partly observed. In fact, young lawyers at many prestigious firms make a point of being seen to be in their offices night and day. In the previous story these employees should want to hide the fact that they are working hard, so that their employers will think their remarkable output is the result of exceptional ability, not hard work. Thus, they should leave the office *early*, carrying sports equipment, but with work that they will do at home hidden in their gym bags!

However, a variation of the model can account for this. Suppose that what employers are trying to discern is not ability as much as a sense of responsibility and a willingness to work hard, and that this differs among individuals but is unobservable. In that case, early in their careers, people will have an incentive to try to build reputations for putting in long hours because they will be perceived as willing to work harder than others in the future as well. Staying in the office longer than would otherwise be optimal could signal this trait, and the observed pattern would emerge. Again, of course, if these incentives are recognized, no one is fooled, and yet no individual can afford to relax for fear of being seen as lazy. Also, these incentives are greatest early in a person's career, for the same reasons we discussed in the first variation of this model.

to perform at the higher level needed to get promoted whereas less able people will not. These are the key elements in generating the equilibrium modes of behavior under the assumed system.

If the number of rungs in the job ladder, the pay and performance levels attached to each job, and the promotion standards at each level are all set properly, employees will be motivated to work for promotions until each reaches a level that is "appropriate" in light of his or her (privately known) abilities. At this point he or she is willing to perform well enough to keep the current job but unwilling to work hard enough to win another promotion: The promise of higher pay but harder work once promoted is not enough to make earning the promotion worthwhile. Thus, the employees sort themselves on the basis of their private information, with those who find it easier to work hard being motivated to do so.

In this theoretical system, the "Peter Principle" is subtly changed from a problem to be avoided into an engine of sorting and motivation. In this system, people are not promoted to their levels of incompetency. Instead, people are repeatedly promoted out of jobs for which they are overqualified until they reach ones where the job demands are well suited to their individual ability levels.

Moreover, if the system is properly designed there will be no shirking. Those who are still striving for promotion will exceed the minimum performance standards, and those who have reached the level appropriate to their abilities will find it worthwhile to meet the standards required so as not to be fired. With no shirking, there will also be no one fired, except those who do not make the cut in the try-out, entry position.

PROPERTIES OF THE SYSTEM   The system explained by this model mimics a remarkable number of the features of actual job ladders in internal labor markets. In the model, an employee's pay depends only on his or her current job assignment. Even those who perform at the extraordinary levels needed for promotion are not directly paid anything more: Their reward is the extra pay they get after being promoted. Salary and responsibilities increase as an employee moves through promotions from one rank to another, and abler people end up reaching higher levels of responsibility in the firm. All hiring is through a single port of entry at the bottom; otherwise, unqualified people would enter at the high level, shirk, collect their pay, and leave. After an initial tryout, employees stay with the same employer in what is effectively a long-term relationship. Firings are rare (they occur only when someone makes a mistake, gets promoted to a too high-level job, and finds it is not worthwhile to meet the job's performance standards), as are quits (these would happen only if an earned promotion were denied, which would be a mistake on the firm's part).

Another interesting feature is that the firm receives no rents on employees who have risen as far as they are going to go in the company: They are paid the value of what they produce. In contrast, the firm does earn rents or quasi-rents from the employees who are still trying for promotions because they are working to a higher level than are other people in the same job but are paid no more. Thus, "rising stars" will be treasured, and firms will compete to identify and attract the most promising new job candidates. (The quasi-rents earned on rising stars may be viewed as a return to these recruitment investments.)

One feature of many real job ladders that is missing here is that actual hierarchies are often pyramids, narrowing towards the top, whereas nothing in the model ensures that there will be more people at lower levels than at higher ones. Although it is true that managerial hierarchies do tend to be pyramids, this is not a universal property of all job ladders, especially when those at higher levels are not responsible for supervising people below them. For example, higher performance might mean being responsible for more tasks in a production process, or more unusual tasks, or serving a larger territory, rather than supervising more people. Then there may well be more people at the higher levels than at lower ones. For example, there are more people at the rank of Secretary IIS on the staff of the Stanford Business School than at the Secretary II level. The same pattern also holds in many professional partnerships, such as law firms, where there are usually more partners than associates, and in universities, where there will often be more full professors than assistant or associate professors.

Within this model, as in many economic models, ability is a one-dimensional quality. Some people are simply more productive than others. In reality, people differ on a much wider array of characteristics, such as temperament, stamina, communication skills, analytical ability, and so on, that make job assignments a complex and subtle task. The next model recognizes some of these complexities.

INFLUENCE COSTS, INCENTIVES, AND JOB ASSIGNMENT

A fundamental conflict can arise when promotions are used both to provide incentives for performance in the current job and to assign the best-qualified people to key jobs. As already noted, the best performer in one job may not be the person who is best qualified for a promotion. An obvious solution would seem to be to separate promotions and performance incentives. We have already suggested some problems with this approach, especially those of defining and measuring performance and of motivating managers to do the sort of careful evaluations that are often needed to use pay as a motivator. Even putting these aside for the moment, however, this solution may not be efficient. Influence costs can arise when it is possible for employees to divert valuable time to affect their apparent qualifications for promotion and when employees' time allocations are not observable. Handling these costs may lead the firm to use promotions as incentives even when it could use performance pay.

Pay Differences, Hierarchies, and Tournaments

An important element of the rewards to being promoted in a hierarchy is that you are positioned to try for further promotions to yet higher levels with even greater status, pay, and perquisites. In essence, job ladders in hierarchies are **elimination tournaments**, where the prize to winning at one stage is the immediate reward (higher salary and other direct benefits) plus the value of the option to continue competing.

The higher a person rises within a firm, the fewer opportunities remain for further promotions. Other things being equal, this reduces the incentives to seek promotion because the second part of the reward to promotion—the opportunity to keep on advancing and to try for yet further prizes—is diminished. This means that to maintain the incentives to compete for advancement, the direct monetary gains to promotion must increase as the person rises through the hierarchy. Consequently, the difference in pay associated with promotion should increase as one rises in the hierarchy. Also, once the person becomes CEO, there are no more prizes to win, so the jump in pay associated with this final promotion should be especially large.

A recent empirical study has tested these predictions.[*] The results generally support the theory. The study examined five job levels, from plant manager through corporate CEO, in a sample of over 300 large U.S. firms in a variety of different industries. The median pay (salary plus bonus) at the plant-manager level was $21,000 (in 1967 dollars), at the next level it was $37,000, at the third level it was $43,000, at the fourth it was $60,000, and at the top, CEO level it was $130,000. The increase associated with a one-level promotion was thus, on average, $16,000, $6,000, $17,000, and $70,000. This aggregate pattern is broadly consistent with the theory. More significantly, examination of the pay differentials between ranks within each individual company gave very strong support for both predictions: Pay gaps widen moving up the hierarchy within a firm, and the promotion to CEO brings an extraordinary jump in pay relative to other promotions. These tests are especially significant because they control for differences in the number of ranks used in different companies and the differences between the sizes of organizational units across companies.

---

[*]Richard A. Lambert, David F. Larcker, and Keith Weigelt, "Tournaments and the Structure of Organizational Incentives," draft, The Wharton School, University of Pennsylvania (1989).

A Job-Assignment Problem

To illustrate this problem and to see how responding to it can influence the policies of the organization, consider a hypothetical situation in which a firm must promote one of two workers to fill a "key" job, which might be a supervisory or leadership position, for example. Its defining property is that if the person holding the key job were to quit, the firm would suffer an extraordinary cost in replacing the employee or in having the job temporarily empty. Both candidates for promotion are currently assigned to a job in which their individual efforts are productive in that more effort increases the probability of a good outcome (say, making a big sale or achieving a breakthrough in a research project). There is no difference between the two workers in their abilities to produce successfully in the base-line job, but they may differ in their abilities to perform in the key job. Although one candidate might be better qualified for the key job (in the sense that total profits will be higher if that person is promoted), the firm does not know initially which candidate that is.

The employees can spend time on the job in two ways. They may each devote time to improving the chances of a successful outcome in their current assignments, or they may devote time to developing evidence about their qualifications for the key job. The workers, however, have no inherent like or dislike for either activity. Without incentives to do otherwise, they are willing to allocate their efforts in any way that the firm's management may direct.

Two observability problems complicate the situation. First, the attractiveness of any competing offer that the person who is ultimately promoted may receive is not observable by the firm. Second, the firm cannot observe the workers' choices in allocating their current time and effort, nor can it tell if a worker is suppressing unfavorable information he or she may have obtained about his or her qualifications for promotion. Under these circumstances, a worker who increases the share of time on the job spent developing information about his or her qualifications and then hides any unfavorable results will likely produce stronger "credentials." He or she is likely to appear better qualified for the promotion than otherwise would have been the case. However, the diversion of attention to building credentials reduces the probability of the worker achieving a good outcome in the current job.

THE IMPACT OF LIMITED OBSERVABILITY Without these observability difficulties, the firm's optimal policy would be simple. It would trade off the value of increasing the quality of information about the candidates' qualifications for the key job against the cost of reducing the expected output in the current jobs, and then it would direct the workers to allocate their time between production and information development accordingly. The workers would be paid a fixed wage for their time in the current job, so that pay is unrelated to performance, and the firm would promote the one who appeared better qualified. The pay that the workers subsequently receive would be independent of their job assignments unless the one assigned to the key job gets an outside offer, in which case the firm would match this offer as long as that is cheaper than losing the worker.

The firm's inability to evaluate outside offers makes the offer-matching strategy infeasible. We saw in Chapter 10 that one solution is to pay a premium wage to the worker who is promoted, as a kind of insurance against losing him or her and suffering the resultant costs. The result of this would be to make the key job more attractive than the other one because the promoted worker would not have to get a good outside offer to earn more.

If the workers' allocations of effort could be perfectly observed, the pay differential associated with being promoted would not cause any further problems. Even if the workers can hide unfavorable information, the firm may be able to allow for this in evaluating their credentials and still make the right promotion decisions. If the allocation of effort cannot be directly measured, however, there is a moral hazard problem. Without any direct incentive to devote effort to production, workers would find it in their interest to spend all their time developing their credentials, trying to win promotion to the better-paying job. The loss of current output occasioned by this diversion of attention could be very costly to the firm. These costs are influence costs, as the workers use resources to attempt to influence which of them will gain the rents that result from being promoted.

Organizational Responses

There are a number of ways that the firm can respond to the incentive difficulties that it creates when it pays more to the promoted worker. It can reduce the difference in pay between the key job and the other. It can introduce performance pay, paying more if the worker's output is high than if it is low. It can reduce the importance of credentials in the promotion decision by promoting on other criteria, such as seniority, perhaps even not gathering the information that the workers develop regarding their qualifications. More directly, it can make performance a criterion in the promotion decision, even though performance in the current job carries no information about qualifications for the key job.

OPTIMAL PAY AND PROMOTION POLICIES   Just which mix of these is best depends in part on the importance of promoting the worker who actually is better qualified. At one extreme, if the profits of the firm crucially depend on whether the better-qualified person is assigned to the key job, it is very important that some information on qualifications be generated and that this information be used to identify and promote the better candidate. In this case, unless the firm wants the workers simply to ignore their current jobs and to spend all their time generating information, some sort of incentives must be provided to get the workers to pay attention to their current responsibilities.

Because the gap in pay between the two jobs creates the incentives for workers to misallocate their time, an obvious possibility would be to narrow this gap. This alone will not help, however, unless the gap is completely closed. As long as there is no reward for current performance, the existence of *any* gap means that the incentives are to ignore productive activity entirely because it is costless to the workers to do so. Thus, some sort of performance incentives are needed, even though employees are (by assumption) not averse to working hard. The appropriate way to provide these in this case is by paying a bonus for success in the current job. Promoting in part on the basis of current performance would also provide the desired incentives, but the extreme importance of promoting the better-qualified candidate makes this alternative unattractive. Once performance incentives are in place, however, it is also useful to reduce the size of the pay differential associated with promotion, thereby reducing the amount of rents and the incentives to try to influence their ultimate distribution.

At the opposite extreme, if it really does not matter which one is promoted because the output in the key job is largely insensitive to the qualifications of the person holding it, then the solution is simply to promote the one who performed better in the current job. (If their performance is indistinguishable, then some other criteria such as seniority might be used, or a random choice could be made: The important point is that their credentials should not be a factor in the decision.) No direct performance pay is needed, nor is there any need to close the pay gap between the worker who is promoted and the one who is passed over. This promotion policy will induce the workers to spend all their time on productive activities, as is optimal.

Finally, when making the right assignment to the key job is of middling importance, it may be worthwhile to provide performance incentives by a mix of methods involving performance pay and the promotion criteria. Promoting on the basis of a mix of performance and qualifications allows production incentives to be maintained without having to offer high levels of direct performance pay. Thus, promotions may be made on criteria that have nothing to do with ability or likely success in the key job. At the same time, it can again be valuable to reduce the pay differential associated with promotion.

More generally, to the extent that the firm limits the linkage between promotions and apparent individual performance or qualifications, influence costs may be reduced.

This possibility gives a reason to apply a seniority rule that only the most senior workers at a given level will be considered for promotion. Such a rule limits the set of people who are effectively competing for a promotion at any given time and so may reduce the total resources wasted in influence activities.

COMMITMENT PROBLEMS   A policy of promoting on seniority, performance, or other criteria other than apparent qualifications may run into a commitment problem. If the firm has the information that has been generated about the worker's qualifications, it will sometimes believe that it is promoting the less-qualified person when it promotes on past performance. This would be especially galling because (at least in the current model), past performance has nothing to do with future productivity in the key job.[8] Because there is no further need to provide incentives (at least in the simplified framework considered here), there will be a temptation to renege and promote the better-qualified person. The alternative is to throw away future profits by adhering to the promise to promote on performance.

If the basis of performance measurement is reasonably objective, so that other workers can observe the firm reneging on its policy, then this problem may not be too serious. Concern for its reputation will prevent management from violating its commitments in a wholesale way. When performance measurement is subjective, however, the temptation to ignore performance and to promote on the basis of perceived qualifications for the job may be irresistible.

Of course, if the workers believe that the firm will not adhere to its announced promotion policy but will instead promote the person with the better credentials, then the announced promotion scheme will be irrelevant to their decision making. In such circumstances, the firm might prefer not to allow employees to present their credentials, even if they are best positioned to do so and have spent resources creating a polished presentation. By refusing to allow such presentations, they avoid the temptation to cheat on their promises and help provide proper incentives to employees.

TENURE AND UP-OR-OUT RULES

Two aspects of the promotion policies of many organizations present especially interesting puzzles: tenure and up-or-out rules in promotions. Someone with formal *tenure* cannot be fired except for serious cause, and then usually only through a demanding process. An *up-or-out rule* means that those denied promotion must leave the organization; they cannot stay on in their original jobs, even if they were doing quite well.

Often these two practices are linked. Tenure is most familiar in universities and colleges, which also have an up-or-out rule that a faculty member who is denied tenure must leave. However, these practices are used in many professional partnerships in law, accounting, and other fields as well. Professional employees are reviewed for partnership at a definite point in their careers, and those who are not admitted to partnership are let go. Meanwhile, attaining partnership has usually meant that the person effectively cannot be fired.[9] The practices are not always linked, however. For

---

[8] In fact, given the incentives in the model and the behavior they would induce, which worker had the higher performance is purely a matter of luck. Both will devote the same time to productive activity, so their expected outputs will be the same. The realized differences in their outputs will reflect only random noise.

[9] In early 1991, however, the large international public accounting firm of Peat Marwick announced that it was planning to lay off 14 percent of its approximately 1,800 partners, and a number of large law firms were reported to have similar plans. These were newsworthy events that caused great discussion and, no doubt, real consternation. Apparently the partners' tenure was not as secure as outside observers (and the partners) had believed.

example, tenure (in the form of partnership) is used without an up-or-out rule at the investment banking firm of Goldman Sachs, where those who are unsuccessful in making partner in a particular year are often encouraged to stay on and try again. In contrast, the U.S. armed forces have a repeated up-or-out rule for officers—those in each cohort at each rank who fail to win promotion to the next rank must retire—but no tenure system.

The puzzle regarding up-or-out rules is this: Why would the firm find it worthwhile to keep someone employed for several years, often at a handsome pay rate and with major job responsibilities, and then the next day refuse to keep them on for any kind of professional work at any compensation level? One possibility is that these lower-level positions are valued for more than just the output that their occupants produce. They provide a training ground for new workers, an opportunity to observe and evaluate employees' capabilities, and a way to bring fresh perspectives and ideas into the firm, all of which are important for maintaining the firm's vitality.[10] However, the very importance of turnover among employees throws into even sharper focus the puzzle associated with tenure: Why does the organization commit itself to keeping on senior employees whose abilities and performance may be much lower and ideas much staler than those of their potential replacements? There is no fully satisfactory, unified explanation available for these practices, but separate, partial explanations based on informational asymmetries and commitment problems have been advanced.

Tenure

The nominal reason for academic tenure is to protect academic freedom: Job security is supposed to make professors less afraid to espouse unpopular positions. More generally, tenure may make professors willing to take risks on new and daring research directions that are likely to fail but might lead to great breakthroughs. This explanation does not seem particularly applicable to professional partnerships, however. In any case, the rigidities and inefficiencies of the tenure system seem to make it an expensive and clumsy way to protect free speech or encourage risk taking.

An "Expertise" Explanation for Academic Tenure   One analysis that explains the practice of tenure is based on the idea that only the current faculty in a university department has the expertise and information sources to evaluate potential new hires, although management (the administration) is able to recognize the quality and measure the productivity of people once they are in the organization. Given some constraint on the number of faculty that can be employed in the institution, the incumbent faculty's fear is that the university will replace them with younger, better qualified, more productive people. The only way that this could happen, however, is if such people are identified by the incumbents and then brought into the system, whereupon the administration can judge their quality relative to their older colleagues. This means that unless the incumbents are unconcerned that identifying good people will endanger their own welfare, they will have an incentive to misrepresent the qualifications of candidates, attempting to ensure that tough competitors are weeded out and that only weak candidates who are no threat to them are allowed to enter the system.

One potential way to remove the incumbents' fear of being replaced would be

---

[10] This argument and the evidence for it is developed in two research papers by Brendan O'Flaherty and Aloysius Siow, "Up or Out Rules in the Market for Lawyers," Discussion Paper 90-10, Economics Research Center, National Opinion Research Center, Chicago (September 1990), and "On the Job Screening, Up or Out Rules, and Firm Growth," Discussion Paper 90-11, Economics Research Center, National Opinion Research Center, Chicago, (September 1990).

to give enough severance pay to senior people who are let go that they are indifferent between keeping their jobs and losing them. Determining the necessary amount of compensation may be extremely difficult, however, and the bargaining costs that would be incurred make this approach very problematic.

A tenure system presents a simple alternative solution. People who have met the tenure criteria cannot be fired simply because their talents or performance levels have deteriorated or their particular area of expertise within the field is no longer in demand. Thus, they have no reason to fear the hiring of people who are better qualified than they are and no reason to misrepresent the quality of candidates.

This explanation is consistent with other aspects of universities' employment and governance procedures. Tenured professors can in fact be fired if their performance is bad enough, but the standard that must be met is painfully low and unresponsive to changing conditions. This is necessary to prevent firing for cause from becoming a masquerade for replacing less qualified professors, which would destroy incentives. Moreover, when financial pressures necessitate a reduction in faculty size beyond what can be accommodated by releasing untenured faculty, a common practice is to eliminate whole departments or schools, rather than individual tenured faculty from across several units. To do otherwise and release people based on their abilities would encourage the senior faculty to stock their departments with mediocrities. In contrast, closing whole units encourages the faculty to make their departments as strong as possible to protect themselves against wholesale dismissal.

Applicability to Other Contexts. The basic idea that tenure is a system that encourages professionals not to misrepresent their evaluations of new job candidates out of the fear of losing their jobs to the newcomers also has applicability in law, accounting, and other professions where partnerships are common. Surely the tax or bankruptcy attorneys in a law firm are especially well positioned to evaluate potential hires in their areas of expertise, and the firm must thus rely largely on their appraisals of candidates. To the extent that, without tenure, the senior people would be concerned about the possibility of their colleagues replacing them with superior younger people, they would have an incentive to screen out the best candidates. This danger would seem to be especially severe in larger firms and in firms that share profits on a seniority basis. In these situations, the costs of having less able people are spread widely across the organization. In smaller firms or those that divide profits according to departmental performance, the costs of having mediocre colleagues fall more directly on those responsible. Thus, their incentives to hire weak people are lessened.

A LEARNING EXPLANATION   An alternative explanation for tenure applies more broadly and seems to have more applicability to situations where acquired professional expertise is not a major factor. Suppose for simplicity there are just two basic types of jobs, one in which productivity is largely insensitive to innate ability and another in which ability or talent plays a key role in determining success. Bureaucratic office work or many jobs in the secondary sector might be examples of the former, and executive positions or artistic work could be examples of the latter type of employment. Efficiency requires that low-ability people should be assigned to the jobs where ability is unimportant and high-ability people should be placed in the ability-sensitive jobs where they are more productive. Suppose too that peoples' ability levels are not directly observed by anyone, including the individuals themselves. Then an efficient allocation of individuals to jobs is not immediately achievable.

If an individual tries the sensitive job, his or her realized output in any period generates a signal about his or her ability. The more successful the individual is in any period, the more likely that he or she is actually well matched in the job, and the more periods in which he or she is successful, the more certain it becomes that the ability-sensitive job is the right one for this person. Eventually, after enough experience, the quality of the match may be almost completely learned, and the person will either move to the other type of job or become permanently matched in the ability-sensitive job. In this case, the person effectively has tenure in the ability-sensitive job. Even if he or she performs very poorly in the future, the estimate of ability will still remain sufficiently high that his or her expected productivity is still higher in the sensitive job.

The same idea can be extended to multiple jobs with differing sensitivities to different kinds of talent and to there being some initial information about abilities. The argument would also work if the match between different jobs and personal tastes differed. The pattern that will emerge is some early experimentation, followed by an eventual settling down with effective tenure. This pattern is in fact quite common in actual careers.

Up-Or-Out Rules

One explanation for up-or-out rules starts from the observation that tenure (or partnership) is usually associated with a quantum jump in earnings (monetary and otherwise), often with no major increase in responsibilities, except for a greater role in governance. Assistant professors have essentially the same job responsibilities as do full professors, and senior associates in law firms do much the same work as partners. Yet the junior people are typically paid much less than senior ones. The average assistant professor makes about half as much as the average full professor in major research universities, and the ratio of associates' pay to partners' earnings in law firms is probably even lower. Apparently, then, the organization collects rents on the junior people. Their reason for staying on, despite being paid less than they are contributing, is the chance to get promoted and then receive their share of the organization's profits and the rents to be earned on later junior people.

In this context, promotions have little effect on the output of the organization, but they mean that the rents and profits must be shared among more claimants. The obvious temptation would be to turn down people who come up for partner or tenure, so that the available rents do not have to be shared with extra people, but to offer them a chance to stay on at competitive wages. Even more attractive would be to try to get the unsuccessful candidates to stay on at their substandard pay with the promise that they will be reconsidered in the near future.

Of course, junior people who recognize these incentives would not play this game. They would not work hard in hopes of promotion; they would not invest in firm-specific human capital whose value would not be reflected in their pay but only add to the rents that the tenured people collect; and they would not work for less than their market wage.

The up-or-out policy imposes costs on the firm when it turns someone down for promotion: It loses the returns that the person brings, and the only way to capture any of the returns is to award tenure or partnership. The firm will then not be tempted to deny people promotions in hopes of exploiting them, and so the incentives that the chance of gaining tenure provides can be effective.

The basic idea that up-or-out rules are a means of imposing costs on the decision makers yields a complementary explanation: Tenure coupled with up-or-out rules forces those doing evaluations to take them seriously because the decisions are made much more important when these practices are in place. This helps overcome the reluctance to bear the costs of doing careful reviews of subordinates that we noted earlier.

SUMMARY

A majority of the workers in developed countries becomes attached to a single employer in a long-term relationship that commonly extends 20 years or more. Although the classical theory of employment arrangements continuously buffeted by changing labor market conditions provides a reasonable description of short-term employment in the *secondary sector* of advanced economies, the long-term jobs in the *primary sector* are insulated to a considerable degree from conditions in the external labor market. Instead, an *internal labor market* develops to assign people to appropriate jobs within the firm and to determine their pay.

One of the distinctive features of traditional internal labor markets is that, to a considerable degree, wages are determined by job classifications rather than by individual qualifications. Table 11.1 illustrates this proposition, but it also illustrates that there is still latitude for individual wage differentials within jobs. More experienced workers and workers with unusually high performance ratings tend to move toward the tops of the categories, whereas less experienced workers tend to be nearer the lower end. As long as job requirements and tasks remain unchanged over fairly long periods of time, this system can be effective, but with changing technologies and products firms may wish to encourage their workers to become flexible, paying wages based on skills rather than on the job actually being done. This system is quite prevalent in Japan and is found increasingly in other parts of the world as well.

Given the advantages associated with worker mobility and the relatively high wages paid in the primary-sector jobs, there must be significant advantages to long-term employment to offset the loss of mobility that it entails. Among these advantages are the acquisition of *firm-specific human capital*, which enables a worker in the primary sector to become especially productive in his or her job; the use of *efficiency wages* and of *implicit, relational contracts*, in which the promises of loyalty and fair treatment are enforced by internal mechanisms within the firm and by the desire of each party to maintain a good reputation in its long-term relationship; and *informational advantages*, especially the superior knowledge that an employer has about its employees' abilities that permits giving more effective incentives and making more productive assignments of workers to jobs.

Jobs within internal labor markets are arranged in hierarchies with the result that employees doing similar work may sometimes have higher or lower rankings. The higher-ranking employees may be more experienced and therefore better able to handle exceptional conditions, to train or advise others about what actions are required, and so on. Extra duties, extra responsibilities, and greater reliance of the organization on the higher-ranking employees' judgments help account for the higher pay and the tendency to assign these jobs to more talented, experienced people. In these kinds of jobs, the use of promotions to reward productivity is relatively unproblematic.

In other jobs, the use of promotions for rewards are a much more nettlesome problem because promotion involves a qualitative change in responsibilities. There is no guarantee, nor even a great likelihood, that the best or most experienced machinist will also be the best supervisor and teacher, or that the best researcher in an R&D laboratory will make the best R&D manager. It may be most productive to retain the machinist and researcher in their original jobs and promote someone whose performance was less outstanding.

Why, then, not use cash bonuses to reward individual good performance rather than promotions? Promotions from within have the advantage that they resemble *tournaments*, which have three important advantages for providing incentives. First, tournaments require only comparative, *ordinal* information about who did better rather than the much costlier *cardinal* information about how much better a party has performed than some absolute standard. Second, even when the quality of each performance is separately and objectively measurable, *relative performance evaluation* may be a better basis for compensation if common factors affect the performance of all the participants. Third, because the bonus pool in a tournament is set in advance, the employer has no incentive to disparage or misrepresent the workers' performance in order to save having to pay performance bonuses: A source of moral hazard is eliminated. In addition to these advantages, attaching pay to jobs and using promotions for incentives mitigates the need to bargain with individual employees over their salaries. Such bargaining is a time-consuming, disruptive, and personally costly process, incurring high *influence costs.*

One model that explains many of the features of internal labor markets in a unified fashion emphasizes that workers vary in their abilities, that their efforts are subject to moral hazard, and that their performance can be judged only by insiders and so cannot be a basis for contracts enforceable in court. The firm creates an internal labor market with entry only at the bottom of the hierarchy, pay in each rank that is insensitive to performance, higher pay and performance requirements being associated with higher-level jobs, and higher levels of performance being required to be promoted than merely to avoid being fired. This leads workers both to select levels of effort that are at nearly efficient levels and to sort themselves among jobs so that the abler ones are eventually promoted to the jobs best suited to their abilities.

When promotions are based partly on forecasts of future performance rather than on past performance alone, candidates acquire an incentive to build credentials for good jobs and to manipulate the decision makers' perceptions, instead of simply being productive. These activities are more examples of influence costs, and they can degrade the performance of the organization. Organizations can reduce these costs in various ways, including the introduction of pay for performance to create an offsetting incentive, increasing the weight given to past performance in promotion decisions, and limiting the input that employees have to the decision process. A decision to establish any policy other than promoting the best qualified person, however, creates a *problem of commitment*—management will not want to carry out the policy when the time comes to do so. If the basis of the decision is observable, then concern for its reputation may lead management to adhere to its policy, but the problem becomes a serious one when the proposed alternative basis of evaluation is highly subjective.

The use of *up-or-out* rules in promotions and the institution of permanent job *tenure*, both of which are common in many professional hierarchies, including law firms, accounting firms, and universities, are puzzles requiring explanation. Junior accountants and associates at law firms and assistant professors at universities work under contracts with limited job security, whereas the partners (at law and accounting firms) or tenured professors (at universities) have an effective employment guarantee. At some point, the young workers must either be promoted and given permanent job security or face termination of their employment. These up-or-out and tenure rules appear to serve a variety of functions which have been the basis for a number of theories. One possibility is that the low-level jobs are continually turned over to allow the organization to import fresh ideas and perspectives from outsiders or to allow the organization to evaluate closely potential candidates for higher-ranking positions. To the extent that only professionals are able to evaluate one another's performance, tenure rules might be designed to encourage professionals to identify the best candidates—candidates who are so good that their appointment might otherwise threaten the recommender's own job. Up-or-out rules force the organization to promote candidates or lose their services. Because junior people in organizations employing these rules are a source of rents to the organization, the temptation would be to try to hold them in the lower-level jobs, but this would destroy incentives and make recruiting difficult.

■ BIBLIOGRAPHIC NOTES

Peter Doeringer and Michael Piore's landmark 1971 study, *Internal Labor Markets and Manpower Analysis,* made clear the usefulness of this concept in understanding employment policies. It remains a basic reference. Richard Edwards suggested the subdivision of the primary sector discussed in the text. Mace Mesters' dissertation explores theoretically the emergence of primary and secondary sectors and the allocation of workers between sectors based on ability. Masahiko Aoki's book (especially Chapter 3) discusses Japanese internal labor market and human resource management systems.

The analysis of tournaments as incentive schemes was begun by Edward Lazear and Sherwin Rosen. Bentley MacLeod and James Malcomson developed the model of an internal labor market as a solution to the problems of moral hazard in effort provision and of inducing self-selection on the basis of ability. The treatment of the job-assignment problem in the presence of influence costs is drawn from our own research.

The "expertise in judging applicants" explanation of tenure originated with H. Lorne Carmichael, and the "learning" explanation is based on the work of Milton Harris and Yoram Weiss. The rationale for up-or-out rules is due to Ronald Gilson and Robert Mnookin.

■ REFERENCES

Aoki, M. *Information, Incentives and Bargaining in the Japanese Economy* (Cambridge: Cambridge University Press, 1988).

Carmichael, H. L. "Incentives in Academics: Why is There Tenure?" *Journal of Political Economy,* 96 (1988), 453–72.

Doeringer, P., and M. Piore. *Internal Labor Markets and Manpower Analysis* (Lexington, MA: D.C. Heath, 1971).

Edwards, R. *Contested Terrain: The Transformation of the Work Place in the Twentieth Century* (New York: Basic Books, 1979).

Harris, M., and Y. Weiss. "Job Matching with a Finite Horizon and Risk Aversion," *Journal of Political Economy,* 92 (August 1984), 758–79.

Gilson, R., and R. Mnookin. "Coming of Age in a Corporate Law Firm: The Economics of Associate Career Patterns," *Stanford Law Review,* 41 (1989), 567–95.

Lazear, E., and S. Rosen. "Rank Order Tournaments as Optimal Labor Contracts," *Journal of Political Economy,* 89 (October 1981), 841–64.

MacLeod, W. B., and J. Malcomson. "Reputation and Hierarchy in Dynamic Models of Employment," *Journal of Political Economy,* 96 (August, 1988), 832–54.

Mesters, M. *Technology and Management of Human Capital,* unpublished dissertation, Stanford University Graduate School of Business (1990).

Milgrom, P., and J. Roberts. "An Economic Approach to Influence Activities in Organizations," *American Journal of Sociology* 94 (Supplement), 1988a: S154–S179.

EXERCISES

Food for Thought

1.   Suppose you were put in charge of promotion and pay determination for the faculty members in your school or department. What criteria would you use in making your decisions? What information would you want? How would you try to get it? Would you eliminate tenure?

2.   Most "permanent" employees in large Japanese firms face mandatory retirement at about age 58 (the most senior executives are exempt). However, social security benefits from the state do not begin until age 65. Contractual, employer-provided pensions were rare until recently, but companies typically made substantial cash grants to retiring workers. Retired workers often seek jobs in smaller, less prestigious firms at lower rates of pay. These firms are sometimes ones with which the original employer has a business relationship, in which case the employer might help the retiring employee find the job. What might be the rationale for these practices? Why not let employees stay with their original employers until they reach 65? Why subject them to the uncertainty about how much retirement pay they will receive? Why force them to look for another job?

3.   David Jacobs[11] has identified two sorts of jobs depending on the relationship between individual and organizational performance. In the first sort of job, individual failures are extremely costly for the firm, but above-average performance has little marginal impact on overall performance. Examples are being an airline pilot or an inspector in a nuclear power facility: A mistake is disastrous, but doing an especially good job has little impact. In the other sort of job, organizational performance is largely a matter of exceptional individual performance, with individual failures being of far less consequence. Examples are jobs in sales and scientific research. What differences would you expect between the human resource policies designed to deal with the two sorts of jobs? Why?

4.   In the late 1980s and early 1990s, the airline industry in the United States was going through a major "shake-out." A number of lines went bankrupt, and several of these either ceased operations entirely or reduced their scale considerably, selling some of their aircraft, routes, and ground facilities to other lines. Meanwhile, the successful lines were expanding rapidly: American Airlines, for example, was hiring almost a thousand pilots a year. Many of these were experienced airline pilots who had lost their jobs at other carriers.

Airline pilots move up through a job ladder that involves three ranks—flight engineer, copilot, and pilot—with increasing responsibilities and that also differentiates by the type of aircraft involved, with larger, more complex airplanes ranking higher. However, the skills and knowledge required to fill a particular role in a particular aircraft are essentially the same across airlines: Being a copilot on a particular type of Boeing 727 with United Airlines involves the same human capital as it does with Delta Airlines.

The airlines used a strict system of hiring only at the bottom of the job ladder. They maintained this policy, which the union supported, even when hiring very experienced pilots from other carriers: a senior pilot who had been flying the most advanced, wide-bodied aircraft on international routes would be required to start over

---

[11] David Jacobs, "Toward a Theory of Mobility and Behavior in Organizations: An Inquiry into the Consequences of Some Relationships Between Individual Performance and Organizational Success," *American Journal of Sociology*, 87 (1981), 684–707.

at the bottom if he or she changed airlines, despite all the non-specific human capital he or she had accumulated. Given this, a number of pilots instead left the industry, finding other work. This policy seems very wasteful. How would you account for it?

5. When labor market supply is tight and it is hard to find qualified workers, firms may be tempted to lower the standards they normally use in accepting applicants who would not be hired under normal circumstances. This is especially problematic for firms with internal labor markets and more-or-less permanent employment policies. What measures would you expect such firms to take to minimize the costs of hiring less-qualified people?

6. Empirically, the probability of a worker being fired from or quitting a particular job in any unit of time is a decreasing function of the length of time he or she has already been in the job. How would you account for this?

7. A number of management consultants in the late 1980s argued that companies should not have any jobs from which an employee, simply by being in them, could not rise to become chief executive officer: If there were jobs and activities whose requirements and focus did not connect this closely to the firms' main business, they should be placed outside the firm and the corresponding goods or services purchased from outside suppliers. What merits do you see in this? What are the difficulties?

8. In a number of technology-based companies (including, for example, Hewlett-Packard), employees move frequently across jobs and even across functions. There are many "lateral" moves that do not involve a promotion in the average employee's career path. What advantages do you see to this? What problems does it create? How might these be mitigated?

12

COMPENSATION AND MOTIVATION

A thorough understanding of internal incentives is critical to developing a viable theory of the firm, since they largely determine how individuals behave in organizations.

George Baker, Michael Jensen, and Kevin Murphy[1]

Compensation has many roles in the organization. One of the most important is to provide proper and effective motivation. This chapter focuses on compensation as a means of motivation, building on the basic theory of incentive pay developed in Chapters 7 and 8.

THE FORMS AND FUNCTIONS OF COMPENSATION

Differing Forms of Pay

Within an organization, compensation can take many forms and can depend on the hours of work, the performance achieved, or other indicators. Production workers are usually paid an hourly wage or, less commonly, a monthly salary. Alternatively, they may be paid a fixed amount, or **piece rate**, for each unit they produce. Office workers usually receive a monthly or semimonthly salary. If they are paid extra for overtime, it will typically be at a higher rate than their implicit hourly wage. Salespeople may receive a straight salary or a commission based on the number of units sold, the amount or revenue generated, or the profit generated by the sales; or some combination of these.

---

[1] "Compensation and Incentives: Practice vs. Theory," *Journal of Finance*, 43 (1988), 593.

Employees in each of these categories may receive bonus payments in addition to their regular pay. These bonuses might be implicitly or explicitly tied to performance at various levels—individual, group, plant, division, or the organization as a whole—and, in each case, performance may be defined in different ways. For determining an individual bonus, performance might be measured in a relatively objective fashion based on skills acquired, individual production, or revenue or profit generation, or instead it may be evaluated subjectively on the basis of a supervisor's determination of the employee's merit and overall contribution. Bonuses for a work group or plant might be based on productivity improvements, reaching quality or output goals, or meeting budgets. For a research and development team, bonuses might accrue for filing new patents or developing new products, or they might be determined as a function of the group's direct contribution to measured profitability. At the level of the business unit or division, bonuses might be based on meeting plans for sales or productivity growth, or budgets for costs and profits, or targets for return on investments. At the level of the organization as a whole, profit sharing may be the basis for extra compensation.

Rewards for good performance need not always take the form of current compensation. It is common to reward salaried employees by giving merit raises that increase base salary in all future periods. In this way, the rewards for current performance are spread over the remainder of the employee's career with the firm. More directly, life insurance agents may receive commission payments known as "renewals" that continue after the first year that a policy is in force, even if they have no further contact with the client and sometimes even if the agent no longer works for the insurance company. Many organizations also make contributions to pension funds on their employees' behalf. These are all essentially deferred cash compensation, with the extra feature that their receipt may be conditional on the employees' remaining with the firm for a specific period of time.

Other examples do not involve direct monetary compensation, but they increase the employees' buying power and so function like pay. For example, many firms give their employees discounts on buying the employers' products or services, and corporations often subsidize their employees' purchase of the firm's common stock. These firms may also pay some part of total compensation in stock directly, often putting restrictions on the employees' sales of these shares. Employee Stock Ownership Plans are an increasingly popular vehicle for this in the United States, where they are replacing contributions to regular pension funds to some extent.

Employers also provide a variety of fringe benefits that involve an element of noncash compensation: health, dental, and medical insurance, disability and life insurance, company cars that might substitute for employees' privately purchased vehicles, computers to use at home, health club memberships, and so on. They also may repay various expenses incurred by the employees, even though some (or all) of the benefits of these expenditures may have accrued to the employees. Examples include reimbursing educational expenses for employees (and, at many private universities, for their children), generously defined moving expense allowances, payment of professional association dues, license fees, and the costs of business publications, and the provision of liberal, loosely monitored expense accounts are examples.

Further variety and richness are found in executive compensation. Besides receiving salaries, bonuses, and all the multitude of indirect forms of compensation that are provided to lower-level employees, executives may also have access to special dining rooms and washrooms, company airplanes and apartments, and membership in exclusive clubs and associations. They are especially likely to receive deferred cash compensation, they may be awarded large amounts of company stock, and they frequently receive *stock options*—rights to buy the company's shares at a predetermined price, which may often turn out to be less than the market price of the stock. Executives being recruited by the firm may receive large signing bonuses that are rarely offered to regular employees. If they lose or leave their jobs after a merger, takeover, or other change in corporate control, they may receive large guaranteed severance payments (*golden parachutes*). Even after retirement they may be paid to work as consultants to the company, or they may be kept on the board of directors, receiving handsome fees for their time.

The complexity of individual compensation is compounded when we examine how pay changes over time and how it varies within and across organizations. Explaining this complexity and variety is a serious challenge to social scientists. Certainly, the classical economic model of determining wages and hours worked by supply and demand is inadequate to the task. For managers, the problem of selecting pay policies and forms and of determining individual compensation is both important and urgent. Their own personal success and the success of their organizations depend crucially on these choices. In this chapter, we seek an economic explanation of the observed diversity and complexity, in part in the hope of providing a better basis for managerial decisions.

The Objectives of Compensation Policy

A large part of the explanation lies in recognizing that compensation policy has a variety of roles to play in an organization and that, even holding the total payment constant, the form in which compensation is received can affect the extent to which these differing goals are met. Well-designed pay policies, forms, and levels can help attract employees to the organization and retain those that the organization wants to keep; they may also play a role in discouraging undesirable candidates and prompting unwanted employees to leave. As accentuated in Chapter 10, pay policies should help employees deal with uncertainties in their earnings opportunities. Pay should also signal what the organization values and what behavior and attitudes it wants to discourage, and it should help employees decide how to allocate their time and effort among competing ends. It should reward accomplishments and successes (and perhaps punish failures), and it should provide motivation for behavior that contributes to organizational success. Finally, it should do all this efficiently, meeting employees' needs for material consumption, equity, or status at the minimal expense consistent with realizing organizational goals.

As we have seen, these goals may not be consistent. For example, in Chapter 7 we saw that providing motivation may require basing pay on performance. However, this may prevent realizing the gains that would come from insulating employees against income risks. As another example, many fringe benefits are not treated as taxable income for the employees, but the costs of providing them are deductible for the employer. This leads firms to provide noncash compensation when, taxes aside, the same outlay paid as cash would allow employees to allocate the funds as they individually deem best and achieve higher levels of satisfaction. As a further example, if employees value "fairness" (interpreted as approximate equality of pay within ranks and "appropriately" small pay differences across ranks) or if visible pay differences give rise to undesirable influence activities, then responding by reducing pay differences may mute incentives and increase quits among valued employees with good alternative job opportunities. If, at the same time, employees in higher-level positions value status and enjoy being visibly differentiated from their colleagues, there are direct conflicts in meeting employees' desires. Conflicts among the different objectives of compensation policy are widespread, and balancing the pursuit of different objectives in light of the attendant difficulties helps account for the patterns of observed compensation we see.

INCENTIVES FOR INDIVIDUAL PERFORMANCE

Throughout this text, we have consistently treated the individual as fundamental. It is individuals who decide and act, and it is individuals who ultimately must be motivated. Thus, although group incentives are empirically important, we first focus on individual incentive compensation.

What to Motivate?

In our treatment of the theory of incentive contracting in Chapter 7, the problem was to induce the agent to provide "effort" of various sorts. There we viewed effort as a broad metaphor, representing whatever the employee might find onerous that was valuable to the employer. In analyzing and designing actual compensation systems, however, we need to be more specific about what it is that the employer wants from employees and what they must be motivated to supply.

In some jobs, the metaphor fits reasonably well because effort in the usual sense is in fact the key to success. Productivity in heavy manual labor, such as ditch digging, hod carrying, or stevedoring (loading or unloading ships) is directly a matter of how much physical effort is exerted throughout the work period. Even in these jobs, however, there are right and wrong ways to do things, and the workers' contribution is greater when they use some wit and skill in approaching tasks. In other jobs, what is primarily needed is diligent application of the employees' mental capabilities— knowledge, attention, and skills. A bookkeeper needs to record figures accurately in the right accounts and to ensure that the calculations are correct. Here, "effort" becomes the care and attention devoted to doing the job well. In still other jobs, physical exertion again is hardly a factor, but the employer desires higher-level intellectual activity from the employee, such as sustained, difficult reasoning focused on intricate and perhaps boring details from a lawyer, or timely creativity from an advertising copywriter. To the extent that the employee finds delivering these activities onerous, at least at the level that the employer desires, any of them could be interpreted as "effort" that must be motivated.

Nevertheless, what the employer wants from the employee is rarely representable by some simple, one-dimensional construct. A rich variety of employee attitudes and behavior affect the organization's success and might be induced or deterred by the motivation system. Production workers in a factory obviously can affect the total volume of output by how hard they work, and they must be motivated to supply effort in this sense. But they also affect many other important variables in different ways. They influence product quality through their attention to their tasks; the physical condition of the machinery they use by the care they devote to maintaining it; raw material costs by their economizing on inputs and reducing waste; and plant safety by their attention to those matters. By suggesting improved work methods, acquiring new skills, and cooperating with the introduction of new technologies, workers can have a major impact on aggregate productivity, and they can improve one another's individual productivity by helping out in emergencies, pacing themselves relative to other workers, and training less experienced employees. Motivating effort in each of these domains should also be a concern.

Managers' jobs may be even more multifaceted. They have to supervise and motivate those reporting to them and win the cooperation of people in other parts of the organization. They may have to develop organizational structures, implement plans to carry out routine operations, and devise responses to unforeseen opportunities and difficulties. They may be responsible for identifying, evaluating, and implementing new investments, forecasting the moves of competitors, and developing competitive strategies. They also may need to deal with suppliers, customers, regulators, and the public. How well managers communicate, how effectively they deal with people, how imaginatively, intelligently, and diligently they work, how efficiently they allocate their time and attention among all the competing demands, and, ultimately, how honestly and loyally they devote themselves to their employers' interests are all important to organizational success.

Effective compensation and reward systems recognize that employees' contributions occur along many dimensions and motivate the employees both to exert themselves mentally and physically and also to allocate their efforts in the ways that serve the organization's interests.

Explicit Incentive Pay

In some contexts, explicit incentive contracts linking pay and measures of individual productivity or performance are used to motivate employees. Examples are piece rates for production workers, commissions for salespeople, and stock options for executives. Other examples from outside a strict employment relation are the commissions paid to real estate agents as a fraction of the sales price of the property, lawyers' contingency fees computed as a fixed share of any amount won at trial, and fees to investment bankers in takeovers that are tied to the eventual price paid per share. Such contracts can provide very strong incentives. However, explicit incentive contracts are not nearly as widely used in employment relations as simple theory might lead one to expect. We have already seen some reasons for this in Chapters 10 and 11. To understand more deeply why this is so and why other measures are substituted for such contracts, it is important to examine some of the circumstances where such explicit individual monetary incentives are used successfully.

Piece Rates

Piece-rate systems involve paying employees a specified amount per unit produced. They are often applied at the individual level where, for example, an agricultural worker might be paid a fixed amount per basket of strawberries picked, a lathe operator might be paid a fixed amount per piece of metal shaped, a knitter might be paid a fixed amount per sweater, or a typist might be paid by the page. They can also be used for groups of employees. In California, for example, teams of fruit pickers are paid based on the number of trees picked cleanly. In a factory, a team of workers might be made responsible for producing a part, assembly component, or finished product, with a fixed amount per unit produced being divided among the team members.

THE ADVANTAGES OF PIECE RATES   Piece rates are simple and easily understood. They give individual financial recognition to more productive or harder-working employees, who are thus encouraged to perform to their potential. They tie pay very directly to performance and so can provide excellent incentives for employees to exert themselves to produce output and generate revenues for the firm: Various studies have found productivity increases of 15 to 35 percent when such incentive pay plans have been introduced.[2] Compared to a system of hourly wages, piece rates differentially attract people who are more productive or harder working. They can encourage employees to improve their skills. They may also reduce the need for complicated performance

---

[2] These studies are cited by Edward E. Lawler, III, *Strategic Pay: Aligning Organizational Strategies and Pay Systems* (San Francisco: Jossey-Bass Publishers, 1990), 57–58.

Piece Rates at Lincoln Electric Company*

The Lincoln Electric Company is renown for its long-standing, very extensive use of explicit incentive pay. Since their adoption in the 1930s, Lincoln's systems have produced spectacular productivity for this Ohio-based manufacturer of arc-welding equipment and fluxes, making it both exceptionally profitable and the market-share leader in its industry. Its labor productivity has been estimated to be three times higher than that of other firms in comparable manufacturing settings; it has an exceptional reputation for the quality of its products; and it has gone almost 60 years without losing money in any quarter.

Lincoln's factory workers are paid piece rates rather than hourly wages or salary. Over the years management has established a credible policy by which rates will be adjusted only when a change in work methods or technology is instituted. The workers are also eligible for yearly bonuses that, on average, have roughly doubled their earnings. The distribution of bonuses is based on merit ratings of the workers on such factors as their dependability, quality, output, ideas, and cooperativeness. In addition, the name of the worker who produced a machine is stencilled onto it. If a quality problem is discovered, the worker responsible must correct it on his or her own time. Further, if a machine proves defective after its delivery to a customer, the worker's annual bonus is reduced—by as much as 10 percent if the problem is a particularly serious one.

Lincoln also has a permanent-employment policy. After two years with the firm, a worker is guaranteed at least 30 hours work a week. In fact, Lincoln has had no layoffs for over 40 years. It also has long encouraged close communication between workers and management. The workers own almost half the stock in the company, with much of the rest held by the Lincoln family.

Lincoln is a model for successful use of incentive-pay systems. Each year hundreds of visitors from leading companies and their unions come to see how Lincoln manages its compensation and motivation schemes.

---

*For further information, see "The Lincoln Electric Company," Case 376-028, Harvard Business School, Boston, 1975, as well as Nancy J. Perry, "Here Come Richer, Riskier Pay Plans," *Fortune* (December 19, 1988), 50–58.

reviews and evaluations that are necessary with other systems to determine individual merit or performance pay. Finally, pay is determined by relatively objective measures, and so it is less subject to manipulation, politicking, or favoritism.

DISADVANTAGES OF A PIECE-RATE SYSTEM   Against these very clear advantages of piece rates stands a variety of difficulties. First, even in the most favorable circumstances, the basis of piece-rate compensation may not be completely uniform. In fruit picking, the measure of performance is usually the number of trees picked cleanly. If some trees are larger, more laden with fruit, or more distant from the truck where the picked fruit must be loaded, then the effort required for picking trees can vary. That introduces possibilities for favoritism and manipulation of the performance measure.

Second, piece rates introduce a variety of sources of randomness into worker incomes. For example, the breakdown of a machine that the worker uses or the failure of suppliers or workers at earlier stages to deliver inputs on time means that the piece-rate worker cannot produce and will not be paid. Poor-quality inputs can further affect the rate of production, even for workers who are exerting themselves fully.

Variability in the demand for outputs creates a special problem because some mechanism must be put in place to reduce output in bad times. One solution is to reduce the piece rate and with it the amount of effort exerted. This not only imposes income risks on the workers, it also can present a dangerous temptation for opportunistic misrepresentation on the part of the employer to try to cut rates when times are actually relatively good. Another approach is to maintain the rate but to ration the amount of output that will be "purchased" or, alternatively, the amount of time the employees are allowed to work. Both of these again load risk on the worker. The first also eliminates many of the attractive incentives of piece rates, and the second may fail to control the actual volume of output adequately because workers may increase their pace in an attempt to maintain their incomes. A further possible response is to attempt to manage demand so that its variability is reduced. This may be both difficult and costly because, for example, it may entail failing to meet customers' orders in peak times.

Third, the incentives provided by individual piece rates are of little value in a traditional transfer-line production system, where one employee cannot increase his or her output independent of the others, or in other contexts where individual variations in the pace of work are not feasible. (It might be possible, however, to use team piece rates in such contexts.) For individual piece rates to work, each employee must be able to set and vary his or her own pace.

Even when allowing this individual flexibility is technically feasible, it may require adapting other elements of the organization's policies and structure. For example, it may be difficult to economize on inventories by adopting Just-in-Time (JIT) methods and still allow employees to set their own pace. This problem arose when a General Electric Company plant producing thermocouples tried to introduce JIT methods.[3] The workers in the plant were paid piece rates, both before and after the adoption of the new methods, which called for leveling the production schedule to produce a constant number of units per day so that input requirements could be more easily forecast and buffer inventories reduced. The employees resisted this change because they feared that the leveling of production would limit their pay and probably reduce it.

Fourth, as the equal compensation principle indicates, paying for output alone encourages employees to ignore other valuable activities. Piece-rate workers will be tempted to reduce quality to increase measured quantity. They will be unlikely to help other workers if it means reducing their own measured output. Unless they are "charged" for inputs, they will not be careful about economizing on their use. Moreover, unless they own the tools, equipment, and machines they use, they may fail to maintain these as well as the firm would desire because doing so takes them away from producing output.

The quality problem can be mitigated by close quality inspection, coupled with charging workers for flaws and failures and/or making them personally responsible for reworking defects on their own time. The extra inspection is costly, however, and in any case final quality may still be lower than it would be if compensation did not focus so much on quantity. Meanwhile, holding the workers responsible for flaws and defects again subjects them to costly risks, for it may be unclear who is responsible

---

[3] "General Electric—Thermocouple Manufacturing," Harvard Business School Case 9-684-040, (1984).

for the defect or whether it actually resulted from something beyond the worker's control. Systems may have to be changed so that each worker is responsible for a distinguishable unit in order to permit assigning individual accountability for defects.

The difficulties in eliciting cooperation among piece-rate workers and in motivating them to maintain equipment can be reduced by maintaining stability in the labor force and in job assignments. Having the same people work together over long periods makes them more willing to lend one another a hand because there is greater mutual dependence in the group and more opportunities to acquire status and repay favors. In addition, having individual workers in the same jobs for long periods means that if they fail to maintain the machines and equipment they use today, they will bear part of the costs tomorrow when breakdowns occur and they cannot produce and earn. Nevertheless, if the workers do not bear the full costs of maintaining, repairing, and replacing machines and equipment, there will still be an incentive to misuse or overuse them. This is especially problematic when machines and equipment must be used by several different workers, as occurs when there are multiple shifts or when a particular machine's capacity is very large compared to a single worker's usage of it. In these circumstances there is a free-rider problem among the workers on top of the moral hazard problem. The solution of having the workers own the machines (perhaps by owning the company itself) is costly and often infeasible. At a minimum, it imposes the risk of fluctuations in asset values on the employees.

IMPLEMENTING AND MANAGING PIECE RATES   Many compensation systems involve a base salary plus piece rates. Even where individual output can be measured with reasonable precision, both setting the base salary and the piece rates and adjusting these as circumstances change represent major problems.

The incentive-intensity principle indicates that piece rates ought to be higher the higher are the additional profits that accrue from extra effort, the less risk averse are the employees, the greater the extent to which measured output accurately reflects individual effort, and the greater the opportunities for the employees to respond to increased incentives. Once the piece rate is determined, the base pay should then be set to make the entire package competitive with other employers' offers. In actuality, each of these factors must be estimated in determining the base salary and the piece rate. As discussed in Chapter 7, a crucial step in this is setting a standard for how much a worker should be able to produce under normal conditions. The higher the standard, the lower the worker's income from any given level of effort and production.

The workers' interests typically are in having the standard set low. Thus, they may have an incentive to work slowly when standards are being established, misrepresenting the difficulty of the task to gain higher income in the future. This is an instance of the ratchet effect. A second instance of the ratchet effect arises if piece rates can be adjusted based on experience. We have already described several examples of this, such as the Soviet chemical combine (Chapter 7) and the General Motors panel stamping plant in Flint, Michigan (Chapter 5). In each of these cases, providing stronger incentives led to dramatic and unexpected increases in productivity, and authorities responded by raising the standard, declaring that the previous one was too low. Unless management can commit itself to let workers keep the promised share of their increased output, piece rates are more likely to cause bitterness and resentment than permanent increases in output. The fear that management may continually raise the standards in a piece-rate system has been suggested as the source of organized labor's long-standing opposition to the system.

A related difficulty is that the workers may have an incentive to hold down production, even after standards are set, in hope that the standards will be lowered if they prove difficult to meet. Edward Lawler cites an example in which a secretary was asked during a strike to take on a factory job that was paid on a piece-rate basis. Despite having no previous experience, she was breaking production records by 375 percent within days. The worker who normally held the job had been in it for ten years and regularly complained that the standard was too demanding.[4]

Potential problems of setting the rates arise anew with every change in economic conditions. The introduction of new machines and methods, for example, calls for recomputation of standards and rates. Demand changes, which are unlikely to be observed by the employees with the same precision as they are by the firm's management, present the special difficulties to which we have already alluded. Theory suggests that rates be lowered when marginal revenue falls, as it might in the face of reduced demand. Suppose, however, that the workers are enjoying quasi-rents in the firm, so that they will not immediately leave for other employment if their earnings are reduced. Then management will have an incentive to misrepresent demand conditions, claiming they are worse than they actually are, in order to justify lower pay. In response to this problem, the usual remedy is to fix piece rates without regard to demand conditions, but this raises the question of how levels of output are to be controlled.

The restricted range of applicability of piece-rate systems and the difficulties of managing them have limited their use. Apparently many companies find that there are other, more effective methods of motivating production workers—especially direct monitoring of effort, perhaps combined with some form of group incentives. At the same time, these companies find that individual incentive pay is effective with employees in other types of jobs.

Sales Commissions

Incentive pay based on explicit formulas is very widely used in compensating salespeople, who regularly receive part or all of their pay through commissions. Greater sales result directly in higher pay for the salespeople, thus motivating them to focus more energy, diligence, and imagination on their jobs. As with piece rates, commissions also induce self-selection. Salespeople who perceive themselves to be particularly talented, dedicated, or energetic and who are less risk averse are attracted by the high earnings possible under a commission scheme, whereas the more risk averse and those who see themselves as less effective salespeople will prefer a job paying a straight salary.

As with piece rates, the first cost of a commission system is that employees' incomes vary not just with their efforts but also with all the random factors that might influence sales success. This means that their average income will have to be higher to compensate for the risk as well as for the extra effort that is induced. When combined with the self-selection effect noted earlier, this effect may explain the difficulties that a number of major U.S. department store chains, including Sears', Dayton Hudson, Bloomingdale's, and Macy's, have experienced in instituting or increasing the importance of commissions for retail salespeople. Unless the new system raises expected total income significantly, the risk-averse salespeople who were attracted to the salaried positions will be worse off. Moreover, those who perceive that they are not especially effective will foresee that they will have great difficulty meeting targets, maintaining their incomes, and keeping their jobs. They will naturally oppose the shift in the compensation system.

Commissions are in fact much more commonly used for field salespeople who operate on their own, away from the direct monitoring of their managers, than for

---

[4] Lawler, *op. cit.*, 58.

retail salespeople selling in stores. The possibilities for monitoring employees in the field are quite limited, so providing incentives through direct supervision is problematic. In contrast, store managers can more easily observe employees' direct provision of effort. They can then provide incentives without subjecting the employees to the income risk inherent in a commission scheme. Along these same lines, commissions in retail selling seem to be more prevalent where there is a greater opportunity for the salespeople to influence sales by difficult-to-monitor activities, such as the quality of advice given. Such advice is very important in selling major appliances, upscale clothing, and consumer electronics, and commissions tend to have a relatively larger role in compensating people selling these items. (Note that this pattern is consistent with the recommendations of the theory of incentive contracting: If profits are more responsive to effort, then the commission rate should be higher.)

The risk that a commission system imparts to employees' incomes is an important determinant of the desirability of using commissions at all. When the risks are relatively small, a large fraction of the worker's total income can be based on commissions. Selling shoes in a retail store, wholesale groceries, or standard industrial supplies and materials are examples. But when sales are large and infrequent, such as billion-dollar contracts to build nuclear power stations, then paying exclusively on a commission basis would make the employee's income unacceptably variable. In such circumstances, the options are to seek out salespeople who are especially risk tolerant or to ignore commissions all together, by paying a salary and providing incentives by other means.

Even when commissions are valuable, they share another difficulty with piece rates: They may cause salespeople to slight other activities that are valuable to the firm. For example, if the sales force is a potentially important source of information about customers and competitors, paying commissions may cause them to focus excessively on sales and to ignore information gathering. One logical possibility is to reward information acquisition as well. As the equal compensation principle indicates, if pay is to motivate gathering information, then the reward at the margin for time devoted to this activity must be equal to that for time devoted to direct sales activity. Performance in information gathering may be exceptionally hard to measure, however, so basing pay on measured performance on this dimension (if it is possible at all) will add a large measure of risk to sellers' incomes. This extra risk might well make this approach unattractive. The solution instead may be to reduce or eliminate the sales commission, relying more on straight salary, so that the salespeople's allocation of their time is more in line with the firm's interests.

The same sort of problems arise when the sales force is expected to provide customer education and after-sale service. If a salesperson serves the same customers and territory for extended periods, his or her concern with future sales and the resulting commissions may alleviate this problem. When there is high turnover and service is important, however, it may be better to reduce the role of commissions.

SETTING COMMISSION RATES: THEORY AND EVIDENCE   Setting commission rates in different selling environments is a central issue in sales force management. Two marketing professors, Rajiv Lal and Venkantaraman Srinivasan, have used the model presented in Chapter 7 to address this issue.[5]

They considered first the case in which the salesperson handles a single product. Suppose that the *sales response function*, which relates the expected number of units

---

[5] Rajiv Lal and Venkantaraman Srinivasan, "Compensation Plans for Single- and Multi-Product Salesforces: An Application of the Holmstrom-Milgrom Model," draft, Stanford University, Graduate School of Business (1991).

sold to the sales activity, is given by $h + ka$, where h is a constant representing the expected unit sales if the salesperson does the job making no special effort, and k parameterizes the responsiveness of sales to individual sales activity a. The corresponding expected contribution to profits is $m \times (h + ka)$, where m is the markup (price minus marginal cost) on the units being sold. Finally, suppose that the personal cost of effort born by the agent is given by a quadratic function:

$$\text{Cost} = b_0 + b_1 a + \tfrac{1}{2}ca^2$$

The theory of Chapter 7 can be applied to this problem by defining effort in a particular way: let $e = ka$. Then the cost of effort $C(e)$ is just the cost of the corresponding level of sales activity $a = e/k$, which is $b_0 + b_1(e/k) + \tfrac{1}{2}c(e/k)^2$. With this definition of effort, the model used by Lal and Srinivasan corresponds exactly to the model of Chapter 7, so we can use the incentive intensity principle to determine the optimal commission rate.

According to the incentive intensity principle, the commission rate should depend on four factors: the marginal profitability of effort, the employee's risk aversion, the significance of random factors in determining measured performance, and the responsiveness of effort to increased incentives. The formula for the optimal commission rate is $m/[1 + r\sigma^2 c/k^2]$, where r is the coefficient of absolute risk aversion, σ^2 is the variance of unit sales for any given level of effort, and c/k^2 is $C''(e)$. The commission rate applied to unit sales should be an increasing function of the margin m and the coefficient k of the sales response function and a decreasing function of the salesperson's risk aversion and the magnitude of uncontrolled and random factors in determining sales. In particular, the commission rate should not depend on the level of base sales h. The base sales h should affect only the performance standard or, equivalently, the salesperson's base salary.

The researchers found general empirical support for the theory using data from studies of several different firms: The theory's qualitative recommendations tend to match actual pay practices. Moreover, the predictions of the theory have been tested more directly using sales-force compensation data from an unnamed large U.S. firm selling computer-related services and hardware.[6] The company uses a variety of combinations of salary and commissions for its various product lines. The data used in the study were obtained from a questionnaire completed by sales managers. The questionnaire itself was partially framed in terms of concepts and issues with which these managers usually concern themselves, such as the importance of team selling, advertising, product quality, firm reputation, and service, as well as some of the factors directly figuring in the theory. To test the theory using this data, it was necessary to interpret the managerial variables in terms of the variables in the theory, and this creates potential difficulties in matching the empirical results to the theoretical predictions. Nevertheless, as interpreted by the researchers, the agency model did a good job of explaining the determinants of sales-force compensation in this firm.

When a salesperson sells several products, the salesperson's ability to affect sales by increased effort, the gross margins, and the variability of sales may differ across items in the line, and the salesperson must decide not just how hard to work but also how to allocate his or her total sales effort among products. Lal and Srinivasan, using the logic of the equal compensation principle, developed recommendations on how the commission rate should vary across products. Other things being equal, the commission rate on unit sales volume should be higher for products with higher gross

---

[6] Rajiv Lal, Donald Outland, and Richard Staelin, "Salesforce Compensation Plans: An Empirical Test of the Agency Theory Framework," draft, Stanford University, Graduate School of Business (1990).

margins, greater responsiveness of sales to selling activity, and less randomness in sales outcomes. Again, it should be independent of the level of base sales.

These last recommendations conflict with some conventional wisdom in marketing management, so it would be especially useful to test these predictions using empirical evidence. Unfortunately, such tests have not yet been conducted.

Individual Incentive Pay in Other Contexts

More and more companies are experimenting with formalized individual performance pay for a variety of different employees. For example, although the bonuses paid to Salomon Brothers investment bankers are normally determined by subjective evaluations, *The Wall Street Journal* reported that in 1990 the bond-arbitrage group at Salomon was paid by a strict formula giving them 15 percent of the profits they generated.[7] This group uses mathematical models to estimate equilibrium price relations between bonds and other securities. When the models indicate there are even very small disparities in actual relative prices, the group simultaneously buys the underpriced securities and sells the overpriced ones. If the models are right, this yields a riskless "arbitrage" profit; if they are wrong, immense losses are possible. Reportedly, the head of the group received $23 million for 1990 (some of which probably was paid in the form of company shares that he could not access for 5 years—see Chapter 1). Others in the group reportedly got huge bonuses under the formula as well. A similar formula linking pay to performance resulted in the $550 million that Michael Milken, the "Junk Bond King," was paid by Drexel Burnham Lambert in 1987. Apparently he had been promised 35 percent of the profits generated by his group when he began trading in high-risk bonds in the early 1970s, and this arrangement stayed in effect even as the profits soared.[8]

PAY FOR SKILLS   Among regular employees, pay-for-skills programs are a form of incentive pay that rewards and motivates employees' investments in skill acquisition and development rather than their direct on-the-job performance. These programs are common in large Japanese firms and are being tried elsewhere in North America and Europe. In these programs, an employee's pay depends not on his or her particular job assignment but instead on the skills he or she has acquired and his or her level of mastery. For example, in a Japanese manufacturing firm, the company might identify several different machines that a particular group of workers might conceivably learn to operate. Each worker is then graded on his or her level of expertise on each machine: Can the worker operate the machine at all? Can he or she operate it without regular assistance and close supervision? Does he or she have enough expertise to help others in using the machine? Has he or she actually achieved enough expertise to be able to teach other workers? Higher grades result in higher pay. On the one hand, such schemes encourage human capital investment, and they facilitate valuable flexibility in work-force assignments. On the other hand, they may require paying people for skills that they may rarely use.

PERFORMANCE PAY FOR SCIENTISTS AND ENGINEERS   Pay-for-performance schemes also have been used with scientific and engineering personnel. For example, Applied Materials Inc., a $500-million California-based producer of equipment for manufacturing semiconductors, gives employees who develop successful new products a percentage of the resulting sales revenues. Under this plan, the physicist who led the team that

---

[7] Randall Smith and Michael Siconolfi, "Roaring '90s? Here Comes Salomon's $23 Million Man," *The Wall Street Journal* (January 7, 1991), C-1.

[8] Connie Bruck, *The Predators' Ball* (New York: Penguin Books, 1989), 31–2.

developed one especially successful product received more than $800,000 in 1989 in incentive pay. He thus ended up earning considerably more than the corporation's chief executive officer. Such plans directly reward and encourage creativity and innovation, and they also help motivate researchers to be concerned with the ease with which their products can be manufactured and sold. They are especially attractive in the high-tech industries of California's Silicon Valley because they help hold engineers and scientists who otherwise would be lured away to new, start-up, firms, where they can have more independence and a significant ownership stake.[9]

MANAGERIAL PERFORMANCE PAY   The most widespread use of formula-based incentive pay is probably for managers. Often this takes the form of the manager receiving a bonus that is a straightforward percentage of sales or profit (or changes in these) in the manager's unit, but sometimes they can be much more complicated. McDonald's provides an excellent example of such complex schemes.

The fast-food restaurant chain has used explicit performance compensation systems for decades to reward and motivate its restaurant managers.[10] Over the years, McDonald's has experimented with a variety of managerial incentive-pay formulas. Beginning in 1967 managers' and assistant managers' base salaries were tied to their meeting corporate standards of quality, service, and cleanliness (QSC) in their restaurants, and quarterly bonuses were based on "controllable" profit contribution: sales revenue less those costs that the manager was expected to be able to control. This scheme apparently did not effectively reward cost-control efforts, however, and it also proved unpopular. In 1972 it was replaced by a system in which starting salary was based on local costs of living and adjusted annually according to overall performance, and bonuses depended on a number of factors. Meeting labor expense targets and negotiated paper and food cost targets each yielded a bonus of 5 percent of salary. QSC performance, which was graded on a three-point scale, contributed up to another 10 percent of salary to the bonus. Further, the manager received 2.5 percent of any sales increase, up to another 10 percent of salary. (If extenuating market conditions limited sales growth, the manager's supervisor could award up to a further 5 percent in place of the share of revenue growth.)

This scheme was further revised two years later. Under the 1974 plan, the bonus depended on measured QSC performance, cost control, revenue generation, and training of personnel, with the weights attached to each negotiated between the manager and the manager's supervisor. The training factor was added because McDonald's was expanding rapidly and faced a shortage of managers. Similar factors are still used, although the pay scheme continues to be adjusted.

These schemes are designed to motivate the managers to devote themselves to their jobs and to allocate their attention among various tasks in ways that support corporate objectives. They also try to recognize differential market conditions (via the salary figures), the managers' knowledge of local conditions (through having some targets negotiated), and the extent to which different observables are reflective of managerial effort (by treating various elements of performance separately and giving them different weights).

Eliciting Employees' Private Information

Often employees have information that is not available to their superiors about their own personal circumstances or interests, what performance is possible on the job, or

---

[9] Valerie Rice, "Tying Pay to Sales Puts Inventor at Top," *San Jose Mercury News* (July 16, 1990), D-1.

[10] See W. Earl Sasser and Samuel H. Pettway, "The Case of Big Mac's Pay Plans," *Harvard Business Review* (July–August 1974), 30ff.

Figure 12.1: Which contract gives the highest expected pay depends on the level of expected sales.

the returns to various activities that the firm might undertake. For example, a division manager is apt to be much better informed about the opportunities for enhancing performance in his or her division than is the central management staff, and an experienced salesperson is likely to know more about the market potential of his or her territory than is the sales manager. In such cases, it can be useful to tap this information in setting objectives and rewarding activity. The potential difficulty is that unless the system is designed appropriately, the employees have incentives to withhold the information they have or to distort their reports.

To overcome this problem and gain access to the information, the organization must be careful not to punish honest reporting. In general, this may be difficult, especially because it may mean committing not to use the information fully. As an extreme example, suppose a new airplane crashes during a test flight, but the pilot survives. The manufacturer will be tremendously interested in learning what caused the crash. Suppose the pilot knows that an error on his or her part was partially responsible but that this cannot be discovered unless he or she confesses. If the manufacturer is to get the right information, it must not treat the pilot worse if he or she accepts responsibility than if he or she keeps quiet. Yet upon learning the pilot's culpability, there will be a strong temptation to fire him or her.

Two common mechanisms can be interpreted as means of using employees' private information. One is to offer a *menu of contracts*, a variety of different methods of determining pay among which employees can choose. This has been done, for example, at IBM in compensating the sales force. The second is the practice of *management by objectives*, under which the employee and his or her supervisor negotiate the criteria and standards against which the employee's performance will be judged. Versions of this system are extremely common and are used at multiple levels within numerous organizations.

MENUS OF CONTRACTS   Different contracts in a well-designed menu offer different combinations of salary and incentive pay—for example, commission rates—with lower salary attached to higher commissions in such a way that each contract offers the highest pay over some possible range of performance. The basic idea is illustrated in Figure 12.1 with a menu that involves three contracts. In the figure, the three sloping lines represent alternative contracts that the salesperson may choose. The slope of each line represents the commission rate and the y-axis intercept represents the salary paid when no sales are made. As shown in the figure, contract 1 offers the highest salary (S_1) and the lowest commission rate, contract 2 offers a lower salary (S_2) but a higher commission rate, and contract 3 offers a still lower salary (S_3) and a still higher commission rate. Contract 1 yields the highest income if sales are less than S'; contract 2 is the most lucrative in the region from S' to S''; and for sales levels above S'', contract 3 yields the greatest income.

To see how this can be useful, suppose that the sales potential of various territories varies significantly and that the person best informed about the potential of any particular territory is the salesperson who works there. If a simple commission scheme is used, then each salesperson will be motivated to underestimate the sales potential of his or her territory. In that way, he or she can make the sales target and earn bonuses and commissions without having to work very hard. The question is how to motivate salespeople working in promising territories to accept and try to meet higher sales goals. The menu of contracts illustrated in Figure 12.1 provides the answer. Faced with such a menu, the salespeople will engage in self-selection: Those expecting low sales will select contract 1, those expecting a moderate level of sales will take contract 2, and those expecting high sales will take contract 3. In this way, strong incentives can be provided for salespeople in promising territories, whereas those in weaker territories can be protected from the consequences of low sales by being compensated principally by salary.

MANAGEMENT BY OBJECTIVES   Offering the same menu of contracts to each employee is optimal only when the employee's report is the only source of information about achievable performance. In general, the proper standard may be better determined in conference between the employer and employee, enabling the parties to use all the available information. Just as in the case of the menu of contracts, to ensure that employees have no incentive to conceal their information, the employer needs to offer more attractive performance rewards to those who accept higher performance goals.

Implicit Incentive Pay

Most often, pay is not linked to individual performance by any simple formula. Instead, supervisors decide on pay, raises, and promotions according to some unarticulated and perhaps subjective or ill-defined criteria. Yet there may still be incentive aspects to the compensation system. At a minimum, those who perform especially badly may be fired, and in most situations this is a spur to attempting to perform acceptably. Beyond this, people who are judged to be doing a better job tend to be treated better, and, understanding this, employees are motivated to perform in the ways that they perceive the organization values and will reward.

THE RATIONALE FOR IMPLICIT INCENTIVE PAY   Implicit incentive schemes represent highly incomplete contracts. Their prevalence results from two factors: the difficulty of specifying desirable performance in advance and the difficulty of adequately measuring performance after the fact.

Except for the most routine jobs, it is rarely possible to foresee all the various significant contingencies that might arise and to determine in advance the responses that would define good performance. For example, a manager has to deal continually with all sorts of emergencies, new opportunities, and unfamiliar situations. If it were possible to foresee all these, describe them, and specify the right behavior in each event, there would be no need for managers as we know them: The responsibility and discretion that mark managerial positions would be eliminated. Generally, if the employer and employee cannot specify in advance what will constitute good performance, they obviously cannot enter a contract that explicitly ties pay to performance.

Yet these difficulties in specifying in advance what constitutes good performance do not automatically prevent the use of explicit incentive contracts because there may still be good proxies for overall performance. Consider, for example, the chief executive officer of a firm. It would be ridiculous to try to specify in advance what the CEO should do in all the situations that might arise and on all the dimensions on which he or she might need to act. Yet from the stockholders' point of view, the change in the value of the company's stock may be a quite adequate "summary statistic" for the CEO's performance, and an explicit compensation contract could be based on stock-price performance.

More often, however, there are no such simple, objective indicators for performance that can be easily observed within a reasonable time frame. What understandable measures could adequately and unambiguously summarize the performance of a secretary, a cost accountant, or a high school principal? Both the employer and the employee may know well what constitutes good performance, in any given situation, and yet describing this performance in advance and measuring it in a quantifiable way after the fact are both impossible. Generally, when no easily quantifiable, credible summary measures for performance exist, explicit performance contracts will be impractical. Instead, performance will have to be evaluated after the fact, on many dimensions, often subjectively, against standards and criteria that were not and could not have been articulated beforehand, and that may remain ill defined. Correspondingly, any incentives that are given through the compensation system will have to be implicit.

Moreover, even when a few aspects of performance are measurable, it may be undesirable to use those measures in explicit pay formulas. Paying for performance on only some of the dimensions that matter encourages employees to slight the other dimensions of their jobs, and the result may potentially be worse than if there were no explicit incentives given at all. This observation is just another application of the equal compensation principle. Sometimes, this problem can be overcome by mixing explicit and implicit incentive pay. For example, Lincoln Electric uses piece rates to reward the direct production of output and the associated provision of effort and attention, but the size of an individual's bonus depends in part on the firm's evaluation of his or her performance on less tangible dimensions, such as reliability, cooperativeness, and the quality of the individual's ideas. As long as the employees understand the factors that figure into the bonus determination and believe that their pay will depend on these, they will be motivated to pay attention to these aspects of their performance, even though there is no explicit formula linking pay to performance.

PERFORMANCE EVALUATION

At the heart of any incentive system is a system for performance evaluation. The more intensively the employer rewards measured performance, the more important it is to measure performance accurately. The monitoring intensity principle discussed in Chapter 7 is a formal version of this dictum.

Performance Evaluation with Explicit Performance Pay

When pay is to be based on an explicit incentive formula, it is especially important that the right measures be used. For example, suppose a firm wants to motivate executives by paying for increasing profitability. How should profitability be measured? Using accounting profits invites manipulation of the accounting procedures, for example, recognizing revenues and costs (recording them on the firm's income statement for the period) at times that are opportune for the executives. More crucially, it may cause them to emphasize investments that raise revenues and measured profits in the near term and to avoid even better investments that do not contribute to immediate accounting returns. They may also hang on to losing operations to avoid having to recognize losses and take write-offs that hurt reported profits. Presumably, stock prices are harder to manipulate and, at least in some conceptions of how the market works (see Chapter 14), these prices give appropriate weight to changes in both the long- and short-term earnings prospects of the firm. Of course, the price of the stock may be very insensitive to the actions of any individual manager below the highest executive levels in the firm, and so it may not be a very effective measure either.

Another issue is whether to measure individual performance on an absolute basis against some given, immutable scale, or relatively, in comparison to others' performance. The latter has the advantage that, if done right, it can help sort out some of the variations in performance that are not due to the employee's efforts but rather to outside influences over which he or she had no control. For example, a given level of sales probably reflects a greater effort by a salesperson when the salespeople in other districts generated low sales volumes than when they were very successful. The idea is that the low general level of sales suggests that demand is weak or that the product is overpriced, so that achieving a given level of sales probably required more effort than would have otherwise been needed. Evaluating the salesperson's performance relative to others' performances in such situations removes some of the risk in the individual's pay and should thus be valuable. The informativeness principle indicates when such comparative performance evaluation is useful and how much weight to give to relative versus absolute performance.

One difficulty with comparative performance evaluation is that the evaluations may be manipulated by the group of employees who are being compared: If they all conspire to take it easy, then none looks bad in comparison. Such a conspiracy is especially threatening when pure relative performance schemes are used. Tournaments, where only the ranking of the contestants matters and not their absolute level of performance, are thus especially vulnerable, particularly if the employees have some way to share the prizes among themselves.

A second problem is that comparative performance evaluation damages the incentives for employees to help one another because taking time to help is then doubly costly: It reduces the helpful employees' own absolute performance and, by improving the other person's performance, it worsens the helper's relative standing. In fact, relative performance evaluation can even create incentives for employees to sabotage one another. For both of these reasons, comparative performance evaluation and tournaments tend to be used only with individuals and groups who are isolated from one another and do not require one another's help.

Performance Evaluation in Subjective Systems

As we discussed in Chapter 11, managers and supervisors seem to find subjective performance evaluation difficult and unpleasant. It is not easy to have to tell someone about their failings. The task becomes even less pleasant in the ambiguous environments that lead to implicit incentive pay because the employee can, perhaps legitimately, dispute the supervisor's evaluation. In fact, many employees perceive that their performance evaluations are neither appropriate nor useful, and they do not trust their supervisors to evaluate them fairly and accurately. Further, differentiating among employees on subjective, ambiguous, debatable grounds invites employees to try to manipulate the perceptions and decisions of the supervisor to their benefit. These factors may help account for some important empirical patterns.

In many companies, supervisors are expected to rate employees' performance on a common, predetermined scale. A first guess would be that the actual ratings should be spread more or less symmetrically across the scale. A more sophisticated

Table 12.1 Distribution of
Performance Ratings of
Managers at Two
Manufacturing Firms

Percentage of Sample
Receiving Rating

COMPANY 1:	
Not Acceptable	0.2%
Acceptable	5.3%
Good	74.3%
Outstanding	20.2%
COMPANY 2:	
Unacceptable	0.0%
Minimum Acceptable	0.0%
Satisfactory	1.2%
Good	36.6%
Superior	58.4%
Excellent	3.8%

estimate would predict that scores ought to be somewhat skewed towards the high end. If the company gets rid of employees who fall in the lower categories or helps them improve, then performance should be improving over time. Assigning employees to those jobs that best suit their tastes and abilities would have the same effect, as would any learning the employees gain through experience. Then, if the standards of performance needed to reach any rating level are not being raised over time, the actual ratings should have a tendency to clump in the higher levels.

Yet the amount of skewness that supervisors' actual rankings show seems extreme. For example, one study documented the performance ratings given to managers at two (unnamed) manufacturing firms in the 1970s.[11] The first company rated 4,788 managers on a four-point scale; the second rated 2,841 managers on a six-point scale. The results are summarized in Table 12.1. In the first company, 94.5 percent of the managers were rated in the top half of the scale ("Good" or "Outstanding"). In the second company, the corresponding figure was 98.8 percent, with essentially no one being rated in the bottom two categories! Either these companies had an absolutely remarkable group of managers working for them or, more plausibly, the people doing the evaluations were reluctant to assign anyone to the lower performance levels. In effect, the evaluators were using a two-point scale at the first firm rather than the official four-point one and a three-point scale at the second rather than a six-point one. They thus made much less differentiation among employees' ratings than they could or than they were apparently expected to make.

Also, in many systems that nominally are based on merit pay, there seems to be very little difference in the pay actually awarded to top performers relative to those rated lower. For example, at the first of the two companies in the study just cited, a manager rated "Outstanding" was, on average, paid only 7.8 percent more than one whose performance was rated "Not Acceptable." At the second company, an "Excellent" rating corresponded to only 6.2 percent higher pay than the lowest rating actually

---

[11] James L. Medoff and Katherine G. Abraham, "Experience, Performance and Earnings," *Quarterly Journal of Economics*, 95 (December, 1980), 703–36.

given.[12] Thus, unless these managers are extremely sensitive to relatively small variations in pay, the pay scheme does not seem to give very strong performance incentives.

Not differentiating very much among employees in the ratings given them or in the pay that results fits with the observations that managers find performance evaluations difficult and unpleasant, that the employees do not have much faith in the evaluations, and that differentiating sharply among employees on subjective grounds invites costly influence activities. If managers dislike having to do performance evaluations, they may not be very conscientious about them, and if giving negative evaluations is especially unpleasant, they will be tempted not to give low ratings. (Note that it is difficult for the managers' supervisors to verify the quality or accuracy of managers' evaluations of their subordinates.) As we noted in Chapter 11, this tendency may be accentuated if the managers themselves are graded on the quality of people they have attracted to work for them and how well they get their people to perform. In that case, a negative evaluation of a subordinate reflects badly on the supervisor. Also, to the extent that there may be limited budgets for salary increases (as happens at least in bureaucracies), a manager may be tempted to overstate the quality of his or her subordinates to increase the share of the limited budget allocated to his or her group for raises.

Employees who do not trust their superiors' evaluations of their performance are perhaps especially likely to view influence activities as legitimate. After all, the evaluations look inaccurate and even random; making one's self look better is thus just correcting a misperception, not misleading anyone. Further, given that the evaluations seem arbitrary, employees may well believe that they can be affected by politicking. In these circumstances, using the evaluations to set large differences in pay will simply ensure that the organization will bear large influence costs.

Furthermore, if evaluations are not in fact very informative, then the gains to the firm from basing large salary differences on them are likely to be small. Of course, with so little in fact riding on the evaluations, managers are hardly encouraged to take them very seriously or to absorb much discomfort by giving negative evaluations.

PROMOTIONS AND SUBJECTIVE EVALUATION SYSTEMS   In systems where performance evaluation is subjective, it seems likely that much of the monetary incentives are provided by the opportunity for promotion to a better-paying job in the hierarchy. As noted in Chapter 11, promotions are rather blunt incentive devices. Also, to the extent that good performance in one job does not necessarily mean that the individual is well suited for the next level in the hierarchy, promotion-based incentive systems may fail to assign the best people to important jobs. Still, they have advantages in dealing with managers' distaste for doing performance evaluations and reluctance to give low evaluations to anyone, as well as with employees' associated incentives to engage in influence activities.

Promotion decisions are important ones, especially in managerial hierarchies. They determine who will make the key operating and strategic decisions instrumental to the organization's success. This may give managers reason to do more careful evaluations in connection with promotion decisions than they would if only a few dollars in raises were at stake. Further, by making the salary change associated with promotions large, companies can both provide incentives to employees to attempt to win promotion and strengthen the incentives for those making the promotion decisions to treat them seriously.

---

[12] George P. Baker, Kevin Murphy, and Michael Jensen, "Compensation and Incentives: Practice vs. Theory," *Journal of Finance*, 43 (May 1988), 593–616.

In this regard, one study found that vice presidents in large U.S. corporations get average annual pay raises of 18.8 percent on promotion, compared to an average raise of 3.3 percent in years that they stay on in the same job.[13] In the same study, vice presidents promoted to chief executive officer averaged a 42.9 percent increase in salary plus bonus. Finally, because a promotion will often place the employee under the supervision of a new manager (who may well be the superior of the former supervisor), it is easier to monitor the quality of the evaluations done for promotion decisions than those done for salary setting.

Of course, with so much riding on the promotion decision, there may be very strong incentives to try to exert influence over the evaluations that determine the choice. The competition for promotions can be quite fierce, and this competition does not simply take the form of hard work. Candidates instead may spend huge amounts of time and ingenuity trying to impress their bosses and even more time worrying about how they are doing and whether they will succeed. However, evaluations for promotions may be less subject to manipulation because they are done more carefully. Moreover, once a promotion decision is made, it is largely irreversible, so the period over which the influence costs are absorbed has a natural limit. In contrast, salary decisions are more easily adjusted or offset over time and so the influence activities to which they can give rise may be unending.

THE FREQUENCY OF EVALUATIONS   The frequency with which employees are evaluated seems to vary significantly across jobs. University professors receive full-blown performance reviews only rarely during their careers—perhaps only when they are hired and again when they come up for promotion or tenure—although they may have less extensive reviews occasionally in connection with salary setting. Lawyers and accountants in large professional firms are similarly subject to infrequent systematic evaluations. In contrast, investment bankers are effectively reviewed very frequently, receiving annual bonuses based on their measured performance. What accounts for these differences?

Performance evaluations are costly. Even if the evaluator does not dislike doing them, they require developing information and transmitting it, both of which take time and resources. Thus, unless they are going to be used for a specific purpose, they should be avoided. We have accentuated their use in performance pay and promotion decisions. These uses, however, would not seem to be sufficient to justify frequent reviews. Incentive payments could presumably be based on very infrequent reviews, with correspondingly large payments. This would even have direct advantages in contexts where the full impact of decisions is not immediately evident. Evaluations for promotions should be necessary only when there is an actual promotion decision to be made.

Another value to reviews, however, is in indicating to employees how they are doing, so that they can change their behavior to match more closely what the employer wants or find another job for which they are better suited. More frequent reviews thus provide useful information to employees earlier, and they should value the increased options that result.

The optimal frequency of review balances the largely fixed costs of the review with the benefits of having information available sooner and being able to act on it. Thus, reviews should be more frequent when they are less costly and when it is more likely that the information they provide affects behavior. For example, academic performance is hard to measure, whereas the quantity and quality of a typist's output

[13] Kevin J. Murphy, "Corporate Performance and Managerial Remuneration: An Empirical Analysis," *Journal of Accounting and Economics*, 7 (April 1985), 11–42.

is relatively easily determined. Thus, a professor should be evaluated less frequently than his or her secretary. In businesses where there is a high probability that any particular individual hired will not have the talent and ability needed for success, there is increased value in employees' learning early how they are doing: If they learn that things are going badly they can move sooner to a different job where they may do better. Thus, evaluations should be more frequent. This may explain the pattern in investment banking. Also, in occupations where employees develop large amounts of firm-specific human capital, it is unlikely that, once this capital is acquired, the employee would be better suited to a job with a different organization. Thus, there is less likelihood that the information from a performance review will be useful, and so reviews should be infrequent. This may explain the pattern in law and accounting firms, where the professionals have developed significant expertise regarding their particular firm's clients.

JOB DESIGN

Most jobs entail a variety of responsibilities. The issues of how many different projects any one person should work on, how tasks should be allocated among individuals, and whether one or more people should be involved in carrying out a particular task are complex, and different organizations resolve them differently. For example, production workers in North American factories traditionally have not been responsible for repairing the machines they use. Instead, the firms employ specialists whose jobs consist solely of doing repairs, and the production workers are supposed to leave the repair work to them. In contrast, Japanese production workers often are expected to repair breakdowns themselves. As another example, the accompanying box on the management consulting firms McKinsey & Company and Bain & Co. illustrates how job design differs between these two companies in ways that fit their differing business strategies.

Many factors influence job design. In the example from management consulting, the nature of the particular projects in which each company has chosen to specialize seems to be a major factor in determining job design. In a manufacturing firm, the decision to adopt a modern manufacturing strategy accentuating flexible equipment, frequent and rapid new product development, high product quality, and speedy response to customer needs has often been associated with complementary decisions to redesign jobs. For example, product-design engineers will be expected to work in teams with manufacturing people to ensure that new products can be produced easily and cheaply; production workers will be encouraged to learn multiple skills so that they can move among tasks and machines as requirements change; and salespeople will be expected to report to the firm on customers' needs to help design a useful product rather than just focusing on making sales. The organization's scale of operations is another influence on job design: If the organization is small, then a single manager may adequately oversee both sales and marketing, whereas in a larger organization, these tasks may be split. Finally, external factors, especially demographic changes, can be important. For example, the increasing role of women of child-bearing age in many countries' labor forces has led some companies to design jobs that facilitate parents' caring for their children.

Rather than attempting a full analysis of the job design problem, we concentrate here on the interaction between job design and incentive pay. We focus on two issues: the grouping of tasks into jobs and the determination of how much discretion employees should be given in allocating their time and attention among tasks and, in particular, between job responsibilities and personal concerns.

Competitive Strategy and Job Design
at McKinsey and Bain

McKinsey & Company, Inc., and Bain & Co., are major management consulting firms that provide expert advice to companies on strategy and organization. In recent years they have usually hired large numbers of new college graduates to work for them for a couple of years before pursuing MBA degrees. These jobs are very much in demand: They are quite well paid, the opportunity they afford to learn about business is highly valued, and some believe that gaining admission to competitive MBA programs is easier for people with experience in the major management-consulting companies. At the same time, the two firms compete directly for students.

At each firm, the new hires (called "business analysts" at McKinsey and "associate consultants" at Bain) work in teams on projects for client companies. The teams are led by more senior consultants, who supervise and evaluate the junior people. Although the work is quite similar between the two firms, there are two important differences. First, at Bain, an associate works on two to six projects simultaneously, whereas a McKinsey analyst normally focuses on a single project at a time. Second, the average work week at McKinsey is reputed to be about 70 to 80 hours, whereas that at Bain is closer to 60 hours.

A single key difference in the strategies of the two firms can account for these differences in their human-resource policies. McKinsey has traditionally focused on projects whose final output is a set of recommendations to meet the client's needs. Bain, in contrast, seeks projects that involve both its formulating recommendations and staying on to help implement them. Consequently, whereas a typical McKinsey project lasts 4 to 6 months, Bain projects last about 18 months. McKinsey projects are conducted largely at the client's site. Bain projects involve less time on the road, with more of the work being done at the team's home office.

The difference in hours worked per week is consistent with a recognition that the two firms' employees face different opportunity costs on their time. In effect, extra working hours are less costly to McKinsey people, who are usually on the road, living in hotels where they eat and get their laundry done. Bain people are more often at home, where they face the usual time demands of normal life and presumably also have greater opportunities for a social life.

Regarding the difference in the number of projects being worked on, suppose that Bain were to adjust its team sizes to have its associates work on only one project at a time, as at McKinsey. This might be directly inefficient if there is an uneven time-pattern to the work and if a team needs to be of a certain size to function effectively. But it would also mean that a new graduate joining Bain would see at most a couple of companies up close before returning to school, whereas the McKinsey analyst would see four to six different firms. Given that a major reason to take these jobs is to learn about business and businesses, Bain might then be at a competitive disadvantage in the labor market. On the other side, if a McKinsey analyst were assigned to several projects at once, the extra travel costs and loss of focus would be highly inefficient. Each firm's job design fits its business strategy.

Based on interviews by A. C. Chidambaram and Kaare Holm with former Bain and McKinsey employees at the Graduate School of Business, Stanford University, Fall 1990.

Job Design and Incentive Pay

Suppose there are four tasks that need to be done and each task requires enough time be devoted to it that any two of them would constitute a full-time job. Suppose there are no important physical complementarities between the tasks that make it efficient to group particular ones together. This might, for example, rule out a situation where one task is using a tool for production and another is maintaining the tool in good condition because the ease of maintenance might depend on how the tool is used.

Ruling out physical complementarities focuses attention on how job design may alter the effectiveness of a system of incentive pay. There are two important effects to consider. First, a proper assignment of tasks to workers can make it easier to assess responsibility for good or bad outcomes. For example, suppose a product may fail to meet quality standards if either of two components is inserted incorrectly during assembly. In this case, assigning the same person to install both components makes it clear who to hold responsible for any product failure.

In managerial work, this task assignment principle is manifested as the *principle of unity of responsibility*. When the success of a project or operation depends on the coordinated execution of several separate tasks in a way that makes it difficult to assess performance separately in each, then it is usually best to make a single individual responsible for all the related tasks. For example, when the Du Pont corporation, originally an explosives manufacturer, decided after World War I to begin manufacturing fertilizers, it suffered losses for a period while a committee administered the two businesses together. To solve the problem, Du Pont became the first firm to implement a modern multidivisional structure, in which the two kinds of products were made in separate factories, sold by separate sales forces, and administered by separate offices, with a single person responsible for the performance of each separate division. Partly for the same reason, many Japanese companies have rejected the traditional separation between design, process, and production engineering, arranging for the engineers who design a product to move with the product as it progresses through the start-up phase and into the production phase, achieving a valuable unity of responsibility.

To isolate the second incentive issue, let us now further suppose that performance in the tasks involved can be separately measured and assessed, but that the accuracy of the individual assessments may vary. Suppose in particular the tasks differ systematically in the difficulty of measuring performance accurately: Tasks 1 and 2 have a low error variance in measuring effort provision, whereas tasks 3 and 4 have a high variance. How should the difficulty of measurement enter into the determination of job design? Should one worker be assigned to do the two tasks where performance is hardest to measure, with the other worker taking the other tasks? Or should those tasks hardest to measure be split, with each worker doing one of them?

In terms of our model from Chapter 7, heterogeneity in the tasks that workers are assigned should be avoided because it complicates the problem of providing incentives. The essential insight comes from the equal compensation principle. If incentives are to be provided for the worker to pay adequate attention to both tasks, then the worker's marginal return from time and effort devoted to each must be equal. If an easy-to-measure and a hard-to-measure task are grouped together in the same job, then it will not be feasible to provide the same individual with strong incentives for the first task, in order to elicit great effort, and weak incentives for the second, in order to insulate the employee from risk. Any attempt to do so will only result in the employee devoting relatively too much time and effort to the task where improved performance is more strongly rewarded and too little to the other task.

Grouping tasks according to their ease of measurement avoids this problem. Suppose the two low-risk tasks are grouped together in one job and the two high-risk ones in the other job. Then strong incentives can be provided for effort provision in each task in the first job without imposing too much risk on the employee in this job and without distorting his or her allocation of effort between tasks. Meanwhile, relatively weak incentives can be applied to both tasks in the second job where the randomness in performance measurement means that strong incentives are too costly in terms of the risk they impose on the employee's income. Proper grouping allows giving an appropriate level of incentives for each kind of job.

Job Enrichment Programs and Complementarities Between Tasks

Many firms are experimenting with programs of job enrichment by redesigning jobs to add variety to the tasks that employees are asked to perform and to give them greater responsibility. The hope is that relieving the boredom associated with doing the same thing all the time will increase job satisfaction and productivity. Another possible source of productivity gains is that by learning more about the overall operation (and not just one specific part of it) employees may be able to use their information better to suggest and implement improvements. The most obvious problem is that reducing specialization may actually impede productivity. The analysis in the preceding section points to further considerations.

Suppose that tasks 1 and 2 are identical to one another and similarly that 3 and 4 are the same. Thus, in effect, there are two tasks, each of which is enough to constitute a full job, but it is possible to split the tasks with both employees doing each task. Then, unless the accuracy of performance measurement is similar in each task, one effect of enriching the jobs by mixing the tasks is to create difficulties in using incentive pay. If this effect is important, however, it might be mitigated by devoting resources to improve performance measurement in both tasks. Another effect of splitting the tasks is to create an opportunity for comparative performance evaluation. As we have seen, this can offer substantial advantages, especially for systems where objective, cardinal measures of performance are hard to come by.

If there are complementarities between tasks, so that doing one task improves the employee's productivity in another, then there are direct productivity effects from grouping certain activities together. For example, if doing research in a subject improves a person's ability to teach effective, up-to-date courses in the area, then there are gains from assigning faculty to teach in their areas of research and, moreover, from having people both teach and do research rather than concentrate on only one of these tasks. Similarly, it may be desirable to have salespeople gather customer information, even when sales performance is easily measured and the quality of information collection is hard to measure. In general, grouping tasks into jobs involves balancing several considerations, with the ease of providing incentives being just one.

Responsibility and Personal Business

An important issue in job design is how much discretion employees should be allowed in allocating their time at work between their direct job responsibilities and their personal concerns. The actual pattern we typically see in organizations is that the more "responsible" the position, the greater discretion the employee is allowed in pursuing his or her own interests. Clearly, from the point of view of maximizing total value, it would sometimes be efficient for employees to spend time during the working day taking care of personal business. This will be true whenever the marginal productivity of time spent on the personal matters exceeds that on work. Moreover, to the extent that worrying about their private concerns distracts employees from their job responsibilities, it might even be in the employer's immediate interest to allow employees to take care of their more pressing personal matters on company time. People in "responsible" positions are allowed to do this, whereas lower-level people are not. An executive may disappear for the afternoon with no questions being asked, but a lower-level employee may be limited in the frequency with which he or she may leave the assembly line to go to the restroom.

In part, this difference seems to be a matter of whether (explicit or implicit) incentive pay is an important element of the motivation system. Some employees are monitored directly on their input provision by having to record when they arrive and leave work and by having supervisors directly observe their work. These people typically are paid an hourly wage that does not vary in any obvious fashion with individual productivity, although their pay may be docked for time absent from the job and they may be fired if they are absent too often or if they are caught shirking. Such workers are usually allowed little discretion in determining whether to devote attention to their work or other matters. In contrast, senior executives' allocation of time is apt to be largely unmonitored, whereas their pay may be relatively sensitive to measured performance.

This pattern is explained by a variant of the equal compensation principle. When outside activities are allowed, employees will tend to pursue them up to the point where time spent on them at the margin has the same impact on their welfare as time spent on their job responsibilities. If there were really little or no connection between the attention they devote to their jobs and their pay, they might tend to spend all their time on other matters. Charity collections, personal phone calls, parties to celebrate employees' birthdays, and absences to take sick children to the doctor may absorb the entire working day. If the pay scheme puts an opportunity cost on the employees' diverting their time, effort, and attention away from their job responsibilities, however, then they will choose to allocate their time to other matters only when they are sufficiently important to offset the value of what they could have earned devoting attention to the job. For example, salespeople paid largely on the basis of commissions or freelance journalists paid by articles actually published would regulate their own allocation of time, without the need for explicit monitoring. Similarly, an aspiring lawyer or executive whose next promotion depends on good performance can be allowed considerable latitude in deciding how to allocate his or her time.

Discretion and incentives provide another example of complementarity. For the reasons we have just described, allowing discretion creates more value for workers with intense incentives than for those with weaker incentives. Complementarity is a symmetric relation, so we might also expect to find cases where it is the increase in discretion that is fundamental and the intensity of incentives that is the response. For example, a salesperson who travels a wide territory making sales calls alone must, by the very nature of the job, have great discretion over how the job is done, how many hours to work, and how long to linger with clients who are old friends. The difficulty of monitoring time devoted to personal business in this case raises the value of strengthening incentives.

INCENTIVE PAY FOR GROUPS OF EMPLOYEES

Almost all of the formal theory emphasizes incentives for individuals on the grounds that it is individuals who must be motivated to work. Yet the most common explicit incentive contracts are applied across groups of employees. The performance of the whole group together determines the total incentive payment, and the total is usually divided among individuals according to formulas or criteria that do not depend on individual performance.

Forms of Group Incentives

Tying individual pay to group performance takes many forms. Sometimes implicit schemes are used, as in the case of the bonuses paid to Japanese workers. These bonuses appear to be related to overall corporate profitability, but there is no formula explicitly linking the two. Instead, the bonuses are determined by the companies' boards of directors. In other cases, and probably more frequently in North America and Western Europe, the linkage of pay and group performance is more explicit.

PROFIT SHARING PLANS   The most common form of explicit group incentive pay in the United States is *profit sharing*, which approximately 30 percent of all firms used to some degree in 1988.[14] Under profit sharing, employees are paid annual bonuses that are supposed to vary with profitability (which may be defined at the overall corporate level or at the level of an individual division) but not with their own personal performance. A part of the bonus is sometimes deferred, being paid into a retirement account. Not all employees may be covered by the profit-sharing plan: For example, senior executives almost always would participate, whereas unionized employees would receive bonuses only if the contract with the union specifically called for it. Despite the number of firms using profit sharing, the amount of total employee income received through such plans in the United States is small, perhaps as low as 1 percent. In contrast, Japanese workers receive on average a quarter of their pay through annual bonuses that they perceive to depend on profitability. Profit sharing in Japan typically applies across the whole company.

An extreme form of profit sharing is for the employees to own all, or at least a substantial share, of the company. In that case, their incomes are very closely tied to the company's performance, either through their receiving the profits directly, as in a partnership, or through dividend payments and the behavior of the firm's stock price. Employee ownership is relatively common in certain industries and countries. Partnerships are the norm in a number of fields, including law, medicine, accounting, management consulting, architecture, and, to a lesser and decreasing extent, investment banking (see Chapter 15). In addition, some taxi companies, garbage collection firms, and plywood manufacturers in the United States are organized as employee cooperatives, as is the inter-city bus service in Israel, large parts of the construction business in Italy, and the collection of diverse businesses in the city of Mondragon in the Basque region of Spain (see Chapter 16). These co-ops are owned collectively by the people who work in them. The growth of Employee Stock Ownership Plans in the United States in the late 1980s had a major impact on the extent of employee ownership (see the box entitled "Employee Stock Ownership Plans"). In the United

---

[14] Nancy L. Perry, "Here Come Richer, Riskier Pay Plans," *Fortune* (December 19, 1988), 50–58.

Kingdom, about 1,950 companies have plans that give stock or stock options to employees generally, and 4,700 have plans aimed just at the executives.[15]

GAIN SHARING PLANS   Other types of group incentives are often called *gain-sharing plans*. Under these plans, when a group meets or exceeds predetermined targets, all the members receive bonuses tied to the extent to which goals were exceeded. Targeted variables often include output levels, productivity gains, customer service, quality, or costs. Four examples from U.S. manufacturing firms illustrate these plans.

Dana Corporation   Dana, the largest U.S. maker of truck parts and subassemblies, uses *Scanlon Plans* at a number of its plants. Under these plans, a target is set for the ratio of labor costs to the value of output produced, and when the actual ratio is less then the target, the workers are paid bonuses based on a fraction (perhaps 75 percent) of the savings of labor cost over the standard. If the actual ratio of labor costs to value of output exceeds the standard, no bonus is paid, and in fact the shortfall is recorded and must be worked off before bonuses resume.[16]

Nucor Corporation   Nucor, a U.S. steelmaker, pays its workers weekly bonuses based on the number of tons of steel produced that meet quality standards. These bonuses on average exceed the workers' base pay. Nucor also pays annual bonuses based on return on plant assets to its department managers and on corporate return on equity to plant managers, and it has a profit-sharing plan under which 10 percent of pretax earnings each year are paid out to all employees below the senior executive level. (Corporate officers get a combination of cash and stock.) Nucor produces twice as much steel per employee as do the large U.S. steel companies, and it attributes half this differential to its incentive systems.[17]

Carrier   Carrier, part of the United Technologies conglomerate, is a leading manufacturer of air-conditioning and heating equipment. The company uses a gain-sharing program it calls "Improshare." Under the plan, half the savings on labor costs achieved by producing an increased number of acceptable units of output over a base year are returned to the employees as bonuses. Carrier credits the plan with a 24 percent increase in productivity coupled with a substantial decrease in rejects during the first two years of the program.[18]

Analog Devices, Inc.   Analog Devices, Inc., a Massachusetts-based electronics firm, instituted an extremely complex group-incentive program during a period of very rapid firm growth in the mid-1970s.[19] First, there was a bonus system for managers, which was used differently at the corporate versus the divisional or group levels. Senior executives' bonuses were based on corporate performance only, whereas lower-level managers' bonuses were based half on overall corporate performance and half on the performance of their group alone. There was also a separate scheme for paying bonuses to technical staff involved in developing new products.

Under either plan, a person's bonus was proportional to measured collective performance and to his or her base salary. The bonus was also an increasing function

---

[15] "Economics Focus: Unseen Apples and Small Carrots," *The Economist* (April 13, 1991), 75.

[16] "Dana Corporation: Richmond Camshaft Plant (Condensed)," Harvard Business School Case 9-488-018, (1987).

[17] Drawn from Perry, *op. cit.*

[18] Also drawn from Perry, *op.cit.*

[19] See Ray Stata and Modesto Maidique, "Bonus Plan for Balanced Strategy," *Harvard Business Review* (November–December 1980), 156–63; and "Analog Devices, Inc." Harvard Business School Case 9-181-002, (1980).

Employee Stock Ownership Plans

By the late 1980s over 11,000 U.S. firms had instituted Employee Stock Ownership Plans (ESOPs). Formally, these are employee pension plans, and in many cases they have replaced more standard plans. Under an ESOP, the company acquires an amount of its own stock that it places in trust in the plan. Each year the individual employees are allocated some of these shares, which the ESOP then holds until they retire or leave the firm. In the first half of 1989, U.S. corporations acquired over $19 billion of their stock to establish new ESOPs, and in some cases the employees actually acquire the whole company through the ESOP.

Among the reasons for the surging interest in ESOPs were that they enjoyed apparent tax advantages over other forms of pension plans and that, by putting a large block of stock in "friendly hands," they could be used to defend against attempted hostile takeovers of the corporation. (This was clearly a major reason when Polaroid Corp. set up its $300 million plan.) ESOPs have also been used to sell companies to the employees when the original owners retire and to allow the employees to save their jobs by acquiring divisions or whole firms that were going to be shut down. The Weirton Steel Company, which was a unit of National Steel before being sold to the employees, is a well-known example.

ESOPs are also claimed to have good incentive effects. By making employees into owners, ESOPs are supposed to tie the employees' interests more closely to the firm's success and motivate them better. For example, Avis, the employee-owned car rental company, advertises that its employee-owners care about the firm's future and so will give customers better service.

There are examples (such as Weirton and Avis) where employee ownership has been associated with dramatically improved performance. Yet in other cases there has been no apparent motivational effect. The average employee in a large firm with an ESOP holds at most a minuscule fraction of the firm's stock. Economic analysis indicates that the direct incentive effect of these plans should be similarly tiny. At the same time, having both the employees' retirement incomes and their current earnings be so completely dependent on the fortunes of a single firm seems risky.

Based partly on Myron Scholes and Mark Wolfson, "Employee Stock Ownership Plans and Corporate Restructuring: Myths and Realities," Arnold W. Sametz, ed., *The Battle for Corporate Control: Shareholder Rights, Stakeholder Interests, and Managerial Responsibilities* (Homewood, IL: Business One Irwin, 1991).

of the employee's rank in the corporation's managerial or scientific hierarchies, with this factor ranging from 10 to 25 percent of salary. Performance under the Management Bonus Plan was defined in terms of (moving averages of) realized return on assets (a measure of income generation) and sales growth relative to the firm's objectives and plans. A matrix, and later an explicit formula, embodied the tradeoffs the company made between these two factors and generated bonuses that grew more than proportionately with performance, up to a cap. A similar formula was used to determine performance under the New Products Plan for technical personnel. It embodied the dollar value of orders for new products and return on new product investment relative to goals. It, too, had the feature that bonuses grew exponentially with performance, up to a cap.

This system was very complicated. Indeed, it is unclear that it would have been understood in situations where employees had less mathematical sophistication than those in this high-tech firm. On the other hand, it was tied very explicitly to corporate strategy and to the abilities of people with differing roles and ranges of responsibility to contribute to corporate objectives.

The Effectiveness of Group Incentive Contracts

There are several reasons to suppose that incentives provided to groups of employees may sometimes be as effective, or even more effective, than individual incentive contracts. First, there may simply be situations where determining individual contributions is impossible: How is the contribution of a single member of a design team measured? Then if any direct financial incentives are to be provided, they must be given to the work group as a whole. Second, groups of workers often have much better information about their individual contributions than the employer is able to gather. Group incentives then motivate the employees to monitor one another and to encourage effort provision or other appropriate behavior. In these circumstances, incentives might be further strengthened if the employer can arrange for the employees to determine one another's rewards.

A third factor favoring group incentives is that individual employees may resist their employer's directives if the employer's wishes conflict with those of the work group. By using group incentives to change the interests of the work group as a whole, the employer may make everyone willing to work more effectively and with a higher level of satisfaction. Fourth, people who work together have various ways of helping one another, exchanging favors, covering for one another, and helping out with extra effort when a member of the group is absent. Group incentives encourage such cooperation, and the possibility of withholding help from slackers can be very effective in providing incentives for members of the group to adhere to the group norms. Finally, if the work group is empowered to change methods to improve efficiency, then the ability of a group to be responsive to incentives may be far greater than is possible for an individual employee, making incentives for groups more beneficial.

Several of these factors point to the advantages of making the group whose collective performance is rewarded relatively small, so that mutual monitoring, concern for the group, and exchanges of favors within the group can be effective. Against this must be balanced the costs of measuring performance accurately for small groups and the difficulties that can arise if some groups are getting bonuses whereas others are not. Such a situation invites influence activities, with those not getting bonuses arguing that the successful groups were just luckier, or that their own group's contributions had not been adequately recognized and accurately measured, or that everyone should share in the fortunes to which all contributed, or, ultimately, that they individually should be transferred to one of the successful groups. Of course, the winners will also be tempted to politic defensively to maintain their awards.

RISK SHARING WITHIN THE WORK GROUP   If a work group is sufficiently tightly knit to act as a single individual, and if it can share risks among its members efficiently, then we can apply incentive theory to the whole group of people as if it were a single person. In such cases, no new principles beyond those developed in Chapter 7 are needed.

As we saw in Chapter 7, a group of people who share the total income received efficiently among themselves can be regarded, for risk-bearing purposes, as a single unit whose risk tolerance is the sum of the risk tolerances of the individual members.

Group Incentives and Risk at Du Pont

An experiment with group incentives at E. I. Du Pont de Nemours and Company attracted much attention, both when it was instituted in 1988 and when it was abandoned two years later. It illustrates some of the difficulties with managing such a scheme.

The plan covered nearly all the 20,000 employees in Du Pont's fibers division, which had 1989 sales of almost $6 billion in departments from intimate apparel to floorings to automobile seat coverings. The plan required employees to put some of their annual wage and salary increases in an "at-risk pot," with the intent that eventually 6 percent of their annual pay would be at risk. The at-risk money would not count as base pay for future years. Bonuses were then to be paid on how the division did relative to its earnings growth target of 4 percent after inflation. Just meeting the target would result in the employees getting back their 6 percent. If earnings grew 5 percent, they would get their 6 percent plus an extra 6 percent as bonus, and if earnings grew by 6 percent, they would get the maximum bonus of 12 percent on top of the money they put in. On the downside, if the division did not achieve at least 80 percent of its target, they would lose the money they had put at risk.

Early concerns with the plan centered on its motivational effects. Would tying pay to overall performance have any effect in such a large organization, where any single individual might have little influence on results? Would a blanket plan like this distort incentives in work groups such as research labs, where short-term earnings growth was not a very relevant issue? The unions also expressed concern about how the management would calculate earnings. However, because employees received $19 million more in bonuses the first year under the plan than they would have under the traditional system, these concerns faded.

The problem came in the business slowdown of 1990, when it became clear that the earnings target would not be met and that the employees would lose at least 2 percent of the money they had risked. Complaints mounted and morale was endangered. In the face of this, management canceled the experiment.

Based on Perry, *op. cit.* and Richard Koenig, "Du Pont Plan Linking Pay to Fibers Profit Unravels," *The Wall Street Journal* (October 25, 1990), B-1.

A cost of providing incentives is the extra risk premium incurred as a result of forcing employees to bear the risk of income fluctuations associated with varying levels of performance. With these risks efficiently shared among the group, this cost is inversely proportional to the risk tolerance of the group. This in turn is much larger than the risk tolerance of any individual, and so the costs of risk bearing may be quite low.[20] The issue then is: When might we expect that the allocation of income and income risks within a work group will be approximately efficient?

---

[20] The risk tolerance of the group is $T = \Sigma t_i = \Sigma(1/r_i)$, the sum of the individual risk tolerances, where r_i is the risk aversion index of individual i. The group risk tolerance is always greater and usually much greater than that of even the most risk-tolerant member of the group.

One such circumstance might be where the group decides how to allocate its total earnings among its members and does so efficiently. A possible example may arise in partnerships. For example, a number of not-for-profit clinics and Health Maintenance Organizations (HMOs) that provide prepaid medical and hospital care (including Kaiser-Permanente, the largest such organization in the United States) contract with for-profit partnerships of doctors to provide the actual care. The contracts often provide incentives for the partnerships to generate revenues and control costs. The doctors in a partnership may be able to monitor one another and induce effort provision without explicit incentive contracting. They then would be in a position to share the aggregate risk to their incomes reasonably efficiently. Moreover, even when some incentive contracting is needed within the group, there should be an opportunity for risk sharing that reduces the costs of providing incentives.

The traditional method of dividing profits among law firm partners provides another example. Large law firms involve specialists in many different facets of law, and the possibilities for generating revenues differ among these areas. Traditionally, partners divided firm profits not according to individual contribution, but rather according to formula. The most standard one was for all partners of a given seniority to be paid the same, with the share rising with seniority. Viewing the receipts from different parts of the firm as separate risks, this pattern is consistent with the recommendation of the theory of efficient risk sharing that any individual bear the same share of each risk. Further, if all partners of a given seniority can be considered to have approximately the same risk attitudes, whereas more senior people are less risk averse (perhaps because their accumulated wealth is larger), then the pattern is quite consistent with the recommendation that shares be positively related to risk tolerances. In recent years, however, this pattern of dividing profits has begun to break down under the demands from partners who produce more revenues that they be paid more or else they will leave to join a competitor or start their own practices.[21]

PAY EQUITY AND FAIRNESS

A major potential issue with any system of pay is its perceived fairness. It is often claimed that people value fair treatment in and of itself, and that a pay system that is perceived as unjust will then be dysfunctional. These sorts of preferences are not usually part of the standard assumptions of economic analysis, but if they are actually present, then managers cannot afford to ignore them. Moreover, economists have recently argued that a taste for "justice" might have had evolutionary advantages among early humans and their ancestors, so that we might have such preferences genetically "hard wired" into us.[22] For example, people who had a sense of when they had been mistreated and a taste for exacting revenge, even when it was costly of their time and resources, would have developed reputations that would have prevented further mistreatment and made them more successful in the competition to reproduce.

What fairness means in any context is a subtle matter. At a minimum, it could mean that individuals are concerned about how they themselves are treated relative to some reference group against whom they compare themselves, and that they feel worse off if they perceive themselves to be mistreated. At a higher level, there could be a sense of injustice when some group is seen as being badly treated, even when the concerned individuals are not affected directly. Finally, there could be an extreme

---

[21] See Ronald Gilson and Robert Mnookin, "Sharing Among Human Capitalists: An Economic Inquiry into the Corporate Law Firm and How Partners Split Profits," *Stanford Law Review*, 37 (1985), 313–92.

[22] See Robert H. Frank, *Passions Within Reason: The Strategic Role of the Emotions* (New York: W. W. Norton, 1988).

version that leads individuals to complain when they believe they are being treated too well, and that they would prefer to be treated just the same as others are.

The last form is not unknown, but does seem limited in its scope. People do give to charities, but managers rarely hear requests from employees that their pay be cut to permit increasing others' wages.[23] Still, if employees are altruistic in this sense, then pay differences should surely take account of this taste: Reducing inequality will reduce the total that needs to be paid to be competitive. The middle level (a general concern with equity) is of little direct significance unless it leads to some manifested desires. When it does, it becomes operationally similar to the case in which people are concerned about their treatment relative to others. A given level of pay may be viewed as good or bad, acceptable or unacceptable, depending on the compensation of others in the reference group, and as such may result in different behavior.

When people do compare their pay, properly applied and understood incentive pay inevitably leads to invidious comparisons. Under a well-designed scheme, equally talented people who are motivated to work equally hard will be paid differently as a result of chance variations that affect their measured performance. Understanding this, people might be less happy than they would be if their pay were more nearly equalized. This is a constraint on the use of any sort of incentive pay. Moreover, if people tend to misperceive their own value and systematically to overestimate their contributions, as some evidence suggests, then feelings of injustice and mistreatment associated with differential pay levels may be accentuated.

Of course, in this latter case, those who end up being well paid will view this as their rightful due. Equalizing pay then hurts them, even if they otherwise have a taste for equality, and managing this situation becomes very complex. This may be a reason to attempt to keep individual compensation figures confidential.

Yet even when people are purely selfish, judging their welfare solely on absolute grounds and without regard to how others may be paid, differences in treatment can be costly to the organization. Differences in realized pay point out what is possible and invite attempts to influence the distribution of rewards by political means. Resisting these may be quite difficult, especially when luck rather than talent or effort plays a part in generating the differences (as occurs under a well-functioning incentive scheme). Avoiding the costs of these influence activities can be a strong constraint on the use of incentive pay. In such a context, pay differentials may be limited, or directly profitable investment projects may not be accepted if they impose too great costs on some groups or divisions. These policies may be interpreted even by those within the organization as reflecting a concern for equity in treatment, whereas in fact their sole role is to limit costly influence activities.

---

[23] It was news when, in 1991, Los Angeles Lakers basketball star "Magic" Johnson took a voluntary pay cut to allow the Lakers to hire another player (Terry Teagle) while staying within a league-imposed salary limit.

Summary

The ways people are paid vary tremendously. This reflects the variety of different objectives that compensation policy must serve, as well as the different circumstances in which organizations operate. Nevertheless, the role of compensation in motivating employees is always a significant element in its design, and many aspects of pay policies can be understood in terms of their incentive effects.

Incentive pay can be applied at the level of the individual employee or at the group level. The purest forms of individual performance pay are *piece rates* and *sales commissions*. Each of these has clear advantages but carry costs and disabilities. They are strong motivators, they elicit self-selection, and they are easily understood. They can, however, distort employees' allocation of their time and effort away from the efficient patterns when there are concerns other than sheer volume of output or sales—for example, product quality, machine maintenance, cooperation with fellow workers, customer service, or information gathering. They also require a system in which individual employees can work at different paces for extended periods of time and that there be some means to allow the firm to limit production during periods of limited demand. Finally, pay that depends on output exposes employees to greater risk than would a fixed wage contract, with attendant costs. Nevertheless, where piece rates and commissions are used, actual practice fits quite well with the recommendations of theory.

Individual incentive pay is used in other contexts as well, especially for managers. (Executive and managerial incentives and compensation are the subjects of Chapter 13.) In all these contexts, there is an advantage in making use of employees' knowledge about their own personal characteristics and the environments in which they work. The problem is to motivate them to reveal this information. *Menus of contracts*, which allow employees to choose the scheme under which they are paid, and *management by objectives*, under which employees help set their performance goals, are two common methods of eliciting this information.

Often, however, the difficulties of defining and measuring good performance and of determining who is responsible for results mean that it is infeasible to set up explicit incentive plans linking pay and performance through simple formulas. In this case, there may still be *implicit incentive pay*, with employees being rewarded after the fact for good performance.

Either sort of incentive pay requires *performance evaluations* to determine what pay is due. With explicit incentive schemes, the key issue is to link pay to the appropriate measures of performance. Ideally, these should reflect the actual objectives of the organization and should not be able to be manipulated by either side. Performance evaluation in implicit pay systems is full of ambiguity and open to dispute. It is also apparently onerous for supervisors. Actual evaluations do not tend to be very informative, and employees do not believe in their accuracy, fairness, or usefulness. This helps account for the apparent low sensitivity of pay to performance found in many organizations.

The provision of incentives can interact importantly with *job design* and with the *discretion* accorded employees in allocating their time between job responsibilities and other interests. Other things being equal, incentive considerations argue for grouping tasks in ways that facilitate assigning individual responsibility for good or bad performance. When groupings do not affect the quality of information and incentive pay is used, there are advantages to grouping together tasks that are similar in their difficulty of performance evaluation. In this way, relatively intense incentives

can be used for all the well-monitored tasks without running afoul of the equal
compensation principle, and weaker incentives can be used for the other tasks.
Employees who are given strong incentives to perform can be given broader discretion
in allocating their time between work and other concerns because they will take better
account of the opportunity costs of their time than will those for whom pay is only
weakly related to performance. In a complementary fashion, those whose jobs demand
more discretion should be given stronger performance incentives so that they will
more fully internalize the overall impacts of their individual decisions.

Incentives for groups of employees are very common, and a variety of different
schemes are used. These include both explicit schemes linking pay to productivity,
profits, or other measures of performance and implicit schemes, such as the systems
used in Japan, which award bonuses that seem related to profits but that are determined
at the discretion of the directors of the firm. Group incentives derive their effectiveness
from the ability of small groups of employees to monitor and enforce good behavior
among themselves. When employee groups can change production methods, the
responsiveness of groups to incentives can be greater than the responsiveness of
individuals, further contributing to the efficacy of the group incentive approach.

Finally, any scheme that differentiates among people in a group may raise
questions of *fairness*. Whether people actually have a taste for justice in pay, or care
about their relative standings, or have altruistic concerns about how others are treated,
or whether instead they are purely selfish but willing to practice influence activities
to affect the distribution of pay, well-designed policies will tend to limit the
discrepancies among rewards. Thus, an apparent concern with pay equality can arise
from a simple concern for efficiency.

■ BIBLIOGRAPHIC NOTES

The basic references on the theoretical issues in performance pay are given in
Chapters 5 through 8. A standard textbook treatment of compensation management
is provided by David Belcher and Thomas Atchison, while Edward Lawler gives
an up-to-date review of behavioral and managerial research in the area and its
implications. Economic discussions of a broad range of issues and puzzles in the
area of compensation and motivation are given by George Baker, Kevin Murphy,
and Michael Jensen and by Edward Lazear. The analysis of the frequency of
evaluations is drawn from Lazear. The treatments of job design and of responsibility
and discretion are based on work by Bengt Holmstrom and Paul Milgrom.

■ REFERENCES

Baker, G., M. Jensen, and K. Murphy. "Compensation and Incentives: Practice
vs. Theory," *Journal of Finance*, 43 (1988), 593–616.

Belcher, D., and T. Atchison. *Compensation Administration*, 2nd edition
(Englewood Cliffs, NJ: Prentice Hall, 1987).

Holmstrom, B., and P. Milgrom. "Multi-task Principle Agent Analysis: Incentive
Contracts, Asset Ownership and Job Design," Working paper 6, Stanford Institute
for Theoretical Economics (1990).

Lawler, E. *Strategic Pay: Aligning Organizational Strategies and Pay Systems*
(San Francisco, CA: Jossey-Bass Publishers, 1990).

Lazear, E. "Labor Economics and the Psychology of Organizations," *Journal of
Economic Perspectives*, 5 (Spring 1991), 89–110.

EXERCISES

> ### Food for Thought

1. Adam Smith, in his *Wealth of Nations* (Book 5, Chapter 1, Part 3, Article 2), argued that university teachers should not be paid salaries but rather that they should have to rely on the fees they can collect from the students they teach. What would be the advantages of this system? What difficulties do you see with this proposal to pay piece rates to faculty?

2. In harvesting some crops, such as lettuce in the Imperial Valley of California, the pickers are hired and paid piece rates as a team. The team then decides the allocation of the receipts among group members. If the team members can monitor one another, there may be no moral hazard problem within the team, and they ought then to be able to allocate their income efficiently. At the same time, the farmers may need to provide incentives to the team as a whole and so they use piece rates.

    However, it seems that the team members in fact usually divide the receipts equally. Moreover, in some other situations (such as celery picking in Ventura County, California, and asparagus harvesting in San Joaquin County), team piece rates are used, but the farmer divides the pay among the workers, giving each an equal share. This is not evidently consistent with efficient allocation of income risks in general. What factors might account for this, and what might mitigate any apparent inefficiency?

3. Firms often have trouble with their performance pay systems when a business downturn means that no incentive payments are made: Du Pont's experience is a relatively common one. How would you account for this? What would you do as an employer in such circumstances?

4. To avoid the problems created by supervisors' reluctance to assign low evaluations, some firms (for example, Merck and Co., Inc., the very respected pharmaceutical company) have experimented with requiring that a certain fraction of the people being evaluated be assigned to each of the various possible grades or performance-evaluation levels. What problems do you see with such a scheme?

5. General Motors' new Saturn automobile line was a completely new design that was built by a specially-recruited workforce in a new factory constructed specifically for the Saturn. To market the new car, which GM hoped would help it learn to become competitive again on a world scale, it set up separate dealerships and announced that the sales people in these organizations would not be paid on a commission basis, as is common in the industry. Instead, they were to be salaried. What might be the advantage of this pay policy?

13

EXECUTIVE AND MANAGERIAL COMPENSATION

O*n the one hand, they [executives] say that intense foreign competition requires sacrifice, restraint, and discipline. Yet they then turn around and demonstrate none of those qualities by awarding themselves more personal compensation for a year's effort than could be spent in several lifetimes.*

Owen Bieber[1]

It [CEO compensation] just seems to get more absurd each year. What is outrageous one year becomes a standard for the next.

Edward E. Lawler, III[2]

Make your top managers rich and they will make you rich.

Robert W. Johnson[3]

This chapter deals with special problems associated with compensating the decision makers and senior leaders in firms. In recent years, executive compensation has become a focus of public concern and debate, especially in the United States, where the compensation of CEOs in large firms has grown much faster than the gross national product (GNP), corporate earnings, or the average worker's pay. Each year, *Fortune, Forbes, Business Week,* and other business publications carry featured stories reporting on the pay received by the CEOs at leading firms, and even the daily newspapers cover these stories. Part of the general interest in executive earnings may be pure jealousy about the spectacular sums received or curiosity about other people's incomes, but there are substantive issues involved as well. Does senior executives' pay motivate them to do a good job running the companies entrusted to them? Or are the huge amounts that they often receive in fact the result of managerial moral hazard, with the CEOs lining their pockets at the expense of their firms' owners?

---

[1] As quoted in John A. Byrne with Ronald Grover and Todd Vogel, "Is the Boss Getting Paid Too Much?" *Business Week* (May 1, 1989), 49. Bieber heads the United Auto Workers' Union.

[2] As quoted in John Byrne, "The Flap over Executive Pay," *Business Week* (May 6, 1991), 90. Lawler is an expert on compensation.

[3] As quoted in *Money Talks*, Robert W. Kent ed. (New York: Facts on File Publications, 1985), 320. Johnson was the CEO of Johnson and Johnson Corporation.

Data on the pay of top-level corporate executives in the United States are publicly available through required reports to shareholders. These list the compensation of the five most highly paid executives in each firm. The actual details of the contracts under which this pay is generated are not public, however, and systematic information on executives' pay in other countries and at lower levels in U.S. corporations is also not so easily obtained. This differential availability of data has helped focus researchers' attention on senior executive compensation, but the size and behavior of the amounts involved are responsible for much of the public's interest.

CEO Compensation in Large U.S. Firms

Each year, *Business Week* publishes a survey of the pay of the two top executives in each of 365 of the largest publicly-held corporations in the United States. According to the 1991 survey (covering 1990 earnings), the total compensation of the CEOs of these firms grew 212 percent during the decade of the 1980s. This was four times the growth in pay of the average factory worker (whose pay rose 53 percent over the period) and three times the income growth of the average engineer. In the same period, earnings per share—the returns to the firms' owners—grew 78 percent.[4] The average salary and bonus of the CEOs in the *Business Week* survey reached $1.2 million per year in 1990, and when long-term compensation through stock options and other plans is included, average total compensation was $1.95 million. It would take the average factory worker 85 years at 1990 pay rates to earn this amount, and the average engineer 45 years.

Other studies reached similar conclusions. In *Forbes'* survey of 1990 compensation of the CEOs of 800 large American firms, average total compensation was $1.635 million, of which 43 percent came from various long-term incentive elements and the rest from salary and annual bonuses.[5] In another study of 200 companies the average CEO total compensation for 1990 was $2.8 million.[6]

Hidden in these average compensation figures are some truly exceptional sums of money. According to *Forbes*, Stephen M. Wolf received $18.3 million in 1990 as CEO of UAL, the parent company of United Airlines. Of this figure, $1.12 million was salary and current bonus, with the rest coming through realized gains on stock-based, long-term incentive plans. John Sculley of Apple Computer earned $16.7 million in 1990, $2.2 million of which was salary and annual bonus. Paul Fireman of Reebok, the athletic shoe company, received $14.8 million, all of it in current salary and bonus. These figures are dwarfed, however, by the $78 million paid by Time Warner to Stephen J. Ross, its chairman and co-CEO. Most of this was a $75-million bonus awarded in connection with the merger of the publishing company Time Inc. with Warner Communications, the entertainment company Mr. Ross headed, to create Time Warner. Even more spectacular was the $186 million received by Donald A. Pels when LIN Broadcasting, the company he headed, was merged into McCaw Cellular Communications and he exercised his stock options. Overall, the 25 best-paid executives on the *Forbes* list averaged over $12 million a piece in 1990.

Of course, with such huge sums included in the calculations, the (arithmetic) average pay figure is larger than the median—the amount received by the CEO half-way down the list. Moreover, the reported long-term incentive component of pay

---

[4] John A. Byrne, "The Flap Over Executive Pay," *Business Week* (May 6, 1991), 90–96.

[5] "What 800 Companies Paid Their Bosses," *Forbes* (May 27, 1991), 237–89.

[6] Testimony by Graef Crystal to the United States Senate Subcommittee on Oversight and Government Management, May 15, 1991, as reported in Kevin G. Salwen, "Executive Pay May Be Subject to New Scrutiny," *The Wall Street Journal* (May 16, 1991), A-3.

Forms of Senior Executive Compensation

Salary: An amount paid over the course of the year and fixed in advance. Salary may be adjusted regularly based on length of service, competitive conditions, the cost of living, performance, or other considerations.

Bonus: A nominally variable amount, often paid as a lump sum, at the discretion of the firm's directors. May be tied to performance, either implicitly or through an explicit formula. If so, performance is usually measured on a short-term basis, such as the previous year's accounting profits or earnings growth, or the extent to which these exceed targets.

Stock Options: Rights given to the executive to buy stock in the firm at a prespecified price during a specific period of time. The price is usually at or above the current price of the stock when the options are awarded, and the time period is usually several years. No actual cash is received until the executive actually buys the stock. Then the compensation is the difference between the market price of the stock and the exercise price (the amount paid by the executive).

(Restricted) Stock Awards: Shares in the firm given to the executive or sold to him or her at a deep discount. Often the ability of the executive to sell this stock is restricted, at least until certain conditions are met (for example, meeting certain growth or profit goals or the executive's retirement). Number of shares awarded may depend on past performance (a "performance share plan").

Phantom Stock Plans: Units that correspond to common stock but carry no ownership claims. These entitle the executive to receive the share price appreciation and dividends that would have been received on actual stock.

Stock Appreciation Rights: Rights to collect the amount of any share price appreciation on a specified amount of common stock over time.

tends to be highly variable because the entire amount is reported in the year in which the gains are realized, even though they may be the result of several years' performance. For example, Michael D. Eisner, the head of Walt Disney Company, received $32.6 million in 1988 from stock options that became valuable because the company had become successful under his leadership in the preceding three years. In 1989 and 1990 he received no long-term compensation. His average annual pay was just short of $20 million per year over the period, but over $40 million was recorded in one year. Because the news stories tend to focus on the highest-paid executives in any year, this method of recording long-term compensation tends to bias the apparent income levels upward relative to the corresponding steady flows. Still, there is no question that these CEOs receive significant amounts of money. Table 13.1 lists the ten best-paid CEOs in the United States from 1986 to 1990.

Patterns and Comparisons

The pay patterns and levels for CEOs in the largest U.S. corporations differ radically from those of the CEOs of comparable firms in other countries and the heads of smaller (but still substantial) U.S. firms.

INTERNATIONAL DIFFERENCES IN CEO COMPENSATION   The average CEO of a very large Japanese firm (the equivalent of $30 billion in sales) earns about 17 times what

Table 13.1   The Ten Best-Paid U.S. CEOs: 1986–1990

Executive and Company	5-Year Compensation
Steven J. Ross, Time Warner	$137,254,000
Charles Lazarus, Toys 'R' Us	91,095,000
Michael D. Eisner, Walt Disney	71,069,000
Paul B. Fireman, Reebok International	69,356,000
Lee A. Iacocca, Chrysler	49,197,000
Martin S. Davis, Paramount Communications	37,380,000
Dean L. Buntrock, Waste Management	33,003,000
John Sculley, Apple Computer	32,310,000
Saul P. Steinberg, Reliance Group	32,183,000
Richard A. Manoogian, Masco	27,802,000

Source: *Forbes* (May 27, 1991), 218.

the average Japanese worker does. For comparable firms in France and Germany, the figure is about 24 times. In the United States, it is 109.[7] An extreme example comes from the oil industry. In 1987 Exxon and Royal Dutch/Shell had about equal sales and equal profits. Both firms are among the leading international petroleum companies and are involved in a similar range of activities. The head of U.S.-based Exxon was paid $5.5 million; the CEO of its European competitor received $500,000. Another example comes from the Sony Corporation. As with most Japanese firms, Sony's board of directors is made up almost exclusively of executives in the firm. In Sony's case, 34 of the board members and statutory auditors in 1989 were full-time employees of Sony or its subsidiaries. As a group, they were paid $8.2 million in salary and bonuses (calculated at 1989 exchange rates), an average of about $242,000 a piece. Had the entire $8.2 million instead been paid to the Sony CEO, he still would not have been among the ten top-paid American executives.

CEO COMPENSATION IN SMALLER FIRMS   In smaller U.S. firms, CEOs are still paid more than their Japanese or European counterparts, but the differences are much less extreme. According to surveys by Towers, Perrin, Forster & Crosby, a compensation consulting firm, the CEO of the average U.S. firm with sales of $250 million receives about $600,000 a year (including an estimated value of various benefits and perquisites). The head of a comparably sized Japanese or European firm receives about half to two thirds as much. Another Towers Perrin study indicated that the average Canadian CEO receives about 65 percent of the pay of a typical U.S. chief executive.

THE ROLE OF LONG-TERM INCENTIVE PLANS   The chief difference between the compensation of the heads of major U.S. firms and their counterparts in large foreign firms and in smaller U.S. firms is the element of long-term incentive compensation tied to stock prices. Such plans became almost universal in large U.S. firms in the 1980s but are rare abroad and in smaller companies.[8] Executives in smaller U.S. firms usually receive a salary, plus perhaps a bonus that may be based on annual accounting measures such as current profits or return on investment.[9] The same is

---

[7] Crystal, *op. cit.*

[8] The chief exceptions are entrepreneurial firms, where the founder is still CEO and retains a significant ownership share.

[9] New firms, especially in high-technology areas, such as electronics and biotechnology, are often an exception. In such "start-up" firms, executives typically receive ownership claims that will become extremely valuable if the company succeeds and goes public, selling its stock to outside investors.

true in continental Europe and Japan (where the executives get bonuses in the same spirit as all other company employees); the various long-term incentive-pay schemes afforded to heads of large U.S. corporations are essentially absent. This is especially the case in France, where a number of the largest firms are state-owned and their executives are (at least by U.S. standards) paid quite modest amounts. In the United Kingdom, however, there has been more of a move towards long-term incentive pay, and large performance-based incentives are common in Hong Kong.[10]

Because it often seems that large U.S. firms add various long-term incentive pay components to their CEOs' compensation packages without obviously decreasing any of the other elements, knowledgeable observers of executive compensation consider these long-term programs the source of the relative jump of CEO pay in the 1980s. In 1980 the relative pay of CEOs, engineers, and factory workers were all in about the same relationship to one another as they had been 20 years before: All three figures had increased about three and a half times over the two decades. In the 1980s the pay of the engineers and factory workers grew at essentially the same rate, whereas that of the CEOs grew four times as fast.[11] Direct performance pay now accounts for the bulk of compensation for CEOs of large U.S. companies, with annual bonuses contributing 25 percent and long-term incentives accounting for 36 percent of total compensation.[12]

Middle-Level Executives

Much less systematic information exists about the pay of middle-level executives. All receive salary, and some form of incentive pay is common in the United States, whether based on individual, divisional, or corporate performance. During the 1980s salary increases in U.S. firms generally seemed to lag behind inflation, but increased use of incentive pay helped total managerial compensation keep up with the cost of living. Increasingly, executives are rewarded for measured performance in the units for which they are responsible. Still, the importance of incentive pay in total compensation seems to be quite a bit lower for middle-level managers than for those at the top of the hierarchy.

DOWN-SIZING AND THE DETERMINANTS OF BASE PAY   A recent key factor in managerial compensation in the United States has been a trend to redefine the criteria for determining base pay. This has accompanied the reduction that many firms have sought in the number of layers of management in their organizational hierarchies and the size of their white-collar staffs.

Given the difficulties of measuring performance, a significant portion of pay for middle-level managers is often tied to the breadth and significance of their responsibilities. These in turn are often measured in part by the number of people reporting to the manager. This system leads to perverse incentives. The only way for a manager to get a substantial raise is to increase his or her responsibilities. One obvious way to do this (apart from winning a promotion to a higher level) is to increase the number of subordinates, particularly the number of higher-level ones. This creates incentives to add staff.

These incentives might be nullified by the resistance of higher-level executives who have profit-and-loss responsibility and are paid for organizational performance. These people have a hard time telling whether extra staff in some function or office

---

[10] See Shawn Tully, "American Bosses Are Overpaid. . .," *Fortune* (November 7, 1988), 121–36.

[11] In after-tax terms, the disparity may have been even larger, because the U.S. personal income tax rate structure became less progressive over the decade.

[12] *The Wall Street Journal* (April 17, 1991), R-5 (Special Report on Executive Compensation).

is actually worthwhile, however, especially when output is hard to measure and everyone is clearly working hard. Here a second perverse effect enters: Each extra staff person creates work that justifies hiring still others! A manager whose staff is overwhelmed by the demands of writing memos, preparing reports, replying to proposals, and so on, may win approval to hire another staff person to help. This person in turn will generate more memos, reports, and proposals. Then other offices can no longer keep up, and they need to add staff, who in turn generate even more work. Thus, massive staffs come into being, with everyone working very hard for long hours, busy keeping one another busy.

To counter these tendencies toward bureaucratic expansion, many firms are attempting to divorce managers' base-pay levels from the sizes of staffs reporting to them. They are also seeking to increase the role of incentive pay tied to measured performance, for example through management-by-objectives plans, where control of staff costs are explicit goals figuring into the determination of the bonus.

PROMOTION TOURNAMENTS AND THE ROLE OF INCENTIVE PAY   Perhaps the major incentive for most middle-level managers, however, still comes through the possibility of promotion. Firms' removal of layers of management has reduced the frequency with which promotions can be gained and the number of promotions that can be won. As we noted in Chapter 11, some of the incentives provided at each stage in elimination tournaments come from the opportunity to continue to be considered for further promotions. The leveling of organizational hierarchies has also probably increased the number of people at the lower rounds and, correspondingly, decreased the chances of winning promotion at these rounds. Both of these effects might well have adversely affected the incentives for middle-level managers. Any such negative incentive effects may have been offset by the impact of the recent increases in CEO compensation, however. Higher pay at the top of the hierarchy has increased the prize attached to winning in the last rounds and becoming an extremely well-paid senior executive, and thus may have increased middle-level managers' incentives to keep competing for promotions.

At the top of the hierarchy, there are no more promotions to win. This means that if there are to be any financial incentives for CEOs, they must come from direct performance pay. Thus, the theory also suggests that explicit incentive pay should become more important at the top of the hierarchy, as is observed in practice. This conclusion is also consistent with the recommendations of the theory of performance contracting, which indicates that the intensity of incentives should be higher when the marginal productivity of effort is higher and when the potential responsiveness to incentives is greater. The quality of the job done by the top executives typically has a greater impact on overall organizational performance than do the efforts of people in lower-level positions. At the same time, the broader discretion and responsibilities accorded the top-level people mean that they have more ways in which they can be responsive to increased incentives. Both of these factors thus suggest that direct performance incentives should be stronger and performance pay a more important part of total compensation at higher levels in the hierarchy than for middle-level executives.

THE EFFICACY OF INCENTIVE PAY FOR MIDDLE MANAGERS   Although performance pay is (and should be) less significant for middle-level managers than for senior executives, its importance is increasing. This raises the issue of whether it is effective in improving these managers' performance.

The publicly available evidence on the efficacy of incentive plans aimed at middle managers is very limited, because employees' individual performance evaluations are extremely confidential. What evidence does exist, however, indicates that incentives do work at these levels. For example, a study of 92 middle- and upper-level managers in an unidentified midwestern U.S. manufacturing firm found that managers' bonuses were sensitive to their performance, with the sensitivity being higher for those at higher levels in the hierarchy, those working in the head office rather than a plant, and those with shorter job tenure. More to the point, greater sensitivity of the bonus to performance tended to increase future performance to a statistically significant extent. This effect remained even after controlling for current performance and, indirectly thereby, for such factors as differing ability.[13]

MOTIVATING RISK TAKING

Large public corporations, with their large numbers of shareholders, can often spread the risks they face so widely that they ought to be virtually risk neutral.[14] Then, assuming they can raise any needed investment funds, they should be willing to make large investments and risk large losses if the expected returns on the investment, taking into account the possible gains and losses, are positive.

Some companies do in fact take immense risks. Together, oil firms in the late 1970s and early 1980s paid billions of dollars to the U.S. federal government to purchase drilling rights in the Baltimore Canyon, an area beneath the Atlantic Ocean off the eastern coast of the United States. They then spent hundreds of millions more dollars for the actual drilling in the ocean floor. No commercializable deposits of hydrocarbons were ever found, however, and eventually the oil companies let their rights expire without developing any of the property. Risks of this magnitude need to be undertaken if the oil producers are to make giant finds like those in the North Sea or Alaska's Prudhoe Bay.

Very large investments were also made in the early 1980s in biotechnology. By the end of the 1980s, these investments had yielded few profitable products, leading many of the early start-up companies to go out of business and others to reduce their scale of operations. In contrast, a small number of the biotech firms had become remarkably successful. In 1990, for example, Hoffmann-La Roche, the giant Switzerland-based pharmaceutical firm, paid $2.1 billion for a 60-percent share of Genentech, which had sales of $383 million and profits of $44 million. The price indicates the buyer's confidence in Genentech's future growth. More recently, the Lockheed Corporation and its allies, the Boeing Company, General Dynamics Corporation, and United Technologies Corporation, spent approximately $1 billion of their own funds developing the prototype of the F22 fighter jet that, in 1991, won a U.S. Department of Defense contest that could lead to between $60 and $100 billion in sales over the coming decade. Another group of firms, led by McDonnell-Douglas, spent a similar amount developing the losing alternative design, the F23, which will likely never be produced. As a final example, Haloid Corporation, a small photographic paper manufacturer, spent over a dozen years trying to develop patents that were already a decade old when it started before it finally launched the plain-paper copier in 1959 (and changed its corporate name to Xerox).

The Puzzle

As these examples indicate, some companies have managed to encourage risk taking on a major scale. Nevertheless, observers of the business world often comment

---

[13] Lawrence M. Kahn and Peter D. Sherer, "Contingent Pay and Managerial Performance," *Industrial and Labor Relations Review*, 43 (February 1990), 107S–120S.

[14] Strictly speaking, this applies only to "unsystematic risks" that are idiosyncratic to the firm itself and can be effectively diversified away by stockholders adjusting their portfolios of investments. (See Chapter 14 for a more detailed treatment of portfolio choice and securities pricing.) Companies need not be risk

critically on the reluctance of managers in some companies to undertake profitable projects where large losses are possible. Assuming that this is true, the issue is: Why should managers exhibit risk aversion in the investment decisions they take on behalf of their firms? After all, it is the stockholders' money that is being put at risk, not their own, and the stockholders ought to be approximately risk neutral. Thus, they should want decisions to be based solely on expected returns—the mean of what might occur if things work out well or badly—without regard to the risk involved. If managers shy away from profitable but risky investments, then the interests of the stockholders are not being served and economic efficiency is not being realized.

One reason managers might be risk averse in their investment decisions is that their pay might be closely tied through incentive contracts to the results of the investments they make. They would then face the investment risks themselves, and unlike the stockholders they would not easily be able to diversify this risk away through their portfolio decisions. Yet, empirically, this does not seem to be the right answer. Relatively few managers have such contracts; further, managerial risk aversion and timidity seem more prevalent in large, bureaucratic organizations, where explicit incentive contracts are especially rare. Even in the absence of explicit linking of pay and investment performance, however, the managers' future incomes might still effectively be tied to the outcomes of the investments they undertake. This in turn can induce risk aversion in their decisions about corporate investments.

Managerial Investment Decisions and Human Capital Risk

In western economies, successful managers are able to move from firm to firm, commanding a salary on the basis of their past performance. Good past performance that suggests that a manager is talented, hard working, or lucky therefore has a positive market value, which is part of the manager's human capital. For many of these people, their human capital is by far the most valuable asset they own. It is also an asset that is essentially nontransferable, so there is little hope of diversifying away risks that attach to it.

When managers undertake a risky investment, they put their human capital at risk. The success or failure of the investment is likely to reflect on the managers who proposed and oversaw it, affecting (current and potential) employers' estimates of their ability and thus their value in identifying and implementing future investments. A good outcome may help their reputations and increase their future earning potential, but a bad outcome will also be attributed at least partly to the managers' talents (or lack thereof) rather than entirely to random bad luck. If the project performs badly, future salaries, jobs, and promotions may be endangered. Thus, even if pay is not directly and explicitly linked to the performance of the investments for which a manager is responsible, in fact the market mechanism may create such a linkage.

Without some incentive for risk taking, managers may sensibly be reluctant to put the value of their human capital at risk: Career concerns will make managers risk averse about corporate investments. The key problem is that the returns to the investments are not solely the financial ones accruing to the risk-neutral owners of the firm but also the effects on the risk-averse managers' human capital. Then it may be necessary to devise special incentive plans to induce desirable risk taking.

THE IMPORTANCE OF THE MARKET FOR EXECUTIVE TALENT   As our analysis in Chapter 11 suggests, the ideal solution would be for the firm to insure the value of the managers' human capital. If the managers' future pay were fully insulated from the

---

neutral in their evaluation of the risk of economic downturns, oil price increases, or other risks that have an economy-wide character.

success or failure of the investment projects they recommend and manage, they would have no reason to be concerned about risk.

In Japan, where successful managers typically spend their entire careers employed by a single company and where salaries vary much less from job to job than is common in North America or Europe, the risk to a manager's human-capital value from recommending or undertaking a risky project is relatively lower. In essence, the pay promised by the firm is the only relevant consideration, and the firm can insulate the manager from the risk inherent in the investments that are undertaken. Moreover, the practice of obtaining consensus on major decisions spreads responsibility and reduces the risk to individual managers. For such firms, no special incentive plan may be required to encourage risky undertakings.

Western firms operate in a different managerial and market environment that makes the Japanese solutions less effective. The active executive recruitment market means that managers whose investments have performed well and who are thus seen as talented *must* be compensated accordingly or else they will be hired away. This means that firms operating in this environment cannot provide the full insurance that would otherwise be optimal and that Japanese firms are better able to offer.

Inducing Risk Taking

Successful firms have a variety of devices for encouraging risk taking in this context. Generally, they follow the pattern suggested by our analysis in Chapter 11 of optimal policy when labor mobility makes full income insurance infeasible: Give as much insurance as possible, which basically means reward people for success and try not to have them bear the costs of failures. Note that charging them for failures would accentuate the risk they already face and make them even more reluctant to recommend projects.

Giving stock options to managers has this effect because successes are rewarded and there is no direct cost to failures. The asymmetry in financial payoffs helps to offset the greater weight that risk-averse managers give to the decrease in the value of their human capital that follows a failure than they give to the increase that follows success and that thus leads them not to want to take risks.

Similarly, many firms in the oil industry give shares in the income generated by successful wells to the petroleum engineers and geologists responsible for their development without charging them for unsuccessful ones. This financial incentive offsets the human-capital risk involved in proposing and developing a project. These companies also consciously aim to attract "high rollers"—people who are less risk averse than the average manager. Many also use a system of approval for risky investments. This has the same effect as does the consensus system in Japan. Decisions to drill in difficult terrain, such as on the ocean floor or in the Arctic, are recommended by *teams* of geologists and explorationists and then must be approved by a management team, relieving the individual experts at each level of some responsibility for the decision. Further, the budget for bidding on oil-bearing lands is typically proposed by management, but it must be approved by the board of directors.

Similar systems of shared blame or responsibility are used in other industries, where major expenditures must be approved by higher-level managers than those who identify and manage the projects and where truly large risks must be approved by the board of directors.

Paying for Investment Proposals

If these review processes are effective, that is, if they reveal a large part of the basis of the expert's recommendation, then one measure of the employee's performance is the number of his or her recommendations that are accepted. How many attractive prospects for drilling did the geologist find? How many attractive biotechnology projects did the scientist propose and successfully defend?

According to the informativeness principle, if the final profitability of an investment is affected by random factors that could not be known when the investment decision was being made, then compensation ought not to be based solely on the outcomes of the investment. Instead, employees ought to be rewarded just for making and successfully defending suggestions for investment projects. Moreover, rewarding employees for getting projects adopted (rather than on the basis of the projects' success or failure) offsets the tendency to conservatism by providing a return to counter the risk to a person's reputation that is necessarily involved when recommending a project.

Of course, paying for accepted projects and giving employees a share of the "upside" on the projects in which they are involved, with no punishment for failures, provide an incentive for successfully promoting projects. This may lead to employees' recommending dubious projects, being overly-optimistic in evaluating prospects, and withholding negative information. For these reasons, a company that adopts such policies will need to set higher standards for project approval than would otherwise be necessary and will need to use more independent auditing of information and other such devices to protect itself. Having different people or groups within the firm responsible for proposing projects and for approving and monitoring them facilitates this.

DEFERRED COMPENSATION

We have already seen instances of deferred compensation that might apply to any of the employees of a firm. For example, the explanations of the positive relationship between pay and age or experience in terms of incentives for effort and discouraging turnover imply that pay is deferred from early in an employee's tenure with a firm until later. Deferred compensation should be especially important, however, in rewarding managers.

The simple compensation formulas involved in piece rates and linear commission schemes are appropriate for motivating steady performance in routine work, where the variations in outcomes that might occur as a result of any single decision or action by the employee are small and performance information on which pay can be based is available quickly. At the highest levels of the firm, where decisions must be made about massive, indivisible, and nonrecurring issues such as acquisitions and divestitures, major investments, and corporate reorganizations, the arguments favoring pay according to simple linear compensation formulas do not apply. Moreover, reasonable measures of performance emerge only over a period of many years for these kinds of decisions, when the profitability of major investments and strategic changes becomes clearer. These information lags make it difficult to compensate executives for taking a long-term view and make it necessary to base compensation on the long-term performance of the firm.

Deferred compensation formulas, when properly designed, can help to achieve that objective. For example, deferred payments that are tied to the firm's future performance will help encourage managers to take a long-term view rather than to concentrate excessively on short-term results. Payment in stock that cannot be sold immediately or in options that cannot be exercised before a certain date would be examples. This is the essence of the plan adopted at Salomon Brothers which was described in Chapter 1.

Many actual compensation programs cannot be described in such simple terms, however. Often, managers will have moved on to other jobs long before the full effects of their decisions become known, and their compensation in the new assignments is largely or completely unaffected by the unfolding results of their previous efforts.

Deferred compensation schemes also have roles other than promoting a long-term view. Compensation is deferred to provide incentives through bonding or to discourage turnover. Under a system of progressive income taxation, deferred compensation may also serve to postpone income not needed today into a period of time after retirement, when income and taxes may be lower. Other tax considerations are important in compensation design, but because the tax laws vary from country to country and even within countries over time, a proper treatment of this subject would be quite lengthy.[15]

Commitment Problems

A complication in using deferred compensation for incentive purposes is that the practice invites renegotiation. Suppose an executive has taken an action whose results will not be evident for some time and that the incentive system deferred part of the executive's compensation until the results of the action become known. Once the action has been taken, however, there is no further reason to subject the executive to the income risk inherent in the incentive contract, especially if the executive is retiring or leaving the firm. In fact, by renegotiating to eliminate the risk, the parties can increase total value by the amount of the risk premium the executive assigns to the income risk. Of course, if this incentive is foreseen and the contract is expected to be renegotiated, then the original contract will be nothing but the starting point for the renegotiation. In this context it may affect the split between the executive and the firm of whatever surplus is available, but it cannot normally be expected to provide appropriate incentives. Thus, providing incentives through deferred compensation requires the ability to make commitments and stick to them.

PERFORMANCE PAY FOR CEOS?

The key issue in managerial compensation is the pay of senior executives, especially CEOs. Some CEOs are paid immense amounts, but even so, their earnings are usually a trivial fraction of the earnings of the firms they head. From the perspective of total value creation, the important question is not how much they are paid; that amount is just a transfer and, consequently, without significance for efficiency. Rather, the more important issue is whether CEOs' pay provides them with the appropriate incentives to maximize value. The sheer magnitude of pay might have some effect here. For example, various observers have asserted that the growing gap between the earnings of senior executives and the pay of average working people in the United States is destructive of employee morale and of the trust that is needed to make businesses run efficiently. If this is true, the highly publicized examples of CEOs' pay skyrocketing while the companies they head flounder, losing money and laying off people, certainly are destructive of value. Yet the overwhelming evidence is that, on average, CEOs' pay and wealth are responsive to company performance. The issue is whether they are appropriately so.

Setting CEO Pay

The compensation of the senior executive officers of a corporation is set by the firm's board of directors. Shareholders have no direct say in the matter, and the U.S.

---

[15] Readers interested in a study that treats tax and incentive issues together are referred to Myron Scholes and Mark Wolfson, *Taxes and Business Strategy: A Global Planning Approach* (Englewood Cliffs, NJ: Prentice Hall, 1991).

Securities and Exchange Commission's policies have generally allowed companies to keep compensation issues from being the subject of shareholder votes. The directors usually appoint a compensation committee charged with recommending executive compensation to the board as a whole. Often, but not always, the compensation committee is composed exclusively of outside directors, who are not officers of the corporation. Nevertheless, the CEO is usually a member of the committee *ex officio* (by virtue of his or her office). Corporate officers are not supposed to have a role in the compensation committee's nor the board's deliberations and decisions regarding their own pay. Instead, the CEO makes recommendations to the compensation committee regarding the other officers' compensation and then is supposed to leave the room while the committee decides on these and on what the CEO should be paid as well.

Frequently, compensation consultants are hired (often by the CEO) to advise the board on compensation. These consultants are often firms—such as Towers Perrin—that specialize in this line of business, although some general consulting firms also have a compensation practice. The consultants have access to information on compensation forms and levels at other firms, and they often have statistical models relating pay to performance, firm size, and other possibly relevant variables. The information they provide is used in setting pay and in designing compensation packages.

The Debate on Executive Compensation

Many knowledgeable critics of executive compensation see this mechanism as having been captured by the executives themselves for their own benefits. The board of directors is supposed to represent the interests of the stockholders, but there are real questions about whether and how well they can do this when the shareholders' interests are in conflict with the CEO's.

Even the outside directors (members of the board who are not employees of the corporation) are likely to have close ties with the officers. They are effectively nominated by the CEO, they must rely on the executives for most of the information they receive, and they need good relationships with the officers if they are to function well in guiding corporate policy. Often, directors share similar backgrounds and interests with the firm's executives. Frequently, they themselves are senior executives in other firms. Moreover, outside directors who are not CEOs of other firms may well derive a significant portion of their incomes from their directorships.

According to Korn/Ferry International, an executive recruiting firm, in 1990 the average outside director of a major U.S. firm was paid over $32,000 as a retainer and for attending board meetings, and many firms were even more generous. For example, Pepsico paid each of its outside directors $78,000 in 1990.[16] Most firms paid extra for serving on board committees, and many firms made stock grants to their directors, gave them insurance and retirement benefits, and even gave them free samples of the company's product, for example, a new car every six months at General Motors. The results could be substantial: The dean of Northwestern University's Kellogg School of Management was reported to earn at least a third more in direct compensation from his service on several boards than he did from his regular job.[17] In this context, critics wonder how much weight compensation committees, even

---

[16] Judith Dobrzynski, "Directors' Pay Is Becoming An Issue Too," *Business Week* (May 6, 1991), 94.

[17] Joann S. Lublin, "While Outside Directors' Pay Increases, Independence From Managers May Fade," *The Wall Street Journal* (April 22, 1991), B-1.

when composed of outsiders, give to stockholders' interests compared to those of the executives whose pay they are setting.

On the other side of the argument are some who claim that CEOs "are worth every nickel they get."[18] These observers claim that CEOs can have a tremendous effect on the performance of their firms and that they in fact collect a very small part of the gains that are generated when they make the firms perform well for stockholders.[19] These observers worry that corporate CEOs are in fact not adequately compensated, both in absolute terms (compared with alternative opportunities in such fields as investment banking or entrepreneurship) and, more importantly, in terms of the explicit incentives they receive to improve corporate performance.[20]

Research results indicate that the stock markets respond very positively to the adoption of both short-term and long-term incentive programs for senior executives.[21] Those who doubt that CEO incentives are adequate point to the fact that sophisticated, knowledgeable investors bid up the stock of firms that strengthen incentives as showing that the senior executives' incentives are important for the performance of the firm. This position is reinforced by the fact that, when ownership becomes concentrated in the hands of professional owners running leveraged-buyout firms, the new owners tie executive compensation very closely to results by giving management significant ownership shares. The observers then argue that management incentives actually provided in most large corporations are too muted to be optimal. Evaluating these opposing positions requires considering what sort of behavior needs to be induced from senior executives and what sort of temptations they might be subject to, as well as examining the evidence on the actual strength of incentives and their impact.

The Tasks and Temptations Facing Senior Executives

Senior executives have remarkably broad responsibilities and great latitude and discretion in determining their behavior and the objectives and policies their firms will pursue. A system that seeks to provide incentives to senior executives therefore may need to be concerned not just with any single dimension of their behavior, such as how hard they work, but also with how they allocate their time and attention among different concerns. What will executive decisions accentuate? Market share? Growth of sales, assets, or employment? Stability of employment and earnings? Accounting rates of return on assets or stockholders' equity? Long-term stock price appreciation? Or any of a multitude of other considerations? What trade-offs will be made among these? Will concerns with the environment, with the communities in

---

[18] Kevin J. Murphy, "Top Executives Are Worth Every Nickel They Get," *Harvard Business Review* (March–April 1986), 125–32.

[19] On average, even the 25 highest-paid executives in *Forbes'* survey of 1990 pay took away only $2.26 for every $1,000 in revenues their companies received, and $30.20 on every $1,000 in profits. Recall that these were the *highest-paid* executives for the year and that the compensation of the highest-paid individuals in any year tends to be inflated by recognition of the gains taken on long-term compensation.

[20] See, for example, the comments of Michael C. Jensen in "A Roundtable Discussion of Management Compensation," *Midland Corporate Finance Journal* 2 (Winter 1985), 32; and Michael C. Jensen and Kevin J. Murphy, "CEO Incentives—It's Not How Much You Pay, But How," *Harvard Business Review* (May–June 1990), 138–53.

[21] Hassan Tehranian and James Waegelein ["Market Reaction to Short-Term Executive Compensation Plan Adoptions," *Journal of Accounting and Economics*, 7 (April 1985), 131–44] found that stock prices jump 11 percent on announcement of the company's first executive compensation plan tying pay to accounting returns, and James Brickley, Sanjai Bhagat, and Ronald C. Lease ["The Impact of Long-Term Managerial Compensation Plans on Shareholder Wealth," *Journal of Accounting and Economics*, 7 (April 1985), 151–74] found that adoption of a long-term incentive plan gave stockholders a direct 2 percent return.

which the firm operates, or with national policy absorb the executives' attention and influence corporate policies? The appropriate choices on any of these matters are not immediately obvious, even if one believes that the firm ought to be run in the interests of the stockholders.

Even when the desired behavior may be clear, there are issues about whether it will be pursued. Will hiring and promotion decisions be driven by efficiency, or will favoritism rule? Will excessive costs and unprofitable activities be eliminated, even though doing so may require tough decisions that make the CEO appear hard or even heartless? Will risks be taken when the rewards to the corporation make them worthwhile, and only then? Will the executives deny themselves perks that cannot be justified on economic grounds? Will they forego making investments and acquisitions that increase their empires at the expense of profitability? Will they meet value-maximizing takeover attempts with honest efforts to get the best terms possible, even though the change of control might cost them their jobs, or will they oppose the change out of self-interest, seeking to entrench themselves in their jobs?

With so many relevant dimensions, there is an obvious difficulty in attempting to shape executives' behavior: There simply would not seems to be enough different instruments available for the task.

Value Maximization and Incentives

The principle of value maximization actually makes the task of motivating senior executives appear relatively simple: Executives should be guided to maximize value. Furthermore, under a frequently made assumption, determining whether they are doing this is also straightforward.

Suppose that the capital markets efficiently aggregate information in the sense that securities prices fully reflect everyone's information to the extent that it is relevant to forecasting future returns. (This presumption is called the *strong form efficient market hypothesis* and is discussed more fully in Chapter 14.) Weaker forms of this hypothesis, which posit that all public information is reflected in prices, have considerable formal empirical support: The prices at which shares trade are determined primarily by the best estimates of skilled, knowledgeable investors who specialize in evaluating firms' plans and prospects and making recommendations to investors. Under this hypothesis, the market's reaction to various moves that the firm makes is the best available measure of their effect in creating economic value: If the market sees a new policy or strategy as increasing total value, then it will bid up the market value of the firm correspondingly. Under these conditions, executive incentives should be structured to encourage *maximizing the market value* of the firm.

Assuming such strongly efficient markets and assuming that the conditions of the principle of value maximization hold, the prescription to maximize the market value of the firm has obvious appeal. No matter in whose interests you believe the firm should be run, the appropriate thing to do is to make the total pie to be divided among the claimants as large as possible, and if the market freely signals whether the total pie has been augmented or reduced, then follow the market's dictates.

But suppose that transfers are difficult, or that bargaining is constrained by informational asymmetries and other transactions costs, or that executive decisions are based in large part on private information that the market cannot assess. What then? Clearly, market-value maximization may not be efficient if the market ignores some of the managers' private information. Market-value maximization may also be inefficient if bargaining costs prevent the value from representing all the interests affected by management decisions.

Of course, the issue is much clearer if the firm *should* be run in the interests of its owners. Then, still assuming that the market value of the firm at any point

Golden Parachutes and the Stock Market

Golden parachutes are contracts that give large severance payments to senior executives who lose or leave their jobs following a merger or takeover. They became very widespread in the United States during the 1980s, especially as the perceived threat of successful hostile takeovers loomed larger as the decade progressed. The largest golden parachutes generated huge sums for their possessors: F. Ross Johnson, the former CEO of RJR Nabisco, received $53.8 million following the leveraged buyout of the firm by Kohlberg, Kravis and Roberts, and the vice-chairman received another $45.7 million.

Golden parachutes have often been attacked as another example of executive greed being catered to by compliant boards of directors. They have also been seen as weakening managerial incentives by reducing the threat posed by the prospect that an ill-run company will be taken over and the nonperforming managers fired. In contrast, they have been rationalized as being useful in aligning executives' and stockholders' interests. The severance pay helps deter executives from resisting takeover attempts that would be costly for them personally but advantageous for stockholders.

One possible way to decide between these competing views is to consider the reaction of the stock market to adoption of a golden parachute provision. A study focusing on the period from 1975 to 1982 found that the share prices of firms announcing such plans in fact rose around the announcement dates relative to what would otherwise be expected.* Thus, at least in this early period, the market responded favorably to the adoption of golden parachute plans. A comparable study covering later periods has not been done.

The favorable market reaction does not necessarily imply that golden parachutes are actually in stockholders' interests, however. The difficulty is that the adoption of a golden parachute might be taken by the market to mean that the firm's executives and board had received private information that the company was a likely target of a takeover attempt. Given that shareholders in firms that were acquired in hostile takeovers in the early 1980s realized average gains on their stock holdings of 40 to 50 percent, any indication that a takeover was more likely ought to have driven up stock prices, even if the parachute provision itself were contrary to shareholder interests.

*Richard A. Lambert and David F. Larcker, "Golden Parachutes, Executive Decision-Making, and Shareholder Wealth," *Journal of Accounting and Economics*, 7 (April 1985), 179–204.

reflects the best estimate of the future cash flows that the firm will generate, market-value maximization is again the proper test of performance. Tying the CEO's pay to the value of the firm would direct attention exactly where it belongs.

The Evidence on Performance and Pay

The presumptions that executives should seek to maximize the market value of the firm and that incentive systems should be structured to encourage this behavior in a cost-efficient manner underlie much of the systematic empirical work on executive performance and pay.

PAY AND ORGANIZATIONAL SIZE   The best-established empirical regularity concerning executive compensation is that pay rises with the size of the unit or organization the executive heads. In study after study the same result appears, and the magnitude of the effect is remarkably stable across firms, industries, countries, and time periods: A 10 percent increase in sales results in about a 2 to 3 percent increase in salary plus bonus.[22] Larger firms pay more, and when a firm grows, its pay rises to the level corresponding to its new size. In fact, after surveying the evidence from different studies, one observer has gone so far as to suggest that a new "universal constant" has been found.

This size-pay effect has been interpreted by some as giving managers an incentive to focus on sales volume and growth rather than value, on the presumption that larger size will mean more pay. Causation need not flow in this direction at all, however. In particular, if the marginal value of having more able people increases with organizational size (because their talents can influence more people and decisions), and if the allocation of executives is efficient, then larger organizations will pay more because they have more able people who have a larger economic impact. Thus, the size-pay correlation is hardly conclusive evidence that pay is not tied to performance.

PAY AND PERFORMANCE   In fact, it is statistically well established that pay for senior executives is sensitive to firm performance. It is certainly easy to find individual examples where there is little apparent connection between the two, particularly in the numerous stories in the business press on executive compensation. A CEO's compensation may rise, year after year, often from an already high level, whereas the firm's profits erode and its stock price falls from sight. In contrast, examples of very explicit linkage between pay and performance can also be found. The box on Michael Eisner of Walt Disney presents one example. In any case, the general pattern is that pay responds to performance.

When performance is measured by *accounting rates of return* (accounting profits divided by the accounting value of total assets, expressed as a percentage), the estimates are that top executives' pay increases between 1 and 1.25 percent when the accounting rate of return rises 1 percentage point. An alternative measure of performance is *shareholder rate of return* (dividends plus any change in the stock price over the year, divided by the price of the stock at the beginning of the year, again expressed as a percentage). With this measure, the magnitude of the effect is lower by a factor of 10, but it is still statistically significant and, again, remarkably stable across data sets. An increase in shareholder returns of 1 percentage point raises the CEO's salary plus bonus by 0.1 to 0.16 percent.[23]

THE INTENSITY OF CEO PERFORMANCE INCENTIVES   For a CEO earning $1 million in salary and bonus in a firm that has been yielding 10 percent market returns to its shareholders, increasing the return to 11 percent is thus statistically associated with an increase in pay of between $1,000 and $1,600. If the value of the company's stock was, say, $1 billion, then the 1 percent gain in returns translates into an increased

---

[22] Sherwin Rosen, "Contracts and the Market for Executives," National Bureau of Economic Research working paper 3542 (1990).

[23] Rosen, *op. cit.* Of course, the shareholder return might be dominated by changes in the share price that are not so much attributable to anything specific to the company but rather to the overall behavior of the stock market. This suggests that relative performance evaluation should be used in setting executive compensation, so as to help filter out the elements of stock returns that are not attributable to the individual firm's performance. The evidence on whether boards of directors in fact do this is mixed, although there is some suggestion that it is becoming more prevalent. See Robert Gibbons and Kevin J. Murphy, "Relative Performance Pay for Chief Executive Officers," *Industrial and Labor Relations Review*, 43 (February 1990), 30S–51S.

A CEO Performance Contract That Performed

In the early 1980s the Walt Disney Company was in disarray. Managed by family members of its brilliant but deceased founder, it had few worthwhile movie production projects, its profits and stock price were substandard, and it seemed to be wasting its resources. It even paid $31 million in *greenmail* to a hostile raider, paying him above-market prices for the Disney shares he had accumulated in return for a promise not to attack again.

In 1984 Disney hired Michael D. Eisner to become its CEO. Mr. Eisner had formerly been at Paramount, another entertainment industry giant. Mr. Eisner's compensation contract with Disney gave him a base salary of $750,000 per year, a very modest amount by Hollywood standards. However, it also entitled him to an annual bonus of 2 percent of all profits in excess of a 9 percent return on equity (ROE). The 9 percent figure was above what the company was earning when he joined. He also received options on 2 million shares of Disney with an exercise price of $14.

Eisner reinvigorated the failing company. Under his leadership, the return on equity jumped to 25 percent, and the stock price climbed to $84. In 1988 he realized $32.6 million on his stock options.

In 1989 he entered a new contract with Disney. This left his salary at $750,000 for ten years, but continued to give him 2 percent of the profits over an elevated new standard of an 11 percent ROE. He also got new stock options: 1.5 million at a price of $69, the market price of Disney stock at the date of the new contract, and another 500,000 at $79.

Mr. Eisner received approximately $7.5 million in bonus payments in 1989 and another $10.5 million in 1990. The company enjoyed $820 million in profits in 1990 on revenues of $6 billion.

Based on Graef Crystal, "CEO Compensation: The Case of Michael Eisner," Fred K. Foulkes, ed., *Executive Compensation: A Strategic Guide for the 1990s* (Boston: Harvard Business School Press, 1991), as well as data from the *Business Week* and *Forbes* surveys.

shareholder wealth of $10 million. The CEO's salary plus bonus rise by about 10 to 16 cents for every extra $1,000 created for the shareholders. These may not seem like very intense incentives. Moreover, a recent noteworthy study by Michael Jensen and Kevin Murphy has argued that the incentives facing CEOs in large firms are even more muted.[24]

Rather than estimating the responsiveness in percentage terms of CEO compensation to stockholders' returns, Jensen and Murphy estimated the change in salary plus wages as a linear function of the change in shareholder wealth, which is essentially the sum of dividends paid during the year plus the change in the market value of the firm's common stock. Their estimate was that an extra $1,000 of shareholder wealth created was associated with only 1.35 cents more pay to the CEO. Comparing this estimate with the figures in the preceding paragraph, we see that it is an order of

---

[24] Michael C. Jensen and Kevin J. Murphy, "Performance Pay and Top-Management Incentives," *Journal of Political Economy*, 98 (April 1990), 225–64.

magnitude smaller than those found using the regression of the change in pay on the rate of return.

Of course, there are many other elements of personal financial concern to a CEO than just the current salary and bonus. To take account of these, Jensen and Murphy estimated the effect of changes in total stockholder wealth (as defined previously) on the change in CEO wealth (defined to include the salary and bonus plus the change in the value of stock options), as well as the value of any of the firm's stock held by the CEO and an estimate of any lasting effects that increased current compensation might have on future pay and retirement benefits. Even allowing for the impact of performance on the probability of being fired, the largest figure they could generate was that CEO wealth rose just $3.25 for each $1,000 increase in shareholder wealth. Moreover, the sensitivity was much lower for the larger firms in the sample. Averaged over the firms in the top half of the sample (ordered by market value), the sensitivity was only $1.85 per $1,000, whereas it was $8.05 for the firms in the bottom half of the size distribution. Most of the sensitivity actually came through the CEOs' holdings of stock in their own companies, whose value is of course perfectly correlated with total shareholder wealth. This accounted for $2.50 of the total figure of $3.25, and the fact that the CEOs of the smaller firms tended to hold a much larger fraction of their firms' stock accounts for most of the difference in sensitivity between large and small firms. In the sample as a whole, the sensitivity of the factors that the board of directors control—salary and bonus, stock options, and likelihood of performance-related dismissals—amounted to only 75 cents over a lifetime per $1,000.

ARE CEOs' INCENTIVES INADEQUATE?   Jensen and Murphy argue that these sensitivity figures are too small to provide adequate performance incentives. For example, consider a CEO contemplating whether to use $1 million of the firm's resources on some pet project—perhaps an endowed chair to support research and teaching at the university the CEO attended. Ignoring risk aversion, the median CEO in the sample—the one relative to whom half get stronger incentives and half get weaker—would find it directly worthwhile to give away the shareholders' $1 million if the project brought $3,250 in personal pleasure to the executive. If the CEO had no substantial ownership stake in the firm, the breakeven occurs at $750. This is less than a single morning's pay for the median executive in the sample. Ethical considerations aside, it might be quite tempting to spend the shareholders' money this way. Of course, the same sort of calculations apply even to less worthy diversions of funds.

Jensen and Murphy also consider a variety of factors that theory would suggest would tend to limit the intensity of incentives provided to CEOs. Risk aversion should lower the intensity of incentives, and CEOs' limited wealth also restricts the intensity of incentives that can be given. The imperfections that arise in performance measurement because stock prices are influenced by much more than the efforts of the CEO are another reason to deemphasize shareholder wealth. Other possibilities are that nonfinancial incentives are adequate or that CEOs' concerns with their market value as managers or with the threat of hostile takeovers are sufficient to induce them to pursue the stockholders' interests diligently. Jensen and Murphy do not find any of these compelling, however. They then argue for tying CEOs' wealth much more to stockholders' welfare to improve corporate performance, essentially by greatly increased use of restricted stock awards.[25]

---

[25] Michael Jensen and Kevin Murphy, "CEO Incentives—It's Not How Much You Pay, But How," *Harvard Business Review* (May–June, 1990), 138–53.

THE COUNTER ARGUMENTS   Jensen and Murphy's analysis and recommendations have attracted attention and criticism from both academics and practitioners. The academics have tended to concentrate on econometric and theoretical issues. Cogent arguments suggest that at least the first of the Jensen-Murphy estimations—the one relating the change in salary plus bonus to shareholder returns—may have assumed an inappropriate functional form relating the two variables, and that this accounts for the order-of-magnitude difference between the estimate they obtained and those generated in earlier studies.[26] Perhaps more tellingly, however, are the arguments that the multidimensional nature of the CEO's job may mean that the incentives tied to stock-price movements optimally should not be too strong.

Tying pay to stock performance certainly discourages excessive perks and unprofitable empire building. There is, however, more to worry about and motivate than these "effort" decisions. Even assuming efficient capital markets, it appears that short-term returns influence market perceptions of long-term prospects and thus stock prices.[27] In that case, tying pay to share prices may invite executives to favor investments that are too short-term oriented. (Of course, if markets are not efficient, then the attractiveness of share prices as measures of performance is even more questionable.) Tying pay too closely to share performance also can have harmful effects on executives' willingness to undertake risky but profitable investments. The use of stock option plans mitigates this somewhat (because the executive does not bear the financial losses that result when investments do not work out but does share in the successes), but these plans may encourage taking excessive risks. Further, accounting measures can be useful in controlling a tendency to take too many perks, and so they should also be used in determining compensation, rather than just stock prices alone. As the equal compensation principle indicates, providing strong incentives for some activities risks distorting executives' choices about others that may be as important. It may be that a low level of sensitivity to stock prices is appropriate in this context.[28]

The other criticism of the Jensen-Murphy position comes from those who are already concerned that executive pay is often excessive and ineffective. It starts from the apparent tendency of boards to add new items to CEOs' compensation packages without adjusting the size of the existing ones. Given this, a recommendation to increase the linkage between CEO and shareholder wealth through stock awards amounts to an invitation to bestow large amounts of stock on the CEOs, giving away even more of the shareholders' money to already well-paid executives.

Does CEO Pay Affect Performance?

Of course, giving stock to executives could still be worthwhile if it would increase performance enough to offset the dilution of share values. This raises the fundamental issue: *Do executive incentives actually work?* Pay may be sensitive to performance, but this is not the real issue. The important question is whether providing incentives to CEOs improves corporate performance. This turns out to be a very subtle issue to decide empirically. Relatively few studies have addressed this question, and the results appear mixed.

STATISTICAL ANALYSES   Jensen and Murphy have presented some limited evidence that the stock-market performance of the 25 companies in their sample which provided

---

[26] Rosen, *op. cit.*

[27] See Chapter 14.

[28] Bengt Holmstrom, "Comment on S. Rosen: 'Contracts and the Market for Executives'," draft, Yale University, School of Organization and Management (1990).

the strongest incentives exceeded the performance of the firms that gave the weakest incentives by a substantial, statistically significant margin.[29] Working with the entire Jensen-Murphy data set, however, Graef Crystal found that differences in the strength of incentives had little or no power in explaining the variation in performance among companies.[30]

These results are not necessarily inconsistent. Pay may affect performance both in fact and statistically (that is, in the sense that the two are more closely linked in the data than is plausibly the result of pure chance), and yet the influence of other variables on performance may totally dominate that of pay. Then, increasing the sensitivity of pay to performance will improve performance in a probabilistic sense, but the effects may quite possibly be drowned out by other factors. Nevertheless, when only the extreme cases are considered, the relationship might show through.

Moreover, there are also subtle issues in interpreting the response of stock market prices to pay systems. For example, if the market believes the adoption of an innovation in CEO pay will improve future performance, then the stock price will immediately be bid up to reflect the expected magnitude of this effect. Subsequently, share performance should not be exceptional because all the gains were realized at the outset when the stock price adjusted to make the anticipated return on holding the firm's stock just competitive with other investment opportunities. Thus, it may be hard to see any difference in stock price performance between firms using high-powered incentives and those that do not unless the data cover the period when the plans were instituted.

More fundamentally, however, neither the Jensen-Murphy calculations nor Graef's regression analyses are really the best way to test whether incentives affect performance. A better test would be to look at changes in the intensity of incentives and the changes in subsequent performance. This has been done in a recent study by John Abowd of some 16 thousand executives in 250 large U.S. corporations in the period from 1981 to 1986.[31] His study indicated that increasing the sensitivity of changes in salary and bonuses to current corporate performance increases future performance in a statistically significant fashion: increases in the sensitivity of either the executives' annual raises or their bonuses in a given year to current shareholder rate of return were associated with an increase in the shareholder rate of return for the next year. Abowd's study did not, however, take account of long-term incentive plans or examine their impact. Doing so would be desirable, but would involve a massive effort to assemble the data.

INTERNATIONAL COMPARISONS   An entirely different approach to the question of whether CEO incentives affect performance and are worth their cost arises from the observation that German and Japanese CEOs receive few or no long-term performance incentives of the kind common in the United States and yet large companies in these countries are generally seen as performing much better than their American counterparts. For example, W. Edwards Demming, the American statistician whose quality-control methods are a key feature of Japanese manufacturing, criticizes most incentive plans as being dysfunctional. Demming sees them as focusing executives'

---

[29] Michael C. Jensen and Kevin J. Murphy, "Letter to the Editor," *Harvard Business Review* (July–August, 1990), 190–1.

[30] Graef Crystal, "The Great CEO Sweepstakes", *Fortune* (June 16, 1990), 94–102; and *The Crystal Report on Executive Compensation*, 2 (May/June 1990). (Mr. Crystal is the former head of a major compensation consulting firm who now teaches at the University of California, Berkeley. The *Crystal Report* is a newsletter he publishes in Napa, California.)

[31] John M. Abowd, "Does Performance-Based Managerial Compensation Affect Corporate Performance?" *Industrial and Labor Relations Review*, 43 (February 1990), 52S–73S.

attention on narrow numerical goals rather than on the long-term health of the company. Various senior Japanese executives have also been highly critical of American executive compensation practices.[32]

There is certainly a nice irony, as well as an important puzzle, in the apparent negative correlation internationally between the prevalence of performance incentives and the level of realized performance. Nevertheless, moving to a Japanese pay system does not seem obviously desirable in the North American context. First, the job of the CEO in a Japanese firm is markedly different from that of a U.S. company's chief executive. Japanese firms traditionally push decision-making power and responsibility down the hierarchy. They rely on consensus, with plans and proposals originating at low levels and working their way up to the executive offices. They do not go outside to hire hot-shot executives to turn the company around. The CEO in this system is supposed to represent the company and its values, not run it in the American sense. Second, Japanese firms are not run in the interests of their shareholders. Indeed, Japanese CEOs do not even profess to believe that they should be: The interests of the employees (in job security, opportunities for advancement, and so on) are seen as being of at least equal importance. This means that the "long-term health of the company" about which Demming worries is a prime consideration in Japan. Yet it is not obvious that it is the appropriate measure of performance to be pursued, at least in the North American context. Third, the period when American industry got into its worst trouble and lost so much of its international competitive position was before the now-popular long-term incentive plans were adopted. At that time, U.S. executives' pay was much less closely aligned with shareholder concerns. Is there any reason to believe that going back to the practices of that era would be an improvement?

Implications and Conclusions

It is very hard to decide whether CEO pay provides appropriate and adequate incentives. Is $3.25 per $1,000 an adequate incentive? Or is the real issue the millions of dollars that top executives are paid to sit in fancy offices, ride in corporate jets, and decide the fates of hard-working people they do not even know exist? Indeed, it is even hard to figure out how to decide this issue.

Even if high pay is well explained as a motivator in average cases, one still might be concerned about the individual cases where it clearly is not. The general pattern may be that executives' pay is responsive to performance and that performance in turn is positively affected by the incentives that corporate leaders receive. It may even be the case that executive compensation systems on average are quite appropriately designed and calibrated. Nevertheless, there are certainly plenty of examples in which whatever performance incentives were in place did not motivate the chief executives in question to pursue much of anything other than their own narrow interests. Moreover, the boards of directors have often sat by as these CEOs led their companies to decline and even ruin, all the while giving them handsome raises.

The question that arises is whether there are other mechanisms that might ensure that such examples are rare and transient. Of course, if the conclusion is that presently prevailing pay schemes do not give CEOs adequate motivation but instead just pay them exorbitant amounts, then the question of the possible existence of other discipline devices is even more pressing.

---

[32] Dana Weschler Linden with Vicki Contavespi, "Incentivize Me, Please," *Forbes* (May 27, 1991), 208–12.

SUMMARY

Executive compensation involves a number of specific issues beyond the general ones addressed in the preceding chapter on pay and motivation. Many of these relate to the form and level of CEO compensation in large U.S. firms.

During the 1980s CEO compensation in the largest U.S. corporations grew four times as much in percentage terms as did the pay of the average employee. Much of this seems to be attributable to the proliferation of long-term incentive provisions that link the executives' pay to the stock-market performance of the shares in their firms. Such schemes are rare in smaller companies (except entrepreneurial ones where the founder is CEO and still retains a substantial ownership share). They are also rare in Europe and Asia. In any case, the absolute level of total CEO pay in large American corporations is approaching $2 million per year, and the ratio of the CEO's total compensation to the pay of an average worker is several times larger than the comparable figure in other leading industrial countries and in smaller U.S. firms.

Pay for middle managers has not risen nearly as fast as for their bosses. Performance-based incentive pay seems to be playing an increasingly important role for these managers, but it is still much less a factor than at higher levels in the corporation. This relative pattern is in line with the predictions of both the tournament theory of promotions as incentive mechanisms and the theory of incentive contracting. The former suggests that direct incentives need to replace promotion incentives as the employee reaches the top of the hierarchy. The latter suggests that incentives should be more intense where the employee's efforts have a bigger marginal impact on profitability and where the employee has greater opportunity to respond to increased incentives. Both these conditions seem more likely to hold at higher levels in the firm. Another major trend in middle-management compensation has been to redefine the basis for determining salary to avoid some of the perverse incentives to expand staff, which are occasioned by basing managers' pay on the number of people they directly supervise.

Deferred compensation can be especially important in providing proper motivation for executives because the results of many of the major decisions and actions they take do not become evident for extended periods. In fact, however, there is some question about the extent that managers are held responsible for these choices: Often it seems they have moved on long before the results become known, and they are never held accountable. This tendency may actually reflect a commitment problem. Once the decisions are made and the actions taken, but before the results become known, an efficiency gain can be realized through insuring the manager by removing the dependence of pay on results.

Motivating executives to take appropriate risks, especially in investment decisions, is complicated by the fact that such decisions put not only the financial capital of the firm's owners at risk but also the human capital of the managers associated with the project. Again, success reflects well on the managers' talent and dedication, and failures hurt their market value. A possible response is to use explicit contracts that pay the managers for successful investments but do not punish them for failures. This asymmetric payoff pattern can help offset the managers' risk aversion about the value of their human capital and motivate them to take on the risks inherent in investing. Stock options have these essential features, as do the contracts used by oil companies to reward professionals involved in developing petroleum deposits. In this context, it may also be useful to pay simply for having proposals adopted. Both of these measures may, however, give excessive incentives to try to get projects funded, and this may necessitate close scrutiny of investment proposals and the use of more demanding criteria for undertaking investments than would otherwise be employed.

A major debate concerns the pay received by the CEOs of large U.S. firms. Some observers see the high levels of pay as unjustified: They see them as the outcome of managerial greed unfettered and even abetted by compliant boards of directors. Others worry that executives are not paid enough to attract the best talent to corporations rather than to such fields as investment banking, consulting, and entrepreneurship. An additional concern is that CEO pay may not provide adequate financial incentives for these executives to pursue stockholders' interests with sufficient diligence. Evaluating the arguments in this debate involves dealing with some subtle issues. The evidence currently available suggests that, on average, CEO pay responds to firm performance and that the intensity of CEO performance pay positively affects firm performance (at least in the context of U.S. firms). Whether the sensitivity of pay to performance is great enough, and whether the improved performance is worth the cost is less clear.

■ BIBLIOGRAPHICAL NOTES

Sherwin Rosen gives an excellent (although somewhat technical) survey of the economic issues in executive compensation. The annual feature stories that appear in *Business Week, Forbes*, and *Fortune* during the late spring and early summer provide up-to-date information on executive compensation, as well as the criticisms of pay excesses. The explanation of how increasing staff size in a bureaucracy increases the work load is due to Jane Hannaway. The analysis of managerial risk aversion in investments is based on the work of Bengt Holmstrom and Holmstrom and Joan Ricart i Costa. The special February 1990 issue of the *Industrial and Labor Relations Review* contains a number of excellent papers on executive compensation and its connection to firm performance. The paper by Baker, Jensen, and Murphy and the book by Lawler referenced in Chapter 12 also have discussions of executive compensation, and the volume edited by Fred Foulkes contains a number of useful papers on the subject.

■ REFERENCES

Foulkes, F., ed. *Executive Compensation: A Strategic Guide for the 1990s* (Boston: Harvard Business School Press, 1991).

Holmstrom, B. "Managerial Incentive Problems: A Dynamic Perspective," in *Essays in Economics and Management in Honor of Lars Wahlbeck* (Helsinki, Finland: Swedish School of Economics, 1982).

Holmstrom, B., and J. Ricart i Costa. "Managerial Incentives and Capital Management," *Quarterly Journal of Economics*, 101 (1986), 835–60.

Rosen, S. "Contracts and the Market for Executives," National Bureau of Economic Research working paper 3542 (1990).

EXERCISES

Food for Thought

1. Senior executives often appear to have effective partial control over the form of their compensation in that they can opt to receive a greater amount in stock

and other performance pay and less in straight salary (although they probably cannot so easily switch risky income into safe receipts). Why might allowing the sort of freedom that executives seem to have be advantageous to stockholders?

2. The study cited in the text of middle managers' pay indicated that the sensitivity of pay to performance tended to be higher for those assigned to the corporate head office than for those working in plants away from head office. How would you account for this pattern?

3. When a company undertakes a massive risky investment whose failure would endanger the company's survival, it puts at risk not only the value of the stock held by its shareholders, but also the earnings of its employees, the profits of its suppliers and of the customers who count on it, and the general welfare of the communities in which it operates. Should this affect investment decisions? If so, how?

4. Consider two CEOs who head similar companies. The two executives are similarly situated except that one has a large holding of the stock in the firm he or she heads and the other does not. How should the compensation contracts of the two differ in theory? What problems do you see with implementing such a recommendation?

5. We accentuated the negative role that career concerns can have by inducing managers to be risk averse in the investment decisions they make for firms. In contrast, concerns with their market value might also provide positive incentives for managers to try to make sure that their organizations do well because the success of their firms will reflect well on them and improve their market opportunities. What implications does this have for the optimal strength of explicit performance contracts at various stages in a manager's career? How would you test this?

6. Suppose you have decided that executive and CEO performance incentives are important. You then note that managers in the not-for-profit sector (for example, university administrators) typically receive straight salaries. Although their raises might possibly depend on performance, they get no bonuses and certainly no long-term incentive pay. Is this a problem for these organizations? If so, how would you seek to overcome it?

Mathematical Exercises

1. Suppose that the change in stock market value X of a firm with annual sales of S is equal to $f(S) + S^{1-a}e + S\epsilon$, where e is the "effort" expended by the CEO, ϵ is earnings variations associated with uncontrolled random influences, and $f(S)$ is some function of the firm's size. An important part of the dispute over proper types and levels of executive compensation is the argument about how much effect an executive can have on the performance of a large organization. In our model, this effect is represented by the elasticity parameter a. For $a = 0$, the impact of executive efforts is proportional to the size of the organization; for $a = 1$, the impact is fixed independently of the size of the organization. For intermediate values of a, the executive's ability to affect profits grows by about $a\%$ every time the organization's size grow's by 1%.

Use the analysis of Chapter 7 to determine the optimal rate at which the executive's earnings should increase with the company earnings. Assume that the CEO's cost of effort is $C(e) = \frac{1}{2}e^2$. (Hint: Use the earnings X to construct an appropriate statistical estimate of e. Compute the incentive intensity β using this estimate and then restate the answer as a function of X.) For S large, how does the answer depend upon a?

14

THE CLASSICAL THEORY OF INVESTMENTS AND FINANCE

October. This is one of the particularly dangerous months to speculate in stocks in. The others are July, January, September, April, November, May, March, June, December, August and February.

Pudd'nhead Wilson[1]

The previous four chapters have investigated the relationships between a firm and its employees. This chapter and the next deal with the relationships with another crucial constituency: the providers of capital. We introduce the subject in this chapter by focusing on the basic theory of classical financial economics, obtaining its central results. At the heart of this theory is a view of the firm as a simple flow of financial streams from investments and an assumption that the way that a firm finances its investments does not affect the investment returns themselves. The resulting theory, which is probably used more in actual business than any other part of economics, is valuable for several reasons. First, it leads to a practical and useful account of how investments ought to be evaluated: The theory of net present value. The Fisher separation theorem clarifies a common confusion about when an owner's personal preferences might matter for investment decisions. The celebrated Modigliani-Miller theorems eliminate another confusion, with their surprising assertion that if capital structure (the way in which the firm is financed) and dividend decisions affect neither the firm's underlying cash flows nor investors' perceptions of them, then they cannot affect the firm's value. The theory of portfolio choice and the resulting capital asset pricing model not only provide explanations of the equilibrium pricing of securities,

---

[1] Mark Twain, Pudd'nhead Wilson (1894).

they also indicate how to calculate the cost of capital to the firm. Finally, augmented with the perfect (or efficient) markets hypothesis, the theory provides a basis for evaluating managerial performance.

As valuable as this theory is, it leaves important questions unanswered. We need a richer theory if we are to understand why and how capital structure can affect the firm's value. The classical analysis views financial instruments as streams of returns promised to lenders and investors. These returns may depend on the stream of earnings of the firm, but, in the classical analysis, financing decisions can affect neither the firm's earnings themselves nor investors' expectations about them. More modern analyses recognize both possibilities: Financial structure can alter management's incentive to work hard on behalf of the firm's owners, and it can also affect investors' beliefs about likely future profits. As well, it can affect the possibilities for changing ownership and control of the firm. All of these relationships affect the firm's market value. Allowing for these possibilities is a key element of Chapter 15.

THE CLASSICAL ECONOMICS OF INVESTMENT DECISIONS

The classical economics of finance is characterized by the assumption that managers and investors have no conflicting interests, or at least that the financial decisions of the firm play no role in any such conflict. Even if you recognize the potential for conflict, the classical assumptions remain useful to the extent that any managerial incentives that can be provided using financial structure might be equally well provided by explicit incentive compensation contracts or by rules limiting managerial discretion that are unrelated to the firm's financing. The modern parts of the theory are still unsettled, but there is little disagreement that the classical theory provides important theoretical and practical insights that are well worth learning.

In classical economic theory, the firm is conceptualized as a set of possible production plans from which the most profitable one is chosen. Classical finance is rooted in this theory. It treats a firm as a set of potential investments from which some are chosen. The questions to be studied concern which investments ought to be undertaken, how the funds needed to pay for the investments ought to be raised, and how investors determine what prices to pay for shares of stock and other securities.

The Fisher Separation Theorem

Suppose that the owner of a shop is considering opening a second outlet in a nearby suburb. He or she must rent a building, hire staff, acquire an inventory, and invest in initial advertising and promotions to inform local consumers that the shop is there. Over a period of perhaps ten years, the owner expects to reap rewards from this investment in the form of additional sales and profits. After accounting for all the costs, the owner expects to earn profits of P_1 in the first year, P_2 in the second, . . ., and P_{10} in the tenth year. Suppose that these numbers are certain, or that the investor is risk neutral and that these are the expected returns. Is the investment worthwhile?

If the owner must finance the shop out of personal savings because there are no developed financial institutions to lend the needed cash, then the answer to this question depends on what else he or she could do with the money. If our entrepreneur had been eagerly looking forward to buying a new sailboat with the money, he or she might be discouraged from investing by the prospect of having to delay that purchase. *When individuals finance an investment entirely with personal funds, the decision depends on personal preferences about the timing of consumption.* This conclusion changes when the investment can be financed with borrowed money, however.

450

Finance:
Investments,
Capital Structure,
and Corporate
Control

INVESTMENTS FINANCED BY BORROWING   Suppose the owner can borrow the money needed to open the shop at an interest rate of r per year. Suppose also that the loan agreement stipulates that the store's entire **cash flow**—its sales revenue after payment of operating expenses—will be used to pay the interest due and to reduce the balance on the loan until it is fully repaid. Further, if the loan is not repaid by the end of ten years, or if the store closes before then, the owner will be responsible for paying whatever loan balance remains from personal funds.

In evaluating the investment when it is financed by borrowed money, the owner will conclude that the investment is worthwhile if the loan can be repaid using the store's cash flow, with something left over. This is because the owner profits by keeping what is left over after the loan is repaid. If the loan cannot be repaid out of the store's earnings, then the owner would do better not to open the new store because he or she would have to turn over all the store's earnings, plus some private savings, to the lender.

Although useful, this preliminary account of how the owner should make this investment decision is thin in several respects. One important omission is the cost of the owner's time in setting up the store and contributing to its operation. This is not a serious conceptual problem, however. To account for the owner's time, we simply ask: Will the revenues be sufficient both to pay the opportunity cost of the owner's time and to repay the loan, with something left over? The investment is worthwhile if, and only if, the answer is yes.

Notice the important contrast between this conclusion and the case we first analyzed in which the owner financed the investment using personal savings. When the markets for borrowing and saving operate perfectly, there is no necessary connection between the timing of income from the investment and the timing of the owner's personal consumption. In that case, the question of whether an investment should be undertaken is transformed. It is no longer a decision based on personal preferences; it becomes instead an objective business decision based only on projected earnings and interest rates.

INVESTING WHEN THERE ARE PERFECT CAPITAL MARKETS   A more realistic case is the one in which the owner can decide whether to finance the investment using any personal savings, to finance by borrowing, or to use some combination of these two means. Suppose the interest rate at which the owner can borrow is the same as the rate he or she could receive by lending to others: This is one aspect of a condition known as *perfect capital markets*.[2] In this case, the owner's opportunity cost of using savings is just the same as the cost of borrowing, so it is correct to analyze this investment as if it could be financed only by borrowing. The conclusion of this logic is summarized by the following:

> **Fisher Separation Theorem:** When there are perfect capital markets, the owner's decision about whether to invest will depend only on the returns he or she forecasts from the investment and on the interest rate. It will not depend on his or her preferences regarding personal consumption or its timing.

This theorem is named for economist Irving Fisher, who developed this logic in the first decade of the 20th century. The term *separation* in the name of the theorem reflects the conclusion that an owner can *separate* the decision about whether to invest from the decision about how to arrange consumption over time. The first

---

[2] More generally, perfect capital markets obtain when all parties, whether they are buying or selling, transact at the same terms and these terms are unaffected by the amounts any one party transacts.

Table 14.1   Calculating the Present Value

Year t	Cash Flow C_t	Accumulation Factors $A_t = (1 + r)^t$	Present Value C_t/A_t
0	—	1.000	—
1	99	1.100	90.00
2	121	1.210	100.00
3	100	1.331	75.13
		Total Present Value	265.13
		Initial Investment	220.00
		Net Present Value	45.13

decision depends on earnings forecasts and interest rates; the second depends on interest rates, wealth, and personal preferences.

SIGNIFICANCE OF THE SEPARATION THEOREM   This separation of investment decisions from personal preferences is very important for the analysis of firms. For example, in a joint business venture, if the partners agree on their forecasts of investment returns, and if they both know what rates of interest are offered by the bank for its loans, then they should agree about whether to undertake an investment, even if their personal circumstances are quite different. To take a particular case, if one partner is near retirement and wants to start spending some of the wealth he or she has accumulated over a lifetime, that is no reason not to invest, provided the investment can be financed with loan proceeds. Without perfect capital markets, this difference of interests between the partners could be a source of disagreement and conflict.

The conclusion about separation is important because it helps to justify the common practice of thinking about firms, especially large firms, as being separate entities from their owners. For small firms, the conclusion may be different because the perfect capital markets conditions is not a good approximation of reality: The owner cannot borrow and lend at (nearly) the same rate of interest. In that case, it may be optimal for a retiring owner to forego making new investments in the business.

Net Present Values

To complete our description of the owner's optimal investment policy, we now show how to calculate whether the loan used to finance the investment can be repaid from the forecasted sequence of cash flows, after deducting the cost of the owner's time and all other relevant costs. The way to do that is to calculate year by year how much of the loan can be repaid using just the earnings generated in that year and then to add these figures to find the largest loan that can be repaid from the earnings of all the years together.

The size of the loan that can be repaid from any year's cash flow is called the **present value** of the cash flow. This concept is very important in practical financial calculations. Table 14.1 illustrates how present value is computed, using both numbers and formulas. To keep matters simple, we assume that all payments are made at the ends of years, though similar calculations could be done using monthly or quarterly payments.

Let us focus first on the column labeled "Accumulation Factor." A debt of 1 (dollar, or thousand yen, or whatever) at an annual interest rate of 10 percent grows, or *accumulates*, after one year, to a debt of 1.10. If unpaid, that debt grows by 10

452

Finance:
Investments,
Capital Structure,
and Corporate
Control

percent again in the next year; that is, it is multiplied again by 1.1 to become a debt of $1.1 \times 1.1 = 1.21$. The numbers in the accumulation column show how much is owed at the end of each year if the $1 loan is allowed to accumulate over the years, with interest compounding annually at 10 percent. The number for each year is computed by multiplying the value for the previous year by 1.1, starting with the number 1.000 in the row for year 0.

Interest rates are commonly quoted in percentage terms; that is, we speak of rates of 3 percent, 10 percent, or 35 percent. For writing formulas and doing calculations, it is more convenient to express interest rates as the decimal fractions: .03, .10, or .35. In general, if the interest rate is r, the accumulation factor A_t corresponding to year t is the result of multiplying by the number $(1 + r)$ by itself t times, or $(1 + r)^t$, as indicated in the column heading. This sort of calculation is easy to program on a personal computer using any of the popular spreadsheet programs. It is also preprogrammed into many hand-held calculators, especially business and financial calculators.

At the end of year 1, the second column of the table shows the owner's forecast that the cash available for servicing debt (paying interest and principal) will be 99, after first paying the necessary operating expenses of the business. That sum is just enough to repay a loan of 90 made at the beginning of the year, if the annual interest rate is 10 percent. The reason is that, using the accumulation factors, a loan of 90 accumulates in a year to $90 \times 1.100 = 99$. The proper procedure for computing the figure to be entered into the present value column is to perform this operation in reverse. In this case, the maximum loan that can be repaid by 99 is 99 divided by the accumulation factor of 1.100. Similarly, the 100 present value for year 2 is calculated by dividing the forecasted cash flow of 121 by the accumulation factor of 1.210.

In general, a loan of L accumulates with interest at rate r after t years to a balance of $L(1 + r)^t$. If the available funds or cash flow C_t are just sufficient to pay the loan, then $C_t = L(1 + r)^t$; therefore, $L = C_t/(1 + r)^t$. In terms of the table, this means that the present value of the cash flow can be computed simply by dividing the cash flow in the second column by the accumulation factor in the third column. The result is the present value reported in the fourth column.

After having computed the present value of the available cash in each year, the total present value of the stream of cash payments is calculated by adding up the entries in the fourth column. This is justified because the reduction to present values expresses all of the flows in the common unit of money today: We are not adding today's dollars or marks or yen to tomorrow's, which are different things with different value. In our sample calculation, this total present value is 265.13. The initial expenditure required for this project is 220, and the *net present value* of the whole project is 45.13 (= 265.13 − 220). That is, the project is expected to generate enough cash to justify loans of 265.13, but only 220 must be borrowed today to finance the project, so there will be surplus cash generated by the project beyond what will be needed to repay the loans. If the only options are either to undertake a project or to reject it, then the project should be undertaken only if the net present value is positive. Generally, *when deciding among several mutually exclusive alternatives, the best one is the one with the highest net present value*, because that is the one that leaves the most additional funds beyond those necessary to repay the lenders who finance the project.

THE COST OF CAPITAL IN THE CLASSICAL FRAMEWORK   The interest rate r used in this calculation is called the **cost of capital**. It represents the lowest rate a business must pay to raise the necessary financing for the project. One of the important practical problems businesspeople face in trying to use this theory is to determine what the actual cost of capital is. The tax deductibility of interest payments, the restrictive clauses in loan agreements, the use of interest rates that vary according to the security of the collateral, and the use of mixed sources of financing involving different terms and interest rates for different parts of the same project all affect the real cost of borrowing. Add to this the possibility of taking in partners for equity financing, and it becomes very difficult to pin down the number that corresponds to the theoretical *cost of capital*. In addition, the returns that investors require from any particular investment depend on the risks they incur in financing it, so it would be incorrect simply to use the average cost of capital in a company to evaluate the attractiveness of each investment the company makes. Finance textbooks contain lengthy treatments about how to compute the cost of capital.[3]

APPLICATION: "SHORTSIGHTED" MANAGEMENT AND THE COST OF CAPITAL   The cost of capital is one of the principal ingredients in determining whether to undertake an investment. When it is high, investments become less attractive. For example, consider an investment of 100 today that is certain to return a cash flow of C in two years but nothing until then. If the interest rate is 6 percent ($r = .06$), then C must be at least 112.36 for the investment to be profitable because a loan of 100 at that interest rate would accumulate after two years to a debt of $100 \times 1.06^2 = 112.36$, and this debt must be repaid from the cash flow. If the interest rate is 10 percent ($r = .10$), then the cash flow must be at least 121 ($= 100 \times 1.10^2$) for the investment to be profitable. The cash flow after two years on an investment of 100 needs to be 7.7 percent ($= (121 - 112.36)/112.36$) higher when the interest rate is 10 percent instead of 6 percent, and the returns net of the initial investment must be 69.9 percent more [$(21 - 12.36)/12.36$].

The difference in required returns grows dramatically as the period of investment grows longer. The cash flow required after ten years to repay a loan of 100 today is 179.08 if the cost of capital is 6 percent, but the corresponding figure is 259.37 if the cost is 10 percent—a difference of almost 45 percent. If the period of investment is 20 years, the corresponding figures are 320.71 for the 6 percent cost of capital and 672.75 for the 10 percent cost of capital. In order to be profitable at a cost of capital of 10 percent, a 20-year investment must generate more than double the cash flow than would be needed if the cost of capital were only 6 percent. Expressed another way, the difference in required cash flow is more than 3.5 times the original investment of 100!

One of the popular explanations of the relatively poor performance of North American manufacturing industries during the 1970s and 1980s was the "shortsightedness" of their managers. According to critics, U.S. managers refused to make investments for the long term at a time when international competitors in Europe and Asia (especially in Japan) were making heavy investments in new equipment and new technologies that would guarantee their competitiveness over long periods of years.

A look at the data on the cost of capital (adjusted to account for the different tax policies of different countries) helps to explain this phenomenon. The cost of capital in the United States was arguably higher throughout this period than was the corresponding cost in countries like Germany, and much higher than in Japan. Indeed, according to one study, when the after-tax cost of financing a new plant in

---

[3] See, for example, James C. Van Horne, *Financial Management and Policy* (Englewood Cliffs, NJ: Prentice Hall, 1989).

454

Finance:
Investments,
Capital Structure,
and Corporate
Control

Japan by issuing equity was 6 percent in 1988, the corresponding figure for an investment in the United States was about 10 percent,[4] this was the basis for the particular numbers illustrated earlier. One reason for this large difference was the much lower savings rate in the United States compared to Japan; another was the different tax rules that applied in the different countries.

TECHNOLOGICAL SHORTSIGHTEDNESS   It would be incomplete to cite these differences in the costs of capital as a full explanation of the different patterns of investments in the different countries. Many scholars believe that differences in management practices also account for part of the difference.

In practice, analysts within firms compute net present values using estimates of the quantifiable cash flows generated by an investment. Benefits that are difficult to quantify are likely to be ignored. However, many of the benefits of investments in new technology are of this very kind: They maintain and improve the company's standing on the frontiers of advanced technology. A technologically advanced company benefits by being better able to incorporate advanced features into its products, to take advantage of new materials, or to duplicate product or process innovations initiated by its rivals. Companies that are run by managers trained in financial analysis but untrained in the relevant technologies may place too little value on these benefits because they may seem too difficult to quantify and to justify later if the investment does not turn out well. They may also fail to distinguish technologies that offer these important benefits from ones that do not. Although evidence on this point is scanty, some observers believe that a major reason that many U.S. firms have made poor decisions about investments in new technologies is that their managers have weak technical training and place too much emphasis on "objective" but incomplete financial analyses.

Strategic Investments as Design Decisions

More broadly, there are whole categories of investment decisions which are complicated by the fact that some of their most important benefits are difficult to quantify. The most important of these is probably the *strategic investments* category. Strategic investments are those whose benefits are likely to accrue to many parts of the organization, including especially units not involved in making the investment. The problem with strategic investments is that middle-level managers, compensated on the basis of their own unit's performance, will be inclined to invest too little in projects whose benefits accrue largely to other units.[5]

DESIGN ATTRIBUTES   An important example of a strategic investment decision is a firm's decision about whether to build a new factory that will use a new technology to manufacture an existing product. In principle, this investment should be undertaken if the net present value of the cash flows that the firm expects to receive would be higher than if it continued to use the old technology. In practice, however, managers who must defend their estimates are likely to focus on a narrow set of "hard" benefits. For example, the manager might use an official sales forecast to determine how many units of the product will be made and how much it will cost to make that number of

[4] B. Douglas Bernheim and John B. Shoven, "Comparison of the Cost of Capital in the U.S. and Japan: The Role of Risk and Taxes," Center for Economic Policy Research Publication No. 179, Stanford University (September 1989).

[5] The idea of *strategic effects* used here corresponds to the idea of *positive external effects* in market economies. The standard analysis in the latter case is that individuals and firms will be inclined to invest too little effort in activities that benefit others but that cannot be sold to the beneficiaries.

units in a new or existing factory using either the new or old technology. This limited approach can give the wrong answer if the new technology has other important benefits, such as (1) increasing the flexibility of the factory and thereby increasing the range of products that can be profitably made in the future, (2) demonstrating new production techniques, the best of which can be selectively adopted at other plants in the company, (3) developing new skills and capabilities among the company's managers and workers, which can be effectively used in planned new products, (4) enabling the firm to increase the specialization of its other plants, leading to greater economies of scale, or (5) discouraging aggressive growth by competitors, who might seize on any delay or inaction by the company to expand their own capacities and their shares of the product market. The monetary value of these strategic aspects of the investment depends on the firm's plans: What kinds of new products does the firm plan to introduce? What core competencies does the firm plan to develop? What are the key sources of advantages that the firm plans to achieve over its principal competitors?

When the firm's decision about whether to invest in the new technology is tightly linked to other parts of the company strategy, it is one with *design attributes*. The significance of these strategic, design attributes is that the benefits of the investment cannot be evaluated in isolation, using only the day-to-day knowledge of the product and the factory available to lower-level managers. The firm's long-term plans about competition, technology, and new products all must enter as premises into the evaluation. As we explained in Chapter 4, the optimal way to take into account all of the relevant information in this sort of context is often for the top management, after suitable information gathering, to specify the "design premises" or "design parameters" for the decision. These might include the capacity of the new plant, a timetable for the project, and objectives for the degree of flexibility of the plant. Subject to these premises, local managers may be permitted to make decisions among various alternatives on the basis of technical feasibility and net present value comparisons.

CONFLICTING MANAGERIAL INTERESTS   In organizing any kind of decision, it is important to recognize that the interests of the lower-level decision makers may not all coincide with those of top management. For example, if the factory manager is compensated on the basis of factory costs, he or she may not be eager to advocate a new technology that leads to higher costs this year in order to reduce the costs at other factories in future years. The effect could also be in the opposite direction. Divisional managers, who commonly find their salaries tied to the size of the division units they manage, are likely to spend more time thinking about the advantages of large investments in their own units than about the associated risks. Similarly, technology managers may seek to justify their own jobs by finding reasons to adopt new technologies. When the choice is between alternative technologies and does not affect the level of total investment in the division, then these *influence costs* associated with the decision are likely to be small. When the future size and importance of the division is at stake, however, the top management will often want to gather information from its own independent sources to reduce the informational bias it faces.

An effective system of capital allocation, then, must meet a diverse set of challenges: It must ensure that major investment decisions are consonant with the company strategy, that they are financially well-justified, that the evaluation of investment projects are not excessively tainted by the personal and career interests of the managers involved, and that the process taps the knowledge of those who are best informed. These individuals are often the very same people whose personal interests are most affected by the decision.

456

Finance:
Investments,
Capital Structure,
and Corporate
Control

CLASSICAL ANALYSES OF
FINANCIAL STRUCTURE DECISIONS

So far our analysis has focused on how managers make investment decisions inside the firm. The other part of financial economics concerns how managers can acquire the funds they need to make investments and how much it will cost to raise those funds. This cost of capital, expressed as an interest rate, is then used in the net present value calculation.

Suppose, for example, that management plans to undertake a project that requires an initial investment of 100. Suppose, too, that the returns on the investment are uncertain and that the whole of the 100 must be raised from outside investors. Management will wonder: If we borrow 50, how much will investors be willing to pay for a share of the earnings that remain (assuming that first claim on any returns must be paid to the lenders)? Could the cost of raising the required funds be reduced if the amount borrowed were greater than 50, with the balance raised by selling shares in the financial results of the venture? To serve the interests of its existing owners, the decision should be made in a way that maximizes the amount of money received for whatever claims on the project returns are assigned to investors. Here we explore this decision using a conceptual model that is richer in two ways than the one considered earlier in the chapter: We allow that investments may be risky and recognize that there are multiple kinds of financing. Also, we focus on companies whose stock shares are publicly traded.

The Modigliani-Miller Analyses

For most of our analysis, we suppose that the firm relies on only two kinds of financing: borrowing from a bank (or from other investors by issuing bonds) and selling shares of stock in the company. We suppose further that the chief difference between debt (loans) and equity (shares of stock) is that the firm's lenders must be paid in full before the shareholders can be paid anything. After the debt has been paid, the owners of shares in the firm divide any remaining earnings among themselves in proportion to the numbers of shares that they own. (The box on corporate liabilities discusses some of the other sorts of financial claims and securities that firms actually use.)

To make things even simpler, let us focus on the case where any loans made to the firm are perfectly secure. That is, although the earnings of the firm are uncertain and subject to fluctuation, let us suppose the financial resources are always at least adequate to repay any outstanding loans, even if very little is left over for the shareholders. If the total earnings of the firm is some random amount X, and the amount the firm has borrowed is B, then the shareholders will receive the residual return $X - B(1 + r)$, that is, whatever earnings are left after the lenders have been paid $B(1 + r)$—the principal and interest on their loans. The amount P that the shareholders will pay to acquire this claim on earnings is denoted by $P[X - B(1 + r)]$ to indicate its dependence on the portion of the cash flow that the shareholders acquire. The total amount that will be paid by the lenders and shareholders to the firm in exchange for the firm's promise to pay them each their appropriate parts of the earnings X is $B + P[X - B(1 + r)]$—this is called the firm's *value*. What we want to know is how the firm's choice of B affects its value.

To understand the answer to this question, it is crucial to recognize that the lenders and the shareholders need not be different people. On the contrary, investors frequently *diversify* their holdings, spreading their investments among the debt and equity of various companies as well as government bonds, real estate, and other assets. To the extent that investors are rational, they do not evaluate investments in isolation, but as part of their larger portfolio of investments.

Corporate Liabilities and Financing

Firms have a variety of ways of financing their operations, and corporations in particular may issue a rich array of financial claims against themselves. It is common to speak of debt and equity, but these terms encompass more than just simple loans and shares of stock, and actual financial claims may mix elements of each.

A broad range of financial claims are labelled as **debt**. All share the property that they are obligations to pay specific amounts or the firm can be forced into bankruptcy. The simplest are accounts payable, bills from suppliers that have not yet been paid. Mortgage and equipment loans are secured by a particular real asset that can be seized for nonpayment. Similarly, a firm's inventory might be pledged to secure a loan of operating capital to finance production and distribution in advance of sales receipts. In other cases, an asset may be pledged as security for a loan even though it has no direct connection with how the loan proceeds are to be used. For example, the bank that financed Japanese tiremaker Bridgestone's purchase of Firestone Tire & Rubber put a lien on one of Bridgestone's Japanese factories, giving it the right to seize the factory if the loan were not paid. Some companies also issue *unsecured debentures*, which are bonds protected only by the general creditworthiness and cash flow of the company. Debentures may differ in the priority they are assigned when the company is unable to meet all its obligations: *Junior* or *subordinated debentures* rank behind more *senior debt* in their claims on the firm's assets. Lenders whose loans are secured by particular assets have a priority in making a claim against those assets in the event of default or bankruptcy.

Equity is distinguished by the fact that it does not have to be repaid and so is junior to debt. It too comes in several varieties. Holders of common stock are the firm's ultimate residual claimants: They are entitled to get what is left after everyone else is paid. Holders of *preferred stock* receive dividends before any are paid to common stockholders, but preferred shares do not carry voting rights. *Convertible preferred stock* can be traded for common stock at a specified rate.

Some kinds of debt have equity-like features. For example, *convertible bonds* can be exchanged at the lender's option for common stock at terms specified in the contract. They offer the protection of debt but the option to share in the "upside" if the company does especially well. Because the option to convert is valuable, these bonds usually carry lower interest rates. Other equity-like securities include *warrants*, which are rights issued by the firm (often in connection with bonds) to purchase shares of its stock on specified terms. They differ from *call options* in that the latter are issued by outsiders rather than by the firm itself. (*Put options* are rights to sell at a specified price.)

458

Finance:
Investments,
Capital Structure,
and Corporate
Control

THE INVESTORS' PERSPECTIVE   To gain perspective on how the problem looks from the investor's side, suppose there are two similar firms: One issues shares of stock but does not borrow at all, whereas the other both issues shares and borrows some positive amount B. A person who wants to receive, say, the return $.05 \cdot X$ can accomplish this by buying 5 percent of the shares of the first firm. Alternatively, he or she can buy 5 percent of the shares of the second firm for $.05 \cdot P[X - B(1 + r)]$ and 5 percent of the debt of that firm for $.05 \cdot B$. The alternative strategy will yield an income of $.05 \cdot B(1 + r)$ from the bonds plus $.05 \cdot [X - B(1 + r)]$ from the stock, for a total income of $.05 \cdot X$. Because the two strategies would lead to the same cash income for the individual investor, if anybody is to buy shares of the first firm, the first alternative strategy must not be more expensive than the second. This implies

$$P[X] \leq B + P[X - B(1 + r)]$$

Now consider an investor who wishes to receive 10 percent of the returns $X - B$ $(1 + r)$. The investor's first alternative is to purchase 10 percent of the shares of the second firm. Alternatively, if the investor can use his or her shares as collateral to borrow on the same terms as the firm, then he or she can buy 10 percent of the shares of the first firm and then borrow 10 percent of the amount B at interest rate r, leading to net receipts of 10 percent of $X - B(1 + r)$, which is just the same as the first alternative. If anybody is to buy the shares of the second firm, the alternative portfolio with the same cash return must not be cheaper:

$$P[X - B(1 + r)] \leq P[X] - B$$

Together, these two inequalities imply that $P[X] = B + P[X - B(1 + r)]$. Evidently, the value of the firm is the same in both cases; it does not depend on how the firm finances itself.

The crux of this argument is that the firm's choice of B has no effect at all on the return streams that investors could acquire by manipulating their portfolios. Consequently, it cannot affect either the returns that investors eventually acquire in constructing their portfolio of investments or investors' willingness to pay for those returns. The conclusion of this line of reasoning, which was first developed by Franco Modigliani and Merton Miller, is one of the most celebrated propositions in the theory of financial markets:

> **Modigliani-Miller Theorem #1**. Suppose that the total return X available for distribution by a firm is unaffected by the firm's financial decisions and that investors can borrow on the same terms as the firm by pledging the firm's stock as security. Then the firm's financial structure decisions cannot affect its value.

In the classical representation of markets, a firm's financial policy can never, by itself, affect the firm's value. The firm can borrow massively from banks or issue junk bonds, and there will be no consequences in terms of the value of the firm. Something else, besides the simple workings of classical markets, must account for the effect that financial structure seems to have on what investors are willing to pay.

TAXES, BANKRUPTCY, AND CAPITAL STRUCTURE   The Modigliani-Miller (MM) theorem itself directly suggests several possibilities. In some countries, debt and equity are treated differently for tax purposes. Most notably, interest paid by firms to lenders in the United States is treated as an expense that is deductible for the firms in determining the base for their corporate income tax, but dividends paid to individual shareholders are not. This gives a very substantial advantage to debt financing in the United States, but it cannot explain the use of debt financing in the era before it had any tax advantages or in other countries where the tax laws treat the two forms of financing symmetrically. In the U.S. context, where the corporate income tax rate hovered around 50 percent for half a century until it was cut to 34 percent in 1986, the tax advantages of debt led some to wonder why firms issue any shares at all. One possible answer is that firms that have too much debt incur an increased risk of bankruptcy, and that bankruptcy destroys value. However, we shall find that the richer conception of financial structures given in the next chapter provides a more convincing account of the purposes of debt and equity.

DIVIDEND POLICY IN THE CLASSICAL MODEL   The ideas used in the Modigliani-Miller analysis can be applied to other financial decisions besides the choice between debt and equity. An argument very like the one presented earlier can be applied to all the diverse and complicated financial instruments that are used in modern financial markets, including options, warrants, callable bonds, convertible bonds, and so on. In each case, the argument is that the investor can put back together the parts of the return that the firm has separated. The investor does that by purchasing some of each kind of financial instrument that the firm issues.[6] Such **arbitrage** arguments (ones based on the requirement that equilibrium security prices do not leave room for surely profitable trades that take advantage of pricing discrepancies among assets) form the crucial logic in financial economics.

The same ideas can also be applied to analyze a firm's dividend policy, provided we continue to assume that the firm's investment decisions are given and thus too its (random) cash flow. In this case, the funds for the dividend must come essentially from issuing new securities. Suppose then that a firm pays a dividend D that it finances by issuing shares. Shareholders who prefer not to consume this dividend can undo the firm's decision by using the dividend to buy additional shares. If the firm finances the dividend by borrowing, then the investors can use the dividend to purchase debt of the firm, effectively neutralizing the impact of the firm's decision on their own financial returns. Just as in the case of the firm's debt-equity decision, we find again that the investor can undo or neutralize the effect of the firm's dividend decisions on his or her own financial returns. Because the investor's opportunities do not depend on the firm's dividend policy, the amount he or she is willing to pay for his or her investments also does not depend on the firm's policy. This conclusion about dividend policy is regarded as so important that it is the basis of a second major MM proposition:

> **Modigliani-Miller Theorem #2.** Suppose that the total return X available for distribution by a firm is unaffected by financial decisions and that investors can buy and sell securities on the same terms as the firm. Then the firm's policy for paying dividends can have no effect on its value.

The MM theorems provide a useful point of departure for thinking about financing and dividend policies. Their essential message is that a firm can no more change its value by divvying up its earnings differently than increase the weight of a cake by cutting the pieces up in different sizes and shapes. Only by changing the ingredients, that is, by changing the total return X that is available for distribution, can the firm create value.

The Allocation of Investment Capital by Markets

The preceding analysis leaves us with something of a puzzle. Champions of free markets sometimes claim that the capital markets funnel limited investment funds to

---

[6] Alternatively, if the firm has failed to take the pieces of return apart by issuing a variety of financial obligations, then investors can do that for themselves, by issuing *derivative securities*, as real investors

460

Finance:
Investments,
Capital Structure,
and Corporate
Control

the most productive companies by making it easy for those companies to raise capital while penalizing companies that perform poorly. The puzzle is: How can capital markets direct capital at all if the firms' analysis of investments is separate from the analysis of financing?

In actuality, there is nothing in the classical theory of markets to justify these claims for capital markets. In the classical theory and in life as well, so long as the security offered for a loan is adequate, the lender has no interest in ensuring that the funds themselves are well invested. For example, the willingness of a bank to lend might depend on the quality of the collateral offered or on the overall prospects of the borrower. If the collateral and overall prospects are strong, then the bank's decision would not depend at all on its independent evaluation of the planned new investment project.

A variation of the same argument begins from the premise that firms that have performed well and that have the prospect of continuing to perform well will have higher share prices.[7] From this premise, the advocates claim that firms with profitable investments find it cheaper to raise funds, but this conclusion is without any warrant in logic or reality. Share prices for a firm depend on the *average* profitability of its investments because the shares are claims on the whole cash flow of the firm, not the returns from any one of its investments. However, the question of how new capital should be allocated depends entirely on the returns to new, *incremental* investments.[8]

When correctly interpreted, the classical theory of capital markets holds that investment funds are allocated efficiently throughout the economy precisely because all the profit-maximizing firms face *exactly the same cost of capital* for any investment project. It is for this reason, according to the theory, that worthwhile projects are undertaken *regardless of the investor's identity* and projects that are not worthwhile are rejected. In the classical theory, the firms that invest most are not those with the lowest cost of capital but those with the largest number of attractive (positive net present value) investments to make.

INVESTMENT RISK AND THE COST OF CAPITAL

In principle, the proper interest rate to use for evaluating an investment is the actual cost of raising money to finance that particular investment. By an extension of the Modigliani-Miller analysis, a firm cannot create value by undertaking a project that investors would be unwilling to finance on its own because the total market value of the firm is just the same as if a separate company were formed to undertake each of the firm's projects. In the classical financial model, the returns on a proposed investment are high enough only if they would be high enough to be attractive to "the market," that is, to investors who buy and sell shares of the various financial assets exchanged in securities markets. Determining the rate of return that the market will demand requires taking a closer look at the way sophisticated investors evaluate risky investments.

Risk and Return

An individual investor may face many possible investments: stocks, bonds, real estate, mutual funds, bank accounts of various kinds, fine art, trading cards, and so on.

---

sometimes do. The description of these, however, would take us too far afield. For more details, see, for example, William Sharpe and Gordon Alexander, *Investments* (Englewood Cliffs, NJ: Prentice Hall, 1990).

[7] Though reasonable, the premise is hardly indisputable. See the following discussion of the efficient market hypothesis.

[8] This same concern of investors also leads them to gather information about average returns on existing projects, rather than about returns on new projects, to the detriment of the capital allocation system.

Some of these are quite safe but offer returns that have, at least historically, been much lower than those available from riskier investments. Other kinds of investments have had higher average rates of return in the past but have sometimes incurred huge losses for investors. Within any single class of risky investments, there can be enormous variation regarding the actual returns. For example, in the class of high-technology small company stocks, the value of shares in a small computer company may be rising at just the same time that the value of shares in a software systems company is falling. Given these risks, what should the investor do?

It would be a mistake for the investor to pose the question as: Which investments are most attractive? This phrasing of the question is too limiting. By combining investments appropriately, the investor can create a *portfolio* (collection of assets) that can achieve the same level of expected return as any single asset but with a less variable pattern of returns. Instead, the investor should ask: What portion of my total portfolio should be invested in each of the various kinds of assets?

MEAN-VARIANCE ANALYSIS   The traditional analysis of this question is based on three main assumptions. First, the investor dislikes risk and likes high expected levels of return, where the risk is measured by the variance of the investment returns or their standard deviation (the square root of the variance). These are just the sort of preferences assumed in the analysis of incentive contracting in Chapter 7. Second, there exists a riskless bond paying a safe rate of return r. Finally, capital markets are *perfect*; that is, an investor can buy or sell as much of any security as he or she likes without affecting the security's price and without incurring significant buying or selling costs.

The basic data of the investor's problem are taken to be a set of J assets of which shares are traded. A typical asset j yields an uncertain rate of return R_j. These returns are usually expressed in percentage terms, like interest rates.

In the standard mathematical representation, a portfolio is defined as a list (vector) of numbers $(\alpha_1, \ldots, \alpha_J)$ indicating what fraction of the total funds available is to be invested in each asset. These fractions must, of course, add up to 1. ($\Sigma_{j=1}^{J}\alpha_j = 1$). In real financial markets, it is possible (within limits) to promise future delivery of assets that are not owned today but will be bought later to fulfill the contract. This practice is called **short selling**; it amounts to having some of the α_j's be negative. With or without short sales, the investor's realized return from the portfolio is equal to $\Sigma_{j=1}^{J}\alpha_jR_j$. It is the mean and variance of this return that the investor cares about.

Figure 14.1 depicts the set of combinations of mean returns and standard

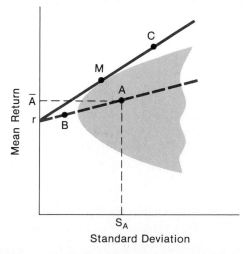

Figure 14.1: Points on the line through M, r, and C show the highest possible mean return for any level of risk.

462

Finance:
Investments,
Capital Structure,
and Corporate
Control

deviations that the investor can attain by choice of some portfolio. The shaded set shows the combinations that can be attained by portfolios of the risky assets alone. Each point in this region represents the return and risk from some single asset available in the market or from a portfolio of assets. The point on the vertical axis at height r is the risk-return pattern given by investing only in the riskless security. The figure is drawn assuming that there are investments that have higher expected returns than r, although these returns are risky.

By investing a fraction $1 - ß$ of his or her wealth in the riskless bond and the remaining fraction $ß$ in the risky portfolio A with mean $\overline{A}$ and standard deviation S_A, the investor creates a new portfolio with mean $(1 - ß)r + ß\overline{A}$ and standard deviation $(1 - ß) \cdot 0 + ßS_A = ßS_A$.[9] For example, the risk-return combination B can be attained by investing one third in portfolio A and two thirds in the riskless bond. If the investor can borrow at interest rate r, then $ß$ can take on values larger than 1. For example, the point C can be attained by borrowing at rate r and investing all the proceeds in portfolio M.

How should investors combine risky and riskless assets to assemble a portfolio? As the figure illustrates, for any level of standard deviation, the highest mean return obtainable by any portfolio lies on the solid line connecting M to the riskless rate r. This rate of return is achieved by investing a fraction of the available funds in the riskless bond and the remaining fraction in the portfolio M. This leads to a key conclusion of portfolio theory:

> **The One-Fund Portfolio Theorem**. For any investor who cares only about the mean and variance (or standard deviation) of returns, the optimal portfolio consists of some mix of the riskless bond and a portfolio of risky assets that has the expected return and standard deviation associated with the point M in Figure 14.1.

The one-fund portfolio theorem gets its name from the fact that if there were a mutual fund whose portfolio had the risk and return profile corresponding to point M in the figure, then no investor need ever invest in any asset except that mutual fund and the riskless bond. In the analysis that follows, we use R_M to denote the (uncertain) returns on the one fund.

A PRICING FORMULA   An important implication of the theorem just described is a pricing formula indicating how the returns from buying any of the assets available in the market must be related to R_M. Let R denote the uncertain returns on any asset. Then its *excess return*, $\overline{R} - r$, which is the expected return on the asset in excess of the riskless rate of interest, is given by the following equation:

$$\overline{R} - r = \frac{\text{Cov}(R, R_M)}{\text{Var}(R_M)}(\overline{R}_M - r) \qquad (14.1)$$

Intuitively, the expected return on any investment in financial securities can be decomposed into a riskless rate of return plus an excess return, which is to be understood as compensation for the risk that the investment entails. Using the expected rate of return suitable for the asset, the appropriate asset price can be determined by

---

[9] To verify this mathematically, if the return on the portfolio is R, note that $E[ßR + (1 - ß)r] = (1 - ß)r + ßE[R]$ and $\text{Var}[(1 - ß)r + ßR] = ß^2\text{Var}(R) = ß^2S_A^2$.

computing the present value of expected cash flows. In a one-period model, today's price is equal to tomorrow's expected return divided by $(1 + \overline{R})$. For example, if the expected returns tomorrow are \$132 and $\overline{R}$ is 10 percent, then today's appropriate asset price is \$120 $(= \$132/1.10)$. Because the rate of return $\overline{R}$ determines the asset price, Equation 14.1 is called a *pricing formula*.

The pricing formula may initially seem surprising. Given our other assumptions, you might have expected that the risk for an individual investment would be measured by something like its variance, Var(R). This is not the case, however: The excess return to compensate for risk does not depend on Var(R) at all. Instead, the compensation is proportional to Cov(R, R_M), the covariance of the return to the security with that of the fund;[10] this is the only term on the right-hand side of the equation that depends on the investment R.

The mystery is resolved when you remember that the investor is concerned not with the risk associated with individual investments, but with the risk associated with the portfolio as a whole. For example, if an asset has a negative covariance, its returns tend to be highest just when the returns on the other assets in the portfolio are lowest. When added to the portfolio M, such an asset tends to *reduce* the variability of portfolio returns. Risk-averse investors will regard this reduced variability as something valuable and will be willing to accept an even lower return on the asset than they would demand from the riskless bond, regarding the difference as a kind of insurance premium paid for reduced variability of the returns to the overall portfolio. Similarly, when Cov(R, R_M) is large, the asset is one whose returns fluctuate significantly and tend to be high when the rest of the portfolio is enjoying high returns and to be low

when the rest is suffering low returns. Holding such an asset tends to amplify swings in portfolio returns, making the whole portfolio riskier. Investors will purchase such an asset only if its expected returns are high enough to compensate for these swings.

Notice how different these conclusions are from what you would obtain if you had made the easy mistake of evaluating the assets individually. From such a perspective, assets whose returns have the same variance would appear equally risky, and it would appear that the investor should demand a correspondingly high excess return. Evaluated as part of a portfolio, the two assets are quite different, and the excess return on the asset with the negative covariance should actually be negative. The portfolio perspective is a necessary part of any sound investment theory.

Mathematical Proof of the Pricing Formula

Given the uncertain return R with mean return $\overline{R}$, define ß to be the number that solves $BR_M + (1 - ß)r = \overline{R}$. Finding ß amounts to finding the combination of the fund and the riskless bond that has the same expected return as R. (If $\overline{R}$ exceeds $\overline{R}_M$, as it might if the asset has higher risk than the fund and so corresponds to a point in the shaded region above and to the right of M, then ß must exceed 1. This means that the coefficient on r is negative and that the desired combination entails selling short the riskless security.) The mean and standard deviation of this new portfolio lie on the solid line through M in Figure 14.1. By inspection of the figure, it follows that this portfolio has the lowest possible variance for the given level of return, $\overline{R}$.

---

[10] Recall that the covariance of two random quantities, x and y, is the expected value of the product $(x - \overline{x})(y - \overline{y})$ and is a measure of how the two move together (see the appendix to Chapter 7).

464

Finance:
Investments,
Capital Structure,
and Corporate
Control

Consider now a composite portfolio consisting of a fraction γ invested in asset R and a fraction $1 - \gamma$ invested in the fund $\beta R_M + (1 - \beta)r$. Because each component of this composite portfolio has expected return $\overline{R}$, its expected return is $\gamma\overline{R} + (1 - \gamma)\overline{R} = \overline{R}$. Consequently, its variance must be at least as high for all values of γ as the variance of the portfolio $\beta R_M + (1 - \beta)r$. That is, the variance of the returns on the γ-weighted portfolio must be minimized when $\gamma = 0$. The variance is:

$$\text{Var}[\gamma R + (1 - \gamma)(\beta R_M + (1 - \beta)r)] \tag{14.2}$$
$$= \gamma^2\text{Var}(R) + (1 - \gamma)^2\beta^2\text{Var}(R_M) + 2\gamma(1 - \gamma)\beta\text{Cov}(R, R_M)$$

The minimum is calculated by taking the derivative with respect to γ and requiring that it be equal to 0 when γ equals 0. When the resulting expression is solved for β, it yields:

$$\beta = \frac{\text{Cov}(R, R_M)}{\text{Var}(R_M)} \tag{14.3}$$

However, β was initially defined so that $\overline{R} - r = \beta(\overline{R}_M - r)$. Hence,

$$\overline{R} - r = \frac{\text{Cov}(R, R_M)}{\text{Var}(R_M)}(\overline{R}_M - r) \tag{14.4}$$

which is just the pricing formula that was asserted earlier.

The Capital Asset Pricing Model

The significance of the pricing formula just derived is that it holds the promise of resolving the question about how risk should be accounted for in business investment decisions. The pricing formula expresses the expected rate of return $\overline{R}$ on a new project in terms of r and $\overline{R}_M$. This is the cost of capital to use in computing the present value of the new investment, rather than, say, some rate of return corresponding to the overall collection of assets in the firm. For this formula to be useful, however, you must be able to identify the portfolio corresponding to M. The first and most prominent attempt to identify M is the Sharpe-Lintner **capital asset pricing model** (CAPM, pronounced "cap-em").

Suppose all investors were to invest in a way consistent with the one-fund portfolio theorem. Because the investors together own all the assets, if each owns a (possibly different) fraction of the same fund, then each must own a fraction of the portfolio of *all* assets, so the point M corresponds to the *market portfolio*, or the portfolio consisting of all the financial assets. Even when investors hold different portfolios of risky assets, all consistent with the point M, it is still true that the market portfolio is among those corresponding to M, so it can be used for the calculations in the pricing formula.

The number β, computed according to Equation 14.3 using the return on the market portfolio for R_M, is known as the security's **beta** among financial economists and sophisticated investors. According to the CAPM, the excess return on a security should be proportional to its beta computed in this way. This predicted relationship, known as the security market line, is depicted in Figure 14.2. The intercept is at r, the risk-free interest rate, because the beta of a riskless bond is zero. The line is upward sloping because higher values of β mean that the security adds risk to the portfolio and so must bring returns above r to be attractive enough to hold. The actual slope of the line is determined by the total risk tolerance of investors and the overall variance of market returns.

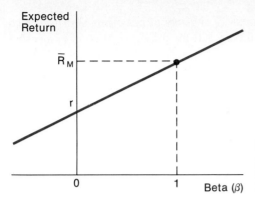

Figure 14.2: The expected return depends linearly on beta and not at all on the variance of the security's own return.

THE FIRM'S EVALUATION OF RISKY INVESTMENTS   For investment decisions by individual firms, the significance of the CAPM is that it identifies a theoretically correct way to account for the riskiness of its projects in computing present values. According to the CAPM, the only measure of risk that matters is the beta. The parts of the randomness or uncertainty in the returns on a project that are **idiosyncratic** or **unsystematic**, that is, that are unrelated to variations in returns for the market as a whole (the **systematic risk**), are irrelevant according to the CAPM for determining the interest rate used to evaluate investments. They will thus not need to be paid for it, nor should it be considered when evaluating investments because investors will not actually bear it.

There are two important caveats to add to the theoretical proposition that idiosyncratic risk does not matter. Both involve recognizing that even though such risks may not matter directly to outside investors, they can have important consequences within the firm. One way this can happen is when the firm uses performance incentives to motivate its managers. Like any other source of risk, idiosyncratic risk in an investment project is a part of the project return that is outside the manager's control. All such risks make it harder to evaluate a manager's performance and more difficult and costly to motivate superior performance. Worse, unlike systematic risks that affect all similar projects, idiosyncratic risks cannot be mitigated by using comparative performance evaluations. It is proper for firms to account for these costs in evaluating potential investments.

Second, if the project can be abandoned or scaled up as uncertainty about the investment resolves, then uncertainty can actually increase value. For example, doing research into synthetic fuel (synfuel) technology may be uneconomical if energy prices follow their expected pattern over time. If there were no uncertainty about energy prices, this research should not be undertaken. In reality, however, there is uncertainty about future energy prices, and that may make the synfuel research investment worthwhile. With increased uncertainty, investments that increase the decision maker's options may have great value, even if the individual options are valueless under the most likely scenario.

The same effect is present for individual investors who own warrants or other rights to purchase shares of stock at a preestablished price. These rights might be valueless if the shares do not fluctuate much in their value but could become quite valuable if share prices are highly uncertain because this uncertainty increases the chance that the options can be exercised at a large profit.

CRITICISMS AND EXTENSIONS OF THE CAPM   The CAPM was the first sophisticated theory of how asset risks affect security returns, but it is hardly the last word on

466

Finance:
Investments,
Capital Structure,
and Corporate
Control

the subject. The theory has been subjected to a variety of criticisms that have provided the impetus for variations of the theory and for the emergence of competing theories.

One major criticism is that because the set of all traded assets includes some whose returns are not readily observed, like housing and other real estate, the pricing formula using the market portfolio for R_M is not testable using available data. This is a cogent objection to the theory, mainly because the needed data are unlikely ever to be available.

Other criticisms of the CAPM focus on the assumptions of the theory. What, in reality, plays the role of the riskless bond? Even a government bond that carries no chance of default is risky if it is denominated in **nominal** (money) terms—as is almost always the case—because unpredictable changes in the price level make the **real** value of the returns uncertain. What happens if some investors consider their human capital as a risky asset in evaluating their portfolio? This is certainly a rational and reasonable thing for many people to do because, for many, the human capital acquired through years of education and experience is the most valuable asset they own. What if some investors do not behave rationally, in the form assumed by the theory? The argument that R_M corresponds to the market portfolio assumes that all investors invest rationally.

Economic researchers have continued to explore all these issues and how they affect the conclusions of theories, but no new consensus has yet emerged.

Expectations, Asset Pricing, and Efficiency

The CAPM and most other pricing theories place great reliance on the mathematical notion of *expected* rates of return. When we try to match the model with the world, however, a serious issue arises: Whose expectations should be used in applying the model? Expectations about how firms will perform are hardly uniform among investors. Managers of firms have their own expectations about how their decisions will turn out, and these are frequently more optimistic than those of outside investors.

To give the theory empirical content, we use the metaphor of *the market* as a single investor whose expectations are a kind of weighted average of the expectations of real investors, with the weights depending on the amounts invested by different individuals. Empirical tests of the theory proceed by investigating whether the market's expectations provide a reasonable and accurate estimate of the future returns of the firm.

Though the whole issue of the market's expectations may seem abstract, it actually has an immediate, practical importance for both business and public policy. If share prices are truly determined according to the pricing formula where the market's expectations are based on sound analysis of everything that investors and managers may know, then the cost of raising capital for various investment projects will be similarly well founded and firms will be encouraged to undertake the right investments. Managers will not fear that good investments made today in the hopes of a long-term return will depress the market price, harming current shareholders and making the company more vulnerable to takeovers. Also, as we discussed in Chapter 13, when stock prices are an accurate indicator of value, stock price changes can be an effective basis for evaluating executive performance and determining executive compensation. Conversely, if the expectations reflected in market prices are not well founded, then even the best-managed companies may be among those most subject to takeover attempts, and compensation based on stock market prices may encourage executives to manipulate investor expectations rather than to create value. For all these reasons, it is of great importance to determine just how well share prices mirror the fundamental values of firms.

INFORMATION AND THE PRICES OF FINANCIAL ASSETS

What an investor expects depends on what the investor knows. For example, a drug company employee who knows that the company is about to announce the discovery of a new AIDS vaccine, or that next quarter's income statement will show sales and profits larger than anyone had forecast, or that the company has been approached about a merger with a larger company at very attractive terms, would normally expect a higher return to holding the company's shares than would other investors who lacked this information. The question of how well share prices mirror fundamental values can thus be decomposed into two parts: What information does the market use in valuing firms, and how accurately does it use that information?

Forms of the Efficient Market Hypothesis

The most optimistic answers to these questions are the various forms of the **efficient markets hypothesis**. All of these affirm that securities' pricing depends on investor expectations and that investors make good use of available information in forming these expectations. They differ about what information, at a minimum, is used in determining those expectations. The *weak form efficient markets hypothesis* holds that the relevant expectations are based at least on information about past and current stock market prices. In other words, an investor who knew only the pattern of past prices for shares of stock in various corporations could not, on that basis alone, pick stocks that would on average have higher excess returns than predicted by the pricing formula. The ability to make such choices would be evidence against the theory; it would mean that market prices do not accurately reflect the best predictions of value, using all the information contained in the present and past prices. If the weak form efficient markets hypothesis is correct, then those who advocate *technical analysis*—using charts based on past price movements to predict future price movements—are mere charlatans whose predictions should not be trusted. There should be no patterns to price changes over time, so that the best estimate of future prices is just today's prices.

Two stronger forms of the hypothesis have also been proposed. According to the *semistrong form efficient markets hypothesis*, the market's expectations are those based on a set of information that includes, in addition to the past prices, everything else that is public information, such as financial statement information and press reports about business events (earnings announcements, new products, takeovers, changes in the executive suite, and so on). The semistrong form of the hypothesis does not, however, require that information that is not generally known be reflected in prices: In the example of the AIDS vaccine, the price of the firm's stock would not necessarily move when the discovery was made, but only when it became publicly known. At this point, however, prices should adjust rapidly to incorporate the new information. According to this form of the hypothesis, it is impossible for an investor who tries to pick stocks using only past prices plus earnings reports and similar public information to form a portfolio that will on average perform better than predicted by the pricing formula. In this case, a strategy of buying and holding a diversified, market portfolio is optimal.

Finally, the *strong form efficient markets hypothesis* posits that market prices reflect even information that is available only to executives and managers inside the firm but that has not yet been publicly announced. This might happen, for example,

468

Finance:
Investments,
Capital Structure,
and Corporate
Control

Insider Trading and Market Efficiency

Insider trading is considered unlawful in the United States, and in recent years the Securities and Exchange Commission (SEC) and federal prosecutors have brought criminal (rather than just civil) cases against alleged insider trading. Unfortunately, just what constitutes insider trading has never been specified in the law or in government regulations. The basic idea, however, is that those whose positions give them access to private information relevant to forecasting stock returns and prices should not be allowed to trade on this information. For example, a corporate officer should not be allowed to buy the firm's stock after seeing unexpectedly good earnings reports that have not yet been released or, perhaps worse yet, tell shareholders that earnings are down when they are actually good and then take advantage of the temporary fall in the stock price to buy shares. (It was just such an instance in 1942 that led to the SEC's adoption of its Rule 10b-5, on which insider trading cases are based.)

Most of the discussion in business and government about insider trading has to do with exactly what behavior by whom should be forbidden. However, there is also an active debate among legal, financial, and economic scholars about whether any restrictions should be placed on insider trading at all. This debate was initiated by Henry Manne in the mid-1960s and continues to this day.

There are basically three arguments against prohibiting insider trading. First, allowing insider trading should mean that information will be embodied in market prices more quickly, and so security prices would become better reflectors of fundamental value. Second, if firms want to compensate their employees by letting them trade on inside information, why not allow them to write these contracts? The logic here is that the information belongs to the firm, which should be able to determine how it is used. Third, insider trading is apparently very widespread anyway, the prohibition is unenforceable, and actual enforcement is capricious and unfair. The evidence for this last point is the frequency with which stock prices start moving before information is publicly released but after it becomes available to insiders. This pattern is so common that scholars doing "event studies," measuring the market reaction to events and announcements, automatically include several days before the information is officially made public in the studies: Otherwise, they would miss much of the reaction.

The counterarguments are often couched in fairness terms, but insider trading can be criticized on efficiency grounds as well. First, the most that allowing insider trading on the basis of insider information might accomplish is to make prices reflect information a few days earlier, which has only trivial consequences for the efficiency of investment decisions. More significant is the efficiency-destroying adverse selection problem that insider trading creates. If ordinary traders in the market are dealing with informed insiders, they face a no-win situation: The insiders will trade only when their private information indicates that being on the other side of the trade is a losing proposition. This could deter others from making trades, leading to less trade and more difficulty in executing trades quickly. Efficiency would hardly be enhanced by that.

if informed insiders—like a drug company employee who knows about the AIDS vaccine—trade on the information themselves, or if the inside information is leaked to analysts or to friends and family members of company insiders. Their buying or selling based on this information will tend to move stock prices to reflect the information and its effects on future returns. The box on insider trading explores the social-efficiency implications of this kind of activity.

HOW PRICES COME TO INCORPORATE INFORMATION   The theoretical arguments in favor of the efficient markets hypotheses are largely based on a simple theory of investor behavior. If the expectations manifested in the prices did not accurately reflect available information about future returns, then investors who used the available information would be led to buy the stocks with the highest expected returns relative to their prices. This extra demand would drive the stock price up and hence drive down the rate of return. Similarly, investors would sell over-priced stocks, driving their prices down and their expected rates of return up. Provided there are enough sophisticated investors who pay attention to the relevant information and act upon it, prices can never be too far out of line, or so the theory goes.

A careful study of portfolio theory provides only partial support for this argument. It is true that other things (such as the beta) being equal, investors will tend to buy more shares of those stocks on which they expect a higher rate of return. Demand by sophisticated investors will tend to push prices toward levels consistent with their expectations. However, the extra demand from sophisticated investors will only be proportional to the expected extra return. The pricing error that remains will depend on the fraction of investors who are knowledgeable and sophisticated and on the risks they incur in reducing the diversification of their portfolios to take advantage of the pricing error. The market's expectations remain a weighted average of the expectations of all investors, weighing the expectations of sophisticated investors (only) in proportion to the magnitude of their investments.

If the vast bulk of market trades are made by sophisticated investors, then prices would reflect their well-informed expectations. Suppose, however, a significant fraction of the trading volume is by market participants who buy and sell not because their rational forecasts indicate that asset prices are misaligned but because they are following the advice of some television or newspaper investment advisor who tells them when and how to trade based on "fundamentals," or because they are following (or running counter to) the herd of other investors, or perhaps because they are trying to behave like the "smart money" but simply have the models wrong. Then, the weighted average may not reflect the best available information and may be more volatile than is justified by changes in underlying economic conditions. Fads, booms, and sudden crashes can be the result. To distinguish between these competing accounts of how prices are determined, we must turn to an assessment of the evidence.

Evidence on the Efficient Markets Hypotheses

In the first years after the efficient market hypothesis was introduced, the custom was to test it by focusing on short-term price changes. The return to a stock earned by an investor over any period of time consists of the dividends paid in that period plus the increase in the stock price. This is converted into a rate of return, and then a statistical analysis is performed to see if the rate of return in any given period depends on the rate in the preceding periods. If the weak form efficient markets hypothesis holds, there should be no such dependence: The change in a stock price today should be uncorrelated with its change yesterday. When it was introduced, this was regarded as a bold prediction, but the repeated findings of a series of studies were consistent with

470

Finance:
Investments,
Capital Structure,
and Corporate
Control

it.[11] Similarly, studies of the semistrong form efficient markets hypothesis failed to find any public information that was useful for predicting short-term price movements.[12]

Evidence that market prices reflected more than just public information (as predicted by the strong form efficient markets hypothesis) was found by using a technique called *event studies*. (These involve using CAPM or some other asset pricing model to estimate how a stock's price would have moved over some period in the absence of new information and then comparing this to its actual behavior during a period in which some event, such as an information release, occurred.) For example, if the earnings reported by a company were less than had been forecast by stock analysts or by the company itself, then you might expect the news to cause the price of the company stock to fall relative to the market as a whole. Evidence, however, shows that although low earnings do lead to lower prices, much of the price decline occurs in the few days *before the earnings are publicly announced*. This is typically the period between the time that the first draft of the earnings report is prepared by company employees and the time of public announcement.[13] The run-up of stock prices before merger announcements is also suggestive of inside information being reflected in stock prices.

As a result of these studies, by the late 1970s, there was substantial consensus among finance scholars on the general validity of at least the weak form efficient markets hypothesis, a belief that one of the semi-strong form might also hold, and some willingness to consider the strong form.

NEGATIVE EVIDENCE   Two papers published in 1981 shattered the consensus and raised serious questions about the consistency of the efficient markets hypothesis with the observed behavior of aggregate stock prices.[14] These papers appeared to show that variations in stock prices were much too large to be explained as responses to changing expectations about future dividends. Later statistical analysis of longer-term price movements showed large negative correlations of prices over periods of three to five years that were inconsistent with the elementary versions of the theory that had been used in earlier empirical studies.[15] The most recent econometric studies tend to support the view that the Weak Form Efficient Markets Hypothesis is not fully consistent with the evidence, but that the deviations from pricing efficiency are not so great as to contradict the hypothesis "grossly."[16]

The worldwide stock market crash of October 19, 1987 gives perhaps an even more cogent reason to question whether the hypothesis is valid. It is still hard to see

---

[11] See Eugene Fama, "Efficient Capital Markets: A Review of Theory and Empirical Work," *Journal of Finance*, 25 (May 1970), 383–417.

[12] This research is surveyed in Burton Malkiel, "Efficient Markets Hypothesis," *The New Palgrave: A Dictionary of Economics*, J. Eatwell, M. Milgate, and P. Newman, eds. (London: The Macmillan Press, 1987), Volume 2, 120–23, and, more completely but also more technically, in Stephen LeRoy, "Efficient Capital Markets and Martingales," *Journal of Economic Literature*, 28 (December 1989), 1583–1621.

[13] See George Foster, *Financial Statement Analysis* (Englewood Cliffs, NJ: Prentice Hall, 1986), 380. A confounding element in this is that the information may appear to become publicly available before it appears in *The Wall Street Journal*, but researchers often take the date of the *Journal* story carrying the news as the release date for their studies.

[14] Stephen F. Leroy and Richard D. Porter, "Stock Price Volatility: Tests Based on Implied Variance Bounds," *Econometrica*, 49 (1981), 555–74; and Robert J. Shiller, "Do Stock Prices Move Too Much to be Justified by Subsequent Changes in Dividends?" *American Economic Review*, 71 (June 1981), 421–36.

[15] Eugene Fama and Kenneth French, "Permanent and Temporary Components of Stock Prices," *Journal of Political Economy*, 96 (April 1988), 246–73.

[16] N. Gregory Mankiw, David Romer, and Matthew Shapiro, "Stock Market Forecastability and Volatility: A Statistical Appraisal," *Review of Economic Studies*, 58 (May, 1991), 455–78.

what news of the day could have justified a downward revision by almost a third in expected future returns and thus in stock prices between Friday and Monday.

Shortsighted Markets and Shortsighted Management

The first kind of criticism of the efficient markets hypothesis was a criticism of its empirical validity. There is evidence to challenge the assertion that the semi-strong form or even the weak form efficient markets hypothesis is true. The second kind of criticism applies regardless of the evidence on these matters: Unless the strong form efficient markets hypothesis is also true, maximizing stock market value may not be a proper objective for the firm's managers. In general terms, when the strong form of the hypothesis is not true, the firm's own executives have better information about the value of various alternatives than do investors, and it would contribute to efficiency if they could be induced to use that information in selecting among activities for the firm, regardless of how those activities are accounted for in the market price. This is a special problem for the many firms that explicitly compensate top executives on the basis of share-price performance, but it is also a problem for other firms where executives may believe that their job security depends on good share price performance.

Generally, investors find it easier to gather and evaluate information about some determinants of the firm's fundamental value, such as short-term earnings performance or the sales of existing products, than about others, such as the market potential of new products or the stage of development of a secret new product. Market prices naturally will be more sensitive to the sources of value that the market can see, such as the levels of quarterly sales and earnings, than to things like investments in promising new technologies, which investors find harder to evaluate. Consequently, an executive who is compensated based on share-price performance will be tempted to put too much emphasis on activities that boost short-term performance compared to those whose benefits will be hidden from investors for a long period of time.

Worse, this problem can be self-reinforcing. Short-term investors are inclined to gather the information that is most valuable for forecasting short-term price changes. Realizing that short-term performance is the prime determinant of prices, these investors will then be inclined to devote even more resources to getting early and accurate information about earnings, neglecting the difficult, costly, and time-consuming task of assessing long-term prospects.

A FORMAL MODEL   Most of these points can be illustrated using a principal-agent model of the kind introduced in Chapter 7 that also incorporates a model of how share prices are determined. In the model, the value of the firm depends on top managers' allocation of effort to creating current and future earnings. Management's information advantage over investors is that it alone knows how much effort it has devoted to short- and long-term activities. Investors attempt to infer the current and future earnings by gathering information about each, and the value they put on the firm accurately reflects their estimates of these. Thus, stock prices accurately reflect all public information, and yet it turns out that management will devote too much effort to improving short-term returns and not enough to long-term earnings. The key to the analysis is that management's allocation of effort is governed by the equal compensation principle.

The Mathematical Analysis of the Model

Suppose there is a firm whose fundamental value V is the sum of the values of the current and future earnings of the firm. Current earnings are themselves the sum of two components. One of these, $C(t_C)$, depends on the time and

472

Finance:
Investments,
Capital Structure,
and Corporate
Control

effort t_C applied by the firm's top managers to boosting these earnings. The second, V_C, represents all the other unknown factors that affect near-term earnings, whether due to history, environment, or chance. Future earnings similarly consist of the sum of a term, $F(t_F)$, that depends on the time and effort management devotes, and a second term, V_F, that represents all the other factors affecting value. Thus, the total value is:

$$V = C(t_C) + V_C + F(t_F) + V_F$$

Investors are unable to observe these components of value directly, but they are able to gather imperfect information about them. In our model, we express the investors' initial uncertainty about the two components of value by treating V_C and V_F as random variables that, for illustrative purposes, we take to be normally distributed with means $\overline{V}_C$ and $\overline{V}_F$ and variances equal to $1/\rho_C$ and $1/\rho_F$. (The amounts ρ_C and ρ_F are the *precisions* of the investors' initial estimates of the components of value.) The information investors observe about these prospects is represented by $C(t_C) + V_C + \epsilon_C$ for current earnings and $F(t_F) + V_F + \epsilon_F$ for long-term ones. The terms ϵ_C and ϵ_F are random errors in the information the investors obtain. They provide a way to represent the idea that some information is gathered but that the information is imperfect. We assume that these terms have mean zero and variances $1/\pi_C$ and $1/\pi_F$. Finally, we assume that investors expect managers to allocate time $\overline{t}_C$ and $\overline{t}_F$ to the two kinds of activities.

A statistical calculation shows that after observing the relevant information, the investors' estimates of the current and future components of value are, respectively:

$$\hat{V}_C = [\rho_C(C(\overline{t}_C) + \overline{V}_C) + \pi_C(C(t_C) + V_C + \epsilon_C)]/(\rho_C + \pi_C) \text{ and}$$
$$\hat{V}_F = [\rho_F(F(\overline{t}_F) + \overline{V}_F) + \pi_F(F(t_F) + V_F + \epsilon_F)]/(\rho_F + \pi_F)$$

In the expression for $\hat{V}_C$, the term $C(\overline{t}_C) + \overline{V}_C$ represents the investors' prior expectations based on their original beliefs about both how managers will behave and what the underlying values are. Similarly, the term $C(t_C) + V_C + \epsilon_C$ is the estimate they would form based solely on the newly observed, imperfect information. Their actual estimate is a weighted sum of the two, with weights determined by the precision of each information source. A similar interpretation applies to the expression for $\hat{V}_F$.

Under the CAPM, for any fixed beta, the price of the stock is proportional to the investors' expectation about total returns, $\hat{V}_C + \hat{V}_F$. Other models of stock prices yield this same conclusion. Thus, the total stock price is proportional to:

$$\hat{V}_C + \hat{V}_F = \frac{\rho_C(\overline{V}_C + C(\overline{t}_C)) + \pi_C(V_C + C(t_C) + \epsilon_C)}{\rho_C + \pi_C}$$
$$+ \frac{\rho_F(\overline{V}_F + F(\overline{t}_F)) + \pi_F(V_F + F(t_F) + \epsilon_F)}{\rho_F + \pi_F}$$

If the top management receives a bonus that is proportional to the share price change, then its marginal reward for efforts (t_C) to boost current earnings is proportional to: $C'(t_C)\pi_C/(\rho_C + \pi_C)$ and for future-oriented efforts (t_F) to $F'(t_F)\pi_F/(\rho_F + \pi_F)$. In each case, the expression is proportional to the marginal contribution of efforts to the component of value multiplied by the weight accorded by investors to the affected information. That weight is the relative precision of the new information compared to whatever information existed before.

According to the equal compensation principle, if the top managers are to be motivated to devote some time and effort to both activities, then their returns to both kinds of efforts must be equal:

$$\frac{\pi_C}{\rho_C + \pi_C}C'(t_C) = \frac{\pi_F}{\rho_F + \pi_F}F'(t_F)$$

Efficiency, however, requires that the marginal value created by effort in each activity be equal: $C'(t_C) = F'(t_F)$.

We have hypothesized that more weight will be placed on the current performance measure. The statistical condition that ensures this is:

$$\frac{\pi_C}{\rho_C + \pi_C} > \frac{\pi_F}{\rho_F + \pi_F}$$

This inequality means that there is less error in forecasts of current performance than in more distant future earnings (each measured relative to the error of prior information).

The inequality, combined with the immediately preceding equation, implies that $F'(t_F) > C'(t_C)$: The effort allocation is inefficient. The marginal increase in value resulting from additional efforts to boost long-term earnings is greater than that for current earnings. Fundamental values could be increased if the top managers could be induced to ignore the market valuations and turn some of their efforts away from activities oriented to the near term and toward more future-oriented activities.

LESSONS FROM THE MODEL   The mathematical formulation clarifies three points. First, the responsiveness of prices to information about current and future returns depends not only on the precision of the information but also on the precision of what was known about returns before the information was received. If long-term performance is highly uncertain, it is not clear that even relatively poor information about those prospects will not elicit a substantial response. Second, the problem is not caused by any mistaken special concern by investors for promoting short-term performance. Rather, the whole matter hinges on the fact that managers have better information than investors do about how their efforts are being directed to increase value. If investors could observe the managers' actions and their impacts—$C(t_C)$ and $F(t_F)$ in the model—directly, then they would correctly reflect the management's performance in the share price. Understanding the problem is the first step in constructing better solutions, as we see in the next chapter. Finally, the argument applies regardless of the correctness of the investors' expectations about fundamental values ($\overline{V}_C$ and $\overline{V}_F$) or about managerial efforts ($\overline{t}_C$ and $\overline{t}_F$). Indeed, in the formal model, these quantities do not even enter into the incentive calculation. If investors use new information in the way the model describes, then they will place more weight on short-term performance measures than on long-term ones. That, according to the model, is what encourages managers to place more emphasis on short-term performance and less on long-term performance than is desirable for maximizing the fundamental value.

Implications of the New Theories for Organizations

The new theories discussed here challenge both the various forms of the efficient markets hypothesis and the business and policy conclusions based on the hypothesis. First, according to these theories, all forms of the efficient markets hypothesis must be false because there are many unsophisticated investors whose ill-informed beliefs and volatile expectations create inaccurate and excessively volatile prices. That the hypothesis is false does not mean that none of its implications are true, however. The

474

Finance:
Investments,
Capital Structure,
and Corporate
Control

presence of some sophisticated investors still implies limits on how severe the mispricing among various kinds of assets can be, and these limits may explain the evidence that it is difficult to earn excess risk-adjusted returns over short periods of time using just public information. That appears consistent with the efficient markets hypothesis.

The failure of the hypothesis also does not imply that firms cannot benefit from taking public actions to enhance their long-term profitability. Indeed, there is evidence that stock prices do rise in response to companies' announcements of increased R&D expenditures and other long-term investments, even when these might be expected to depress cash flow in the short run.[17] Sophisticated investors, and even naive ones, may react to these investments by raising their expectations about the firm's total value, thereby raising the firm's price.

Investors may also raise their expectations on the news that companies have improved their incentive compensation plans for top managers, for example by increasing the weight of long-term earnings in compensation. Applying this conclusion requires making a careful examination of the changes. Increasing the intensity of top management's incentives transfers risk to the affected managers, raising their risk premium, and requiring higher pay. A proper incentive plan needs to balance the demands of short- and long-term performance incentives and to keep the risks transferred to a bearable level.

The theories of shortsighted management indicate that even if the semi-strong form efficient markets hypothesis is true, there may still be validity both to the complaints that managers give too much weight to the short term and the retort that stock market pressure makes them behave that way. Managers who attempt to maximize the market value of the firm's shares will not be led to make socially efficient decisions. Instead, to the extent that their actions are unobserved or based on private information, they will be tempted to focus their efforts on attempts to boost current earnings while devoting too little effort to the business of managing for the long term.

This theoretical prediction raises important issues about whether alternative institutions might perform better. For example, might economic systems perform better when stocks are held primarily by long-term investors who will not sell on the first bad earnings report? This pattern of ownership has been the norm in Japan, where a large fraction (70 percent) of the shares of most major companies are held by other firms that will not normally sell them and by financial institutions that have traditionally held stocks for long periods rather than actively trading them. Firms in Germany obtain about 90 percent of their financing from banks, who in turn are represented on the firms' supervisory boards. The relationships between banks and the firms they finance are long-term ones.

There are signs that a similar pattern may be emerging in the United States. A large fraction of all U.S. stocks, especially those of the larger firms, are held by **institutional investors**, such as insurance companies, mutual funds, and pension plans. It has often been claimed that institutional investors are especially fickle and impatient, and their rise has been blamed for the short-term performance pressures that managers claim to feel. By the early 1990s, however, many of these investors were finding that it was unprofitable to manage their portfolios actively, buying and selling in response to market developments, not only because they found that they did not have enough inside information to create profitable trading strategies but also because their holdings were so large that their transactions had too great an impact

---

[17] Office of the Chief Economist, United States Securities and Exchange Commission, "Institutional Ownership, Tender Offers, and Long Term Investment," 1985, and John J. McConnell and Chris J. Muscarella, "Capital Expenditure Decisions and Market Value of the Firm," *Journal of Financial Economics*, 14 (1985), 399–422.

began to adopt buy-and-hold strategies and to attempt to put pressure on managers in the firms they owned to manage more efficiently.

The move in the United States in the 1980s toward companies going private, with most financing from debt and with ownership concentrated among managers and a small group of outsiders, had the same effect of insulating managers from the temptations to worry about short-run stock market pressures and to neglect long-run returns. It also strengthened their incentives to maximize the firm's fundamental value.

The new theories also challenge the traditional economic notion that firms ought to be managed to maximize the value of currently traded shares. It may better serve the interests of efficiency to serve the more basic objective of maximizing fundamental value. The problem with this latter objective is detecting whether managers actually are adopting it rather than following their own agendas. Even if the market is not a perfect indicator of managerial performance, without an alternative way to evaluate and motivate management, it may be better to motivate them to follow the dictates of share prices than to give them no motivation at all.

Another issue is the interpretation and evaluation of takeovers. If market prices accurately reflect the value of the firm in the control of its current managers, then a takeover can be profitable only if it can make the firm more valuable. If it is possible for corporate raiders to gather better information than other investors, the issues become more complex. The raider may simply be buying an underpriced company and evicting a competent management, destroying value in the process. Alternatively, it may be that raiders are the investors most highly motivated to assess the long-term value of the company, and their activities may help make share prices more accurate estimates of the fundamental values of companies. Takeovers raise a number of other issues as well, which we treat in more detail in the next chapter.

476

Finance:
Investments,
Capital Structure,
and Corporate
Control

SUMMARY

The classical economics of finance is based on a model of the firm as a flow of income and expenses. Managers must decide which flows represent good investments, whether to finance those investments by borrowing or issuing stock, and what portion of the firm's earnings should be paid to shareholders in the form of dividends. Investors must decide how much of which companies to buy. Their combined actions determine the demand for various securities and consequently the relationship among the returns on different kinds of investments. Finally, in the classical theory, the whole system can be evaluated to determine the efficiency with which it allocates capital among potential investments.

We examined a number of major results from the classical theory. First, in the idealized situation where the firm can borrow and save at the same interest rate, the firm's investment decisions can be evaluated separately from any consumption decisions made by the owners and without reference to the owners' preferences. This first result is called the *Fisher separation theorem*. Second, an investment is profitable and should be undertaken exactly when the *present value* of the cash flows it generates, which is defined to be the largest loan that could be repaid using these cash flows, exceeds the amount of the initial required investment. An equivalent statement is that the *net present value* of the cash flows ("net" of the initial investment expenditure) must be positive. Third, for *strategic* investment decisions, a correct single-project net present value calculation using only local information about the direct cash flows from the project lead to the wrong answer because a large part of the value of the project may come from its indirect effect on other units or projects in the organization.

The fourth conclusion of the classical theory is that if investors can borrow and save on the same terms as firms, and the firms' financing decisions do not affect their total cash flow, then the firms' choices between debt and equity and their dividend decisions have no effect on their total market value. These propositions about capital structure and dividends are known as the *Modigliani-Miller (MM) theorems* and are often captured by the words: "Capital structure and dividend policies cannot create value unless they affect the total returns."

Fifth, when the Fisher separation theorem applies, investment throughout the economy is efficient because all firms face the same cost of capital on their investments and the only investments that are undertaken are those that can repay the cost of capital while still leaving something for the owner.

Several additional conclusions are obtained when it is assumed that investors care only about the mean and variance of the returns on their portfolios of investments and there is a riskless bond available. There then exists a single portfolio of assets such that any risk-averse investor would optimally invest a portion of his or her wealth in the riskless asset and the remaining fraction in the identified portfolio. The *pricing formula* then asserts that the expected rate of return on any investment is equal to the riskless rate plus an amount that is proportional to the *beta* of the asset, which is the covariance of the asset returns with the returns on the identified portfolio divided by the variance of the return on that portfolio. The capital asset pricing model (CAPM) adds the assumption that all investors optimize in this way and concludes that the identified portfolio coincides with the *market portfolio*, the portfolio of all assets available for investment.

The *efficient markets hypothesis* has three variants. The *weak form* holds that past prices contain no information that can be used to predict future price changes. The *semistrong form* holds that published public information also cannot be used to predict price changes. Finally, the *strong form* holds that even insider information cannot be used to predict price changes. The weak and semistrong forms of the hypothesis formerly had wide acceptance, but even the weak form has been challenged in recent empirical and theoretical work. There is now significant doubt about its general validity.

An important implication of the strong form of the hypothesis is that maximizing the fundamental value of the firm to its shareholders is equivalent to maximizing the value of the firm's shares. The reason is that the market's reaction to strategies and events will embody the best possible estimates of any value they created or destroyed that can be made from currently available information. Some newer theoretical work emphasizes that these same conclusions cannot be derived from the weak and semistrong forms. In particular, even if markets use all public information perfectly to forecast efficiently, that information may still reflect more fully efforts that boost short-term earnings than ones that increase long-term values. Consequently, executives whose pay or job security depends on share prices may be led to neglect long-term concerns in favor of increasing short-term performance measures.

◼ Bibliographic Notes

The subject of finance has evolved into a tremendously active field of research beginning in the late 1960s. The field now supports several specialized journals devoted exclusively to the topic, and our reporting in this chapter has been even more selective than in the other chapters. For the selection of results reported here, a few names stand out. Irving Fisher's 1907 book laid the foundations for present value analysis by treating interest rates as prices and cash flows as amounts that could be priced. His later book is, however, better known and somewhat clearer.

Franco Modigliani and Merton Miller's main work is described in the text. An excellent discussion of the MM results and their impact over the 30 years since they were developed is given by Miller's paper in the *Journal of Economic Perspectives* and the comments that follow it by Modigliani, Sudipto Bhattacharya, Stephen Ross, and Joseph Stiglitz.

The capital asset pricing model (CAPM) is the creation of William Sharpe and John Lintner, building on the portfolio theory analyses of Harry Markowitz and James Tobin. Jan Mossin is also an important early developer of this line of work. Douglas Breeden developed a major extension of CAPM which responds to some of the criticisms levelled against it, and Stephen Ross has developed a major competing alternative model of asset pricing. The asset pricing analysis of Robert Lucas has also been very influential. Bengt Holmstrom emphasized that incentives create a reason for firms to care about idiosyncratic risk, even when the CAPM applies.

Paul Samuelson provided the theoretical underpinnings for the efficient markets hypothesis. An excellent discussion of it and its implications is provided by Burton Malkiel's classic, A *Random Walk Down Wall Street*. Markowitz, Miller, Modigliani, Samuelson, Sharpe, and Tobin have all been awarded Nobel Memorial Prizes in Economic Science.

The challenge to the efficient markets hypotheses began with empirical papers by Robert Schiller, and by Stephen Leroy and Richard Porter. The papers in the *Journal of Economic Perspectives*' 1990 "Symposium on Bubbles" address the possibility and some of the implications of systematic deviations from market efficiency. Especially useful is the paper by Andrei Shleifer and Lawrence

478

Finance:
Investments,
Capital Structure,
and Corporate
Control

Summers. A survey of the efficient markets hypothesis is provided by LeRoy. Our mathematical model of short-sighted management and short-sighted markets is based on the work of Timothy Bresnahan, Paul Milgrom, and Jonathan Paul, who also develop the basis for our discussion of the role of financial markets in allocating capital for investments. Related models of myopia have been developed by Jeremy Stein and by Richard Zeckhauser and John Pound. Henry Manne inaugurated the debate on insider trading.

One of the most important elements of the classical theory of finance that we have not treated is the pricing of derivative securities, such as options and futures, that are derived from other, more fundamental securities, such as stocks. The breakthrough in this area came with the work of Fisher Black and Myron Scholes on options pricing. A review of this material is provided by Mark Rubinstein. The accompanying paper by Hal Varian examines the importance in financial economics of the arbitrage arguments originated by Miller and Modigliani.

Excellent textbooks in the aspects of finance discussed here include those by Richard Brealey and Stewart Myers, James Van Horne, and Sharpe and Gordon Alexander.

■ REFERENCES

Bhattacharya, S. "Corporate Finance and the Legacy of Miller and Modigliani," *Journal of Economic Perspectives*, 2 (Fall 1988), 135–48.

Black, F., and M. Scholes. "The Pricing of Options and Corporate Liabilities," *Journal of Political Economy*, 81 (May 1973), 637–54.

Brealey, R., and S. Myers. *Principles of Corporate Finance* (New York: McGraw-Hill, 1991).

Breeden, D. "An Intertemporal Asset Pricing Model with Stochastic Consumption and Investment Opportunities," *Journal of Financial Economics*, 7 (September 1979), 265–96.

Bresnahan, T., P. Milgrom, and J. Paul. "The Real Output of the Stock Exchange," in *Output Measurement in the Services Sector*, Zvi Griliches, ed. (Chicago: University of Chicago Press, 1991).

Fisher, I. *The Rate of Interest* (New York: Macmillan, 1907).

Fisher, I. *The Theory of Interest* (New York: Macmillan, 1930).

LeRoy, S. "Efficient Capital Markets and Martingales," *Journal of Economic Literature*, 27 (December 1989), 1583–1621.

LeRoy, S., and R. Porter. "Stock Price Volatility: Tests Based on Implied Variance Bounds," *Econometrica*, 49 (May 1981), 555–74.

Lintner, J. "The Valuation of Risky Assets and the Selection of Risky Investments in Stock Portfolios and Capital Budgets," *Review of Economics and Statistics*, 47 (February 1965), 13–37.

Lucas, R. "Asset Prices in an Exchange Economy," *Econometrica*, 46 (November 1978), 1429–45.

Malkiel, B. A *Random Walk Down Wall Street* (New York: W. W. Norton, 1991).

Manne, H. *Insider Trading and the Stock Market* (New York: The Free Press, 1966).

Markowitz, H. "Portfolio Selection," *Journal of Finance*, 7 (March 1952), 77–91.

Miller, M. "The Modigliani-Miller Propositions After Thirty Years," *Journal of Economic Perspectives*, 2 (Fall 1988), 99–120.

Miller, M., and F. Modigliani. "Dividend Policy, Growth and the Valuation of Shares," *Journal of Business*, 34 (October 1961), 411–33.

Modigliani, F. "MM—Past, Present, Future," *Journal of Economic Perspectives*, 2 (Fall 1988), 149–58.

Modigliani, F., and M. Miller. "The Cost of Capital, Corporate Finance and the Theory of Investment," *American Economic Review*, 48 (June 1958), 261–97.

Mossin, J. "Equilibrium in a Capital Asset Market," *Econometrica*, 34 (October 1966), 768–83.

Ross, S. "An Arbitrage Theory of Capital Asset Pricing," *Journal of Economic Theory*, 13 (December 1976), 341–60.

Ross, S. "Comment on the Modigliani-Miller Propositions," *Journal of Economic Perspectives*, 2 (Fall 1988), 127–34.

Rubinstein, M. "Derivative Assets Analysis," *Journal of Economic Perspectives*, 1 (Fall 1987), 73–94.

Samuelson, P. "Proof that Properly Anticipated Prices Fluctuate Randomly," *Industrial Management Review*, 6 (Spring 1965), 41–49.

Schiller, R. "Do Stock Prices Move Too Much to be Justified by Subsequent Changes in Dividends?" *American Economic Review*, 71 (June 1981), 421–36.

Sharpe, W. "Capital Asset Prices: A Theory of Market Equilibrium under Conditions of Risk," *Journal of Finance*, 19 (September 1964), 425–42.

Sharpe, W., and G. Alexander. *Investments* (Englewood Cliffs, NJ: Prentice Hall, 1990).

Shleifer, A., and L. Summers. "The Noise Trader Approach to Finance," *Journal of Economic Perspectives*, 4 (Spring 1990), 19–34.

Stein, J. "Efficient Capital Markets, Inefficient Firms: A Model of Myopic Corporate Behavior," *Quarterly Journal of Economics*, 104 (November 1989), 655–70.

Stiglitz, J. "Why Financial Structure Matters," *Journal of Economic Perspectives*, 2 (Fall 1988), 121–26.

Tobin, J. "Liquidity Preference as Behaviour toward Risk," *Review of Economic Studies*, 25 (February 1958), 65–86.

Varian, H. "The Arbitrage Principle in Financial Economics," *Journal of Economic Perspectives*, 1 (Fall 1987), 55–72.

Zeckhauser, R., and P. Pound. "Are Large Shareholders Effective Monitors? An Investigation of Share Ownership and Corporate Performance," *Asymmetric Information, Corporate Finance, and Investment*, Hubbard, R. G., ed. (Chicago: University of Chicago Press, 1990), 149–80.

EXERCISES

Food for Thought

1. A stock mutual fund is a company that invests in shares of the stock of other companies. These funds exist to make it possible for small investors to pool their

480

Finance:
Investments,
Capital Structure,
and Corporate
Control

Table 14.2 Calculating Present Values in an Economy with Inflation

Year t	Nominal Cash Flow C_t	Inflation Factor $I_t = (1 + i)^t$	Real Cash Flow C_t/I_t	Accumulation Factors $A_t = (1 + r)^t$	Present Value C_t/A_t
0	—	1.000	—	1.000	—
1	124	1.250	99	1.100	90.00
2	?	1.563	121	1.210	100.00
3	195	?	?	1.331	?
				Total Present Value	?
				Initial Investment	220.00
				Net Present Value	?

money in order to hold a widely diversified portfolio of investments. In an *open-end* fund, shareholders can redeem their shares and demand to be paid the corresponding fraction of the value of the fund's shareholdings. In a *closed-end* fund, shareholders can obtain cash for their shares only by selling them to others. It is common for closed end funds to sell for prices lower than the actual value of company's holdings. How can one account for that? Under what circumstances would a closed-end fund be preferred to an open-end fund? See *The New York Times*, MONEY, (Sunday, July 15, 1990): "Close Ties at a Closed-End Fund," F13.

2.   Suppose the preferences of individual investors depend on more than just the mean and variance of asset returns. Which aspects of the discussion of individual investments would you expect to be most affected? How would you expect them to change?

3.   What kind of information advantage would you expect insiders to have over ordinary investors? Is it reasonable to suppose that they know more about the prospects of long-term investments? About imminent earnings reports? How does each kind of information advantage damage the efficient functioning of a system of finance based on securities markets? Which effect is most important?

Quantitative Problems

1.   Suppose a graduating student from a U.S. community college expects to earn $20,000 per year for 5 years and $60,000 per year for the subsequent 30 years until retirement. Assume that the income arrives at the end of each year. What is the present value of the student's future incomes, using a 5% rate of interest? How does your answer change if the income arrives instead at the beginning of each year? The middle?

2.   Show (using calculus) that if a firm produces positive profits in every future year, then the present value of the profit stream decreases when the interest rate used in the calculation rises. To see that the conclusion is different when the stream has both positive and negative elements, compute the present value of the stream $(-50, +190, -100)$ at interest rates of 3%, 5%, and 7%.

3.   The accompanying table (Table 14.2) shows a present value calculation for a country that is suffering inflation of 25% per year when the company's real cost of capital is 10%. Fill in the missing figures. Show that the resulting present value is the same as if the calculation followed the pattern of Table 14.1, but using the *nominal* cost of capital of 37.5%. [The nominal cost of capital n is determined from

Table 14.3

Value of Bonds Issued	Firm's Payoff	Bondholders' Receipts	Stockholders' Receipts
(A) 50	100	50	50
	300	50	?
	Expected	50	?
(B) 100	100	?	?
	300	?	?
	Expected	?	?
(C) 150	100	?	?
	300	?	?
	Expected	?	?

the formula $1 + n = (1 + r)(1 + i)$ where r is the real cost and i is the rate of inflation.]

4. A firm is about to be sold by its founder. The firm's future earnings from its operations are uncertain. They may be either 100 or 300, each with probability one-half. Investors are risk neutral, so they would be willing to buy the firm for its expected return of 200. The founder, however, wants to consider whether a higher total price could be obtained by selling the claim to the firm's earnings as some combination of bonds and stocks, in which the bondholders have first claim to the firm's earnings up to the amount of the bonds. The bond amounts considered are 50, 100, and 150. In Table 14.3, fill in the amounts that the stockholders and bondholders receive in each contingency and determine the price that will be paid in each case. Does the Modigliani-Miller conclusion hold for this example?

5. Suppose a particular investor can allocate his or her investments among three assets only. The first is a riskless asset that generates a certain net return of 5 for every 100 invested. The second is a risky asset that generates an expected net return of 9 for every 100 invested but where the variance of that return is 64. The third is another risky asset that generates an expected return of 7 per 100 invested with a variance of 100. Suppose the returns on the two assets are statistically independent: (a) Compute the mean and variance of a portfolio invested 80% in the riskless bond and 20% in the first risky asset; (b) Compute the mean and variance of a portfolio invested 75% in the riskless bond, 15% in the first risky asset, and 10% in the second risky asset; (c) Why isn't the third asset, with its lower expected return and greater risk always worthless to the investor?; (d) Use calculus to determine the fraction of the One Fund that should be invested in each of the two risky assets. (Observe from Figure 14.1 that the One Fund is the portfolio of risky assets for which the ratio of expected return to the standard deviation of return is maximized.)

15

FINANCIAL STRUCTURE, OWNERSHIP, AND CORPORATE CONTROL

T*he Raiders' Creed: "Give me your undervalued assets, your plants, your expenditures for technology, research and development, the hopes and aspirations of your people, your stake with your customers, your pension funds, and I will enhance myself and the dealmakers."*

Robert Mercer[1]

As we discussed in the preceding chapter, the classical theory of finance is extremely useful, but also seriously incomplete. The classical theory regards financial securities simply as claims on streams of net receipts whose magnitude and variability are exogenously given. For example, a share in a firm simply entitles its owner to a fraction of the revenues remaining after the firm pays its contractual obligations. The theory allows that these receipts may be uncertain, but their likely magnitude (and investors' beliefs about these) are assumed to be unaffected by the firm's financial structure. There are at least three significant elements that make the classical theory misleadingly simple.

First, the forms and patterns of financing can actually affect the returns generated by the firm by affecting the incentives and behavior of various parties and the probability of incurring the costs of bankruptcy. Second, because a firm's managers often know more than investors do about the firm's likely prospects, some investors will scrutinize management's financial decisions for indications about its business forecasts. For example, a reduction in dividends may convince investors that management expects the firm to be short on cash. By affecting investor beliefs,

---

[1] As quoted in Donald B. Thompson, A Hollow Victory for Bob Mercer, *Industry Week* (February 23, 1987), 48. Mr. Mercer was CEO of Goodyear Tire & Rubber Company from 1983 to 1989.

financial decisions can affect stock prices. Finally, financial securities are not just claims on return streams: They also give their holders certain rights concerning decision making and control. As we saw in Chapter 9, a proper joint allocation of decision rights and returns can have important consequences on economic performance and consequently on the firm's share prices.

In this chapter we develop these ideas and use them to examine the differences in the patterns of financial structure between countries, the changes in financing that took place during the 1980s, and the dramatic contests for corporate control that arose in that decade.

CHANGES IN CORPORATE CONTROL: PATTERNS AND CONTROVERSIES

Although businesspeople have long wondered about the best ways to finance their operations, the seemingly arcane subject of corporate finance took on a new urgency in the 1980s. Dramatic changes took place in corporate financial structure, ownership, and control, and these changes sparked great public debate and led to a new awareness of the international differences in financial practices.

Corporate Control Changes in the 1980s

The decade of the 1980s was marked by a wave of changes in corporate ownership and control in North America and the United Kingdom that involved some of the world's largest and most prominent firms. Many of these changes were precipitated by hostile takeover attempts, that is, attempts to buy control of a company despite active resistance by the top management of the target firm. Some were **management buyouts** (MBOs), in which the firm's managers purchased its outstanding shares themselves in order to gain ownership control. In many cases, these financing changes were accompanied by other structural changes, particularly the breaking up of large firms into smaller, independent operating units.

MERGERS AND ACQUISITIONS   The scale of the takeovers in the 1980s was unprecedented and involved many well-known corporations. For example, Chevron Oil bought Gulf Oil for $13.3 billion in what was then the largest-ever combination of two industrial firms. Marathon Oil was bought by U.S. Steel, and Mobil Oil merged with retailer Montgomery Ward. Four years later, Montgomery Ward reemerged as an independent but **privately held corporation**, that is, one whose ownership shares are not publicly traded. Olympia & York Development, the giant international real estate firm, bought Gulf Oil of Canada and Hiram Walker, a distillery and resource firm, but let the liquor business go to Allied-Lyons, the British food, brewing, and liquor concern. General Electric Company bought RCA, acquiring the National Broadcasting Company (NBC) television network in the process. R.J. Reynolds, the tobacco company, bought Nabisco Brands, the bakery and food concern that had recently been formed in the merger of Nabisco and Standard Brands. General Motors bought both Electronic Data Services (EDS) and Hughes Aircraft. Bridgestone, the Japanese tire and rubber company, acquired U.S. tire maker Firestone, and French tire maker Michelin bought Uniroyal Goodrich. Sony bought CBS Records and Columbia Pictures, and Matsushita then bought entertainment giant MCA. Thomson Corporation, owner of the largest number of U.S. and Canadian newspapers and British regional papers, became the largest Canadian retailer when it acquired the venerable Hudson's Bay Company.

The list goes on and on. In 1986, at the height of activity, there were 3,336 announcements in the United States of mergers and acquisitions involving transfers of ownership of at least 10 percent of a company's assets or equity and with a price

484

Finance:
Investments,
Capital Structure,
and Corporate
Control

of more than $500,000. The dollar value of these transactions was $173 billion, up from $44 billion at the start of the decade. By 1988 the number of transactions had fallen, but their total value reached a quarter of a trillion dollars.[2]

HOSTILE TAKEOVERS   The 1980s were also the era of the hostile takeover. Many of the offers to buy the shares of corporations in the face of opposition from management and their boards of directors came from corporate raiders. T. Boone Pickens, Jr. of (relatively) tiny Mesa Petroleum went after Unocal, the giant oil company. Sir James Goldsmith, who earlier had acquired Crown Zellerbach and had bid for Goodyear Tire and Rubber,[3] launched the biggest takeover attempt in the United Kingdom when he went after B.A.T. Industries. Ronald Perelman gained control of Revlon and attacked Salomon Brothers. The Walt Disney Company paid Saul Steinberg $31 million more than the market value of his stockholdings (greenmail) to leave the company alone. Robert Campeau acquired both the largest and the fifth-largest department store groups in the United States, giving him control of some 250 stores in 33 chains, including such famous names as Brooks Brothers, Bloomingdales, Bonwit Teller, Donaldson's, Filene's, I. Magnin, and Rich's. Alan Bond acquired breweries, hotels, publishing, broadcasting, mining, and real estate operations on five different continents. Carl Icahn bought Trans World Airlines.

Yet other hostile offers were launched by corporations. For example, AT&T's offer to buy NCR, a computer manufacturer, in a deal that was realized in early 1991 was initially strongly opposed by NCR's management. When Mobil Oil attempted a takeover of Marathon Oil, U.S. Steel played the role of a **white knight**, rescuing it by making a bid that Marathon's management favored and finally accepted.

MANAGEMENT BUYOUTS   Often the fear of corporate raiders led firms' managers to institute management buyouts, in which they and their allies acquired their companies' outstanding stock, thereby ending public trading of the shares. For example, the management of Safeway, the world's largest food retailer, fought off an attempted takeover by the Haft family by executing a management buyout with the assistance of Kohlberg, Kravis, Roberts & Company (KKR), a buyout specialist.

There were other motives for MBOs as well. For instance, initially the management of RJR Nabisco proposed a buyout because they professed to believe that the stock was undervalued and that a buyout would allow stockholders to realize the underlying value. (The senior executives themselves stood to gain substantially as well.) Eventually, the firm was restructured, but not by management: They lost out to a bid from KKR.

DECONGLOMERATION   Many of these transactions (mergers, acquisitions, takeovers, and buyouts alike) in the 1980s were followed by **bust-ups**, in which a firm's businesses and divisions were sold to other companies, or **spin offs**, where units were separated as independent companies and shareholders received stock in the new companies in proportion to their holdings in the original concern. In a large number of bust-ups, the businesses were acquired by firms already having interests in the same or related industries.[4] The result was a large-scale undoing of the conglomerate mergers of the 1960s and a refocusing of corporations on a narrower, better-defined range of

---

[2] Data from W.T. Grimm & Company, *Mergerstat Review*, Chicago.

[3] Thereby provoking the quotation with which this chapter opened.

[4] Sanjai Bhagat, Andrei Shleifer, and Robert W. Vishny, "Hostile Takeovers in the 1980s: The Return to Corporate Specialization," *Brookings Papers: Microeconomics 1990*, 1 (Washington: Brookings Institution, 1990).

businesses. (See the box on focus, productivity, and corporate control for more on this phenomenon.)

The Rise of Debt

Many of these control changes in the United States were accompanied by vast changes in the financial structures of the firms involved. The source of financing for the American corporate raiders and many of the management-led buyouts alike after mid-decade were **junk bonds**—bonds deemed by a major rating agency to have a high risk of default.[5] These bonds were used to increase the firm's **financial leverage**—the ratio of the firm's total value to the underlying amount of equity capital invested by stockholders (the rest of the capital coming from debt financing). This pattern became so common that the going-private transactions came to be called **leveraged buyouts** (LBOs). Other firms also greatly increased their leverage by taking on debt to finance acquisitions or to buy their own shares to put into Employee Stock Ownership Plans (ESOPs) and by simply buying back their shares in "leveraged recapitalizations." For example, Polaroid bought 22 percent of its shares and put them into a new ESOP when threatened by a raider, and GenCorp (the former General Rubber and Tire) issued debt to pay for acquiring half its outstanding stock. The $25 billion leveraged buyout of RJR Nabisco by KKR resulted in RJR's having $23 of debt for each $1 of equity. It had to pay out $3.34 billion to service its debt in 1989 alone. Between 1980 and 1989 the ratio of long-term debt to total corporate assets rose by almost half, from 16.6 percent to 24.2 percent.[6]

Correspondingly, as firms were acquired or merged out of existence, repurchased their shares, or went completely private, stockholders' equity declined. Between 1980 and 1989 the ratio of stockholders' equity to total assets on the balance sheets of U.S. manufacturing firms fell from 49.6 percent to 40.5 percent, and the ratio of long-term debt to equity went from 34 per cent to 59 per cent. These balance sheet trends were mirrored in the markets as well. In 1984 and 1985 alone nearly 10 percent of the market value of U.S. shares outstanding were retired.[7]

By 1990 the trend to increasing corporate debt in the United States had stopped, at least temporarily. In part under government pressure that forced the savings and loan associations to sell the junk bonds they had bought and in part under the impact of the conviction of Michael Milken on securities charges and the bankruptcy of Drexel Burnham Lambert, the market for new junk bonds had largely disappeared.

At the same time, the takeover and LBO waves collapsed. The volume of LBOs fell from $54 billion in 1989 to one tenth as much in 1990, and the dollar volume of takeovers was almost cut in half. Many of the firms that had taken on exceptionally high levels of debt in buyouts began reducing their debt loads by selling assets or

---

[5] These bonds were backed by the target company's cash flow, but because so much of the firm's total financing was from debt, there was a significant chance that there would not be enough money to meet required interest payments.

[6] The data on debt and equity relative to assets come from the U.S. Department of Commerce *Quarterly Financial Report*, 1980 through 1989. These are so-called "book values," the numbers appearing on companies' balance sheets. Balance sheets list the book value of assets (often their historical cost less accumulated depreciation) against liabilities (short-term plus long-term debt), with the difference being stockholders' equity. Thus, the figures need not be in any close relation to the market value of the assets or of the firms' shares.

[7] Henry Kaufman of Salomon Brothers Inc., quoted in J. Fred Weston, Kwang S. Chung, and Susan E. Hoag, *Mergers, Restructuring, and Corporate Control* (Englewood Cliffs, NJ: Prentice-Hall, 1990), p. 123.

486

Finance:
Investments,
Capital Structure,
and Corporate
Control

Focus, Productivity, and Corporate Control

The merger wave of the 1980s was only the latest of several that have occurred over the last century in the United States. The preceding one, in the 1960s, featured the "conglomerate merger," under which unrelated businesses were brought under common ownership. Although the most obvious result of this was the emergence of the conglomerate firm exemplified by Tenneco, ITT, and United Technologies, in fact most large companies expanded the scope of their activities very broadly. The rationale offered for these mergers was twofold. First, management was thought to involve a generic set of talents and skills such as budgeting, financing, procurement, personnel management, and so on, so that industry expertise was unnecessary and firms would be most efficient by having them run by the especially good managers that the conglomerates had or could attract. Second, it was argued that professional managers were better than investors at the tasks of directing capital to its best uses and diversifying risks among businesses.

Although the stock market at the time generally reacted favorably to conglomerate mergers and acquisitions, in fact both arguments now appear flawed. As was noted at the time, stockholders can achieve diversification for themselves by adjusting their investment portfolios, so they hardly need it to be done for them by firms. Moreover, despite their better information, managers have other objectives and face other pressures than do shareholders who are investing their own money. Since the 1960s it has also become evident that there are real advantages in managers being more than casually acquainted with the businesses they run, and there is accumulating evidence that more focused, less diversified firms perform better. For example, Birger Wernerfelt and Cynthia Montgomery found that more focused firms had higher values of "Tobin's q" (defined as the ratio of the market value of the firm to the replacement value of its assets and a measure of the value being created in the firm) than did more diversified firms. Frank Lichtenberg found that plant productivity fell significantly with increases in the number of different lines of business in which the firm owning the plant was engaged. By the 1980s many diversified firms' stock-market values were less than their apparent bust-up values—the total for which the separate pieces could likely be sold.

The control changes in the 1980s in part undid the diversification of the 1960s. Companies spun off unrelated lines of business as separate organizations or, in the relaxed antitrust environment of the period, sold them to firms with related interests. Some of this was done by existing management teams under conscious strategies of refocusing, but often it followed bust-up takeovers designed to take advantage of the difference in the value of the firm and its pieces. LBOs also contributed to the reduced diversification, as businesses were sold to generate cash to pay down debt.

The result was a significant decrease in overall diversification. Lichtenberg found that firms that ceased to exist in the second half of the decade tended to be more diversified than average, new firms that emerged in the period were much more focused, and the firms in his sample that continued through the period tended to reduce significantly the number of different industries in which they were active. Overall, the mean number of industries in which the firms operated fell 14 percent, whereas the fraction of highly diversified firms (defined as operating in more than 20 different industries) in his sample fell 37 percent and the fraction of highly focused firms operating in a single industry rose 54 percent.

Combining the increase in focus with the connection between focus and productivity, we should expect that the changes in control should have increased productivity. There is some direct evidence for this: Lichtenberg and Donald Siegal found that productivity, measured at the plant level, rose relative to the industry mean in the following year in manufacturing plants involved in ownership changes in the 1970s and also in plants involved in LBOs in the 1980s. Further, in the 1980s stocks of firms outperformed the market in years that the firms became more focused, and did worse than the market in years in which they became more diversified.

Based on John G. Matsusaka, "Takeover Motives During the Conglomerate Merger Wave," mimeo, University of Chicago, 1991; Cynthia Montgomery and Birger Wernerfelt, "Tobin's q and the Importance of Focus in Firm Performance," *American Economic Review* 78 (March 1988), 246–50; Frank Lichtenberg, "Industrial De-Diversification and Its Consequences for Productivity," National Bureau of Economic Research (NBER) Working Paper 3231 (January, 1990); Lichtenberg and Donald Siegal, "Productivity and Changes in Ownership of Manufacturing Plants," *Brookings Papers on Economic Activity* 3 (1987), 643–73, "The Effects of Takeovers on the Employment and Wages of Central-Office and Other Personnel," NBER Working Paper 2895 (September 1989), and "The Effects of Leveraged Buyouts on Productivity and Other Aspects of Firm Behavior," NBER Working Paper 3022 (June 1989); and Gregg Jarrell and Robert Comment, "Corporate Focus and Stock Returns," mimeo, University of Rochester, 1991.

issuing new stock, and more firms were issuing new shares of stock to raise money for new investments. Between the fourth quarter of 1989 and the fourth quarter of 1990 the ratio of long-term debt to assets in manufacturing fell slightly to 23.9 percent, although the ratio of equity to assets also continued its decline.

The Debate

All this activity caught the public attention and sparked much debate. The need to generate cash to service the new debt led highly leveraged firms to trim staff and divest or close various parts of their businesses, often throwing long-time employees out of work. Critics worried that firms burdened with heavy debt would be forced to curtail investments in new products, new equipment, and new technology and would then be condemned to a future of obsolescence and decline. They also worried about the increased likelihood of bankruptcies in a recession, a concern that proved to have some validity in the recession that began in the summer of 1990. They saw corporate managers as being totally absorbed by financial dealmaking and by defending against irresponsible raiders bent on bust-up takeovers. They feared that foreign competitors, with no such distractions, would seize total market dominance, leaving those Americans who were not investment bankers with nothing but badly-paid jobs with no future— "flipping burgers at McDonalds."

Not everyone shared this assessment, however. Advocates cheered the corporate

488

Finance:
Investments,
Capital Structure,
and Corporate
Control

Michael Milken, Drexel Burnham Lambert, and Junk Bonds

High-yield junk bonds played an important role in the LBOs and takeovers of the 1980s. They played an even more important role in the public perceptions of the financial activity of the period—both the LBOs and takeovers and the S&L disaster. Michael Milken of Drexel Burnham Lambert was personally the creator and center of the junk-bond market.

Corporate bonds with high risk and high promised returns are not new: There have always been "fallen angels," bonds issued by major firms that were initially regarded as safe but that became risky when the firms ran into trouble. The key innovation, developed by Milken in the late 1970s, was for Drexel to underwrite and make a market in debt issued by firms which previously would not have been able to sell bonds to the public because they would not have been rated as sufficiently safe investments by the rating agencies. These deals were immensely profitable for Drexel, which charged fees of four or five times what other investment banks charged for underwriting more standard debt issues. Drexel came to dominate the junk market, which grew immensely in the early 1980s as more established firms began to issue junior, subordinated debt in it, and, because his operation generated a huge share of the firm's profits, Milken dominated Drexel.

Junk bonds became very popular investments for many S&Ls attracted by their yield-risk mix. When the public began to become aware of the impending S&L debacle in the late 1980s, many were quick to blame junk bonds and Milken for the industry's problems.

In 1982 Drexel began to help finance MBOs with junk bonds, and shortly thereafter, partially as a means to break into the booming business in mergers and acquisitions, it began using its junk bond operation to finance hostile takeover attempts by such raiders as Carl Icahn, Ronald Perelman, Boone Pickens, and Saul Steinberg. Drexel and Milken raised hundreds of millions, and even billions, of dollars at a time to finance takeovers, much of it in bonds to be backed by the target companies' cash flows in specific deals but some for "war chests," funds to bankroll future raids.

In 1981, new issues of junk totalled $1.3 billion; by 1986 they were $32.4 billion, and the total junk market involved $125 billion. Despite the attempts of other investment banks to enter the business, Drexel—through Milken—still dominated it, and for the first time Drexel was attracting "blue-chip" companies as investment banking clients. Drexel made immense profits on its junk-bond business. Milken also made millions for himself: $550 million from Drexel in 1987 alone, plus hundreds of millions more on his own account.

Although Milken and Drexel made money, they also made enemies of those who saw the junk-bond, bust-up takeover as a fundamental threat to American business and probably to America's future. Milken's pronouncements that he and his associates were rescuing American business from overly conservative, incompetent, self-serving managers did not add to his popularity in these circles. At the same time, others in business, the press, and Congress saw them as heroes.

The fall of Milken and Drexel began in 1986, when arbitrageur Ivan

Boesky, a Milken client, pleaded guilty to insider trading and began cooperating with the government in investigating others who had violated the securities laws. It became clear that Drexel and Milken were targets in these investigations, and this limited the firm's opportunities and weakened it abilities to raise funds and force takeovers. Still, it did back Perelman in his attempted takeover of Salomon Brothers in 1987, and it was the sole manager on the junk offering for the gigantic KKR takeover of RJR Nabisco.

Finally, in 1988, the government filed criminal and securities law charges against Drexel and Milken for insider trading, manipulating stock prices, making false filings with the SEC, falsifying records and documents, and defrauding clients. Drexel pleaded guilty to felony charges, paid $650 million in fines, and agreed to cooperate in the government's case against Milken. Facing potentially huge liabilities in civil suits and without the source of its revenue and power, Drexel soon went bankrupt.

In 1990 Milken entered a plea bargain, admitting guilt in six "narrow" felonies. He was, however, given an unprecedentedly severe sentence: 10 years in jail, three years required community service, and a $600 million fine. Many viewed this, for good or ill, as a "verdict on a decade of greed."

Based largely on Connie Bruck, *The Predator's Ball* (New York: American Lawyer: Simon and Schuster, 1988), as well as news reports. The quotations are from Chris Welles and Michele Galen, "Commentary: Milken is Taking the Fall for a 'Decade of Greed'," *Business Week* (December 10, 1990), 30.

raiders, arguing that the target firms had become bloated and complacent. Why else were savvy investors willing to pay an average of 40 to 50 percent more than the market price of shares for the opportunity to replace existing management and boards? Acquired firms were usually thoroughly reorganized to create units more focused around single businesses, with the top management of each business having a larger ownership share and with the providers of capital having greater power to remove top management if it performed poorly. The raiders and leveraged buyouts were shaking business from the self-satisfied lethargy into which it had fallen after World War II in the easy environment of limited international competition, and the new debt levels just reproduced financing patterns that were common in other industrialized countries.

International Patterns of Financing and Ownership[8]

The heavy reliance on equity financing that marked U.S. firms before the rise of debt in the 1980s differed considerably from the traditional patterns of financial structure in other industrialized economies, which themselves were also changing in this decade. In France in 1980, for example, bank loans provided 71 percent of companies' external financing, with the rest split between shares and corporate bonds in approximately a 3 to 1 ratio. Debt slightly exceeded two-thirds of the value of assets, and it peaked at 72 percent in 1982. Then equity financing became much more attractive after the large banks were nationalized (making bank loans a less attractive

[8] This section draws heavily from Bill Emmott, "The Ebb Tide: A Survey of International Finance," *The Economist* (April 27, 1991), which is also the source for most of the data quoted.

490

Finance:
Investments,
Capital Structure,
and Corporate
Control

means of financing) and the stock market's rules were liberalized. The volume of new issues of stock rose sixfold between 1984 and 1990, reaching the equivalent of $42 billion, and about 30 percent of firms' funding came to be through shares. Banks became significant purchasers of these shares, as did mutual funds, most of which were bank subsidiaries. By 1988, bank borrowing accounted for only 53 percent of the financing of French nonfinancial firms, and debt had fallen to 63 percent of the value of assets.

Japan experienced a similar, but stronger, move away from bank loans and toward equity and other sources of financing in the 1980s. At the start of the decade, the average debt-equity ratio among major, publicly-traded firms was 2.75 to 1, and 64 percent of their external financing was from bank loans. Then Japanese firms began to seek financing elsewhere. First they raised funds in the international bond markets, then on the booming Tokyo Stock Exchange, and later still through convertible bonds (debt that could be converted into common stock) and bonds with warrants (rights to buy the firm's stock at a prespecified price) attached. By 1990 the overall debt-equity ratio was almost 1 to 1, interest-bearing debt was only about 75 percent of the value of equity (whereas it had been more than twice the value of equity in the mid-1970s), and the ratio of debt to assets was less than 30 percent. Firms retired bank loans and built up hordes of cash. Toyota Motors, for example, was jokingly called "Toyota Bank," because in 1990 it held over ¥1.36 trillion (about $10 billion) in cash and cash-equivalents, and another ¥.84 trillion in short-term investments.

In Germany, bank loans provide over 90 percent of firms' external financing. This fraction changed relatively little between 1970 and 1990, despite some increase in the importance of equity. In part, the new equity replaced corporate bonds, which have ceased to be a noticeable source of financing. Few German firms' shares are publicly traded, however. Of the approximately 360,000 German firms whose shareholders have the limited liability for the firm's debts that marks the U.S. corporation, only 2,300 are established as *Aktiengesellschaften*, whose shares could potentially be publicly traded, and of these only 619 actually are traded on the different German stock exchanges.[9] Moreover, most new issues of stock are sold through negotiated private placements rather than general offerings to the investing public. The banks are close to the firms they finance, and they normally have places on the firms' supervisory boards—the second board that German firms are required to have by law and that also must include workers' representatives. Often a banker chairs the board and can wield great power.

The hostile takeovers that were so prominent in the English-speaking countries in the 1980s were rare in France and essentially absent in Japan and Germany. In part, the patterns of financing and ownership explain this. In France, there are different types of shares with different voting rights, and Germany carries this even further by allowing companies to limit the share of voting rights that any single stockholder can have. In both countries, banks' stock holdings would not normally be for sale to a raider. These holdings can be significant: Deutsche Bank, for example,

---

[9] The *Aktiengesellschaften* are identifiable by the letters "AG" after the company name, while the private corporations (*Gesselschaften mit beschränkter Haftung*) are denoted by "GmbH." Examples of the former are the chemical firm Bayer AG and the electronics firm Siemens AG. The private firms tend to be smaller and less well known internationally, but Sony's wholly-owned European subsidiary is such a firm. The parallel designations in the United Kingdom are the letters "plc," for "public limited company," and "ltd," indicating a privately owned firm. Again, the large firms—for example, British Petroleum plc and the international conglomerate Hanson plc—tend to be organized as public limited companies, while smaller ones are private. Notable private companies are such publishers as the Macmillan Press, Ltd, and many British securities firms.

holds more than 25 percent of the shares in five different major German companies, including auto-maker Daimler-Benz. It reputedly organized resistance to the attempt by Italian tire maker Perelli to take over Continental, a German tire firm. These factors make winning a takeover bid difficult, and the fact that most companies in Germany are private removes them completely from the threat of raiders inviting stockholders to tender their shares. Of course, the key distinctive feature of ownership patterns in Japan is the cross-ownership of shares by other firms sharing business relations. Some 24 percent of the shares of major Japanese industrial and financial corporations are held by other corporations, and the figure reaches a full 70 percent when the stockholdings of non-corporate financial institutions (such as mutual insurance companies and investment funds) are considered.[10] The shares held by other corporations would not be offered to a raider because doing so risks breaking the economic alliances they help cement, and the financial institutions have also traditionally been friendly to management. Nevertheless, there have been very active mergers and acquisitions markets in Europe (and to a lesser extent in Japan) throughout the 1980s and into the 1990s, with control of businesses changing hands in friendly transactions.

The events of the 1980s, as well as the international differences and trends, have puzzled many observers. Were the takeovers necessary to revitalize the target organizations? Does it really matter whether firms finance their investments by issuing stock or by borrowing? What determines the firm's choice between these two options? Why do the patterns differ so much internationally? What effect does the choice have on the efficiency of the firm and of the economic system? What are the implications for business in the 1990s and beyond?

FINANCIAL STRUCTURE AND INCENTIVES

The Modigliani-Miller—MM—analysis of the irrelevance of financing and dividend decisions begins with the premise that financing decisions do not affect the cash flow stream itself. We have already observed that debt financing can reduce the firm's tax obligations and, in that way, it can transfer value from the government to the shareholders. The effects that the diverse tax treatments of dividends, capital gains, and interest payments have on firms' decisions can be detected statistically by studying the differences in firm's financing decisions in different jurisdictions with different tax rules. Although the way firms respond to incentives created by tax rules is an important subject of study for both public policy makers and businesspeople, it is too lengthy and involved for a detailed treatment here. The interaction of business decision making and taxation merits has received its own book-length treatment.[11] The main focus of our attention here is on how capital structure can affect value by changing the incentives of managers, by affecting the conflicts of interest that can arise between stockholders and creditors, by influencing the probability that the costs of bankruptcy will be incurred, and by providing incentives for equity investors and lenders to monitor management and limit its excesses.

Conflicting Interests: Managers Versus Owners

Capital structure can affect two broad sets of conflicting interests: managers versus equity owners, where the issues are basically the familiar problems of managerial

---

[10] Jack McDonald, "The *Mochai* Effect: Japanese Corporate Cross-Holdings," *Journal of Portfolio Management*, 16 (Fall 1989), 90–5.

[11] Myron Scholes and Mark Wolfson, *Taxation and Business Strategy: A Global Planning Approach* (Englewood Cliffs, NJ: Prentice-Hall, 1992).

492

Finance:
Investments,
Capital Structure,
and Corporate
Control

moral hazard in controlling costs and maximizing value, and existing creditors versus other suppliers of capital, where the issues revolve around the choice of investments.

Consider the case of a small, growing firm whose founder wants to "go public," that is, to sell shares to outside investors to raise money for additional investments. The founder must decide how many shares to sell to outside investors and what share of ownership to keep for himself or herself. This decision is not one that outside investors can neutralize through financial market transactions as in the MM propositions. The fraction of the firm that the founder keeps is determined fully by the number of shares sold versus the number retained.

As we have seen in several earlier chapters, ownership affects incentives. In the present case, selling part of the firm to outside stockholders can adversely affect the owner-manager's incentives for maximizing profits. If the founder retains a specific percentage share in his or her firm, then he or she enjoys that share of the financial benefits and incurs that share of the financial costs of his or her decisions. This alone causes no distortions because the decisions and actions that maximize a fixed fraction of the benefits less that fraction of the costs also maximize the difference between the total benefits and total costs. To the extent that the decisions have nonfinancial costs and benefits that are not easily observed and contracted over, however, the owner-manager is likely to bear these directly. In that case, maximizing the net benefits that accrue to the owner-manager is not the same as maximizing total net benefits.

For example, an owner-manager who holds a 50 percent stake in the firm and who decides to fly first class, to stay in expensive hotels, to have a luxurious company car, and to invest the firm's resources in pet projects that are of dubious value bears half the financial costs of these decisions, but gets all the benefits. The temptation to indulge in this type of behavior may be limited by a 50 percent ownership stake, but the attractiveness of such decisions is much greater if the manager retained only 5 percent of the firm because 95 percent of the costs are paid by the outside stockholders. Small shareholdings by the top managers of the firm also reduce their incentives to be diligent in monitoring the performance of others within the firm, controlling costs and increasing revenues. The box on executive behavior and ownership stakes illustrates two recent examples of such conflict between management's and shareholders' interests.

Generally, when management owns only a small fraction of the outstanding shares in a firm, several sources of conflict may exist. First, managers will be more interested than shareholders in the growth and longevity of the company. Growing companies provide more opportunities for promotion, and top managers in larger companies tend to earn higher salaries. Meanwhile, when companies close, become bankrupt, or are sold or taken over, lucrative jobs are often lost, especially in the management group. Second, management will be tempted to spend too much on perks for themselves and, possibly, for their subordinates or other employees because they enjoy these perks but bear only part of the cost. Finally, management prefers independence from outside interference, both for its own sake and because independence contributes to job security and allows managers to set higher rates of pay in their own ranks. All of these problems become worse as the managers' equity stake in the firm becomes smaller.

These tendencies may be exacerbated when the firm has a large **free cash flow**. Cash flow amounts to revenues less direct outlays, or, equivalently, profits plus depreciation allowances. Free cash flow is the cash flow in excess of the amount that can profitably be reinvested in the firm. For efficiency, these funds should be returned to stockholders, for example by increasing dividends or repurchasing shares of stock. The stockholders then can put the money to whatever use they think best in consumption or other investments. Managers and their boards may be severely tempted

Executive Behavior and Ownership Stakes: Armand Hammer and F. Ross Johnson

Occidental Petroleum and RJR Nabisco provide two recent extreme examples of CEOs with few shares being apparently less-than-frugal with corporate resources (and of the firms' boards failing to restrain them). Occidental Petroleum was built and led by Armand Hammer, who served as CEO and Chairman of the Board until his death in 1990 at age 92. He pursued a variety of acquisitions and business strategies that were widely criticized, including money-losing businesses in the USSR and China (Hammer had been one of the first western businessmen to meet with Lenin, and he kept in contact with the succeeding generations of communist leaders) and meat-packing and seed-research operations. He also kept the company's dividend high and stable at $2.50 per share whereas in 1990 earnings were only $1.03 and the company had to borrow to pay the dividend. During the last decade of his leadership, the firm's share price fell by a third while oil company shares on average tripled in value. Discontent with Hammer's strategies and the firm's performance led most institutional investors to abandon the stock.

Over his lifetime, Hammer had acquired a large personal art collection (some of it allegedly with corporate funds), and he decided it should be seen by the public. He therefore had the corporation undertake building the Armand Hammer Museum of Art and Cultural Center in Los Angeles to house his collection. Suits attempting to stop this diversion of corporate funds were settled without going to trial, and the museum was built at an eventual cost to the corporation's shareholders of as much as $120 million.

Hammer held less than 0.5 percent of Occidental Petroleum's stock, although he had once owned nearly half the company. The Occidental board included his grandson and two of his lawyers. After his death they renounced many of Hammer's strategies that outsiders had criticized.

F. Ross Johnson was CEO of RJR Nabisco until the KKR buyout in 1988. As the head of Standard Brands and then of Nabisco Brands, Johnson had already built a reputation for spending corporate money lavishly. He doubled executives' salaries at Standard Brands and provided them (and himself) with company apartments, a private box at Madison Square Garden, and multiple country club memberships. He also put a variety of former athletes on the payroll. He was quoted as saying "Give me a guy who can spend creatively, not one who is trying to squeeze the last nickel out of the budget," and he expressed admiration for the executive he put in charge of entertainment and "extravaganzas" for being "the only man who can take an unlimited budget and exceed it."

These patterns continued at RJR Nabisco. He also handed out $1,500 watches, hired former U.S. president Gerald Ford to play in a golf tournament the company sponsored and Frank Sinatra and Bob Hope to entertain guests, expanded the company's stable of athletes (a number of whom apparently did nothing for the retainers of up to $1 million a year they received), authorized extremely luxurious office furnishings, company-provided Cadillacs, Mercedes, and even Rolls Royces with chauffeurs, and hired 36 pilots for the company's ten corporate jets. The planes of the "RJR Air Force" were

494

Finance:
Investments,
Capital Structure,
and Corporate
Control

available for executives' use under any pretext of a business reason, and sometimes allegedly even when there was none.

Johnson held 60,000 of RJR Nabisco's 247 million shares, or 0.02 percent. Until the board accepted KKR's bid over his, he seems to have had its full support. He was quoted as saying "One of the most important jobs a CEO has is the care and feeding of the directors."

Based on "Wife's Heir Sues Armand Hammer," *The New York Times* National Edition, (July 15, 1990), 8Y; "Occidental Petroleum: Taking a Sickle to Hammer's Empire," *The Economist*, (January 19, 1991), 64–65; Nell Minow, "Shareholders, Stakeholders, and Boards of Directors," mimeo, Institutional Shareholder Services, Inc.; and Bryan Burrough and John Helyar, *Barbarians at the Gate: The Fall of RJR Nabisco* (New York: Harper & Row, 1990). Burrough and Helyar are the source of the material in quotation marks; the direct quotations of Johnson are from pages 25 and 26 of their 1991 Harper Perennial edition.

to use these resources within the firm, however, carrying out new investments that (by definition) are not profitable and not in the shareholders' interests. They may also be more inclined to indulge themselves in excessive perks and to share the wealth with the employees.

Despite the problems that arise from small managerial shareholdings, we cannot conclude that the net effect is beneficial when the managers retain a large share of ownership in the firm. Sometimes the problem of the top management owning a minor share of the equity is unavoidable. For example, few managers have the personal wealth to purchase a large share of a major automobile company, and it is not obviously in the shareholders' interest simply to give large shareholdings to repeated generations of managers. Even if the company in question is small enough and the owner wealthy enough to avoid this first problem, there may be a second one: A manager whose wealth is entirely tied up in a single firm bears too much of the firm's risk personally. Risk-averse managers may then be too cautious about risking their entire personal fortunes in aggressive company investments that would be desirable if the risk could be optimally shared. Some diversification of their investments would both reduce the risk premium that is incurred and make the managers more willing to take appropriate risks.

Of course, it may be possible to provide incentives for managers through explicit and implicit compensation contracts rather than through shareholdings directly, and concern with their professional reputations and consequent market opportunities may also discipline their choices. Yet neither of these mechanisms is perfect, so the ownership position of managers may still play a role.

Conflicting Interests: Current Lenders versus Other Capital Suppliers

If the needed funds are not raised by issuing shares, then the primary alternative is to finance company investments by borrowing. However, this can give rise to conflicts between the interests of shareholders (perhaps including management) and those of the firm's creditors. In general, unless those who select the firm's investments own equal shares of the firm's debt and equity, they will not be financially motivated to select the investments that maximize the total value of the firm.

CEO Shareholdings

Michael Jensen and Kevin Murphy have assembled data on U.S. CEOs' holdings of their companies' stock.* The data are from the 1987 *Forbes* survey of executive compensation and concern 746 executives.

The mean value of the CEOs' holdings across the whole sample was $41.0 million, which represented 2.42 percent of the outstanding shares. The distribution was quite skewed, however, because some CEOs (often the companies' founders or their heirs) had very large holdings, whereas 80 percent of the CEOs held less than 1.38 percent of the stock in their firms. The median holdings were only $3.5 million, representing 0.25 percent of the shares outstanding. The total value of the shares of the median firm was $1.2 billion.

In firms below the median size in the sample, the CEOs held an average of 3.05 percent of the shares, representing a value of $19.3 million, but again the medians were much lower: 0.49 percent or $2.6 million. In the larger half of the firms, the CEOs' percentage holdings were smaller, but the values were bigger. The averages were 1.79 percent of the shares, worth $62.6 million, whereas the medians were 0.14 percent of the total shares, with a value of $4.7 million.

---

* "Performance Pay and Top-Management Incentives," *Journal of Political Economy*, 98 (April 1990), 225–64.

EXCESSIVE RISK-TAKING   One problem between shareholders and creditors is that of asset substitution, which we emphasized in Chapter 5 in our discussion of the savings and loan crisis. When a firm has too much debt compared to its equity, the owners may be too ready to undertake risky investments. This is because the owners of shares enjoy virtually all the benefits if returns on the risky investments turn out to be high, but the lenders suffer a major portion of the losses if the returns turn out to be low. For a given expected net present value to the investments, the parties' interests are in direct conflict: Any increase in risk that reduces the expected return to creditors results in an equal increase in the expected return to shareholders. As we saw in the savings and loan example, shareholders may even prefer risky investments with negative net present values to safer ones with positive total returns. This inefficiency is a cost of debt.

Lenders ought to forecast that the firm's owners will have these incentives to make inefficient investment choices (or to direct or motivate managers to make them). This means that the amount they are willing to lend will be less or the return they will demand will be increased. Consequently, the expected costs of the inefficient investment choices will fall on the shareholders. This in turn will give them incentives to try to find ways to commit themselves not to undertake risky investments. For example, they may agree to place covenants in the debt contract that restrict their ability to make risky investments, or they may use short-term bank debt, allowing the lender to withdraw the loan in case of excessive risk taking.

DEBT OVERHANG AND UNDERINVESTMENT   A second problem arises particularly when the firm currently does not have enough cash to pay its current debt obligations but does have profitable investment opportunities. As an extreme example, suppose the firm has an outstanding debt of $10 million more than the value of its assets and that

496

Finance:
Investments,
Capital Structure,
and Corporate
Control

it then obtains an opportunity to make an investment of $5 million yielding a sure gross return of $12 million for a guaranteed net profit of $7 million. If the debt covenants give the current debt priority for repayment, then no new lender or investor will be willing to finance the investment because the first $10 million accrues to holders of its existing debt, leaving only $2 million in returns for the $5 million of new investment. As a result, the profitable investment may not be undertaken and value may be lost.

This is a particular case of **debt overhang**, the inability of a company with profitable investment opportunities to finance them because it has excessive levels of debt relative to its assets. Debt overhang has been a newsworthy issue in the context of Third World economic development. Like firms, countries that are deep in debt may be unable to borrow money to finance promising new industrial development projects because any profits may have to be paid first to existing lenders. (The problems may be even more severe for these countries than for firms because their very sovereignty may prevent nations from committing themselves using loan covenants that restrict their activities.)

The fact that value is lost from the underinvestment caused by debt overhang means that the outcome is inefficient and there is some other arrangement that everyone would prefer. In our example, the failure of the firm to make the investment will lead to losses of $10 million for the lender. If the firm and its lender can agree to reduce the debt by $5 million, then the investment can be undertaken profitably, the reduced loan can be repaid, and the new investors can earn profits of $2 million. The debt reduction reduces the loan losses suffered by holders of existing debt from $10 million to $5 million.

In view of the advantages of being able to renegotiate debt contracts in case earnings are low, it might seem that the parties would want to ensure that renegotiation is possible. For example, concentrating the debt in the hands of a few lenders would make it easier to renegotiate the debt, creating additional value, if the firm experienced hard times. The error in this logic is that the very act of protecting owner-managers against the consequences of bad outcomes reduces their incentives to act diligently to ensure good outcomes and reinforces their already excessive incentive to engage in risky activities.

When the holders of debt are many in number and holdings are diffuse, the threat of debt overhang without the possibility of debt renegotiation favors limiting the level of debt. When debtholdings are concentrated in the hands of a few parties, so that debt renegotiation is more likely, incentives are created for managerial misbehavior. In either case, high levels of debt carry a significant risk of destroying part of the firm's value.

FREE CASH FLOW AND DEBT FINANCING   Balancing these negative effects of debt are direct, positive effects on managers' incentives not to waste free cash flow. Replacing equity by debt commits and compels managers to pay out cash to meet debt service requirements or risk losing control of the company in bankruptcy. Equity financing brings no such direct, unavoidable pressure, and unless the board is very responsive to stockholder interests and well positioned to ensure that perquisites are kept in check and empire building is avoided, there may be little effective pressure of any sort to turn over free cash flow to investors. A missed dividend may anger and upset shareholders, but they may be powerless to do much about it. In language sometimes heard among financiers: "Equity is soft; debt is hard."

Owners' Incentives for Monitoring

The board of directors is supposed to ensure that the interests of shareholders, and perhaps of other stakeholders, are represented in the firm's major decisions. However, the creation of a board of directors just drives the issue one level deeper: What disciplines the behavior of the members of the board? Who monitors the monitors? Ultimately, someone with an ownership interest is needed to ensure that the management does not squander the shareholders' investments. Yet individual investors with relatively small holdings have little incentive to bear the costs of monitoring management's performance or the board's diligence.

For example, suppose you held 1,000 shares of IBM in June 1991. At the stock prices then prevailing, that holding would have been be worth over $98,000 dollars. Because there were over 592 million shares of IBM stock outstanding, however, your ownership claim would have been only 0.000168 percent of the total. Thus, if you exerted enough effort in monitoring to increase the profitability of IBM by $1, you would have gotten back only .000168 cents. You would clearly have been unwilling to do this unless you are motivated by very different considerations than we have assumed. Only investors with a relatively large stake will be inclined to do significant amounts of monitoring. Thus, the concentration of share ownership can affect a firm's value.

CONCENTRATED SHAREHOLDING   Among the 500 largest U.S. industrial concerns in 1980 (the "Fortune 500"), in only 15 cases was there no investor holding at least 3 percent of the shares of the company. On average, the largest investor owned 15.4 percent of the shares and the five largest owned 28.8 percent, which are significant fractions of the total.[12] In smaller companies, the concentration of ownership is even greater.

Large shareholders who have large sums at stake can play an important role in disciplining management. These shareholders have little personal interest in unprofitable growth for growth's sake because the new career opportunities and higher salaries for top management that accompany growth do not accrue to them. The very takeovers that threaten managerial jobs hold the promise of lucrative sales of shares for the large shareholders. Sometimes, these shareholders may be willing to incur the expense of filing lawsuits to protect their interests. If they are represented on the company boards of directors, they may be able to fire managers who are performing badly, replacing them with more effective managers. The threat of being fired from a lucrative job (one that provides rents to the manager) can be a very effective incentive for good performance.

In Japan, the other companies that hold a corporation's stock to cement business relations between them can also serve as monitors. They have a very direct and pressing interest in the success of the firm, and the close relationships among them may facilitate their taking an active role in monitoring. The Japanese practice of executives from major firms becoming CEOs of smaller, related firms may help in this.

An important issue has been the extent to which large institutional investors— pension funds, mutual funds, and insurance companies—have been willing and able to play an active monitoring role. Pension funds alone control 30 percent of the shares of major publicly traded firms in the United States and the United Kingdom, and in at least 20 percent of the cases noted previously, the concentrated ownership comes from institutions' holdings. The professional money managers hired to run the institutions' portfolios are not necessarily especially able monitors of management. Moreover, in the past, institutional investors' policies were usually to avoid "interfering" in the companies' management and simply to sell their holdings if they were dissatisfied

---

[12] These data were reported by Andrei Shleifer and Robert Vishny, "Large Shareholders and Corporate Control," *Journal of Political Economy*, 94 (1986), 461–88.

498

Finance:
Investments,
Capital Structure,
and Corporate
Control

The Efficiency of Ownership Patterns

The extent to which ownership of a corporation's shares is concentrated varies widely across American business. For example, in a sample of 511 large corporations from 1980, the fraction of the total stock held by the five largest shareholders ranged from 1.27 percent to 87.14 percent, with a mean of 24.81. What accounts for the variation?

Harold Demsetz and Kenneth Lehn suggest that efficiency provides one answer. * They argue that ownership should be more concentrated where the net returns to concentration are higher. Large firms, they argue, should have more diffuse ownership for three reasons. First, it is more expensive to increase one's percentage of ownership in a larger firm. Second, a given fractional shareholding will give more influence in a larger firm than in a smaller one. Third, risk aversion among investors implies that higher concentration imposes increasing risk premia as the firm becomes larger. Size, however, is not the only variable that affects net returns to increased concentration. Greater firm-specific uncertainty increases the opportunity to add value by careful assessment of the firm's performance. Greater government regulation limits the firm's range of action (thereby reducing both management's discretion and owners' options), reducing the returns to concentration. Finally, they suggest that in some types of firms there may be consumption value in determining the nature of the firm's output. The two examples they highlight are professional sports, where there may be an extra thrill to seeing your team win when it really is "your team," and the media, where the benefit is in having your opinions broadcast and influencing public opinion.

They tested these predictions by regressing measures of ownership concentration on variables representing the elements listed previously. Each turned out to have the predicted sign and to be statistically significant. Moreover, the extra concentration for media companies came almost entirely from individual and family holdings rather than institutional investors, consistent with the idea that it is the personal consumption value of control that accounts for the effect.

---

* Harold Demsetz and Kenneth Lehn, "The Structure of Corporate Ownership: Causes and Consequences," *Journal of Political Economy* 93 (December 1985), 1155–77.

---

with performance. As noted in Chapter 14, however, there are indications that this pattern may be changing. We will return to this point later.

An additional problem comes from the fact that being a large shareholder in a large firm necessitates holding a very unbalanced portfolio unless the investor is extremely wealthy. What additional returns accrue to the large investor to offset the costs of being poorly diversified? Perhaps the fear of adversely affecting the stock price deters large stockholders from selling their holdings (except to others who are willing to take a comparably large position), but this issue is as yet not well understood.

A third question involves the influence that a large stockholder actually can exert in the face of management's resistance. Anecdotes suggest that this resistance can be very effective. For example, Ross Perot became General Motors' largest shareholder and a member of its board after he sold EDS to the automotive giant.

He was in constant conflict with Board Chairman Roger Smith over policy and was extremely critical of what he saw as GM's institutionalized bureaucratic lethargy. Yet he seemed unable to make any difference, and eventually he agreed to be bought out. In the late 1980s Carl Icahn was by far the largest shareholder in USX (the former U.S. Steel), with a 13.3 percent stake. He sought to have the firm divide its steel and oil businesses into separate entities, but management resisted. Icahn sold his shares in 1991 after only limited success. That same year T. Boone Pickens gave up trying to win a seat on the board and redirect the strategy of Koito Manufacturing, an auto lighting supplier to Toyota. Pickens had acquired 26 percent of the shares in this Japanese concern, making him the largest shareholder, but he was systematically rebuffed in attempting to influence its policies. Indeed, he was even denied access to the company's accounting books, and when he won the legal right to examine them, he could not find a Japanese accounting firm willing to assist in this task.

There is also some limited systematic evidence on the efficacy of large shareholders as monitors, which suggests a more positive inference.[13] We might hypothesize that an outsider would be a more effective monitor in firms with relatively little firm- and manager-specific capital than firms where capital is very largely firm- or manager-specific, because in the latter case it will be harder both to analyze investment decisions and to change them usefully if performance seems lacking. For example, it might be more difficult for an outsider usefully to redirect an R&D-intensive computer company than an oil or steel company. In fact, across 11 industries where capital is generally unspecific (as measured by a low ratio of R&D to sales), the presence of a single entity owning 15 percent or more of the stock had a very significant positive effect on the ratio of stock price to current earnings, implying a higher than normal expected growth in future earnings. No such effect showed up for firms in industries with high ratios of R&D to sales.

LBO ASSOCIATIONS AND ACTIVE INVESTORS   The problem of inadequate monitoring by owners is a *free-rider problem*; it arises because any individual bears the full cost of any monitoring effort but shares the benefits with all the other owners. If concentrating the ownership in one single entity is difficult because the value of the firm's equity is high, one obvious solution is to replace much of the equity by debt and then to have the debtholders organized to monitor management intensively to avoid the problems described earlier. This pattern is the essence of what Michael Jensen has labelled the **LBO association**.[14]

Typically, LBOs are financed with 80 to 90 percent debt. Much of the financing may be arranged by a buyout firm such as KKR or Forstmann, Little & Company, or by the LBO fund of an investment bank. They provide the bulk of the equity for the buyout and arrange for the loans (and, in very large deals, any needed equity partners) to finance the rest. They then have very strong incentives to make sure that the firm performs. They do this by careful monitoring, as well as by giving management very strong incentive compensation (including a share of the equity). The other members of the association are the institutional investors who invest in the LBO firm or fund, providing the resources to buy the equity in the LBOs, and the banks and other investors who make the needed loans and purchase the debt. Their monitoring

---

[13] Richard J. Zeckhauser and John Pound, "Are Large Shareholders Effective Monitors? An Investigation of Share Ownership and Corporate Performance," R. Glenn Hubbard, ed., *Asymmetric Information, Corporate Finance, and Investment* (Chicago: University of Chicago Press, 1990), pp. 149–80.

[14] Michael Jensen, "The Eclipse of the Public Corporation," *Harvard Business Review* (September–October 1989), 61–74.

500

Finance:
Investments,
Capital Structure,
and Corporate
Control

of the buyout firm, and its incentives to maintain a good reputation so that it can do further deals, are additional support for performance.

More generally, concentrating equity holdings gives the usual strong incentives of ownership. The common pattern of success among such active investors as the Hanson Group in the United Kingdom and Clayton & Dubilier and Berkshire Hathaway in the United States, despite their very different styles of dealing with the companies in which they hold major stakes, is evidence of this.[15]

VENTURE CAPITAL   For start-up companies in some areas and industries, **venture capitalists** play much the same role that large shareholders do for established firms. These investors provide the financing that start-up companies need and also monitor their activities closely to ensure that the funds they have supplied are well used.

One of the main problems that venture capitalists face in financing start-ups is that the customary kinds of financial data are of little use for evaluating the firm's performance. In the early years of a new firm's existence, it may have to invest enormous sums in new products and systems before there are any sales or production data that can be compared with competitors' results or other standards to give a reasonably objective assessment of the new firm's performance. For example, Alza Corporation, a California-based drug company, took seven years of testing of its products to obtain approval from the U.S. Food and Drug Administration before its first product could be marketed.

Without the benefit of objective measures, those who provide financing to new firms must stay close to the business, keeping track of the kind of detailed, subjective information that only an insider could know. Venture capitalists, who install their own employees in high positions in the firm (often as chair of the board of directors), continue to finance the start-up firm until it reaches a stage where there is enough objective performance information to convince public investors to buy its shares.

Monitoring Incentives for Lenders

Venture capitalists, like the large shareholders discussed earlier, are essentially equity investors in the firm.[16] It is not only equity investors, however, who can be usefully enrolled as monitors of the firm. There can also be incentives for lenders to monitor firms in a way that improves the borrower's economic performance.

BANKS   Most firms that borrow obtain their money from a bank, which monitors the firm's financial health and only lends funds if it judges that repayment is likely. Short-term loans for working capital based on anticipated revenues are the major business of commercial banks. For example, a bank might make a seasonal loan to a farmer to hire workers for a harvest, expecting to be repaid when the harvest is sold. Similarly, the bank might lend to a toy manufacturer to finance a build-up of inventories in anticipation of Christmas sales. In the months before Christmas, the manufacturer needs money to pay wages, to acquire supplies, to pay rent on the factory building, and so on. From the banker's point of view, the chances that the firm can repay the loan after the Christmas season may appear to be good, especially if the firm has received advance orders from retailers and if it has successfully marketed its toys in the past.

Longer-term bank loans are an important feature of business in other countries,

---

[15] See "Punters or Proprietors: Survey of Capitalism," *The Economist* (May 5, 1990).

[16] In fact, in return for their investments venture capitalists typically receive preferred stock that can, at their option, be converted to regular common stock. This conversion is usually made when the firm sells its stock to the public. Until then, the venture capitalists' preferred stock gives them the protection of having a prior claim on the firm, ahead of the holders of common equity.

where they often represent the bulk of external financing, even for large firms. In these cases, each firm typically has an ongoing relationship with a "main bank." This bank may have a representative on the firm's board of directors and will have close, ongoing contacts with management. It may also hold some stock in the firm. It is thus in a good position to monitor the firm's health and the safety of its loans.

BONDHOLDERS   When lenders are simply the purchasers of the firm's bonds in the debt markets, they have less direct access to information and less direct say in operating decisions. In this case, they may insist on covenants in the bond contracts which limit the actions that the firm can take. Such covenants are designed to protect the value of the bonds against opportunistic behavior by managers (on their own behalf or in the interests of shareholders). For example covenants may limit the firm's right to issue new debt of equal or greater seniority in order to prevent undercutting the value of the existing bonds by giving other borrowers higher priority on the firm's cash flow. Other covenants may limit investments in totally new lines of business or might restrict the sale or pledging of major assets to ensure that they are available to secure repayment of the bonds.

The bondholders in RJR Nabisco, for example, suffered very large losses— estimated at perhaps $1 billion—on the market prices of their bonds when the firm went through its LBO because the huge debt load it took on made their claims much more uncertain: Essentially, the highly rated bonds became junk. The assets the company then sold to meet immediate debt service requirements arguably turned this risk into reality and became the basis of a lawsuit by the Metropolitan Life Insurance Company, which held RJR Nabisco debt with a face (nominal) value of a quarter of a billion dollars. These events illustrate the value to lenders of including appropriate covenants in bond agreements.

LONG-TERM LENDERS   Long-term loans are sometimes granted by banks and other lenders (such as insurance companies) to finance the purchase of specific major assets, which are then used as security for the loan. Mortgages on real estate are a familiar example, but other assets can also be financed in this way. For example, an airline might borrow to purchase an airplane, with the plane being subject to seizure by the lender if the airline fails to make its payments of interest and principal. New airplanes are especially popular security for loans because there is an active secondary market for planes and the planes are easily relocated to the airline where they are most valuable.

A popular variation of this practice is the use of a long-term lease, in which the lender buys an asset from a company and then leases it back to the company to use in its business. Once again, airplanes are a popular example. The lease agreement may also stipulate that after a fixed period of time, the airline company has the right to purchase the plane for some bargain price. Such a lease is almost the same as a loan because the airline is committed to pay the amounts in the contract over a period of years and stands to lose the plane if it defaults. Among the main differences are the tax treatment and the treatment in bankruptcy: Leased airplanes do not belong to the airline. In 1991 Trans World Airlines faced the prospect that its planes might be seized just as its peak summer season approached because it had failed to meet scheduled payments on a number of its aircraft and jet engines.

Default and Bankruptcy Costs

Sometimes firms are unable or unwilling to meet their loan payments on schedule, and the lenders then must choose between extending the time allowed the borrower to repay the loan or forcing the borrower into bankruptcy to collect what they can. Both options are costly. If the lenders extend the loan, the firm may sink deeper into

502

Finance:
Investments,
Capital Structure,
and Corporate
Control

financial problems and become still less able to pay. There may also be adverse reputation effects with other borrowers. Forced bankruptcy usually means that the firm is liquidated. The firm is then nothing more than a collection of used physical assets that may have to be sold at a deep discount. In contrast, if it stays in operation, the firm has much more: As a going concern it has a team of knowledgeable managers and employees, trademarks and brand names, business systems, and established supplier and customer relationships that are all needed if the assets are to generate any income. Some of these values may be lost in bankruptcy, and the employees may be thrown out of work, at least temporarily. In the interim, the firm's managers are distracted from running what is left of the business.

Bankruptcy proceedings also create legal and administrative costs that may, if the lawyers are effective maximizers, absorb a huge fraction of the net value left in the company. Further, the conflict between management and lenders is intensified in bankruptcy proceedings, leading to additional losses of value. Influence costs are incurred as the claimants to the firm's resources—creditors of various sorts, workers, governments (if taxes are owed), shareholders, and the lawyers representing each group—struggle to claim as large a share as possible.

Even the prospect of bankruptcy can be costly. If employees and managers are encouraged to develop firm-specific human capital by the promise that they will share in the returns it generates, then the fear that bankruptcy will deprive them of the promised quasi-rents may lead to inadequate investment. Also, when the firm is in financial difficulties, management may be led to take unwise risks. If these turn out well, the employees' and managers' jobs will be saved, whereas the chances are that they are lost if the risks are not taken. Moreover, suppliers of a firm that is in financial trouble will be reluctant to extend credit and, estimating that their relationships with the firm are less valuable because it may fail, they will be less willing to invest in maintaining these relationships and may cut quality, be slow with deliveries, and so on.

The larger the amount of debt relative to equity financing, the greater is the probability of the firm's being unable to meet required payments, and the greater is the expected value of the costs that are incurred in bankruptcy.

CHAPTER 11 BANKRUPTCIES   These costs of forced bankruptcy and liquidation help explain the existence of the Chapter 11 provision in U.S. bankruptcy law and similar provisions in other countries. Firms that declare Chapter 11 bankruptcy are given protection from their creditors (that is, the creditors cannot seize assets or force immediate liquidation for nonpayment), and current management is allowed to try to reorganize the firms' activities to make them profitable again. This means that a plan is put forward to pay the creditors only part of their claims, with any debts incurred after declaring Chapter 11 getting first priority. The creditors ultimately must approve the planned reorganization for it to be accepted by the courts, and if they cannot or do not agree, then forced liquidation follows. Typically, however, management has at least six months at least to come up with a plan, and in fact the firm may continue in Chapter 11 almost indefinitely.

Without this institution, firms that were basically healthy but suffering from short-term cash-flow problems would be at the mercies of their creditors. A single creditor among many, fearing for its loan or refusing to renegotiate terms when other lenders are willing, could force liquidation of the firm. The result might be that good firms would be liquidated, with all the attendant costs, when they optimally should have continued in business.

INFORMAL "WORKOUTS"   Although Chapter 11 reorganizations in bankruptcy may save on the costs of forced liquidations, they too have their costs. In particular, lawyers' fees can be immense, eating up more than ever flows through to claimants. A particularly disturbing example involves the U.S. asbestos manufacturers that declared Chapter 11 bankruptcy when the immense claims against them as a result of incidents of asbestos-related diseases began to emerge. In these cases, legal costs were $1.70 for every $1 that the plaintiffs received.[17]

In response to these costs of bankruptcy, **informal debt workouts** have emerged. Under these, the firm and its creditors bargain over rescheduling debt payments and over the amounts that ultimately are to be repaid. We have already discussed how, in the presence of debt overhang, it can be beneficial for a lender to reduce its claim, and the same principles apply when bankruptcy is threatened. Although the courts are not directly involved in these negotiations, the possibility of Chapter 11 bankruptcy lurks in the background and influences the bargaining, as does the ultimate threat of forced liquidation.

This bargaining results in shifts of gains and losses among claimants relative to their contractual claims. Under forced liquidation, the holders of senior debt have absolute, contractual priority on the available funds (after the bankruptcy lawyers, the taxing authorities, and wage earners). Junior or subordinated debt comes next in line, then preferred shares, and, finally, common stock. The courts typically enforce these priorities. However, the costs of bankruptcy mean that it may be advantageous to give up some claims in Chapter 11 negotiations to save the dissipation of value that would result from pushing for forced liquidation. Meanwhile, the rules under Chapter 11 give junior debt, preferred stock, and common equity some say in accepting or rejecting a proposed reorganization. These rules in turn give them bargaining power in the negotiations in workouts. In each case, it may be better to have a slice of a larger pie than all of a smaller one.

Over the course of 41 Chapter 11 bankruptcies examined in a recent study, junior claimants managed to extract $878 million that contractually was owed to senior debtholders.[18] Of this $878 million, junior debtholders gained more than half and the owners of common stock gained a third, despite their arguably having no valid claim at all. In 47 workouts examined in the same study, senior debt gave up almost $1.4 billion to which it was contractually entitled. Most of this went to common stock: Although it had no legal claim, it had the power to declare Chapter 11 bankruptcy.

STRATEGIC ASSET DESTRUCTION   The equity holders and managers of a firm in financial distress may actually face incentives to destroy the value of the firm's assets to improve their bargaining position in negotiating with the firm's creditors. To see how such perverse incentives could arise, consider a firm with assets and liabilities of $10 million, so that there is just enough value in the firm to satisfy its creditors' claims arising from the resources they have provided, leaving nothing for the shareholders. If management destroys part of the firm's value, the entire cost falls on the creditors. By threatening such asset destruction, management might be able to win concessions from the creditors for itself and the shareholders. For example, if management is in a position to destroy $2 million in value, the creditors are better off abandoning up to $2 million of their claims in return for not having the assets destroyed.

Of course, the same sort of incentives exist if the firm's assets are smaller than

---

[17] James S. Kakalik, et.al., "Costs of Asbestos Litigation," (Santa Monica, CA: Institute for Civil Justice, Rand Corporation, Publication R-3042-1CJ, 1983).

[18] Julian Franks and Walter Torous, "How Firms Fare in Workouts and Chapter 11 Reorganizations," London Business School working paper (May 1991), as reported in "Economics Focus: The Kindness of Chapter 11," *The Economist* (May 25, 1991), 83.

504

Finance:
Investments,
Capital Structure,
and Corporate
Control

its liabilities, although the bankruptcy court may be able to provide creditors with some protection. More strikingly, there can be incentives for asset destruction even when the firm is solvent. For example, suppose that the firm has liabilities of $10 million but assets worth $10.1 million and that it is still possible to destroy $2 million in value. If management now destroys $100 thousand in value and threatens to destroy the remaining $1.9 million, the creditors find themselves in much the same situation as in the previous paragraph. It is distinctly possible that they then will be willing to make enough concessions to management and the equity holders that these groups are better off than when the assets were intact. Of course, if all sides recognize these incentives, it may be possible to exact concessions without ever destroying the assets' value. On the other hand, some asset destruction might be needed to make the threat credible.

The obvious way to avoid this problem is to ensure that the firm's assets are so much larger than its debt obligations that it will never be worthwhile to destroy value as a bargaining ploy. This means that there must be some minimal share of equity in the firm's financial structure.

Financial Structure, Incentives, and Value

The incentive and rights aspects of financial structure provide ample reason to challenge the Modigliani-Miller theorems' conclusions that financial decisions cannot affect value. A firm's capital structure affects the incentives and behavior of its managers, lenders, and equity holders, as well as the likelihood of incurring the costs of bankruptcy. Changing the financing of the firm changes incentives, and the resulting real changes in behavior affect the returns that are generated. These in turn determine what the firm is worth to outside investors, and consequently what they will be willing to pay.

However, it is not just simple financial indicators like the debt-equity ratio that determine these incentives. The number of shares held by the management team, the concentration of ownership among large outside investors, the composition and powers of the board of directors, the restrictive clauses in loan agreements and bond contracts, and the anticipated sharing of available resources in the event the firm gets into financial trouble all affect incentives and behavior.

A first pass at a theory of the optimal financial structure of the firm would recognize the complex, interacting incentive effects of different financing decisions and the tradeoffs that must be made. It would then recommend that structure that balances these tradeoffs in a manner that is value-maximizing in the context of the particular firm in question. For example, other things being equal, highly profitable firms in markets that have little growth potential should carry more debt and have less equity financing in order to deal with the incentive problems of free cash flow. A prime example here might be the tobacco business in the United States because the industry generates immense cash flow but its market is shrinking. The oil business in the late 1970s and early 1980s may be another because, at least at that time, the industry was highly profitable but overexpanded. As another example of the trade-offs, debt should be lower in firms with largely intangible assets that may be particularly susceptible to being opportunistically destroyed by management acting in its own interests or those of the equity holders during debt renegotiations. In this regard, it is notable that physical-capital intensive industries, like public utilities, airlines, and steel producers, are heavily debt financed, although avoiding the costs of bankruptcy would argue for low debt in volatile industries like the latter two. In contrast, industries where assets are less tangible, such as high-tech firms and advertising agencies, are primarily financed by equity.

Although the incentive and rights aspects of financial structure are surely important, there is even more to be considered.

SIGNALING AND FINANCIAL DECISIONS

It is well established empirically that increases in the amount of equity the firm issues lower the firm's share price (and decreases in the number of shares increase their price), whereas increases in debt tend to increase the share price. Further, in transactions involving more complex securities (such as preferred stock or convertible debt) or simultaneous buying and selling of different securities (such as borrowing to finance a share repurchase), the more "equity-like" is the security being issued, the more negative is the effect on share prices.[19] A variety of signaling models will explain these patterns.

Regardless of how diligent investors may be in monitoring their investments, the management of the firm will usually be much better informed about the firm's prospects than will most outside investors: Managers and investors are asymmetrically informed. As we have discussed in earlier chapters, conditions of asymmetric information create incentives for the relatively uninformed parties to draw inferences from the choices made by the better-informed parties. The informed parties, if they recognize that their actions are being interpreted as signals, may attempt to manipulate the signals to convey a particularly favorable message. Financial decisions can serve as just this kind of signal.

Debt and Equity

Suppose managers gain when the stock price of the firm is higher and that they lose personally if the firm goes bankrupt. The former effect might arise from their having personal stock holdings or incentive contracts. Management could lose in bankruptcy because they enjoy quasirents in their current employment in the form of high pay, perks, status, and independence in their decision making about the firm's activities or because their professional reputations are harmed by failure. Debt financing is costly for these managers because the higher the level of debt, the higher the probability of having to suffer the costs of bankruptcy. However, managers whose firms have higher expected cash flows face a lower probability of bankruptcy than do those with otherwise similar earnings distributions. Finally, assume that the market values higher earnings distributions but cannot observe them directly, but that the managers can.

A signaling equilibrium in this context involves managers with higher distributions of earnings adopting higher debt levels. A higher debt level then signals a better distribution of returns to the market, which responds by assigning a higher value to the firm. This higher value is sufficient to compensate managers with good return distributions for the increased risk of facing bankruptcy that comes with increased debt. It is not enough to induce managers whose returns are poor to take on the same level of debt, however, because the same amount of debt is more likely to lead them into bankruptcy.

According to this theory, when a firm's earnings prospects improve significantly, it will be led to change its financial structure, increasing the role of debt. The market will then read this as signaling the underlying change in the managers' private information about returns and will bid up the value of the firm. In contrast, worsened

---

[19] See J. Fred Weston, Kwang S. Chung, and Susan E. Hoag, *Mergers, Restructuring, and Corporate Control* (Englewood Cliffs, NJ: Prentice-Hall, 1990), p. 125, for a more precise statement and Milton Harris and Arthur Raviv, "The Theory of Capital Structure," *Journal of Finance*, 46 (March 1991), 297–355 for a variety of references to the original studies that found these patterns.

506

Finance:
Investments,
Capital Structure,
and Corporate
Control

prospects will lead managers to want to issue more equity because the risk of bankruptcy is now too high. New equity issues will signal bad news to the market, and it will respond by marking down the value of the firm.

A related model uses managerial risk aversion as the source of the differences in the costs of signaling across differently informed managers that is needed to support a signaling equilibrium. More leverage allows insiders to keep more of the equity for themselves, which is most beneficial when management expects high earnings. Risk aversion means that holding risky equity is costly, but the cost of risk bearing is the same regardless of the level of expected returns. Thus, management that expects higher returns is inclined to issue more debt and less equity, so sophisticated investors would interpret a debt issue as a signal of high anticipated earnings. This implication for stock price reactions to changes in financing is again consistent with the observed pattern.

REAL EFFECTS   The investor reactions described in this section represent a problem for firms trying to raise equity capital. The very act of selling shares drives down the share price, to the detriment of the firm's founders. The signaling analyses suggest that the problem is worst for young firms, when the uncertainty about the firm's quality and prospects is greatest, because it is then that the insiders' information advantage is likely to be greatest. This perspective helps to explain the reliance of young firms on bankers and venture capitalists, who invest resources to acquire information about the firm, its prospects, and its operational needs, and use that information to form their own judgments without needing to rely extensively on management's signals. All of this is expensive, of course, and adds to the firm's cost of raising capital. Once the firm has an established record of performance, reducing the uncertainties facing individual investors, these losses can be significantly reduced.

Dividends, Monitoring, and Signaling

Just as incentive and signaling arguments can provide a basis for understanding the choice of financial structure and some of the empirical regularities regarding actual capital structure patterns, so too can they give insight into dividend policy. Dividends present a puzzle that goes beyond the Modigliani-Miller irrelevance proposition. In many countries, capital gains (wealth changes arising from increases in the value of assets) are taxed much less heavily than are dividend receipts. For example, some countries have no tax on capital gains at all, whereas dividends are taxed as ordinary income. In the United States, capital gains are now taxed at the same rate as regular income, but only when they are realized by selling the asset. This allows the taxpayer to defer the tax liability. Further, given the peculiarities of U.S. tax laws, it may be possible for people to avoid the tax altogether by passing the appreciated assets on to their heirs. This suggests that firms would increase (private, if not social) value by returning earnings to investors in other forms than dividend payments, such as repaying debt or buying back some outstanding shares. Yet not only do firms pay dividends, but the market on average reacts favorably to increases in dividend payments.

An immediate objection to the suggestion of not paying dividends is that some shareholders look to them for current income. However, this need could be met by selling a portion of the appreciating portfolio. The firm could even offer to repurchase the shares. Unless the transaction costs of selling shares are very high, the puzzle remains.

A variety of signaling models can help rationalize the practice of paying dividends, with dividends again signaling management's private information about future cash flows. One, mentioned earlier, is that a firm that anticipates a future cash flow problem may try to conserve its current cash resources by cutting its dividend.

Similarly, a firm that anticipates an improving cash flow may be willing to increase its dividend. Investors, reading these changes as signals about insiders' well-informed expectations, may respond by bidding up the price of a firm that raises its dividend and bidding down the price of a firm that cuts its dividend.

Dividends may also serve incentive roles. Paying them removes resources from the firm and so helps overcome some of the difficulties of free cash flow: Shareholders who might have a difficult time monitoring management's investment decisions and expenditures can easily tell if they are getting the dividends that they demand. This incentive effect argues for dividends being higher in slow-growth industries than ones with good investment opportunities. Dividends also force firms to go to the capital markets more frequently than otherwise would be necessary. This in turn may facilitate investors' monitoring management's performance and putting checks on bad investments that would otherwise be difficult to prevent if retained earnings could be used for financing.

Objectives in Selecting Financial Structure

Given these theories and the evidence that capital and ownership structures affect value, the next step is to ask how they will be chosen. Will the capital structure be chosen to maximize the market value of the firm, that is, the total amount that the founders of the firm can collect for all the claims to the firm's assets? The strongest theoretical argument favoring this conclusion is that a firm's founders will want to extract as much value as possible when they sell the firm, and consequently would choose the capital structure that maximizes the firm's market value. Any other choice means that the amount the founders can realize from the firm is less.

More generally, however, if the firm's founders expect to participate actively in the firm's management even after the financing is completed, they might value their independence as managers to make the choices they prefer as well as the cash they receive from selling claims to the firm's earnings. If the investors in the firm buy shares and make loans in competitive markets, then they can expect to gain nothing from the transaction because this investment opportunity will be priced to be equally as good as their next best opportunity. Because capital structure decisions will not affect the welfare of new investors, an efficient choice of capital structure entails the founder-managers' most preferred combination of personal control and net proceeds received from loans and the sale of shares.

After the departure of the founder, control of the firm will typically pass to professional managers operating under the oversight of a board of directors. Will these parties be motivated to continue to make the capital structure choices that are value-maximizing as circumstances change? More generally, will the choices they make on the whole variety of issues confronting the firm be the ones that shareholders would want? What mechanisms ensure that firms that are not being run well are redirected, with managers who are not performing and with boards that do not provide the proper incentives being replaced by ones who will?

CORPORATE CONTROL

Financial securities are not just claims on return streams. They also give decision and control rights. For example, stockholders have the right to elect boards of directors to represent them in monitoring, motivating, and disciplining managers and in overseeing strategy. They can also vote to replace directors who are not performing these tasks to their satisfaction. Furthermore, in many countries the corporation cannot sell off the bulk of its assets or merge itself out of existence without a shareholder vote. Creditors can typically force a firm that is in default to liquidate assets, and in the

508

Finance:
Investments,
Capital Structure,
and Corporate
Control

United States they have the right to approve or reject any reorganization plans under Chapter 11 bankruptcy. They can also sue to enforce restrictions on the debtor's behavior which are written into the debt contracts. These powers, even when not actually exercised, can affect economic performance.

The transferability of securities (especially equity shares) and the rights they give are also the basis for the **market for corporate control**. The functioning of this market can be another important determinant of managerial and corporate performance. Assets that would be more valuable under different management can be purchased, and control of them can be vested with those who can use them best. In particular, corporations with poorly performing management teams whose boards have failed to discipline them are subject to having a controlling block of their shares acquired by investors who will replace the incumbents with new managers who will realize the firms' potential and new directors who will ensue that they do this.

This market for corporate control was especially active in the 1980s, with mergers and acquisitions, takeovers, and leveraged buyouts. During that period, managers and boards discovered many ways to protect their companies from irresponsible raiders and themselves from market discipline. The market has quieted since then, although it remains a force. The protective measures remain, however. The diminished disciplinary role of the market for control coupled with the increased power of incumbents to entrench themselves has led a number of institutional investors to look for new methods to increase their abilities to monitor and discipline management.

The Mechanics of Control

Two options are open to dissatisfied shareholders: "exit"—sell their shares—and "voice"—vote against the current board.[20] Neither of these is a perfect solution. Selling means suffering the low price that attaches to the shares of a poorly performing firm. Casting a vote against management may be a futile gesture. This is especially the case because management and the board typically control the processes for nominations in board elections and for putting resolutions to a shareholder ballot. There may simply be no alternative to vote for. Tender offers and proxy contests are responses to these problems.

TENDER OFFERS   In a tender offer, the person or entity making the offer invites shareholders to sell (tender) their stocks at an announced price. The offer may be for some or all the stock, and it may or may not be conditional on a certain number of shares being tendered for sale. It may also be a "multitiered" offering, at least in the United States, with a certain fraction of the shares being offered one price and the remainder being paid lower prices. (The United Kingdom's Takeover Code bans paying less to minority shareholders once 30 percent of the shares have been acquired.) Firms themselves might make tender offers to buy back their own stock in recapitalizations that decrease retained cash or increase debt while lowering equity. This is how management buyouts and other going-private transactions are accomplished. The other use of a tender offer is for outsiders to gain control of the firm in a takeover, whether friendly or hostile.

The idea in a hostile tender-offer takeover is that the raider, having obtained the firm's stock, will vote it to replace the existing board. The new board will then order management to implement a new strategy designed to generate better performance. Often, the current management will be replaced and new management

---

[20] These terms are due to Albert Hirschmann, who has applied the concepts much more broadly. See his *Exit, Voice and Loyalty* (Cambridge, MA: Harvard University Press, 1970).

brought in to implement the strategy, or the firm may be merged into one already held by the buyer.[21] The promise of the better performance means that the raider can bid more than the current price of the shares.

PROXY CONTESTS AND SHAREHOLDER RESOLUTIONS   Few shareholders in a large, broadly held firm find it worthwhile to attend the annual shareholders' meeting at which directors are elected and other shareholder votes are taken. Instead, they give a *proxy* to someone else to vote on their behalf. Management includes a form soliciting proxies for itself when it sends notice of the annual meeting and normally receives the vast bulk of the proxies. In a proxy contest, another entity seeks to obtain shareholders' proxies in order to vote them against management and the current board. This allows changing control without the expense of having to acquire a controlling block of shares from the current owners. However, proxy contests are expensive and difficult to organize and win, and the gains from reorganization are broadly spread among all the stockholders. Thus they may suffer from a free-rider problem.

A shareholder resolution is a measure requesting or instructing the board and management to follow particular policies. Examples might be to renounce a previously adopted poison pill[22] or to avoid using animals in research. They represent stockholder attempts to direct the affairs of the corporation without replacing the board or management. Shareholder resolutions are restricted by law in many countries. For example, under U.S. Securities and Exchange Commission rules in effect through 1990, shareholders had no right to vote on executive compensation issues, which were deemed to be an ordinary business decision that is reserved for the board of directors. This particular rule was, however, revamped in 1991 in light of the popular concern and complaints about excessive CEO pay.

BANKRUPTCY AND CONTROL   In bankruptcy, the control structure of a corporation shifts. In an involuntary bankruptcy (a Chapter 7 bankruptcy in U.S. law), the court appoints a receiver or trustee to wind up the business and liquidate its assets. Management and the board, as representatives of the most junior claimants, the stockholders, lose control, and to the extent that any business decisions are made, they are supposed to be taken in the interests of the more senior claimants. Under Chapter 11 voluntary reorganization bankruptcies, current management retains some control: It is allowed time to develop a plan to reorganize the firm, pay some fraction of its debts as settlement of the claims against it, and reposition it to be profitable. For a plan to be accepted, two-thirds of the creditors, of the preferred stockholders, and of the shareholders must each vote for it. If no agreement is ultimately reached, then the creditors can force the firm into Chapter 7 bankruptcy and liquidation. Meanwhile the firm continues to operate. If the creditors believe that management is wasting the existing value of the firm and further depleting the resources available to meet their claims, they may seek to have the court appoint a trustee to take over operations. This is unlikely to happen, however, until management has had reasonable time to develop a plan and have it win approval unless the depletion of assets is too egregious. For example, the creditors of now-defunct Eastern Airlines complained bitterly but with little effect about the additional losses it incurred during its extended period of operating in bankruptcy.

---

[21] Even if only a majority of the shares are purchased, then the acquired firm may still be merged into another by vote of the new board. The stockholders in the acquired firm whose stock was not purchased originally must be compensated for their holdings when the firm ceases to exist, but they are largely unable to prevent the merger.

[22] These are described in Chapter 6.

510

Finance:
Investments,
Capital Structure,
and Corporate
Control

Takeovers and Restructurings in the United States in the 1980s

Although the market for corporate control was especially active throughout the 1980s, there were some real differences in the sorts of transactions pursued over the course of the decade. In the early period much of the activity involved oil companies' buying one another, acquiring other firms in a continuing pattern of diversification, and being subject to hostile attacks themselves—sometimes from other oil companies. Food, lumber, banking and finance, and insurance firms were also heavily involved in the activity in this period. Later, there was much less industry specificity, and towards the end of the decade it seemed that any firm might be a target. However, it does seem that targets tended to be firms with low market valuations relative to the replacement costs of their assets.

Junk bonds were not a factor until the middle of the 1980s, when Michael Milken showed their potential and created a large secondary market in them. Earlier, financing was by cash, stock, or private placement of subordinated debt. LBOs also were not a major factor in the early part of the decade, but they became so in the second half. The nature of the LBOs changed as well. Early on they tended to be relatively small and to involve divisions of corporations or firms in a single business. Until 1985 the organizations involved in buyouts by KKR averaged only 6,351 employees and $834 million in revenues.[23] Then came the Beatrice and Safeway deals. With the continuing flow of smaller buyouts, these raised the averages through early 1988 to 37,000 employees and $4.8 billion in revenues. However, Safeway alone had more revenues and almost as many employees as all of KKR's previous buyouts together. The RJR Nabisco deal of course dwarfed them all. This pattern was not unique to KKR. There were still some buyouts of small, single product firms, but the later part of the decade also saw transactions involving huge, diversified companies. This activity continued, at a much slower pace, into the 1990s.

Throughout the period, despite all the attention focused on hostile takeovers, they were actually a small part of the activity in the corporate control market. For example, in 1986, there were only 40 hostile tender offers out of the 3,336 transactions listed in the W.T. Grimm *Mergerstat Review* series. There were another 110 tender offers unopposed by management, and the rest were negotiated transactions agreed to by management (although perhaps with the threat of a hostile tender offer in the background).[24]

TAKEOVER PREMIA   In the average control change, the existing shareholders received a price that was 30 to 50 percent higher than the price at which their shares had previously been trading, and sometimes this **takeover premium** was over 100 percent. For example, shares of RJR Nabisco stock had been trading in the mid-forties before the bidding war that began after management proposed a buyout. The final price paid by KKR was $108 a share: $80 in cash, with the rest in preferred stock and debentures. Similarly, when Bridgestone Tire launched its bid to take over Firestone, the total market value of Firestone's shares was about $1 billion. The final price paid was $2.6 billion. Firestone's shareholders thus enjoyed a takeover premium of about $1.6 billion, or 160 percent. There is some evidence that the magnitude of premia rose over the decade, and they were much higher than in the 1960s. Over the ten-year period up to 1986, the premia paid to selling-firm shareholders totaled $346 billion

---

[23] William F. Long and David J. Ravenscraft, "The Record of LBO Performance," Arnold W. Sametz, ed., *The Battle for Corporate Control* (Homewood, IL: Business One Irwin, 1991).

[24] Michael C. Jensen, "Takeovers: Their Causes and Consequences," *Journal of Economic Perspectives*, 2 (Winter 1988), 21–48.

(in 1986 dollars), which was equal to almost 45 percent of the value of corporate dividend payments over the same period.[25]

In contrast, the shares of acquiring firms on average did not change in value or fell slightly during these transactions.[26] This average, however, masks some significant variability. For example, the shareholders of Occidental Petroleum lost $365 million when their firm acquired Midcon as a white knight, and Marriott's stockholders lost $162 million when their firm acquired Saga in a hostile takeover that paid Saga's shareholders a premium of $148 million.[27] In the 29 hostile takeover attempts in the United States from 1984 through 1986 with values over $50 million where the change in bidding firms' stockholder wealth could be computed, there were losses in 16 cases and gains in 13. The losses totalled $1.25 billion; the gains totalled $508 million. On average, the buyers' stockholders lost $15 million, but this is negligible next to the average transaction value of $1.74 billion.[28]

The stockholders at the time of the transactions thus did very well in total, with most of the gains apparently accruing to the stockholders in the acquired firm. But do their gains represent value creation and increased efficiency or something else? What accounts for the takeover premia?

POSSIBLE SOURCES OF THE GAINS

Overpaying.   One obvious possibility is that the buyers paid too much. This might have occurred as a result of "hubris," with the acquirers' overestimating their ability to add value, but it would have been especially likely when the management of the acquiring firms were intent on building empires, diversifying, or pursuing other strategies that were not in stockholders' interests. This certainly cannot account for the whole of the premia, however, because if it were we should have expected to see bidders' stock prices fall approximately one-for-one with the rise in the targets' prices when they attempted acquisitions. Nevertheless, it may have been a factor, at least in some cases: There is evidence that bidders' stock prices did tend to decline when the acquisitions appeared to be motivated by managerial considerations.[29]

Stock Market Mispricing.   Some critics claim that the premia were simply evidence that stock market valuations are highly inaccurate and that the buying firms were acquiring underpriced firms whose long-term strategies were not properly understood and valued by the market. This is why they could afford to pay the premia. The accuracy of stock market valuations remains a hotly disputed topic, and it is certainly

---

[25] *Ibid.*

[26] Michael Bradley, Anand Desai and E. Han Kim, "Synergistic Gains from Corporate Acquisitions and their Division Between the Stockholders of Target and Acquiring Firms," *Journal of Financial Economics*, 21 (1988), 3–40.

[27] Sanjai Bhagat, Andrei Shleifer, and Robert W. Vishny, "Hostile Takeovers in the 1980s: The Return to Corporate Specialization," *Brookings Papers: Microeconomics 1990* (Washington: Brookings Institution, 1990). These figures are based on estimating (via CAPM methods) what the price of the stock in question would have been on the date the transaction was completed versus what it actually was. Such losses were not unique to North American takeovers. A similar calculation done by Evan Davis and Graham Bannock ["The Nestle Takeover of Rowntree," David Hume Institute Paper 31 (1991)] indicates that the shareholders in the Swiss firm Nestle lost £500 million in stock market value when their firm acquired Rowntree, the British candy company, for £2.6 billion, or about 2.7 times what its market value had been ten months earlier.

[28] Bhagat, Shleifer, and Vishny, *op. cit.* These acquisitions were by publicly traded companies; the returns to raiders operating through private companies could not be computed.

[29] Randall Morck, Andrei Shleifer, and Robert W. Vishny, "Characteristics of Hostile and Friendly Takeover Targets," Alan J. Auerbach, ed., *Corporate Takeovers: Causes and Consequences* (Chicago: University of Chicago Press, 1988), pp. 101–29.

512

Finance:
Investments,
Capital Structure,
and Corporate
Control

possible that this argument is correct. However, the available evidence indicates that LBOs and takeovers were concentrated on firms and industries that were not R&D-intensive and that firms with high R&D expenditures were not more vulnerable to takeovers, as this undervalued stock theory would suggest they should have been.[30] The takeover targets in the United States between 1977 and 1987 had accounted for less than two percent of total U.S. R&D spending even before the takeovers occurred.[31]

A related argument is that the raiders diverted firms from a proper long-term focus to an emphasis on short-term performance, which the market is asserted to value relatively too highly. However, except in the oil business (which was arguably overexpanded anyway), there is little evidence of cutbacks in R&D or other investments following mergers or takeovers as would be expected if the buyers were intent on short-term gains. There is, on the other hand, evidence of cutbacks in R&D and other investments after management buyouts.[32] This is hardly support, however, for an argument that management had previously been producing unrecognized value by aiming for the long term, for when managements' ownership stake increased, it reduced investment.

A separate line of evidence regarding the possible mispricing of target shares involves the fact that when takeover attempts were defeated, the share price of the former targets tended to drop back to essentially their levels before the attempt. Given the close attention paid to firms when they are "in play," if there were really significant information that had not previously been incorporated in the share price, one would expect it to come out and for the stock price to have adjusted permanently to reflect it.

A stronger version of the underpriced-assets theory claims that the raiders were not even paying the full value of the firms they acquired. Thus, management had a duty to resist. The buyers in these takeovers did not obviously enjoy especially high returns after the takeovers, however, as might be expected if their purchases were a bargain (although performance does seem to have improved in many LBOs). In fact, as competition in the market for control intensified and court rulings forced companies "in play" in effect to conduct auctions, allowing and even encouraging competing bids, we might expect to see some overpaying for firms because of the "winner's curse" (see the box on the winner's curse for an explanation of this phenomenon.)

Transfers and Breach of Trust. Other critics argue that part of the premium represented not an increase in total value but transfers of value away from others with claims of the firms' cash flows. Control changes sometimes resulted in reductions in employment and wages. For instance, the reduction in total wages when Carl Icahn took over TWA in 1985 was about $200 million, which in itself was enough to justify the takeover premium. In Youngstown, Ohio, the layoffs that followed the 1979 takeover of Youngstown Sheet and Tube were followed within a year by a reduction in the median home sale price of 23 percent.[33] The holders of the targets' bonds or

---

[30] Abbie Smith, "Corporate Ownership Structure and Performance: The Case of Management Buyouts," draft, University of Chicago Graduate School of Business (1989); Bronwyn H. Hall, "The Effect of Takeover Activity on Corporate Research and Development," Alan J. Auerbach, ed., *Corporate Takeovers: Causes and Consequences* (Chicago: University of Chicago Press, 1988); and U. S. Securities and Exchange Commission, Office of the Chief Economist, "Institution Ownership, Tender Offers, and Long-Term Investment" (1985).

[31] Bronwyn Hall, *op. cit.*

[32] Stephen N. Kaplan, "The Effect of Management Buyouts on Operating Performance and Value," *Journal of Financial Economics*, 24 (October 1989), 217–54.

[33] These last two calculations are reported by Andrei Shleifer and Lawrence Summers in their paper, "Breach of Trust in Hostile Takeovers," A. Auerbach, ed., *Corporate Takeovers: Causes and Consequences* (Chicago: University of Chicago Press, 1988).

The Winner's Curse

Auctions are often used for the sale of properties of unknown value. Uncertainty is present whether the object of the bidding is drilling rights on an unexplored tract of land (Is there oil? How much?), timber rights to an area of forest (How many board feet of each type of wood is there?), or shares of a company (What is the profit potential of the widget division?). Bidders do their best to deal with that uncertainty by gathering information and making estimates of the underlying values. Because the factors underlying these estimates are themselves subjective and uncertain, there can be considerable variation among the bidders' estimates of the true underlying value.

This variation in estimates has an interesting consequence that has come to be called the *winner's curse*. A bidder is more likely to win when its estimate is too optimistic and it bids high than when its estimate is too pessimistic and it bids low. On average, then, the winning bidder tends to be one who has overestimated the value of the object being sold. In a similar fashion, contractors who bid for jobs may find that their bids are most likely to win when they have been too optimistic about the cost of doing the job. A bidder ignores these tendencies at its peril: Naive bidders may pay too much for the items they buy at auction or ask too low a price for the services they sell.

The winner's curse of overbidding was first noted by professionals in the oil industry. It shows up repeatedly in experimental settings. Experimental subjects are asked to bid for an envelope containing an amount of money after each has been given an unbiased estimate of the amount actually in the envelope. Predictably, the winner bids more than is actually in the envelope because his or her estimate was higher than the true amount and he or she failed to account for the fact that he or she would tend to win only when this was the case.

In the context of takeovers where several bidders are competing to acquire a firm, the winner's curse would mean that the successful bidder would frequently be one that overestimates what the target firm is worth and consequently pays too much for it.

preferred shares also might have lost if the value of their assets was reduced in the takeovers, with the gains being captured by target stockholders. Certainly, the value of RJR Nabisco's bonds were adversely affected in its takeover. Other takeovers resulted in reductions in taxes paid to the government because the increased debt reduced corporate tax liabilities, the upward revaluation of assets after the takeovers permitted greater deductions for depreciation and did not require payment of corporate capital gains taxes, and previous tax losses in one firm could be applied against the profits of the other after a merger.

Under the hypothesis of no wealth effects, simple transfers do not affect efficiency directly. Nevertheless, if the transfers are the returns from reneging on implicit contracts, there can be long-term costs. Employees, for example, may be much less willing to invest in firm specific assets and to remain loyal to the firm if they fear that the implicit promise to reward these sacrifices will be broken after some future change in control.

514

Finance:
Investments,
Capital Structure,
and Corporate
Control

According to recent studies, however, these transfers can account for only a fraction of the increase in the market value of firms. It is difficult to get any systematic evidence on wage changes, particularly relative to industry trends, but the one study to examine this issue found that wage cuts would explain a trivial percentage of the premium.[34] Bhagat, Shleifer, and Vishny found that layoffs occurred in only a fraction of all hostile takeovers and that they tended to be concentrated in the white-collar staff, particularly at corporate headquarters. Furthermore, layoffs were on average three times as large a fraction of the work force when the target successfully resisted as when the bidder was successful, and two-thirds larger when target management found a white knight to acquire the firm rather than its falling to the hostile bidder. In some cases the savings from labor are a significant part of the premium, but those cases are a small fraction of the total.[35] In any case, if the organization were inefficiently overstaffed, the reallocation of labor might increase efficiency. Similarly, transfers from bondholders and holders of preferred shares may have been substantial in some cases where there were not covenants in place, but it seems that bondholders on average did not lose from buyouts (at least in the early part of the period)[36] or hostile takeovers. Finally, tax considerations were clearly a factor in some control changes, especially where leverage increased significantly, but again they are not enough to explain more than a fraction of the premia on average.[37]

Value Creation. According to Bhagat, Vishny and Shleifer, the majority of the increase in the case of hostile takeovers was accounted for by the high prices paid by the final buyers of the divisions being sold, either in the original transaction or in the asset sales (bust-ups) that often followed. In most cases, these buyers were other firms in the same industry who used the purchases to expand their own operations. Advocates of takeovers argue that these buyers, firms that are specialists in the industry where they are buying, were better able to manage the divisions they acquired than the conglomerate firms had been, and that improved management accounted for the increase in value.[38]

These factors may also have been central in other control changes, but there are at least three other possible sources of value. First is simply the possibility that incompetent or self-serving managers were replaced. Second is the increased intensity of incentives that the LBOs typically provided: Managers came to hold a much higher fraction of the equity in the firm, were subjected to the performance pressures from the high debt levels, and—where a buyout firm was involved—were made subject to intense monitoring. Finally, in the oil and tobacco businesses and perhaps some others, the premia may have been simply a matter of returning free cash flow to the shareholders, with value being increased by managers' being unable to waste the corresponding resources on economically unjustified investments and diversification.

---

[34] Joshua Rosett, "Do Breaches Explain Takeover Premiums: The Evidence on Union Wages" (1990), as cited in Sanjai Bhagat, Andrei Shleifer, and Robert Vishny, "Hostile Takeovers in the 1980s: The Return to Corporate Specialization," *Brookings Papers: Microeconomics 1990*, 1 (Washington: Brookings Institution, 1990).

[35] Bhagat, Shleifer and Vishny, *op. cit.*

[36] Kenneth Lehn and Annette B. Poulsen, "Sources of Value in Leveraged Buyouts," M. Weidenbaum, ed., *Public Policy Toward Corporate Takeovers* (New Brunswick, NJ: Transaction Publishers, 1988).

[37] Bhagat, Shleifer and Vishny, *op. cit.*

[38] Critics sometimes contend that even this portion of the increase in value is partly a transfer, resulting from increased market power that enables the larger firm to charge higher prices rather than from any real social gain, but they offer no evidence to support this thesis.

Takeover Defenses

Various practices were spawned in the 1980s as the boards and management of potential target firms sought ways to defend their firms and themselves against attempted hostile takeovers. Some of these seem justified as devices to defend legitimate interests in an efficient way against threats by corporate raiders or to strengthen management's bargaining position to allow it to get the best possible price for the shareholders when the firm is eventually sold. Others, however, raise disturbing ethical and public policy questions.

INADEQUATE AND COERCIVE OFFERS   At first glance, it may be hard to see why there would be any need for takeover defenses at all, other than to protect entrenched managers and their allies on the board. If a takeover bid is below the underlying worth of the company, shareholders presumably will reject it. However, matters are actually somewhat more complicated.

First, it may be difficult for shareholders to know how much the firm is worth. They may thus be tempted to accept an offer when they might actually be able to get a better one. If management and the board of the target are working in their shareholders' interests, they should try to ensure that the firm is sold for the highest possible price. However, finding out how much can be obtained, even from the current bidder, may take time. For example, it might be necessary to find another bidder, so that competition could generate the highest possible price. Takeover defenses that allow management and the board to delay the process can thus provide value for shareholders.

Also, offers may actually be **coercive** in the sense that individual shareholders might feel pressure to sell even when they know that as a group they would be better off rejecting the bid. It is easiest to see how this can happen by considering a conditional offer to buy only a controlling stake in the firm. (Similar coercion could be felt by small stockholders in other forms of takeover bids.) Suppose that a raider makes a tender offer for 51 percent of a firm's shares at some price p_1, with the offer conditional on at least 51 percent of the shares being tendered. If the target is acquired, the buyer can vote to merge the target into another firm it owns, paying some lower amount p_2 for any outstanding shares that were not acquired initially.

Consider now the incentives facing a small shareholder—one small enough to ignore the impact of his or her tender decision on the likelihood the 51 percent level of tendering is reached. If the fraction of shares tendered is less than 51 percent, then it does not matter whether the individual tenders because no transactions will take place anyway. If 51 percent or more are being tendered, then the individual gets p_2 by not tendering but has some chance of receiving p_1 if he or she tenders. Thus, tendering is a "no-lose proposition": only by tendering can the shareholder have a chance of receiving the high price, p_1. Yet, there is no guaranty that p_1, let alone p_2, has to be an attractive price. In the United States, state laws would ensure that p_2 could not be too low relative to the pre-merger price of the target's stock, but both p_1 and p_2 might be much less than the stockholders thought the firm was worth, and they would still feel compelled to tender their shares![39]

---

[39] Strikingly, if the bidder simply attempts to buy a controlling interest and cannot prevent shareholders who do not tender from enjoying the full value of their share of the firm after the takeover, then the best strategy is for the small shareholders not to tender unless they are offered the full post-takeover value of their shares. Again, if no control change is going to occur, it does not matter what any individual does. If a change will occur even if the individual does not tender, then by tendering he or she gets the offered price, p. By not tendering, he or she gets v, the value under the new ownership. As long as $p < v$, it is better never to tender. Thus, takeover bids would succeed only when $p = v$, which would

516

Finance:
Investments,
Capital Structure,
and Corporate
Control

Although such coercion is theoretically possible, note that it depends on there being only a single bidder. Thus, its empirical significance and the justification it gives for takeover defenses is questionable. In particular, a management-led buyout would seem to eliminate the threat of coercion (unless the original bid is from management itself!).

TYPES OF DEFENSES   The variety of defenses developed is truly remarkable.[40] Poison pills (discussed in Chapter 6) raise the cost of a takeover by giving current shareholders extra claims if a control change occurs or even if a single entity acquires a threatening large holding of stock. **Differential voting rights** can give extra votes to shares that have been held for extended periods, so that a recent buyer of half the shares has only a small fraction of the votes. **Scorched earth policies** of various sorts deliberately reduce the firm's value to the bidder, even if it reduces value to shareholders in the process. For example, in resisting Mobil's takeover attempt, Marathon Oil gave USX an option to acquire its "crown jewel," the Yates oil field, at a bargain price if some other company gained control of Marathon.

A related but less-extreme technique involves **restructuring** the firm to make it harder for the raider to finance the debt taken on in the merger. For example, the firm might spin off attractive divisions that the raider might have counted on selling after the merger to raise funds for debt repayment. It might also reduce corporate cash holdings that also would facilitate servicing the post-takeover debt. Share repurchases are one possible way to accomplish this; another is to buy other companies at possibly inflated prices. **Classified** or **staggered boards**, where only a fraction of the members are up for election each year, and **supermajority rules**, which require as much as 90 percent of the votes to effect a control change, make it more difficult to gain control after buying what would otherwise be a controlling interest. These can be supplemented by putting a large block of shares in an Employee Stock Ownership Plan, on the assumption that the shares will be voted for management because employees will be worried about losing their jobs in a takeover. **Antitakeover statutes** passed by the state government where the firm is incorporated, such as those passed by Minnesota to protect Dayton Hudson, are also a possibility, and the firm can also move its **state of incorporation** to one with protective rules. This list just scratches the surface.

Each of these would be just a means for entrenching managers but for the fact that, for many of them, their application can be waived at the option of the board of directors. This means that they can be used to strengthen the board's bargaining position as well as to thwart an unwelcome offer. Of course, they are waived when the board and management is positively disposed to the offer. To get a flavor of the effects of these different sorts of measures, we consider three in more detail.

GOLDEN PARACHUTES   As discussed in Chapter 13, a *golden parachute* is a clause in a compensation contract providing for very attractive benefits in the event that a manager leaves after a control change. Among the most important arguments that have been advanced in favor of golden parachutes is that career executives have a legitimate right to expect protection of the rewards that have been earned by years of hard, skillful work. Moreover, without adequate protection, executives would mount fierce resistance against any attempt to undermine those rights, making worthwhile

---

leave no return for the bidder (even to cover its costs) unless it were able to obtain some block of shares before making the tender offer

[40] See J. Fred Weston, Kwang S. Chung, and Susan B. Hoag, *Mergers, Restructuring and Corporate Control* (Englewood Cliffs, NJ: Prentice Hall, 1990), Chapter 20 for a much more complete discussion.

Paramount and Time Warner: In Whose Interests?

Time Inc., the largest U.S. magazine publisher (*Time*, *Fortune*, *People*, *Sports Illustrated*) acquired Warner Brothers, the movie, television production, and record company (Warner/Reprise and Atlantic) in early 1990, but most observers regarded the transaction as a Warner takeover of Time. Time and Warner were in merger negotiations, a transaction that the shareholders would have had to approve, when Paramount Communications (movies and sports plus publishing—it owns Prentice Hall) made a $200 a share, all-cash offer for all of Time's stock. Backed by a landmark court ruling that a board had a right to "just say 'no'" to a takeover offer without consulting shareholders, Time bought Warner, paying what knowledgeable observers regarded as a hefty premium. Carrying out the transaction this way meant it did not have to go to a vote of Time's shareholders, who might have preferred to sell their shares to Paramount.

Time's management argued that its intrinsic worth in combination with Warner was about $250 a share, so that the Paramount offer of $200 was totally inadequate. However, the market price of Time Warner never got above $125, and in June 1991, Time Warner's efforts to eliminate much of the debt acquired in the merger sent its price plummeting to less than $85 per share.

For further information and analysis, see Gregg A. Jarrell, "The Paramount Import of Becoming Time-Warner: A Present-Value Lesson for the Lawyers," *The Wall Street Journal* (July 13, 1989), A-14.

---

takeovers less likely to succeed, blocking smooth transitions, and diverting attention from value-creating activities.

The two arguments are readily construed in terms of efficiency: Executives may be unwilling to invest in their careers without some assurances that the return on their investments will not be easily appropriated by outsiders. Moreover, unless their investments in their careers are protected, managements' efforts to resist takeovers will divert their attention from the business, lead them and the raiders to incur huge legal and professional fees, and generally use up resources in a way that is wasteful because it produces no increase in output. These latter costs are influence costs; they arise from a process in which individuals fight to defend their unprotected rents.

In outline, these arguments in favor of golden parachutes are just the same as the other arguments we have made about the advantages of secure ownership rights. It is difficult to make a general evaluation of arguments like this because the premises of the argument need to be verified in each case. Generally, if we suppose that executives have made a valuable specific investment, it is curious that raiders would so often be eager to dismiss them. It seems more reasonable to suppose that raiders dismiss managers who are performing badly and who will vigorously resist the takeover because there is no other firm willing to offer comparable employment terms with so little evidence of good performance.

In any case, golden parachutes are typically given only to the most senior executives, who have already made most of the investments in firm-specific capital that they might ever undertake. The incentive arguments in terms of encouraging investments, at least by these individuals, thus seem irrelevant.

518

Finance:
Investments,
Capital Structure,
and Corporate
Control

The first objection to golden parachutes is that they defend entrenched managers, not the firm, and that they are costly for stockholders. Moreover, if they are too large, managers may be too ready to encourage a control change and may not defend the stockholders' interests well. Further, they might encourage valuable managers to leave the firm after a control change, and this would make desired takeovers less likely.

GREENMAIL   The main problem with defensive measures undertaken to fend off corporate raiders is that they can also be used to defend an incompetent management or to defend management's interests even when they are in conflict with the interests of shareholders and others. One of the most ethically troubling examples of this is the case of *greenmail*, which is essentially (though not legally) a bribe paid to raiders by a firm's managers, using the shareholders' money, to induce them to break off the raid.

An example of greenmail is the case of Walt Disney Productions. In early 1984 the price of Disney stock was in the range of $50 to $55 per share. Raider Saul Steinberg began buying shares and prices began to rise. On June 4 of that year, an article in *Forbes* magazine estimated that the company's assets, if sold separately, would fetch a total price of $110 per Disney share. On June 8 Steinberg offered to buy 37 percent of Disney's shares at $67.50 per share. After three days of negotiations, Disney Productions agreed to buy Steinberg's shares from him at $70.83 per share, plus $28 million for his "investment expenses." The price of Disney shares promptly plummeted to less than $50 per share.

From a small shareholder's point of view, greenmail is company money that has been paid to a raider by company management to leave things just as they were before the raid was begun. Someone in this tale is a villain, but who? Should Disney's management be condemned for spending the shareholders' money to protect its own position of control? Or should they be congratulated for keeping a productive organization intact despite the reckless machinations of greedy financiers? Those who believe that a company's share price represents the best available estimate of its value (including most mainstream financial economists) will believe that Disney management destroyed value by its actions, as evidenced by the plunge in price after the greenmail was paid. Those who distrust market evaluations, thinking them too much subject to fads and manipulations, may think that the company was undervalued all along and that Disney management was actually acting in the interests of its long-term shareholders. The evidence on the accuracy of share prices as an estimate of value is mixed, and the debate rages on.

VOLUNTARY RESTRUCTURING   Many executives were convinced by the successes of the 1980s takeover wave and the associated increase in share prices that the organizational strategies of the corporate raiders—tighter focus, higher debt, and increased incentive pay—actually did add value. Some firms implemented programs of voluntary restructuring that were intended to duplicate the benefits of leveraged buyouts while avoiding their costs. In these reorganizations, stock was repurchased with debt financing, and sometimes the changes went deeper, with management teams in operating divisions being given a larger stake in the divisional returns. In effect, corporate headquarters became the lender to the divisions, and the divisions became increasingly leveraged, even though the firm itself retained a more traditional debt-equity ratio that allowed it to weather economic downturns without cutting back too severely on its long-term investments.

Another aspect of restructuring was the sale of unrelated divisions. Conglomerate firms come under intense pressure from insiders to provide subsidies to declining divisions in order to reduce the hardships suffered by employees. Companies have long sought ways to isolate unprofitable divisions to mitigate this pressure. One example we cited earlier was in 1974, when increased oil prices made the Japanese aluminum industry unprofitable. Mitsubishi Chemical, Sumitomo Chemical, and Showa Denko separated the unprofitable subsidiaries "to isolate the problem and the losses."[41] In general, spinoffs have been of underperforming units. This makes economic sense if others could manage them better or if keeping them in the firm leads to large influence costs. One of the major aims of restructuring is to create focused units, with fewer opportunities for managers to gain by competing for shares of a fixed pool of resources.

Preempting a raider is also an excellent defense. A problem is that many of the steps involved in a genuine restructuring are difficult for shareholders to distinguish from scorched earth policies designed to thwart the raider while maintaining control for the current incumbents. There is also a question of why, if the restructuring is a good thing for shareholders, management waited until threatened by a takeover to implement it. Influence costs provide a possible explanation. Restructuring reallocates rents within the firm and would normally be strongly resisted. A raider threatens to take some of the rents for itself and pass some to shareholders. This would severely diminish the amounts that would be available to current claimants. In this context, resistance to management's restructuring, which may keep more rents in the firm than the raider would leave, may be lessened.

The Aftermath

The U.S. takeover boom went bust in 1990. TWA defaulted and faced repossession of a large share of its fleet; Drexel Burnham Lambert went bankrupt; and Michael Milken was sentenced to ten years in a federal penitentiary for securities law violations. Corporate bankruptcies exploded, the volume of merger and acquisition activity was cut in half, and LBOs all but disappeared. Dozens of troubled companies that had taken on high debt in the 1980s sought to negotiate away their high interest obligations, replacing junk bonds with equity or lower-yield debt. Other, more successful, leveraged companies reduced their debt loads and even successfully issued new equity. Meanwhile, the Federal Deposit Insurance Corporation and the Resolution Trust Corporation, charged with cleaning up the Savings and Loan debacle, sued Milken and seven pages worth of other defendants, charging that the junk bond market had been a fraud that had duped the S&Ls into disaster.

Many people clearly hoped that the threats, costs, and discipline of the market for corporate control were gone for good. Others, however, were worried about exactly the same possibility.

ACTIVE INVESTORS AND CORPORATE GOVERNANCE REFORMS   The takeover boom clearly produced excesses and inefficiencies. Yet the threats of takeovers also made management much more conscious of shareholders' interests. The collapse of the market for corporate control in the recession of 1990, coupled with the strong takeover defenses that had been erected through the decade, led some investors to seek alternative means of protecting their interests.

A number of institutional investors, and especially the public employee pension plans of states such as Wisconsin and California, were leaders in this. They reasoned that attempting an active investment strategy designed to beat the market was futile both because they had no special access to information that was not already available to other sophisticated investors and because their shareholdings were so large that

---

[41] James C. Abegglen and George Stalk, Jr., *Kaisha, The Japanese Corporation* (New York: Basic Books, 1985), p. 25.

520

Finance:
Investments,
Capital Structure,
and Corporate
Control

their purchases and sales of companies' shares affected prices. Thus, the only way they could really improve the performance of their portfolios was to improve the performance of industry overall. If they could not rely on the pressure of takeover threats to keep management focused on shareholder value, they would have to become more active monitors of management.

With this objective, they began introducing shareholder resolutions to dismantle various defenses corporations had put in place and to shift their states of incorporation away from ones that had enacted especially restrictive antitakeover measures. Although many of these failed to win shareholder approval when actually put to votes, others were accepted by management and the corporate boards in negotiations with the institutional investors. They also used the leverage they possessed in the control contests that did occur to win concessions from management. For example, Lockheed Corporation's management agreed to nominate a number of outside directors suggested by the institutional investors to its board and to meet regularly with large shareholders in order to win their support in a control battle it faced with investor Harold Simmons. Various proposals were also put forward to facilitate proxy fights and successful shareholder resolutions, and the institutional investors lobbied the Securities and Exchange Commission and Congress to adopt these.

A major element of these reform efforts was to redefine the functioning of the board to make it more effective as the agent of the shareholders. One interesting proposal was that the institutional investors should identify and develop a cadre of professional board members. Each of these would be elected to serve on several boards, making a full-time job out of these responsibilities, and would be evaluated by a group representing the large shareholders at reelection time.[42] CalPERS, the California state public employees retirement system, was actively investigating this proposal in 1991 with the support of some of the corporations of which it held shares.

ALTERNATIVES TO THE PUBLICLY HELD CORPORATION

The problems of corporate control stem from many of the same features that are recognized as particular strengths of the corporate form. This fact raises the question of whether some alternative organizational form might be more efficient.

The free transferability of ownership shares permits extensive risksharing and facilitates raising capital. This feature also encourages homogeneity of interests among the owners of the firm, who will generally tend to favor increasing its market value, and thus avoids the political costs of disagreements over policies. The fact that the firm is not obligated to repurchase the shares it issued to raise capital and, as a legal entity separate from its owners, can in principle continue in existence long after its founders have died facilitates its taking on long-term projects and building valuable reputations with other parties. Limited liability for shareholders frees them from having to risk more than they have invested, and so they do not need to monitor the firm's operations nearly as closely as would be prudent if their entire personal assets could be claimed to settle the firm's debts. This further facilitates efficient diversification and permits investors to leave the day-to-day operations of the firm to full-time professionals. Further, lenders do not have to be concerned with the personal creditworthiness of the firm's owners because they have no claim against the owners' other assets. The practice of having the board oversee management, with shareholders

---

[42] This idea was put forward in Ronald Gilson and Reinier Kraakman, "Reinventing the Outside Director," draft, Stanford University Law School (1990), and was endorsed editorially by *The Economist* ["Redirecting Directors" (November 17, 1990), 19–20].

Time Warner's Rights Offering and the Shareholder Movement

In June, 1991 Time Warner announced a novel plan to obtain additional equity that would permit it to retire some of its debt. Current owners of the firm's 57.8 million shares were to be given the right to purchase up to 34.5 million new shares of the firm's stock. Such "rights offerings" are common, at least in the United Kingdom, but the unorthodox element in Time Warner's plan was that the price that investors would have to pay would depend on the fraction of them that accepted the offer. If only 60 percent of them accepted, then they would pay only $63 a share, about half the price at which Time Warner was trading at the time of the announcement. On the other hand, if there was 100 percent participation, the price would be $105. The offering was to have been the largest equity issue in Wall Street history. Also unusual was that the investment banks behind it, notably Merrill Lynch, would collect up to $145 million in fees although they would not take the normal risk of underwriting the issue.

Stockholders reacted very negatively. They objected to not knowing what the securities were going to cost them and to the investment banks' fees, and they decried the plan as "coercive." An "avalanche of protest" from institutional and individual investors followed, and the stock price fell by over 25 percent in a matter of days. Eventually, Time Warner's executives gave in to the pressure and did not appeal an SEC ruling against the plan. In its place they announced a fixed-price offering at $80 that would be underwritten, largely by Salomon. The stock price quickly fell toward this new level.

Observers saw the episode as potentially a watershed event for the shareholder-power movement: A company that two years before had gone to court to prevent its owners from considering the Paramount offer had been forced to back down by shareholder pressure. Moreover, a month later it decided to scrap its antitakeover poison pill rather than face an embarrassing vote at its annual meeting. Nevertheless, it retained another poison pill that would come into effect in case of a successful proxy fight.

For more details, see Judith H. Dobrzynski, Dean Foust, and Blanca Reimer, "Time Warner Feels the Force of Shareholder Power," *Business Week* (July 29, 1991), 58–59.

having only limited direct involvement in decision making (for example, in voting on sales of all or most of the firm's assets), further reduces the need for investors to expend resources to stay well informed, as would be necessary if they were called on to play a more active role. Yet these strengths also contribute to ownership being widely dispersed among small shareholders who may have little reason to care about anything but the stock price and dividends and few incentives to monitor the performance of management, to the ability of an entrenched management to pursue its own objectives with the shareholders' money, and to boards that may identify with and defer to the managers they are supposed to monitor and discipline.

522

Finance:
Investments,
Capital Structure,
and Corporate
Control

We have already seen some alternatives to the publicly held corporation at various points throughout this text. Privately held firms (including LBO associations) and employee ownership are two, and we will examine another—cooperatives—in the next chapter. Here we consider two others: partnerships, and the not-for-profit form. Each of these forms is widespread in certain industries.

Partnerships

The dominant mode of organization in professional services industries (apart from sole proprietorship) is partnership. The biggest international accounting firms, most major law practices, many consulting and architectural firms, the best-known medical clinics, and some investment banks are organized as partnerships, rather than as corporations.[43] Moreover, some of these partnerships are huge: the largest accounting firms have more than a thousand partners, and the biggest investment banking partnerships carry out billions of dollars in transactions. What explains this choice of organizational form in these industries?

Partnerships involve an association of two or more persons to carry on a business, sharing gains and losses. They are not generally legally distinct from the individuals comprising them, and the partners jointly own the partnership. They are free to determine their membership, internal decision procedures, and organizational structures, and rather than having perpetual life, they exist only so long as the partners maintain the relationship. Partners typically have the right to remove their assets from the partnership at any time but cannot sell or otherwise transfer their ownership claims except with permission of the other partners. If a partner withdraws or dies, the partnership ceases to exist (unless a clause in the partnership agreement provides otherwise, as it normally does in large partnerships). Most crucially, the partners are each individually responsible for the entire liabilities of the partnership, and each of the partners individually, so long as they are acting within their authority as partners (either as set by law or defined in the partnership agreement), can take actions that expose all the partners to unrestricted liability. This liability extends to the partners' personal assets, including bank accounts, stocks and bonds, houses, and cars.

The risk of ownership in a corporation is divisible and transferrable; that in a partnership is not. This limits the possibilities of diversification of risk. Thus the partnership form is at a clear disadvantage relative to the corporation in regards to risk sharing and the consequent ability to raise capital. It might seem that involving third party investors as passive partners would solve this problem, but that raises the problem of unlimited liability of partners.

UNLIMITED LIABILITY   Without limited liability, investors have to be concerned that they would lose most or all of their wealth if the firm cannot pay its bills. This leads them to expend extra resources on monitoring the firm and its managers and it might well deter some from investing at all (especially investors who would own only a small share and have little to gain from the firm's successes). This factor constrains partnerships from expanding the number of partners and reducing the amount invested by each to permit better diversification. Similarly, it makes it expensive for partnerships to expand into different lines of business or into new geographical markets because such moves increase the cost of monitoring.

The potential advantage of unlimited liability is that it represents the posting of a bond, with the individuals' private wealth serving as collateral against the debts of the organization. Bonding can be useful in situations with either moral hazard or

---

[43] In some cases these organizations are legally "professional service corporations." For our purposes, however, this form is largely indistinguishable from the partnership.

adverse selection. The cost of posting a bond is lower for businesspeople whose private information about their honesty and competence and about the quality of the firm's earnings opportunities indicates that they are unlikely to have to forfeit the bond. The danger of having to forfeit a bond also improves incentives for working hard at controlling costs and enhancing revenues. This same danger encourages the partners to monitor one another to prevent one of them from incurring losses for the partnership that the others will have to make good out of their own private wealth.

The predominance of the corporate form for organizing all but the smallest businesses suggests that the relative disadvantages of the partnership form normally outweigh the advantages. Special features of the businesses in which partnership is common reverse the ranking in these particular cases.

ADVANTAGES OF THE PARTNERSHIP FORM   First, except perhaps for the investment banks (which have largely switched to the corporate form in any case), the most important specialized input in partnerships is typically the knowledge and abilities of the workers, that is, their human capital. Human capital is not easily tradable, and if the residual returns on that capital belong to the humans who embody it, then the usual arguments about ownership rights suggests that the residual control should be assigned to them, too. Moreover, the need for physical and financial capital in large professional partnerships is often small, reducing the value of outside financing to share the asset value risk.

Perhaps even more important is the nature of the work done by professional partnerships, which makes effective, timely monitoring by outsiders very difficult. In particular, outside directors and professional managers are poor monitors of the quality and quantity of the crucial inputs. Is that doctor doing too many hysterectomies, or is the number a result of the patient mix? Are the contracts the lawyer has drafted air-tight? Are that architect's ideas breathtakingly original or naively impractical? Other professionals are in a much better position to judge these matters than is anyone else, and even they find the judgments difficult.

In addition to the problem of monitoring, there is a problem of bonding: What assets does the firm make available as a bond to guarantee its good performance? As we have already seen, a professional partnership requires few physical or financial assets to do business, so the direct partnership assets against which a dissatisfied client could make a claim are meager. However, the damages that a professional can cause by his or her poor performance can be very large, indeed: The patient dies after minor cosmetic surgery, the building falls down, investors are defrauded out of millions, or an innocent person is convicted.

Professional partnerships help to solve both the monitoring problem and the bonding problem. The partners personally are legally responsible for one another's work, and this provides powerful incentives for mutual monitoring. Their unlimited liability also provides the necessary large bond even though the actual capital required to run the firm is small. Unlike shares of stock, partnership interests are not tradable because the wrong pattern of ownership could destroy incentives and reduce the bond and because outside investors would fear adverse selection in purchasing profit-shares from partners who have much better information about the state of the firm.

Finally, with regard to the choice of the partnership form, some of the decision-making costs that would otherwise be incurred are reduced by the relative homogeneity of the partners. All are doing similar sorts of work, and they share common educational backgrounds and a common professional orientation. This does not mean there will not be conflicts and disputes, but these are likely to be less than would be found in organizations where the work is more varied and the workers less homogeneous in their outlooks and interests.

524

Finance:
Investments,
Capital Structure,
and Corporate
Control

Charitable Activities and Not-for-Profit Organizations

The same themes that govern the analysis of control of for-profit organizations arise in the not-for-profit sector. For example, following the earthquake in northern California in 1989, the Red Cross appeal for donations to its relief fund was so effective that the agency made an unannounced decision to divert some of those funds to its other programs. When donors discovered how their contributions had been diverted, the organization was pressured to reverse its decision. More serious scandals involving misappropriation of funds for personal use have also occurred, even in organizations headed by religious leaders. Jim Bakker, charismatic leader of a Christian evangelist organization known as the PTL, Father Bruce Ritter, founder and inspirational leader of Covenant House, a New York home for homeless and runaway teenagers, and the Indian guru Bhagwan Shree Rajneesh, whose Oregon commune promoted love and spiritual awareness, were all embroiled in financial scandals in the 1980s. In 1991 Stanford University, a large not-for-profit institution, was raked by allegations that U.S. federal government research funds had been used for such nonresearch purposes as maintaining a large yacht and purchasing an Italian fruitwood commode for the university president's house. Whenever large sums of money are being managed, inattention to financial controls creates temptations and the risk of large financial losses.

Not-for-profit organizations in the United States provide food and social services to the poor, bring art into the community, support or undertake research into alleviating killer diseases, produce and distribute noncommercial radio and television programming, provide a large fraction of education at all levels from kindergarten through graduate school, and generally provide a wide variety of goods and services at prices that do not cover the full costs of operation. It is not unimaginable that all of these services could be provided by profit-making organizations. Most drug research is a for-profit activity; popular music, films, television, and videos are provided predominantly by for-profit firms; and housing for the poor is often built, with the help of government subsidies, by private, profit-making firms. Yet food giveaways, social services, art museums, and many other activities are most commonly conducted on a not-for-profit basis. Why are not-for-profit organizations so important in these fields?

THE ROLE OF VOLUNTARY DONATIONS   One major part of the answer has to do with the fact that, in the United States, these activities are funded in significant part by voluntary donations from private individuals. A chief characteristic of charitable activities is that those who provide money to support the activities find it difficult to ascertain if their money has been well spent. Either a large portion of the revenues of the organization are not provided by those who receive the services (as when donations go to help feed the poor) or the marginal impact of an individual's donations is nearly impossible to determine (as when the money supports a public television station). This fact means that the monitoring that occurs naturally in a normal market (where buyers refuse to pay unless the supplier performs acceptably) cannot be nearly as effective in disciplining the providers of charitable services. This problem is compounded by the fact that, like most service activities, performance in the charitable services "business" is often very difficult to measure. It is therefore hard for the donors, and especially small donors, to check that services they are paying for are being properly delivered.

Organizing as a not-for-profit provides some assurance to donors.[44] The key fact

---

[44] Of course, under current tax laws, not-for-profit status often also gives the donors tax deductibility for their donations. However, this cannot be the dominant motivation for the form, which existed even before the adoption of the income tax.

about a not-for-profit is that no individual has a legal claim to the residual returns: There is no owner in this sense. If revenues exceed costs, the surplus must remain in the organization. Nor does anyone have the right to sell the assets of a not-for-profit and pocket the proceeds. This eliminates one major source of potential conflict between those who finance the organization (donors) and those who run it. It explains why organizations that rely on voluntary donations would so often be organized as not-for-profits.[45]

MORAL HAZARD IN NOT-FOR-PROFITS   Adopting a not-for-profit form does not solve all the problems associated with the revenue providers and the service receivers being different people. The danger is that, with the ownership incentives for cost-control missing, the decision makers and employees of the organization may still appropriate the donations for their own use, although probably not by pocketing residual returns directly. In scandals like those cited earlier, the top managers of the not-for-profits paid themselves high salaries, lent large sums at low rates of interest to friends or family members, enjoyed expensive residences and cars supplied by the organization, as well as plush offices and surroundings, business trips to exotic locales, short hours, and frequent vacations.

These moral hazard problems are not unique to not-for-profits, of course. However, the competitive pressures from the output and input markets and from the market for corporate control that help control them in for-profit organizations are weaker in not-for-profits. The recipients of the goods and services are not paying the bills and so cannot easily turn to more efficient providers; the donors who provide revenues are unable to monitor their use cheaply; and the impossibility of claiming the returns that would result from increased efficiency removes the incentives to take over and improve the performance of inefficient not-for-profits. Donors' recognition of these problems would endanger the flow of donations, and so it becomes important (and in the interest of those involved in the not-for-profit) to establish other mechanisms to control them.

One of these mechanisms is that managers of not-for-profits are held to stricter legal standards in their operation of the firm than are the hired managers of private, for-profit firms. A second widely used mechanism is to recruit employees who have a strong, manifested interest in advancing the objectives of the organization and so are less likely to misuse its funds. Volunteers are clearly of this sort, and the extensive practice in many charities of relying on volunteer labor and favoring former volunteers when hiring for paid staff positions can be understood in this light. A third is to vest responsibility for oversight of the organizations' operations in a board whose members are not legally permitted to gain personally from their service and who might be expected to want the interests of the donors to be pursued efficiently. Thus, large donors are in themselves excellent board candidates, both because they have a demonstrated personal interest in seeing that the funds are well spent and because the size of their donations indicates that they can afford to divert time from earning money to serve in a voluntary capacity. Other good candidates are well-known public figures whose names small donors will recognize, whose past accomplishments give indication of their ability to provide effective control, and who can be expected both to be free of any personal interest in profiting from the activity and to be concerned with maintaining their own personal reputations by preventing misbehavior during their watch.

This analysis suggests a reason why university boards of trustees historically did

---

[45] It also explains why governments might prefer to fund provision of services through not-for-profits, as is common in the Netherlands, rather than profit-making firms. Why governments use not-for-profits to provide the services rather than doing it directly themselves is another issue, to which we will return.

526

Finance:
Investments,
Capital Structure,
and Corporate
Control

not include faculty and current students among their members and even now do not have more than token representation from these groups, despite the fact that the faculty and students are among those most affected by the board's decisions. The board's role is to guard the long-run viability of the university by protecting its reputation and revenue sources. To do so, it must protect the outside contributors (whether private donors or taxpayers) from having their money used to promote private benefits rather than the public weal that they presumably wanted to support. The parties who have presented the greatest threat of misappropriating these contributions have historically been the faculty and students because until quite recently they were the only significant interest groups within the institution. An effective board must not be led or too greatly influenced by those who are to be monitored, and so student and faculty participation has been severely limited.

In recent years, however, a number of universities have developed large cadres of professional managers in addition to the academic support staff. This former group in particular represents an independent threat to misappropriate contributed funds. They too do not typically have board representation, but because most of the information that the board must use for its decisions is developed and presented by the professional administrators, there is the real possibility of their influencing board decisions to their private benefit. Of course, to the extent that the board must rely on some group within the university to provide this information, the possibility of attempts at influence is unavoidable, although collecting information from different interested groups might allow the board to sort out the facts better.

GOVERNMENT FUNDING   In most countries, private donations (except to religious organizations) are rare, and the government funds social, charitable and cultural activities. At least in some of these situations, however, the government-financed services are provided through not-for-profits. This is especially common in the Netherlands. Even in the United States, many not-for-profits are financed jointly by government funds and private donations. For example, a large amount of basic research is paid for by the federal government through grants and contracts to private, not-for-profit universities whose employees produce the actual research. The arguments already given explain why governments might prefer to supply these services through not-for-profits rather than profit-oriented firms, but why might they choose to have activities they finance be provided through not-for-profits rather than by government organizations?

Several reasons for this pattern exist, although none is fully satisfactory. One is that the government may be able to avoid various constraints by using this mechanism. For example, government wages may be higher and work rules more restrictive than in the private sector, and in this case a not-for-profit may enjoy lower costs than would the government. Similarly, use of the not-for-profits may allow paying higher wages than are politically acceptable for public servants but which are necessary to attract the sort of people needed. What is unsatisfying about this is that it leaves the existence of the crucial constraints unexplained.

A second possibility is that this pattern helps insulate the provision of the services from direct political interference; for example, the government cannot simply dismiss the directors of an independent foundation. To the extent that this interference is aimed at distributional considerations (serving the elected officials' supporters rather than some other group) but has efficiency-reducing side-effects, insulation enhances efficiency. The problem here is to explain why influence costs should be less when a client organization is used rather than a branch of government. For example, an effective civil service organization might well accomplish the same objective.

A final possibility is that this pattern accommodates differences in tastes and encourages innovation better than a government-run program, which will tend to produce uniformity. This is of course just a version of the standard arguments for federalism: The different jurisdictions can pattern what they do to local situations, and successes (or failures) in one can be a lesson to others. This too has a ring of truth. For example, in the province of Ontario taxpayers can indicate whether they want their school taxes to go to support the nondenominational public schools or instead the schools run by the Roman Catholic church: The point is to provide a level of funding while still permitting some responsiveness to differences in preferences. However, again the crucial question arises: Why can't government provide the desired diversity while producing the services itself?

This last question is closely related to the question of why firms ever rely on independent suppliers to provide them with inputs. There is not yet a consensus answer to that question, but some tentative answers are supplied in the next chapter.

528

Finance:
Investments,
Capital Structure,
and Corporate
Control

SUMMARY

In this chapter, we enrich the classical theory of finance by adding three ideas. First, managers, lenders, and shareholders may all have different interests, different from those of the firm's lenders or shareholders, and financial arrangements may affect how different those interests are and what decisions management will make. Second, managers may be better informed than investors about the firm's prospects, so the financial decisions they make may affect investors' beliefs and therefore the price of the firm's shares. Third, financial securities are not just claims to part of a firm's net receipts; they also give the security holder certain rights. Just as in the theory of ownership, a careful matching of rights and returns can create incentives that increase total value. The chapter closes by considering the control problems in partnerships and not-for-profits, where some of the same issues of motivation and control arise.

The financing patterns of firms vary significantly among developed countries, with more equity financing having been used traditionally in the United States, Canada, and the United Kingdom than in many of the other industrial countries. The huge wave of takeovers in these countries in the 1980s often involved refinancing firms using large amounts of debt and concentrating equity ownership in the hands of fewer large investors, who could exercise more effective control. Because these transactions increase the firm's ratio of assets to equity or *leverage*, these deals are called *leveraged buyouts* or LBOs. Especially noteworthy were the *management buyouts* (MBOs), in which ownership was concentrated in the hands of the firm's managers and, often, the shares of the firm ceased to be publicly traded, and *hostile takeovers*, in which individuals and firms attempted to acquire control of companies against the wishes of the firm's management. When the target firms were conglomerates with many different businesses, the changes in control were frequently followed by *bust-ups*, in which the various businesses were separated and sold to other investors, leading to a significant deglomeration of the industries in the affected countries. All this activity casts doubt on the conclusion of the Modigliani-Miller analysis and leads us to ask anew: How can capital structure matter?

Given the relative payment priorities, increasing the riskiness of cash flows tends to transfer value away from the holders of debt to the holders of equity. This occurs because when favorable outcomes occur, the equity holders enjoy all the extra returns, whereas debtholders suffer part of the loss when the most unfavorable outcomes occur. Consequently, when equity holders control management, high levels of debt encourage excessive risk taking.

A second kind of cost arises when high levels of debt combine with a run of operating losses. This can lead to *debt overhang*, in which a firm with profitable investments is unable to finance them because the suppliers of new financing fear that part of their investment will be diverted to satisfy the demands of existing lenders and debtholders. Debt overhang thus leads to *underinvestment*. The problem of debt overhang can sometimes be overcome by *debt renegotiation*, in which existing lenders agree to reduce their claims in order to encourage others to supply new capital, but renegotiations are difficult when there are many debtholders who must agree to the deal. Moreover, even the option of renegotiation may damage incentives because it protects equity holders and managers from some of the losses from risky investments.

When renegotiations are unsuccessful, a third cost of debt is that default may lead to *bankruptcy*, even if the current operations of the firm are fundamentally sound. Even if bankruptcy leads only to a reorganization of the company's affairs, rather than to an actual liquidation of its business, the bankruptcy event can be profoundly disruptive to the firm's operations. Suppliers of goods, fearing that they may not be repaid, may no longer be willing to ship supplies on credit. Suppliers of capital engage in legal battles among themselves and between them and management, which divert the attention of management from the pressing need to reinvigorate the firm. Partly to avoid these costs, suppliers of capital may engage in informal *workouts*, agreements made without the assistance of the court to avoid the costs of bankruptcy.

Against these three disadvantages, debt has the important advantage that it compels management to return earnings to investors, rather than retaining them for its own purposes within the firm. This prevents managers from using the firm's *free cash flow*—the amount of cash generated by the firm in excess of what can be profitably reinvested, to enlarge their units (unprofitably), decorate their offices, and so on. Moreover, given that managers have limited resources, high levels of debt make it possible to concentrate a higher fraction of the equity ownership in the hands of the management than would otherwise be possible. This leads to better incentives for managers to increase value in the event that the firm does not default on its loans.

The *LBO association* is a form of organization that attempts to enjoy these advantages of high levels of debt while avoiding its worst disadvantages. Using capital provided by outside investors, the association sponsors LBOs to improve management incentives, concentrates financial control in a few hands, actively monitors the firm's management, and stands prepared to replace its managers or to inject new financing as circumstances demand.

The LBO association illustrates the benefits of concentrated ownership. There is considerable concentration of ownership in many companies, even without this form of organization. Individuals and funds that supply *venture capital* to new companies perform a similar function, monitoring the performance of management during the start-up of the new venture. In many countries, where relatively high leverage is the norm, the principal lender to a company serves a similar monitoring function, often having a representative on the company's board of directors. Bondholders and long-term lenders attempt to protect their investments by other means, such as by requiring collateral for loans or writing *loan covenants* that restrict the management's ability to sell assets or encumber the security for existing loans.

These considerations indicate how financial structure can affect the parties' incentives in a way that alters the total value of the firm.

The second class of theories we considered are the signaling theories, according to which financial decisions can affect what investors believe about the firm's prospects. One of the most robust empirical conclusions is that attempts by a firm to refinance in the direction of increased equity reduces the total market value of the firm, whereas refinancing in the other direction increases it. Similarly, reductions in dividends lead to a decreased value, whereas increased dividends have the opposite effect. According to the signaling theories, these simply represent optimal responses by investors who are interpreting the actions of the firm's managers, who are better informed than the investors. Managers with an ownership stake in the firm, acting in their own interests, will want to sell equity when they think it is overvalued and to buy equity when they think it is undervalued. They will want to replace debt by equity when they expect the firm to have too little cash to meet its future obligations. Increases in dividends and stock repurchases indicate the managers' confidence that the firm's future cash flow will be adequate to meet its needs. Reacting to these indicators, it is rational for investors to bid up the price of the firm's share when the firm announces its intention to repurchase its stock, whether the repurchases are to be financed by debt or retained earnings, and when the firm announces a dividend increase, and to do the opposite when the firm announces a new stock issue or a dividend reduction.

Financial structure can also affect value by the way it allocates rights. Stockholders

530

Finance:
Investments,
Capital Structure,
and Corporate
Control

have the right to elect corporate directors and to vote on certain major changes in the organization's charter, but not to interfere with the discretion of the board of directors in ordinary business decisions. These voting rights are useful to those who wish to effect a change in control of the company. They may engage in a *proxy fight*, soliciting a proxy to vote on behalf of other shareholders to place their own representatives on the board of directors. They may also purchase shares to be used together with any proxies and the shares of their allies to elect directors.

In the United States in the 1980s these takeovers led to huge increases in the market values of the target firms, but essentially no change in the value of the acquiring firms. On average the *takeover premium*—the amount by which the takeover price exceeds the earlier market price—was 30 to 50 percent, but it sometimes exceeded 100 percent. It appears that most of this value was created by selling or reorganizing divisions of the target firm to create more focused firms operating fewer businesses. Recognizing the value of these reorganizations, many other companies undertook *voluntary restructurings*, in which the corporation itself became the lender to its divisions, which could be highly leveraged and in which the division managers could own substantial shares.

Management devised a number of means to defend themselves against the corporate raiders. *Golden parachutes*, which provided generous payments to managers displaced in control changes, were justified as means to reduce managerial resistance to takeover attempts and protect their investments in firm-specific capital. *Greenmail*, in which a firm repurchases a raider's shares at a special price, fends off the raider with the shareholder's money, leading to no improvements in operational efficiency. This tactic has been widely condemned, but commentators disagree about whether it is the raider or the management that is the proper object of the condemnation.

In 1990 takeover activity was substantially diminished as the market for new bonds below investment grade, known as *junk bonds*, had virtually disappeared. Some large public investors began to press companies to adopt the reforms that had increased value during the takeover wave and to eliminate some of the takeover defenses, to provide discipline over themselves, and some companies complied with these requests. In the first half of 1991 takeover activity began to increase again, though on a much smaller scale than found during the peak of takeover activity in 1986 through 1988.

The issue of who controls a large organization and monitors its activities is not limited to public corporations. Groups of professionals, such as doctors, lawyers, accountants, architects, and others are usually organized as partnerships. The major assets of these businesses are the skills and reputations of the partners, which are human-capital assets, and a matching of residual returns and residual control would suggest the desirability of a partnership form, in which the professionals own the firm. Moreover, because professional work is so hard to evaluate, outside monitoring is likely to be ineffective compared to a system in which the professionals monitor one another. The heads of these organizations are virtually always other professionals because nobody else would be qualified to evaluate and criticize the professional's work.

Charitable and not-for-profit organizations often handle significant sums of money. There have been many scandals in which donations were used to finance fancy cars and residences, pay high salaries, make loans to directors and officers, and so on. In addition, the priorities of those who run the organizations may not coincide with those of the donors, so moral hazard remains an issue. Organizations that receive voluntary donations are usually organized as not-for-profits to counter the obvious problem that an owner might neglect providing services to increase profits. This is most problematic when there are many small donors or when services are especially hard to measure. Boards of directors consisting of volunteers, who are also often principal donors, helps to resolve the monitoring problem and to ensure that directors do not have financial interests that conflict with the organization's goals.

One of the puzzles of not-for-profit organization arises when funding for the organization comes from a government. The question is: Why doesn't the government provide the services itself, rather than relying on an independent organization? Although a number of answers suggest themselves, none treats the fundamental issue of why the government can't organize within itself a unit that duplicates, in all essential respects, the attributes of a not-for-profit. This is the same issue that arises in connection with vertical integration in the private sector, and some answers are offered in the next chapter.

■ BIBLIOGRAPHIC NOTES

Michael Jensen and William Meckling published the first systematic economic analysis of how inadequate managerial equity holdings might reduce managerial incentives for effort and innovativeness and how debt might encourage excessive risk-taking. Stewart Myers first analyzed the debt overhang problem, suggesting that excessive debt can lead a firm to bypass profitable investments. Michael Jensen developed the free cash flow hypothesis and accentuated the role of the debt and LBO associations in dealing with free cash flow problems. Andrei Shleifer and Robert Vishny, Harold Demsetz and Kenneth Lehn, and Richard Zeckhauser and John Pound all present both theory and evidence for the proposition that large shareholders add value by monitoring their firms.

Signaling theories in financial economics were pioneered in 1977 by Hayne Leland and David Pyle (who hypothesized that high levels of share ownership by management signaled high value per share) and Stephen Ross (who argued that a high debt-equity ratio signaled valuable equity shares). Stewart Myers and Nicholas Majluf further advanced this theory. Sudipto Bhattacharya developed the first models of dividend signals, which were later refined by Kose John and Joseph Williams. Frank Easterbrook championed the role of dividends in providing incentives. The danger of strategic asset destruction and its implications for financial structure were pointed out by Yaacov Bergman and Jeffrey Callen. Milton Harris and Artur Raviv provide an excellent survey of research on financial structure emphasizing incentive considerations.

Henry Manne first accentuated the importance of the market for corporate control in increasing efficiency. Jensen has been a prominent proponent of this interpretation of takeovers. Richard Roll proposed the "hubris theory" to explain takeover premia, and Shleifer and Lawrence Summers accentuated breach of trust and transfers. The formal analysis of coercive offers was first developed by Lucian Bebchuck, while Sanford Grossman and Oliver Hart pointed out the free-rider problem in tender offers. The Symposium on Takeovers in the *Journal of Economic Perspectives* (with an introduction by Hal Varian and papers by Shleifer and Vishny; Jensen; Gregg Jarrell, James Brickley, and Jeffry Netter; and F. M. Scherer) provides a very accessible introduction to economic research on this question. A textbook treatment of these matters is given by J. Fred Weston, Kwang S. Chung, and Susan Hoag.

The choice of organizational form has been analyzed by Eugene Fama and Michael Jensen and by Henry Hansmann, among others. A survey of the economics of the not-for-profit firm is given by Estelle James and Susan Rose-Ackerman.

532

Finance:
Investments,
Capital Structure,
and Corporate
Control

■ REFERENCES

Bebchuck, L. A. "The Pressure to Tender: An Analysis and a Proposed Remedy," in J. Coffee, Jr., L. Lowenstein, and S. Rose-Ackerman, eds., *Knights, Raiders and Targets* (New York: Oxford University Press, 1988), 371–97.

Bergman, Y., and J. Callen. "Opportunistic Underinvestment in Debt Renegotiation and Capital Structure," Working Paper 90-24, Brown University Department of Economics (1990).

Bhattacharya, S. "Imperfect Information, Dividend Policy, and 'The Bird in the Hand' Fallacy," *Bell Journal of Economics*, 10 (Spring 1979), 259–70.

Demsetz, H., and K. Lehn. "The Structure of Corporate Ownership: Causes and Consequences," *Journal of Political Economy*, 93 (December 1985), 1155–77.

Easterbrook, F. "Two Agency-Cost Explanations of Dividends," *American Economic Review*, 74 (1984), 650–59.

Fama, E., and M. Jensen. "Agency Problems and Residual Claims," *Journal of Law and Economics*, 26 (1983), 327–49.

Fama, E., and M. Jensen. "Organizational Forms and Investment Decisions," *Journal of Financial Economics*, 14 (1985), 101–19.

Hansmann, H. "The Ownership of the Firm," *Journal of Law, Economics, and Organization*, 4 (Fall 1988), 267–304.

Hansmann, H. "When Does Worker Ownership Work? ESOPs, Law Firms, Codetermination, and Economic Democracy," *Yale Law Journal*, 99 (June 1990), 1751–1816.

Harris, M., and A. Raviv. "The Theory of Capital Structure," *Journal of Finance*, 46 (March 1991), 297–355.

Grossman, S., and O. Hart. "Takeover Bids, the Free-Rider Problem, and the Theory of the Corporation," *Bell Journal of Economics*, 11 (Spring 1980), 42–64.

James, E., and S. Rose-Ackerman. *The Nonprofit Enterprise in a Market Economy* (Chur, Switzerland: Harwood Academic Publishers, 1986).

Jarrell, G., J. Brickley, and J. Netter. "The Market for Corporate Control: The Empirical Evidence Since 1980," *Journal of Economic Perspectives*, 2 (Winter 1988), 49–68.

Jensen, M. "The Eclipse of the Public Corporation," *Harvard Business Review* (September–October 1989), 61–74.

Jensen, M. "Agency Costs of Free Cash Flow, Corporate Finance and Takeovers," *American Economic Review*, Papers and Proceedings, 76 (May 1986), 323–29.

Jensen, M. "Takeovers: Folklore and Science," *Harvard Business Review*, (November–December 1984), 109–121.

Jensen, M. "Takeovers: Their Causes and Consequences," *Journal of Economic Perspectives*, 2 (Winter 1988), 21–48.

Jensen, M. and W. Meckling. "Theory of the Firm: Managerial Behavior, Agency Costs, and Capital Structure," *Journal of Financial Economics*, 3 (1976), 305–60.

John, K., and J. Williams. "Dividends, Dilution, and Taxes: A Signaling Equilibrium," *Journal of Finance*, 40 (1985), 1053–70.

Leland, H., and D. Pyle. "Information Asymmetries, Financial Structure, and Financial Intermediation," *Journal of Finance*, 32 (1977), 371–88.

Manne, H. "Mergers and the Market for Corporate Control," *Journal of Political Economy*, 73 (1965), 110–20.

Myers, S. "The Determinants of Corporate Borrowing," *Journal of Financial Economics*, 5 (1977), 147–75.

Myers, S., and N. Majluf. "Corporate Financing and Investment Decisions When Firms Have Information that Investors Do Not Have," *Journal of Financial Economics*, 13 (June 1984), 187–221.

Roll, R. "The Hubris Hypothesis of Corporate Takeovers," *Journal of Business*, 59 (April 1986), 197–216.

Ross, S. "The Determination of Financial Structure: The Incentive Signalling Approach," *Bell Journal of Economics*, 8 (Spring 1977), 23–40.

Scherer, F. "Corporate Takeovers: The Efficiency Arguments," *Journal of Economic Perspectives*, 2 (Winter 1988), 69–82.

Shleifer, A. and L. Summers, "Breach of Trust in Hostile Takeovers," *Corporate Takeovers: Causes and Consequences*, A. Auerbach, ed. (Chicago: University of Chicago Press, 1988).

Shleifer, A., and R. Vishny. "Value Maximization and the Acquisition Process," *Journal of Economic Perspectives*, 2 (Winter 1988), 7–20.

Shleifer, A., and R. Vishny. "Large Shareholders and Corporate Control," *Journal of Political Economy*, 94 (June 1986), 461–88.

Varian, H. "Symposium on Takeovers," *Journal of Economic Perspectives*, 2 (Winter 1988), 3–6.

Weston, J. F., K. Chung, and S. Hoag. *Mergers, Restructuring, and Corporate Control* (Englewood Cliffs, NJ: Prentice Hall, 1990).

Zeckhauser, R., and J. Pound. "Are Large Shareholders Effective Monitors? An Investigation of Share Ownership and Corporate Performance," in R. G. Hubbard, ed. *Asymmetric Information, Corporate Finance, and Investment*, (Chicago: University of Chicago Press, 1990), 149–80.

EXERCISES

> Food for Thought

1. A stock mutual fund is a company that invests in shares of the stock of other companies. These funds exist to make it possible for small investors to pool their money in order to hold a widely diversified portfolio of investments. In an *open-end* fund, shareholders can sell their shares and demand to be paid their pro rata share of the value of the fund's shareholdings. In a *closed-end* fund, shareholders can obtain cash for their shares only by selling them to others. It is common for closed-end funds to sell for prices lower than the actual value of company's holdings. How can one account for that? Under what circumstances would a closed-end fund be preferred to an open-end fund?

2. Firms frequently establish long-term relationships with a single bank. If the firm is large, the single bank may then enlist other banks to meet any especially large loan needs for their customer. What are the advantages of such an arrangement? For example, why do individuals not make small loans to firms directly, rather than depositing their money in a bank and having the bank lend the money? Why does the firm not deal with the individual banks separately? Would it be better if, in the

534

Finance:
Investments,
Capital Structure,
and Corporate
Control

United States, there were fewer, larger banks to make loans to large companies rather than the multitude of small banks that actually exist?

3.   What inferences might investors draw when a company announces an increase in its quarterly dividend? What would you expect to happen to share prices following such an event? What are the associated problems of commitment? How might those problems be resolved?

4.   In 1990, American Telephone and Telegraph, the giant telecommunications company with sales of $36 billion a year from long-distance telephone service (60 percent) and sales of telephone equipment, launched an attempted takeover of NCR Corporation, a major U.S. computer manufacturer. AT&T had long tried to establish itself in the computer business but had been unable to produce and market successfully competitive machines. It was estimated to have spent $2 billion on this effort in six years and still to be losing $200 million a year on its computer business. It had also attempted to buy its way into the market by acquiring equity stakes in other computer firms, but had failed. AT&T offered to acquire NCR (formerly called the National Cash Register Company) for $90 a share. This was about 15-times NCR's earnings per share, which were falling, and it put a value of $6.1 billion on the target firm. Before the AT&T offer, NCR shares sold at $48.

NCR's board and managers rejected the offer. AT&T persisted, making the offer hostile, and NCR resisted strenuously, adopting a tougher poison pill, establishing an ESOP, and invoking a state law that forbid buying more than 10 percent of a firm without its directors' approval. The senior managers, whom AT&T wanted to retain, also threatened to quit if AT&T gained control. AT&T then launched a proxy fight. In response, NCR changed its by-laws to make it extremely difficult to remove a majority of the board in such a fight. All this was done despite strong shareholder pressure to accept the offer, which AT&T had increased. The NCR chairman claimed he was willing to sell the firm, but demanded $125 a share. Eventually, after almost six months from the time AT&T made its initial offer to NCR, NCR agreed to an offer of $110, with the managers of NCR taking over AT&T's computer operations.

How would you judge if NCR was a worthwhile investment for AT&T? How would you judge whether NCR's leaders were pursuing their own interests or those of their stockholders? What further information would you want?

5.   In 1991, General Motors announced its intention to raise additional equity capital by issuing a new form of hybrid securities it called "preference shares" or "perks." The preference shares were to be issued at the same price as GM's common stock, but were to offer an expected dividend yield of twice what the firm's common stock had been returning. Although the perks could fall in value, just like the common stock, their dividends would have to be paid before those on the common stock. They would automatically convert after three years to common stock on a 1 to 1 basis. Meanwhile, GM was free to redeem them at any time at a predetermined price. This limited their possible appreciation. Why would anyone buy these rather than regular stock? Why would GM want to sell them?

6.   In recent years, the large accounting firms have expanded into the field of management consulting, bring non-accountants into the firms for this purpose. Many of these consulting businesses have grown very fast and are now apparently very profitable. What problems would you expect this to create in these partnerships?

7.   The venture capital industry is predominantly organized through limited partnerships. Venture capitalists establish limited partnerships to invest in new businesses, with themselves as the general partners. Investors supply the bulk of the money for investment by buying limited partnerships in the funds. The general partners put up about one percent of the funding, but typically receive 20 percent of the disbursements. They choose the actual investments, while the management

companies that they own make recommendations to the partnership on possible investments and charge the partnership for these services. How do you account for these practices? What possible problems do you see?

8.   In the United States there are both for-profit and not-for-profit hospitals. What differences in policies and practices would you expect to see between the two forms?

9.   In the United States in recent years there has been a great increase in the number of malpractice suits against professionals (doctors, lawyers, etc.) and in the size of the awards. Malpractice insurance, which pays legal fees and the costs of any awards to plaintiffs, dulls the incentives of unlimited liability, but may be "necessary" to get people into these industries. What form should it take?

Quantitative Exercise

1.   Suppose firms differ in their possible cash flows. High-cash-flow firms have cash flows which might take on any value in the interval $[0, H]$ with equal probability, while the cash flows of low-cash-flow firms are uniformly distributed over the interval $[0, L]$, where $L < H$. Each manager knows what kind of firm he or she has, but investors do not have this information: All they know is that some fraction of the firms have high cash flow and the rest have low. They do, however, observe the amount D of debt that the firm issues.

Suppose each manager chooses a value of D and is paid in such a way that he or she seeks to maximize a weighted average of the current value of the firm V_0 and its expected value in the next period (at which point the cash flow is realized and becomes publicly known) less a bankruptcy penalty, P, that is incurred by the manager (not the firm's owners) if earnings turn out to be less than D. This occurs with probability D/H for high-cash-flow firms and D/L for low ones. The expected value of the firm's next period is just its expected cash flow, $L/2$ or $H/2$. The current value may depend on D because through investors' inferences. Thus a manager of a firm of type t, $t = H$ or L, who selects a debt of D receives a payoff (proportional to)

$$(1 - \gamma)V_0(D) + \gamma(t/2 - PD/t),$$

where γ is the weight.

Under the assumption that managers in the two types of firms pick different levels of D, investors will infer firm's values from the choices. Thus, if a firm has debt D_L it will be thought to be worth $L/2$ in the first period, and similarly for D_H, no matter what its true type. Thus, V_0 is determined: $V_0(D_H) = H/2$, and $V_0(D_L) = L/2$. However, the firm's value next period will be determined by its actual type.

Show (using the appropriate incentive constraints) that D_H must exceed D_L: More profitable firms issue more debt. Show that if D_L is set at zero and D_H is set as low as possible to meet the incentive constraints, then D_H decreases as P increases: Higher bankruptcy costs decrease the amount of debt and the probability of bankruptcy.

Part
VII

THE DESIGN AND DYNAMICS OF ORGANIZATIONS

16

THE BOUNDARIES AND STRUCTURE OF THE FIRM

T*he make-or-buy decision that occasioned so much debate in mass production firms struck Ohno and others at Toyota as largely irrelevant, as they began to consider obtaining components for cars and trucks. The real question was how the assembler and supplier could work together smoothly to reduce costs and improve quality, whatever formal, legal relationship they might have.*

James Womack, Daniel Jones and Daniel Roos[1]

This chapter is concerned with the positive ("what is") and normative ("what should be") analysis of the design of the firm. How do firms determine their vertical boundaries and arrange their relationships with suppliers and customers? When should a firm use the market to acquire the goods and services it needs? When should it undertake to provide these for itself? And when should it seek to develop some hybrid organizational arrangements to conduct a transaction? How do firms decide on their horizontal scope—what activities to undertake and what businesses to be in? How should they structure their internal mechanisms for coordination and motivation, allocating decision-making power and responsibility for different activities, and what is the relationship between scope and the firm's internal structure? How have the choices that firms actually make on these dimensions changed, and what has motivated these adaptations? What principles ought to guide these decisions?

These questions are centrally important to the economics and management of organizations, and entrepreneurs and managers have been exceptionally innovative over the last century in devising new answers. Systematic understanding of the strengths and weaknesses of the alternative organizational forms has not always kept

---

[1] *The Machine That Changed the World* (New York: Rawson Associates, 1990), p. 58.

538

up, although study of these issues is one of the most active and promising areas of research in economics and management.

In our analysis, we continue to regard organizational forms as being chosen by people who enter into relationships that are efficient for themselves. The first step in determining what the efficient forms of organization are must be to identify the feasible organizational alternatives. These have changed over time, but we largely limit attention here to modern practices. The alternatives are multifaceted, and part of the problem is to review the complementarities among the parts; that is, how the pieces of the organization fit together into a coherent design. The second step is to identify the qualitative costs and benefits of alternative forms. What is gained and what resources are used by each form of organization? What causes these costs and benefits to vary over time? Finally, differences in costs across segments of the economy, across countries, and over time are used to analyze differences in the choices that have been made.

THE CHANGING NATURE OF THE FIRM

Any serious attempt to explain actual business organization must grapple with the historical fact that the nature of the firm has changed tremendously over the last century and a half.

Emergence of the Industrial Enterprise

Before 1850 hierarchical structures were virtually nonexistent outside the episcopal churches and the military. The Hudson's Bay Company had a primitive managerial hierarchy, with the heads of each trading post directing the local employees while taking orders from London, and the East India Company had a well-developed bureaucracy. Both companies enjoyed the quiet life of the monopolist, however, and when the HBC was faced with competition, it came close to failing. Manufacturing was generally conducted on a small scale. One person, or perhaps a small group of people, hired all the employees and directed all the activities of the business, and thus each business was limited to a scale that an entrepreneur could personally supervise. The small scale of operations generally fit the markets of the time. Bankers and traders had operated over long distances for centuries, and the industrial revolution in Great Britain had seen the development of some national and even international markets in industrial products, but most markets remained local, and business was adapted to this pattern.

Three crucial technological developments changed all this. The steamship permitted scheduled, predictable ocean shipping. The railroad allowed speedy transportation of people, goods, and information over continental distances. The telegraph initiated near-instantaneous communication. Together, these developments made it possible to conceive of doing business on a scale never before possible. By the end of the nineteenth century, larger enterprises had emerged to sell their products on a nationwide scale and even in international markets. No longer limited by the size of their local markets, firms began to use new methods of production, designing specialized tools and introducing mass-production methods. These developments allowed firms to produce larger quantities of higher-quality products at lower cost.

These strategic changes were accompanied by equally revolutionary changes in organization. As we saw in Chapters 3 and 4, the price system, which can be so effective for coordinating trade in standardized commodities, is much less useful for coordinating activities that exploit economies of scale. The growing scope and complexity of business overwhelmed the capacity of owners to manage their operations, requiring them to hire supervisors and middle managers who would oversee parts of the business, increasing the span of the firm's activities and the number of people who could be monitored and motivated.

With the owner no longer personally and directly overseeing all the crucial activities, it became necessary to create information and reporting systems to guide, control, and evaluate the managers who carried out these tasks. Traditional *financial accounting* systems were refined to provide investors and lenders with information to help them assess the firm's creditworthiness and prospects and, eventually, the performance of its hired managers. In addition, *cost accounting* systems were designed to provide information about the costs of making specific products in particular factories. The information generated proved valuable in setting prices, deciding which products to make, identifying sources of any cost increases over time, and pinpointing the activities where cost reductions would be most valuable.

Along with the new information systems, new financing arrangements emerged. In the United States, the demands of railroads and other large enterprises exceeded the financial capabilities of local banks, leading to the development of bank syndicates and bond markets and to the great expansion of stock markets and contributing to the emergence of an insurance industry. Other countries resolved the large-scale financing problem in other ways. In Canada, Germany, and Japan, for example, giant banks played a dominant role in financing growing firms.

As industrialization proceeded, the profitable monopolies of local producers were challenged by competition from national and international firms. Businesses responded in part by being innovative in their collusive organizations. Trusts and cartels of national producers conspired to maintain high prices. In the United States, most major manufactured goods were brought under price-fixing arrangements. Then, when enforcement of the Sherman Antitrust Act (1890) made cartels unattractive, a wave of mergers created many of the giant firms that dominated U.S. industry for the next century. US Steel, for example, was formed in 1901 through the amalgamation of 11 firms in what remains (in inflation-adjusted terms) the second largest merger in U.S. history. Such familiar names as General Electric and Eastman Kodak also appeared in this period. Some of these new organizations were centrally managed and organized on functional lines, but others were simply holding companies, giving unified ownership with little central direction. The business institutions of the early twentieth century were radically different from those in place just 50 years earlier.

The Development of the Multidivisional Form

Change in the organization of firms has continued unabated throughout the twentieth century. An especially important development, however, occurred in the years immediately following World War I, when the multidivisional form of organization was introduced. In this form managers who control individual divisions and are held responsible for their performance report to higher-level managers, who evaluate them, coordinate their activities, and plan the firm's strategy. This multidivisional form became the template for big business in North America and much of the world for most of the twentieth century. Four U.S. firms—General Motors, Du Pont, Sears Roebuck, and Standard Oil of New Jersey—were the innovators in developing the multidivisional form. Given the importance of this innovation, it is worth considering its history in greater detail.[2]

The history of General Motors in the early 1920s with which this book began

---

[2] The story of the emergence of the divisionalized firm is told by Alfred Chandler, Jr., *Strategy and Structure: Chapters in the History of the American Industrial Enterprise* (Cambridge, MA: MIT Press, 1962). We discussed aspects of this story briefly in Chapter 3.

is a story of the simultaneous creation of a new strategy and a new business structure. The strategy entailed a diversification in GM's existing product line, introducing high-price cars with many standard features and low-price ones with few features. The structure was the creation of separate divisions matched with an expanded central office that would monitor divisional performance and coordinate business strategies.

Du Pont, which in the nineteenth and early twentieth centuries had been an explosives manufacturer, had expanded to meet the surge in demand during World War I. Its capacity to make smokeless powders to propel shells exploded from 8.4 million pounds per year in 1914 to 455 million pounds in 1917. Looking for ways to use its excess manufacturing capabilities after the war, Du Pont diversified into the manufacture of chemical fertilizers, which it hoped would exploit its special abilities in nitrogen-based chemistry. However, the production and marketing of fertilizers to farmers was a very different business from making and selling smokeless powder to governments at war. Unlike governments purchasing war supplies, farmers had to be educated individually about Du Pont's products and convinced to buy them. Different farmers' needs varied with the crops they grew and the soil and weather conditions they faced. New distribution channels were also needed. Product developers and salespeople thus needed to be close to their customers and well informed about the products and about farmers' needs and concerns, and the people who supervised and managed them needed similar knowledge. To accommodate the demands of the fertilizer business, Du Pont eventually established a separate division, with its own independent management running its own manufacturing and sales departments, without detailed direction from the central office.

Before World War I, Sears Roebuck had been a highly centralized mail-order catalog business dealing in "hard goods," such as tools. After the war, under the leadership of former army general Robert Wood, it introduced retail stores on main streets in U.S. towns and cities and expanded its product line to include "soft goods," such as clothing. Sears initially tried to maintain its centralized organization. Centralizing procurement and offering a standardized product line in all its retail outlets allowed the company to tempt suppliers with large orders, enabling it to negotiate especially favorable prices. A strategy of standardized product offerings, however, was incompatible with the product-line expansion and was doomed to failure because customer demands varied widely over the nation. For example, during the winter, warm coats would sell well in the cold northern states but not in Florida or Texas. If the organization was to be responsive to local conditions, managers in the different regional markets needed to be given more authority to run their local operations. Ultimately, Sears reorganized its business by establishing divisions on a regional basis so that its managers could exploit some scale economies while still being responsive to regional and local needs.

The fourth firm to develop the multidivisional form was Standard Oil of New Jersey (now called Exxon). When the U.S. Supreme Court dismembered the old Standard Oil Company in 1912 for antitrust violations, gasoline had only recently surpassed kerosene as the major product of the oil industry. In the 13 years that followed, buffeted by war and recession, growing demands for gasoline, and the discovery of huge new oil fields in Texas and Oklahoma, Standard Oil of New Jersey sought to **integrate vertically** all the operations from oil exploration to gasoline marketing in a single huge firm. From its strong oil refining base, it integrated **upstream** (or **backward**) to supply its refineries with oil, establishing its own extensive oil field exploration and development operations, pumping its own crude oil and transporting it through its own pipelines. It also expanded **downstream** (or **forward**), distributing and selling refined products to retail customers. In addition to these vertical expansions, the company spread **horizontally** from its original kerosene refining base, expanding its production of gasoline and lubricating oil and introducing other petroleum-based products. The company reorganized its management several times in attempts to cope with the increasing complexity of its operations. Some of these changes were intended to centralize authority in order to improve coordination within the firm in marketing or manufacturing petroleum products. These changes typically placed individual plant managers under the control of a central office committee. Other changes were intended to reduce the reliance on committees in order to fix responsibility for performance on individual managers and executives. Finally, in 1925 the company began a process of divisionalization. Within two years the company had arrived at a multidivisional structure with individual managers, rather than central office committees, in charge of each unit.

The Multiproduct Firm

As new management methods and systems evolved and improvements in transportation and telecommunications continued, it became possible to include more and more activities within the domain of a single firm, rather than organizing the same transactions through the arm's-length purchasing that characterized traditional market arrangements. At the same time, rising consumer incomes generated demand for larger quantities of a broader array of products and services, and technological and commercial innovations met these demands.

The giant firms of the early twentieth century were narrowly focused: U.S. Steel made steel, Ford made cars (in only one model and color), and Gillette made razors and blades. At Du Pont, General Motors, Sears, and Standard Oil of New Jersey, the years after adoption of the multidivisional form were accompanied by a great expansion in the firms' scope of activities. Exploiting its corporate strengths, Du Pont introduced new fibers like nylon and other chemistry-based products. GM expanded vertically, making most of its own systems and parts and even some of its own basic materials, like steel. It also expanded horizontally, making trucks, refrigerators, air conditioners, railroad locomotives, and other products that exploited its design and manufacturing expertise, as well as into commercial lending to car buyers. Sears, whose special competence was retail marketing, introduced its own brands of durable goods, integrated vertically to a limited degree into manufacturing, and later expanded its horizontal range by introducing insurance and other retail financial products. Standard Oil also continued to expand both vertically and horizontally into all aspects of petroleum-related businesses, becoming the largest corporation in the world.

During the course of the century, firms worldwide took increasing advantage of the multidivisional form to integrate forward and backward, bringing within the firm transactions with suppliers and customers that previously might have occurred in markets. They also greatly expanded the range of unrelated activities that they encompassed. This was accomplished both by entering new businesses themselves and by buying existing firms. This process peaked in the 1960s with the emergence of the giant conglomerates, any one of which might involve businesses from baking through hotels and car rentals to industrial components manufacturing and telecommunications (as ITT did). The extent to which firms could profitably take over the operations of their suppliers and industrial customers and also expand into new activities is highlighted by the following description of the growth of South Korea's giant Lucky-Goldstar *chaebol* or industrial group:

> My father and I started a cosmetic cream factory in the late 1940s. At the time, no company could supply us with plastic caps of adequate quality for cream jars, so we had to start a plastic business. Plastic caps alone were not sufficient to run the plastic-molding plant, so we added combs,

toothbrushes, and soap boxes. This plastic business also led us to manufacture electric fan blades and telephone cases, which in turn led us to manufacture electrical and electronic products and telecommunication equipment. The plastics business also took us into oil refining which needed a tanker-shipping company. The oil-refining company alone was paying an insurance premium amounting to more than half the total revenue of the then largest insurance company in Korea. Thus, an insurance company was started. This natural step-by-step evolution through related businesses resulted in the Lucky-Goldstar group as we see it today. For the future, we will base our growth primarily on chemicals, energy, and electronics. Our chemical business will continue to expand toward fine chemicals and genetic engineering while the electronics business will grow in the direction of semiconductor manufacturing, fiber optic telecommunications, and eventually, satellite telecommunications.[3]

Drivers of Change: Complementarities and Momentum

Organizations change when their environments and the technologies they use change, and as they accumulate information and experience about what kinds of organizations work best for particular tasks. The key environmental change in the United States in the nineteenth century was the development of technologies (the railroad and telegraph) permitting emergence of unified national markets. As we have discussed, this change favored large-scale production technologies, which in turn favored large-scale organizations like those of the railroads and the steel and oil companies, and led to the development of institutions for large-scale finance. The firms involved in this first round of changes improved and refined their methods, which further changed the environment of traditional industries by making it less costly for them to expand their scales, to find managers trained and experienced in the new methods, and to finance their own large-scale operations.

A system of complementary changes, once put in motion, develops a natural momentum as the range of application expands and as firms improve their methods in the course of using them, making the methods even more effective and valuable. (Recall that two activities are *complementary* if the profit or value created by doing both is greater than the sum of the individual profits from doing just one or the other.) The complementarities among changes in technology, demand, and the structure and scope of enterprise continued to generate positive feedbacks on each other through the twentieth century.

The 1980s in particular saw a refocusing, with firms limiting the number of different businesses they tried to encompass and manage. Simultaneously, many firms expanded the number of products they produced in any one line, increased their abilities to develop and market new products, expanded their activities internationally, and searched for new ways of organizing their internal structures to facilitate these strategic changes. They also sought to create new sorts of relationships with other, independent companies, cooperating in some ways while remaining separate in others.

We will return to examine these more recent developments later. First we must examine the factors that figure into the choice of organizational structure and the scope of a single firm's activities.

---

[3] Koo Cha-Kyung, son of the Lucky-Goldstar founder, as quoted in Francis Aguilar and Dong-Sung Cho, "Gold Star Co. Ltd.," Harvard Business School Case 9-385-264, reprinted in *Management Behind Industrialization: Readings in Korean Business*, Dong-Ki Kim and Linsu Kim, eds. (Korea University Press, 1989), p. 426.

The multidivisional form is the dominant model for organizing business. What are the sources of its strengths, and what are the characteristic difficulties entailed in designing and managing a divisionalized operation?

Advantages of the Multidivisional Form

The multidivisional firm emerged in an era when there were only two major alternatives: highly centralized organization, such as that which had previously existed at Sears and Du Pont, and organizations with almost no central control, such as the form that existed at General Motors before the reforms introduced by Alfred Sloan. Compared to those alternatives, the multidivisional form had decisive advantages.

In centralized organizations, top management and its staff try to stay informed enough to control the operating decisions of their many units directly. In the Standard Oil case, for example, there were oil fields, pipelines and shipping, refineries, marketing operations, research laboratories, financial operations, natural gas operations, and so on. In addition to these domestic operations, there were various foreign operations that further increased the complexity of the business. Even with head-office specialists in finance, marketing, production, and the like overseeing the various activities and with staff assistants to gather and cull information, the operations were far too varied and extensive for any single group of executives to manage closely. The members of the central office committees could never be well enough informed about even a small fraction of these operations to participate effectively in making good operating decisions.

The problem was similar to the one the Hudson's Bay Company had faced more than a century before: The people empowered to make decisions were too far removed from the action and could never have the relevant information in a timely fashion. However, an extra dimension had been added by the vastly greater volume and scope of Standard Oil's business compared to the HBC's. Even if all the relevant information could have been quickly and accurately conveyed to head office, its volume and complexity would have overwhelmed the central decision makers.

Comprehensive decision making in a large organization *must* involve considerable delegation of authority to lower levels of the organization. Even if the organization chart calls for a single individual or committee to run everything, the sheer numbers of decisions to be made would overwhelm the process and as a result, a great number of decisions are made at lower levels or not at all. The design of the multidivisional form recognized this reality and sought to put mechanisms in place to ensure that the decisions made at lower levels by those with the relevant local information would be well coordinated and would be guided by proper incentives—the goals that the North West Company's partnership arrangement had realized long before.

IMPROVED INFORMATION AND INCENTIVES In a multidivisional firm, the division manager is empowered to make operating decisions in his or her unit. That manager resides not in the central office, where he or she is forced to rely on second-hand reports, but near the actual production or markets that define the division, visiting the most critical operations to gain first-hand knowledge of how they work, consulting with those on the scene, hearing suggestions, viewing options, *specializing* in the knowledge that is relevant for running that particular division. There is no attempt to convey all this information to the central office. By consulting with the central office when that seems advisable or necessary, the executive can still take advantage of the experience and perspectives of the headquarters staff, but the headquarters does not exercise direct day-to-day control. Decisions can be made quickly by people on the scene with the relevant knowledge.

With decision-making authority goes responsibility as well. Managers are held accountable for the performance of their divisions and rewarded accordingly. This obviously requires that the central office have information by which to judge performance, but at an operating level this can be largely summary data and financial measures that can be simply transmitted and relatively easily evaluated.

The division manager's intimate knowledge of the operation and its suppliers, customers, and competitors also means that he or she is often also uniquely well placed to recognize new strategic options and evaluate at least their local costs and benefits. Involving the division managers in the formulation of plans and strategies then permits their knowledge to be used in these processes. More detailed information may be needed for planning major strategic investments, but this information need not be transmitted continuously.

By separating different parts of the business into distinct divisions with well-specified areas of responsibility and authority, the problems of determining who is responsible for good or bad performance are lessened and the linkage between the efforts of individuals or small groups and measured performance of their unit are tightened. This allows and encourages stronger incentives to be provided, because performance can be more accurately measured. These increased incentives are provided first at the level of the division managers, who are judged on divisional performance, but pay can also be linked to divisional performance for other divisional employees.

ENHANCED COORDINATION AND CONTROL   Some of the organizations that predated the multidivisional form, such as the North West Company's, did have decentralized decision-making authority. However, the broadened range of activities that was undertaken within single firms in the era after World War I brought increased demands for coordination. Before Sloan's reorganization of General Motors, the manufacturing managers of Buick, Cadillac, Chevrolet, Oakland, and Olds operated with sufficient independence but not with sufficient coordination among themselves and with the sales operations. The central office did not have the information it needed to evaluate and coordinate the plans and decisions of independent managers. The separately chosen product strategies of the units led to more competition among themselves than with Ford. Failure to coordinate on design standards also prevented the divisions from taking full advantage of the potential economies of scale in making or purchasing common components, like sparkplugs and bearings. Failure to coordinate sales and production or to charge inventory costs to the division led to production levels that sometimes substantially outpaced sales.

The multidivisional form could resolve these problems because in addition to its decentralized divisions it also had a central office staff to plan strategy, coordinate divisional activities, and assess the performance of the divisions and their managers. At General Motors, the central office was responsible for assigning target market segments to the individual divisions, creating more comprehensive and useful divisional performance measures, and sponsoring group meetings to explore ways to achieve economies of scale in the combined operations. Its success in achieving these objectives led others to mimic GM's structure and strategy.

The head office also took responsibility for raising capital and allocating it among the divisions. Centralizing the dealings with the capital market economized on the skills needed in this function and, in an era before the development of very sophisticated financial markets, may have led to a lower cost of capital than the individual divisions would have enjoyed as separate companies. The allocation of capital among divisions also may have been more efficient than the market could have accomplished because the central executives in the firm had better access to information.

INCREASED ABILITY TO MANAGE DIVERSE BUSINESSES   Adopting the multidivisional form is complementary to engaging in a wide range of business activities. This can be seen either by thinking about how the form affects the value of widely ranging business activities or about how the widely ranging activities affect the form. In one direction, adopting the form is most valuable when the businesses being managed are already diverse, as we saw in the histories of the four companies that innovated the structure. In the other direction, adopting a multidivisional form makes additional expansions into new activities easier to manage and therefore more valuable.

Problems of Managing a Divisionalized Firm

The challenges in efficiently designing and managing a divisionalized firm involve the same dimensions on which the form finds its strengths. First, divisions must be delineated, reporting relationships structured, and activities allocated among the divisions and between them and the head office so that coordination is facilitated. Second, information, decision, evaluation, and reward systems need to be structured to encourage the appropriate behavior. Third, the scope of activities that the firm is going to undertake must be chosen in light of the costs and benefits.

DEFINING DIVISIONS AND REPORTING RELATIONSHIPS   Often there will be a variety of ways in which divisions can be defined: geographically, by the technology employed, by the products produced or the particular market segments being served, and so on. Moreover, there is an issue of how many divisions to establish and where to draw the lines between them. The choices made on these dimensions may be very important to the way the firm functions and its success in coordinating its activities.

No matter how the cuts are made to divide up the company's business, there will inevitably be mismatches between the way problems present themselves and the way the company is structured. If the divisions are defined geographically with, for example, a domestic and a foreign operation, then coordination problems will arise with customers or suppliers who operate in both markets, have not structured themselves this way, and want to deal with one entity, not two. This has been an issue for IBM in dealing with international businesses that use its computers and want to have uniform systems and service across their operations.

Defining divisions technologically facilitates dealing with R&D, design, and especially manufacturing issues, because these are apt to be heavily determined by the technology. Having only a single unit dealing with each technology then means that coordination across divisions is not necessary on that dimension. However, the technology of production may have little to do with customer needs: Du Pont's attempt to operate their explosives and fertilizer business as one unit based on the nitrogen-chemistry underlying both products illustrates that kind of difficulty.

A product-based definition becomes problematic when opportunities are present to make different divisions' products in the same production facilities or to sell the products of different divisions to the same customers. The customers may want to buy a whole variety of different products without having to deal with different divisions. Developing new products in this context can lead to special problems. For example, at one point two Hewlett Packard divisions—one that made hand calculators and one that made minicomputers—were developing personal computers, with the two designs being incompatible. Defining divisions by market segments means that the same problems with suppliers and production will arise across divisions and have to be addressed repeatedly.

Ideally, to avoid the need for coordinating across division boundaries, divisions should be self-contained units. The problem is that being manageably small and also self-contained may be incompatible. Defining the divisions very broadly minimizes

Coordinating the Computer Businesses of Hewlett Packard

William Hewlett and David Packard founded the Hewlett Packard Company (HP) in a Palo Alto garage, where they made scientific and industrial instruments. The company achieved immense success, a superb reputation for high-quality products, and an exceptionally loyal clientele.

HP has a very strong corporate culture. One of its elements is to encourage responsibility and innovativeness by maintaining extreme divisional independence. Its policy has been to keep divisions as small, manageable entities with which their members can identify and whose success depends on their efforts. Consequently, whenever a successful division grew too large ($20 million in sales or 1500 employees was the usual point in the 1980s), it was split up or a new division established.

This degree of independence created coordination problems, even in the instrument business, which is characterized by relatively discrete products. However, with HP's entry into the computer business, these difficulties intensified. The traditional divisions were individually too small to design and produce whole computer systems on their own. Thus, work had to be broken up among divisions, with one producing hard drives, another the input-output systems, a third handling display terminals, and so on, but without a single individual with responsibility for the project's success and authority to match. This division of responsibilities led to serious coordination difficulties for a system whose parts have to fit and work together. The coordination task was further complicated by the rapid pace of change in the computer business, which put a premium on speedy product development and quick response to changing technological, demand, and competitive conditions.

To overcome the resulting conflicts, HP experimented through the 1980s with increasing centralization, assigning single executives more and more responsibility over computer operations, and shifting the structure of reporting relationships to encourage better coordination. The centralizing moves represented wrenching changes for HP and presented a serious challenges to HP's vision of itself.

Based in part on Richard T. Pascale, *Managing on the Edge*, (New York: Simon and Schuster, 1990).

the interactions among them and the need to coordinate these. However, divisions that are too big run into all the problems of firms that are too big: It becomes impossible for the senior divisional managers to keep informed and to find time to deal with all the problems, and measuring individual contributions for performance evaluations becomes too difficult.

A modern solution to these problems is to keep divisions relatively small but to group together those that are likely to need coordination among them. The individual division managers in the group then all report to one senior executive, who is responsible for the group and rewarded for its performance. The largest firms may even have a number of groups, with their presidents reporting to another level of

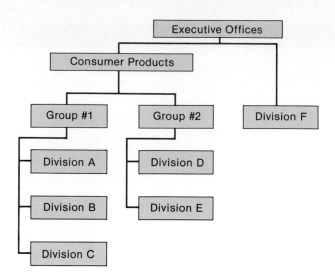

Figure 16.1: The structure of a divisionalized firm with division groupings.

executive below the top levels of the firm. Figure 16.1 illustrates a hypothetical divisionalized firm with a group structure. Divisions A, B, and C are in Group 1 and report to a group president. Divisions D and E are in Group 2 under its president. These two group presidents report through a single executive to headquarters. In the figure, these are groups of consumer products divisions. Division F, which might, for example, be a heavy equipment division with little need to share information or plans with consumer products divisions, reports directly to headquarters.

In this structure, disputes between divisions are ultimately to be settled at the lowest level of the hierarchy to which both divisions report. Thus, a conflict between divisions A and B over which will get a given customer's business would be settled by the group president, but conflicts between C and D over the transfer price that one will pay the other for its output would be settled at the level to which the presidents of the two different groups report. A conflict between E and F would go all the way to the top of the firm.

In general, the problem is to design this structure to reduce coordination problems and to handle those that do arise at the lowest possible level. The higher the level to which decisions must be pushed, the slower is decision making, the greater are the costs of information transmittal, and the greater are the possible influence costs that may be incurred as successive levels of executives campaign for their units' interests.

ASSIGNING ACTIVITIES AND RESPONSIBILITY TO LEVELS   Adapting well to changing local circumstances, using local information well, saving on the costs of information transfer, and making effective use of scarce central management time and attention all argue for pushing decision-making power and responsibility as far down in the organization as possible. Economies of scale of various sorts may mean that not all activities should be pushed down to the division level, however.

For example, almost all firms maintain the finance function at the corporate level. Research and development may be done at quite low levels, where the scientists and engineers are close to the constituencies they serve, or they may be centralized. Hewlett Packard has tended to follow the first model, whereas AT&T, before its court-ordered break-up, centralized at least the more basic R&D for the Bell System in Bell Laboratories. Japanese firms, in which personnel are frequently shifted between divisions and firm-financed investments in human capital are especially important, tend to centralize the human-resource function to facilitate tracking individual employees' progress and managing their career development. In many North American firms, in contrast, personnel management is more decentralized. By separating the sales and distribution functions from the product divisions, many firms seek to gain the economies of scale in distribution and sales, for example, by having one sales representative call on customers or one truck deliver a range of different products. A problem is that the information that salespeople may gather from customers needs to be transmitted to many different units.

INCENTIVE AND CONTROL ISSUES   Decentralizing authority facilitates making good use of local information, but the very fact that decisions are based on information that is not available to headquarters exacerbates the moral hazard problem. Consequently, incentive systems must be put in place, incurring the kinds of costs discussed in Chapters 7 and 8. Granting decision-making authority and assigning financial responsibility for outcomes to the same person are complementary actions: Each is more valuable when done with the other. As we have seen, providing incentives effectively requires creating good performance measures, which is another cost of divisionalization. The spread of divisionalization was promoted in part by the development of accounting and management methods that allowed improved incentives for division managers.

The point that a manager with broader authority should be given stronger incentives is an application of the incentive intensity principle. For example, a division manager who controls sales and marketing as well as production has more ways available in which to improve unit performance and can be profitably given more intense incentives. The relationship, however, is one of complementarity, so the reverse implication also holds: The greater the manager's financial incentives, the greater the proper scope of the manager's authority.

THE TRANSFER PRICING PROBLEM   The need for divisions to transact with one another provides a second way in which incentives can affect the appropriate allocation of activities among divisions. As we discussed in Chapter 3, interdivisional transactions are quite common. They are unavoidable in a vertically integrated company in which one division supplies inputs to others, as in the example of the integrated oil company where the refinery buys crude oil from the pipeline division that in turn buys the oil from the production division. If a company sells systems as well as individual products such as personal computer systems that consist of the actual computer, a display, a keyboard and mouse, a modem for communicating with other computers, and a printer, each of which could also be sold separately, then each of these might sensibly be made in a different division. When sold together they will have to be transferred to the unit selling the system. Because transfer prices determine the revenues received in internal transactions, they are of immense concern to division managers who are paid for division performance.

We saw in Chapter 3 how, if managers have discretion to decide how much they want to buy and sell in interdivisional transactions, wrongly set transfer prices can hurt corporate profitability. Yet allowing managers such freedom gives them greater opportunities to respond fully to incentives and provides competitive pressure for internal suppliers to maintain cost and quality control. This means that the setting of transfer prices is an important issue.

We also saw in Chapter 3 that if there is a competitive market for the product or service being transferred, then the transfer price should equal the market price (perhaps adjusted for any cost advantages of internal supply). However, when the external price reflects monopoly distortions or when the product simply is unavailable outside, then this solution is inappropriate or unavailable.

An alternative is to let the managers involved bargain over the transfer price and the quantities to be transferred. Because each is likely to be privately informed about the costs and benefits of the transaction to his or her department, however, there is the possibility that the sort of bargaining problems discussed in Chapter 5 will create inefficiencies. The supplying division will be inclined to overstate the costs of production in order to get a higher price, and the purchasing division will be inclined to understate the marginal value of the transferred good in order to reduce the price it pays. The result could be that too little is transferred and final output is too low. The same result is likely to occur with other systems as well.

Double Marginalization: The Mathematics of Transfer Pricing

The nature of the difficulty can be seen by assuming that the system in place allows the supplier or *upstream* division to state the price at which it will supply an input to the final producer or *downstream* division, and then the downstream division decides how much to buy. Suppose the downstream division markets the final product directly to customers outside the firm at a constant cost c_F per unit. It faces a demand curve that is downward sloping. Production of a unit of final product requires one unit of the intermediate good, which can be produced at a cost of c_I per unit. Thus, the total cost of the final good to the firm as a whole is $c_F + c_I$, and the firm would want the quantity sold of the final good and thus the amount transferred of the intermediate good to be determined by the condition that the marginal revenue on final sales be equal to $c_F + c_I$.

For example, if the final demand is given by $P = 10 - Q/16$, where Q is the amount sold at a price of P, then total revenue is $10Q - Q^2/16$, and marginal revenue is $MR = 10 - Q/8$ (this can be quickly obtained by differentiating the total revenue function). If the value of c_F is 2 and that of c_I is 1, then the marginal cost to the firm as a whole is 3. Equating MR to marginal cost gives $10 - Q/8 = 3$, or $Q = 56$, which means the final price should be $P = 6.50$. These calculations are shown in the first column of Table 16.1.

To achieve this in a divisionalized firm under the given procedure, the transfer price should be $T = 1$, or more generally, $T = c_I$. Facing this price, the manager of the downstream division will see a marginal cost to his or her division of $2 + T = 2 + 1 = 3$, the actual cost to the firm. He or she will then select $Q = 56$, (where $MR = 2 + T$) and order this many units of the intermediate good from the upstream division. If any other value of T is selected, then the downstream manager will buy and produce an amount that does not maximize corporate profits. If T is set at 4, for example, then the manager downstream will face a marginal cost of $2 + 4 = 6$ and will select $Q = 32$,

Table 16.1 An Example of Double Marginalization in Transfer Pricing

	Integrated Firm	Downstream Division	Upstream Division
Demand	$P = 10 - Q/16$	$P = 10 - Q/16$	$T = 8 - Q/8$
Total Revenue	$10Q - Q^2/16$	$10Q - Q^2/16$	$8Q - Q^2/8$
Marginal Revenue	$10 - Q/8$	$10 - Q/8$	$8 - Q/4$
Total Variable Cost	$3Q$	$(2 + T)Q$	Q
Marginal Cost	3	$2 + T$	1
Quantity	56	$8(8 - T)$	28
Price	6.50	8.25	$T = 4.50$

where MR equals the marginal cost he or she faces. This would lead to less profit for the firm. Entering different values for T in the second column of the table gives the quantities that result.

At a transfer price equal to its constant marginal cost, however, the revenues of the upstream division are just equal to its total variable costs.[4] Its manager, being evaluated on the division's profits, would do better with a higher transfer price, even though this hurts corporate profitability. For example, he or she shows a net division profit of $(4 - 1)32 = 96$ if the transfer price is set at 4.

More generally, the relationship $MR = c_F + T$ defines how much the downstream division will want to sell on the final market and thus how much the upstream division can sell internally at any transfer price T. Equating the marginal cost of $c_F + T$ to the marginal revenue of $10 - Q/8$ leads to $Q = 8(8 - T)$. This formula indicates the amount the downstream division will want to sell as a function of the price it pays for the input and thus the amount of input it will buy. This is effectively a demand curve for the upstream division and is entered accordingly in the first row of the third column. For the upstream division to maximize its profits, its manager will equate the *marginal revenue* facing the upstream division to its marginal cost, c_I. The fact that the upstream division considers the marginal revenue of the firm as its (inverse) demand curve and looks to the curve that is marginal to it in computing the transfer price is the source for the term **double marginalization**.

The inverse demand corresponding to a demand of $Q = 8(8 - T)$ is $T = 8 - Q/8$. This gives a marginal revenue of $8 - Q/4$. With a marginal cost of $c_I = 1$, this yields $Q = 28$, $T = 4.50$ as the optimal choice for the upstream division (see the third column of the table). This gives the upstream division profits of $28(4.50 - 1) = 98$. With only 28 units rather than 56 being transferred, however, final goods' output is half what it takes to maximize corporate profits. Corporate profits, which would have been $56(6.50 - 3) = 196$, are now only $28(8.25 - 3) = 147$, where 8.25 is the price the downstream division charges in the final market when it faces a transfer price of 4.50 and correspondingly chooses to sell 28 units. (We will see this sort of double marginalization problem again later in the chapter.)

Approaches to the Problem.   It is probably unreasonable to expect that the upstream manager would be allowed to set the monopoly price for the intermediate good. Still, there will be a tendency for the upstream manager to select too high a price for corporate profit maximization. Similarly, if the price is left to the downstream manager, with the upstream manager deciding how much to supply, then the downstream manager will have an incentive to take advantage of his or her monopsony position and set *too low* a transfer price. This results again in too little being transferred.

One solution to this problem might be to order the transfer to occur at the upstream division's marginal cost. However, if the head office does not know the actual costs in the upstream division, then the manager of this division may have an incentive to overstate his or her division's marginal costs to get a higher transfer price. This would again result in more revenues and recorded contribution in the upstream division, but lower corporate profits overall. Another might be to make the upstream division a cost center, with transfers at marginal cost and the manager being rewarded for keeping costs down. This will not be easily implemented if the upstream division

---

[4] With constant marginal costs, average variable cost equals marginal cost.

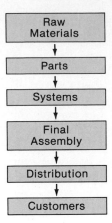

Figure 16.2: A hypothetical single product firm.

also has markets outside the firm, however. A third possibility is to merge the two divisions, but this merely converts a problem between divisions in the firm into one between departments in the division, unless it is accompanied by some other real change in responsibilities and incentives.

DECIDING ON THE SCOPE OF THE FIRM   The multidivisional firm is able to take on and manage a much wider set of activities than would be possible under a less decentralized form of organization. As Coase accentuated, the costs of administering transactions internally versus the transaction costs of conducting them through markets determine the boundaries of the firm. The innovation of the multidivisional form lowered the costs of internal administration. This means that the range of transactions optimally brought within the firm should increase. Which activities should the expanded firm undertake? That is the subject of the next two sections.

VERTICAL BOUNDARIES AND RELATIONS

We begin our study by examining a highly simplified version of the problem of producing and distributing one single kind of good. Figure 16.2 illustrates the usual conception of this process. Production begins upstream, for example, with the extraction of ores to be processed into the raw materials from which the good will be made. Using hired labor and machinery of various kinds, the firm and its suppliers convert these raw materials through a sequence of steps into parts and systems before assembling the various systems into a final product. At the last stage, the product is distributed to customers. For example, among the materials used in the production of an automobile are steel, aluminum, rubber, plastics, foam, and so on, which are made into parts like frames, padding, and covers for seats, as well as chassis, dashboards, and other parts. These parts are in turn assembled into systems. For example, seat systems may incorporate frames, levers, springs, padding, covers, and so on. Finally the several systems are assembled into the product, which must be distributed downstream to the customer.

Figure 16.2 highlights the many steps involved in the creation of a product and its delivery to the final consumer and hints that there may be many ways to divide responsibility for the steps. At one theoretical extreme, each activity might be carried out by a separate firm, which buys inputs from the firm one step upstream and sells its product to the next firm downstream. At the other extreme, a fully vertically integrated automobile company would own mines from which to obtain raw materials, smelters and mills to create usable rolls of steel, and aluminum mills, plastics factories, rubber plantations, tire plants, die makers, and so on, providing the capabilities for operations from the digging of the raw materials to the final assembly of the product.

It would also be integrated further into downstream operations, owning trucks, rail cars, and cargo ships with which to distribute its cars to the dealerships, which it would also own. Its own employees would also provide the various staff services it needs. Its law department would handle contracts and litigation. Its accounting, engineering, and advertising departments could provide those services without relying on outside suppliers. Its finance specialists would handle its relations with the capital market, and its senior executives would plot strategy and its implementation on their own, without relying on outside consultants.

A strategy based on extreme vertical integration was tried by Ford Motor Company before World War II, but was later abandoned. In modern times, few firms even approach the pattern of complete vertical integration. The question is: Why not? What alternatives does the firm have for organizing its activities? Why does it rely on independent suppliers for some services and its own divisions for others? What determines which services are (or should be) purchased from outside suppliers and which the firm provides for itself?

Advantages of Simple Market Procurement

For many of the inputs that a company uses, actual market conditions pretty well approximate the idealized competitive market model of Chapter 3. As long as the firm's scale of purchases is too small to make it profitable either to design highly specific inputs for its own particular needs or to make standardized products at an efficient scale, firms tend to rely on independent suppliers. For example, even the largest, most highly integrated firms rarely make the paper clips, ballpoint pens, and coffee pots used in their offices, nor do they make the furniture, file cabinets, and office equipment. Most do not maintain construction divisions to build their buildings and factories or maintain fleets of aircraft to transport employees. The reason is that these are standard goods and services for which there are many suppliers, so the firm buying inputs can enjoy the many advantages of the competitive market system without fear of a hold-up problem.

ECONOMIES OF SCALE   One significant advantage of using independent suppliers arises when scale economies are important in producing the input the firm needs but its own level of usage of the input would not allow the firm to achieve the minimum efficient scale. For example, airlines are most efficiently run at a large enough scale to enable regular flight scheduling. Even the largest industrial companies benefit by buying air transportation services provided as part of a system serving many customers rather than providing the services for themselves.

Companies do sometimes maintain their own small planes for executives whose time is so valuable that it is efficient to schedule special flights to meet their needs. They may also own planes for highly specialized transportation needs. For example, a company exploring for oil in the Arctic might provide its own specially equipped aircraft and prepare its own landing sites. Even in this case, however, if other companies need a similar service and there are economies of scale or scope in providing it, the service might be provided by an independent firm. Alternatively, the firm might set up an operation to serve its own needs and also market the service to others. For example, the Kimberly-Clark paper company, which has production facilities in a number of small towns in Wisconsin, started an air service for its personnel that developed into Midwest Airlines.[5]

---

[5] Milton Moskowitz, Robert Levering, and Michael Katz, *Everybody's Business* (New York: Doubleday, 1990), p. 501.

ECONOMIES OF SCOPE   Even when the scale of the supplier's production of any particular product or service is small, the supplier may enjoy economies of scope by engaging in activities that are unconnected with the buying firm's business. An example comes from gasoline retailing, where it is often profitable to sell convenience foods or to provide car washing or repair service at a gas station. In this business, oil companies frequently purchase retailing services from independently owned gas stations. They also sometimes handle retailing themselves through company-owned outlets managed by employees. Theory suggests that the choice between these two patterns of organization should depend on whether the outlet provides services other than gasoline sales.

Even though the provision of these other services does not directly affect oil company profits from gasoline sales, these extra activities can affect the relationship between the oil company and the retail gas station manager. A business with multiple activities has an effort allocation problem, requiring that incentives be devised so that the station manager will devote the proper amount of time and effort to each aspect of station operations. As we saw in Chapter 7, it is more expensive to provide contractual incentives to agents engaged in multiple activities. The problem becomes more severe when measuring performance in some of the activities is relatively hard or when accurate performance assessments can be made only over long periods of time. In these cases, it is advantageous to deal with an independent owner rather than an employee.

In automotive repair, performance is hard to measure over short periods of time because shoddy service may increase short-run profits while eroding sales and profits (both in repair work and in gasoline sales) only over a much longer period of time. This implies that the managers of stations providing repair services should tend to be residual claimants rather than oil company employees so that they will have an owners' incentives to care for the long-term value of the station. The relative ease of hiding and misappropriating revenues from repair business works in the same direction. The evidence supports this prediction. One recent study found that among stations offering automotive repair services, 96 percent of outlets in the sample were not owned by the affiliated oil company but were instead operated as franchises.[6] Another study used a different sample in which 83 percent of all outlets offered automotive repair services. Only 25 percent of the outlets owned by the oil companies offered such services, however.[7]

CORE COMPETENCIES   We have previously explained that core competencies are a kind of economy of scope connecting products made at different points in time. For example, the costs that a firm incurs in developing an ability to design, manufacture, or market a certain group of products may be recouped from sales of all the products in the group. A firm may choose to rely on an independent supplier even when there are no economies of scale in manufacturing the current generation of the product and no economies of scope among existing products because the supplier has developed a special competence to improve the product or to incorporate quickly the latest manufacturing innovations to keep production costs low. The box on EDS and Continental Airlines illustrates such a decision: EDS has a core competence in

---

[6] J.A. Brickley and F.H. Dark, "The Choice of Organizational Form: the Case of Franchising," *Journal of Financial Economics*, 4 (1987), 401–20. In a franchise arrangement, the franchisee (the service-station owner) makes contractual payments to the franchisor (the oil company) for use of its name, but remains the residual claimant. A fuller discussion of franchising is given later.

[7] Andrea Shepard, "Contractual Form, Retail Price and Asset Characteristics," working paper, MIT, (1990).

EDS and Continental Airlines

System One is a subsidiary of the U.S. carrier, Continental Airlines. The subsidiary owns the airline's computer reservations system, which provided services to nearly 20 percent of the airline reservation agents in the United States. Until 1991 the subsidiary also provided various data and computation services, such as air traffic scheduling, to about 170 different airlines.

In 1991 System One signed a ten-year contract with Electronic Data Services (EDS), a subsidiary of General Motors Corporation, to perform the airline services function. EDS, with 1990 revenues of $6.1 billion, was already a leading supplier of information services to the energy and banking industries. It contracted to provide the information service at a lower cost than Continental could achieve and agreed to accept 1,860 System One employees as part of the bargain.

There are economies of scale in providing information services to airlines, which arise from writing the programs and maintaining the data bases. Many of the services EDS will provide, such as route scheduling, are standard services that require no specific investments. These facts clarify why smaller airlines do not provide the information services function for themselves, but not whether Continental Airlines or EDS would be the most efficient provider. EDS has developed special skills useful for running its information service businesses, but it has limited knowledge of the operation of airlines. By hiring System One employees as a group, it may be purchasing the necessary airline expertise.

Source: Agis Sapulkas, "G.M. Unit Will Run Airline Data Service," *The New York Times,* (April 24, 1991), C4.

computerized information services and that Continental cannot match. Alternatively, a firm might undertake production of a good itself even when outside procurement would be directly cheaper because the firm wants to build or maintain a competency.

The magnitude of economies of scope and the nature of core competencies are particularly important for decisions about the horizontal extent of the firm, so we postpone most of our discussion of them, including our examples, to that section of this chapter.

INDEPENDENT, COMPETITIVE SUPPLIERS   As a buyer in a competitive market for a standard input, a firm need not show favoritism to any particular supplier. It can purchase the input from the supplier willing to meet its needs at the lowest price. When technical innovations occur, even if they are adopted by only some of the suppliers, the buyer typically enjoys some of the extra value that is created, in the form of either higher quality or a lower price.

If the buyer had its own supply division that was less innovative than the competition, the buyer might face pressure to continue to purchase supplies from its own unit to maintain employment and employee morale. Even if the firm successfully resisted the influence attempt, it would suffer influence costs as employees spent their energies trying to protect their jobs. It is also possible that these pressures would succeed in forcing the company to incur extra costs to maintain an inefficient unit.

Compounding these problems is the fact that if the supply division anticipates this protection, its employees will feel less pressure to be innovative.

Generally, for standardized inputs that can be supplied by competitive firms earning only normal profits, there is little that the firm can gain by making the product itself. Owner-operated suppliers in a competitive market are driven to be innovative by the desire to realize even temporary cost advantages and earn an increased profit. A similar force drives them to be responsive to customers' other needs. Accumulating experience as they run their own businesses, owner-managers have the knowledge, motivation, and authority to make decisions that maximize value. The buyer cannot do better producing on its own from scratch. The alternative of buying out the independent supplier and bringing it into the firm as division exposes its manager (the former owner) to being held up, with the new boss reneging on promises.

The same qualitative advantages are present even in firms that are not owner operated, though usually to a smaller degree. The top executives of an independent firm usually capture a larger portion of the value they create by making good business decisions than do divisional managers within a larger firm. Indeed, large organizations tend to emphasize distributional equity to avoid organizational politics and the resulting influence costs. The greater claim by top executives on their business profits strengthens incentives and contributes to improved performance.

COMPETITIVE BIDDING   Even when the needed supplies are specialized and are not available through simple competitive market transactions, many of the advantages of competitive markets can sometimes be enjoyed by soliciting competitive bids. For example, an office building may have to be built at a particular time and place and according to a particular design, but the service of constructing the building may still be a general skill for which there are many qualified suppliers. By relying on an independent supplier, the firm takes advantage of the best available resources and, provided there is adequate competition, pays only the real economic cost of the service. From the perspective of the economy as a whole, hiring the contractor and subcontractors with available resources avoids leaving crews idle and creates value, some of which is captured by the purchasing firm.

Advantages of Vertical Integration

As we have seen, the advantages of simple market procurement are greatest when particular circumstances prevail. These include the use of standard inputs, the presence of several competing suppliers, economies of scale in the supply firms that are too large to be duplicated by the buyer, economies of scope that would force the vertically integrated firm into unrelated businesses, and the absence of specific investments on the part of either the buyer or the seller. When these conditions fail, vertical integration can enjoy significant advantages over simple market procurement.

IMPROVED COORDINATION AND BETTER PROTECTION OF INVESTMENTS   In modern economies, firms frequently use components and services that are highly specialized. In the area of marketing services, for example, a company selling a new medical imaging system would need to train the sales force in the uses of the product so that they can explain how the product can be used and why it is advantageous to use it. This knowledge would then also permit the salespeople to report back effectively on customer reactions, needs, and suggestions. Using an independent distributor would require close coordination in the development of training materials and a routine for transferring information from customers back through their firm to the producer. The training itself would constitute a specific investment, and some arrangements would have to be made to protect that investment. The box on the Rolm Corporation reports

Strategic Business Decisions at the Rolm Corporation

The Rolm Corporation was founded in 1969 as a manufacturer of computers made to military specifications. By 1973 the company was profitable on sales of about $3 million annually. Looking for additional ways to apply technology, the company's founders saw an opportunity to market the first computer-controlled private branch exchange (PBX) systems. PBXs are the systems used in private businesses to switch incoming telephone calls among employees, to manage internal office telephone communications, and to direct outgoing calls to an available "trunk" connected to the public telephone system.

The product that Rolm proposed to make had several advantages over existing PBX units. It introduced new features, like call transfer, multiparty conference calling, speed dialing, restrictions on toll calls from particular phones, accounting records for calls from individual phones, and so on, all of which were beyond the capability of the older electromechanical switching equipment. In addition, using the computer to route calls in the cheapest way could reduce phone bills. Despite these advantages, Rolm's decision to enter the PBX business was regarded skeptically by industry observers. Rolm's own consultants had argued that computer technology would be too expensive for use in telephone switching and that it was foolhardy for such a small company to use technology to compete with AT&T and its world-famous Bell Laboratories research subsidiary. Spurning this advice, Rolm decided to proceed with the project.

The decision to develop and market this new product required that Rolm make a number of choices. First, should the system be designed to use existing telephones or new ones better suited to a computer-controlled system? Using existing telephones would reduce the technical capabilities of the system. However, making special telephones would either stretch the company's engineering and production resources or force it to coordinate with a specialized telephone supplier, which might lead to delays or other problems. Rolm decided to use standard telephones for its first system.

Second, should the company build its own sales force to market the new system to businesses? Or, should it instead rely on some existing sales force? At the time, AT&T held a 78 percent share of the national market, with General Telephone and Electronics (GTE) and United Technologies as its nearest competitors, but there were also some smaller companies providing installation and service of imported PBX systems.

Building its own sales force to sell to a national market would be time consuming and costly and would not make the best use of the company's strengths, which lay in its engineering capabilities. Accordingly, Rolm decided to rely on eight existing regional PBX sales and service organizations. To enable installers trained in the older electromechanical technology to install its computer-controlled systems, Rolm compromised its design so that the external connections on the new PBX resembled those on the older systems. To protect the selling organizations' specific investments in training, Rolm offered them exclusive territorial franchises.

The first PBX units were shipped in 1975, leading to sales of $1.3 million for that year. These grew to $10 million in 1976, and $20 million in 1977. In 1978 GTE signed up to become a Rolm distributor and Rolm began to internalize part of the marketing function by adding three marketing companies of its own. By 1980 annual sales were $200 million, with half coming from Rolm's own sales force.

Source: Lecture by Rolm cofounder Robert Maxfield, Stanford University, May 21, 1991.

how one high-technology company made and managed its decision to use independent distributors.

Buying inputs for manufacturing raises similar difficulties. In simple market transacting, the downstream firms with knowledge of customer demand decide what to make and sell and then buy the materials, parts, systems, or services they need from upstream firms. Taking into account quoted prices plus shipping costs and other terms, they seek to acquire the needed inputs as inexpensively as possible. They may solicit competitive bids or negotiate with suppliers over prices and features, especially for nonstandard inputs. Soliciting bids to provide a good at the best possible price requires that the characteristics of the desired product be specified in great detail, with drawings and performance specifications prepared before the bidding can begin. Otherwise, the bidders can only guess at the costs involved and may refuse to make any price commitments. This problem is especially severe for new products and for companies that engage in frequent product redesign. Moreover, if producing the desired input efficiently requires that the supplier make highly specific investments, the necessary investments may be blocked or diminished by the threat of a subsequent hold-up.

Vertical integration alleviates all of these problems. In the integrated organization, planning entails consultation between those who sell the product, those who make it, and those who supply parts or systems for it. Together they forecast capacity needs and identify product improvements and investments in specialized equipment that promise higher quality or lower production costs. If the investment is highly specific, vertical integration alleviates the hold-up problem by eliminating the opportunity to negotiate over the price paid to the owner of the newly created asset.

It would be a gross exaggeration, however, to suppose that vertical integration completely eliminates these incentive problems. As we have already seen, even in an integrated organization, individual managers have different interests. The manager of the sparkplug unit may still haggle over the transfer price of sparkplugs because this number affects the unit's recorded revenues and the manager's measured performance. Unlike the owner of an independent firm, however, the inside manager cannot threaten to withhold supply and bring downstream production to a halt if he or she is unhappy with the established transfer price. This ability to continue performing disputed services while deferring any settling up until later is more limited in ordinary market procurement.

REDUCING THE NEED FOR STRONG PERFORMANCE INCENTIVES   An independent supplier makes its own decisions about how to allocate its time and effort among various activities, including supplying profitable services to other customers. According to the equal compensation principle, to induce this supplier to pay adequate attention to the firm's needs, appropriate financial incentives are needed. The more difficult it is to

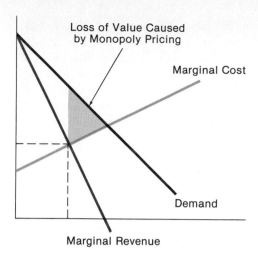

Figure 16.3: Monopoly losses.

measure performance and hence to provide financial incentives, the more costly it is to use an independent supplier for the service.

The importance of this factor was confirmed by a recent study of the choices that electronic components manufacturers face about whether to use their own direct (employee) sales agents or to rely on independent manufacturers' representatives who would also represent other firms.[8] Examining 159 U.S. sales districts of 13 manufacturers, the study found that the two principal determinants of vertical integration into sales were the difficulty of evaluating performance and the importance of nonselling activities. When performance is difficult to measure, providing strong incentives is costly, whether they are given to employees or independents. Weaker incentives can be used for employee agents, however, without the fear that they will emphasize selling the products of others, as an independent representative would if faced with low commissions. Similarly, because nonselling activities by sales agents in the field are especially hard to evaluate, the equal compensation principle suggests that the commissions for sales by these agents should be set low to avoid inducing an overemphasis on selling versus nonselling activities. Again, using weak incentives with independent representatives risks their shifting effort to other firms' products.

AVOIDING MONOPOLY DISTORTIONS   A principal cost of using an independent supplier when the input market is not competitive is that the supplier may try to exercise monopoly power, driving its price up above marginal cost. Figure 16.3 recaps the standard economic analysis, in which the higher price may lead to an inefficiently low use of the input and a real loss of value. This outcome is not assured because the parties may negotiate a price-quantity agreement between themselves to avoid some of the inefficiency. In general, however, bargaining will be imperfect and some value losses will remain.

Simply integrating into the supply business to eliminate the monopoly distortion is hardly a costless solution. As indicated earlier, independent firms enjoy a number of significant advantages. The buying firm could try to offset these advantages by increasing its own scale and selling to others (as Lucky Goldstar did). Alternatively, it could acquire the supplier and maintain its scale of operations. It could then use an incentive contract to motivate the formerly independent manager, but this involves incurring costs of the kind we analyzed in Chapters 7 and 8.

---

[8] Erin Anderson, "The Salesperson as Outside Agent or Employee: A Transaction Cost Analysis," *Management Science*, 4 (Summer 1985), 234–54.

If both a firm and its independent supplier have some monopoly power, then the tendency of each is to add a monopoly profit margin to its costs. This can lead to an excessively high price for the buyer's output, a price even higher than the level that would maximize the two firms' total profits. A vertically integrated firm that sought to maximize its profits would charge a lower price, resulting in both higher profits and happier consumers. This *double marginalization* is the same phenomenon that we studied in transfer pricing, and we can illustrate it with the same example.

A Numerical Example of Double Marginalization

The data and calculations are essentially those summarized in Table 16.1, except that now the first column should be interpreted as the choices that would be made in an integrated firm that maximized overall profits, whereas the second and third columns refer, respectively, to the downstream and upstream firms when there is no vertical integration. The (inverse) demand for the final product is $P = 10 - Q/16$, where again Q is the number of units that will be purchased if the price is P. The upstream firm produces the component needed by the downstream firm at a marginal cost of $1 per unit, and it charges a price T for it. Besides the price that it pays to the upstream firm, the downstream firm incurs additional costs of $2 per unit that it makes. Thus, as in the transfer-pricing discussion, the actual cost of making the product is $3 per unit, but the downstream firm's marginal cost is $(2 + T)$.

If the two stages of production are combined under the control of a single firm (without affecting the cost of production), the total variable cost of production is $3Q$, with marginal cost 3. The integrated monopolist's marginal revenue is $10 - Q/8$. Equating the marginal revenue to the marginal cost of 3 leads, as before, to the conclusion that the optimal quantity is $Q = 56$. Then, from the demand equation, $P = 6.50$.

Suppose the upstream sets a price of T for its component if the two stages of production are not integrated. Then the downstream firm's cost per unit is $2 + T$, which is also its marginal cost. Equating this to the marginal revenue of $10 - Q/8$ leads, as before, to $Q = 8(8 - T)$ as the demand facing the upstream firm. Solving for T, the inverse demand facing the supplier is $T = 8 - Q/8$. Because the upstream firm's marginal cost is 1, this leads to the conclusion that T will be set so that Q equals 28—only half as much as the output of an integrated monopolist. Substituting into the consumer demand function, this quantity implies that the consumer price must be $8.25, even higher than the price charged by an integrated, profit-maximizing monopolist!

Note, however, that these calculations assume that the integrated firm is a profit maximizer that somehow solves the transfer pricing problem. This is not an innocuous assumption. Without it, the problem is not really solved by integration: It is merely converted into a problem of transfer pricing.

CAPTURING SUPPLIERS' RENTS   There are various reasons that suppliers could earn above-average profits in providing inputs to the buying firm. We discussed one important reason in Chapter 8: It may not be possible to induce a supplier to sustain the quality of its production without giving the supplier something to lose. That something generally takes the form of a stream of extra earnings, or *rents*, from the supply relationship. These rents imply that the price the firm pays for its inputs must exceed the supplier's full economic cost of production, including a normal return on the supplier's capital. Vertical integration provides a way for the firm to capture some or all of these rents.

For any of the reasons described earlier, it may not be possible for the firm to match its supplier's performance. The vertically integrated firm will need to provide incentives to managers of the supplying division, who may then earn rents as managers rather than as owners. The firm could alleviate that by substituting monitoring for rents, reducing total value but increasing the firm's profits. Extra monitoring is sometimes easier to impose on employees, over whom the employer has discretionary authority, than on an independent supplier. Even if the firm cannot quite match the technical efficiency of its formerly independent supplier, however, it may still be able to produce for itself at a lower cost than the price it formerly paid. Note, of course, that there will be incentives to avoid value-reducing vertical integration that is aimed solely at capturing rents. It may still happen, however, if contracting problems between separate entities prevent costless reallocation of rents.

ENTRY DETERRENCE   Sometimes an advantage of vertical integration from the narrow point of view of the integrating firms is that it creates a barrier against future entry by firms that may want to compete in the same market. This gain exists, however, only provided that the entry would reduce the combined profits of the two integrating firms. For example, if the vertical integration eliminates an important potential source of supply to a downstream competitor, then any new competitor would have to arrange an alternative source of supply. There is no guarantee that such a source would exist. Even if it did, the problem of bringing the necessary production capacity on stream in a pair of new enterprises is more difficult than entry at just one stage of the vertical chain. That extra difficulty might deter the competitor from even trying.

The proviso that entry must reduce the combined profits of the two integrating firms is important, for otherwise the arrangement would not be total value maximizing. For example, suppose the potential entrant is a competitor for the downstream company. The expansion of the market that would likely follow entry would increase demand for the input supplied by the upstream firm and raise its profits. If this market expansion is expected to increase the upstream firm's profits by more than what the downstream firm loses, then the existing downstream firm will be unable to pay a high enough price to attract the upstream firm to merge with it.[9]

Alternative Vertical Relations

Simple market procurement and vertical integration do not exhaust the important options open to firms in a vertical supply relationship. Modern firms continue to forge innovative organizational arrangements in their attempts to enjoy the incentive advantages of independent firms while still facilitating close planning where necessary, protecting investments from hold-ups, and avoiding monopoly inefficiencies like that of double marginalization. As firms continue to innovate in this arena, the set of options will continue to expand.

We explore three possible options that represent organizational innovations of different eras. The co-op form of organization was an outgrowth of the utopian experimental communities of the nineteenth century. Franchise retailing began to emerge as an important form in the first half of this century. The last example is the supplier organization used by Japanese automobile companies, which is an organizational innovation and success story of the second half of this century.

---

[9] The situation becomes more complicated if you consider the further possibility that the combined firms might negotiate with the entrant to buy its technology or its production services, but we omit that possibility here.

COOPERATIVES[10]   Cooperatives (co-ops) are business organizations that are owned by the individuals who transact with them—usually workers or customers, but occasionally suppliers—and that are organized under specific legal rules. Individual members' voting power in co-op decisions is not determined by the amounts of capital they have provided (as it is in a corporation with a one-share/one-vote rule) but instead on a one-member/one-vote basis or, less often, in proportion to the amount of business done with the co-op. Similarly, profits are distributed in the form of reduced prices for whatever services the co-op supplies. Often, only members can transact with the co-op. (In the United States, to qualify legally as a cooperative, at least half the organization's business must be sales to members.) Memberships are sold by the organization only: There is no secondary market for them, and a member who quits may receive nothing or may receive a return of his or her initial capital contribution.

Co-ops play a significant role in some segments of modern economies. Prominent examples of worker co-ops include the diverse set of businesses around the city of Mondragon in Spain, large portions of the construction industry in Italy, and the major bus company in Israel. Many of the new businesses emerging in the Soviet Union were, for legal reasons, structured as co-ops. In the United States, co-op book stores serving college and university campuses supply about 10 percent of the overall book market. In home hardware, retailer-owned supply cooperatives like True Value and Ace account for half the U.S. market. Supply co-ops handle almost one third of wholesaling of groceries to U.S. retailers (excluding firms that are vertically integrated between wholesale and retail). Associated Press, which is owned by the newspapers, is one of two major international news services in the United States. In agriculture, farm supply co-ops serve over 25 percent of the U.S. market and are especially important in manufacturing and distributing petroleum products, feed, fertilizers, and chemicals. Rural electric power is also often supplied by co-ops. Cooperatives are also active in marketing farm products. Among the best-known brands in the United States are Land O'Lakes (dairy products), Blue Diamond (almonds), and Sunkist (citrus). Similarly, co-op grain elevators are a common sight across Western Canada. Finally, consumer co-ops provide a variety of services, especially retailing food and groceries.

Why Are There Cooperatives?   In the early days co-ops had an explicitly social and ideological basis. More recently, government policies to promote cooperatives by providing cheap credit or tax advantages and the development of supporting institutions are partial explanations of the popularity of this form of organization and of regional differences in how it is used. They do not explain why the form is more common in some industries than in others, however. Monopoly power seems to provide such an explanation.

In many cases of thriving supply cooperatives, economies of scale make it difficult for there to be more than one or two suppliers. Co-ops then serve to alleviate problems of monopoly pricing. For example, college students buying textbooks have a highly inelastic demand, making them especially vulnerable to high mark-ups at local bookstores. Economies of scale in handling inventories of the many books professors assign limit the number of competitors. In this case, a cooperative sponsored by a group of activist students can help to cap retail textbook prices, even if the not-for-profit cooperative is not efficient enough to replace its for-profit competitors completely. The coexistence of vertically integrated firms and supply cooperatives for small firms in the grocery and home hardware industries suggests that both forms are aimed at solving the same problem—that of monopoly supply. Consumer-

---

[10] Based in large part on Henry Hansmann, "The Ownership of the Firm," *Journal of Law, Economics, and Organization,* 4 (Fall 1988), 267–304.

co-op grocery stores that compete with for-profit supermarkets have a similar explanation.

Besides alleviating monopoly power, some cooperatives have been formed to create power for their members over consumers. For example, agricultural shipping and marketing cooperatives in California have sometimes set quotas for members, which have the effect of creating monopoly prices.

Generic Problems of Cooperatives. If the membership of the co-op is not too large or heterogeneous, the ability of members to monitor the quality of co-op services and their general agreement about what should be done can make this form of organization quite effective. Nevertheless, cooperative organizations, especially large ones, do suffer from a number of predictable organization problems.

With limited residual claimant status and no concentration of ownership, individual co-op members may have little incentive to keep tabs on the co-op management. If some members expect to participate in the co-op only in the short term, they may not be inclined to vote for investments that benefit the co-op over a longer horizon. Worse, they may promote projects that have short-term benefits but tend to run down the co-op's capital. If the co-op's charter permits it to engage in a wide range of activities, then diverse objectives among its members can lead to damaging influence activities.

An instructive example is the Berkeley Co-op, a consumer cooperative in Berkeley, California, which mainly operates grocery stores but has also sold gasoline, auto supplies, prescription drugs, and clothing. Its membership in the 1980s was quite heterogeneous, reflecting a population that included college students and poor families as well as very affluent individuals and families. This organization saw its very existence threatened by a series of struggles over cross-subsidies among its activities. Should there be low prices for basic necessities, to subsidize poor households? What about upscale products to serve the desires of the wealthier clientele? Free in-store child care? More locations for better accessibility in lower-income areas? These battles tied up the organization and its management in political maneuvering while the stores suffered large losses.

Similar problems would arise if the co-op approach to electric power distribution that is successful in rural America were attempted in cities. The diversity of the set of customers would cause problems in agreeing on the policies to be followed. How should costs be allocated among industrial, commercial, or residential users? Should rates climb rapidly with usage to encourage conservation or more slowly, so that those stuck at home can afford to heat and cool their homes? Should rates be higher at peak times for everyone or just for those identified as putting the extra demands on the system? Rather than crippling decision making in the urban electric co-op by fights over these questions, a pattern of investor ownership is used, with public utility regulation to control the monopoly inefficiencies.

FRANCHISE RETAILING In the United States, automobile dealerships, gas stations, convenience stores, clothing stores, hotels, restaurants, tax preparation services, car rentals, and banking are among the many businesses that are frequently operated on the franchise system. By the mid-1980s over 300,000 establishments in the United States operated as franchises, with an average of about half a million dollars in annual sales each,[11] and North American firms were expanding their overseas franchising rapidly: There are McDonald's outlets on the Champs-Elysées in Paris and Red Square in Moscow, for example.

---

[11] James A. Brickley, Frederick H. Dark, and Michael S. Weisbach, "An Agency Perspective on Franchising," *Financial Management*, 20 (Spring 1991), 27.

The franchisee owns and runs a retail business using the franchisor's brand name, often buying inputs or goods for resale from the franchisor. The franchisor collects fees and royalties from the franchisees for the use of the brand name and commonly also provides training, advertising, and other services. Franchisors also generally maintain rights to set and enforce standards on the franchisee. For example, a clothing franchisor may require that the retail store operator maintain a specified number of varieties or a minimum level of inventories. An oil company may require a station operator to remain open for certain hours and days, even when the additional hours are not profitable for the franchisee. Franchise restaurants must typically submit to inspections, with penalties for failing to maintain cleanliness and food quality standards. They may even have their franchise revoked if they refuse to acquiesce to the franchisor's demands.

This kind of arrangement takes advantage of owner-operators' incentives to keep costs low, attract customers, and care for the premises. In this respect, franchising arrangements share the advantages of ordinary market arrangements. At the same time, the control exerted by the franchisor adds value by overcoming a variety of problems arising from specific assets, free riding by franchisees, and economies of scale in marketing and perhaps in purchasing. When these additional sources of value are important, franchise contracts can have important advantages over spot market contracting.

Specific Assets and Incentives. Consider the case of McDonald's Corporation, which serves customers in approximately 6,900 restaurants in the United States and hundreds more in other countries. Approximately 5,300 McDonald's restaurants in the United States are run by franchisees who own and operate the individual restaurants. In these arrangements, one specific asset is the restaurant building itself, which is typically specially designed and equipped to be a McDonald's restaurant and would be less valuable in other uses. In addition, the owner-manager makes a specific investment in learning the company systems. At McDonald's, this is done partly by working for a period without pay as an apprentice at another restaurant and partly by attending Hamburger University, as the company calls its restaurant manager training center. From McDonald's point of view, the franchisee's expenditure of time and money signals his or her commitment to the business. From the franchisee's perspective, it is an investment that is vulnerable to hold-up.

The unusual architecture of the buildings in which McDonald's restaurants are located would cause a potential hold-up problem if the franchisees were to own the buildings. Thus, unlike many other franchisors, McDonald's owns the individual structures. More generally, the potential for hold-ups by the franchisor is a serious matter in many franchise businesses. A common complaint by franchisees is that, after they have invested in developing a market, the franchisor holds them up by establishing another (competing) franchise in the same market area. The franchisor may claim that the market has now grown to be too large to be most profitably served by a single franchise. Automobile franchisees have been particularly active in seeking legislation to prevent such an encroachment on their markets, and franchisee organizations often work with franchisors to establish mutually agreed standards for how many franchises an area can support, in order to reduce this potential for conflict.

Like other franchisors, McDonald's values its brand name reputation, which in this case promises customers clean premises and surroundings and hot, fresh food, served quickly and cheerfully, as well as certain specific menu items, like the Big Mac. The overall reputation is a valuable asset that a local franchisee could damage by failing to live up to the franchise standards. In fact, the individual franchisee has an incentive to free-ride on the general brand reputation, skimping on service and quality, because all the cost savings accrue directly to the individual franchisee, but the damage is spread among all the outlets and the franchiser. The rights of the franchisor to insist upon the franchisees' following certain procedures, to inspect to ensure that these requirements are being met, and to exact punishments (including termination of the franchise) if they are not are important for managing this incentive problem and protecting the valuable asset.

Franchising has been less common in Europe than in the United States, and the European Economic Community, as part of its efforts to establish uniform business standards, has been hostile to franchisors' control of franchisee operations. In 1989, however, McDonald's won a ruling that protected some of its rights to regulate franchisees: "While McDonald's Corporation may still tell its European franchisees how big a dollop of ketchup to put on each Big Mac, it can't make them sell Coca Cola" in preference to other brands.[12] This ruling reflects the European Community's attempt to balance the goals of efficient contracting and local control of European businesses.

Coordination Issues.   Another kind of problem that franchise systems need to anticipate is the conflict that frequently accompanies changes in systems or in the product line. In many franchise situations, uniformity in what is offered at different outlets is important for marketing: People value knowing that they can get what they expect. If McDonald's and its franchisee group seek to reposition their image around healthier foods, or Exxon and its franchisees decide as a group to increase their advertising expenditures or to build a reputation for clean bathrooms, there needs to be a way to enforce these standards across all the outlets without incurring excessive bargaining costs. There can also be economies in having uniform operating systems. For example, if Bennetton introduces a new computerized inventory tracking system, then the fixed costs of developing and running the system and the economies of scale achievable in implementing it may imply that total value is maximized when every outlet participates in the change. Such universal participation would be practically impossible if it were necessary to negotiate with the franchisees individually about their costs and benefits of implementing the system in order to subsidize those stores for which conversion is especially costly. When these kinds of changes are introduced, there is usually a need for close coordination and a mechanism to enforce decisions on individual franchisees. These coordination problems arising out of the economies of scale create an additional reason for giving the franchisor the authority to intervene in the franchisees' operations.

Authority and Its Limits.   Of course, franchisees seek to protect themselves against excessive demands or penalties imposed by the franchisor, for example, by forming associations of franchisees to bargain with the franchisor. Because the parties cannot foresee the circumstances and proposals that will arise over time in these relationships, the processes by which decisions are to be made become the focus of the contract. Accordingly, franchise agreements specify some of the rights and responsibilities of the various parties in the conduct of their business. Routines developed in the course of doing business also provide guidance regarding what is normal and expected behavior. Such arrangements are fundamentally different from the cash-for-product contracts that characterize simple market transactions.

SUPPLIER RELATIONS IN THE JAPANESE AUTOMOBILE INDUSTRY   In ordinary markets, the firms that are most successful in meeting customer needs at low cost are rewarded

---

[12] Philip Revzin, "European Bureaucrats Are Writing the Rules Americans Will Live By," *The Wall Street Journal* (May 17, 1989), 1.

Franchises or Company-Owned Outlets?

Typically, franchisors themselves own about 20 percent of the outlets, hiring managers to run them. What factors should enter the decision between establishing a particular unit as a franchise or keeping it company owned?

First, agency considerations suggest that the extent of franchising should increase and company ownership of units decrease, where monitoring managers is more difficult. Second, franchises should be more common when repeat business at a particular outlet is greater because the free-rider problem should be less acute. Third, franchising should be less common where the capital requirements of the business are higher because of the increased costs of inefficient risk sharing. Fourth, as new laws and regulations have made it more difficult for franchisors to terminate franchise agreements, there should be a tendency in recent years to reduce the extent of franchising relative to company ownership.

We have already cited evidence regarding the first of these in connection with the greater frequency of franchising among gas stations that provide repair services versus those that do not. More generally, recent empirical work tends to bear out all three of these predictions.

One puzzle appears in these studies, however. We would expect from free-rider considerations that units located along freeways would be more likely to be company owned because they should get less repeat business, but this does not appear to be the case. We know of no satisfactory explanation for this.

See James A. Brickley, Frederick H. Dark, and Michael S. Weisbach, "An Agency Perspective on Franchising," *Financial Management*, 20 (Spring 1991), 27–35, and the references given there for additional details.

with increased sales. The North American automobile manufacturers have traditionally tried to take advantage of these market incentives by selecting suppliers by competitive bidding. Where specific assets were involved or where few qualified bidders could be found, the usual solution was to arrange for the specific assets to be owned by the automobile company, often through a process of vertical integration.

How U.S. and Japanese Practices Differ.   Japanese automobile companies have been innovative in creating ways to achieve the advantages of market incentives even where specific investments are required for efficient production. As we described in Chapter 9, the Japanese auto firms have been much less vertically integrated than the American ones and have instead purchased fully assembled systems from a relatively small number of suppliers. For example, General Motors used some 35,000 different suppliers in 1986, whereas in that same year Toyota made virtually all of its purchases from its core group of 224 suppliers, a ratio of more than 150 to 1.[13] The Japanese and U.S. figures are not precisely comparable, however, because of differences in the definition of "supplier" used in data sources. Excluding GM's smallest suppliers closes

---

[13] These data and those that follow in this section are drawn from Banri Asanuma, "Japanese Manufacturer-Supplier Relationships in International Perspective: The Automobile Case," Working Paper No. 8, Faculty of Economics, Kyoto University (1988).

the gap somewhat but still leaves a remarkable difference between the companies: General Motors' 5,500 largest suppliers accounted for only about 80 percent of that company's purchases. By any reasonable calculation, Toyota relied on a far smaller number of suppliers than did GM. Toyota's practices set the pattern for other Japanese automobile companies.

Japanese management of supplier relations differed from U.S. practices in other ways, as well. The Japanese made much less extensive use of competitive bidding to obtain low prices from their suppliers. Instead, suppliers were evaluated according to how well they had performed on earlier contracts, with the top performers being rewarded with additional orders. This reward system leads to long-term relationships, which in fact characterized the Japanese pattern. Systems based on competitive bidding typically require that the bidders know in advance exactly what is to be supplied, so contracts can be bid only after detailed drawings of the desired parts are prepared. Because they did not rely on competitive bidding, Japanese companies could select suppliers before the parts specifications were made final, making it possible to exploit the suppliers' expertise in design engineering, to design parts to fit the capabilities of the suppliers' existing equipment, and to allow suppliers more time to plan and prepare for production. The most reliable and technically sophisticated suppliers could even be trusted to design their own parts completely, subject to general design specifications provided by the automobile manufacturer.

The Performance Appraisal Problem.   A system like this would appear to have two important potential disadvantages. The first concerns performance appraisal. Without a competitive bidding stage, how does the automobile maker know how much the input should cost to produce? Were the supplier's costs really as low as they should be? Was its quality as high? Could another supplier have produced the same component or system with better quality and at a lower cost? The second problem is one of specific assets. Once the firm and its supplier have committed themselves to a contract in which, say, headlamps for Toyota Corollas are to be supplied, how is the price to be determined? Who determines the delivery schedule? Can orders be canceled if sales of the car are disappointing? If the company's own work force is not fully employed, can it choose to take over production of headlamps to ensure that its employees are kept busy?

To manage the first problem, Toyota has a *two supplier policy*: Except for products produced exclusively in house, there must always be at least two suppliers for each category of component. If supplier A makes headlamps for model X, then a different supplier B will make the headlamps for some other model Y. Having just one supplier for the headlamps of a single model allows the supplier to take full advantage of economies of scale in making the lamp. Guaranteeing the supplier that it will continue to make the part throughout the life of the model helps to protect any specific investment the supplier makes. Having a different supplier for the other model allows Toyota to use comparative performance evaluation to assess how well each supplier is performing. The reward for good performance in making headlamps may be contracts to make headlamps and taillamps on the next model, or headlamps on two different models (provided the two-supplier policy is not violated). If the supplier demonstrates technical prowess, the reward may be an *upgrading* that qualifies the supplier to make more complex parts.

Because suppliers make complete systems, it is practical to hold them responsible when a system fails, without endless arguments about which supplier is responsible. The system maker must accept responsibility for the cost of any necessary repairs. This practice also encourages suppliers and the core firm to cooperate in identifying problems and fixing them.

The Hold-Up Problem.   The second kind of problem of determining prices and avoiding hold-ups is less easily resolved. The long-term, mutually beneficial nature of the relationship does help to mitigate this problem by providing both sides with an incentive to find mutually acceptable terms. Even though they do foster goodwill, long-term relationships cannot themselves determine prices or resolve real differences of opinion. Initial prices can be set in light of the planned cost of production, based on the company's experience with other similar parts. Profits are then based on the supplier's ability to produce at a lower cost than previous suppliers, by seeking improvements in their production systems. The supplier earns additional points in the supplier rating system for codifying methods so that they can be used by other suppliers, leading to lower costs for the core firm. The objective is continuous improvement in productivity by all of the core firm's suppliers.

A complex relationship such as this holds opportunities for hold-ups besides price renegotiation. For example, a supplier may fear not getting proper credit for its innovations, which are transferred to competing suppliers. Resolving the ever-changing issues in the relationship between the firm and its suppliers appears to be one of the roles of the supplier associations. In this regard, it is illuminating that Toyota maintains an association for parts suppliers (*Kyohokai*) and for suppliers of tools, equipment, and construction services (*Eihokai*), but no associations for the supply of basic materials like oil or steel, where specific investments are much less important. A similar pattern is found at other Japanese automobile companies.

Advantages.   This system of managed supplier organization has formidable advantages over the system of competitive bidding among independent suppliers. It allows the core firm to assess supplier performance accurately, to ensure that the suppliers with the best performance records get most of the contracts for the next car models, to take advantage of suppliers' design capabilities and the peculiarities of their equipment, and to allow longer lead times for design and planning. Contracts extending over the life of a car model promote cost-reducing specific investments. The system encourages suppliers to be innovative but also promotes rapid communication of valuable information among competing suppliers—an achievement that would not be possible with more traditional supplier relationships.

The more relevant comparison, however, is not with simple market transactions, which are unlikely to be viable when there are the kinds of advantages that exist in the auto industry to making specific investments. Rather, the issue is how the Japanese system compares with a system of vertical integration used in North America. Both systems allow for creation and protection of specific assets, with the Japanese relying on reputations and repeated dealings rather than ownership.[14] One significant advantage of the Japanese system is that it may be easier to break relations with a supplier who fails to perform than it is to stop obtaining supplies from a badly performing division. The influence costs that would be involved in closing a division and going to outside suppliers, or even in replacing the managers of the division, might be substantial. The two-supplier system potentially sacrifices some economies of scale, but this is not a great drawback if the minimum efficient scale is not too large relative to demand. In return, it allows comparative performance evaluation and creates competition that keeps prices low and quality high. It would be possible, in

---

[14] There are occasional complaints that the major Japanese firms hold up their suppliers, however. American firms that have obtained supply contracts have alleged this: See, for example, Dana Milbank, "Culture Clash: Making Honda Parts, Ohio Company Finds, Can Be Road to Ruin," *The Wall Street Journal* (October 5, 1990), A1. T. Boone Pickens has claimed that Toyota forces unfairly low prices on Koito, an auto-light supplier in the Toyota group of which Pickens was, for a while, the major shareholder: See T. Boone Pickens, "Pickens to Toyota: I Give Up," *San Jose Mercury News* (April 30, 1991), 7B.

theory, to have competing internal supply divisions, but this seems difficult in practice, again for influence cost reasons. Also, because at least the independent suppliers (those that are not members of the suppliers' associations of any of the major auto manufacturers) can work for any of the large firms, and even members of Nissan's group may supply parts to Toyota, there is flexibility in the system to respond to shifting demands. It would likely be more difficult for GM to act as a supplier to Ford than it is for a separate company to supply either or both as needs dictate.

HORIZONTAL SCOPE AND STRUCTURE

The meaning of the term *vertical structure* is clear in the case of the process depicted in Figure 16.2, where a single, stable product is processed through a fixed series of steps on its way to the final customer. The issue is how the transactions between successive stages are managed: through spot market transactions, through administrative direction after integrating both stages within a single firm, or through a more complex institutional arrangement with a specially crafted governance structure for making decisions and resolving disputes? The choices offered by this vision of the firm are useful, but they are far too simple and narrow to describe the scope of modern business organizations.

Competitive Strategy and Organizational Innovation

Recall the quotation describing the development of Lucky Goldstar. Unable to find caps of adequate quality for its jars of cosmetic cream, Lucky (as it was then called) decided to make them for itself. In our simple conception of the firm, the decision was one of vertical integration, and it was arguably the right choice. Presumably Lucky might have been able to arrange for some other Korean firm to develop the expertise and make the physical investments to meet its needs. However, with only Lucky demanding such high-quality plastics, the investments would be specific, at least until a larger market developed. There would thus be a bilateral monopoly supply relation between Lucky and its supplier, and this favored vertical integration. On the negative side, however, the scale of the molding operation would be too small to enable production at an efficient scale; it might be cheaper to rely on a foreign firm that could produce at an efficient scale, provided the South Korean government would allow such an import.

Some of the problem of scale could be overcome by making other molded plastic products: toothbrushes, combs, and soap boxes, for example. Because Lucky toothpaste had a virtual monopoly in the toothpaste market, the firm already had a distribution system that could handle these new products. The resulting expansion into plastic molding was thus both vertical—into a new stage of cosmetic cream business—and *horizontal*—into a new set of consumer products.[15]

In plastics, Lucky sought to expand its market to achieve the advantages of scale. It grew by making electric fan blades and telephone cases. It increased the demand for those products by entering the electrical and telecommunications equipment businesses as well. This might be thought of as a vertical move into another stage of the production of fans and phones, but it is probably more useful to think of it as another horizontal extension.

The field of **corporate strategy** or **competitive strategy** focuses on one of the questions that the Lucky Goldstar story raises: What businesses should a company be

---

[15] Our use of the term *horizontal* conforms to the use in business writing, where it refers to activities that are not vertically related. In the literature of antitrust law and economics, the term *horizontal merger* is used to mean something different, specifically, merger between two firms in the same market.

in? To put the same question another way, what should be the horizontal boundaries and scope of the firm? To address this question broadly would take us much too far afield. However, one aspect of it is central to our concerns: How does the extent of activities that a firm undertakes affect the way it structures itself, and how do the mechanisms it puts in place for information gathering, decision making, implementation, and evaluation affect the range of activities that it can successfully undertake?

Directions of Divisional Expansion

As several of the examples in this chapter suggest, the direction of business expansion has often been determined by considerations of scale, scope, and core competencies. The Lucky Goldstar story is one of (somewhat opportunistic and even haphazard) expansion through effective exploitation of complementarities and economies of scale and scope. Firms often avoid expansion even into related businesses where these kinds of economies are absent. For example, Sears, with no special competence in manufacturing, relied primarily on independent suppliers to make its store brands. As argued previously, there are real advantages in relying on independent suppliers, especially when there are several competitive ones and the product being purchased is a standard one, like hammers or tires. More recently Sears has expanded into retail financial services, including insurance, real estate, and credit card businesses. It gambled that it could use its retailing experience to sell those services like other consumer products, but it has so far found only meager success.

The takeover by Electronic Data Service (EDS) of Continental Airlines' airline information systems business (see earlier box) illustrates a horizontal expansion by EDS. Here, EDS's bet is that the competencies it has developed by managing computerized data bases in energy and banking give it an advantage managing a system for airlines as well. Another interesting example is the Sony Corporation's purchase of CBS Records and Columbia Pictures. Sony's videocassettes in the technologically superior Beta format lost the competition to Matsushita's VHS format partly because rental movies were initially less available in the Beta format. Sony's digital audio tape (DAT) format for sound recording and reproduction, introduced in 1987, was opposed by the record companies and achieved only limited market penetration. With its new purchases, Sony hoped to ensure coordination between any new entertainment hardware technology that it may introduce and the development of entertainment software in a corresponding format. For example, the former CBS Records was expected to offer music in Sony's Mini Disc (MD) format as soon as the format became commercially available, and Columbia was to produce feature entertainment using Sony's High Definition Video Systems.

CORE COMPETENCIES AND BUSINESS STRATEGY   Generally, firms seeking profitable expansion are most likely to be successful by identifying the areas of their own special competencies, investing to build those competencies, and introducing products where the competencies give them a cost advantage or a marketing advantage. Often, this involves a measure of guesswork. Sears guessed that many of its department store customers would want to buy financial services in the same retail stores where they bought pajamas and bicycles; Continental Airlines initially guessed that its status as a major airline with a leading computer reservations system gave it a competency in providing information services for airlines; GM guessed that the marketing and manufacturing skills it honed in making and selling automobiles would be valuable in making other consumer durables, like refrigerators and air conditioners; Walt Disney guessed that the characters it successfully created for movies could be the basis for a successful set of theme parks.

Evidently, not all such guesses work out well. Sometimes, even if the concept is correct, a strategic expansion may fail because the timing is wrong. For example, since the early 1980s, it has been widely believed that the marriage of data transfer and data-processing technologies is inevitable. The extensive use of networking among individual computer work stations illustrates the close connections between these kinds of technologies. Some of the largest computer and telecommunications companies have invested heavily in this vision of the future, suffering large losses, and many continue to make new investments pursuing this vision. For example, IBM entered telecommunications in the 1970s by investing in Satellite Business Systems, purchased 16 percent ownership in MCI in the early 1980s, and then entered a joint venture with Canada's Mitel Corporation. In 1984 IBM acquired Rolm Corporation, a rapidly growing and innovative maker of telephone switching equipment, for $1.5 billion. After pumping nearly another $1 billion into Rolm to cover losses and pay for new investments, IBM sold Rolm's manufacturing operation and half of its marketing operation to Siemens just four years later. IBM is not alone in these strategic investment attempts. Japan's NEC has invested similarly and, in 1991, the U.S. telecommunications giant AT&T purchased NCR Corporation, a computer maker, to build in a competency in this technology that AT&T sees as key to future competitive success.

Disadvantages of Horizontal Expansion

As several of these examples illustrate, some mergers and horizontal extensions do fail. What are the disadvantages that attend integration? Given the multidivisional form, it might seem that a large organization can do anything a small firm could do by just duplicating the style, incentives, and authority structure that are present in the small firm within a small division. It might even do better because the small division can call upon the resources of a large corporation in times of growth—resources that may be unavailable to a small, independent company. The debate about what costs are incurred by horizontal integration is one of the most active in modern economic theory.

PROBLEMS OF INFORMATION AND COORDINATION One important effect is that an organization that gets too large tends to suffer from poorer coordination and decision making. As the size of the firm increases, either each division becomes bigger or the number of divisions is increased. In the latter case, the amount of information coming in from the divisions to the head office increases. Top managers become overloaded. They may respond by adding staff to support them or by further decentralizing, pushing more decisions to lower levels and perhaps adding levels of management between the top executives and the divisions, but both these responses bring costs. Providing staff with the proper incentives is especially hard because their performance is very difficult to measure. Decentralizing more decisions means sacrificing control and coordination across these decisions, and the additional layers of management slow decision making, act as filters in information transmission, and are themselves directly costly. If the growth comes with a given divisional structure, the individual divisions start to become too big to manage. Then they in turn must be decentralized, again creating extra layers of management and the attendant problems.

Expansion into unrelated fields creates additional problems because central decision makers cannot become or stay adequately informed about the peculiarities of the technologies of the individual businesses and the markets in which they operate. This means that they have more difficulty evaluating the performance of different divisions and the proposals they make for new investments. More and more reliance is necessarily placed on financial data in making decisions, and inadequate attention

The Failed Merger of Rolm and IBM

Rolm Corporation epitomized the small, fast-growing companies of Silicon Valley, projecting a relaxed corporate culture but maintaining a sense of mission. There were no dress codes or fixed working hours, but the parking lot would often be full at 6:00 on Fridays and on weekends. The company had a gym and swimming pool that employees could use in the middle of the day, and lunchtime barbecues were common. Stock options for key employees allowed some to get rich as the value of Rolm stock rose, and a 2 percent rate of commission on top of a $24,000 salary in the mid-1980s allowed typical salespeople to earn $60,000 per year.

To maintain the small company atmosphere, even as it grew, Rolm subdivided its operations into many divisions, with separate divisions selling to specific markets like banking, education, government, health care, hotel/motel, and retail. Another division handled distribution to phone companies and interconnect companies. The manufacturing operations were also subdivided. A set of four planning groups were set up to ease coordination among the groups in the areas of strategic planning, product maintenance, product development, international sales, and procurement.

Rolm's principal competitors were the telecommunications giants AT&T and Northern Telecom, which were able to devote more resources to product development than Rolm could generate. It therefore encouraged IBM to invest in its operations, and eventually to become full owner of the company. IBM declared it would exercise a hands-off policy in managing the company in order to allow it to maintain its entrepreneurial spirit. Problems soon surfaced, however.

Organized along regional lines, Rolm's sales force would sometimes offer different deals to the same corporate customer in different regions of the country. IBM, which sold using uniform terms nationally, found itself subjected to pressures from its customers to offer uniform terms in its communications products, too. Succumbing to the pressure, it tried to enlist Rolm salespeople to participate in national marketing, which created pressure on the compensation scheme. Were Rolm salespeople to be paid a higher commission than IBM people even when selling to the same clients? Moreover, national sales are more complex and take more time to close than do sales to smaller regional clients, threatening to reduce the incomes of Rolm salespeople in the short term. IBM responded by raising base salaries and reducing the rate of commission. The lower commission rates had the largest effect on the best salespeople, leading some to quit.

It was not only in sales that IBM dampened Rolm's incentives. Rolm engineers, previously motivated by stock options in Rolm Corporation, were now given stock options in IBM instead. Although their successes in developing a new product could make a substantial difference in Rolm's fortunes and the price of its stock, nothing they could do would have much effect on the value of IBM stock, so performance incentives were muted.

By January 1986 Rolm co-founder Kenneth Oshman had quit, triggering the departure of other key executives. With the passage of time, IBM executives gained increasing control of Rolm's operations, trying to stem the tide of losses the company was incurring. Finally, in 1988, IBM sold Rolm's manufacturing divisions and a 50 percent interest in the marketing divisions to Siemens.

Even this did not end the problems. Rolm Systems (the manufacturing arm) and Rolm Company (the marketing arm) battled over whether the salespeople should be allowed to be full-service suppliers, carrying the products of other companies where Rolm Systems product line was incomplete. The manufacturing company wanted the marketing company to keep it informed of product developments in advance, so it could design and make products to meet all its customers' demands. The marketing company believed it could perform best if it could serve its customers' complete needs, even if that sometimes meant selling a Rolm competitor's product.

is given to important but nonquantifiable information. Excessive reliance on accounting numbers is often cited as a problem at General Motors.

Another problem is that performance measurement may become more costly as the scope of the organization grows. Consider two separate firms of comparable size, each big enough to have access to the equity markets. Investors will follow both firms, and the prices they put on the firms' shares will reflect their estimates of the earnings that will be generated by their managers and the strategies they adopt. The performance information in the stock price is free to the firms' owners. If the two companies merge, then there is only one share price, and the separate information about performance of the constituent parts is lost. Moreover, there will now be only one set of financial accounting reports rather than two, so again less information is available for judging performance.

INFLUENCE COSTS   Influence costs arise from attempts to reallocate and protect rents and quasi-rents within the organization. Presumably, the larger the organization, the larger are the rents in total and the more people competing for them. If the bigger prizes and greater numbers of contestants result in greater competition for these rents, a larger firm will suffer more than proportionally higher influence costs. The following example is too simplified to be realistic, but it does show how these effects can come about.

A Mathematical Example of Competition for Rents

Suppose the rents that can be reallocated through influence are a function $P(n)$ of firm size n, where we measure size by the number of employees. Consider for simplicity a winner-take-all contest, in which the successful person gets the whole prize $P(n)$. This might represent the political aspects of the competition to become CEO, with $P(n)$ representing the extra income, perks, and status that accrue to being the head of a company of size n. Empirically, it appears that all of these are increasing in n. Individual contestant i can expend resources s at a personal cost cs on influence, and if the different contestants $i = 1, 2, \ldots, n$ each expend s_i, then the chance of any one of them winning is s_i/S, where S is the resources expended by everyone in total. To decide how hard to try to win, individual i considers the extra costs of increasing s_i, which are c, and equates this to the increase in the benefits from increasing the chance of winning the prize. This can be computed to be $\{(S - s_i)/S^2\}P(n)$.[16] If each contestant forecasts correctly how hard the others will try (so that each correctly forecasts the value of $S - s_i$) and chooses his or her expenditure accordingly, then they will all choose a common level $s(n)$ which satisfies the equation

$$\frac{(n - 1)s(n)}{n^2(s(n))^2}P(n) = c$$

or, $\{(n - 1)/n\}P(n) = ncs(n)$. The right-hand side of this expression is the total cost of the influence activities to the contestants. The left-hand side approaches $P(n)$ as n becomes large. Thus, even if the prize does not grow as the size of the firm does, the total influence costs will. Moreover, if $P(n)$ also grows with n, then the costs increase more than proportionally with the size of the prize. In the limit, the entire rents are absorbed in influence costs. Of course, if the contestants can use firm resources rather than their own in the contest, they may well value them at much less than they are worth to the organization. In this case, the personal cost cs may be much less than the actual cost, and the resources spent may actually exceed the value of the prize!

SPECIAL PROBLEMS OF ACQUISITIONS AND MERGERS   A firm that has decided to expand its scope has two choices: to develop the business itself from scratch, hiring new people, investing in new capacity, and developing new suppliers and new distribution channels; or to acquire another company already in the business, along with the expertise its employees already have and the capacity and relationships it has already developed. The latter may seem appealing, but there are special costs incurred when an independent organization becomes integrated into a larger firm that arise to a smaller degree, or not at all, in transactions between the independent entities. The costs have been described in various ways by different observers. There may be conflicts of *corporate cultures*, political battles leading to *influence costs*, or misbehavior by the central office of the acquiring firm, which *reneges on promises* made to managers and employees of the formerly independent subsidiary. Because all these occur together in most of the cited examples, we shall not try to distinguish sharply among them.

These problems can arise when similar-sized organizations are brought together. Shearson American Express experienced great difficulties integrating the investment bankers from Lehman Brothers Kuhn Loeb into its operations, which were primarily in the retail stock brokerage business. As well, computer maker Unisys has experienced major organizational difficulties since its formation in a merger of Burroughs and Sperry. Part of the trouble is attributed to differences in styles between the organizations. Burroughs' formal, no-nonsense style contrasted with Sperry's relaxed one, while the cost-conscious retail brokers at Shearson were often appalled by the lavish style of the investment bankers of Kuhn Loeb. In each case, many employees had chosen the work environment they preferred and resisted attempts at change.

The problems of conflicting cultures seem most intense, however, when a large company takes over a smaller one in hopes of taking advantage of complementarities in their technological capabilities and the smaller firm's entrepreneurial flair. We saw examples of this in earlier chapters, particularly Tenneco's acquisition of Houston Oil and Minerals in Chapter 6, and in the boxed accounts in this chapter of IBM's purchase of Rolm and GM's purchase of EDS. In each case, the acquiring firm

---

[16] The calculation is done as follows. Let S_{-i} be the resources spent by everyone except individual i. Then i's payoff is $s_iP(n)/(s_i + S_{-i})$. The expression in the text is the derivative of this with respect to s_i.

promised to keep the smaller one independent, with its original management, procedures, and style. In each case, this proved impossible.

The smaller, entrepreneurial firms were organizations that emphasized and rewarded initiative with large bonuses. High performance led to high levels of pay, and poor performers dropped by the wayside. These firms did not specialize in activities that called for reliable, routine service, and they did not reward reliable, routine performers. Their key employees were risk takers, gambling on new technologies, new industries to service, and new oil fields.

Once integrated into a larger organization, the compensation and perquisites accorded employees of the entrepreneurial units were regarded as special deals and became a source of jealousies. GM managers were angry about the bonuses paid to EDS employees for cost reductions. "If you paid me that much and allowed me that much discretion and staff resources to use in cutting costs, I'd find you even greater savings." IBM employees were jealous of the commissions and bonuses paid to their Rolm counterparts. At Tenneco, the pressure to maintain pay equity throughout the company forced the firm to integrate Houston's operations with its own, destroying the unique identity of the Houston Oil unit. Sony Corporation executives report feeling similar pressures over the salaries and bonuses paid to executives in their entertainment business subsidiaries, but are determined to resist them.

As long as the central office of the firm maintains some control over its divisions, the political pressures within the organization to equalize pay and opportunities will be large. In purely economic terms, unequal treatment leads employees to divert their attention from productive work, instead conniving ways to get the good jobs for themselves. Of course, there are other costs—not all economic—to having to deal with angry and jealous employees.

A different set of issues arose in the recent conflict within Sears over its joint venture with IBM, the Prodigy system. Prodigy is a network system for home computer users, which incorporates electronic games, mail, news, shopping services, and more. Users connect their home computers to the Prodigy system using ordinary telephone lines. Among the services offered by Prodigy is a discount brokerage service called Personal Control, in which investors manage their own portfolios, transmitting their own buy-and-sell orders electronically to Personal Control, which is managed by Donaldson, Lufkin and Jenrette. A problem for Sears is that the commissions charged by Personal Control are approximately 75 percent below those charged by Sears's own Dean Witter Reynolds brokerage unit. Dean Witter is a full-service brokerage house, and its fees must cover its cost for research, sales, and order entry—costs that are avoided by the Personal Control system. If Sears had no control over Prodigy, Dean Witter employees could hardly complain about its fee structure and would spend their energies competing as effectively as possible. Because Prodigy is partially owned by Sears, however, considerable anger and energy are channeled within the Sears organization, and the trust between Sears management and its subsidiary's employees is undermined.

Effective legal boundaries between firms can avoid attempts at influence within the firm, limit top management's ability to renege on agreements, and isolate the conflicting cultures of different units. These can be important advantages of independent firms.

BUSINESS ALLIANCES

In our discussion of vertical structure, we have already noted that there are many more alternatives than just simple market procurement and full vertical integration. The nature of links between firms can be subtle and complex, and the way the transaction is managed depends on all the key dimensions of the transaction (see

General Motors and EDS

When General Motors purchased Ross Perot's Electronic Data Systems (EDS) in June 1984 for $2.55 billion in cash and stock, expectations were high on both sides. EDS was an entrepreneurial company that had thrived by taking over clients' computer operations and promising to offer better service at lower cost than the clients could do for themselves. Because EDS's own profits depended on its employees' ability to gather business and cut costs, it rewarded them directly for doing that, paying bonuses in the form of EDS stock for outstanding performance. Paying bonuses in stock also gave the top performers a vested interest in the success of the company.

The giant automobile manufacturer under Roger Smith had dedicated itself to the introduction of high technology in its operations, intending to lead the world with its computer-integrated manufacturing and electronic order processing technologies. What better way to begin than by purchasing EDS?

GM was committed not to tamper with EDS's style of doing business. Within GM, EDS was to be an agent of change, introducing new computer technology where it saw fit and collecting a fraction of the cost savings as EDS earnings. EDS employees would still be rewarded with EDS stock, but now that EDS stock would be listed as a special "class E" General Motors stock. At the same time, EDS founder Ross Perot would become a major GM shareholder and a member of the board of directors, bringing his valuable computer experience to GM's inner circle.

In 1985, largely as a result of its work with GM, EDS revenues surged by 400 percent. As GM made more money available for computer services, EDS employees took credit for the benefits of the improved systems, to the chagrin of GM's managers. Disputes arose over how much of the savings that EDS employees claimed they achieved were really attributable to them. Meanwhile, bitter arguments arose between Ross Perot and Roger Smith, who Perot believed was reneging on his commitments to EDS's people. By December of the following year, GM purchased Ross Perot's shares for $750 million and Perot parted company with GM.

Source: Doron Levin, *Irreconcilable Differences: Ross Perot versus General Motors* (New York: Penguin Books, 1989).

Chapter 2). Various special arrangements, especially nonexclusive ones, between separately owned companies are called *business alliances*. The arrangements between IBM and Mitsubishi and between Rolm and GTE discussed in boxes in this chapter are examples, as is the alliance between IBM and Apple discussed in Chapter 9.

The use of business alliances varies greatly among firms. General Motors, for example, has used alliances to transform its business. In the 1960s GM had a vertically integrated organization that tried to be self-reliant. By the late 1980s it had developed an extensive network of relationships with automobile companies and suppliers in Europe and Asia as well as North America. Some alliances were to improve foreign marketing; others involved sharing technologies for such things as robotics to be used in automobile manufacturing; still others were to add models to the weakest parts of

Mitsubishi Electric Selling IBM Computers

IBM Corporation has traditionally relied on its own sales force for all its sales of large business computers. Having a full line of computers from personal computers through large mainframe computers and networks to hook them all together, IBM's strategy was to provide products to serve companies of all sizes relying exclusively on its own products. Sales representatives from manufacturers who do not make large mainframe computers are put at a disadvantage by this strategy, because they cannot generate as much revenue per visit as an IBM representative. So it was news when in 1991 IBM agreed to allow Mitsubishi Electric Corporation to sell an IBM mainframe computer under its own name. The machines being sold cost between $1 million and $5 million, and Mitsubishi hoped to sell 900 of them during the three years after the agreement.

According to theory, a deal like this should occur only if the two companies can create more total value combined than they could achieve separately, that is, if the two can supply complementary resources. What might these be?

IBM, the world's largest computer maker, has been trying hard to increase its sales in Japan. Its 1990 Japanese revenues were 1.3 trillion yen, or about $9.6 billion. It faced resistance in expanding its sales into some segments of Japanese industry, however. Mitsubishi Electric, a core member of the Mitsubishi *keiretsu* (group of firms), is the fifth largest computer vendor in Japan, and lacks the scale necessary to make all its own machines at low cost. It was in danger of falling behind its larger Japanese competitors because of its inability to supply a complete line of computers. The Mitsubishi *keiretsu* is the largest industrial group in Japan, which allows Mitsubishi Electric salespeople to open doors that had been closed to IBM. If this alliance is moderately successful, it could benefit both IBM and Mitsubishi Electric. If it is very successful, it may help Mitsubishi Electric to build its own mainframes, improving its ability to compete directly with IBM in the future.

Source: Andrew Pollack, "IBM Model to Be Sold by Mitsubishi," *The New York Times* (April 29, 1991), 17.

GM's product line. A notable example is GM's joint venture with Toyota, establishing New United Motors Manufacturing, Incorporated (NUMMI). In this venture, an old GM automobile plant in Fremont, California became a showcase for Japanese automobile manufacturing methods applied in a North American environment (see the box entitled "New United Motors Manufacturing, Incorporated"). Unlike its integration decisions in which GM purchased an ownership share in suppliers or other automobile companies, this joint venture was explicitly a temporary alliance, during which GM hoped to learn about Toyota's production methods and Toyota hoped to establish a production foothold in its North American market and learn about doing business in the United States.

Business alliances often arise when each participating company has some special resource or competency that the other lacks. We have already seen several examples of two-party alliances of this kind, but multiparty alliances are also possible. For

New United Motors Manufacturing, Incorporated (NUMMI)

In 1984 Toyota and General Motors established NUMMI to build Chevrolet Novas and Toyota Corollas in a closed GM plant in Fremont, California. Built in the 1960s, the Fremont plant had been a money loser for GM and had been plagued by labor problems. Absenteeism rates of 22 percent and drug and alcohol abuse in the factory had created a nightmare for management. Employees were equally unhappy, with some 2,000 formal grievances still unresolved when GM had finally closed the factory.

For GM, the new agreement promised a way to learn about Japanese management practices from Toyota, a master and principal innovator of the system. The top management of the new plant would be Toyota executives, but GM could place up to 16 managers of its own in the plant where they would learn about Toyota's methods in order to transfer what they had learned to other plants in North America and around the world. But what could Toyota hope to gain?

Toyota had been the last of the Japanese automobile companies to build facilities in the United States. With increasing pressure from trade negotiators to reduce Japan's enormous trade surplus with the United States, Honda and Nissan had responded quickly by building U.S. plants. One thing that Toyota needed was a way to begin production in the United States quickly, and GM's existing Fremont plant offered a quick solution. As it prepared for its expansion, Toyota wanted to begin building a network of North American U.S. suppliers and to gain experience dealing with North American workers and their union, the United Automobile Workers (UAW). One statistic stands out as a special indicator of its success: Although 85 percent of its work force came from former GM Fremont plant workers, the absentee rate at Toyota was only 2 percent.

The arrangement was, by agreement, a temporary one. Indeed, the U.S. antitrust authorities insisted that the agreement expire by 1996 in order to thwart the possibility of an international automobile cartel. The labor arrangements set a pattern that deeply affected the 1987 negotiations between GM and the UAW, in which GM obtained greater flexibility in assignments in exchange for much greater job security for workers. GM also patterned many of the labor and manufacturing practices at its new Saturn subsidiary on its NUMMI experience. Toyota took similar advantage of what it had learned about American workers, who demanded more autonomy and more information than Japanese workers and who did not always participate in "voluntary" company programs. Based on the confidence and experience it had gained, Toyota built large new automobile plants in Canada and the United States.

example, in 1990 Hewlett Packard and EDS each purchased a portion of Ask Computer Systems to help it finance a purchase of Ingres, a data base software company. The four companies plan to team up to develop and sell factory automation systems.

In many alliances, the greatest danger is that one of the participating companies may learn enough about the other's operations to duplicate its routines and special competencies and become an effective competitor. For example, Boeing, in order to participate in the development of a Japanese fighter aircraft, agreed to conduct the project as a joint venture with Japanese partners, but it excludes those partners from its manufacturing facilities to protect its trade secrets and special competencies in aircraft manufacturing and technology. Learning methods and technology can also be the reason for an alliance, as in the NUMMI example.

Economies of scale can be an important stimulus to joint projects for the same general reason that they can favor the development of cooperatives. For example, the International Telecommunications Satellite Project (INTELSAT) is a joint project whose members are governments who contribute capital and own shares in proportion to their intended usage of the system. Similarly, U.S. semiconductor firms have formed a research consortium, Sematech, to promote large-scale research in semiconductor manufacturing technologies. It is estimated that the cost of a state-of-the-art, efficient-scale semiconductor manufacturing facility may reach $1 billion to $2 billion by the year 2000. This price tag is far too high for the firms each to maintain separate facilities, and the firms fear having to deal with a monopoly supplier and especially one wedded to a foreign competitor.

Economies of scope in marketing can be another reason for an alliance. For example, the Lenscrafters chain which sells eyeglasses has arrangements with a variety of optometrists, who run a completely separate eye examination business in the same stores. The operations of the two parts of the store are quite distinct and independent; the purpose of the alliance is to provide more convenient service to the shared customers.

Keiretsu

An especially interesting kind of alliance and one of great importance in the modern world is the Japanese *keiretsu*, or groups of related firms. These groups, which dominate the Japanese economy, consist of independent firms with close links and often a shared name. The biggest of these is the Mitsubishi group, with 1990 aggregate sales of approximately $175 billion. With 28 core companies and hundreds of other affiliates, the members of the group produce and deliver thousands of different products and services.

Members of the *keiretsu* are linked financially in two major ways. First, companies in the group commonly own shares in the other members. On average, about 24 percent of the shares of the largest Japanese companies are owned by other, related companies. Nevertheless, because it is rare for any one company in a group to own more than 10 percent of another, the companies do not automatically direct purchases to related companies unless these other companies offer the best economic deal.

A distinctive role of the group of companies is as an information network and source of joint venture partners. The presidents of member companies meet together regularly to hear presentations, share business ideas, and cement personal relationships. At Mitsubishi, the meetings occur twice a month. To promote information exchange and business dealings among employees below the presidential level, there are clubs and restaurants reserved for employees of *keiretsu* members. The central offices of the member companies are all located in close proximity to one another in one area of Tokyo to make attendance and interactions easy. These practices combine with an expectation that the member companies will support one another in projects that make economic sense to create a powerful ability to move into promising new businesses with an instant market for one's product. For example, all 28 of Mitsubishi's core companies participated in establishing Space Communication Corporation, a satellite communications company. The clear expectation is that the members would become early customers of the new company, helping it become established and profitable quickly. In a world where business alliances to exploit special competencies are frequent, having a regular group of partners who encompass all the important competencies and who are ready to deal can be an important advantage.

Although the *keiretsu* do not have the same central structure as a multidivisional firm, there remain some important similarities. Just as the GM central office had to direct its divisions not to compete among themselves in the product market, the trading companies may play a similar role in the *keiretsu*. For example, Mitsubishi Heavy Industries and Mitsubishi Electric both make industrial air-conditioning equipment. Mitsubishi Corporation, the trading company often considered to be the central Mitsubishi firm, distributes its products to export markets and works to prevent these two separate companies from bidding against one another. In addition, capital for new investments beyond that generated within the division is often allocated by the central office in multidivisional firms, which reviews competing requests for funds. In the *keiretsu*, the main group bank plays a related role, as well as serving as a central, well-informed agent that can make opportunities for cooperation within the group known to the member firms.

Summary

Business organization has changed enormously over the past 150 years and continues to change in important ways. From the small, family-owned firms of the early nineteenth century, the development of national and international markets linked by improved transportation and communication led to larger-scale firms, which required complementary innovations in management and finance. These innovations in turn favored the development of similarly large firms in other industries. Experimentation and complementary innovations give a momentum to change and stamp a consistent pattern on it.

An especially important development was the creation of the multidivisional form of organization, which was pioneered by Du Pont, General Motors, Sears, and Standard Oil of New Jersey in the years following World War I. This form balanced the needs of decentralized decision making, in which authority for decisions was placed on those with local knowledge about operations, with the need for joint planning to exploit economies of scale. As the form evolved, businesses found they could handle larger numbers of divisions by organizing them into groups of related divisions. Before the introduction of this form, most firms were either controlled from a central office or operated as a holding company, in which the role of the central office was little more than to provide financing and receive profits. Compared to centralized organizations, the multidivisional firm had the advantages of decentralized decision making. The manager in command was better informed about operations than a central office committee could be and, being held responsible for performance, could be motivated more effectively. The multidivisional firm was also better able to expand into new businesses without overextending the few top executives of the central office than were more centralized organizations. Compared to the holding company, the multidivisional form could adopt a more coherent strategy and could sponsor joint projects that enhanced the overall competitiveness of the divisions.

Implementing a multidivisional form requires deciding on how activities should be grouped into divisions and resolving certain problems that are particular to this form. Generally, the economic principles governing the divisions and their groupings are that activities that require close coordination should be grouped together closely to facilitate coordination, that division managers should be given wide latitude to allow them to be fully responsive to performance incentives, and that divisions should be small enough that those in control can have meaningful individual effects on the division's performance.

The multidivisional form also gives rise to the transfer pricing problem as the problem of determining the price at which trades between divisions will occur. If a division makes a good for which there are competitive suppliers, then the competitively determined price leads, theoretically, to efficient decisions. Otherwise, the double marginalization issue arises, and the upstream will be inclined to set too high a price leading not only to a transfer of earnings from the downstream firm but to a loss of total profits as well.

The success of the multidivisional form leads to the question: What limits the size of the firm? We address this question in two parts, focusing first on the vertical and then the horizontal structure of the firm.

An early and still common abstract conception of the firm is as a maker of a single product, occupying some part of the vertical chain in which raw materials are processed into parts and systems and finally assembled into products for distribution to consumers. According to Coasian transaction costs economics, the chain will tend to be divided into firms in the way that minimizes the total costs of managing the transactions between successive stages. Two successive stages will be vertically integrated if the advantages of doing so outweigh the advantages of simple market contracting. The latter include the benefits of competition among suppliers and ownership incentives for them and any economies of scale and scope (including core competencies) that may be unavailable to a small integrated firm. Compared to simple market procurement, vertical integration allows for better coordination and better protection of specific investments, permits the firm to capture any rents its supplier is earning, avoids distortions like double marginalization that are associated with monopoly supply, and may help to deter entry by potential competitors.

Vertical integration and simple market procurement, however, are not the only available alternatives. New forms are continually developed among which we have reviewed three. Cooperatives allow the members to reap the advantages of scale economies while avoiding monopoly distortions in their purchase of supplies (buyers' cooperatives) and marketing services (sellers' cooperatives). Lacking a large owner, however, these cooperatives may suffer from insufficient monitoring of management, conflicting objectives of members, and political infighting. Franchise retailing is another form that maintains the powerful incentives of ownership for the franchisees while allowing the franchisor to protect its brand-name reputation and to force cooperation when close coordination is needed. The danger is that a powerful franchisor may exploit franchisees, the mere threat of which discourages specific investments. However, franchisee organizations to negotiate with the franchisor can mitigate that problem.

A third new arrangement is that used by Japanese automobile manufacturers to manage their suppliers. Using comparative performance evaluation instead of competitive bidding to pick suppliers, the system rewards efficient suppliers by awarding them additional supply contracts. This promotes good performance and allows suppliers to participate in product design, encouraging designs that are easy to manufacture. To encourage innovation and the rapid diffusion of new ideas, the automobile maker gives points to its suppliers in the internal rating system for any cost-reducing innovations they share. To achieve economies of specialization and scale, the supply contracts extend over the whole period for which the part or system is made. This practice also protects any specific investment the supplier may make. The supplier organizations contribute an additional layer of protection.

The identification of a firm with the product it makes is a tenuous notion even in a static context, and it becomes quite untenable in an environment characterized by constant product change. An alternative conception of the firm is as an organization that musters and organizes the resources it controls to exploit appropriate business opportunities. The way a firm operates its existing businesses helps it to acquire certain core competencies. These competencies as well as opportunities to exploit other economies of scale and scope are a major factor in determining the most profitable directions of business expansion.

Multidivisional firms may also incur costs that the same divisions would not incur if operated as separate companies. A clash of corporate cultures, based on differing routines and expectations in different divisions, can cause friction as divisions attempt to impose their standards on other parts of the organization. High levels of incentive pay in small entrepreneurial organizations have often caused jealousies in larger, more traditional organizations, leading to destructive influence activities such as lobbying efforts for "pay equity."

Alliances between independent business firms can arise for several reasons. A common one is that the participating firms have different competencies or special resources that can be usefully combined for some new business venture. Alliances can also be created to facilitate learning or to exploit economies of scale in research or supply operations.

Japanese business is dominated by a unique organization form: the *keiretsu*, or group of firms. The independent companies that are the members of these groups are bound together by mutual ownership arrangements, frequent meetings of the company presidents, physical proximity, common financing and direction from a main bank and trading company, and a complex web of social relations among their employees. The exchange of business information among group members and the ready availability of qualified partners and financiers for economically sensible joint ventures give these groups an unusual ability to identify opportunities and to respond quickly and flexibly to them.

■ **BIBLIOGRAPHIC NOTES**

Most of the theoretical ideas used in this chapter are developed at more length in other chapters, with contributors cited there. The other major influence on this chapter is the writing of business historian Alfred Chandler, who has emphasized the changing character of business organization, researched and told the stories of the companies that invented the multidivisional form, emphasized that changing business strategy drives organizational change and that new organization structures affect the business's subsequent strategy, and insisted that the relentless pursuit of economies of scale and scope were historically the key to business success.

■ **REFERENCES**

A.D. Chandler, Jr. *Strategy and Structure* (Cambridge, MA: MIT Press, 1962).

A.D. Chandler, Jr. *The Visible Hand: The Managerial Revolution in American Business* (Cambridge, MA: The Belknap Press, 1977).

A.D. Chandler, Jr. *Scale and Scope* (Cambridge, MA: Belknap Press, 1990).

EXERCISES

Food for Thought

1. In 1991, Wal-Mart Stores overtook Sears as the leading retailer in the United States, and its rapid growth appeared to be continuing. Wal-Mart's computerized inventory tracking systems allow it to keep close track of its stocks and alert its suppliers to coming orders. Concerned about its own reputation among customers, Wal-Mart pays close attention to its suppliers' quality and prices and engages some of its suppliers in long-term relationships making unique brands, such as its Liberty brand children's wear. What kinds of problems would you expect Wal-Mart to face in coordinating with its suppliers? How would this affect the kinds of contacts between the companies? Compare the costs and benefits of this system with those of an arms' length supply relationship or a system of vertical integration in which Wal-Mart would manufacture its own store brands.

2. In recent years, the leading Japanese producers of consumer electronics have purchased leading U.S. producers of entertainment "software" like records and movies in an effort to improve coordination in new product introduction and marketing. For example, Sony purchased the former CBS Records and Columbia

Pictures Entertainment and Matsushita purchased MCA. What are the likely advantages of this sort of horizontal integration? Could these consumer electronics companies have achieved substantially the same results by entering into long-term relationships with the software suppliers? Could arrangements for new product introductions be worked out equally well on a product-by-product basis?

3. Prudhoe Bay near the Arctic Circle in Alaska is one of the largest oil fields in North America. Shipping access to the Bay is blocked by ice during large parts of the year, so a pipeline was built to transport oil across Alaska to the Port of Valdez, where tankers can be loaded year-round. The eight large oil companies with major holdings in the area formed a joint venture, Alyeska, to manage the operation of the pipeline. Each oil company has a transportation subsidiary that owns a fraction of the capacity of the pipeline and charges a fixed amount per barrel for shipping oil. Expenses for operating the pipeline are allocated among the companies according to a formula that Alyeska employs based primarily on volume. What problems would you expect from a system of this kind? What might happen if a company's share of ownership differed significantly from its share of the oil being pumped? Identify alternative ways to organize oil transportation and compare their advantages and disadvantages for shipping Alaskan crude oil.

4. Honda Motor Company is one of three companies that the public generally knows as Honda. The Motor company engages in sales and manufacturing of automobiles, but there are also independent Honda companies for engineering and for research. What problems or concerns might have prompted Honda to adopt this unusual form of organization?

5. In the U.S. airline industry, companies often form alliances to expand and coordinate the network of cities they serve and to expand the schedules they offer to customers. For example, the regional air carriers affiliated with American Airlines are called American Eagle carriers, and they schedule their flights to connect with American's longer distance flights, carrying connecting passengers to cities throughout a regional market. In addition, American Airlines maintains relationships with some national and transnational carriers, like Trans World Airlines and British Airways, giving credit in their frequent flyer program for mileage flown on these lines. At the same time, the experience of smaller U.S. national air carriers like Eastern Airlines and Continental Airlines suggests that size really is important for success. Remaining mindful of the possibilities for coordination among independent airlines, discuss the role of scale and scope in organizing airline operations.

17

THE EVOLUTION OF BUSINESS AND ECONOMIC SYSTEMS

B usiness organizations are facing a change more extensive, more far-reaching in its implications, and more fundamental in its transforming quality than anything since the "modern" industrial system took shape in the years roughly between 1890 and 1920. These changes . . . come from several sources: the labor force, patterns of world trade, technology, and political sensibilities. . . . [T]he changes are profound, and they are occurring together.

Rosabeth Moss Kanter[1]

We opened this book by recounting historical episodes—stories of competition among Ford, General Motors, and Toyota, and between the Hudson Bay Company and the North West Company, of compensation reform at Salomon Brothers, and the failures of communism in Eastern Europe and the Soviet Union. The episodes exemplify many of the themes developed in the intervening chapters, but none more clearly than the ongoing drama of organizational change.

As the previous chapter stressed, the scale, scope, and organization of firms have changed massively over the decades as managers have experimented with organizational innovations to solve coordination and motivation problems and to respond to ever-changing markets and technologies. Within the firm, new pay systems and new bases for compensation have emerged. Job definitions and career paths have changed. Financing and ownership patterns have been radically altered. Relationships between suppliers and customers have been restructured, the scope of activities carried out within the firm has shifted, and the patterns of information flows, authority, and reporting within and between organizations have been redrawn.

Recent decades have also seen massive changes in organization at the level of the economy as a whole. In the capitalist world, governments have **deregulated**,

---

[1] *The Change Masters: Innovation and Entrepreneurship in the American Corporation* (New York: Simon and Schuster, 1983), 37–38.

reducing the extent and intensity of regulatory oversight, and **privatized**, selling or transferring firms that were previously government owned to private investors. Many examples of these phenomena can be found in Western Europe, North and South America, and Japan. At the same time, the Soviet Union and the formerly communist nations of Eastern Europe have undertaken a total restructuring of their economic and political institutions, introducing new systems of democratic political decision making and market-oriented economic-resource allocation. In this final chapter, we highlight and analyze some of these changes and the major forces that still drive them.

One theme emerges repeatedly in our analysis: When a group of activities is complementary, changes that increase the effectiveness of some activities in the group promote adoption and improvement of the other activities. Within a group of complements, causation does not work in just one direction. The most successful organizational innovations are often mimicked and copied by competitors and adapted by firms in other industries. Those firms will be led by the logic of complementarities to develop additional technologies and practices that enhance the effectiveness of their newly adopted organizational arrangements. As knowledge of these changes spreads, the new organization becomes even more advantageous, leading to even more widespread adoption and additional improvements. Changes that feed on themselves in this way can generate a snowballing momentum that leads to sustained trends and major shifts in technology and organization.

THE PRESENT AND FUTURE OF THE BUSINESS FIRM

In the late twentieth century, as throughout the preceding 200 years, business organization continues to evolve as companies adapt to new challenges and opportunities. In particular, the rapid pace of technological change combined with falling international barriers to trade have created new strategic and organizational opportunities to which many business firms have responded creatively. These responses have, in turn, encouraged the spread and further development of the new technologies, as well as further reduction in international barriers.

Technological and Organizational Change in Manufacturing

The frontiers of technological advance in the late twentieth century have been remarkably broad, impinging on organizations from many directions. One example is the changing technology for making semiconductors, where the growing importance of economies of scale in both research and manufacturing has changed the face of the industry. The cost of a semiconductor manufacturing facility capable of producing modern memory chips is expected to rise by a factor of about ten from about $200 million to about $2 billion between 1990 and the year 2000, promoting further concentration in the already concentrated chipmaking business. In response, chip users and makers in the United States have initiated joint ventures in semiconductor research and manufacturing (for example, the Sematech R&D venture and the unsuccessful U.S. Memories manufacturing effort). Meanwhile, the world's largest chip maker, IBM, has tried to increase its own scale of production by dropping its long-standing policy of producing semiconductors only for its own internal use and has entered into a series of cooperative efforts with various firms to develop and manufacture new semiconductor-based products. Worldwide, strategic alliances of various sorts aimed at sharing the costs and risks of research and development in the electronics and other industries have become more and more important. The rise of these alliances has blurred organizational boundaries and increased the need to encourage coordination among organizations.

COMMUNICATION AND TRANSPORTATION TECHNOLOGIES   Scale economies are only one way that technology affects organization. A second modern example is the falling costs of telecommunications and rapid air cargo systems, which have reduced the need for many firms to hold high levels of finished goods inventories in local shops and warehouses near their customers. Instead, these firms emphasize gathering and quickly processing information about customer demands, adjusting production to match current demand, and shipping products to arrive only when they are actually needed. For example, Benetton—the Italian clothing manufacturer—collects nightly sales data from retail stores and tries to ship just what is needed from its single central warehouse near Venice. This style of operation reduces the need for high levels of clothing inventories in the stores and economizes on overall inventories by shipping goods only when and where they are most valuable. This style of operations would have been impossibly expensive with the costly data communications, slow and unreliable computing, or slow transportation systems of earlier eras. The style requires standardization of the systems used by the individual stores and close coordination among them on changes to the system, which in turn require a shift in responsibility for systems design from the stores to the system planner. In this case, strategy and organization are tightly linked, and the feasibility of the strategy is a consequence of new technologies.

FLEXIBLE MANUFACTURING TECHNOLOGIES   Another change of the late twentieth century is the increasing use of flexible manufacturing technologies, which allow the same equipment to be used efficiently to make a variety of different products. For example, leading Japanese auto makers are approaching the point where they will be able to serve their local markets on essentially a make-to-order basis, building each individual car to the specifications of an individual customer's order. The contrast with Henry Ford's assembly line, which could produce anything the customer wanted as long as it was a black model T, is remarkable.

The use of these flexible manufacturing technologies is complementary with the use of new telecommunications and transportation capabilities. The case of Allen Bradley, a U.S. manufacturer of electronic controls, illustrates the complementarity. Making hundreds of different models of controls in its Milwaukee factory, the company programs its flexible production equipment to fill each electronically transmitted individual order separately, holding no finished goods inventory, and ships the products by air express within a day of receiving the order. Without the ability to process orders quickly and to ship them expeditiously, the ability to shift production from one model to another in seconds would be much less valuable.

Flexible operations require very different organizational policies and procedures than have been traditional in manufacturing. For example, traditional cost-accounting procedures, devised in an era of mass production systems in which specialized tools were used for each type of product and the important controllable factory costs were those of labor time, have proved less useful for informing decisions about products made in these new ways. When machines are put to multiple uses, the accounting system needs to provide information for deciding among those uses. Companies, such as Hewlett Packard, have pioneered new systems to provide more accurate assessments of the marginal costs of making each product, for example by designing devices to record the time used on each type of machine in a manufacturing process and figuring the cost of each product according to the number of machine hours used. This cost information helps not only in pricing decisions, but also in establishing product designs that can be manufactured at low cost and in creating meaningful measures to evaluate the performance of factory managers.

Flexible production equipment also encourages more frequent product change, which changes the demands on engineering, marketing, and supply, as well as on the assembly plant. For example, frequent product change has forced a reorganization of the product design and engineering functions of firms. In traditional mass production, product designers were aloof from actual factory operations. A product would be designed, then the design would go to engineers who would figure out how to turn it into a physical reality, and then the engineers would pass it on to manufacturing to figure out how to produce the product economically in volume. In an earlier era, this sequential approach caused few problems because a new factory or at least new equipment would be used to produce any new product. With more variety and more frequent product change, modern design engineers need to know more about the costs and capabilities of existing equipment and about what designs can be brought rapidly into production. To achieve this, firms are replacing the traditional sequential pattern of separated specialists with teams of designers, product engineers, and manufacturing experts who work together to develop products that can be made well and efficiently. This pattern is supported by yet another technical development—the introduction of computer-aided design and manufacturing (CAD-CAM) programs and the computer hardware on which to run them. Use of these technologies is complementary to frequent product change because it reduces the costs of product design and facilitates bringing new designs into production quickly and cheaply.

These technologically induced changes are also affecting jobs and career paths. Many engineers are now rotated frequently among jobs to create a deeper understanding of the capabilities and needs of different parts of the company. The same changes affect production workers, who are expected to master a variety of skills and to be willing to move from task to task, often working in teams and being paid for the skills they have mastered rather than for the particular job they are doing. It is the workers' range of knowledge and skills, more than any other single factor, that determines how quickly a firm can work out the bugs in making a new product and how easily it can introduce new technologies and improved methods. Progressive firms, recognizing these facts, are moving to entrust their workers with more responsibility and discretion, allowing them to make better use of the special local knowledge they alone possess.

In industries where the pace of product change is rapid, the individual product market is no longer a suitable focus of strategic decision making. Instead, management must anticipate its customers' needs and invest in building the firm's capabilities to fulfill those needs. The adoption of this new focus entails far-reaching changes. These firms develop systems to maintain effective, ongoing communication with customers to learn about their changing plans and requirements. They develop a capability to design and manufacture new products quickly, and they train and reward workers to be multiskilled. They work to coordinate with suppliers and distributors to ensure coherence of plans and actions in the face of changing circumstances. They may also build alliances with other businesses to gain quick access to capabilities that they lack. All of these changes are promoted by the modern design and manufacturing technologies, and all increase the rate of product change and the demand for further improvements in these technologies.

The Service Industries

Although manufacturing provides the most striking examples of complementary technological and organizational changes, these patterns are present in the service sector as well. Financial services provide a case in point. Easy, high-speed voice and data communication has resulted in increasingly close linking of financial markets around the world. Investors and corporate treasurers in North America can keep abreast of developments on the Tokyo and London stock markets as easily as of those on the New York and Toronto exchanges. This has created new opportunities for securities firms, encouraging them to expand and reorganize to enable them to seek funding and investment opportunities for their local clients on a world scale. The technical changes and the new services offered by securities firms encourage both investors and borrowers to adopt a global approach to their financial decisions. This further increases the flow of information, the demand for global communications, and the changes occurring in the markets and the securities firms.

Globalization of Economic Activity

In nineteenth century North America the falling costs of communication (telegraphy) and transportation (railroads) combined with the constitutional prohibition on the individual states' regulating interstate commerce in the United States and the "National Policy" of conscious government sponsorship of national economic integration and development in Canada to stimulate the growth of national markets and national scale firms. A similar phenomenon is occurring on a global scale in the late twentieth century under similar impetuses.

The spread of jet airline service, fax machines, international overnight parcel services, cheap and reliable international telephone links, wide-ranging scheduled air-freight operations, and computer data links via satellites have made moving information, goods, and people unprecedentedly easy and quick. Among centers of commerce, any place on the globe can be reached in a day from any other spot, and information can pass between any two points at the speed of light. The effects of the huge improvements in the technologies of transportation and communication have been amplified by reductions in economic and political barriers to international movements of goods and capital (and, to a lesser extent, labor). The United States and Canada have agreed to free trade between them, and in 1991 negotiations were under way to include Mexico and to create a North American free trade zone. Western Europe in 1992 would take another major step toward becoming a single, united market in goods, services, capital, and labor. More broadly, trade barriers have been progressively diminished under successive rounds of international negotiations under the General Agreement on Tariffs and Trade (GATT). Together, these developments have resulted in the beginnings of global markets.

Firms already raise money in whatever part of the world they find most attractive: Japanese firms have issued bonds in Europe and arranged for their shares to be traded on the New York Stock Exchange, and the Walt Disney Company has put together limited partnerships of Japanese investors to finance production of its films. Investments and acquisitions occur across national boundaries, as do strategic alliances. A Canadian firm, Olympia and York, was one of the biggest land owners in New York City in 1991 and had undertaken the largest real estate development in London. Western-European and U.S. firms had begun setting up joint ventures and subsidiaries in the former socialist countries of Eastern Europe and the Soviet Union. Apple Computer and Sony were working together, as were GM and Toyota, and Renault and Volvo. Following their clients—and sometimes leading them—consulting and accounting firms and investment and commercial banks were reaching out internationally, establishing themselves around the world. Goods and services markets were becoming global as well. World brands were emerging, with such names as Panasonic, Louis Vuitton, Coca Cola, Gucci, Levi's, Reebok, and Mercedes Benz known and sought worldwide.

As companies develop internationally, they face new kinds of challenges. Products need to be developed to meet the specialized needs of different markets. For example, automobiles need to be adapted to the driving regulations and conditions in different countries—the width, condition, and congestion of the roads, which side of the road traffic moves on, speed limits, safety and fuel-economy regulations, local content rules that prescribe what fraction of any good must be produced locally to receive favorable tax treatment, weather conditions, and so on. At the same time, the gains in productive efficiency from standardization on a global scale can be hard to ignore, even though they conflict with the need to meet local tastes. Attempts to serve a national or regional market by establishing a research center or factory there create a need for developing enough flexibility in procedures to accommodate local patterns of business relations, labor-market practices, and government regulation. Additional demands are imposed on the organization by the need to develop means to coordinate information flows, make decisions, and implement plans across national borders and time zones, to surmount linguistic and cultural differences, and to take advantage of the particular skills and resources that are most prevalent in each region.

Even firms that decide to stick to serving their local or national markets are affected by the growing internationalization of business because their competitors or the lowest cost supplier may be from other parts of the globe. This means that the ability to operate in global markets is of very general value. It also means that there are strong forces driving firms to adopt the strategic and organizational adaptations that help them to operate in international markets. Just what these adaptations may be is not yet clear: These are relatively new management problems, and international firms are experimenting with many kinds of solutions. Whatever solutions do emerge will further promote the globalization of economic activity by lowering the cost of doing business internationally.

Innovations in Ownership, Financing, and Control

Even after allowing for the influences of technology and markets, business organizations evolve in response to organizational entrepreneurship—the development and implementation of new management ideas. As we have seen, the 1980s were an especially active period for innovation in financing and control. In the English-speaking developed countries, for example, highly leveraged firms created by LBOs emphasized incentives for top management and close scrutiny by large investors in an effort to improve business performance. The same ideas lay behind a series of other innovations in financing and incentives that spread in the late 1980s. Some firms now provide an equity stake to their divisional managers, encouraging them to behave like the managers of highly leveraged firms but retaining sufficient resources in the central office to bail out failing divisions in hard times. In the insurance industry, mutual companies that were formerly owned by their policy holders are being demutualized, that is, sold to private investors who will exercise tighter financial control over the managers than the dispersed policy holders were motivated to provide. These trends illustrate how ideas developed in one sector of an economy are adapted to promote change in other sectors.

If the effectiveness of these new organization forms is still unproved, the success of the *keiretsu* in Japan is not. These groups of firms have proven to be extremely agile in responding to new market opportunities and new technologies, transferring information, technology, and financial resources among members, rescuing partners in financial trouble, cooperating in exploiting new opportunities for investment, and maintaining employment and high levels of productivity and growth. In an environment characterized by rapid change, the ability to transfer technology and knowledge is a new aspect of the organization problem, whose importance may equal that of the traditional aspects of coordination and incentives.

Even as firms around the world study Japan's system for hints about its success, that system continues to change. Reliance on debt financing among Japanese firms fell sharply during the 1980s, and some of the most successful Japanese industrial firms have completely escaped their dependence on bank financing. At the same time, the cost of capital rose markedly in the early 1990s, until by some estimates it exceeded that in the United States, while the boom in land and stock-market prices of the 1980s faded and, in the latter case, reversed. Deprived of the capital gains they had enjoyed in the past, institutional investors' returns from holding Japanese corporate stocks became dependent on dividend payouts, which had traditionally been very low. Some observers wondered whether this would lead the institutions to increase pressure on management to generate and distribute current earnings. The likely consequences of these changes in Japan are as hotly debated as are the consequences of the 1980s' financial restructuring in the United States and United Kingdom.

Human Resources

Japan is facing major changes in its labor markets as well. The population is growing older, and many forecast a labor shortage in future years. This might well contribute to the emergence of a very active labor market for experienced workers, similar to that in other developed countries. Further, the lifetime employment system and the employee's devotion to the interests of the employer are being challenged by a younger generation that has grown up in affluence and has been exposed to other countries' ways. As we have argued, the absence of an active outside labor market interacts crucially with other elements of the Japanese employment and human-resource management system. These developments thus raise serious challenges to the Japanese system and to the organizations within it.

In other countries, the increasing role of women in the labor force is forcing reconsideration of old patterns. Traditional career paths were often based on a model of a male employee who focused on his job while his wife stayed home to keep house and raise children, supporting him in his job, and following wherever her husband's career took them. As these patterns change, firms are having to revamp their human-resource policies to account for the needs of dual-career couples and the demands of child care.

In the United States and Canada especially, firms are also concerned that the educational systems are not producing potential employees with the basic skills in language, mathematics, and simple reasoning to meet the demands of the new technologies and methods. Many are increasing their expenditures on training programs, even when the human capital being developed is nonspecific. Meanwhile, although the Japanese educational system has been successful in teaching students facts, it has also been criticized for not encouraging creativity. Japanese critics have called for change on that dimension.

THE PRESENT AND FUTURE OF ECONOMIC RESTRUCTURING IN EASTERN EUROPE AND THE USSR

Although the changes in the structure of capitalist firms and economies in the late twentieth century have been quite profound, they are overshadowed by the pervasive and momentous economic reorganization occurring in the formerly communist states of Eastern Europe and the Soviet Union. The transformation of these economies is not solely a matter of transferring the state-owned means of production into private hands. Rather, one coherent system is being junked, and another coherent system must be found and implemented to replace it. The process is not reform, but metamorphosis.

In Chapter 4 we discussed the possibility that there could be multiple coherent patterns of organization. Within each pattern, the various elements of organizational design and strategy are mutually supporting, and yet one pattern might be much more productive than another in a particular environment. Moreover, mixing elements from two different coherent patterns would not typically yield another coherent pattern, but instead might more likely result in a mismatch that performs miserably. We also suggested that the process of moving from one coherent pattern to another might be quite difficult, especially if there were little relevant experience within the organization about how the pieces in the new solution might fit together and support one another. The discussion in Chapter 4 was at the level an individual firm, but the same point applies with even more force to the restructuring of an entire economy.

The Communist and Capitalist Systems

State ownership, centrally planned resource allocation, authoritarian political decision making, and the monopolization of power by a pervasive communist party together constituted an internally consistent, coherent solution to the general economic problem of organization: It was a system. In later years it became clear that it was not a very efficient system, even from a purely materialistic point of view, and it always involved tremendous costs in terms of human freedom, human dignity, and human lives. Nevertheless, it did perform well on some dimensions. Centralized decision, allocation, and control mechanisms allowed the USSR to focus its physical and human resources with remarkable effect on narrow objectives: the rapid development of heavy industry in the period through World War II and of space rockets and military hardware in the following decades. The overwhelming difficulties created by the inability to use local information appropriately and by the dysfunctional incentives, however, meant that achieving these successes used up inordinate amounts of resources. Moreover, these same problems meant that the resources that remained could never be put to very effective use in meeting the varied needs of consumers: The complexity of the task was too great.

Private ownership, decentralized resource allocation, democratic political decision making, and a distribution of powers among a variety of different institutions and organizations together constitute another coherent system, with the various pieces again mutually supporting one another. These two solutions differ on almost every relevant dimension, however. Moreover, few of the people involved in reshaping the former communist economies have experience with any version of the alternative pattern. This is especially true in the Soviet Union, where there is essentially no one with personal experience and first-hand knowledge of the operation of a market economy and a democratic political system. In the language of Chapter 4, these nations face a *design problem with innovation attributes*: A host of different pieces must be introduced and structured to fit together, and no one has much experience with identifying the relevant pieces and how they fit.

To illustrate, consider only the issue of the ownership of the means of production. As we have seen, the very definition of ownership is a subtle matter. What rights and duties will owners have? What rights and duties will be assigned to workers, managers, and government? The answers given to these questions have very real effects on incentives, behavior, and performance. If share ownership is dispersed, as many of the reformers advocate, how will business organizations be controlled? What mechanisms will ensure they function in a way consistent with efficiency? If ownership is concentrated in mutual funds or other institutions, how will those institutional managers be controlled? Competition in input, output, and corporate-control markets are important parts of the solution in the English-speaking economies. In Japan and continental Europe, however, ownership is not as dispersed, and bankers play a larger role in overseeing corporations. It is important to understand that different control systems are adapted to different ownership patterns and legal structures. Once ownership is established, how will investments be safeguarded? A largely legal approach based on court enforcement of explicit contracts is one possibility. This requires a legal system that is very different from what has been in place. Primary reliance on multifaceted, long-term relationships is more in the Japanese mode. This approach, too, demands a set of legal and institutional supports that are missing in Eastern Europe.

Managing the Transition

We described the move from one system to another as a metamorphosis. Both caterpillars and butterflies are coherent, successfully functioning creatures; the thing in transition inside the chrysalis is neither. Similarly, economies halfway on the transition between communism and capitalism are apt to be monsters, unable to function. It is crucial to go all the way to a new, coherent form and not to dawdle or get stuck *en route*.

During the communist era in Eastern Europe, incentives in the enterprises were blunted because any losses suffered would be financed by the state and most profits would be taken by the state, with only meager rewards for good performance and trivial penalties for failure. In the transition between communism and private ownership, incentives for profitable enterprises have often become even worse. With a change of ownership imminent, any resources that the firm can squirrel away will reduce current profits and taxes and increase the amount eventually available for workers, managers, and the new owners. In Poland, partly as a result of these incentives and partly from the turmoil in the economy, total enterprise profits in 1991 were forecast to be virtually zero. This eliminated virtually all of the government's income from the profits tax, one of its main sources of revenue, and contributed to a massive fiscal crisis. The longer the transition takes, the worse these problems will be. At least in this respect, Poland's radical, "cold turkey" approach seemed wise. Despite serious unemployment and other economic woes, shortages had ceased, and there were signs of economic recovery.

The problems were much worse at the same time in the USSR, largely because decisive action had not been taken. Through 5 years of half-hearted economic reform and major political change, President Gorbachev had attempted to save essential elements of the communist system without any apparent coherent plan as to where *perestroika* would lead and what system would result. Pressures mounted for abandonment of communism and adoption of a thorough-going market system on one side, and for return to tight state and party control of the economy on the other.

By 1991 the state ministries had essentially ceased to function as a means of coordinating economic activity on even the inefficient level they had previously attained. They and their allies were still powerful enough, however, to ensure that well-functioning markets had yet to replace them. Consumer goods of the most basic sort were becoming very scarce in many parts of the country, and there were fears of real hunger during the winter of 1991–1992. The shortages were not just a result of much of the supply being drawn off to the nascent free markets in the richer areas, although the differential between the free-market prices and those paid by the state was more than sufficient to pay the fines imposed for failing to deliver the state's orders. Even more important was that the decrepid transportation system could not get food from the farms to the people: Huge fractions of the crops from the collective farms were rotting in fields. Real output was shrinking rapidly, and inflation was becoming a major problem. Compounding the problem was a deteriorating balance of payments, as the previously captive markets in Eastern Europe were lost and oil production, one of the few major sources of hard currency earnings, fell precipitously. Meanwhile, the threatened political collapse of the Soviet Union and the aftermath of the attempted *coup d'etat* of August 1991 were diverting attention from the crucial tasks of establishing a coherent economic system for coordination and motivation, whether through private ownership and markets or state ownership and central planning.

Throughout Eastern Europe, new systems are being implemented by people with no experience and little understanding of how the system works or what it takes for a capitalist system to succeed. The social experiment of economic transition is an event of great historical importance, but many severe disappointments on the road to capitalism are likely.

THE FUTURE OF ECONOMICS, ORGANIZATION, AND MANAGEMENT

The economic analysis that goes under the label of the "theory of the firm" in traditional microeconomics textbooks is one in which firms act like single decision makers guided by prices and costs, buying labor and other inputs in impersonal spot markets, converting them into output via given and largely unchanging technologies, and selling this production in more impersonal markets. This has proven to be a very useful abstraction for many purposes, but of course the reality of actual firms is very different. Large firms bring together a multitude of individuals with differing information and interests, and it is only through careful design of the incentive and coordination systems that coherent, fruitful action can be achieved. Accommodating the diversity of hundreds or thousands of unique local markets increases these demands because it means that decision making must be divided among many parties. Long-term relations with employees, suppliers, and customers are commonplace and fundamentally important for developing systems in which prices are not the primary guide of individual behavior. With constantly changing technologies and long-term relationships, long-term strategic decisions are based on building the systems, capabilities, and alliances to respond flexibly and coherently to the challenges of a changing and uncertain future. Recognizing all this is crucial to understanding organizations as they really are. This understanding, in turn, is necessary if we are to help structure and manage organizations so that they better serve peoples' interests.

Students and practitioners of management have traditionally been well aware of the actual features of organizations, but they have lacked any unified and powerful framework for organizing and understanding the facts and patterns they observed. Without this, anecdotes too often become the basis for general pronouncements. Theory—a sorting out in a logically consistent fashion of the forces that are important, of how they interact, and of what consequences result—is necessary for a real and useful understanding of the business environment. As this book has demonstrated, economics offers uniquely powerful tools and methods to build such a theory.

This pinpoints yet another complementarity: Theory is enriched and made useful by institutional knowledge, and this knowledge is organized and made generally applicable by theory. Economists have too long ignored the study of how firms and economic systems actually operate in a dynamic, tumultuous environment. Those who have studied these matters and those who have managed organizations in these environments have too long labored without the benefits of useful theories to guide their investigations and their decisions. Bringing the two pieces together will give much more than the simple sum of the parts. The serious study of economics, organization, and management has just begun.

Glossary

Terms in italics correspond to other entries in the glossary.

accounting rate of return (on assets): The rate of return on an investment for a particular period—such as a year—computed by dividing the net income before interest charges for that period from an income statement (prepared according to the applicable accounting rules) by the accounting value of the assets.

accounting rate of return (on equity): The rate of return on an investment for a particular period—such as a year—computed by dividing the net income after interest charges from an income statement (prepared according to the applicable accounting rules) by the accounting value of the firm's equity.

adverse selection: Originally, an insurance term referring to the tendency of those who seek to buy insurance to be a nonrandom selection from the population—more particularly, to be those who expect to have the highest expected claims. Adverse selection now refers also to the kind of *precontractual opportunism* that arises when one party to a bargain has private information about the something that affects the other's net benefit from the contract and when only those whose private information implies that the contract will be especially disadvantageous for the other party to agree to a contract.

agency relationship: As used in economics, an agency relationship is one in which one person (the *agent*) acts on behalf of another (the *principal*). For example, an employee is an agent of his or her employer and a doctor is the agent of a patient. (The term principal-agent relationship has a narrower meaning in law.)

agent: One who acts on behalf of another. See *agency relationship*.

allocation: In the neoclassical model of a private ownership economy, an allocation consists of lists for each consumer and each firm of the amount of each commodity to be bought and the amounts to be sold. More generally, an allocation is a complete specification of how resources are to be used.

antitakeover statutes: Public laws designed to make hostile takeovers more difficult. Many U.S. states have adopted such legislation.

arbitrage: Originally, buying and selling the same item in different markets simultaneously in order to profit from a difference in prices between the markets. A pure arbitrage transaction involves no risk and no net investment. The term is now applied more broadly to trading that takes advantage of discrepancies in pricing among groups of assets that are close substitutes.

asset: A potential future flow of benefits and services. Also, the article giving rise to the stream. For example, shares of stock or machines are assets.

assignment problem: A situation in which efficiency requires that one or more tasks be done and that only a single individual or group do each task. The problem is to ensure first that all the tasks are done without duplication of effort and second that no other assignment of people to tasks yields greater output or incurs lower costs.

authority relation: One in which one party (the superior) has the right to direct the behavior of the other (the subordinate), at least within bounds, and to supervise, monitor, and punish or reward the subordinate.

backward integration: Bringing the supply of an input under the ownership and management of the input purchaser. A form of *vertical integration*.

bankruptcy: A set of legal provisions designed to come into effect when a firm or individual is unable to meet its debt obligations. Under Chapter 7 bankruptcies in United States law, the debtor firm's assets are sold, and the proceeds distributed to claimants in order of their priority. In a Chapter 11 bankruptcy, for which the firm applies to the courts, the firm is protected from its creditors for a period in which it attempts to reorganize and negotiate a settlement of claims with the creditors.

bargaining costs: The *transaction costs* involved in negotiations between or among different parties. These include the time spent on bargaining, resources expended during bargaining or in trying to improve bargaining position, and any losses incurred as a result of failure or delay in reaching otherwise efficient agreements.

beta: The expected percentage change in value of a financial asset when the value of the *market portfolio* of all assets changes by one percent. See *capital asset pricing model*.

bounded rationality: The limitations on human mental abilities that prevent people from foreseeing all possible contingencies and calculating their optimal behavior. Bounded rationality may also include those limitations on human language that prevent perfect communication of those things that are known.

brittleness: The extent to which the performance of an economic system deteriorates when the information supplied to the system is slightly inaccurate.

business judgment rule: In U.S. corporate law, the unwillingness of the Courts deciding in lawsuits against a corporation's board of directors to "second-guess" the board's business decisions and rule that those decisions were unwise or mistaken, provided they were made in good faith and in the honest belief that they were in the best interest of the company.

bust-up: A form of takeover in which the purchaser of a company resells its individual divisions or other assets to other buyers.

call option: A financial contract in which the buyer of the option receives the right (which he or she may choose not to exercise) to purchase some particular asset (often, shares of a particular company) from the seller of the option on a particular date (a European call) or on or before a predetermined date (an American call) at a predetermined price, called the striking price. See also *option*, *put option*, *warrants*.

capital asset pricing model (CAPM): A model of stock market prices according to which the expected or average return to investing in any stock is equal to the rate of return on a riskless investment plus an *excess return* proportional to the *beta* of the stock.

cash flow: Accounting net income plus any allowances for depreciation. Essentially, the amount of money generated by the operation that is currently available for investing, servicing any new debt taken on, or disbursing to owners.

centralization: The vesting of control for individual activities with a higher authority who communicates or imposes the decisions on the individuals. The higher authority might be a person at a higher rank in a hierarchy, or the collectivity of individuals themselves acting through some group decision process. Contrast with *decentralization*, where each of the individuals themselves would make the decisions.

CEO: Chief Executive Officer, the highest ranking officer of a corporation. The CEO is typically either the company president, or chair of the board, or both.

certain equivalent: Given a choice between an uncertain or random income and a certain, nonrandom one, the amount of certain income that would make the chooser just indifferent between the two alternatives. Also called the certainty equivalent.

classical firm: A conception of the firm in which the actions of the firm are those that would be taken if a single individual had decision making authority and paid fixed wages to workers and prices to suppliers and received as profit any excess of the firm's receipts over its expenditures.

classified board of directors: A board in which only a minority of the members are up for re-election by the stockholders in any year, so that the votes of even a majority of the shares cannot immediately replace a majority of the board. Also called a *staggered board*.

Coase Theorem: A proposition that if there are *no wealth effects* and no significant *transaction costs*, then (apart from distributional considerations) the outcome of bargaining or contracting is independent of the initial assignment of ownership, wealth, and property rights and is determined solely by efficiency.

coefficient of absolute risk aversion: Twice the amount that an individual would pay to avoid having to bet $1 on the toss of a fair coin.

coercive tender offer: A tender offer structured so that it is in the best interests of each shareholder to tender, even though he or she believes the offer is for less than the firm is worth.

collateral: Property of a borrower that is contractually forfeited to the lender if the loan payment terms are not met. Also called security for the loan.

common-resource problem: A situation in which several different parties can use a resource for their individual benefit and property rights are not sufficiently well defined and enforced to ensure that individuals bear the full costs of the actions and receive the full benefits they create. Also called a *free-rider problem* (especially in situations where excluding parties who fail to pay for the resource is difficult) or a *public good problem*. The resulting inefficiencies have led to the term *the tragedy of the commons.*

comparative performance evaluation: The practice of evaluating an individual's performance by comparing it to the performance of others doing similar work.

competitive equilibrium: A list of prices, consumption plans, and production plans such that (1) every individual consumes the goods he or she most prefers subject only to the limits of his or her budget, (2) every firm makes goods and uses inputs in the way that maximizes its profits, and (3) the total quantity supplied of each good is equal to the total quantity demanded.

complements: A set of activities with the property that doing more of any subgroup of the activities raises the marginal return to the other activities.

complete contract: A hypothetical contract that describes what action is to be taken and payments made in every possible contingency.

complete markets: A hypothetical set of markets, one for each possible commodity at each future date and for each possible realization of the uncertainty in the world.

conglomerate firm: A firm operating in several unrelated lines of business.

connectedness: The expected loss incurred from failing to coordinate a particular group of decisions.

consumption plan: A pair of lists showing the amounts of every good that a consumer plans to buy and to sell. Actual consumption is calculated by adding purchases and subtracting sales from the consumers's *endowment.*

contracts: Formally, contracts are legally enforceable promises. They may be oral or written, and they typically must involve obligations on each party—for example, to provide a good or service on the one hand, and to pay for it on the other. See *complete contract, incomplete contract,* and *implicit contract.*

convertible bond: A corporate debt instrument which carries the right to convert the obligation to common (or, perhaps, preferred) stock at a contractually specified exchange rate.

convertible preferred stock: Preferred stock with the right to convert the claim to common stock at a specified rate.

cooperatives: A form of commercial organization in which only customers (or sometimes suppliers) are eligible to be among the owners and any earnings are distributed in proportion to sales or membership or through price reductions, rather than in proportion to the owners' investments.

core competencies of the firm: A form of economy of scope that arises out of a firm's ability to carry out some types of activities well. Typically, this refers to the firm's ability to design, make, sell, or distribute a certain kind of product.

corporate control: Authority over the decisions of a firm, typically attained by purchasing alone or with allies a large fraction of the firm's shares.

corporate culture: A set of shared beliefs and values, precedents, expectations, stories, routines, and procedures in a firm that help define that firm's way of doing things and serve as a guide to behavior for those within the firm.

corporate raider: An individual who undertakes *hostile takeovers.*

corporate strategy: The determination of which business activities the firm will undertake. Contrasts with *business-unit strategy,* which is concerned with how the firm will compete in a given business.

corporation: An organizational form that allows the enterprise to act as a legal entity separate from its owners, who enjoy limited liability for the corporation's debts. See also *not-for-profit corporations, public corporations, private corporations.*

cospecialization: A condition of two assets each of which is more productive when used with the other. Cospecialized assets must be unique in some respect and must also be *complements.*

cost of capital: The cost to an organization of obtaining financial resources. Usually stated as an interest rate.

covariance: A measure of the extent to which the realizations of two *random variables* are linked. Measured as the expected value of the product of the deviations of the variables from their means.

debenture: A document indicating that a firm has incurred a debt and setting forth the required interest payments and repayment schedule.

debt overhang: A situation in which a borrower that does not have enough resources to meet its current debt obligations nevertheless has profitable investment opportunities but does not undertake these because its debt makes it unable to obtain financing or because the profits would accrue to the creditors rather than to the borrower.

debt workouts: Negotiations between a debtor and creditors designed to avoid bankruptcy by revising the creditors' claims.

decentralization: See *centralization.*

design problem: A decision problem in which there is a large amount of *a priori* information about the relationship among the variables in an optimal solution and in which failing to achieve the desired relationship is costlier than other kinds of errors.

differential voting rights: A system of corporate governance in which not all common stock has equal voting rights. For example, recently acquired stocks might be accorded fewer votes than those that have been held for an extended period. Used to make hostile takeovers harder to win, because a majority of shares, if newly purchased, will not carry a majority of the votes and so cannot alone unseat the board.

diversification: For an individual investor, the division of invested wealth among a variety of different assets. For a firm, the operation in several different lines of business. In either case, diversification is designed to reduce risk.

double marginalization: The tendency of two firms, one of which supplies the other, to set prices at such a high level as each adds a profit margin to its own marginal cost that their combined profits would be increased if the final price were lowered.

downstream: An activity that follows the reference activity in the sequence of steps from producing raw materials to delivering a finished product to the customer.

economies of scale: The reduction in average cost that is achievable when a single product is made in large quantities.

economies of scope: The reduction in total cost that is achievable when a group of products are all made by a single firm, rather than being made in the same amounts by a set of independent firms.

efficiency principle: The working hypothesis that organizations and institutional arrangements that persist tend to be efficient ones. The logic is that if an arrangement is inefficient, then there are gains to be realized from changing it.

efficiency wage: Higher pay than required to attract and hold workers in the particular employment, provided the higher pay is designed to induce higher productivity. For example, pay in excess of the recipient's market opportunities could encourage greater effort and productivity through the fear of losing quasirents if the relationship is terminated for poor performance.

efficient: An allocation, contract, or organization is efficient if there is no feasible alternative one that everyone finds to be at least as good and that at least one person strictly prefers.

efficient markets hypothesis: The hypothesis that prices in securities markets, and particularly stock markets, fully and accurately reflect all information relevant to forecasting future returns. The *weak, semi-strong,* and *strong form of the efficient markets hypothesis* differ in the specification of what information is asserted to be embodied in prices.

elimination tournaments: A sequence of contests with only the winners at each stage being allowed to compete at the next.

employee-owned firm: A firm in which the providers of labor services hold at least a controlling interest.

employee stock ownership plan: A form of pension plan in which stock in the employing firm is purchased and held in trust for employees as the basis for their retirement incomes.

end-game problem: The difficulty that a person in a relationship that is about to end may face different incentives than in an on-going relationship and may be led to act dishonestly or inefficiently.

endowment: In the competitive equilibrium model, the amounts of various goods that a consumer owns initially, before trade opens.

equal compensation principle: The principle in incentive contracting that if an agent is to allocate effort among different activities, then each must bring the same marginal return to effort. Otherwise, the agent will focus exclusively on the one that yields the greatest impact on his or her income.

equity: (1) The value of real property in excess of any legal claims against it for debts owed. (2) Resources contributed to a firm in exchange for an ownership claim. (3) Securities issued by a firm that represent ownership rights (such as stocks) or that are convertible into such securities (such as warrants).

event study: A statistical and economic methodology under which the market's evaluation of the value created or destroyed by some event or action is estimated by examining abnormal returns to assets whose values might plausibly reflect the effect of the event or action. These abnormal returns are determined by comparing the actual price of an asset around the time of the event with a statistical estimate of what this price would otherwise have been.

excess return: In the *capital asset pricing model,* the expected return above the risk-free interest rate.

expected value (or expectation): The weighted average of the possible realizations of a *random variable,* where the weights are the probabilities.

externalities: Actions of one party that affect the welfare of others and are not mediated through markets.

financial leverage: The use of debt financing to increase the resources available to the firm for a given level of equity provided by owners.

firm-specific capital: Human or physical capital that is less productive when it is used outside a particular firm.

Fisher separation theorem: The proposition that a decision maker who is able to borrow and lend at the same interest rate can base investment decisions solely on a forecast of cash flows and interest rates, without regard to his or her preferences about the timing or composition of consumption.

focus: The extent to which a firm limits itself to a relatively few lines of business.

forward integration: Bringing a *downstream* activity, such as distributing or selling a firm's product, under the ownership and management of the firm.

free cash flow: (1) *Cash flow*, plus after-tax interest expenses, less investments. (2) In Michael Jensen's free cash flow hypothesis, the amount of a firm's *cash flow* in excess of what can be profitably invested in the firm.

free-rider problem: See *common-resource problem*.

functionally organized firm: A firm in which the traditional functions, such as accounting, sales, manufacturing, and so on, are each controlled by a single department, in contrast to the *multidivisional firm*.

fundamental theorem of welfare economics: The proposition that the allocation associated with a competitive equilibrium is efficient.

gain-sharing plans: Compensation plans designed to motivate employees by giving them some fraction of the returns to improved performance.

game theory: A general analytical approach to modeling social situations in which the information, possible actions, and motivations of the actors or *players* and how those actions lead to outcomes are all specified in detail. In contrast, the competitive equilibrium model does not specify what would happen if the demands of consumers exceeded the available supply.

general partners: The members of a *partnership* who have decision-making authority and who have unlimited personal liability for the partnerships' debts.

general-purpose (human) capital: See *non-specific asset*.

goal congruence: A situation in which the objectives of different individuals or organizations are sufficiently aligned that they are led to pursue common goals.

golden handcuffs: Compensation designed to reduce turnover by paying exceptionally large amounts or by giving substantial amounts of deferred pay that would be forfeited if the employee were to leave the firm.

golden parachutes: Contracts that promise large severance payments to employees (usually senior executives) who lose or leave their jobs shortly after a change in corporate control.

greenmail: Payments by a corporation to a potential corporate raider to induce him or her to give up an attempted takeover. Usually involves a targeted share repurchase, in which the firm pays a premium over the market price to buy back the shares accumulated by the raider.

hierarchy: (1) An idealized arrangement of authority in which each person has only one boss and the organization has a single top officer. (2) A system of ranking employees.

holding company: A company which owns several other companies but exercises little or no management control over them.

hold-up problem: The problem that one who makes a relationship-specific investment is vulnerable to a threat by other parties to terminate that relationship. This threat then permits these parties to obtain better terms than were initially agreed.

horizontal integration: (1) In antitrust economics, expansion of a firm by acquisition of or merger with competitors. (2) In business usage, an expansion into a related activity that does not involve vertical integration.

hostile takeover: A change in corporate ownership that is opposed by the current management and board. Usually accomplished by buying a sufficiently large fraction of the shares from the current stockholders to be able to control the election of board members.

human capital: Acquired skills and knowledge that make an individual more productive.

human-resource management: The formulation and administration of human resource policies and of exceptions to these.

human-resource policies: Policies relating to recruitment, employment, training, compensation, employee benefits, job assignments, promotion, and termination.

Hurwicz criterion: A standard for measuring the amount of information required by a decision-making or resource allocation system. The standard measures the number of variables which must be communicated at the last stage of the planning process to check whether the plan is efficient.

idiosyncratic risk: The portion of any financial risk that is independent of the total financial risk born in the economy. Also called *unsystematic risk*, as contrasted with *systematic risk*.

imperfect commitment: Parties' limited abilities to bind themselves to future courses of action, especially to bind themselves to avoid opportunistic behavior.

implementation problem: The mathematical problem of minimizing the cost born by a principal while still inducing a self-interested agent to perform in a particular way. Also called a *minimum cost implementation problem*.

implicit contracts: Shared understandings that are not legally enforceable but that the parties consider to be binding on one another's conduct.

incentive compatibility constraints: Limitations on the set of contracts that can be implemented that arise from the necessity of giving individuals appropriate incentives to induce them to adopt the desired course of action. These constraints are particularly important when there are *informational asymmetries* or *incompleteness*, so that individuals might misrepresent their private information or take unobservable actions that are different from those desired by the other parties.

incentive efficient: Efficient when the constraints implied by the necessity of providing incentives are recognized.

incentive intensity principle: The principle in incentive contracting that the intensity of incentives should increase with the marginal productivity of effort and with the agent's ability to respond to incentives and should decrease with the agent's risk aversion and the variance with which performance is measured.

influence activities: Self-interested activities designed to influence others' decisions. Within organizations, these are often aimed at redistributing rents and quasirents and take the form of political activity or misrepresentation or distortion of information.

influence costs: The costs incurred in attempts to influence others' decisions in a self-interested fashion, in attempts to counter such *influence activities* by others, and by the degradation of the quality of decisions because of influence.

informational asymmetries: Differences among individuals in their information, especially when this information is relevant to determining an efficient plan or to evaluating individual performance.

informational incompleteness: Lack of complete information, especially when the actions of one party may not be observable by others.

informationally efficient: A system for communicating information to support efficient resource allocation decisions is informationally efficient if no other system also results in efficient decisions and requires that less information be communicated. See *Hurwicz criterion*.

informational rent: A return in excess of opportunity costs that accrues by virtue of an individual both having access to precontractual private information. The private information means that the individual must be given incentives not to take advantage of the informational asymmetry, and providing these incentives results in the rents.

informativeness principle: The principle of incentive contracting that holds that payments under a contract should depend on the value of a variable if and only if accounting for that variable allows a reduction in the error with which performance is measured.

innovation attribute: The attribute of a decision problem that the information required for an optimal decision is not directly available to people within the organization.

intensity of incentives: The rate at which expected income changes with improved performance under an incentive contract.

internal labor markets: A complex of administrative procedures and rules governing the allocation of labor, investments in it, and its compensation within an organization. The key idea is that these procedures and rules supplant the operations and directives of the outside labor market.

investment: An expenditure of resources that creates an *asset*.

job ladder: A sequence of jobs of increasing rank through which employees climb by gaining promotions.

junior debentures: Debt that contractually has a lower priority than other, *senior* debt in claims on the firm's assets in bankruptcy. When assets are inadequate to pay all claims,

junior debt has no legal claim until the claims of more senior debt have been met. Also called subordinated debt.

junk bonds: Corporate debentures that are considered particularly risky and so carry a high interest rate. More formally, bonds that are not rated as being of investment grade by one of the bond rating services (Moody's or Standard and Poor's).

just-in-time manufacturing: A production system in which inventories of goods in process are minimized because the required inputs to each stage of manufacturing are delivered to each work station just as they are needed.

LBO association: Michael Jensen's term for the collectivity consisting of the management of a firm that has gone through an *LBO*, the firm that arranged the transaction and purchased the bulk of the equity, the banks that provided loans, and the various purchasers of the firm's debt obligations.

leveraged buyout (LBO): The purchase of the stock in a firm when the resources to finance the purchase come mostly from borrowing that is debt of the firm. The result of the borrowing means that the firm is highly leveraged.

limited liability: The condition of a person whose liability for the debts of a partnership or other organization is limited to the amount of capital that the person has invested.

limited partner: A partner in a limited partnership who supplies financing and enjoys a share of the partnership profits but who exercises no control of partnership decisions and who has limited liability for partnership debts.

limited partnerships: A partnership consisting of both general partners and limited partners.

liquidate: Sell all the assets of a firm.

local nonsatiation: A property of preferences that means that near any consumption bundle there is another one that is strictly preferred.

management buyout: A purchase of a firm by its managers. Often these transactions are also leveraged buyouts because the purchase was financed by heavy borrowing.

management by objectives: A technique for setting performance standards for employees in which the individuals have a role in identifying the objectives they will try to meet.

market failures: Failures of markets to achieve efficient allocations. Sources include *economies of scale*, *externalities*, and *missing markets*.

market for corporate control: Refers to the possibility of changing corporate control through buying the stock of the firm in the securities markets.

market portfolio: A portfolio that contains dollar amounts of different assets in proportion to their aggregate values in the overall economy.

market socialism: A hypothetical economic system in which the means of production would be owned socially (or by the state) but resources would be allocated by prices.

measurement costs: Costs involved in determining the quality of a good or service that a party incurs to improve its bargaining position.

menu of contracts: A system for compensation in which individual employees may choose which of several different formulas will be used to compute their pay.

minimum cost implementation problem: See *implementation problem*.

missing markets: A situation in which no market exists in which to transact in a particular good or service.

modern manufacturing strategy: Any of a collection of manufacturing strategies that seek to exploit the capabilities of flexible equipment and rapid data communication and processing to increase the rate of new product introduction, improve quality and reduce inventories and overhead costs.

Modigliani-Miller theorems: Two propositions in corporate finance theory. The first is the proposition that, but for taxes, the total market value of a firm's debt and equity would be independent of how much of the financing takes each of these forms. The second proposition is that the total market value of the firm's debt and equity is unaffected by its dividend policy, provided its investment policy is held fixed.

monitoring: An activity whose aim is determining whether the contractual obligations of another party have been met.

monitoring intensity principle: The principle of incentive contracting that indicates that more resources should be used to reduce the errors in measuring performance when stronger performance incentives are being given.

moral hazard: Originally, an insurance term referring to the tendency of people with insurance to reduce the care they take to avoid or reduce insured losses. Now, the term refers also to the form of *postcontractual opportunism* that arises when actions required or desired under the contract are not freely observable.

multidivisional organization: A form of firm organization in which there are multiple business units with autonomy to make day-to-day operating decisions and with control over their own functional departments (accounting, marketing, etc). Planning and coordination among these units and performance evaluation of the unit managers are the responsibility of a central office.

mutual insurance company: An insurance company that is legally owned by its policyholders.

Nash equilibrium: A strategic situation in which each decision maker's planned strategy is best from his or her point of view in light of the strategies that he or she expects others to employ, and these expectations are correct.

neoclassical market model: A model of market exchange in which utility-maximizing consumers and profit maximizing firms transact at prices over which each party perceives itself to exercise little control.

net present value: The worth today of a cash flow stream, computed as a weighted sum of the cash flows in each future period, using weights that depend on interest rates.

nexus of contracts: A nexus is a connected group. Armen Alchian and Harold Demsetz have identified the firm as such a connected group of (explicit or implicit) contractual relationships among suppliers, customers, and workers.

nominal: Amounts measured in some currency, rather than in units of actual purchasing power.

non-specific assets: Assets that are equally useful when employed in combination with any of various other assets or in any of several different relationships. See *specific asset*, *firm-specific capital*, and *cospecialization*.

normal form game: A list of players, their available strategies, and the payoffs that each player stands to earn from each possible combination of individual strategies.

not-for-profit organization: An organization (often a corporation) whose net proceeds from operations must remain in the organization and be used to advance the organization's objectives. Often used for organizing the provision of charitable activities. A not-for-profit has no owners in the sense of *residual claimants*.

no wealth effects: The condition on preferences that means that choices among nonmonetary alternatives are unaffected by the individual's wealth or income.

one-fund portfolio theorem: The conclusion that, for investors who care only about the mean and variance of the returns on their investments, the optimum portfolio always consists of shares of a riskless asset with the balance invested in predetermined proportions among the other securities. These predetermined proportions are the "one fund" that underlies every efficient investment portfolio.

opportunistic behavior: Self-interested behavior unconstrained by morality.

option: A financial contract giving a right which need not be exercised unless the holder chooses to do so. See *call option* and *put option*.

Pareto dominated: A situation from which it is possible to increase strictly the welfare of some party without diminishing that of any other party.

Pareto optimal: A situation from which it is impossible to increase the welfare of any party without decreasing that of some other party.

participation constraints: Limitations on contracts or other organizational arrangements arising from the fact that participation is voluntary and so individuals must expect to do at least as well as under their next-best alternatives or they will refuse to participate.

participatory management: A policy of allowing employees to participate in all important management decisions, usually accompanied by arrangements to ensure *goal congruence*.

partnership: A form of organization in which some or all of the multiple owners, the *general partners*, accepted unlimited liability for the organization's debts and exercise management control.

perfect capital markets: A theoretical ideal in which all individuals can borrow and save on the same terms, with these terms being unaffected by the amounts involved.

piece rate: The amount paid for each unit of a product that is produced. Also the system of compensating people in proportion to the amounts they produce.

poison pill: A takeover defense that greatly reduces the value of the firm in the event of a hostile takeover by giving stockholders a right to acquire shares in the firm (or some other financial claim on the firm) at a greatly reduced price in the event of a control change.

postcontractual opportunism: Opportunistic behavior by a party that takes place after a contract is signed. *Moral hazard* and the *hold up problem* are two particular problems of postcontractual opportunism.

posting of bonds: Setting aside a sum of money (a *bond*) to guarantee performance under a contract.

precontractual opportunism: Opportunistic behavior by a party that takes place before a contract is signed. *Adverse selection* is a problem of precontractual opportunism.

preferred stock: Securities issued by a firm which, like common stock, need not be redeemed by the corporation but which do not carry voting rights and must be paid dividends before any dividends can be paid on common stock.

present value: See *net present value.*

principal: (1) The party whose interests are meant to be served in an agency relationship. (2) The initial amount of a loan or investment.

principle of risk sharing: The principle that when many people share in a number of independent risks, with each taking a small part of each risk, the total cost of bearing the risk is reduced.

principle of unity of responsibility: The principle that final responsibility for all the jobs needed to accomplish a particular task should reside with a single person. This policy both clarifies what might otherwise be ambiguous responsibilities and makes it easier to evaluate performance and provide incentives.

principle of value maximization: The principle that in the absence of wealth effects an allocation is efficient if and only if it maximizes the total value obtained by all of the parties.

prisoners' dilemma: A strategic situation modelled as a *normal form game* in which each party or player has a dominant strategy—one that is best no matter what behavior is expected from the others—but play of these dominant strategies results in an outcome that is *Pareto dominated* by an outcome that would be achieved under some other (dominated) strategies.

private corporation: A corporation whose common stock is not offered for sale to the general investing public.

private information: Information that is relevant to determining efficient allocations that is known only to some subset of the parties involved.

privately held corporation: See *private corporation.*

privatization: The transfer of firms from government to private ownership.

production plan: A listing of inputs to be purchased and outputs to be sold by a firm.

profit sharing: An element of a compensation plan in which employees receive bonuses that are in aggregate tied to firm profits.

proxy fight: A contest among competing parties to gain the proxies of a majority of a corporation's shareholders, giving the successful party the right to vote the shares in a shareholder vote. Usually launched as a challenge to management (which normally gets the proxies of shareholders who do not attend shareholder meetings) and the current board of directors.

public corporation: A corporation whose shares are bought and sold through an organized exchange and so may be held by any investor.

public-goods problem: See *common-resource problem.*

publicly held corporation: See *public corporation.*

put options: A financial contract that gives the buyer the right (which the buyer may choose not to exercise) to sell a particular asset at a specified price on a certain date (a European put) or on or before a certain date (an American put).

quality circles: Groups of workers who meet to identify and implement ideas for improving the quality of their product.

quasirent: A return in excess of the minimum needed to keep a resource in its current use.

random variable: An amount that depends on the outcome of an uncertain event.

ratchet effect: The tendency of performance standards in an incentive system to be adjusted upwards after a particularly good performance, thereby penalizing good current performance by making it harder to earn future incentive bonuses.

real: Real, as opposed to *nominal* amounts, represent actual purchasing power by allowing for price changes.

relational contract: A contract that specifies only the general terms and objectives of a relationship and specifies mechanisms for decision making and dispute resolution.

renege: Deliberately choose not to carry out a promise or contract to the detriment of the other party.

renegotiate: Bargain to determine new terms to replace those of an existing contract. If no new agreement is reached, the previous one remains in force.

rent: A return received in an activity that is in excess of the minimum needed to attract the resources to that activity.

reorganization: Redesign of the relationships, authority, responsibilities, and lines of communication in an existing organization. In a reorganization in bankruptcy, the bankrupt firm renegotiates the amount of its debts and the timing of its payment obligations and may also reorganize its activities to allow continued operation.

reputation: The view formed of an individual or organization by another based on past experience, especially as a basis for forecasting future behavior.

residual claimant: One who is entitled to receive the residual return of an asset.

residual return: Income from an asset or business that remains after all fixed obligations are met.

residual right of control: The right to make any decision concerning an asset's use that is not explicitly assigned by law or contract to another party.

resource allocation problem: The problem of using limited resources efficiently or in a way that maximizes some fixed objective.

restructuring (financial): Changing the financial structure of the firm. During the 1980s restructuring typically was designed to reduce the *free cash flow* and thereby improve managerial incentives or to make the firm a less attractive target for *corporate raiders*, or both.

revelation principle: The principle holding that any outcome that can be achieved by some mechanism under the self-interested strategic behavior that is induced by the mechanism can also be achieved by a mechanism employing an honest mediator to whom the parties willingly report truthfully and who then implements the outcome that would have resulted from the original mechanism.

risk aversion: The preferring of a sure thing to a risky outcome with a somewhat higher expected return.

risk neutral: The characteristic of a person who is indifferent between receiving a fixed sum of money or a risky prospect with an expected value equal to the fixed sum.

risk premium: The excess of the expected value of some random income over its certain equivalent.

risk tolerance: A measure of willingness to bear risk. Measured as the inverse of the *coefficient of absolute risk aversion.*

routines: Standardized rules for decision and action that, although they may vary to a limited degree with the particular circumstances, are applied across a period of time without further fine-tuning.

sales response function: A relation indicating how the level of sales is expected to respond to changes in certain variables, such as the salesperson's efforts.

Scanlon plans: An incentive plan in which workers are paid a bonus if the ratio of labor cost to sales is less than some specified target, with the bonus being in proportion to the costs saved.

scorched earth policies: A kind of takeover defense that deliberately reduces the value of a firm to discourage hostile bidders.

screening: Offering a menu of contracts or options with the intention of encouraging *self-selection.*

secured debt or loan: A debt for which a particular asset has been pledged as security. If the borrower does not meet the terms of the contract, the lender can legally seize that asset.

selective intervention: The management practice of allowing divisions or businesses to operate with nearly complete independence, intervening only to correct particular problems characteristic of independent firms.

self-selection: The pattern of choices that individuals with different personal characteristics make when facing a menu of contracts or options. For example, workers who face a choice between a job with a fixed hourly wage and one with piece rate incentives will tend to prefer the former if they expect to be relatively unproductive and to prefer the latter in the opposite case.

semistrong form efficient markets hypothesis: The hypothesis that stock prices (or those of other assets) fully reflect all publicly available information. This hypothesis implies that unless an investor has inside information, he or she cannot expect to earn better rates of return (on a risk-adjusted basis) from any active investment policy than from one of simply buying and holding a fully diversified, market portfolio.

senior debt: Debt which has priority over other, more *junior* debt in its claims on the firm's assets in bankruptcy.

separation of ownership and control: A situation in which the *residual returns* and *residual rights* of control belong to different parties. More particularly, the common condition of modern corporations in which the shareholders are the residual claimants but effective control of decision making lies with the top managers of the firm.

separations: Quits, firings, and permanent layoffs.

shareholder rate of return: The rate of return on holding a stock over a period, calculated as the change in share price plus any dividends received, all divided by the initial price of the shares.

short selling: The practice of borrowing an asset in order to sell it and later repurchasing a similar asset to repay the loan.

signaling: Acting in a way that demonstrates to others the actor's intentions or abilities or some other characteristic about which the actor has private, unverifiable information. For example, a worker who accepts a job that begins with several weeks of unpaid, specific training signals an intention to work for the firm for a long period of time.

specialization: (1) The division of tasks on the basis of comparative advantage. (2) The process of narrowing (and, presumably, deepening) the range of tasks that a particular individual or machine can perform.

specific investment: An investment that creates a *specific asset*.

specific assets: Assets whose value is much greater in a particular use or relationship than in the next-best alternative.

specificity: The extent to which assets are specific. When the *principle of value maximization* holds, specificity is measured by the loss in value entailed in shifting the asset to another use.

spin off: The creation of a separate corporation whose shares are distributed to the original firm's stockholders and into which certain assets are placed.

spot market contract: A contract for the immediate exchange of goods or services at current prices.

staggered board of directors: See *classified board*.

stakeholder: Any individual or group who has a direct interest in a firm's continuing profitable operations (including stockholders, lenders, employees, customers, suppliers, communities where the firm employs workers, and so on).

state of incorporation: In the United States, the state in which a company is legally established and whose laws govern the relationship between the company and its stockholders. Need not be the location of the headquarters of the firm.

statistically independent: A condition holding between *random variables* under which knowledge of the realized value of one variable gives no information about the probability of different realizations of the other.

stock options: In executive compensation, *options* given to the employee by the firm to buy its stock for a specified price during some specified period.

strategic investments: (1) Investments whose benefits partially accrue to parts of the organization not involved in making the investment. (2) Investments made to create or demonstrate commitment and thus alter the behavior of competitors or allies.

strong form efficient markets hypothesis: The hypothesis that stock prices (or those of other assets) fully reflect all information, including both publicly available information and information held by insiders.

strongly complementary: A group of activities is strongly complementary when increasing the levels of some activities in the group greatly increase the marginal returns to the remaining activities. Strong complementarities lead to *design decisions*.

supermajority rules: A requirement in many antitakeover charter amendments that any change of control be approved by more than a simple majority of the voters. For example, a ⅔ or ¾ majority may be required.

synchronization problem: The problem of arranging the timing of activities when close coordination is required.

systematic risk: The portion of the variance of return on an investment that varies directly with returns on a market index. In the *capital asset pricing model*, the systematic risk of an investment is measured by its *beta*. See also *idiosyncratic risk*.

takeover premium: The amount by which the price paid for a firm's shares in a takeover exceeds the total market value of the firm's shares in the absence of a takeover.

team production: A production process in which the individual outputs cannot be separately identified. For such a process, any individual incentives must be based on some measure of the effort or diligence of the workers.

technical analysis: The practice of attempting to identify patterns in asset price movements for use in forecasting future price movements.

tenure: The condition of being protected from termination of employment in a job, regardless of general performance, subject only to meeting certain minimal standards of acceptable behavior.

tournament: A contest in which the prizes received depend only on ordinal ranking (first, second, third, etc.) and not on absolute performance. A policy of promoting the person who is judged best qualified creates a tournament, as do sales contests in which a prize is given for achieving the largest sales volume.

tragedy of the commons: See *common-resource problem*.

transaction: (1) An exchange involving goods, services, or money. (2) The largest unit of economic activity that cannot be subdivided and performed by several different people.

transaction costs: Costs of carrying out a transaction or the opportunity costs incurred when an efficiency-enhancing transaction is not realized.

transfer prices: The prices used for transactions among departments or divisions within a firm.

unlimited liability: The condition of a person whose liability for the debts of a partnership or other organization is not limited to the amounts he or she has invested.

unsecured: An unsecured loan or debt is one which no specific asset is pledged to support repayment.

unsystematic risk: See *idiosyncratic risk*.

up-or-out rule: An employment policy under which employees who are not promoted or made partners must leave the organization.

upstream: An activity that precedes the reference activity in the sequence of steps from producing raw materials from natural resources to delivering a finished product to the customer.

utility function: A numerical representation of an individual's preferences over different possible choices or situations.

variance: A mathematical measure of the amount that a random variable is likely to vary around its mean value. The variance is equal to the expected value of the square of the difference between the variable and its mean.

venture capitalist: An investor who specializes in providing equity funding to new ventures, often also providing advice and practicing active monitoring.

vertical integration: Bringing two or more successive stages in production and distribution under common ownership and management.

warrants: Rights issued by a firm (often in connection with the issuance of new bonds) entitling the holder to buy common shares from the firm at a specified price on or before a specific date. In contrast to *call options*, warrants, when exercised, lead to an increase in the number of shares of the firm that are owned by private investors.

weak form efficient markets hypothesis: The hypothesis that current stock (or other asset) prices reflect fully all the information that is embodied in past prices. An implication is that observing past prices cannot help in forecasting future prices. In particular, price changes should not be correlated over time and should not display any predictable patterns. This implies that *technical analysis* cannot be the basis of a profitable investment strategy.

wealth effects: The variation in the amount a consumer is willing to pay for some object or in the quantity that the consumer may wish to buy at a particular price as a result of a change in the consumer's wealth.

white knight: A merger partner or acquirer sought out by the target's management or board to thwart a *hostile takeover*.

winner's curse: The tendency of the winning bidder in a contracting competition to be one who has underestimated the cost of doing the job, because bidders who overestimate the cost usually bid too high. Similarly, the tendency of the winning bidder in an auction to be one who has overestimated the utility of the object being sold.

Index